A Companion to Soviet Children's Literature and Film

Brill's Companions to the Slavic World

Editor-in-Chief

Oleg Minin

VOLUME 2

The titles published in this series are listed at *brill.com/bcsw*

A Companion to Soviet Children's Literature and Film

Edited by

Olga Voronina

BRILL

LEIDEN | BOSTON

Cover illustration: Petrushka, Source: primary source collection *Children's Leisure* in the series *Mass Culture and Entertainment in Russia*. © Brill.

Library of Congress Cataloging-in-Publication Data

Names: Voronina, Olga, editor.
Title: A companion to Soviet children's literature and film / edited by Olga Voronina.
Description: Leiden ; Boston : Brill, 2020. | Series: Brill's companions to the Slavic world, ISSN 2468-3965 ; Volume 2 | Includes bibliographical references and index.
Identifiers: LCCN 2019032007 (print) | LCCN 2019032008 (ebook) | ISBN 9789004401488 (hardback) | ISBN 9789004414396 (ebook)
Subjects: LCSH: Children's films–Soviet Union–History and criticism. | Avant-garde (Aesthetics)–Soviet Union–History.
Classification: LCC PG3190 .C66 2019 (print) | LCC PG3190 (ebook) | DDC 891.709/92820904–dc23
LC record available at https://lccn.loc.gov/2019032007
LC ebook record available at https://lccn.loc.gov/2019032008

Typeface for the Latin, Greek, and Cyrillic scripts: "Brill". See and download: brill.com/brill-typeface.

ISSN 2468-3965
ISBN 978-90-04-40148-8 (hardback)
ISBN 978-90-04-41439-6 (e-book)

Copyright 2020 by Koninklijke Brill NV, Leiden, The Netherlands.
Koninklijke Brill NV incorporates the imprints Brill, Brill Hes & De Graaf, Brill Nijhoff, Brill Rodopi, Brill Sense, Hotei Publishing, mentis Verlag, Verlag Ferdinand Schöningh and Wilhelm Fink Verlag.
All rights reserved. No part of this publication may be reproduced, translated, stored in a retrieval system, or transmitted in any form or by any means, electronic, mechanical, photocopying, recording or otherwise, without prior written permission from the publisher.
Authorization to photocopy items for internal or personal use is granted by Koninklijke Brill NV provided that the appropriate fees are paid directly to The Copyright Clearance Center, 222 Rosewood Drive, Suite 910, Danvers, MA 01923, USA. Fees are subject to change.

This book is printed on acid-free paper and produced in a sustainable manner.

Contents

Acknowledgements VII
List of Figures VIII
Notes on Contributors X

Introduction. "The Only Universal National Text": On the Centennial of Soviet Children's Literature and Film 1
Olga Voronina

PART 1
Forging a New Children's Culture: (R)evolution, Poetics, Aesthetics

1 Unnatural Selection: A Natural History of Early Soviet Picturebooks 49
Sara Pankenier Weld

2 The Junctures of Child Psychology and Soviet Avant-Garde Film: Representations, Influences, Applications 72
Ana Hedberg Olenina

3 The Dictionary as a Toy Collection: Interactions between Avant-Garde Aesthetics and Soviet Children's Literature 99
Ainsley Morse

4 The Literary Avant-Garde and Soviet Literature for Children: OBERIU in the Leningrad Periodicals *Еж* and *Чиж* 139
Oleg Minin

PART 2
Constructing Socialism, Building the Self: History, Ideology, Narrative

5 Re-imagining the Past for Future Generations: History as Fiction in Soviet Children's Literature 179
Marina Balina

6   Education of the Soul, Bolshevik Style: Pedagogy in Soviet Children's Literature from the 1920s to the Early 1930s   212
Olga Voronina

7   "Be Always Ready!": Hero Narratives in Soviet Children's Literature   250
Svetlana Maslinskaya

8   Unspeakable Truths: Children of the Siege in Soviet Literature   303
Tatiana Voronina and Polina Barskova

PART 3
New Approaches to the Avant-Garde: Reconstructing the Canon

9   Children's Poetry and Translation in the Soviet Era: Strategies of Rewriting, Transformation and Adaptation   341
Maria Khotimsky

10   Under the Hypnosis of Disney: Ivan Ivanov-Vano and Soviet Animation for Children   389
Lora Wheeler Mjolsness

11   Embracing Eccentricity: *Золушка* and the Avant-Garde Imagination   417
Larissa Rudova

12   The Queer Legacies of Late Socialism, or What Cheburashka and Gary Shteyngart Have in Common   440
Anna Fishzon

Bibliography   475
Index   493

Acknowledgements

I wish to extend my thanks to Brill's editorial team, and especially to Ivo Romein and Marti Huetink, for initiating this project and seeing it to completion. A newcomer to the field, I am indebted to Larissa Rudova and Marina Balina, two outstanding scholars of Soviet children's culture, who welcomed this volume with enthusiasm, served as my guides and mentors, and helped bring our dynamic group of scholars together. My gratitude also goes to the volume's authors for their talented contributions, incredibly scrupulous and patient revisions, and valuable criticism, and to Oleg Minin, for his thorough edits. The book would not have been possible without a Research Grant from the American Association of Children's Literature, which helped to offset translation costs and editorial expenses, as well as research funds generously supplied by Bard College, my academic home and also an intellectual and artistic haven that constantly inspires scholarly projects like this one. Having spent many hours at the Russian National Library in St. Petersburg, I cannot but express my admiration for its preservation of rare books and manuscripts, periodicals and graphic art pertaining to the pre-Soviet, Soviet, and Post-Soviet children's literature and film, and the librarians' eagerness to help with difficult research questions. Throughout these years of team-building, essay-writing, editorial regrouping, and endless improvements, my family has been understanding, supportive, provocative, and fun. Mom, dad, and Martin, this book is dedicated to you, with love.

Figures

2.1 Pedologist Abram Gel'mont conducting a psycho-physiological study of children spectators' perception of films in 1929. A pheumograph is recording the girl's breathing patterns, while her finger's rhythmical oscillation is being registered by a kymograph.   74

2.2 Young children in an orphanage supervised by Dr. Durnovo are demonstrating a Pavlovian "goal reflex" (a frame from Механика головного мозга [*The Mechanics of the Human Brain*]).   76

2.3 Nikolaj Krasnogorskij (left) and his assistant operating a control board that administers cookies to a child and taps him on his hand. Their booth is isolated from the child to insure the purity of the experiment (a frame from Механика головного мозга).   79

2.4 Krasnogorskij's assistant peeks out of his booth to check up on the child (a frame from Механика головного мозга).   82

2.5 A small child in Krasnogorskij's experiment looks into the camera (a frame from Механика головного мозга).   83

2.6 A child with a calibrated saliva collector inserted into a fistula on his cheek (a frame from Механика головного мозга).   83

3.1 Cover of О том как старушка чернила покупала (*How an Old Woman Went Shopping for Ink*), by Daniil Charms with illustrations by Eduard Krimmer (1929).   103

3.2 Olga Rozanova's cover of Тэ ли лэ (*Te Li Le*) by Aleksej Kruchenych and Velimir Chlebnikov (1914).   104

3.3 The cover of Трое (*The Three*) by Velimir Chlebnikov, Aleksej Kruchenych and Elena Guro, illustrated by Kazimir Malevich (1913).   107

3.4 A "drawing by 7 year-old M. E." from Kruchenych's Собственные рассказы [*и рисунки*] детей (*Children's Own Stories and Drawings*), 1914. Photograph by Maria Vassileva, courtesy of the Houghton Library, Harvard University.   111

3.5 Vladimir Majakovskij, Советская азбука, 1919.   118

3.6 Конная Буденного (*Budennyj's Cavalry*) by Aleksandr Vvedenskij, illustrations by V. Kurdov (1931).   130

4.1 Back cover ad for Еж 2 (1930).   142

4.2 Nikolaj Olejnikov's photograph from Еж 5 (1929), 36.   150

4.3 Nikolaj Olejnikov as Makar the Fierce. Illustration from Еж 11 (1928), 8.   152

4.4 "Incredible Adventures of Makar the Fierce," in Еж 5 (1929), 31.   153

4.5 "Makar the Fierce (Olejnikov) and Ivan Charmsovich Toporyshkin (Charms). Illustration by Boris Antonovskij from Еж 6 (1929), 23.   154

6.1 Cover of Gleb Pushkarev's Яшка Таежник (*Jashka the Taiga Dweller*, Moscow 1927). Illustration by R. Cherumjan.   213

FIGURES   IX

6.2   Illustration by G. G. Likman to "Яшка Таежник" in Pushkarev's collection *Два Петра Ивановича* (*Two Peter Ivanoviches*, Novosibirsk 1949).   214
6.3   Cover of Innokentij Grjaznov's *Искатели мозолей* (*Callus Seekers*, Moscow 1931). Illustration by M. Rajskaja.   225
6.4   Cover of Anatolij Finogenov *Кто впереди* (*Who is Ahead*, Leningrad 1932). Illustration by M. Gerec.   230
6.5   Cover of Lidija Budogoskaja's *Нулевки* (*Zero-Graders*, 1933). Illustration by Eduard Budogoskij.   233
6.6   Nina Zlatova addresses a group of students and teachers. K. Rudakov's illustration to Boris Vinnikov's *Победа* (*Victory*, Leningrad 1932).   235
9.1   Cover page of Kipling's *Сказки* (*Fairytales*) in Marshak and Chukovskij's translation, Moscow 1923.   354
9.2   Original publication of Marshak's translation of Kipling's poem which concludes the fairytale "The Beginning of Armadillos" ("Как появились броненосцы"), Moscow 1923.   355
9.3   An excerpt from the first publication of "Плюх и Плих," in *Чиж* 11 (1936).   366
11.1 Janina Zhejmo as Cinderella.   427
11.2 Cinderella (Janina Zhejmo) and Prince (Aleksej Konsovskij).   430
11.3 King (Erast Garin) and a page (Igor' Klimenkov).   432
11.4 Vasilij Merkurjev as Cinderella's father.   433
11.5 Faina Ranevskaja as stepmother.   434
12.1 *Винни-Пух идёт в гости*, director Fedor Chitruk, Sojuzmul'tfil'm 1971.   452
12.2 *Малыш и Карлсон*, director Boris Stepancev, Sojuzmul'tfil'm 1968.   457
12.3 *Чебурашка*, director Roman Kachanov, Sojuzmul'tfil'm 1971.   463

Digital images in Chapters 4 and 6 come from the Russian National Library, which provides special digitization service to researchers. Images 1, 5, and 6 in Chapter 3 are courtesy of Cotsen Children's Library, Department of Rare Books and Special Collections, Princeton University, while images 2 and 3 in the same chapter are courtesy of the Getty's Open Content Program. Images 1 and 2 from Chapter 9 have been kindly provided by the Houghton Library, Harvard University. Digital image 3 from Chapter 9 is courtesy of the National Electronic Library of the Russian Federation.

All images used in Chapters 2, 4, 6, 9, and 11 are not subject to copyright under the Civil Code of the Russian Federation because over 70 years have expired since their original publication. Additionally, the publication of all pre-1958 images in the book falls under "fair use," according to the Copyright Law of the United States (Title 17 Chapter 107), because they are used for the purposes of criticism, comment, and research: this is known as "transformative use," which adds "something new, with a further purpose or different character, and does not substitute for the original use of the work."

Notes on Contributors

Marina Balina
is Isaac Funk Professor of Russian Studies at Illinois Wesleyan University, USA. She is the author, editor and co-editor of numerous volumes, among them *Russian Children's Literature and Culture* (with Larissa Rudova, 2008), *Petrified Utopia: Happiness Soviet Style* (with Evgeny Dobrenko, 2009), *The Cambridge Companion to Twentieth Century Russian Literature* (with Evgeny Dobrenko, 2011), and *"Убить Чарскую": парадоксы советской литературы для детей* (*"To Kill Charskaja": Politics and Aesthetics in Soviet Children's Literature of the 1920s and 1930s*, with Valerij Vjugin, 2013). She has published extensively on contemporary Russian life writing and children's literature.

Polina Barskova
is Professor of Russian Literature and Film at Hampshire College. She has published six books of poetry in Russian. Having received a Ph.D. from the University of California at Berkeley, she currently works on the culture of the besieged Leningrad (1941–1944). Dr. Barskova is the author of multiple articles on Vladimir Nabokov, the Bakhtin brothers, early Soviet film, and the aestheticization of historical trauma.

Anna Fishzon
is a psychoanalyst in private practice in New York City and an independent scholar. She has taught history and comparative literature at Williams College, Duke University, and Columbia University. Dr. Fishzon is the author of *Fandom, Authenticity, and Opera: Mad Acts and Letter Scenes in Fin-de-Siècle Russia* (2013), as well as articles on sound recording, celebrity, temporality, and animation. She is the editor of *The Queerness of Childhood: Essays from the Other Side of the Looking Glass* (with Emma Lieber, 2018). She also cohosts the podcast "New Books in Psychoanalysis" and edits *The Candidate Journal: Psychoanalytic Currents*.

Maria Khotimsky
is a Senior Lecturer in Russian at the Massachusetts Institute of Technology. Her research interests focus on the institutional and cultural history of literary translation in Russia, Silver Age Russian Poetry, contemporary poetry, as well as translingual poetry. Dr. Khotimsky is a co-editor and contributor to *The Poetry and Poetics of Olga Sedakova: Origins, Philosophies, Points of Contention* (University of Wisconsin Press, 2019). Her other publications include book

chapters and articles devoted to poetry translation in the Soviet era, the history of the World Literature Publishing House, and translation in the works of major Russian poets ("Cvetaeva and Translation," in *Brill Companion to Marina Cvetaeva*, ed. Sibelan Forrester).

Svetlana Maslinskaya
is Researcher at the Research Center for Russian Children's Literature at the Institute of Russian Literature (Pushkinskij Dom) in St. Petersburg and Senior lecturer at the Department of Literature, St. Petersburg State University of Arts and Culture. Dr. Maslinskaya teaches children's literature, literary theory, and sociology of children's reading and has an extensive publication record in Soviet children's literature, the history of Soviet childhood, and the Soviet Pioneer organization. She has recently published a chapter on Kornej Chukovskij in *Russian Literature of the 20th Century*, eds. N. Lejderman, M. Lipovetsky, and M. Litovskaja (2014). Dr. Maslinskaya is a member of the editorial board of the journal Детские чтения (*Children's Readings: Studies in Children's Literature*).

Oleg Minin
is a Visiting Assistant Professor at Bard College, where he teaches Russian art, literature, and language. He is editor at large of Brill's *Companions to the Slavic World*, author of numerous articles on the visual and literary culture of the Russian Silver Age and the Avant-Garde, and co-editor (with Marcus Levitt) of the 19th volume of the journal *Experiment* (2013) devoted to the study of the satirical press of the 1905 Revolution. Dr. Minin is co-author of *One Hundred and One Photographs: Emil Otto Hoppé and the Ballets Russes* (with John E. Bowlt and Graham Howe, 2018).

Lora Wheeler Mjolsness
is Lecturer and Director of the Program of Russian Studies in the Department of European Languages and Studies, University of California, Irvine. She teaches courses on Soviet and New Russian Cinema and on History of Soviet Animation, including new developments in the Post-Soviet era. Dr. Mjolsness has co-edited a series of papers, "Traditions and Transitions: Russian Language Teaching in the United States," in *Russian Language Journal* (2014), and published several articles on Soviet and Russian animation, including "Vertov's *Soviet Toys*: Commerce, Commercialization and Cartoons," in *Studies in Russian and Soviet Cinema* 2:3 (2008), and "Russian Web Animation from St. Petersburg to Siberia," in *Animation Journal 13* (2005). Dr. Mjolsness is co-author of *She Animates: Gender in Soviet and Russian Animation* (with Michele Leigh, 2020).

Ainsley Morse

is Assistant Professor of Russian at Dartmouth College, and translator. Her book project, *Word Play: Unofficial Poetry and Children's Literature in the Soviet Union*, traces the interactions between Avant-Garde poetics and Soviet children's literature from the early Avant-Garde through the unofficial poetry of the Thaw period. Dr. Morse's published book-length translations include *I Live I See: Selected Poems by Vsevolod Nekrasov* (with Bela Shayevich, 2017), Andrej Sen-Senkov's *Anatomical Theater* (with Peter Golub, 2014) and *Kholin 66: Diaries and Poems of Igor Kholin* (2017). Her other translations from Russian and Bosnian/Croatian/Serbian have appeared in journals and other venues.

Ana Hedberg Olenina

is an Assistant Professor of Comparative Literature and Media Studies at Arizona State University. Her main research focuses on the Soviet Avant-Garde, while her broader interests lie at the juncture of early film history and media theory, with an emphasis on historical configurations of sensory experience, emotional response, embodiment, and immersive environments. Dr. Hedberg Olenina is currently completing a monograph entitled *Psychomotor Aesthetics: Movement and Affect in Russian and American Modernity*. Her essays appeared in *Discourse*, *Film History*, *Apparatus*, and *Киноведческие записки* (*Film Experts' Annals*), as well as several anthologies in the USA and Russia. In collaboration with Maxim Pozdorovkin, she has co-curated two DVD releases of restored Soviet silents (*Miss Mend* and *Early Landmarks of Soviet Film*) by Flicker Alley, Inc.

Larissa Rudova

is Yale B. and Lucille D. Griffith Professor in Modern Languages and Professor of Russian at Pomona College. She is the editor, with Marina Balina, of *Russian Children's Literature and Culture* (2008) as well as co-editor of *Russian Children's Literature: Changing Paradigms*, a special issue of *Slavic and East European Studies Journal* on Russian Children's Literature (49: 2, Summer 2005). Dr. Rudova is the author of *Pasternak's Early Fiction and the Cultural Vanguard* (1994) and of *Understanding Boris Pasternak* (1997). Her current research focuses on Post-Soviet Russian letters, culture, film, and children's literature.

Olga Voronina

is Associate Professor of Russian and Director of the Russian and Eurasian Studies Program at Bard College. She has co-edited and co-translated, with Brian Boyd, Vladimir Nabokov's *Letters to Véra* (2015), as well as published papers and articles on Soviet literature of the Cold War, Post-Soviet transformation of the Russian literary canon, children's literature, and Nabokov's art and metaphysics. Dr. Voronina contributed a chapter on Post-Soviet children's literature to *Современная русская литература (1990-е гг. – начало 21 века)* (*Contemporary Russian Literature (1990s–early 21st century)*), which she co-edited with Svetlana Timina and Vladimir Vasiljev (2005, 2011).

Tatiana Voronina
is a historian and researcher working on social and cultural history of the late Soviet Union, memory studies, and oral history at the Department of East European History of the University of Zurich and the book review editor at *Laboratorium: Russian Review of the Social Studies*. Her current project's title is "The Late Soviet Village: People, Institutions, and Things between the Socialist Cult of Urbanity and the Ruralization of Urban Lifestyles." Formerly a visiting scholar at the International Institute of Social History, Amsterdam, Netherlands, and a Fulbright fellow at the University of California, Berkley, she also served as coordinator and researcher at the Oral History Center at the European University in St. Petersburg. Dr. Voronina has published essays on the history of the Soviet Red Cross, representations of the Siege of Leningrad, the oral history of Bailkal-Amur Mainline Railroad, and aesthetics of Socialist Realism. Dr. Voronina's book, *Помнить по-нашему: Соцреалистический историзм и блокада Ленинграда* (*Remembering It Our Way: Socialist-Realist Historicism and the Siege of Lenigrad*) was published in 2018.

Sara Pankenier Weld
is an Associate Professor in the Department of Germanic and Slavic Studies at the University of California, Santa Barbara, where she teaches Russian and Comparative Literature. Her research interests include Russian literature, comparative literature, and Scandinavian literature; Avant-Garde literature, art, and theory; modernism; word and image; childhood, children's literature, and picturebooks. Dr. Weld's previous publications include articles on a variety of Russian writers, artists, and filmmakers, which have appeared in books and journals, such as *Scando-Slavica, Slavic Review, Slavic and East European Journal*, and *Russian Language Journal*. Her interdisciplinary study of Russian literature, art, and theory, *Voiceless Vanguard: The Infantilist Aesthetic of the Russian Avant-Garde*, was published in 2014. Her second book, a study of word and image entitled *An Ecology of the Russian Avant-Garde Picturebook* (2018), treats the interactions of art, ideology, and censorship.

INTRODUCTION

"The Only Universal National Text": On the Centennial of Soviet Children's Literature and Film

Olga Voronina

1   A Celebration or a Commemoration? Relating to the Soviet Past through the Literary and Cinematic Children's Canon

Kornej Chukovskij's first long poem for children, "Ваня и крокодил" ("Vanja and Crocodile"), later known simply as "Крокодил" ("Crocodile"), appeared in twelve installments in the January-December 1917 issues of the magazine *Для детей* (*For Children*) – a free companion to the popular journal *Нива* (*The Grainfield*), which Chukovskij edited.[1] Its main protagonist saves the city of Petrograd twice: first by overcoming the nasty Crocodile who swallows citizens and their pets, and later by crushing down a revolt of wild animals who take a little girl hostage because they want their relatives liberated from a city-park prison. Vanja Vasil'chikov sets the zoo animals free on the condition that they promise to behave and live peacefully with others. In return, the animals praise him, love him, bake pies for him, and even polish his boots.[2] An echo of the historical events of 1917 rather than a prophetic tale, Chukovskij's story could not hint at the chaos of the early post-revolutionary years or portend the personality cult that would disfigure millions of lives twenty years down the road. And yet, the happy resolution of "Крокодил," with its insistence on the possibility of a radical solution to a political crisis, followed by a mass indoctrination and re-distribution of social benefits, is obviously a nod to the utopian thinking that ushered in the revolution itself.

Although *Нива* folded nine months after its young readers had learned about Vanja's feats, the impact of Chukovskij's *pièce de résistance* is still tangible. The publication of "Крокодил" at the end of the revolutionary year marked a connection between a string of historical events that brought about a new, politically determined, outlook on childhood and the origins of the

---

1   Ben Hellman, *Fairy Tales and True Stories: The History of Russian Literature for Children and Young People (1574-2010)*, Leiden and Boston 2013, 292.
2   Kornej Chukovskij, "Ваня и крокодил," in *Для детей* 1-12 (1917). See also the early edition of the book: Chukovskij, *Приключения Крокодила Крокодиловича*, ills. Re-Mi. Petrograd 1919.

Soviet literature for children. Oriented towards child heroism, internationalism, communal values, and atheism, and replete with references to individuals' struggle for freedom, the new children's literature emerged simultaneously with the post-revolutionary upheaval that led to the formation of the early Soviet state. Soviet filmmaking for children followed the same trajectory. It began in 1918, when the first Soviet film designated for young audiences came out – Aleksandr Arkatov's thirty-minute-long *Сигнал* (*The Signal*). Children's cinematography became a real cultural force a few years later, with the release in 1923 of Ivan Perestiani's immensely popular *Красные дьяволята* (*The Little Red Devils*). The film was based on Pavel Bliachin's eponymous novella (1921) about three underage military scouts who valiantly served "the glorious Red Army, the great guard of free labor." In 1927, sixty percent of young respondents to a question about their favorite film named *Красные дьяволята* as a beloved moving picture that had also informed their belief system.[3]

If the intersection of the hundredth anniversary of the October revolution of 1917 and of the centennial of Soviet literary and cinematic production for the young may seem unsettling due to the brutality of the social upheaval and the violent means of the new Russian government, the concurrence of tragic events in Soviet history and the appearance of some of the most popular children's works in literature and cinema is even more uncanny. For example, the printing of Chukovskij's other bestseller, a tale about the animal kingdom's descent into darkness, *Краденое солнце* (*The Stolen Sun*, 1927), preceded Stalin's notorious collectivization campaign with its alleged ten million peasant victims.[4] In 1937, in the midst of Great Terror, Daniil Charms published, in book form, his translation of Wilhelm Busch's *Plisch und Plum* (*Плюх и Плих*), a series of merry adventures of two obnoxious boys totally oblivious to the danger into which they are putting themselves and others. The Battle of Stalingrad was raging when Samuil Marshak wrote *Двенадцать месяцев* (*Twelve Months*, 1943), a play about a poor, unloved girl who earns a magic ring and overcomes her foes by turning them into sleigh dogs. The releases of Ivan Ivanov-Vano's animated films *Снегурочка* (*The Snow Maiden*, 1951) and *Сказка о мертвой царевне и о семи богатырях* (*The Tale of the Dead Princess and Seven Bogatyrs*, 1952), which celebrated Russianness, took place during the notorious anti-cosmopolitan campaign. There is historical logic in these coincidences, but it may not be immediately noticeable. Moreover, the juxta-

---

3 A. A. Sal'nikova, A. P. Burmistrov, "Советское детское игровое кино 20-х годов XX века и его юные зрители," in *Ученые записки Казанского университета* 156:3 (2014), 134-5.
4 Helen Rappaport, *Joseph Stalin: A Biographical Companion*, Santa Barbara, CA 1999, 53.

position of the political events and creative accomplishments of Soviet children's authors goes against the not uncommon perception of Soviet works for children as a phenomenon that belongs to the sphere of unhindered artistic self-expression.[5] Without detecting the connection between history and Soviet cultural production for children, however, it is hard to know when the oeuvre should be celebrated and applauded – and when it should be mourned as a fragment of the national trauma, which, if left unhealed, will continue to contaminate the present.[6]

When we consider the correlation between the dramatic impact of the 1917 Revolution on the country and its citizens, and the powerful grip in which the "Socialist [...] artistically-bright" children's works have held their audiences, the momentousness of the overlap between the Soviet children's literature and film and the tragic course of Soviet history becomes more pronounced.[7] It was Maksim Gor'kij who, in 1916, prompted Chukovskij to stop merely blaming inept children's authors and publishers and to create a long fairytale in verse, with references to modern-day realities: "Today, one well-made children's book will do more good than a dozen polemical essays," Gor'kij allegedly proclaimed.[8] According to Jurij Tynjanov, "Крокодил" annulled the "Lilliputian" Russian children's literature and opened up new horizons for authors willing to experiment with ideas and form, stop treating youngsters condescendingly, and engage their readers in verbal play.[9] After Chukovskij's little book, a true "insurgency [переворот]" in cultural production for children ensued, Tynjanov maintained, paving the way for other authors' "further development."[10]

---

5   Reviewing *Inside the Rainbow: Russian Children's Literature 1920-1935*, Philip Pullman comments on the "sort of freedom that let [Soviet children's writers and artists] produce work like this [i.e. of great imaginative power]," while recognizing that "there was always an air of threat in the background." Pullman, "How children's books thrived under Stalin," in *The Guardian*, October 11, 2013. This opinion may be currently heard on Russian television and Post-Soviet radio programs, such as Boris Paramonov's *Русские вопросы* (*Russian Questions*) on *Radio Svoboda* ⟨http://modernlib.net/books/paramonov_boris/russkie_voprosi_19972005_programma_radio_svoboda/read_52/⟩ (Accessed August 12, 2018). The perception of children's literature as "pure art [чистое искусство]" made its way into a discussion published in *Детские чтения* journal in 2012, where Ol'ga Maeots marked it as problematic. "Анкета ДЧ," in *Детские чтения* 1 (2012), 171-172.
6   Alexander Etkind, *Warped Mourning: Stories of the Undead in the Land of the Unburied* (*Cultural Memory in the Present*), Stanford, CA 2013, 14-15.
7   Maksim Gor'kij, "Литературу – детям," in *Правда*, June 11, 1933, 1.
8   Kornej Chukovskij, *Об этой книжке: Стихи*, Moscow 1961, 7.
9   Ju. Tynjanov, "Корней Чуковский," in *Детская литература* 4 (1939), 24-25.
10 Ibid.

But just as the October Revolution precipitated the establishment of the authoritarian regime eager to control its citizens' every thought and action, the revolution in children's literature and film led to the creation of a well-organized, state-funded system of ideological manipulation of the country's youngest people – the boys and girls on whose loyalty the regime ultimately depended. A dazzling array of works for the Soviet youth was initially created by the writers and illustrators who first coagulated around more or less autonomous periodicals, writers' unions and publishing houses (Студия детской литературы [The Children's Literature Studio], Радуга [The Rainbow], *Воробей* [*The Sparrow*], *Новый Робинзон* [*The New Robinson*]), and later, around state-controlled institutions, such as the Leningrad Section of Detgiz directed by Marshak or Sojuzdetfil'm, initially electrified by Margarita Barskaja's artistic energy.[11] By the mid-1920s, however, they began to give way to the books and films that combined brilliant form with transparently ideological and heavily didactic content, such as embedded messages targeting enemies of the state. Over the course of almost eight post-revolutionary decades, an immense of creative output by hundreds of talented writers and film directors has accumulated. The importance of this accomplishment is hard to overestimate: it conquered the hearts and minds of Soviet citizens in spite of its "revolutionizing," collectivist, nationalist, and pro-militarist content.

Even of greater consequence is the fact that Soviet literary and cinematic works for children continue to engage a variety of audiences now. Not only several generations of Soviet citizens have been entertained, delighted, consoled, and inspired, as well as taught, morally instructed and ideologically inculcated by Soviet authors and directors, but they have also experienced their favorite books, films, and cartoons more than once: as first-time readers and viewers, as parents, and, possibly, as grand- and great-grandparents. This is why Miron Petrovskij, in his insightful study of Soviet juvenile reading, called children's books produced in the USSR "the only universal national text."[12] People who came of age in the Soviet era eventually transformed children's literature into the "cultural foundation" of the nation, Petrovskij suggested, by mythologizing and re-mythologizing literary works encountered in their youth.[13]

---

11 Detgiz, or Детское государственное издательство (The State Children's Publishing House) was established in 1933, with its offices opening simultaneously in Moscow and Leningrad. Samuil Marshak was its first and most influential editor-in-chief. Sojuzdetfil'm (Союздетфильм, or Советская киностудия детского и юношеского фильма [The Soviet Children's and Youth Film Studio]), was organized in Moscow in 1936.

12 Miron Petrovskij, *Книги нашего детства*, St. Petersburg 2006, 9-10.

13 Ibid.

The value of Soviet children's literature and film as the cultural foundation of the nation is the subject of *The Brill Companion to Children's Literature and Film*, while the deficiency of awareness of its ambiguous impact on the Soviet and Post-Soviet society is the focal point of this introduction. In bringing twelve essays by contemporary scholars who study Soviet cultural production for children to readers' attention, I seek to highlight the conceptual frameworks employed by the authors themselves, as well as the contemporary critical discourse, including responses to the modern-day omnipresence of children's works created under the authoritarian Soviet regime that are generated by Post-Soviet readers, educators, and publishers. I also rely on Alexander Etkind's exploration of historical Soviet trauma, and especially on his study of mechanisms of cultural memory that hamper collective self-reflection. Like most contributors to the *Companion*, I believe that the fear of historical analysis, or the Russian society's perception of its past as fiction, slows down the post-Soviet project of replacing old Soviet children's books and movies with those that explore the harrowing outcome of the twentieth century and deal with difficult subjects of great importance, i.e. state violence, historical trauma, and the impact of totalitarian regime on people's thinking and behavior.[14]

As stated by Etkind, the unanalyzed, improperly mourned past produces "dispersed, fragmented and scary [...] phantoms" that haunt the present.[15] And indeed, every short story geared towards young Soviet readers, and every cartoon produced by a Soviet film studio is stamped with history's finger- or boot-prints. Detecting these traces and reading them as clues of Soviet society's self-understanding and collective identity of child audiences is the principal task of contemporary critics, researchers, teachers, and parents. The approach gains even greater urgency, given the insufficiency of nation-wide efforts to deal with historical truths, such as the idea pointed out by the scholar Elena Prokhorova that "propaganda of Soviet adult achievements aimed at children and the propaganda of happy childhood aimed at adults" was the

---

14 For an illuminating discussion of this project, see "Детям до 16-ти: как цензура пришла в подростковую литературу," in *Lenta.ru*, May 27, 2015, ⟨https://lenta.ru/articles/2015/05/27/teenagers/⟩ (Accessed December 22, 2017). It should be noted that children's books that explore the 20th century historical trauma do appear and are currently making their way into classrooms and personal libraries. Ekaterina Murashova, Dina Sabitova, Mariam Petrosjan, Ol'ga Gromova, Julija Jakovleva, Nikolaj and Svetlana Ponomarev, and Marjana Kozyreva are among the notable authors who address the questions of political terror, displacement, the subjugation of the individual by the totalitarian state, orphanhood, and identity crisis within a rigidly politicized society.

15 Etkind, *Warped Mourning*, 16-17.

essence of Soviet children's literature and film, notable exceptions notwithstanding.[16]

There are plenty of examples of the "dispersed" and "fragmented" perception of Soviet history in modern-day Russia. One of them comes from a 2013 interview with the Russian Minister of Culture, Vladimir Medinskij, a journalist by education, who expresses his strong opposition to the "liberals'" demand for in-depth reflection on tragic events in Soviet history. When his interviewer suggested that the Soviet past remained modern Russian society's main problematic issue, Medinskij replied:

> The only true view of Soviet history, and equally of all national history in general, is simple and obvious: our ancestors, having endured enormous burdens in terms of their labor and colossal losses, left us a great country. We need to know how they have done this, we must cherish and respect their heritage, and we must build our future life, pushing ourselves against [our past].[17]

Medinskij's response is part of the official government position on how Soviet history should be perceived in Russia today, but it can also be seen as an infantile view of the past – or, rather, as a recollection of it by someone who experiences facts as fiction.[18] Russia's leading cultural manager is ready to formulate "the only true view" of history by accentuating his country's glory

---

16 Elena Prokhorova, "A Traditionalist in the Land of Innovators: The Paradoxes of Sergei Mikhalkov," in Marina Balina and Larissa Rudova, eds., *Russian Children's Literature and Culture*, New York and London 2008, 295.

17 The journalist did not merely pose a question about Russia's contemporary views on the Soviet past, but asked the minister to suggest a course of action for healing historical trauma: "According to my observations, the main reason for conflict [главный повод для раздора] in modern Russia is not the last thirteen years, but the Soviet era – people test one another in their relation to it. What can be done about it?.." Elena Jampol'skaja, "Министр культуры РФ Владимир Мединский: 'Без идеологии человек становится животным'" in *Газета "Культура,"* April 9, 2013 ⟨http://portal-kultura.ru/articles/kolonka-glavnogo-redaktora/8642-ministr-kultury-rf-vladimir-medinskiy-bez-ideologii-chelovek-stanovitsya-zhivotnym/⟩ (Accessed November 2, 2017).

18 At a meeting with history students in November 2014, the President of Russia Vladimir Putin, having called himself historians' "colleague," formulated the task for all who work within the discipline. Most characteristically, he stressed the need to manipulate the country's population by persuading the people of the unbiased nature of historical facts which may or may not be objective: "Our goal is ⟨…⟩ to convince the overwhelming majority of the country's citizens of the correctness, objectiveness, of our approaches and present this result to our society. To win minds, to inspire people so that they them-

rather than suggesting guidelines for dealing with people's sacrifice, those "colossal losses" he mentions in passing. Numerous Soviet children's books and films – from Lev Kassil''s *Великое противостояние* (*The Great Opposition*, 1940) to Vasilij Zhuravlev's *Мальчик с окраины* (*A Boy from the Suburbs*, 1947) and from Valentina Oseeva's *Васек Трубачев и его товарищи* (*Vasek Trubachev and His Comrades*, 1947-1951) to Ilja Frez's adaptation of Evgenij Shvarc's *Первоклассница* (*The First-Grader*, 1948) – which Medinskij probably grew up reading and watching – created a similar template for complacent historical self-reflection. Not only did these literary and cinematic works provide a basis for present-day cultural policies and practices, which were introduced and implemented by those who are now between thirty and seventy years old, but they also continue to affect the perception of Soviet history by young people who are still learning about their country's past. Russian publishers have reprinted hundreds of works of children's poetry and fiction written in the 1920s-80s. Who buys them and for what purpose? How well do Russian citizens understand the social practices and ideological clichés that they pass on to their children with each nostalgically cherished Soviet book? What compels managers of TV channels to screen Soviet-era films or cartoons as part of prime time programming for children? And how does Medinskij's stance correspond to the government policy regarding children's literature, with its emphasis on the need to cultivate "lofty civic and moral guidelines" in the current generation of readers?[19]

Some publishers realize that reprinting a Soviet children's book or issuing a literary work that contains references to the totalitarian past requires an act of "estrangement" on the readers' part.[20] They believe that, for a contempo-

---

selves would take an active position based on the knowledge you present as objective [побудить людей самих занять активную позицию на основе тех знаний, которые вы презентуете в качестве объективных]." ⟨http://kremlin.ru/events/president/news/46951⟩ (Accessed December 21, 2017).

19 Russian Book Union, "Национальная программа поддержки и развития чтения в РФ," ⟨http://www.bookunion.ru/doc_news/концепция_блок_ТП%20(1).pdf⟩ (Accessed December 2, 2017).

20 One of the models for such an approach is the Moscow publisher Clever/Клевер. See its recent "Советская серия" ["The Soviet Series"] of children's books, replete with maps, period photographs, and color inserts with propaganda posters, for ex.: Arkadij Gajdar, *Военная тайна. Голубая чашка. Тимур и его команда. Чук и Гек* (*The Military Secret. A Blue Cup. Timur and His Team. Chuk and Gek*), Moscow 2014; Grigorij Belych and Leonid Panteleev, *Республика ШКИД* (*The Republic of Shkid*), Moscow 2014. Another example of a canonical Soviet children's book perceptively introduced in historical context is Chukovskij's *Тараканище* (*The Big Cockroach*, 2013) issued by the Moscow publishing house Vozvrashchenie with illustrations by Nastja Sajfulina and a preface by Elena Chukovskaja.

rary child or adolescent, the Soviet reality appears both tragic and enigmatic, and to traverse its narrative and historical terrains, children would need an elaborate map or a skillful guide. This is why an editor might supplement a reprinted work of fiction with an introduction that explains historical realities of the Brezhnev era, a photographic essay that demonstrates what life was like fifty or seventy years ago, or an insert with pioneer insignia which could be cut out. More often than not, however, the tone of these introductions is either soothing or exultant, while the attitude readers are expected to develop towards the symbols of the Soviet state is playful if not downright nostalgic. Take, for example, Valentin Kurbatov's afterword to Aleksandr Blinov's novella for elementary school students, *Море, бабка и охламон* (*The Sea, the Granny, and the Dumb Kid*, 2017), published by Nigma. It is a recent literary work, and not a re-print of a Soviet book for children, but it does eulogize the Soviet lifestyle in a way that is similar to children's books of the 1950s-80s. Kurbatov mentions Soviet-era monuments and party leaders that appear on the pages of Blinov's book as remnants of the past that may be unfamiliar to contemporary readers. That said, in his understanding, the southern village where "охламон" spends his summers represents an untainted "paradise," no matter what time it was and who presided over the country:

> How blissfully the entire village enters the book, with its sea, reedy banks, clouds, heat, May bugs, constipation in cows, dogs, pigs, ankle-deep dust, stars, and the ever-present Lenin covered in silver paint in front of the House of Culture. He has a cap in his hand, which makes it immediately clear that he is not a local, for one would freeze without a cap in the winter, while it is so hot in the summer that not only intelligent monuments should hide, but silly chickens as well.
>
> The painted Lenin alone lets one guess that this is Soviet childhood and that somewhere Chrushchev is banging on something with his fist, while Brezhnev knits his brows, but they bang and frown in jest, without scaring the village kids who have never heard about these guys.[21]

Kurbatov praises Blinov for his alluding to history by means of hilarious rhetorical and figurative gestures: Chrushchev and Brezhnev are a joke, Lenin is a badly made theatrical prop, while living in the shadow of his monument is a blissful reality, which the grown-up author longingly recalls. This representation may seem innocent, except it is not. The notion of the Soviet past as

---

21   Aleksandr Blinov, *Море, бабка и охламон*, Moscow 2017, 306.

a "paradise" resonates with those who have recently outgrown children's fiction: Russian young adults. A poll of university students conducted by the National Research University Higher School of Economics reveals that those who are eighteen to twenty-five years old today idealize the Soviet Union, seeing in it a fairytale world straight out of a book or a film. Their perception may have been formed by Blinov's portrayal of a southern village with the revolution leader's statue in the middle, a May Day parade described by Sergej Michalkov, or a scene from an animated short produced by Sojuzmul'tfil'm. One of the respondents, who is twenty-four, imagines the Soviet Union as "a land of happy, smiling, laboring people, and policemen who also smile. [...] And there should certainly be a festival somewhere: the folk form a merry crowd [весело толпятся], singing some kind of a soulful song. The people work, but none of them complains at their fate, saying how uneasy their life is. Everyone is happy with everything."[22] Another interviewee, who is eighteen, says that his or her "first association with the Soviet Union is a circle of dancing people [хоровод] wearing various national costumes: they are embracing one another and performing a Russian folk dance. Or simply something with dance, with smiles. In other words, it is some kind of brightness, of vivacity [яркость, бодрость]. What has remained from Soviet films or cartoons: kindness, tolerance – those very important principles which the Soviet Union relied on."[23]

Young men and women in contemporary Russia may not identify with the cheerful folk in the timeless Soviet pastoral, but the poll demonstrates that their collective imaginary is nevertheless contaminated by the ahistorical, infantile visions of the country's recent and not-so recent past – the kind of apparitions that Michalkov's poems, Marshak's plays, and their modern nostalgic renderings generate skillfully and even brilliantly. And although many Soviet children's authors and film directors represented the brave new world and its young citizens' ways of coping with the Soviet historical reality with great nuance – from Grigorij Belych and Leonid Panteleev to Boris Vasiljev and Vladimir Zheleznikov, and from Ilja Frez and Nadezhda Kosheverova to Dinara Asanova and Rolan Bykov – it is the blatantly optimistic qualities of the "universal national text" that seem to be living on in the post-Soviet collective memory. Having received their visions of Soviet "kindness" and "tol-

---

22   Viktoria Voloshina, "Страна счастливых людей и улыбающихся милиционеров," in *Gazeta.ru*, ⟨https://www.gazeta.ru/25_years_without_the_USSR/8274407.shtml⟩ (Accessed November 1, 2017).

23   Ibid.

erance" from the books and animated films created when their parents were children, contemporary young adults may continue to eagerly share the same fare with their children – and thus propagate the Soviet vision of "happiness" that needs to be reconsidered drastically. It is, therefore, not an exaggeration to say that the transmission of the collective Soviet identity in the national children's literature and film produced over the course of the past several decades has never stopped. Moreover, the infantilizing element of Soviet children's culture, embodied by Medinskij and identified by Eduard Nadtochij as its main quality, appears to be the most attractive and thus, most easily transferrable element of the Soviet psyche.[24]

It would be too naïve to suggest, however, that publishers who reprint Soviet fiction at the expense of pre-revolutionary, translated, or critically minded contemporary authors,[25] librarians who recommend Soviet children's books, or adults who choose reading and viewing matter for their offspring, merely invite Russian youth to re-live the country's past as a worry-free time full of wonders and adventure. Nostalgia for the imaginary Soviet happiness is only one motivating factor behind the official endorsement and popular recycling of Soviet children's literature and film. The second impetus is part of Russia's current national idea, with its reversal to the basics of Soviet ideology, such

---

24 The critic calls the infantilism of Soviet children's culture the "fundamental anthropological prosthesis for the construction of social solidarity" within the society dealing with state terror and its aftermath. In Nadtochij's view, the Stalinist regime and its less bloodthirsty, but no less resilient Soviet and post-Soviet clones, owe their longevity to the ideal image of a Soviet paradise. This trope was fashioned by the culture that targeted children but, in actuality, could reach everyone. Eduard Nadtochij, "Тимур и его arcana: социально-антропологическое значение советской 'революции детства' в 1920-30-е годы," in *Социология власти* 3 (2014), 96.

25 Specialists representing a variety of publishing houses and children's periodicals repeatedly articulate the demand for works of contemporary children's authors to appear in print. This means that while the players on the market of children's fiction realize the need to replace the old repertoire of children's books with a new one, they are still restricted by the buyers' choice of a more traditional children's reading – i.e. the books pertaining to the Soviet era. See, for example, the interview with Tatjana Androsenko, editor-in-chief of *Мурзилка* (*Murzilka*), a popular children's journal which was launched in 1924: "If you hear somewhere that there is no children's literature today, do not believe this; we do have children's literature, we have good authors. They simply have to be supported, we must publish them more often, give books by young authors a chance to come out. Publishing houses need to be braver in deciding to publish them, for publishers are still afraid to try." "Интервью с главным редактором," in *Мурзилка*, April 12, 2014, ⟨http://www.murzilka.org/home/about-magazine/smi-o-zhurnale/intervju-s-glavnym-redaktorom/interfaks/⟩ (Accessed December 21, 2017).

as political vigilance and loyalty to the state.²⁶ The continuous readiness to embrace Soviet children's culture thus lies in the present-day administrators', educators', and parents' desire to never let go of the literature and film that inspired patriotism and prompted children to be industrious, well-disciplined, and goal-oriented. Finally, there is a collective longing for "commendable" works for children, the kind of literary and cinematic "golden standard" that would "equally contain classical works, modern, and Soviet literature, as well as some additional branch of the quality literature that teenagers like."²⁷ This idealized list of children's works is currently a subject of heated discussions: most critics and *kulturträgers* require teachers and parents to provide children with specially selected books and films that "educate the soul and develop consciousness and conscience [сознание и совесть]"²⁸ – an imperative that coincides with former guidelines for Soviet children's authors and educators – while only a minority of others reject them as cultural products full of "meaning pushed down from above."²⁹

Nostalgia for a happy Soviet childhood, the recognition of the need to instill the moral and ideological "substance" in Russian youth that would turn them into decent individuals and good citizens, and the shared perception of Soviet children's books and film as "quality" works of art are the three characteristics that have upheld their value in contemporary Russian society. References to them have, for one, dominated the "Campaign for the Unified Reading List" in post-Soviet schools. This is clear from the recent interview of the Russian

---

26   See Rosalind J. Marsh, *Literature, History, and Identity in Post-Soviet Russia, 1991-2006*, Oxford, Bern, New York 2007; *The Post-Soviet Russian Media: Conflicting Signals*, eds. Birgit Beumers, Stephen Hutchings, Natalia Rulyova, New York 2009; Marija Petrova, *Национальная идея России: история и современность*, Izhevsk 2005; Boris Noordenbos, *Post-Soviet Literature and the Search for a Russian Identity*, New York 2016.

27   Roman Harrasov, "Завести тренера по чтению или другие способы приучить детей любить книги," in *My Life*, September 26, 2016 ⟨https://life.ru/t/звук/908442/zaviesti_trieniera_po_chtieniiu_i_drughiie_sposoby_priuchit_dietiei_liubit_knighi⟩ (Accessed December 18, 2017).

28   "Детям до 16-ти: Как цензура пришла…" ⟨https://lenta.ru/articles/2015/05/27/teenagers/⟩ (Accessed December 22, 2017); see also Prime Minister Dmitrij Medvedev's remarks at a round table dedicated to the first literary festival on Red Square: "Книжный фестиваль Красная площадь," June 3, 2016, ⟨http://m.government.ru/news/23262/#ved⟩ (Accessed December 2, 2017). Notably, while the Prime Minister called the Soviet practice of having the government "strictly control what was published from the ideological standpoint" unacceptable, he also said that there was "a definite benefit" resulting from that situation: "It created a chance to produce quality literature. And that, of course, formulated the people's perception ⟨of literature⟩, the children's perception."

29   "Завести тренера по чтению…" ⟨https://life.ru/t/звук/908442/zaviesti_trieniera_po_chtieniiu_i_drughiie_sposoby_priuchit_dietiei_liubit_knighi⟩ (Accessed December 18, 2017).

Minister of Education Olga Vasiljeva, who is working on the "Golden Standard" project in alliance with the Russian Orthodox Church.[30] In a 2016 interview, Vasiljeva recalled that Arkadij Gajdar's *Тимур и его команда* (*Timur and His Team*, 1940) once prompted her to begin reading fiction as a child. She remembered a pioneer leader who read the book to her class artistically, "using different voices." She also spoke fondly of her father, who, having heard about the recital, bought a two-volume edition of Gajdar for his enchanted daughter. Finally, Vasiljeva explained that, in her life, *Тимур и его команда* took precedence over other children's fiction, such as fairytales, which she began to consume later. By telling this story, the minister sent a clear message to teachers and parents about the book which, for her, represented the master text of children's literature as a whole.[31] It is only natural, then, that in discussions that followed the "Golden Standard" initiative, educators began to suggest such ideologically charged novels as Nikolaj Ostrovskij's *Как закалялась сталь* (*How the Steel Was Tempered*, 1934) and Aleksandr Fadeev's *Молодая гвардия* (*The Young Guard*, 1946, 1951). They wanted these "quality," and "ethical" texts to return to the obligatory reading program in middle and high schools, while completely ignoring their undesirable ideological messages.[32]

Post-Soviet critical discourse concerning children's reading and media also reflects the national perception of Soviet children's literature and film as the primary phenomena associated with three loaded notions: "happiness," moral and patriotic "substance," and aesthetic "quality." Darja Bucharova's essay on the value of reprinted Soviet books issued by the publishing house Rech' is a representative example. The critic eulogizes children's literature of the past:

> These novellas and short stories touch the depths of our souls; they make us laugh and cry sincerely. Some of the realities [described in these

---

[30] "Нужен 'золотой канон' для школьной программы по литературе – Патриарх Кирилл," in *Православное Закамье*, May 25, 2016, ⟨http://pravchelny.ru/all_publications/publications/?ID=13872⟩ (Accessed December 21, 2017); Elena Selivanova, "Васильева одобрила список школьной литературы, предложенный патриархом," September 24, 2016, ⟨https://www.opentown.org/news/127309/⟩ (Accessed December 8, 2017).

[31] Aleksandr Milkus, Ksenija Konjuchova, "Министр образования и науки Ольга Васильева: 'В школе будем наводить порядок. Полумер не ждите!'" in *Комсомольская правда*, October 5, 2016, ⟨https://www.spb.kp.ru/daily/26589/3605216/⟩ (Accessed December 8, 2017).

[32] Marija Michajlovskaja, "В Министерстве образования поддержали идею создания обязательного списка школьной литературы," in *Парламентская газета*, November 13, 2016, ⟨https://www.pnp.ru/social/2016/11/13/v-ministerstve-obrazovaniya-podderzhali-ideyu-sozdaniya-obyazatelnogo-spiska-shkolnoy-literatury.html⟩ (Accessed December 8, 2017).

books] are gone forever: there are no pioneer ties, "courtyard" friends have turned into "internet" buddies, and one can always call his or her child on a cell phone. But time has no power over these truly morally good [по-настоящему добрыми] novellas, for they are about children with strong characters, who will unfailingly grow into bigger people, Men with a capital M.³³

Many other Russian cultural practitioners ruminate on the subject of Soviet literature for children with greater nuance than Bucharova who does not see how theological and hagiographic, heroic and didactic aspects of Soviet children's literature defy the intellectual, aesthetic, or spiritual needs of modern young readers.³⁴ And yet, Bucharova's essay is exemplary of the modern-day thinking on the merit of Soviet cultural production for children and its continued existence as the "universal national text." For her, the "moral goodness" of Soviet fiction is true, while its ability to bring up ethical and loyal individuals promises Russia a better future. The notion of "bigger people," which Bucharova relies on, is thick with ideologically loaded historical and literary associations – from Nikolaj Tichonov's people of steel who should be made into "nails" for Socialist construction ("гвозди бы делать из этих людей") to Gajdar's Mal'chish-Kibal'chish, and from extolled party leaders to pioneer heroes.³⁵ Even so, the critic does not explicate these objectionable references in her eulogy, believing that parents who are reading her review have already appropriated the concept. Thus, according to Bucharova, the value of Soviet children's books lies in their ability to facilitate greatness of the future "Men with a capital M." This vague but potent quality seems to eliminate the difference between the pedagogical and political goals of the totalitarian state, under the auspices of which these books were created, and the current-day cultural politics.

The centennial of Soviet cultural production for children reflects a hundred years of very specific "culture wars" – the political and aesthetic fight

---

33 Darja Bucharova, "Машина времени издательства 'Речь,'" in *Материнство*, November 27, 2014, ⟨https://materinstvo.ru/art/9681⟩ (Accessed December 2, 2017).

34 See, for example, "Что читать детям? Беседа с Марией Минаевой о литературе для детей – православной и просто хорошей," in *Православие.ru* ⟨http://www.pravoslavie.ru/90231.html⟩ (Accessed December 21, 2017); Irina Balachonova, "У нас нет книжек, с которыми все ясно," in *Год литературы 2017* ⟨https://godliteratury.ru/projects/u-nas-net-knizhek-s-kotorymi-vsyo-yasno⟩ (Accessed December 2, 2017); Julija Jakovleva, "Состояние литературы: детские книги в России. Круглый стол редакторов на Colta.ru," in *Colta.ru*, May 29, 2015 ⟨https://www.colta.ru/articles/literature/7485⟩ (Accessed December 2, 2017).

35 Nikolaj Tichonov, "Баллада о гвоздях," in *Стихотворения и поэмы*, Leningrad 1981, 116.

for the right to influence the country's youngest citizens. Although the Soviet state is no more, the common perception of its "paradise-like" qualities lingers, reinforced by children's books and films that people continue to read and watch. Refuting the myth of Soviet literature and film for the young as a fictional realm inducing happiness, a series of guidelines for children's moral and civic maturation, and a compendium of recipes that guarantee their audience's commitment to national patriotism is an uneasy, but necessary task. The debunking is already accomplished in a number of remarkable monographs, scholarly volumes, and critical essays. Nevertheless, for researchers bent on studying ideological functions of Soviet children's culture as well as on exploring its relevance to the cultural-historical experience of modern Russians, there is still a lot of work ahead.

2 An Ideal Little Citizen: The Impact of Children's Literature and Film on Collective Soviet Identity

In 1950, Lidija Kon, a prominent party critic and daughter of the head of the Narkompros Arts Department, authored a scholarly volume on Soviet children's literature. Its very first sentence – "All of our literature is the literature of a society standing on the threshold of Communism," – points to the fact that Soviet cultural production for children has always remained a branch of a totalitarian art system.[36] In spite of undisputable poetic innovations and frequent artistic brilliance, it functioned within a rigidly structured and highly symbolic ideological field, which, at the height of Socialist Realism, was based on "pragmatic logic and determinism" imposed from above.[37] Most images, plot twists, and verbal or visual gestures within a literary or cinematic work targeting Soviet children represented the hierarchical relationship between the Bolshevik power and its progeny, future citizens of the promised Communist land. Soviet child protagonists could be inventive and mischievous, as Kolja and Mishka in *Весёлые рассказы и повести* by Nikolaj Nosov (*Merry Stories and Novellas*, 1958), doggedly loyal, as the protagonist of Leonid Panteleev's "Честное слово" ("The Word of Honor," 1941), well-groomed and prim,

---

36 Lidija Kon, *О детской литературе: сборник статей*, Moscow 1950, 5.
37 In her book on Futurism, Nina Gourianova asserts that post-Revolutionary Avant-Garde movements struggled against this concept and, instead, embraced the idea of artistic freedom and poetic chaos. See, *The Aesthetics of Anarchy: Art and Ideology in the Early Russian Avant-Garde*, Berkeley, Los Angeles and London 2012, 88. This is especially true of the early 1920s, the moment of flourishing of the Avant-Garde, which is distinctly different from the late 1920s and even more so from the early 1930s.

as Elena Verejskaja heroines, or ready to teach others how to be good, as the blue-haired Mal'vina in Aleksej Tolstoj's *Золотой ключик, или Приключения Буратино* (*The Golden Key, or Buratino's Adventures*, 1936) and its cinematic adaptation by Leonid Nechaev (1976).[38] In spite of differences in their personalities, these heroes were all models of ideal boys and girls who would eventually cross the border between reality and utopia. In study and in play, the literary and film characters followed Lenin's dictum – learning how "to be participants in the struggle for emancipation from the exploiters" and "to start building the edifice of communist society and bring it to completion."[39] Even Cheburashka, the fuzzy bear-like creature from Roman Kachanov's adaptation of Eduard Uspenskij's novella *Крокодил Гена и его друзья* (*Crocodile Gena and His Friends*, 1966), wanted to join the pioneers, march to the drum, and wear a red tie.[40]

The visionary strategy of the Soviet state affected every aspect of Soviet childhood, from family politics and personal hygiene to pedagogy and entertainment. Because Soviet children were seen as prototypes of the adults who were worthy of their communist future, their literary and cinematic rolemodels strove to turn themselves into more conscientious, morally staunchier, intellectually superior, and even physically stronger individuals than the grown-ups charged with their upbringing. Becoming a better and completely different person ("[…] нужно стать совсем другим человеком"), for example, is a credo of Aleksandr Grigorjev in Veniamin Kaverin's *Два капитана* (*Two Captains*, 1938-1944): at an early age, this character, nicknamed San'ka, realizes that he needs to completely transform himself, which means outgrowing not only his own lack of will, but also the bad example of some of his mentors.[41] Similarly, while learning how to survive under the German occupation, Valentina Oseeva's Vasek Trubachev (and his on-screen alter ego from Ilja Frez's 1955 film) wants to carry out "valiant and audacious plans […], keep the military secrets, entrusted to him by the older party members," and "do any-

---

38   Tolstoj's novella was itself an adaptation of Carlo Collodi's *The Adventures of Pinocchio* (1883). He started working on it when editing Nina Petrovskaja's translation from the Italian, but ended up writing his own version of the tale, significantly reworking the original. See Miron Petrovskij, "Что отпирает 'Золотой ключик'?" in *Вопросы литературы* 1979 (4).

39   Vladimir Lenin, "From the Speech Delivered at the Third All-Russian Congress of the Russian Young Communist League, October 2, 1920," in Julian Rothenstein and Olga Budashevskaya, eds., *Inside the Rainbow: Russian Children's Literature 1920-1935: Beautiful Books, Terrible Times*, London 2013, 77.

40   Roman Kachanov's animated film, *Крокодил Гена* (*Crocodile Gena*), came out in 1969.

41   Veniamin Kaverin, *Два капитана*, Moscow 2004, 83.

thing" for "his native land."⁴² The present-day myth of Soviet children's books' ability to convert modern children into "Men with a capital M" was born in such works.

Soviet children's novels and poems, graphic illustrations and cinematic propaganda were the Bolshevik state's primary tools for promoting its futuristic agenda. They aimed to indoctrinate, rather than soothe, amuse, or distract their readers, in spite of the existence of such deviant phenomena as Chukovskij's early writings, a few purely fun works by the OBERIU poets, and Uspenskij's whimsical creations. In 1928, People's Commissar of Enlightenment Anatolij Lunacharskij proclaimed that the party "had the right to demand that the writer portray positive types, which could demonstrate what the young citizen of our republic should be like" and "should aim at [...] portraying the beat of a communist heart in a purely artistic image."⁴³ Writers responded with works which urged Soviet youth to replicate the thinking and behavior of revolutionary heroes, Civil and "Great Patriotic" war veterans, party leaders, pioneer "martyrs," and winners of socialist labor competitions. By the mid-1930s, film directors also created an array of feature films depicting Bolsheviks and their juvenile supporters and assistants, the beat of whose "communist hearts" was supposed to inspire young viewers: Prestiani's *Красные дьяволята* (1923) was followed, among many others, by Petr Malachov's *Мишка Звонов* (*Mishka Zvonov*, 1925), Vladimir Petrov and Nikolaj Beresnev's *Золотой мед* (*Golden Honey*, 1928), and Abram Narodickij and Naum Ugrjumov's *Отчаянный батальон* (*The Daredevil Batallion*, 1933).

Soviet literary and cinematic child protagonists not only performed heroic deeds, but also were capable of self-reflection: Misha Poljakov in Anatolij Rybakov's *Кортик* (*Cutlass*, 1948) and *Бронзовая птица* (*The Bronze Bird*, 1956); inventiveness: Vitja Maleev in Nosov's novella (*Витя Малеев в школе и дома* [*Vitja Maleev at School and at Home*, 1951]; and poetic creativity: Senja Gaj in Lev Kassil"s *Дорогие мои мальчишки* (1944). That said, they rarely represented real boys and girls, many of whom suffered terrible deprivations and were brutalized by the regime. Instead, the fictional heroes legitimized the existence of the "new type of state" – the state that, having slaughtered millions of its people, could nevertheless produce this miraculously healthy, smart, brave, and morally impeccable progeny.

---

42 Valentina Oseeva, *Васек Трубачев и его товарищи*, Moscow 1961, 342-343.
43 Anatolij Lunacharskij, "Этика и эстетика Чернышевского перед судом современности," in Lunacharskij, *О детской литературе, детском и юношеском чтении: Сборник*, Moscow 1985, 63, 65.

Kassil''s writing exemplifies the relationship between Soviet children's authors and the political system in which they operated. Although his most famous book, *Кондуит и Швамбрания* (*Konduit and Shvambrania*, 1935), "symbolizes the tyranny of the adult world over childhood," as Inessa Medzhibovskaya shrewdly observes, the symbolic focus is readjusted in Kassil''s other works.[44] In *Вратарь республики* (*The Goalkeeper for the Republic*, 1937), *Великое противостояние* (*The Great Opposition*, 1940), *Дорогие мои мальчишки* (*My Dear Boys*), *Черемыш, брат героя* (*Cheremysh, the Brother of a Hero*, 1938), and *Улица младшего сына* (*The Street of a Younger Son*, 1949), Kassil' represents children as little sages who, in spite of their transgressions, have internalized adults' expectations of them as the nation's infallible future. Gaj, for example, is portrayed as a born leader, intrepid fighter, and morally staunch individual. Kassil' first introduces him as he composes and recites incendiary verses:

> A son will replace his father, and a grandson will replace his grandfather,
> The Motherland is summoning us to an exploit and to labor!
> "Valor, Labor, Loyalty, and Victory" is our motto!
> Forward, comrades! Friends, go forth![45]

Every word here is emblematic of the special mission imposed on most child protagonists of Soviet fiction and film – to be useful to the state as individuals who die protecting it or who labor for the country's future success. That said, the most important message of Gaj's poem is in its first line. By celebrating cross-generational loyalty, it reveals the regime's true expectation of Soviet children: in addition to dedicating themselves to hard work and valiant service, they should grow into progenitors who will eventually beget and raise politically devout offspring.

Brought up on this kind of poetic fare, Soviet people ended up feeling stuck in an ideological purgatory between the unprecedented (and unreachable) future, which could be advanced only by the purest of Soviet souls, and the idealized past that required homage, reverence, and a constant reiteration of real and imaginary exploits. In *Children's World: Growing Up in Russia, 1890-1991*,

---

44 Inessa Medzhibovskaya, "Lev Kassil. Childhood as Religion and Ideology," in Balina and Rudova, eds., *Russian Children's Literature and Culture*, 245.

45 "Отца заменит сын, и внук заменит деда, / На подвиг и на труд нас Родина зовет! / Отвага – наш девиз, – Труд, Верность и Победа! / Вперед, товарищи! Друзья, вперед!" Lev Kassil', "Дорогие мои мальчишки," in Kassil, *Собрание сочинений в пяти томах*, Vol. 2, Moscow 1987, 402-403.

Catriona Kelly cites a generic response of some of her interviewees to the images of children's accomplishments and happiness propagated by the Soviet culture: "[I]f 'childhood' is what we were told about in our alphabet books and reading primers, then I never experienced anything like that."[46] The lack of historical verity in the works created in the Socialist Realist mode or the disconnect between the meager lifestyle and political emasculation of the majority of the Soviet population and the well-being, security, fearlessness, confidence, and initiative of the literary and cinematic youth they beheld, are not the only reasons for such a reaction. The bitterness of Kelly's respondent may also be explained by the perilousness of the communist vision and the futility of all efforts to achieve it. In spite of the people's acclaimed heroism, there was no end to their fight for a better future. According to Boris Groys, the state they belonged to could accomplish a balance of power "only in and through permanent struggle, conflict and war."[47] In other words, when there was no frontline, the fight had to be internalized. Thus, Soviet youngsters inhabited a teleologically implausible realm: they lived in a challenging world but were forced to perceive it as either an ahistorical "now" or a paradisiacal time ahead. They were expected to advance the latter by committing acts of valor or by dedicating themselves to the never-ending process of self-improvement.

Soviet literary and cinematic works for young audiences helped create this paradox and consistently contributed to its perpetuation. In the first four post-revolutionary decades in particular, including the years of World War II and the period of postwar reconstruction, children's authors, artists, and directors portrayed a Soviet child as either a capable and resilient archetype of a "builder of Communism" or as a sacrificial victim whose martyrdom guaranteed the inescapability of the nation's imminent bliss. Books and screens flashed visions of young defenders of barricades, resourceful juvenile assistants to commissars combatting anarchists during the Civil War, whistleblowers in knickerbockers and red neckties who exposed grain hoarders, pioneer guerilla fighters, brave teenage internationalists, and innocent casualties of the nation-wide struggle against saboteurs and spies. These wild adventures eventually solidified into a more streamlined, even hagiographic, storylines.[48]

---

46   Catriona Kelly, *Children's World: Growing Up in Russia, 1890-1991*, New Haven and London 2007, 8.
47   Boris Groys, *Art Power*, Boston 2008, 24.
48   See Svetlana Maslinskaya, "Жизнеописание пионера-героя: текстовая традиция и ритуальный контекст," in *Современная российская мифология*, Moscow 2005, 89-123, as well as Maslinskaya's chapter in this volume. Larissa Rudova writes about the heroes of Soviet children in "From Character-Building to Criminal Pursuits: Russian Children's Literature in Transition," in Balina and Rudova, eds., *Russian Children's Literature and Culture*, 23-24.

Their goal was to ensure that children's reading and film remained entertaining while promoting what Kelly has called "the two opposite images of a child as a Soviet national symbol [...] that of a savior and a martyr."[49]

The publication of Тимур и его команда on the brink of World War II became a turning point in Soviet cultural production for young audiences. Timur was a new type of a Soviet hero: Gajdar endowed him with a will to help others and save them, as well as with leadership qualities, such as independence and aptitude for quick decision-making. Besides, Timur possessed vulnerability and empathy – the endearing personality traits that surpassed the standard set of Soviet virtues. Soon to be mirrored by Kaverin's San'ka Grigorjev in Два капитана and Elena Iljina's Gulja Koroleva (Четвертая высота, [The Fourth Altitude], 1945), this character appealed not only to children, but also to adults, some of whom still harbored memories of the peasant "communal spirit" and pre-revolutionary family ethics.

According to Andrej Fateev, whose recent monograph offers one of the most comprehensive analyses of children's cultural production under Stalin, Тимур и его команда became so influential because it supplemented the moral and political guidelines issued by the Communist Party for the country's youngest citizens with the "noble values of human solidarity and mutual support."[50] Expected to rely on these principles for the raising of their children, Soviet people also used them to evaluate the actions of their government. Although Soviet adults received, in Тимур и его команда and other talented works for young readers, a mirror which reflected the government's misdeeds most distinctly, it was not a sufficient reason for curtailing the book's influence, Fateev tells us.[51] Camaraderie and selfless cooperation were essential for the survival of both the Soviet economy and the communist ideology, while Timur's openness to self-improvement inspired readers to change for the better themselves. Thus, the promulgation of "Timurian" virtues by writers and film directors carved a new niche for children's literature and film: now government officials could treat it as a social "medicine" for the country as a whole.[52] In other words, after Тимур и его команда had ascended to fame, Soviet authors began to create works for young audiences with the idea of healing the entire nation's social ills that utopian thinking alone could not eradicate.

Stalin's death did not immediately end political indoctrination by means of sacrificial imaginary. Schematic child heroes, including those willing to

---

49　Kelly, "Об изучении истории детства в России XIX - XX веков," in G. V. Makarevich, ed., Какорея. Из истории детства в России и других странах, Moscow and Tver' 2008, 28.
50　A. V. Fateev, Сталинизм и детская литература в политике номенклатуры СССР (1930-е – 1950-е гг.), Moscow 2007, 90, 93.
51　Ibid., 93.
52　Ibid.

give up their lives for the state, dominated the literary and cinematic production for children until the end of the worst phase of Soviet totalitarianism; in the subsequent decades, they co-existed on screen and in children's books with more believable and morally nuanced heroes. And yet, after 1953, the portrayal of child martyrs gradually ceased to be either ideologically propitious or very entertaining. Raising its head in the late 1950s and especially in the 1960s, Soviet society, inspired by the more humanistic policies of the "Thaw" period, began to realize its readiness for new role models, including those the younger generation could imitate in the process of "moral self-education [самовоспитание]." As Ilja Kukulin convincingly demonstrates, the social chaos, domestic disarray, and plain hunger of the early postwar years caused adults' failure to provide proper moral education to their children at school and, partially, at home. This crisis, in its turn, triggered the need for fictional and cinematic child protagonists who could cultivate their personalities on their own. Children's authors and film directors responded by creating characters capable of setting an example for the nation-wide self-improvement. Not only did these little heroes act independently, but they also made their own ideological and behavioral choices – often with a nod to young guerilla soldiers who had to fight for survival on enemy territory during World War II.[53] Kukulin refers to Vitalij Gubarev's *Королевство кривых зеркал* (*The Kingdom of Crooked Mirrors*, 1951) and the eponymous film by Aleksandr Rou (1963); Nosov's *Витя Малеев в школе и дома* (*Vitya Maleev at School and at Home*), along with Viktor Ejsymont's film *Два друга* (*Two Friends*, 1954) based on this novella; and Anatolij Granik's film *Алеша Птицын вырабатывает характер* (*Alesha Pticyn Builds His Character*, 1953, after Agnija Barto's screenplay) as the works that were teaching children how to achieve moral advancement – if not political maturity – on their own, rather than by relying on adults' counselling or the guidance of their supreme parent, the Soviet state.[54]

The Thaw, with its political reforms, re-evaluation of the Soviet historical experience, and the society's newly discovered shift from collective to individual self-perception, directed Soviet children's literature and film towards identity-seeking, experimentation, and the rediscovery of its Modernist roots. Nevertheless, Soviet writers and film-makers still had to operate within an art system precipitated by totalitarianism. Therefore, they had to continue dealing with ideological paradoxes, some of them perplexing. For example, post-

---

53   Ilja Kukulin, "Воспитание воли в советской психологии и детская литература конца 1940-х – начала 1950-х гг.," in Kukulin, Marija Majofis and Petr Safronov, eds., *Острова утопии: Педагогическое и социальное проектирование послевоенной школы (1940-1980-е)*, 172.
54   Ibid., 183-84.

war Soviet political leaders boastfully declared the nation's almost complete transition to the social relations which were the best in the world ("лучшие в мире общественные отношения"). This assertion led critic T. D. Kornejchik to declare Gajdar's *Тимур и его команда* an unnecessary work for children, since the novella portrayed the fight between a group of good kids and a gang of petty street thieves and hooligans led by one Mishka Kvakin, allegedly an outdated type of child protagonist.[55] The critic's opinion, however, went against that of Joseph Stalin himself. In 1952, the Soviet dictator criticized editors, pedagogues, and journalists for a stilted approach to narratives that denied the existence of "evil" in the postwar Soviet Union.[56] The paradox was resolved in an escapist but productive manner typical of Soviet creators' responses to ideological pressure. Just as in the 1930s-40s, when the Stalinist doctrine of a "New Soviet Man" ushered in literary and film heroes of mythological proportions while the Soviet utopian mentality called for an appropriation of fairytale plots and motifs,[57] the postwar "theory of conflictlessness [теория бесконфликтности]" born out of the government-guided attempts to assert the moral and ideological advancement of the country, stimulated the return of children's authors and directors to "make-believe" aesthetics and the subsequent creation of texts that contained "the imaginary, the fantasy."[58] Fairytale archetypes and narrative devices became especially prominent in such works from the 1960s-70s as Uspenskij's novellas and scripts for animated films, Nosov's Neznajka series and its sequels,[59] and works by Veniamin Kaverin and Vladislav Krapivin.[60] Soviet authors' and film directors' return to

---

55   Cited in Fateev, *Сталинизм и детская литература*, 162.
56   Ibid., 161.
57   Anja Tippner, "Evgenii Shvarts's Fairy-Tale Dramas: Theater, Power, and the Naked Truth," in Balina and Rudova, eds., *Russian Children's Literature and Culture*, 312; Alexander Prokhorov calls this new *Zeitgeist* a "quasireligious ideology transcending the limits of reason." See "Arresting Development: A Brief History of Cinema for Children and Adolescents," in *Ibid.*, 135.
58   Fateev, *Сталинизм и детская литература*, 161-163.
59   Shortly after Uspenskij's novellas appeared in print, they were adapted to the screen. Films about Gena and Cheburashka were directed by Roman Kachanov: *Крокодил Гена и его друзья* (*Crocodile Gena and His Friends*), 1966, 1970. Uncle Fedor cartoons were created by Jurij Klepackij and Lidija Surikova: *Дядя Федор, пес и кот* (*Uncle Fedor, Dog, and Cat*) came out in 1973; its sequels premiered in 1997-2004.
60   Nikolaj Nosov, *Приключения Незнайки и его друзей* [*The Adventures of Dunno and His Friends*, 1954; *Незнайка в Солнечном городе* [*Dunno in Sun City*], 1958; *Нейзнайка на Луне* [*Dunno on the Moon*], 1964-1965); Veniamin Kaverin's *Легкие шаги* (*Light Steps*, 1963); *Летающий мальчик* (*The Flying Boy*, 1969), and Vladislav Krapivin's trilogy *Мальчик со шпагой* (*The Boy with a Sword*, 1972-1976). For the discussion of children's literature of the period, see M. I. Meshcherjakova, *Русская детская, подростковая и юношеская проза 2 половины XX века: Проблемы поэтики*, Moscow 1997, 240.

fantasy and fairytale not only helped resolve the conflict between the regime and its literature and film for children, but also responded to the mass adult reader demand for engaging and emotionally stimulating fiction written in playful and imaginative language.[61]

In the 1960s, the gap between the two tiers of Soviet cultural production for children – the whimsical offshoot of the Russian and European Avant-Garde and the Socialist Realist literature and cinema with their simplified language, cookie-cutter protagonists, and a black-and-white representation of the struggle between good and evil – grew bigger.[62] Following the increase in consumerism, the country's cultural consumption evolved, and so did the government policies regulating culture and political propaganda through the arts. The legacy of Soviet children's literature and film had by then become sizeable and impressive. In addition to the schematic works lacking in thematic and imaginary inventiveness and displaying impoverished, if not fully obliterated, poetic texture, there were also stunning creations produced by talented writers, illustrators, playwrights, actors, and cameramen. Among them were heirs to the Avant-Garde aesthetic, who survived the Great Terror of the 1930s. Their poetic and visual – as well as theatrical and cinematic – output had real artistic value. Even if the government could interpret the political "message" of such works as Shvarc's drama *Дракон* (*The Dragon*, written in 1942-44, first staged in 1962 by Mark Zacharov) or perceive the apolitical quality of Chukovskij and Vladimir Konashevich's collaborative works for children, first produced by the Raduga publishing house, as subversive, it could not fully ostracize talented authors and directors at the height of the Cold War, when an outstanding literary work or film served as a winning bid in the competition with the West for cultural supremacy.[63]

Meanwhile, Communist party officials, authors recruited by the state, and "politically conscientious" critics kept reminding adults responsible for the upbringing of a healthy postwar generation that, albeit victorious, the country still depended on the solicitous attention and hard labor of its youth.

---

61   This demand became apparent as early as in the 1940s, when former peasants – now soldiers serving at the front – began to ask for and consume children's books written in "accessible" language (Fateev, *Сталинизм и детская литература*, 110-111). See also Marietta Chudakova, "Заметки о языке современной прозы," in *Избранные работы*, Vol. 1 (*Литература советского прошлого*), Moscow 2001, 248-252.

62   Evgenij Dobrenko discusses the proximity of the latter to the Socialist Realist canon for adults in *Stalinist Cinema and the Production of History*, Edinburgh 2008.

63   On the value of work by Chukovskij, Vladimir Lebedev and heirs of the Russian Avant-Garde during the Cold War, see David Caute, *Politics and the Novel During the Cold War*, New Brunswick 2009.

Moreover, it appeared that in a socialist society, even fairytale narratives had no chance of promoting the kind of moral and spiritual transcendence that Western folklore spinoffs and fantasy books with a Christian or mythological subtext proffered.[64] Geared towards humanism, with the imaginary serving mostly as a vehicle for attracting readers and viewers' attention, most postwar Soviet works for children continued to rely on a conflict that retained the epic proportions of class struggle, which, in Marxist terms, was historically inevitable.

In his introduction to a 1972 propagandistic pamphlet on Soviet pedagogy and children's culture, bona fide Soviet writer for children Sergej Michalkov explained the Soviet society's constant demand for literature and film that would stimulate the transformation of comfortably housed and well-fed youngsters into fighters and survivors. Writing for the audience of parents and educators who themselves might have never participated in combat, Michalkov first pointed out the lack of actual conflict, including death or starvation, in both the real life and in children's fiction and cinema that reflected the country's peaceful present. Then he demanded that his Soviet writer-colleagues go back to producing children's works of grave social and political urgency:

> Today's teenagers were born after the war. It is very fortunate that they have not seen bombs explode, have not heard the soul-splitting wail of an air raid alarm.
>
> They do not know how scary it is to have lost one's bread ration cards.
>
> They did not have to run barefoot through the snow to a partisan camp, saving themselves from the fascists.
>
> It is fortunate that our children have avoided the horrors and burdens of wartime, but it is bad that nowadays, in a time of peace, some adults, having experienced war and survived it, are trying to shelter their children from [even] minimal difficulties and chores. It is therefore not an accident that their children sometimes grow into consumers of life's benefits, passive observers of life, lazy, vulgar skeptics indifferent to labor, to everything that our heroic people have lived through and suffered.[65]

The author of a series of poems about Дядя Степа (Uncle Stepa), a benevolent giant who symbolizes the state as a parental figure capable of protecting inno-

---

64   Linda C. Salem, *Children's Literature Studies: Cases and Discussions*, Westport, CT and London 2006, 25-26.
65   Sergej Michalkov, *Все начинается с детства*, Moscow 1972, 6.

cent Soviet citizens from the dangers they could neither imagine nor avoid, Michalkov in this essay recommended that "difficulties and chores" be reinstituted as tools of proper socialist upbringing. He also illustrated the dangers inherent in stress-free life and parental pampering by creating poetic and satirical representations of children who grow up in a world without challenges or traumas.[66] These caricatures of lazy or cowardly adolescents were similar to the burlesque portrayals of slackers, alcoholics, and irresponsible spouses in the satirical cinematic and, later, TV program, *Фитиль* (*The Whisk*, est. 1962), which Michalkov edited. Eventually, other ideologues joined him in endorsing "real" conflict in Soviet children's literature and film. Speaking in 1986, at the Eighth Congress of Soviet Writers, Secretary of the Writers' Union Ivan Motjashov criticized literary works which focused on a "narrow circle of purely childish activities and problems" and welcomed books concerning "real problems, serious grief, or powerful evil." According to Motjashov, if "unexposed to grave trials, a child's personality would stop in its development and growth."[67]

In order to avoid the unwanted transformation of a budding ideal Soviet citizen into a pot-bellied drunkard with a three-day stubble or a garrulous housewife in curlers, central radio and TV shows, the pioneer press, and family periodicals, such as the popular magazine *Семья и школа* (*Family and School*), started propagating "education through labor [трудовое воспитание]" and the re-introduction of utopian collectivist movements (for instance, "Young Communards").[68] Most importantly, this nationwide drive towards improving Soviet children's social and moral awareness gave rise to "the education of the senses [воспитание чувств]" campaign. The principles of school and domestic education embedded in this approach aimed at shaking children and teens out of their emotional comfort zone by exposing them to such problems as broken families, economic hardship, harassment by stronger or more successful classmates, and romantic failure.

Michalkov's demand that Soviet adults subject children to situations in which their souls would evolve in the process of overcoming "severe trials"

---

66   See such poems by Michalkov as "Про Мимозу" ("About a Delicate Flower"), "Чудесные таблетки" ("Miraculous Pills"), "Модное платье" ("A Fashionable Dress"), "Лапуся" ("Cutie"), "Как у нашей Любы" ("Our Ljuba Has a Toothache"), among many others.
67   "Материалы VIII Съезда советских писателей," in *Литературная газета* 1986 (July 2), 16.
68   The Commune of Young Communards named after Michail Frunze was founded in Leningrad in 1959. One of its prototypes was Semen Makarenko's school for juvenile delinquents, established in the Ukraine in the 1920s. See Darja Dimke, "Юные коммунары, или Крестовый поход детей: между утопией декларируемой и утопией реальной," in *Острова утопии*, 360-397.

and "serious grief" was not unjustified. It could have been an ideal moment to revisit the nation's dramatic past and start creating factual, if not analytical, works about the revolution and its victims, the wars in which the Soviet Union participated, or the destinies of millions of displaced, declassified, or murdered Soviet citizens. Instead, children's authors and film directors received a "state order [госзаказ]" to produce school novellas about friendship, fiction about teenage love, and films in which the plot owed its intricacy to the complexities of protagonists' emotions. Channeled this way and still severely censored, their creative energy nevertheless flourished. The appearance of novellas by Dragunskij, Viktor Goljavkin and Anatolij Aleksin, poems and translations by Genrich Sapgir and Boris Zachoder, and such films as Andrej Tarkovskij's *Иваново детство* (*Ivan's Childhood*, 1962), Ilja Frez's *Вам и не снилось* (*Could One Imagine?*, 1981), Pavel Arsenjev's *Гостья из будущего* (*A Guest from the Future*, 1985, after Kir Bulychev's "Alisa Selezneva" series), and Rolan Bykov's *Чучело* (*The Scarecrow*, 1982) signified a paradigmatic shift in Soviet cultural production for children and young adults.

Child protagonists who previously played predominantly symbolic roles suddenly emerged as lovers and haters, betrayers and the betrayed, or merely keen observers of reality, capable of registering their feelings and identity crises. Not only did their appearance become more varied and included deviations from the Soviet norm of celebrating neat pioneers and prim school girls, witty peasant children and disheveled war orphans, or denigrating bad kids with sleek hair wearing expensive clothes, but their forms of self-expression also changed. Thus, in Viktor Dragunskij's *Денискины рассказы* (*Deniska's Tales*, 1959), even the speech of the narrator-hero changes as he matures. When Deniska is still a little boy, he describes his experiences in short, emotional sentences, while the interior monologue of his older self includes longer syntactic periods and a more complex vocabulary. Moreover, as critic Ljudmila Dolzhenko notices, Dragunskij's older character begins to speak with a greater degree of self-reflection.[69] In the same vein, Soviet children's film also shifted towards the more nuanced portrayal of Soviet youth. Alexander Prokhorov points out that such films as Julij Rajzman's *А если это любовь?* (*And What if This Is Love?*, 1962) and Stanislav Rostockij's *Доживем до понедельника* (*We'll Live till Monday*, 1969) featured adults who had "lost their unquestionable authority over children" while "rais[ing] the issue of privacy, the realm of human relations where school as a state institution had no business whatsoever."[70]

---

69 L. Dolzhenko, *Рациональное и эмоциональное в русской детской литературе 50-80-х годов XX в. (Н. Н. Носов, В. Ю. Драгунский, В.П. Крапивин)*, Volgograd 2001, 192.

70 Prokhorov, "Arrested Development," 142.

According to Marina Balina, there also appeared a subtler and more varied gender discourse, with adolescent sensuality replacing the "honest friendship" of the 1930s-40s children's fiction.[71]

This transition from the politically charged and emotionally stilted literary and cinematic narratives to literature and film about children's inner life has prompted even the most perceptive contemporary critics to consider the ethical component of Soviet works for children more valuable than their questionable, if not outright detrimental, ideological substance. For example, Evgenija Putilova notices elements of "education of the senses" not only in children's literature of the 1960s-70s, but also in Gajdar's more distant Школа (*School*, 1930) and Дальние страны (*Far-Away Lands*, 1932). Gajdar, Putilova suggests, makes readers work hard to notice the complexity of his protagonists' emotional life as well as recognize the finality of their ethical choices.[72] In her interpretation, when Gajdar permits Boris Gorikov in Школа to remain indecisive at the time of danger, thus forcing him to imperil his friend and mentor Chubuk, the writer achieves two goals simultaneously: he deprives his character of the moral gratification with regard to a successful exploit and breaks the existing literary tradition of a happy ending (Chubuk gets executed). For the critic, this choice demonstrates the essence of Gajdar's "understanding of and responsibility for the fate of a growing individual," rather than exposes the author's reliance on stilted storytelling steeped in autobiographical detail and dominated by ideological clichés.[73]

Marietta Chudakova, whose analysis of Soviet children's literature as a "laboratory" of later Soviet adult fiction is, on the whole, remarkable, also sees great narrative complexity and emotional depth in the writings for children from the 1920s and 1940s. Chudakova is especially attentive to the changes in literary language, characterized by the merging of the "'standard norm' [средняя норма] of the turn of the century belles-lettres vernacular" and "the language of the street," which led to the new type of prose made up of shorter phrases and featuring more energetic tempo as well as truncated transitional links between the narratives' subjects and their impressions.[74] The critic believes that prewar children's fiction played an "evolutionary role" in the development of Soviet literature. When many Soviet authors refrained from

---

71 Marina Balina, "Воспитание чувств a la sovietique: повести о первой любви," in A. S. Obuchova, M. V. Tendrjakova, eds., *Ребенок в истории и культуре*, Moscow 2010, 456.

72 E. O. Putilova, *Детское чтение – для сердца и разума: Очерки по истории детской литературы*, St. Petersburg 2005, 148-162.

73 Ibid., 152.

74 Chudakova, "Заметки о языке современной прозы," 248.

writing for publication because they felt the futility of complying with the regime's political and aesthetic demands or feared political oppression, "it was in children's literature that one could find a [...] variety of psychological collisions and human emotions," Chudakova writes.[75] She also points to Michail Zoshchenko, Boris Zhitkov, Sergej Auslender, Gajdar, and other children's authors of "well-constructed novellas" featuring "quite compelling characters" as principal originators of 1960s-70s "adult" prose, in which Sergej Dovlatov and Venedikt Erofeev shined.[76]

Putilova and Chudakova's research demonstrates how Soviet works for children can be canonized outside of the direct ideological context due to their contribution to the moral education of readers and viewers as well as their artistic qualities. Indeed, when we parse literary and cinematic texts in a careful and compelling, but also strategically one-sided way, it becomes possible to accept the linguistic vibrancy of Soviet children's literature and the intense emotionality of post-war poetry, prose, and film as their predominant and most attractive qualities. This acceptance leads to a continuing affirmation of the high aesthetic properties of Soviet literary and cinematic children's works and, subsequently, to their being re-offered for public consumption. And yet, this ahistorical approach is not only inconsistent, but also detrimental. It introduces a fragmented vision of literary history, which, in its turn, informs a skewed perception of Soviet realities by post-Soviet generations. A case in point is Gajdar's *Школа*: before Boris Gorikov fails to act decisively and thus save Chubuk, he runs away from home and kills his peer, a cadet. Gajdar's protagonist experiences no pangs of regret, because he is acting in self-defense, but also because the cadet is affiliated with the counter-revolutionary White Guards. Thus, the murder acquires the flavor of a political execution, while the episode's psychological intensity, its being one of the tragic elements of the book, wanes. Gajdar offers readers a story of Soviet-style maturation predicated on enhanced class awareness: that is, the protagonist's ability to first tell an ally from an enemy and then to destroy the latter.

At the end of *Школа*, Bolshevik commander Shebalov has to decide whether Gorikov should be punished for his misdemeanors, or whether he could be given another chance. The commander forgives the young man and accepts him into his army detachment, because he considers Gorikov an "unruined" guy: his faults "could be washed off him."[77] Moreover, Shebalov's verdict is based on his recognizing the advantage of Gorikov's youthfulness. The

---

75   Ibid., 360.
76   Ibid., 359.
77   Gajdar, *Школа*, Minsk 1976, 178.

commander sees himself as someone already set in his ways, "a worn-out leather boot, studded with nails," while Gorikov for him is like a leather blank: "Whichever shoe-tree you pull it onto, that's the shape it will be [на какую колодку натянешь, такая и будет]."[78] The characteristic given by Shebalov to Gorikov, Gajdar's alter ego, is precise and symbolic. This is how Gajdar saw himself – a tough, but also malleable apprentice to the revolution – and also how Soviet authors and film directors had to imagine their readers and viewers. Like many protagonists of children's fiction and film, they were supposed to adhere to the socialist mold and retain the acquired shape for life. Current cultural practitioners willing to adopt Soviet children's literature and cinema as desirable fare for contemporary Russian society also accept this agenda. They do it either without fully recognizing the Soviet canon's already firm grip on the collective national identity, or with an acolyte zeal that welcomes the continuation of its impact.

3 From Cultural Myths to Scholarly Analysis: Current Scholarship on Soviet Children's Literature and Film and This Volume's Contents

No matter how misleading myths might be, we embrace them. This happens not because we believe myths to be true, but because they may help us deal with oppression and violence, desire and loss, anguish and exhilaration, poverty and the curse of riches better than rational thinking. Political myths are no exception. They help societies articulate the inexplicable in their existence – as well as accept the unacceptable.[79] This is why it is important to stress that Soviet children's culture owes its current popularity not only to the nostalgic attachment that current publishers and TV producers feel or to the widespread recognition of its moral and patriotic values, but also to the intellectually subtler general perception of Soviet children's literature and film as a zone of creative freedom that occasioned the production of works superior to the politically tainted adult fare. According to this theory, select authors, illustrators, dramaturges and film directors avoided getting sucked into the totalitarian power vortex or learned how to resist the impetus to turn all Soviet people – from the cradle to infantilized adulthood – into recipients of state ideology. Frequently, their stepping out of the precarious relationship with

---

78   Ibid.
79   Henry Tudor, *Political Myth*. New York 1972. See also Christopher G. Flood, *Political Myth: A Theoretical Introduction*. London and New York 2005.

the Soviet state signified either ostracism or death – as it happened, for instance, to Charms and Aleksandr Vvedenskij, Marshak's talented Detgiz editorial team, Grigorij Belych, Vitalij Bianki, Julija Voznesenskaja, Aleksandr Ivich, Lev Kvitko, Andrej Nekrasov, Radij Pogodin, Roman Sef, film director Barskaja, screenwriter Michail Vol'pin, and animator Kirill Maljantovich. Others, such as Chukovskij, Shvarc, Marshak, Kassil', Gajdar, Ovsej Driz, director Elem Klimov, kept balancing on the brink, inventing strategies of ideological draft-dodging which scholars now refer to as "a refuge [убежище]" (Kondakov) or "ideological transgression from within" (Omri Ronen).[80]

Appealing and even reassuring, the view of Soviet cultural production for children as a zone of creative freedom is, nevertheless, rife with contradictions. Balina, for instance, avoids subscribing to this idea, citing convincing evidence that repudiates the relative freedom of children's literature as an institution and an area of artistic self-expression.[81] Natalja Miloserdova and Jeremy Hick are similarly convinced of the impossibility of freedom from ideology in Soviet film for children.[82] Possibly the most resonant clash of opinions on this subject results from Chudakova's opinion about the so-called "loophole" and Fateev's response to it. Chudakova treats the relationship between children's writers and the Soviet state as both these authors' personal choice and a poetic strategy. She suggests, for example, that "one could (and had to) write about pioneers, about Pavlik Morozov, but one could also not do so – a fact that today's observer may overlook."[83] For Chudakova, children's authors continued to experiment with Avant-Garde devices, design forms of language play, and integrate modernist approaches to narrative structures not because they had managed to escape state control, but because their inventions were part of the broader literary process. Fateev disagrees with this view by pointing

---

80   Igor' Kondakov, "'Убежище-2': 'Детский дискурс' советской литературы в 1930-е годы," in *Ребенок в истории и культуре*, Библиотека журнала Исследователь / *Researcher*, Vol. 4, Moscow 2010, 25; Omri Ronen, *Соцреалистический канон*, St. Petersburg 2000, 975. Ronen demonstrates that such authors as Gajdar and Kassil' were capable of overcoming the strict confines of Socialist Realism without fully parting with methods and clichés of totalitarian aesthetics.
81   Balina, "Советская детская литература: несколько слов о предмете исследования," in Balina and Valerij Vjugin, eds., *"Убить Чарскую": парадоксы советской литературы для детей*, St. Petersburg 2013, 8-10.
82   Natalja Miloserdova, "Детское кино," in L. Budjak and D. Karavaev, eds., *Страницы истории отечественного кино*, Moscow 2006, 9; Jeremy Hicks, "Soiuzdetfil'm: The Birth of Soviet Children's Film and the Child Actor," in Birgit Beumers, ed., *A Companion to Russian Cinema*, Malden, MA and Oxford, 2016, 117-135.
83   Marietta Chudakova, "Сквозь звезды к тверниям," in *Новый мир* 4 (1990), 248.

out children's writers' almost complete reliance on the state-controlled literary institutions, which invented, propagated, and enforced ideological clichés. He also cites the commitment of Soviet authors to the communist worldview, stating that most of them considered their political beliefs to be part of "общечеловеческие ценности [universal human values]."[84] It is this understanding that has put the children's writers and filmmakers on equal footing with the state which masterminded their work. In other words, what seems to some critics "a loophole" in the regime-controlled cultural production, may, in fact, be yet another form of alleviating ideological tension by the regime itself. Isaiah Berlin saw in this "creative freedom" a fluctuation between strict counter-dissent measures and the more permissible deviations from the firm political course. In a seminal 1952 essay, Berlin called it the "zigzag path" of Soviet "artificial dialectic" – the dialectic which, in the philosopher's view, had no end and no resolution.[85]

There are several ways to explain the engagement of Soviet children's authors and film directors with the state without downplaying the role of ideology in shaping the pedagogical, socio-political, and artistic discourse directed towards the country's youth. Sara Pankenier Weld's essay in this *Companion*, for example, provides an evolutionary explanation for the Soviet picturebook authors' engagement with – as well as avoidance of – censorship. Another approach, exemplified by the scholars who collaborated on the edited volume *Веселые человечки: Культурные герои советского детства* (*Merry Little People: Cultural Heroes of the Soviet Childhood*), presupposes an in-depth semiotic study of the Soviet cultural output for children, with a particular emphasis on its ability to destabilize the social and political norms, rather than find a secure niche within the totalitarian system. Sergej Ushakin takes yet another analytical course. According to him, the half-human and half-animal protagonists of children's books and animated films produced in the late Soviet period functioned as monstrous hybrids which "materialized the very impossibility of drawing a clear line, [...] regularizing differentiations of the heterogeneous and incongruous parts and qualities within a single figure," be it a representation of the state itself or one of its confused, identity-seeking nationals.[86]

An exploration of the actual impact the Soviet children's literary and cinematic works had on the country and its citizens is one of the most productive

---

84 Fateev, *Сталинизм и детская литература*, 7-8.

85 Isaiah Berlin, "Artificial Dialectic: Generalissimo Stalin and the Art of Government," in Berlin, ed. Henry Hardy, *The Soviet Mind: Russian Culture under Communism*, Washington, DC 2003, 115.

86 Sergej Ushakin, "Пролог," in Ilja Kukulin, Mark Lipoveckij, and Marija Majofis, eds., *Веселые человечки: Культурные герои советского детства*, Moscow 2008, 28.

ways of bringing into perspective their aesthetic merits, political potency, and socio-cultural legacy. This is easier to do now, a hundred years after the publication of Chukovskij's "Ваня и Крокодил" ("Vanja and Crocodile"), than, for instance, thirty years ago, when research in the area of Soviet children's literature and film was just moving from the periphery of literary and cultural studies to the center. That much time had to pass between the collapse of the Soviet regime, the opening of the archives, and the emergence of publications about the totalitarian state's relationship with its children's authors and filmmakers for scholarship to evolve theoretically and methodologically – as well as to become fully grounded in fact. Presently, the history of Soviet children's literature is documented in meticulous studies by Ben Hellman, Irina Arzamasceva, Evgeny Steiner, and Andrej Fateev.[87] In addition to their monographs, several important volumes have come out, edited by Marina Balina, Larissa Rudova, Evgeny Dobrenko, Valerij Vjugin, Marija Majofis, Ilja Kukulin and Petr Safronov.[88] These studies have expanded the field's range, while bringing together scholars, some of whom previously worked on adjacent subjects, such as the Soviet literary canon, narrative theory, gender studies, history of pedagogy, and folklore.

Time was also needed for historically accurate biographies of individual children's authors and film-makers to appear, including Valerij Shubinskij's biography of Daniil Charms and Irina Lukjanova's, of Chukovskij.[89] Meanwhile, new translations of previously unknown literary works and newly available Soviet children's films in English allowed university instructors to make them part of curricular offerings and thus stir interest in Soviet cultural production

---

87　Ben Hellman, *Fairy Tales and True Stories: The History of Russian Literature for Children and Young People (1574-2010)*; Irina Arzamasceva, *"Век ребенка" и русская литература 1900-1930-х годов*, Moscow 2003; Evgeny Steiner, *Stories for Little Comrades: Revolutionary Artists and the Making of Early Soviet Children's Books*, Seattle and London 1999; Andrej Fateev, *Сталинизм и детская литература в политике номенклатуры СССР (1930-е – 1950-е гг.)*, Moscow 2007.

88　Marina Balina and Larissa Rudova, eds., *Russian Children's Literature and Culture*, New York and London 2008; Balina and Evgeny Dobrenko, eds., *Petrified Utopia: Happiness Soviet Style*, London and New York 2009; Balina and Valerij Vjugin, eds., *"Убить Чарскую": парадоксы советской литературы для детей (To Kill Charskaja: Politics and Aesthetics in Soviet Children's Literature of the 1920s and 1930s)*, St. Petersburg 2013; Ilja Kukulin, Marija Majofis and Petr Safronov, eds., *Острова утопии: Педагогическое и социальное проектирование послевоенной школы (1940-1980-е)*.

89　Valerij Shubinskij, *Даниил Хармс: Жизнь человека на ветру*, Moscow 2015; Irina Lukjanova, *Корней Чуковский*, Moscow 2006; Matvej Gejzer, *Маршак*, Moscow 2006; and Clare Kitson, *Yuri Norstein and* Tale of Tales: *An Animator's Journey*, Bloomington and Indianapolis 2005.

for children among a new generation of scholars. *Politicizing Magic: An Anthology of Russian and Soviet Fairy Tales* (ed. Marina Balina, Helena Goscilo, and Mark Lipovetsky, Evanston, IL 2005) and *Russian Magic Tales from Pushkin to Platonov* (trans. Robert Chandler, London 2012) offer Anglophone readers an insight into the extraordinary riches of Russian folklore and elucidate Soviet authors' renderings of fairytale motifs, plots, and magical thinking. Evgeny Ostashevsky's OBERIU: *An Anthology of Russian Absurdism* (Evanston, IL 2006) and translations of children's works by Charms, Vladimir Majakovskij, and Osip Mandel'stam that have come out as picture books brilliantly illustrated by contemporary American artists help reveal the apolitical, imaginative, and experimental side of the formerly little-known Soviet children's literary canon.[90] The four-volume set, entitled *Masters of Russian Animation*, released on DVD in 2000 by Films by Jove, in association with Sojuzmul'tfil'm studios, contains famous and little-known animated films produced in the Soviet Union between 1962 and 1991. This collection is now widely available, along with such Soviet cinematic classics as Nadezhda Kosheverova and Michail Shapiro's Золушка (*Cinderella*, 1947), Vladimir Bychkov's Русалочка (*The Little Mermaid*, 1976), Pavel Kadochnikov's Снегурочка (*The Snow Maiden*, 1968), and Aleksandr Rou's Василиса Прекрасная (*Vasilisa the Beautiful*, 1939).

Although a comprehensive history of Soviet children's film has yet to be written, books by Kira Paramonova, Birgit Beumers, and Evgenij Margolit, as well as numerous essays in journals and online publications have resulted in an in-depth exploration of Soviet cinematic production for young viewers.[91] Among the most perceptive of those surveys are Alexander Prokhorov's "Arresting Development: A Brief History of Soviet Cinema for Children and Adolescents" and Jeremy Hicks' "Soiuzdetfilm: The Birth of Soviet Children's Film and the Child Actor."[92]

---

90   Daniil Kharms, *First, Second*, ill. Marc Rosenthal, trans. Richard Pevear, New York 1996; Daniil Kharms, *It Happened Like This: Stories and Poems*, trans. Katya Arnold, New York 1998; *The Fire Horse: Children's Poems by Vladimir Mayakovsky, Osip Mandelstam, and Daniil Kharms*, trans. Eugene Ostashevsky, New York 2017.

91   Kira Paramonova, *Необыкновенные годы: страницы истории детского кино*, Moscow 2005; Birgit Beumers, *A History of Russian Cinema*, Oxford and New York 2009, and Beumers, ed., *A Companion to Russian Cinema*, Malden MA and Oxford 2016; Evgenij Margolit, *Живые и мертвые: Заметки к истории советского кино 1920-1960х годов*, St. Petersburg 2012.

92   Prokhorov, "Arresting Development," in Balina and Rudova, eds., *Russian Children's Literature and Culture*, 129-152. Hicks, "Soiuzdetfilm," in *A Companion to Russian Cinema*, ed. Birgit Beumers, Malden, MA and Oxford 2016, 117-135. See also Alexander and Elena Prokhorov, *Film and Television Genres of the Late Soviet Era*, New York 2017.

INTRODUCTION 33

Enchanted by the visual magnificence of Soviet books for young readers, contemporary scholars have paid tribute to this phenomenon in exhibition catalogues or lavish editions and their accompanying exhibits.[93] These collaborative projects have sparked interest in the Soviet graphic art for young audiences, which has resulted in comprehensive monographs on comic books and animation as a visual art form.[94] The emergent interest in Soviet children's illustration has also led to the creation of Princeton University's online database of Soviet children's books *Playing Soviet: The Visual Languages of Soviet Children's Picture Books, 1917-1953*.[95]

A more comprehensive understanding of the scope and variety of Soviet cultural production for children has become possible after authors of critical volumes and exhibition curators gained access to collections of original artwork, Glavlit and Sojuzmul'tfil'm archives, transcripts of editorial and censorship committee meetings, and writers' and film-makers' personal files, their NKVD and KGB dossiers included. Another contribution to the field has been made by dedicated historians who discovered Russian and Soviet childhood as a previously unexplored, but resonant and controversial theme. Kelly's *Children's World: Growing Up in Russia, 1890-1991*, is supplemented by a personalized history of the Stalinist era in Orlando Figes's *The Whisperers: Private Life in Stalin's Russia*, while Julie deGraffenried's thorough investigation of Soviet state policies regarding young soldiers and war victims in *Sacrificing Childhood: Children and the Soviet State in the Great Patriotic War* is echoed in Olga Kucherenko's perceptive study of war orphans in *Soviet Street Children and the Second World War: Welfare and Social Control under Stalin*.[96] Lisa A. Kirschenbaum's insightful analysis of early pedagogical efforts by the Soviet

---

93   Peter Noever, ed., *Shili-Byli: Russian Children's Books 1920-1940*, Vienna 2004; Julian Rothenstein and Olga Budashevskaya, eds., *Inside the Rainbow. Russian Children's Literature 1920-1935: Beautiful Books, Terrible Times*, ed., London 2013; Robert Bird, *Adventures in the Soviet Imaginary: Children's Books and Graphic Art* (Vol. 11 of *Exhibition Catalogues, Chicago University Library*), Chicago 2011.

94   David MacFadyen, *Yellow Crocodiles and Blue Oranges: Russian Animated Film Since World War Two*. Montreal 2005; José Alaniz, *Komiks: Comic Art in Russia*. Jackson, MS 2010; Laura Pontieri, *Soviet Animation and the Thaw of 1960s: Not Only for Children*, New Barnet, Herts, UK 2012; Maya Balakirsky Katz, *Drawing the Iron Curtain: Jews and the Golden Age of Soviet Animation*, New Brunswick, NJ 2016.

95   ⟨http://commons.princeton.edu/soviet/⟩ (Accessed December 1, 2017).

96   Catriona Kelly, *Children's World: Growing Up in Russia, 1890-1991*, New Haven and London 2007; Orlando Figes's *The Whisperers: Private Life in Stalin's Russia*, New York 2007; Julie deGraffenried, *Sacrificing Childhood: Children and the Soviet State in the Great Patriotic War*, Lawrence 2014; Olga Kucherenko, *Soviet Street Children and the Second World War: Welfare and Social Control under Stalin*, London and New York 2016.

state in *Small Comrades: Revolutionizing Childhood in Soviet Russia, 1917-1932* (New York 2001), was followed by several important studies of Bolshevik education policies.[97] A number of monumental oral history projects conducted in post-Soviet Russia led to the publication of many informative, but also heartrending, volumes, including Cathy A. Frierson's and Semyon S. Vilensky's *Children of the Gulag* and Svetlana Alexievich's *Последние свидетели: соло для детского голоса* (*The Last Witnesses: A Hundred of Unchildlike Lullabies*).[98] The most valuable feature of these works is the historically accurate depiction of Soviet youth, due to the fact that any analysis of state-controlled production for the young, with its thoroughly distilled and very focused ideological message, would not be feasible without an accurate profiling of the flesh-and-blood, rags-and-bones audiences of Soviet children's literature and films.

Among recent monographs on Soviet children's culture, those volumes stand out which zoom in either on its recipients, or on the authors' power of ideological and aesthetic transgression. Sara Pankenier Weld's *Voiceless Vanguard: The Infantilist Aesthetic of the Russian Avant-Garde* provides a comprehensive examination of the overlap between the Russian Modernism's propensity for verbal play, imaginativeness, and stylistic quirkiness and the linguistic and figurative playfulness of Avant-Garde children's literature.[99] According to Weld, children's culture had a significant impact on Avant-Garde practice from its earliest origins, inspiring the Neo-Primitivist and Cubo-Futurist aesthetics of the 1900-1920s, even before Avant-Garde writers such as those affiliated with OBERIU integrated "infantile" elements in poetic works for young readers. In

---

[97] See, for instance, Megan Behrent's "Literacy and Revolution," in Jeff Bale and Sarah Knopp, eds., *Education and Capitalism: Struggles for Learning and Liberation*, Chicago 2012, 217-241; Matthew D. Pauly, *Breaking the Tongue: Language, Education, and Power in Soviet Ukraine, 1923-1934*, Toronto and London 2014; Evgenij M. Balashov, "The Russian School System and School Students during the Wars and Revolutions of 1914-22," in Murray Frame, Boris Kolonitskij, Steven G. Marks, Melissa K. Stockdale, eds., *Russian Culture in War and Revolution, 1914-1922*, Bloomington, IN 2014; and Vitalij Besrogov, "'If the War Comes Tomorrow': Patriotic Education in Soviet and Post-Soviet Primary School," in Mark Bassin and Catriona Kelly, eds., *Soviet and Post-Soviet Identities*, Cambridge, UK and New York 2012.

[98] Cathy A. Frierson and Semyon S. Vilensky, *Children of the Gulag*, New Haven 2010; Svetlana Alexievich, *Последние свидетели: соло для детского голоса*, Moscow 2007. See also, Cynthia Simmons and Nina Perlina, *Writing the Siege of Leningrad: Women's Diaries, Memoirs, and Documentary Prose*, Pittsburg 2002; and Jehanne Gheith, *Gulag Voices: Oral Histories of Soviet Incarceration and Exile*, New York 2011.

[99] Sara Pankenier Weld, *Voiceless Vanguard: The Infantilist Aesthetic of the Russian Avant-Garde*, Evanston 2014.

a different vein, Kelly's *Comrade Pavlik: The Rise and Fall of a Soviet Boy Hero* (London 2005), traces the emergence and nation-wide dissemination of a cultural myth of a valiant boy whose political outlook and heroic conduct, however implausible, in view of the resurfaced archival data, affected the young Soviet readers' and movie-goers' complete rejection of infantile children's culture, with its familial affection, baby talk, and celebration of innocence. The same fascination with the mythological and mythologizing properties of Soviet and post-Soviet children's culture is manifest in the emergence of the journal *Детские чтения* (*Children's Readings: Studies in Children's Literature*), which began publication in St. Petersburg in 2012 and presently includes fifteen substantial and enlightening installments. Most engaging material appearing in this journal delves into such problems as the literary representation and anthropology of Soviet childhood, the relationship between Soviet political institutions and cultural production for the young, and the ability of Soviet authors to undermine ideological frameworks while creating apparently conformist, if not aggressively propagandistic, literary works for children.[100]

The *Companion to Soviet Children's Literature and Film* complements the vibrant scholarship of the last thirty years by emphasizing the ideological, aesthetic, psychological, and political impact of the Soviet children's culture not only on the USSR's youngest citizens, but also on their Post-Soviet descendants. In "The Queer Legacies of Late Socialism, or What Cheburashka and Gary Shteyngart Have in Common," Anna Fishzon explores the peculiar appearance, behavior, and mannerisms of protagonists of animated films transplanted to the Soviet collective imagination by translators and film directors.

---

100 The journal is edited by Marija Litovskaja, Svetlana Maslinskaya, Irina Arzamasskaja, et al. Among the articles of interest in the context of this volume are: Marina Balina, "Литературная репрезентация детства в советской и постсоветской России," in *Детские чтения* 1 (2012), 43-66; Aleksej Mironov, "Жизнь замечательных игрушек: Трансформация образов животных-игрушек в российской литературе," in *Детские чтения* 3 (2015), 257-272; Svetlana Maslinskaya, "'Пионерская' беллетристика vs. 'большая' детская литература," in *Детские чтения* 1 (2012), 100-116; Evgenij Ponomarev, "Воспитание новых людей. Методика преподавания литературы в советской школе 1930-х годов," in *Детские чтения* 5 (2014), 95-121; Elena Dushechkina, "'Чтобы тело и душа были молоды…': Тема оздоровительной профилактики и здоровья в советской детской песне," in *Детские чтения* 5 (2014), 191-200; Valerij Vjugin, "'…Чистые люди, почти "святые"' ('Мистер Твистер,' Маршак и табу)," in *Детские чтения* 4 (2014), 152-189; Mark Lipoveckij, "Шалуны, враги, другие… Трикстер в советской и постсоветской детской литературе," in *Детские чтения* 6 (2014), 7-22; Igor' Vdovenko, "Мурзилка на фабрике советского (модели присвоения и переозначивания 'чужого' в советской детской литературе)," in *Детские чтения* 10 (2016), 237-269.

In this study, the queerness of Fedor Chitruk's Vinni-Puch and Pjatachok, and of Kachanov's Cheburashka and Gena, is emblematic of the Soviet culture's attempts to deal with the historical trauma of the 1920s-50s. Fishzon draws a parallel between both the child and animal characters' anxieties, as well as the film directors' infantilizing portrayal of the cartoons' "adults" Puch and Gena, and the representation of failure in the relationship between a father and child in *Little Failure*, a memoir by Shteyngart, a contemporary Russian-Jewish American writer. Marina Balina, in "Re-Imagining the Past for Future Generations: History as Fiction in Soviet Children's Literature," approaches the problem of restoring the shattered cross-generational relationships as well as the broken "connection between times" from a different perspective. Although Balina analyses Soviet-era historical prose for children as a prototype of "infantilized" historical fiction for adults, her main argument concerns the relative autonomy and greater originality of the children's version of the genre – two qualities that have allowed young readers to flee into the enchanting realms of ancient classics. According to Balina, it was children's prose that preserved the pre-revolutionary tradition of historical storytelling, and saved generations of young Soviet readers from a heavily politicized perception of historical discourses which adults could not avoid.

One can study the continuity of the Russian children's literary and cinematic tradition from a variety of standpoints. One of them is the recognition of the influence of the Avant-Garde on Soviet poetry, fiction, translation, animation, and film for young audiences. Although the impact has already been well-established, the *Companion*'s authors provide fresh perspectives and new knowledge on the legacy of the Avant-Garde in Soviet children's literature and film. In "The Junctures of Child Psychology and Soviet Avant-Garde Film: Representations, Influences, Applications," Ana Hedberg Olenina examines the way in which early Soviet filmmakers engaged with pedological theories and practices. The Bolshevik investment into the new science of the child in the 1920s gave rise to multiple research institutions, which rivaled each other in the race to create a materialist platform for pedagogy steeped in reflexology and Marxist sociology. Documentaries and feature films from the 1920s have preserved traces of diverse models of a child's psyche articulated by Soviet psychologists. In her first case study, Olenina analyzes Vsevolod Pudovkin's unintentionally harrowing representation of Ivan Pavlov's experiments in reflexology conducted in Soviet orphanages in the *kulturfilm*, Механика головного мозга (*Mechanics of the Human Brain*, 1926). In her second case study, she discusses Sergei Eisenstein's idiosyncratic interpretation of child reflexology, as well as Lev Vygockij and Aleksandr Lurija's cultural-historical theory, which informed some of the stylistic decisions in the director's drama about the

Young Pioneers, Бежин луг (*Bezhin Meadow*, 1935-1937). Overall, as Olenina argues, these cinematic projects reveal just how illusory the Bolshevik ideologues' dream of a consolidated front in child science and its straightforward channeling into the arts was.

Entitled "The Dictionary as a Toy Collection: Interactions between Avant-Garde Aesthetics and Soviet Children's Literature," Ainsley Morse's chapter also addresses the Avant-Garde authors' and illustrators' contributions to the Bolshevik project of building a pristine state and creating an entirely new type of individual. Her lens, however, is linguistic and historical, rather than informed by psychology. By looking into experimental modernist writers' reconciliation of the so-called *beyonsense* (*заумь*) and young children's inventive use of language, Morse convincingly validates the aspiration of the early Soviet children's literature to create a revolutionary poetics – the poetics that is grounded in the right of the youngest Soviet citizens to experiment, break linguistic norms, and be creative.

While Morse's essay focuses on the value of the ground-breaking work of Russian modernist authors and illustrators' in early Soviet literature for children, Oleg Minin's essay, "The Literary Avant-Garde and Soviet Literature for Children: OBERIU in the Leningrad Periodicals *Еж* and *Чиж*," offers a thorough assessment of the contribution to early Soviet literature for children by Russia's last experimental poetic group, "The Association of Real Art." Minin's meticulous analysis of Charms, Jurij Vladimirov, Aleksandr Vvedenskij, Nikolaj Zabolockij, and Nikolaj Olejnikov's contributions to the two literary children's journals, *Чиж* (*The Finch*) and *Еж* (*The Hedgehog*), provides a rare insight into the strategies of both political conformity and creative transgression engendered by the OBERIU authors. By tracing their tragic destinies, Minin reveals the OBERIU's individual and collective failure to survive in the thickening atmosphere of Stalinist terror. His analysis of the poets' playful language and humorous tropes also helps illustrate why even the most politically engaged works by Charms and Vvedenskij continue to attract a sizeable readership today.

Sara Pankenier Weld's "Unnatural Selection: A Natural History of Early Soviet Picturebooks" similarly focuses on the predatory relationship between the state and its children's authors, but her perspective examines the evolutionary dynamic interrelation between writers and illustrators and the Soviet censorship. According to Weld, censorship as an intensive selective pressure, in addition to its obvious negative consequences, had unintentional secondary effects that drove the development of mimicry and "camouflage" in books for children and thus enabled covert communication under adverse conditions. In the late 1920s and the early 1930s, when the extent of censorship became prohibitive, the example of Charms illustrates the life-and- death stakes if and when such covert messages were intercepted.

However vicious the struggle for survival, some of experimental writers and artists of the early 1920s and their later disciples managed to carry the Avant-Garde legacy well into the 1960s and beyond. Both Larissa Rudova and Lora Wheeler Mjolsness examine new approaches to the literary and artistic experimentation by Soviet film-makers. By tracing the artistic biography of Ivan Ivanov-Vano, in her "Under the Hypnosis of Disney: Ivan Ivanov-Vano and Soviet Animation for Children," Mjolsness reveals the renowned Soviet animator's indebtedness to Walt Disney. Her analysis of Ivanov-Vano's transition from purely experimental work in animation, informed by the Avant-Garde experimentation, to ideologically driven fairytale narratives that celebrated Russianness in the midst of Stalin's anti-cosmopolitan campaign and the Cold War reveals a controversial aspect of the director's borrowing from Disney. Mjolsness establishes that Soviet competition with the West was as prominent in the area of cultural production for Soviet children as it was in literature and film created for adult audiences.

Rudova's "Embracing Eccentricity: Золушка and the Avant-Garde Imagination" presents Kosheverova and Shapiro's Золушка (*Cinderella*, 1947) as a work of art that harkened back to the early Soviet cinematic and theatrical experimentation, while foregoing the constraining clichés of Socialist Realist musical comedies. According to Rudova, Золушка is a work of "double estrangement" – it immerses the viewer in a narrative that, in the words of Viktor Shklovskij, "lays bare" the whimsical and utterly non-realist storytelling devices. The film contains hidden references to Avant-Garde artistic techniques and even personalities that could not be openly mentioned on the Soviet screen. With Золушка, Rudova tells us, Avant-Garde experimental cinematic imagination made a triumphal comeback, enchanting traumatized post-war audiences and offering them a dazzling artistic diversion.

Another original feature of the *Companion* is its focus on obscure prototypes of well-known Soviet works for children. In her "'Be Always Ready!': Hero Narratives in Soviet Children's Literature," Svetlana Maslinskaya investigates some of the forgotten texts and films about pioneer heroes, which were enormously influential in their time. Maslinskaya outlines the development of the child hero trope with great historical and textological accuracy, pointing out numerous pre-revolutionary and early Soviet predecessors of the better-known pioneer hero narratives from the 1930s-50s. Her impressive foray into the mass media's representation of valiant young citizens of the Soviet state helps elucidate the influence of newspaper discourse on the construction of a rigid and "hagiographic" image of the Bolshevik child hero. Maslinskaya's study spans Soviet history in its entirety, providing a comprehensive survey both of the heroic genre in children's literature and film and of its protagonists.

Tatiana Voronina and Polina Barskova examine discursive approaches to heroism in children's literature from a different angle. Their "Unspeakable Truths: Children of the Siege in Soviet Literature" engages in a unique investigation of the entire spectrum of the Soviet representation of the Siege childhood – from narratives of denial and concealment, produced during the war, to the more frank and humanistic representation of the starving, frost-bitten, grieving fatalities of one of the war's most brutal atrocities. For Voronina and Barskova, literature about the Siege childhood is still a work in progress, for it is only the brutally honest and psychologically complex works of fiction that contribute to the process of healing the trauma experienced by the city of Leningrad and, in a broader sense, by the entire Soviet people.

As Voronina and Barskova's essay demonstrates, the *Companion's* other distinctive characteristic is its focus on the re-interpretation of Soviet historical reality from the perspective of the child, who could be both an agent of socialist construction and its victim. In "Education of the Soul, Bolshevik Style: Pedagogy in Soviet Children's Literature from the 1920s to the early 1930s," I analyze fictional depictions of children as educators of adults in the context of the pedagogical ideas of prominent Bolshevik leaders. My essay elucidates the early Soviet state's reliance on its youngest, politically "untainted" citizens as efficient catalysts for the country's transition to socialism. I suggest that images of children as educators of adults prevailed in Soviet children's literature only briefly. By the late 1930s, Soviet fiction for children reverted to an authoritarian educational model, which relied on a strict hierarchy of power relations: from the state insistent on firm control over every aspect of learning, to the teacher or parents who implemented this control, and even down to the obedient, hard-working, well-disciplined student. Disobedient child protagonists capable of resisting the authority of their parents and educators re-emerged only through the liberal reforms of the "Thaw" era, when Soviet society began to question the parental functions assumed by the state.

The vibrancy of Soviet cinematic and literary production for the young, as well as the canon's indebtedness to literary translation as an art form and a strategy for circumventing the ideological demands of the state, comes to the fore in Maria Khotimsky's "Children's Poetry and Translation in the Soviet Era: Strategies of Rewriting, Transformation and Adaptation." Khotimsky covers vast historical and poetic terrain by linking early endeavors to transplant European children's poetry to Russian soil and post-war attempts to translate, re-translate, thematically and poetically embellish, cinematize, or set to music literary works written in English, German, Yiddish, and Polish. Her essay connects many dots on the volume's conceptual map by presenting efforts made by Soviet poets to render children's poetry written in other languages into Russian as an attempt to preserve the linguistic and figurative richness of the genre under conditions of strict political control.

It is important to note that the *Companion* conceptualizes translation as an integral attribute of Soviet cultural production for children as a whole. It offers readers a chance to compare the original Soviet literary and cinematic output for the young to works derived from a range of sources, be it poems and novels in other languages, American animation, or pre-revolutionary Russian literature. Moreover, this volume may be metaphorically viewed as a work of translation, because some of the contributors strive to convert aspects of the contemporary discourse on Soviet cultural production for children from the language of overwhelming, but not always thoughtful, public approval in Russia to that of scholarly analysis and historical re-evaluation.

Chukovskij's "Крокодил" may again help us emphasize the necessity – and even inevitability – of translating the past into the language of the present. The story's protagonist, Vanja Vasil'chikov, emerged victorious because he was able to resolve a difficult moral dilemma: instead of killing the escaped predators whose aggressive behavior threatened the peace and security of Petrograd citizens, he liberated and indoctrinated them. Chukovskij's poetically exuberant, captivating tale that immortalized Vanja's exploit, launched Soviet cultural production for children and then remained with Soviet readers for generations. Fun to read and easy to recite, it is likely to live on in Russian families and nursery schools as a Soviet counterpart to the Anglophone children's favorites, *Good Night, Moon* and *The Little Engine that Could*. But unlike these works, it has its share of political conflict, ideological rhetoric and violence. Therefore, reading "Крокодил" today requires reflection, interpretation, and mediation on the part of grown-ups who share it with their children. Many adults may overlook the book's subversive features, lulled by the familiarity of Chukovskij's poetic lines and the sheer vivacity of the story. This does not mean, however, that their offspring will not benefit from a more in-depth, contemplative introduction to the foundational tale of the Soviet children's literary canon. As this *Companion* demonstrates, the literary and cinematic works created in the Soviet Union and Post-Soviet Russia between 1917 and 2017 contain many controversial motifs and images that glorify brutality or eulogize the country's totalitarian culture. Instead of accepting this Soviet children's culture uncritically, the new generation of Russians has a duty to sort out this legacy and re-evaluate the continuity of national cultural production for young readers and viewers.

Works Cited

Primary Sources

Belych, Grigorij, and Leonid Panteleev. *Республика ШКИД*. Moscow 2014.

Blinov, Aleksandr. *Море, бабка и охламон*. Moscow 2017.

Chukovskij, Kornej. "Ваня и крокодил," in *Для детей* 1-12 (1917).

Chukovskij, Kornej. *Приключения Крокодила Крокодиловича*, ill. Re-Mi. Petrograd 1919.

Chukovskij, Kornej. *Об этой книжке: Стихи*, Moscow 1961.

Gajdar, Arkadij. *Военная тайна. Голубая чашка. Тимур и его команда. Чук и Гек*. Moscow 2014.

Gajdar, Arkadij. *Школа*. Minsk 1976.

Kassil', Lev. "Дорогие мои мальчишки," in Kassil', *Собрание сочинений в пяти томах*, Vol. 2, Moscow 1987.

Kaverin, Veniamin. *Два капитана*, Moscow 2004.

Kharms, Daniil. *It Happened Like This: Stories and Poems*. Trans. Katya Arnold. New York 1998.

Kharms, Daniil. *First, Second*. Ill. Marc Rosenthal, trans. Richard Pevear. New York 1996.

Michalkov, Sergej. *Все начинается с детства*. Moscow 1972.

Oseeva, Valentina. *Васек Трубачев и его товарищи*, Moscow 1961.

Panteleev, Leonid. "Честное слово," in Костер 6 (1941), 1-3.

The Fire Horse: Children's Poems by Vladimir Mayakovsky, Osip Mandelstam, and Daniil Kharms, trans. Eugene Ostashevsky. New York 2017.

Tichonov, Nikolaj. "Баллада о гвоздях," in *Стихотворения и поэмы*, Leningrad 1981, 116.

Secondary Sources

"Детям до 16-ти: как цензура пришла в подростковую литературу," in *Lenta.ru*, May 27, 2015, ⟨https://lenta.ru/articles/2015/05/27/teenagers/⟩ (Accessed December 22, 2017).

"Материалы VIII Съезда советских писателей," in *Литературная газета* 1986 (July 2), 16.

"Нужен 'золотой канон' для школьной программы по литературе – Патриарх Кирилл," in *Православное Закамье*, May 25, 2016, ⟨http://pravchelny.ru/all_publications/publications/?ID=13872⟩ (Accessed December 21, 2017).

Alaniz, José. *Komiks: Comic Art in Russia*. Jackson, MS 2010.

Androsenko, Tatjana. "Интервью с главным редактором," in *Мурзилка*, April 12, 2014, ⟨http://www.murzilka.org/home/about-magazine/smi-o-zhurnale/intervju-s-glavnym-redaktorom/interfaks/⟩ (Accessed December 21, 2017).

Balachonova, Irina. "У нас нет книжек, с которыми все ясно," in *Год литературы 2017*, ⟨https://godliteratury.ru/projects/u-nas-net-knizhek-s-kotorymi-vsyo-yasno⟩ (Accessed December 2, 2017).

Balakirsky Katz, Maya. *Drawing the Iron Curtain: Jews and the Golden Age of Soviet Animation*. New Brunswick, NJ 2016.

Balashov, Evgenij M. "The Russian School System and School Students during the Wars and Revolutions of 1914-22," in Murray Frame, Boris Kolonitskij, Steven G. Marks, Melissa K. Stockdale, eds., *Russian Culture in War and Revolution, 1914-1922*. Bloomington, IN 2014.

Balina, Marina. "Воспитание чувств a la sovietique: повести о первой любви," in A. S. Obuchova, M. V. Tendrjakova, eds., *Ребенок в истории и культуре*. Moscow 2010.

Balina, Marina. "Литературная репрезентация детства в советской и постсоветской России," in *Детские чтения* 1 (2012), 43-66.

Balina, Marina. "Советская детская литература: несколько слов о предмете исследования," in Balina and Valerij Vjugin, eds., *"Убить Чарскую": парадоксы советской литературы для детей*. St. Petersburg 2013.

Behrent, Megan. "Literacy and Revolution," in Jeff Bale and Sarah Knopp, eds., *Education and Capitalism: Struggles for Learning and Liberation*, Chicago 2012, 217-241.

Berlin, Isaiah. "The Artificial Dialectic: Generalissimo Stalin and the Art of Government," in Berlin, *The Soviet Mind: Russian Culture under Communism*. Henry Hardy, ed. Washington DC 2003, 98-118.

Besrogov, Vitalij. "'If the War Comes Tomorrow': Patriotic Education in Soviet and Post-Soviet Primary School," in Mark Bassin and Catriona Kelly, eds., *Soviet and Post-Soviet Identities*. Cambridge, UK and New York 2012.

Beumers, Birgit. *A History of Russian Cinema*. London and New York 2008.

Beumers, Birgit, ed. *A Companion to Russian Cinema*. Malden, MA and Oxford, UK 2016.

Beumers, Birgit, Stephen Hutchings, Natalia Rulyova, eds. *The Post-Soviet Russian Media: Conflicting Signals*. New York 2009.

Bucharova, Darja. "Машина времени издательства 'Речь,'" in *Материнство*, November 27, 2014, ⟨https://materinstvo.ru/art/9681⟩ (Accessed December 2, 2017).

Caute, David. *Politics and the Novel During the Cold War*. New Brunswick, NJ 2009.

Chudakova, Marietta. "Заметки о языке современной прозы," in *Избранные работы*, Vol. 1 (*Литература советского прошлого*). Moscow 2001.

Chudakova, Marietta. "Сквозь звезды к терниям," in *Новый мир* 4 (1990), 242-262.

Davydov, Petr. "Что читать детям? Беседа с Марией Минаевой о литературе для детей – православной и просто хорошей," in *Православие.ru*, ⟨http://www.pravoslavie.ru/90231.html⟩ (Accessed December 21, 2017).

Dimke, Darja. "Юные коммунары, или Крестовый поход детей: между утопией декларируемой и утопией реальной," in Ilja Kukulin, Marija Majofis and Petr Safronov, eds., *Острова утопии: Педагогическое и социальное проектирование послевоенной школы (1940-1980-е)*. Moscow 2015, 360-396.

Dobrenko, Evgeny. *Stalinist Cinema and the Production of History*. Edinburgh 2008.

Dolzhenko, L. *Рациональное и эмоциональное в русской детской литературе 50-80-х годов XX в. (Н. Н. Носов, В. Ю. Драгунский, В.П. Крапивин)*. Volgograd 2001.

Dushechkina, Elena. "'Чтобы тело и душа были молоды...': Тема оздоровительной профилактики и здоровья в советской детской песне," in *Детские чтения* 5 (2014), 191-200.

Etkind, Alexander. *Warped Mourning: Stories of the Undead in the Land of the Unburied (Cultural Memory in the Present)*. Stanford, CA 2013, 14-15.

Fateev, Andrej. *Сталинизм и детская литература в политике номенклатуры СССР (1930-е – 1950-е гг.)*. Moscow 2007.

Flood, Christopher G. *Political Myth: A Theoretical Introduction*. London and New York 2005.

Gor'kij, Maksim. "Литературу – детям," in *Правда*, June 11, 1933, 1.

Gourianova, Nina. *The Aesthetics of Anarchy: Art and Ideology in the Early Russian Avant-Garde*. Berkeley, Los Angeles, and London 2012.

Groys, Boris. *Art Power*. Boston 2008.

Harrasov, Roman. "Завести тренера по чтению или другие способы приучить детей любить книги" in *My L!fe*, September 26, 2016 ⟨https://life.ru/t/звук/908442/zaviesti_trieniera_po_chtieniiu_i_drughiie_sposoby_priuchit_dietiei_liubit_knighi⟩ (Accessed December 18, 2017).

Hellman, Ben. *Fairy Tales and True Stories: The History of Russian Literature for Children and Young People (1574-2010)*. Leiden and Boston 2013.

Hicks, Jeremy. "Soiuzdetfilm: The Birth of Soviet Children's Film and the Child Actor," in Birgit Beumers, ed., *A Companion to Russian Cinema*. Malden, MA and Oxford 2016, 117-136.

Jakovleva, Julija. "Состояние литературы: детские книги в России. Круглый стол редакторов на Colta.ru," in *Colta.ru*, May 29, 2015, ⟨https://www.colta.ru/articles/literature/7485⟩ (Accessed December 2, 2017).

Jampol'skaja, Elena. "Министр культуры РФ Владимир Мединский: 'Без идеологии человек становится животным'" in *Газета "Культура,"* April 9, 2013 ⟨http://portal-kultura.ru/articles/kolonka-glavnogo-redaktora/8642-ministr-kultury-rf-vladimir-medinskiy-bez-ideologii-chelovek-stanovitsya-zhivotnym/⟩ (Accessed November 2, 2017).

Kelly, Catriona. "Об изучении истории детства в России XIX - XX веков," in G. V. Makarevich, ed., *Какорея. Из истории детства в России и других странах*. Moscow and Tver' 2008, 8-46.

Kelly, Catriona. *Children's World: Growing Up in Russia, 1890-1991*. New Haven and London 2007.

Kon, Lidija. *О детской литературе: сборник статей*. Moscow 1950.

Kondakov, Igor'. "'Убежище-2': 'Детский дискурс' советской литературы в 1930-е годы," in *Ребенок в истории и культуре, Библиотека журнала Исследователь / Researcher*, Vol. 4. Moscow 2010, 70-117.

Kukulin, Ilja. "Воспитание воли в советской психологии и детская литература конца 1940-х – начала 1950-х гг.," in Kukulin, Marija Majofis and Petr Safronov, eds., *Острова утопии: Педагогическое и социальное проектирование послевоенной школы (1940-1980-е)*. Moscow 2015, 152-190.

Lenin, Vladimir. "From the Speech Delivered at the Third All-Russian Congress of the Russian Young Communist League, October 2, 1920," in Julian Rothenstein and Olga Budashevskaya, eds., *Inside the Rainbow: Russian Children's Literature 1920-1935: Beautiful Books, Terrible Times*. London 2013, 76-77.

Lipoveckij, Mark. "Шалуны, враги, другие… Трикстер в советской и постсоветской детской литературе," in *Детские чтения* 6 (2014), 7-22.

Lunacharskij, Anatolij. *О детской литературе, детском и юношеском чтении: Сборник*. Moscow 1985.

MacFadyen, David. *Yellow Crocodiles and Blue Oranges: Russian Animated Film since World War Two*. Montreal 2005.

Marsh, Rosalind J. *Literature, History, and Identity in Post-Soviet Russia, 1991-2006*. Oxford, Bern, New York 2007.

Maslinskaya, Svetlana. "Жизнеописание пионера-героя: текстовая традиция и ритуальный контекст," in *Современная российская мифология*. Moscow 2005, 89-123.

Maslinskaya, Svetlana. "'Пионерская' беллетристика vs. 'большая' детская литература," in *Детские чтения* 1 (2012), 100-116.

Medzhibovskaya, Inessa. "Lev Kassil. Childhood as Religion and Ideology," in Marina Balina and Larissa Rudova, eds., *Russian Children's Literature and Culture*. New York and London 2008, 241-262.

Mescherjakova, M. I. *Русская детская, подростковая и юношеская проза 2 половины XX века: Проблемы поэтики*. Moscow 1997.

Michajlovskaja, Marija. "В Министерстве образования поддержали идею создания обязательного списка школьной литературы," in *Парламентская газета*, November 13, 2016, ⟨https://www.pnp.ru/social/2016/11/13/v-ministerstve-obrazovaniya-podderzhali-ideyu-sozdaniya-obyazatelnogo-spiska-shkolnoy-literatury.html⟩ (Accessed December 8, 2017).

Milkus, Aleksandr, and Ksenija Konjuchova. "Министр образования и науки Ольга Васильева: 'В школе будем наводить порядок. Полумер не ждите!'" in *Комсомольская правда*, October 5, 2016, ⟨https://www.spb.kp.ru/daily/26589/3605216/⟩ (Accessed December 8, 2017).

Miloserdova, Natalja. "Детское кино," in L. Budjak and D. Karavaev, eds., *Страницы истории отечественного кино*. Moscow 2006, 6-133.

Mironov, Aleksej. "Жизнь замечательных игрушек: Трансформация образов животных-игрушек в российской литературе," in *Детские чтения* 3 (2015), 257-272.

Nadtochij, Eduard. "Тимур и его arcana: социально-антропологическое значение советской 'революции детства' в 1920-30-е годы," in *Социология власти* 3 (2014), 81-98.

Noordenbos, Boris. *Post-Soviet Literature and the Search for a Russian Identity*. New York 2016.

Pauly, Matthew D. *Breaking the Tongue: Language, Education, and Power in Soviet Ukraine, 1923-1934*. Toronto and London 2014.

Petrova, Maria. *Национальная идея России: история и современность*. Izhevsk 2005.

Petrovskij, Miron. *Книги нашего детства*. St. Petersburg 2006.

Petrovskij, Miron. "Что отпирает 'Золотой ключик'?" in *Вопросы литературы* 1979 (4).

Ponomarev, Evgenij. "Воспитание новых людей. Методика преподавания литературы в советской школе 1930-х годов," in *Детские чтения* 5 (2014), 95-121.

Pontieri, Laura. *Soviet Animation and the Thaw of 1960s: Not Only for Children*. New Barnet, Herts, UK 2012.

Prokhorov, Alexander. "Arresting Development: A Brief History of Soviet Cinema for Children and Adolescents," in Marina Balina and Larissa Rudova, eds., *Russian Children's Literature and Culture*. New York 2008, 112-124.

Prokhorov, Alexander and Elena. *Film and Television Genres of the Late Soviet Era*. New York 2017.

Prokhorova, Elena. "A Traditionalist in the Land of Innovators: The Paradoxes of Sergei Mikhalkov," in Marina Balina and Larissa Rudova, eds., *Russian Children's Literature and Culture*. New York and London 2008, 285-306.

Putilova, Evgenija. *Детское чтение – для сердца и разума: Очерки по истории детской литературы*. St. Petersburg 2005.

Rappaport, Helen. *Joseph Stalin: A Biographical Companion*. Santa Barbara, CA 1999.

Ronen, Omri. "Детская литература и социалистический реализм," in Hans Günther and Evgenij Dobrenko, eds., *Соцреалистический канон*. St. Petersburg 2000, 969-80.

Rudova, Larissa. "From Character-Building to Criminal Pursuits: Russian Children's Literature in Transition," in Marina Balina and Rudova, eds., *Russian Children's Literature and Culture*. New York and London 2008, 19-40.

Russian Book Union. "Национальная программа поддержки и развития чтения в РФ," ⟨http://www.bookunion.ru/doc_news/концепция_блок_ТП%20(1).pdf⟩ (Accessed December 2, 2017).

Salem, Linda C. *Children's Literature Studies: Cases and Discussions*. Westport, CT and London 2006.

Sal'nikova, A. A., and A. P. Burmistrov. "Советское детское игровое кино 20-х годов XX века и его юные зрители," in *Ученые записки Казанского университета* 156:3 (2014), 131-141.

Selivanova, Elena. "Васильева одобрила список школьной литературы, предложенный патриархом," September 24, 2016, ⟨https://www.opentown.org/news/127309/⟩ (Accessed December 8, 2017).

Tippner, Anja. "Evgenii Shvarts's Fairy Tale Dramas: Theater, Power, and the Naked Truth," in Marina Balina and Larissa Rudova, eds., *Russian Children's Literature and Culture*. New York and London 2008, 307-323.

Tudor, Henry. *Political Myth*. New York 1972.

Tynjanov, Jurij. "Корней Чуковский," in *Детская литература* 4 (1939), 24-25.

Ushakin, Sergej. "Пролог," in Ilja Kukulin, Mark Lipoveckij, and Marija Majofis, eds., *Веселые человечки: Культурные герои советского детства*. Moscow 2008.

Vdovenko, Igor'. "Мурзилка на фабрике советского (модели присвоения и переозначивания 'чужого' в советской детской литературе)," in *Детские чтения* 10 (2016), 237-269.

Vjugin, Valerij. "'...Чистые люди, почти "святые"' ('Мистер Твистер,' Маршак и табу)," in *Детские чтения* 4 (2014), 152-189.

Voloshina, Viktorija. "Страна счастливых людей и улыбающихся милиционеров," in *Gazeta.ru*, ⟨https://www.gazeta.ru/25_years_without_the_USSR/8274407.shtml⟩ (Accessed November 1, 2017).

PART 1

Forging a New Children's Culture:
(R)evolution, Poetics, Aesthetics

∴

CHAPTER 1

Unnatural Selection: A Natural History of Early Soviet Picturebooks

Sara Pankenier Weld

1 Introduction

When Charles Darwin describes the principle of natural selection in his landmark treatise *On the Origin of Species* (1859), he bases his groundbreaking new theory of what occurs in nature on what people have long witnessed "in the hands of man":

> Can the principle of selection, which we have seen is so potent in the hands of man, apply in nature? I think we shall see that it can act most effectually. [...] Let it be borne in mind how infinitely complex and close-fitting are the mutual relations of all organic beings to each other and to their physical conditions of life. [...] Can we doubt (remembering that many more individuals are born than can possibly survive) that individuals having any advantage, however slight, over others, would have the best chance of surviving and of procreating their kind? On the other hand, we may feel sure that any variation in the least degree injurious would be rigidly destroyed. This preservation of favourable variations and the rejection of injurious variations, I call Natural Selection.[1]

In this chapter I propose to examine the fierce censorship that reigned in the Soviet Union and exerted an undue influence on the publication and survival of works of literature as a form of intensive selective pressure, although in this instance it more appropriately might be termed 'unnatural selection.' This chapter studies a process of unnatural selection through a closer look at the evolution of one particular literary organism – the early Soviet picturebook

---

[1] Charles Darwin, *On the Origin of Species by Means of Natural Selection or the Preservation of Favoured Races in the Struggle for Life.* London 1859. Though this article opens with reference to Darwin, the "evolutionary" processes it describes might also be compared to the theories of Jean-Baptise Lamarck, which do not require successive generations for their functionality, or epigenetics today.

in the 1920s and 1930s – which itself amounted to a newly evolved hybrid form, bringing together image and text and uniquely combining Avant-Garde aesthetics and an ideological investment in the child as audience that was motivated by revolutionary ideals.

In considering the role of this unnatural selection on the development of the early Soviet picturebook, this chapter builds on the work of Lev Loseff, who authored the scholarly study *On the Beneficence of Censorship: Aesopian Language in Modern Russian Literature*.[2] In his work, Loseff explores the prevalence in Russian literature of Aesopian language, which cloaks forbidden ideas behind a simpler surface in order to escape the notice of censors. I here contend that censorship, if considered apart from its obviously negative impact and often devastating consequences for writers, exerts an influence on the literary organism that may be productively compared to evolutionary pressure, which, if not causing outright extinction, might drive innovation and invention and even increase the vigor of the literary work, literary environment or sophistication of the audience. Moreover, I also show that evolutionary models, such as protective camouflage and notions of mutualistic and antagonistic coevolution, can inform our understanding of the dynamic interrelations of censorship and early Soviet children's picturebooks. I propose that one might consider early Soviet literature as part of a dynamic system where the conceptualization of the interplay of art and censorship can be informed by concepts and metaphors reappropriated in an interdisciplinary fashion from naturalistic study, evolutionary biology, and models of the relations of predator and prey. The unique evolution of early Soviet picturebooks and their unnatural selection thus offers a uniquely telling example of the natural history of literature.[3]

2 A Natural History of Literature

In this same time period, Russian Formalist theorists were applying scientific terminology and evolutionary thinking to literature as they sought to take a more scientific approach to literary study and consider its development over time. For instance, in "О литературной эволюции" ("On Literary Evolution,"

---

2 Lev Loseff, *On the Beneficience of Censorship. Aesopian Language in Modern Russian Literature*. München 1984. The fact that Loseff was a poet, son of a poet, critic, and children's magazine editor all inform his study and make him uniquely suited to explicate the mechanics of Aesopian communication.

3 Material published in this chapter appears also in the introduction to Sara Pankenier Weld, *An Ecology of the Russian Avant-Garde Picturebook*, Amsterdam 2018.

1929) Jurij Tynjanov wrote, "In order to fully become a science, the history of literature must claim reliability. All of its terminology [...] must be reconsidered." He displayed such new scientific and naturalistic terminology in his own use of the term 'evolution' in his title and statements such as "The main concept for literary evolution is the *mutation* of systems."[4] Such examples show that natural history and the influential concept of evolution played a key role in early Formalist thinking. For the purposes of this study, Russian Formalism offers an early precedent for the reapplication of naturalistic terminology for literary study.

More recently scholars and theorists have applied Darwinist models to literary studies in so called literary Darwinism, practiced by Joseph Carroll and other scholars, or evocriticism espoused by Brian Boyd more recently in *On the Origin of Stories*, although some of this work may be critiqued as reductivist.[5] My goals here, however, are different, since rather than seek Darwinism in the texts themselves or in their portrayal of human nature, for instance, I wish to employ an ecological model to consider literature and literary techniques as part of a dynamic system, the understanding of which may be informed by naturalistic models that relate the relationship of censor and literary work to that of predator and prey. To my knowledge, no one has looked at censorship or the literary system in this particular way or from this particular perspective. Nor has anyone applied any of these approaches to children's literature systematically or to the mechanics of how children's literature functions in a dynamic system.[6] One notable exception is Lev Loseff, who considers Censor, Author, and Reader as part of a system and, in one section of his book, accounts for the relationship of children's literature and literature for adults as a result of the influence of censorship. This chapter is deeply indebted to Loseff's work even as it moves in new directions.

The positive aspects of the evolutionary process and advantageous adaptation to adversity which is implied in natural or unnatural selection finds an echo in Loseff's account of "the beneficence of censorship." He observes that, "with the return of an unremitting censorship, what is more, writers would

---

4 Ju. N. Tynjanov, "О литературной эволюции," in *Поэтика. История литературы. Кино*. Moscow 1977, 270-281. Its earliest version dates to 1927: Ju. N. Tynjanov, "Вопрос литературной эволюции," in *На литературном посту* 10 (1927), 42-48.
5 Joseph Carroll, *Evolution and Literary Theory*. Columbia, MO 1995; Carroll, *Reading Human Nature: Literary Darwinism in Theory and Practice*. Albany, NY 2011. See also the collection *The Literary Animal: Evolution and the Nature of Narrative*. Eds. Jonathan Gottschall and David Sloan Wilson, Evanston, IL 2005, and Brian Boyd, *On the Origin of Stories: Evolution, Cognition, and Fiction*, Cambridge, MA 2009.
6 Boyd does include what he calls an evocritical discussion of Dr. Seuss's *Horton Hears a Who* in *On the Origin of Stories*, 370-378.

sometimes entertain the paradoxical thought that, like it or not, censorship had become a factor in the creative process, owing to which an Aesopian manner was not artistically detrimental, but beneficial."[7] Loseff cites the nineteenth century Russian writer and thinker Alexander Herzen's trenchant insights on this subject:

> Censorship is highly conducive to progress in the mastery of style and in the ability to restrain one's words [...] The word implied has greater force beneath its veil and is always transparent to those who care to understand. A thought which is checked has greater meaning concentrated in it—it has a sharper edge [...] Implication increases the power of language.[8]

Herzen here articulates a metaphysical Russian idea succinctly expressed by the poet Fedor Tjutchev, in the poetic line from "Silentium": "Мысль изреченная есть ложь" ("The thought that is uttered is a lie").[9] Loseff also cites Brodskij's observation that "the machinery of constraint, of censorship, of suppression turns out to be—this is a paradox—useful to literature."[10] He further notes that "In their observations the masters of Aesopian language directly link a writer's formal virtuosity to the censorship and the necessity of avoiding its snares."[11] With the metaphor of the snare, and in rejecting "the traditional comparison between hangman and victim" and instead proposing comparison of the situation with "one with ecological import: wolves are needed to keep the deer in top form," Loseff moves in the direction of this study.[12]

Among principles deriving from natural history, the concept of protective camouflage, which evolves through dynamic interrelation and perhaps even in antagonistic coevolution between "predator" and "prey," also might be applied in a literary context and in the particular situation of Soviet children's literature. For instance, the oppositional relations of writers/artists and censorship

---

7   Loseff, 11.

8   From A. I. Gercen, *Избранные сочинения*, Moscow 1937, 400-401. Cited in Loseff 11, 248n.

9   From Fedor Tjutchev, "Silentium," in Tjutchev, *Полное собрание сочинений и писем в 6 томах*, Vol. 1, Moscow 2002, 123.

10   This quote is taken from an interview Brodskij gave to V. Rybakov published in I. Brodskij. "Язык – единственный авангардист," in *Русская мысль* 3188 (26 January, 1978), Paris, 8. Cited in Loseff, 12, 248n.

11   Loseff, 12.

12   Ibid. That Loseff taught and did his graduate work in Michigan is perhaps not entirely coincidental, since this was also the location of the famous study at Isle Royale which established that the presence of wolves was to the benefit of the population of moose on the island.

function in a dynamic interrelation where survival, and the successful transmission of an encoded message, may depend on escaping detection. From the perspective of evolutionary biology, camouflage can be defined as the concealment of animals by a number of methods that help them escape notice, such as by avoiding observation or detection, which is called crypsis, or by mimicking something not of interest to the observer, which is termed mimesis. Both principles of protective camouflage, I would argue, are relevant for the discussion of early Soviet children's literature under the selective pressure of censorship.

Russian writers found in children's literature a kind of camouflage that to some extent allowed them to escape notice and to continue to produce novel and creative work or disseminate messages disguised within children's literature but intended for other audiences. Comparing the upsurge in translation activity in the Soviet era "to a heightening of ideological censorship which had pressed writers out of original writing," Loseff writes, "no one further dared draw attention to the analogous, and perhaps even more revealing, situation in Russian children's literature to which, ever since the 1920s and by reason of similar imperatives, the most prominent writers had extended their energies."[13] Loseff goes so far as to devote an entire chapter to "Aesopian Language as a Factor in the Shaping of a Literary Genre (From the Experience of Children's Literature)," although children's literature scholars today would cavil at the characterization of the diverse genres of children's literature as one genre.[14]

This idea of mimetic camouflage applies on various levels of analysis, including as regards the audience. For instance, in his systematic classification of Aesopian devices on the level of intended audience (sender and receiver), Loseff includes the example of an apparent audience of children, while the actual audience is adults.[15] The actual audience (adults) in this way is mimetically camouflaged as children, just as literature for adults may be mimetically camouflaged as children's literature. What might appear a simple story for children to the censor, for example, may reveal itself to be something else entirely when subjected to closer scrutiny by its actually intended audience – skilled Aesopian readers.

In this case, mimetic camouflage disguises one audience as another, thereby bifurcating Wayne Booth's idea of the implied reader.[16] This type of situation recalls Zohar Shavit's analysis of the child as pseudo addressee in an ambiva-

---

13   Loseff, 194.
14   Ibid., 193-213.
15   Ibid., 60-61, 86.
16   Wayne Booth, *The Rhetoric of Fiction*, Chicago 1961.

lent work designed to appeal to adult audiences,[17] or later children's literature scholarship which develops the notion of dual audience.[18] Similarly, on the level of language itself, one might consider how an Aesopian work might appear to be one thing, such as a harmless children's story that succeeds in passing the censor, while it simultaneously offers something else entirely, i.e. a clandestine communication to adults that would be opposed by the censor, if it were to be intercepted. Such ambivalent children's literature uses mimetic camouflage to bypass the censor and transmit an alternative meaning to its audience.

By the same token, the Aesopian language which children's writers use also offers a kind of cryptic camouflage, or crypsis, that makes its hidden messages harder to see, thereby defeating the censor, who here serves as a kind of predator. Successful Aesopian language, which Loseff views through the perspective of information theory, manages to bury a covert message within the noise, which information theory posits is contained in any channel of communication.[19] In short:

> An Aesopian text will make its way successfully from author to reader if what is in actual fact an Aesopian device is perceived by the censor as a lapse in the author's command of his craft (as noise outside the competence of the censorship) and by the reader as the express indication of an Aesopian text which awaits decoding. The skill of the Aesopian author lies in his ability to arrange such a successful transaction.[20]

To put it another way, the author or artist of a picturebook engages in crypsis, or cryptic camouflage, just as prey does in relation to a predator, in order to avoid detection by the censor. These cryptic layers of communication evolve under the selective pressure of censorship. Paradoxically, censorship necessitates their existence, hastens their evolution, and, thus, encourages them to flourish.

---

17 In her discussion of "the ambivalent status of texts" and the notion of dual address, Zohar Shavit writes, "In such a way, unlike other texts that assume a single implied reader and a single (though flexible) ideal realization of the text, the ambivalent text has two implied readers: a pseudo addressee and a real one. The child, the official reader of the text, is not meant to realize it fully and is much more an excuse for the text than its genuine addressee." Zohar Shavit, *Poetics of Children's Literature*, Athens, GA 1986, 71.

18 For a collection of scholarly approaches to dual audience, see Sandra Beckett, ed., *Transcending Boundaries: Writing for a Dual Audience of Children and Adults*, New York 1999.

19 Loseff, 42-43.

20 Ibid., 44-45.

If one views such interactions in an evolutionary context over time, the dynamics become still more complex. Here the naturalistic model of coevolution may be applied, since the antagonistic relations of censor and works or writer/artist, which might be described as a form of antagonistic coevolution, may lead to reciprocal effects and development. As a result of censorship, alterations occur, thereby encouraging new methods of disguising cryptic messages once one code has been cracked. In a kind of antagonistic coevolution, new methods necessarily evolve once one adaptive avenue closes down. At the same time, however, the evolving ability of authors to communicate with their audience by circumventing the censors, and of the audience to comprehend these messages, might be regarded as a form of mutualistic coevolution, since the nature of communication between Author and Reader also evolves over time.

In this respect, children's literature also represents the next generation of readers and acts upon their evolution as individuals and as readers. In this sense, as Loseff notes, "The function of Aesopian literature with respect to the former [children] is, of course, the gradual nurturing of a future Aesopian reader."[21] Aesopian children's literature trains the next generation of readers to become discerning and initiated interpreters of subtle textual details. In this way Aesopian literature and Aesopian readers coexist in a kind of mutualistic coevolution. Moreover, these same texts, despite the restrictions of censorship, have the opportunity to contribute to the creative and intellectual shaping of the individual as reader or writer,[22] as Juliet Dusinberre avers in *Alice to the Lighthouse*, where she claims that Lewis Carroll shaped a generation of Modernist writers.[23] Similarly, Aesopian children's literature breeds future generations of Aesopian readers and writers in the dynamic context of evolution and coevolution.

3 The History of Censorship in Russian Literature and Children's Literature

Censorship in Russia dates back to centuries of autocratic times under the tsars. For example, in 1804, the Russian imperial statute on censorship read,

---

21 Ibid., 213.
22 Of course, circumstances would also encourage censors to evolve in their sophistication or in response to costly mistakes, their own or others'.
23 Juliet Dusinberre, *Alice to the Lighthouse. Children's Books and Radical Experiments in Art*, Basingstoke, HA 1987, 1-5.

in part: "1. The Censor has the duty to consider all manner of books and essays that are presented for public consumption. 2. The primary object of this consideration [is] to bring to the public books and essays that contribute to true education of the mind and the formation of manners, and to remove books and essays of ill intent. 3. Pursuant to this end, no book or essay shall be printed in the Russian Empire except following review by the Censor."[24] Such statements illustrate the fundamental assumptions regarding censorship that far preceded Soviet censorship and derive from Russia's imperial history. In this sense, the establishment of Soviet censorship only continued a venerable Russian tradition. Yet it was not always so, as Herman Ermolaev notes in his book *Censorship in Soviet Literature, 1917-1991*:

> In March 1917 the Provisional Government abolished all censorship except that of the military. The Bolsheviks, however, viewed freedom of expression as a direct threat to their ideology and dictatorship. The persecution of the press commenced on the first day of the October Revolution.[25]

So when the Council of People's Commissars set up the organ of the censorship Glavlit in 1922, it continued a venerable Russian tradition dating back to centuries of autocratic times under the tsars, the momentary relaxation of censorship notwithstanding.

As regards books for children, they had close ties to autocracy dating back to the earliest days of Russian literature for young readers, when printed children's works were created specifically for future rulers. Early examples include Karion Istomin's primer for the tsar's children, Букварь (*Primer*, 1694), and Catherine the Great's tales for her grandsons (1781, 1783).[26] As Russian children's literature developed into its own established field in the nineteenth century, and came to flourish in the twentieth century, its relations with censorship became more complex as well.[27] At the time when the new Soviet state

---

24 N. G. Patrusheva and N. A. Grinchenko, eds., "Устав о цензуре.' 1804. 9 июля. Нижегородское отделение Российского общества историков-архивистов." ⟨http://www.opentextnn.ru/censorship/russia/dorev/law/1804/⟩ (Accessed November 1, 2017).
25 Herman Ermolaev, *Censorship in Soviet Literature, 1917-1991*, Lanham, MD 1997, 1.
26 Karion Istomin, *Букварь составлен Карионом Истоминым гравирован Леонтием Буниным отпечатан в 1694 году в Москве*, Leningrad 1981; Jekaterina II, "Сказка о царевиче Февее"; "Сказка о царевиче Хлоре," in *Сочинения Императрицы Екатерины II. Произведения литературные*, St. Petersburg 1893, 373-80; 367-73.
27 For a more detailed history of children's literature in this period that includes some attention to the political environment and censorship, see Ben Hellman, *Fairy Tales and True Stories: The History of Russian Literature for Children and Young People (1574-2010)*, Boston 2013.

was established, children's literature and picturebooks were coming into their own, a tide which continued in the early Soviet period, particularly as there was a major investment in the field due to its political importance for indoctrinating the young. Ben Hellman cites, for example, a 1918 article in *Правда* tellingly entitled "Забытое оружие" ("The Forgotten Weapon") in reference to children's literature.[28] The official interest in children as an audience proved double-edged. Now impolitic influences were to be kept out. For instance, in 1923, the Soviet Union officially barred from importation, among other things, "children's literature containing elements of bourgeois moral and lauding old conditions of life."[29] Ermolaev summarizes the changing tenor of censorship at this time:

> In the 1920s the prohibitive role of censorship was supplemented by an educative one. The censor not only banned the offensive text but also made, or suggested, additions in order to further political, ideological, or moral upbringing of the reader in tune with the immediate goals of the ruling Communist Party.[30]

Though Ermolaev here discusses literary censorship in general, the shift to an actively propagandistic mission has added import for children's literature. The next decade provided new challenges; "In comparison with the 1920s, Soviet censorship during the 1930s and early 1940s intensified and spread."[31] In 1931 Lenin's widow Nadezhda Krupskaja gave a keynote speech at the First All-Russian Conference on Children's Literature entitled "Детская книга—могущественное орудие социалистического воспитания" ("Children's Book—a Mighty Weapon of Socialist Education"), where she acknowledges the significance of childhood impressions and the power of children's books and calls for Soviet communist books.[32] By 1933, the authorities took full control of children's publishing houses.[33]

---

28 Hellman, 294. L. Kormchij, "Забытое оружие," in *Правда*, February 17, 1918, 3.
29 Arlen Bljum, *За кулисами 'Министерства правды': Тайная история советской цензуры*, 1917-1929, St. Petersburg 1994, 194.
30 Herman Ermolaev, *Censorship in Soviet Literature, 1917-1991*, Lanham, MD 1997, 259.
31 Ibid., 51.
32 N. Krupskaja, *Педагогические сочинения в десяти томах*, Vol. 3. Moscow 1959, 439-442. Cited in Hellman, 361.
33 Alena Tveritina, "Soviet Children's Literature: The Struggle Between Ideology and Creativity," in *Russia Beyond the Headlines*, ⟨http://rbth.com/literature/2014/06/27/soviet_childrens_literature_the_struggle_between_ideology_and_creativity_3776⟩ (Accessed November 1, 2017).

History shows that censorship has often been applied even more rigorously to literature for children, even in places where censorship has not conventionally been regarded as existing. The question of managing influences on children, as opposed to giving them freedom to determine what to read themselves, often characterizes the paternalistic relations of adults with children, particularly in a "neontocracy" such as prevails in much of the Western world.[34] In a totalitarian state, these principles apply even more strongly since the political payoff for indoctrinating the young, who assume outsized importance in building, for example, a new communist world,[35] looms even larger and proves characteristic of the paternalistic and infantilizing attitude of autocratic leadership.

Ironically, however, this ideologically motivated investment in children's literature by the state also provided a new niche for creative energies that were being stifled elsewhere and were diverted by censorship into writing for children in a kind of trophic cascade. Paradoxically, the ideologically motivated investment in children's literature by the state first led to creative opportunity and only later suffered from close scrutiny and increasing censorship. If Yuri Lotman spoke of the periphery being "the area of semiotic dynamism,"[36] then children's literature offered precisely this kind of periphery, which also was further from scrutiny, and thereby served as a site of experimentation, as result of the greater freedom it provided, for a time.[37] As a result, twentieth century Russian children's literature benefited from the productive synergy brought by the combined contributions of specialists diverted from a variety of other realms. For instance, Ben Hellman describes how Marshak managed to recruit to children's writing such figures as Boris Zhitkov, Vitalij Bianki, and Michael Iljin, who had scientific and technical backgrounds, as well as established writers and poets like Evgenij Shvarc, Viktor Shklovskij, Nikolaj Aseev, Nikolaj Tichonov, Osip Mandel'shtam, and Boris Pasternak.[38] In children's literature these creative individuals found a new frontier to explore and no doubt inspired one another in this flourishing new ecological niche. But eventually,

---

34 I borrow the term neontocracy from David F. Lancy's *The Anthropology of Childhood: Cherubs, Chattel, Changelings*, Cambridge, UK 2008.

35 For a discussion of the uses of childhood in this era, see Lisa A. Kirschenbaum *Small Comrades Revolutionizing Childhood in Soviet Russia, 1917-1932*, New York 2001. See also Catriona Kelly. *Children's World: Growing Up in Russia 1890-1991*, New Haven and London 2007.

36 Yuri Lotman, *Universe of the Mind. A Semiotic Theory of Culture*, trans. Ann Shukman, Bloomington, IN 1990, 134.

37 Lotman argues that it is the periphery of the semiotic sphere that "is the area of semiotic dynamism." Ibid.

38 Hellman, 301.

as Lotman also noted, the periphery itself moves to the center and, in this particular case, also into the focus of the censor.

4 Exploiting a New Niche: The Rise of the 20th Century Russian Picturebook

The evolution of the Soviet picturebook thus began as the exploitation of a new niche that appeared as a result of a constellation of circumstances in the early Soviet period. In the aesthetic realm, the exquisitely produced experiments of the World of Art had established a rich new tradition of picturebook production at the beginning of the twentieth century, as manifest in Ivan Bilibin's ornate illustrations of classic Russian folk tales and Alexandre Benois's exquisite illustrated alphabet.[39] In this sense, the picturebook as genre already stood poised for continued development at the beginning of the twentieth century.

As a result of cataclysmic cultural developments and the 1917 Revolution in Russia, this potential and the picturebook form, which had arisen during prerevolutionary times for a privileged audience, instead came to be reappropriated for new functions and evolved to fill a new niche of mass-produced literature for young children.[40] Post-revolutionary educational policies offered a new audience of readers, and soon considerable resources were channeled into publishing children's literature for new Soviet subjects. In subsequent years, major writers and artists turned their energies to this new area, which led to a successful wave of innovation where burgeoning Avant-Garde aesthetics, a newly created and acknowledged audience, and an ideologically motivated investment in future Soviet subjects worked together synergistically to produce new experiments and aesthetic achievements in the early Soviet picturebook.

Russian children's literature was experiencing a resurgence and rebirth thanks to the influence of Kornej Chukovskij, whose contributions to it proved transformative.[41] Likewise, the children's poet Samuil Marshak would become

---

39 Aleksandr Benua, *Азбука в картинках*, St. Petersburg 1904.
40 At this very juncture of old and new we see hybrid creations like the immediately post-revolutionary Christmas collection *Елка* (*The Christmas Tree*, 1918), which uncomfortably straddles aesthetics old and new as embodied by illustrators from the World of Art, such as Benois, and new illustrators whose day was yet to come, such as Vladimir Lebedev, and begins to navigate the new themes of the revolutionary era. Aleksandr Benua and Kornej Chukovskij, eds., *Елка. Сборник. Книжка для маленьких детей*, Petrograd 1918.
41 Hellman, 311.

an editor of great influence in children's literature publishing. Picturebooks based on texts for children written by Chukovskij and Marshak and illustrated by Vladimir Konashevich and Vladimir Lebedev, respectively, abounded in the ensuing decades. Following in the footsteps of these significant early influences and shepherded by Maxim Gorky, who played a central role in 1920s Soviet children's publishing, early Soviet picturebooks underwent a creative explosion and rapidly evolved to fill this new niche where much energy, investment, and capital were being expended.

5 A Case of Mutualistic Coevolution: The Soviet Avant-Garde Picturebook

In the 1920s, early Soviet picturebooks benefited from a kind of hybrid vigor as a result of a synergy of different energies being brought to the genre and combining in new ways. For example, Lebedev drew upon his experience as a painter and in producing propaganda posters for the the Russian Telegraph Agency, when he engaged in multiple aesthetic experiments in the picturebook. Drawing upon Avant-Garde and primitivist influences, Lebedev produced innovative works, such as the infantile and primitivist *Приключения Чуч-ло* (*The Adventures of Scare-Crow*, 1922), the indigeneity-inspired primitive of *Охота* (*The Hunt*, 1925), and the folk-inspired primitive of *Золотое яичко* (*The Golden Egg*, 1923) and other folk tales.[42] Lebedev's early experiments hit upon a successful new approach in his illustrations for *Слоненок* (*The Elephant's Child*, 1922), a translation of Rudyard Kipling's *The Elephant's Child*.[43] This Avant-Garde tour de force came to be regarded as "the manifesto of a new approach to children's book graphics," and offered a radically new evolutionary direction that numerous subsequent picturebooks would follow.[44] Here Avant-

---

42 Vladimir Lebedev, *Приключения Чуч-ло*, Petrograd 1922; *Охота*, Leningrad 1925; *Золотое яичко*, Petrograd 1923. Other picturebooks by Lebedev inspired by folk stories and themes include *Медведь* (*The Bear*), *Три козла* (*Three Goats*), and *Заяц, петух и лиса* (*The Hare, the Rooster, and the Fox*), in addition to *Золотое яичко*. All four books were published in Petrograd by Mysl' in 1923-1924. The latter three books can be found in complete reproductions in V. Lebedev, *Десять книжек для детей*, ed. G.I. Chugunov, Leningrad 1976.

43 Rudjard Kipling, *Слоненок*, trans. Kornej Chukovskij, ill. Vladimir Lebedev, Petrograd 1922.

44 Evgeny Steiner, *Stories for Little Comrades: Revolutionary Artists and the Making of Early Soviet Children's Books*, trans. Jane Ann Miller, Seattle 1999, 42. See also Evgenij Shtejner, *Авангард и построение нового человека. Искусство советской детской книги 1920 годов*, Moscow 2002.

Garde aesthetics enrich the established artistic form of the picturebook. Even the cognitive material of Kipling's story participates in the deconstruction of the image in an Avant-Garde Cubist fashion. It also evinces infantile aspects insofar as it playfully breaks the image into component parts, like a puzzle or toy. In this it also resembles constructivist aspects of El Lissickij's *Про два квадрата: супрематический сказ в 6-ти постройках* (*Suprematist Tale of Two Squares in Six Structures*, 1922).[45] In itself, *Слоненок* exemplifies the synergy of forces resulting in creative innovations that filled this new niche.

In their Avant-Garde aesthetic, these early Soviet picturebooks were, like the propaganda posters of the Russian Telegraph Agency, ideally designed to be mass-produced, as evident in their simple lithographic design and limited palette of colors, which distinguishes them very much from their World of Art predecessors. For example, Lebedev's *Азбука* (*Alphabet*, 1925) is printed in black and white using simple lithographic block print that dramatically expands each simplified letter until it dwarfs the visual representations of the sound.[46] The simple and visually dramatic compositions are surrounded by blank space. Here the new pedagogical project of universal education and Soviet enlightenment marks a dramatic shift from Bilibin's fairytales; now elaborate illustrations producing works of art for an audience of elite children give way to mass-produced pamphlets for an egalitarian audience of proletarian children. In these texts ideology is present largely behind the scenes, in the motivation for their existence, their revolutionary aesthetic, and production values. The subjects themselves lack an ideological component. By this point, the new educational project becomes very apparent, as is a revolutionary paring away of old aesthetic trappings.

In the next phase of the evolution of the early Soviet picturebook, the ideological component emerges detectably in picturebooks that still straddle Avant-Garde aesthetics and Soviet ideology. Examples by the productive collaborators Marshak and Lebedev include the satirical *Багаж* (*Baggage*, 1926), which mocks the abundance of material possessions belonging to an old lady; the ideologically framed but aesthetically Avant-Garde opposition of the trappings of present and past in *Вчера и сегодня* (*Yesterday and Today*, 1925); moments of subtle ideology interspersed with carnivalesque and early twentieth-century world culture in *Цирк* (*Circus*, 1925); and the weakly propagandistic *Мороженое* (*Ice Cream*, 1925), whose overindulging antagonist resembles the capitalist villains of propaganda posters, just as its everyday heroes resemble the schematized depictions of workers in Lebedev's Telegraph

---

45 El Lissickij, *Про два квадрата: супрематический сказ в 6-ти постройках*, Berlin 1922.
46 Lebedev, *Азбука*, Leningrad 1925.

Agency posters.[47] Also figuring here are Vladimir Majakovskij's picturebooks, which often combine Avant-Garde aesthetics, both poetically and visually on the basis of their illustrations, with ideologically inflected content motivated by Majakovskij's own revolutionary ethos. For example, Majakovskij's *Что ни страница, – то слон, то львица* (*Not a Page without an Elephant or a Lioness*, 1928) contains only moments of ideology presented playfully in an Avant-Garde visual display, as does *Эта книжечка моя про моря и про маяк* (*This is My Book About the Seas and about a Lighthouse*, 1927), while the later *Сказка о Пете, толстом ребенке, и о Симе, который тонкий* (*The Story about Pete, the Fat Child, and about Simon, who is Thin*, 1925) delivers a critique of bourgeois ideology in a form adapted for an audience of children.[48] In this moment in the evolution of early Soviet picturebooks these seemingly disparate influences come together in a kind of mutualistic coevolution as the uneasy bedfellows of Avant-Garde aesthetics and Soviet ideology come together to produce hybrid creations of lasting force.

6 Adaptation and Antagonistic Coevolution: Ideology vs. Aesthetics

Gradually, however, the comparatively free development and hybrid vigor of these unexpectedly successful interacting forces and influences in the 1920s gave way to increased restrictions as the political aims became more explicit in the 1930s. In response to these fiercer selective pressures, the experimental picturebooks that had evolved in a creative explosion following *Слоненок* as a precursor were compelled to accommodate further. At this time, censorship began to winnow out works and writers or artists who deviated from ideologically defined goals, and the ecological niche of the early Soviet picturebook shrank demonstrably as an ideological bottleneck formed. Ultimately those writers who made accommodations to censoring pressures and altered their style and substance to conform to this unnatural selection were the only ones to survive.

A process of antagonistic literary coevolution occurs when increasing restrictions begin to compromise texts, so that censorship drives rapid and di-

---

47 Samuil Marshak, *Багаж*, ill. Vladimir Lebedev, Leningrad 1926; *Вчера и сегодня*, ill. Vladimir Lebedev, Leningrad 1925; *Цирк*, ill. Vladimir Lebedev, Leningrad 1925; *Мороженое*, ill. Vladimir Lebedev, Leningrad 1925.

48 Vladimir Majakovskij, *Сказка о Пете, толстом ребенке, и о Симе, который тонкий*, ill. N. Kuprejanov, Moscow 1925; *Что ни страница, – то слон, то львица*, ill. K. Zdanevich, Tiflis 1928; *Эта книжечка моя про моря и про маяк*, ill. B. Pokrovskij, Moscow 1927.

vergent literary evolution. At this point, Russian Avant-Garde aesthetics as regards the visual aspect of these books started to lose their place beside increasing ideology. For example, consecutive editions of Marshak and Lebedev's *Мистер Твистер* (*Mister Tvister*, 1933)[49] demonstrate increasingly realistic depictions of the human figure, for instance, alongside decreasing degrees of stylization and visual innovations.[50] The same development transpires in consecutive editions of *Почта* (*The Mail*, 1932) by Marshak and illustrated by Michail Cechanovskij, who was deeply influenced by Lebedev and who may be considered to be his aesthetic successor.[51] In such transitional texts and editions, the dictates of Socialist Realism at first combine uneasily with Avant-Garde aesthetic features, for instance, the addition of three dimensions to two-dimensional images.[52] Eventually, however, even these uneasy compromises are no longer possible, and the early Soviet picturebooks of Marshak and Lebedev give way completely to Socialist Realism, thereby forsaking the Avant-Garde heritage and experimental approach that had characterized their early evolution and creative peak. Both Marshak and Lebedev were compelled to adapt to the new environment in order to ensure their own survival and that of their art. As a result of this process of unnatural selection, their later works take an entirely unrecognizable form when compared to their earlier Avant-Garde picturebooks.

7 Protective Camouflage as Adaptive Strategy

If the evolution of the picturebooks of Vladimir Lebedev demonstrates the increasing influence of ideology and censorship, other early Soviet picturebooks display more specific adaptive strategies. For example, cryptic camouflage using Aesopian language represents another adaptive strategy for getting a message across to an intended audience, despite the ideological demands of the

---

49 Samuil Marshak, *Мистер Твистер*, ill. Vladimir Lebedev, Moscow 1933.
50 For detailed comparison of successive editions of *Мистер Твистер* and *Почта*, see Sara Pankenier Weld, "The Obliteration of the Avant-Garde Aesthetic: Comparative Study of 1930s Picturebooks by Samuil Marshak," in *Детские чтения* 2:6 (2014), 187-198.
51 Samuil Marshak, *Почта*, ill. Michail Cechanovskij, Leningrad 1932. Cechanovskij offers an interesting example of sublimated energies reappearing elsewhere, since his picturebook *Pochta* whose Avant-Garde aesthetic fell out of favor, also morphed into an innovative animated film. Animation proved an avenue where Avant-Garde picturebooks continued to evolve in a different form, through bridging figures such as Michail Cechanovskij.
52 Weld, "The Obliteration of the Avant-Garde Aesthetic," 187-198.

environment or policing of literature by the censor. Russian children's literature as a whole may be considered an example of mimetic camouflage, since works frequently may appear to be children's literature when they are not. Daniil Charms offers many examples of this, since his creative energies were entirely sublimated into children's literature. In fact, by the late stage of his career, no other publication avenues were open to late successors of the Avant-Garde such as Charms. An example of literary mimicry is Charms's short children's poem "Из дома вышел человек. Песенка" ("A Man Had Left His Home One Day. A Song," 1937), which seems a simple poem resembling a folk tale.[53] Yet it violates the obligatory morphological script of a folk tale by lacking any homecoming, since the man disappears.[54] Broaching a dangerous topic during the height of the purges and Stalinist repression, this clandestine commentary on contemporary events was intercepted and caused the arrest of Charms as well as future publication difficulties for the imperiled writer.[55] This example also displays a case of fateful code-breaking. The censors' interception of the subsurface content, belied by the simple surface, had serious consequences for the author. As a result of this interception, even Charms's Aesopian avenues of communication in children's literature were closed. Eventually, he paid with his life for this and other brave refusals to adapt his aesthetics to the standards of censorship. Charms was arrested again in 1941 and died in 1942. His example illustrates the life and death stakes involved in the interception of covert communication in this most repressive period. It also signals the end of a period of experimentation and hybrid vigor, as censorship became overwhelming even within children's literature.

Examples of cryptic camouflage that succeeded in passing the censors include Osip Mandel'shtam's earlier picturebook *Два трамвая: Клик и Трам* (*Two Tramcars: Klik and Tram*, 1925) illustrated by Boris Ender.[56] This work also displays mimetic camouflage, since it appears to be children's literature and directed at children. The real audience is actually adults with the ability

---

53 Daniil Charms, "Из дома вышел человек. Песенка," in Charms, *Собрание сочинений в трех томах*, Vol. 3., St. Petersburg 2000, 53-54.

54 I refer here to the structural features of folktale identified in Vladimir Propp's *Morphology of the Folktale*. See Vladimir Propp, *Morphology of the Folktale*, trans. Laurence Scott, Austin, TX 1975, 60.

55 N. Gernet recalls that it was the publication of this poem that caused the authorities to recommend that children's magazines *Finch* and *Hedgehog* not publish the works of Charms. N. Gernet. "О Хармсе," in *Нева* 2 (1988), 204. Cited in V. N. Sazhin, "Примечания," in Charms, *Собрание сочинений в трех томах*, Vol. 3, St. Petersburg 2000, 239.

56 Osip Mandel'shtam. *Два трамвая Клик и Трам*, ill. B. Ender, Leningrad 1925.

and knowledge to decode its Aesopian message embedded in the text through cryptic camouflage.[57] The encrypting of Aesopian language takes place here in the sense that this story of a tramcar (Tram/Mandel'shtam) searching for his lost and injured friend (Klik/Nikolaj Gumilev) actually offers Mandel'shtam's covert commentary on the loss of Gumilev, who was arrested and executed by the authorities in 1921.[58] In this case, Mandel'shtam's cryptic camouflage succeeded and perhaps too well, since the poet's message was not necessarily intercepted by all intended audiences and his children's books were commonly dismissed as insignificant.[59] Beneath the cryptic camouflage, however, and within its Aesopian subsurface layers, Mandel'shtam's picturebook offers poignant commentary on the loss of a prominent poet, a traumatic and symbolic event for the literary community as well as for Mandel'shtam personally.

8 Adaptive Coevolution: The Uses of Ambivalent Discourse

Examples of adaptive coevolution, though highly rare, also might be found in the natural history of the early Soviet picturebook. Here the works of Jurij Olesha, both for children and for adults, exemplify a surprisingly successful ambivalent discourse that succeeded even under harsh conditions of censorship. Its success may lie in its very ambiguity and its use of both cryptic and mimetic camouflage; ambivalent discourse might always appear to be something else, even its own opposite, and encodes any critical messages in cryptic communication. Here it is not so much Aesopian language as a kind of Aesopian discourse that occurs. Olesha's revolutionary fairytale *Три толстяка* (*The Three Fat Men*, 1924),[60] like his similarly ambivalent Soviet novella *Зависть* (*Envy*,

---

57 For more detailed analysis of these Aesopian levels, see Sara Pankenier Weld, "Delad läsekrets och dubbelt seende: Aisopiska djup i Osip Mandel'stams *Två sparvagnar*," in *Tidskrift för litteraturvetenskap* (Journal of Comparative Literature) 2, trans. Maria Andersson, Stockholm 2014, 49-67. See also Weld, "Удвоенная аудитория и двойное видение: Эзоповские глубины *Двух трамваев* Осипа Мандельштама," in M. Gronas and B. Scherr, eds., *Лившиц/Лосев/Loseff*, trans. Vladimir Kutcherjavkin, Moscow 2015.
58 As I discuss in the above articles, Nikolaj Gumilev was the author of the poem "Заблудившийся трамвай" ("The Lost Tramcar") which Mandel'stam's story refers to, obliquely. See Gumilev, "Заблудившийся трамвай," in *Стихотворения и поэмы*, Leningrad 1988, 331-332.
59 Elena Sokol, for instance, makes no mention of this subtext in her brief discussion of the work, which is dismissive of the children's poetry of Mandel'shtam. Sokol, *Russian Poetry for Children*, Knoxville, TN 1984, 172-173.
60 Jurij Olesha, *Три толстяка*, ill. Mstislav Dobuzhinskij, Moscow 1928.

1927),[61] is a case in point, since it appears to conform ideologically to the revolutionary themes of its time and to remain ideologically correct. In this sense, it succeeds in its subtle usage of mimetic and cryptic camouflage.

At the same time, however, under closer scrutiny, the symbolism of *Три толстяка* proves remarkably ambivalent and double-sided, such that the opposite meanings also can be read into it. For example, despite the revolutionary fairytale it puts forward, it also expresses the plight of the intellectual in revolutionary times or that of the child who is held captive by ideology. It even offers an apologia and defense of the fundamental independence and inviolability of the human heart. Even the idea of revolution or the instability of an autocratic regime, such as that embodied by *Три толстяка*, also contains a critique of any totalitarian regime, however revolutionary it may have been at the outset or how ideologically correct the framing might seem. The secret of Olesha's success lies in his cryptic and mimetic camouflage, which is accomplished through the ambivalent and ambiguous tone for which he is famed.[62]

Unfortunately, such examples of successful adaptive coevolution, where independence of expression can be retained under trying circumstances of censorship, prove rare. Instead, the constraints in the literary environment only increased and to a prohibitive level; Aesopian messages were intercepted; Aesopian authors were silenced by censorship, repression, or death; and Aesopian avenues, even in Soviet children's literature, were effectively closed down. Eventually, conditions became hostile for any kind of creative innovation and, as a result of a most unnatural selection, ultimately only one aesthetic option remained – the officially prescribed Socialist Realist pseudo-aesthetic, in image and in text. By this time, picturebooks, children's literature, and children's writers faced a manmade evolutionary bottleneck as a result of the fierce depredation of censorship. To survive these increasingly harsh conditions, they had only one viable option remaining – adaptation and accommodation.

9   Conclusion

In the case of early Soviet picturebooks, this unnatural selection, driven by censorship, plays a role in determining the development of the early Soviet picturebook before its unique and innovative features are driven to extinction.

---

61   Olesha, *Зависть. Три толстяка. Рассказы*, Moscow 1998.
62   For a discussion of the widespread ambivalence in Olesha's work, see, for example, Victor Peppard, *The Poetics of Yury Olesha*, Gainesville, FL 1989.

In fact, censorship contributed to the diversion of literary energies from elsewhere into children's literature, which was an officially supported and safer environment for a longer time than literature for adults. It is here where the selection proves unnatural. But once the literary creation has lost the freedom to evolve and adapt within the official literary realm, and even within children's literature, as scrutiny, restrictions, and censorship in this area also increased, it ceases to function in an ecological balance with its environment, or to be a "living" or dynamic entity: the literary work loses all creative adaptive capability within government sanctioned print media. At that point, literary innovation is driven out of official discourse, though it may still reemerge in unofficial discourse, such as samizdat, or clandestine self-published circulation;[63] or be diverted into safer areas like animation or translation.[64] In the face of these severe environmental circumstances, the only option is complete adaptation and to such an extent that any originally distinctive and characteristic qualities may be lost. At this point, the early Soviet picturebook was compelled to evolve into an entirely new shape – Socialist Realist children's literature – the only form able to survive the increased censorship and ideological control of the 1930s.

At the same time, however, these creative impulses do not entirely disappear, but simply bide their time, lying latent in the genetic code, as it were, until restrictions are loosened. In this regard, one might think of the recurrence theorem of dynamical systems posited by Henri Poincaré, which holds that certain systems will, after a sufficiently long but finite time, return to a state very close to the initial state. Early Soviet Avant-Garde picturebooks first evolved to exploit a new niche and flourished in the dynamic synergy of intersecting influences. They then became endangered under fierce censorship and selective pressure, and finally were driven to extinction. Yet, despite being forcibly and artificially deprived of natural successors or direct descendants, due to this process of unnatural selection by means of censorship, the extraordinary achievements of these years were not lost forever. After a sufficiently

---

[63] For an introduction to samizdat, see F. J. M. Feldbrugge, *Samizdat and Political Dissent in the Soviet Union*. Leyden 1975. For a more recent essay collection, see Friederike Kind-Kovács, *Samizdat, Tamizdat, and Beyond: Transnational Media During and After Socialism*, New York 2013.

[64] Judith A. Inggs explores the relationship between the multiple forces at work in the translation of children's literature under conditions of censorship, concluding that censorship provides fertile ground for the creative manipulation and appropriation of texts. Inggs, "Censorship and Translated Literature in the Soviet Union: The Example of the Wizards Oz and Goodwin," in *Target. International Journal of Translation Studies* 23:1 (2011), 77-91. Loseff earlier makes this observation about translated literature in general, including its exposure by Efim Etkind (*On the Beneficience of Censorship*, 193).

long but finite time, these achievements again came to be recognized and, once the environment proved adequately conducive, they reappeared in later incarnations.[65] As such, and by maintaining a place in the latent lineage of artists and writers, despite the vagaries of censorship and environmental circumstance, they have exerted and continued to exert an influence on contemporary generations of artists and writers.

That Henri Poincaré developed his theories of dynamical systems and understanding of their evolution out of the study of the three-body problem seems appropriate, since Loseff, whose work inspires this chapter, himself began his elucidation of these principles by considering the interactions of three bodies, namely "Author, Reader, and Censor."[66] Out of the complex interactions of these three bodies, the dynamical system and evolution of early Soviet literature is revealed. This example also illustrates the complexity of the literary ecosystem of the early Soviet period, Russian children's literature, and early Soviet picturebooks in particular, both of which flourished in a new ecological niche and suffered under the fierce predation of censorship, whether subjected to external or internal censorship.[67] Clearly, the evolution of early Soviet picturebooks under these harsh circumstances of severe and unnatural selection, is anything but simple and proves to be very dynamic. But it is also uniquely revealing insofar as the natural history of the early Soviet picturebook abundantly displays how, as R. Franck summed it up as early as 1694, "Art imitates Nature, and Necessity is the Mother of Invention."[68]

Works Cited

Beckett, Sandra, ed. *Transcending Boundaries: Writing for a Dual Audience of Children and Adults*. New York 1999.

---

65   For example, many of the most significant and innovative early Soviet picturebooks, such as S. Marshak and V. Lebedev's Багаж (*Luggage*), Как рубанок сделал рубанок (*How a Plane Made a Plane*), and Охота (*A Hunt*) appeared in color reproductions along with a critical apparatus in the 1970-80s series Художник делает книгу: Избранные детские книги советских художников by the publisher Sovetskij Khudozhnik (Moscow, 1978, 1982) and edited by Jurij Gerchuk. Interestingly, these titles are listed in the Sacharov Center Library, for example, under the category of "репрессированное искусство."
66   Loseff, 5.
67   As Ermolaev notes, writers were also forced "to engage in a humiliating self-censorship to secure publication or reprinting of their works. Even before putting down a single word, the author had to weigh what would be passed or tabooed by his editors or Glavlit." *Censorship in Soviet Literature*, 260.
68   R. Franck, *Northern Memoirs, calculated for the Meridian of Scotland. To which is added, The Contemplative & practical angler*, London 1694.

Benua, Aleksandr and Kornej Chukovskij, eds. *Ёлка. Сборник. Книжка для маленьких детей*. Petrograd 1918.

Bljum, Arlen. *За кулисами 'Министерства правды': Тайная история советской цензуры. 1917-1929*. St. Petersburg 1994.

Booth, Wayne. *The Rhetoric of Fiction*. Chicago 1961.

Boyd, Brian. *On the Origin of Stories: Evolution, Cognition, and Fiction*. Cambridge, MA 2009.

Brodskij, I. "Язык – единственный авангардист," in *Русская мысль* 3188 (Paris), 26 January 1978, 8.

Carroll, Joseph. *Evolution and Literary Theory*. Columbia, MO 1995.

Carroll, Joseph. *Reading Human Nature: Literary Darwinism in Theory and Practice*. Albany, NY 2011.

Charms, Daniil. "Из дома вышел человек. Песенка," in Charms, *Собрание сочинений в трех томах*, Vol. 3. St. Petersburg 2000, 53-54.

Darwin, Charles. *On the Origin of Species by Means of Natural Selection or the Preservation of Favoured Races in the Struggle for Life*. London 1859.

Dusinberre, Juliet. *Alice to the Lighthouse. Children's Books and Radical Experiments in Art*. Basingstoke, HA 1987.

Ermolaev, Herman. *Censorship in Soviet Literature, 1917-1991*. Lanham, MD 1997.

Feldbrugge, F. J. M. *Samizdat and Political Dissent in the Soviet Union*. Leyden 1975.

Franck, R. *Northern Memoirs, calculated for the Meridian of Scotland. To which is added, The Contemplative & practical angler*. London 1694.

Gercen, A. I. *Избранные сочинения*. Moscow 1937, 400-401.

Gernet, N. "О Хармсе," in *Нева* 2 (1988), 204.

Gottschall, Jonathan and David Sloan Wilson, eds. *The Literary Animal: Evolution and the Nature of Narrative*. Evanston, IL 2005.

Gumilev, N. S. "Заблудившийся трамвай," in *Стихотворения и поэмы*. Leningrad, 1988, 331-332.

Hellman, Ben. *Fairy Tales and True Stories: The History of Russian Literature for Children and Young People (1574-2010)*. Boston 2013.

Inggs, Judith A. "Censorship and Translated Literature in the Soviet Union: The Example of the Wizards *Oz* and *Goodwin*," in *Target. International Journal of Translation Studies* 23:1 (2011), 77-91.

Istomin, Karion. *Букварь составлен Карионом Истоминым гравирован Леонтием Буниным отпечатан в 1694 году в Москве*. Leningrad 1981.

Jekaterina II. "Сказка о царевиче Февее," in *Сочинения Императрицы Екатерины II. Произведения литературные*. St. Petersburg 1983, 373-380.

Jekaterina II. "Сказка о царевиче Хлоре," in *Сочинения Императрицы Екатерины II. Произведения литературные*. St. Petersburg 1983, 367-373.

Kelly, Catriona. *Children's World: Growing Up in Russia 1890-1991*. New Haven and London 2007.

Kind-Kovács, Friederike. *Samizdat, Tamizdat, and Beyond: Transnational Media During and After Socialism*. New York 2013.

Kipling, Rudjard. *Слоненок*, trans. Kornej Chukovskij, ill. Vladimir Lebedev. Petrograd 1922.

Kirschenbaum, Lisa A. *Small Comrades Revolutionizing Childhood in Soviet Russia, 1917-1932*, New York 2001.

Kormchij, L. "Забытое оружие," in *Правда*, February 17, 1918, 3.

Krupskaja, N. *Педагогические сочинения в десяти томах*, Vol. 3. Moscow 1959, 439-442.

Lancy, David F. *The Anthropology of Childhood: Cherubs, Chattel, Changelings*. Cambridge, UK 2008.

Lebedev, Vladimir. *Азбука*. Leningrad 1925.

Lebedev, Vladimir. *Десять книжек для детей*, ed. G.I. Chugunov. Leningrad 1976.

Lebedev, Vladimir. *Охота*. Leningrad 1925.

Lebedev, Vladimir. *Приключения Чуч-ло*. Petrograd 1922.

Lebedev, Vladimir. *Золотое яичко*. Petrograd 1923.

Lissickij, El. *Про 2 квадрата: супрематический сказ в 6-ти постройках*. Berlin 1922.

Loseff, Lev. *On the Beneficience of Censorship. Aesopian Language in Modern Russian Literature*. München 1984.

Lotman, Yuri. *Universe of the Mind. A Semiotic Theory of Culture*, trans. Ann Shukman. Bloomington, IN 1990.

Majakovskij, Vladimir. *Что ни страница, – то слон, то львица*, ill. K. Zdanevich. Tiflis 1928.

Majakovskij, Vladimir. *Эта книжечка моя про моря и про маяк*, ill. B. Pokrovskij. Moscow 1927.

Majakovskij, Vladimir. *Сказка о Пете, толстом ребенке, и о Симе, который тонкий*, ill. N. Kuprejanov. Moscow 1925.

Mandel'shtam, Osip. *Два трамвая: Клик и Трам*, ill. B. Ender. Leningrad 1925.

Marshak, S. and V. Lebedev. "Багаж," in *Избранные детские книги советских художников*, ed. Ju. Gerchuk. Moscow 1982.

Marshak, S. and V. Lebedev. "Как рубанок сделал рубанок," in *Избранные детские книги советских художников*, ed. Ju. Gerchuk. Moscow 1978.

Marshak, S. and V. Lebedev. "Охота," in *Избранные детские книги советских художников*, ed. Ju. Gerchuk. Moscow 1978.

Marshak, Samuil. *Багаж*, ill. Vladimir Lebedev. Leningrad 1926.

Marshak, Samuil. *Мистер Твистер*, ill. Vladimir Lebedev. Moscow 1933.

Marshak, Samuil. *Мороженое*, ill. Vladimir Lebedev. Leningrad 1925.

Marshak, Samuil. *Почта*, ill. Michail Cechanovskij. Leningrad 1932.

Marshak, Samuil. *Цирк*, ill. Vladimir Lebedev. Leningrad 1925.

Marshak, Samuil. *Вчера и сегодня*, ill. Vladimir Lebedev. Leningrad 1925.

Olesha, Jurij. *Зависть. Три толстяка. Рассказы.* Moscow 1998.

Olesha, Jurij. *Три толстяка,* ill. M. Dobuzhinskij. Moscow 1928.

Patrusheva, N. G. and N. A. Grinchenko, eds. "Устав о цензуре.' 1804. 9 июля. Нижегородское отделение Российского общества историков-архивистов." ⟨http://www.opentextnn.ru/censorship/russia/dorev/law/1804/⟩ (Accessed November 1, 2017).

Propp, Vladimir. *Morphology of the Folktale,* trans. Laurence Scott. Austin, TX 1975.

Sazhin, V. N. "Примечания," in Daniil Charms. *Собрание сочинений в трех томах,* Vol. 3. St. Petersburg 2000, 239.

Shavit, Zohar. *Poetics of Children's Literature.* Athens, GA 1986.

Shteiner, Evgenij. *Авангард и построение нового человека. Искусство советской детской книги 1920 годов.* Moscow 2002.

Sokol, Elena. *Russian Poetry for Children.* Knoxville, TN 1984.

Steiner, Evgeny. *Stories for Little Comrades: Revolutionary Artists and the Making of Early Soviet Children's Books,* trans. Jane Ann Miller. Seattle 1999.

Tjutchev, Fedor. "Silentium," in Tjutchev. *Полное собрание сочинений и писем в 6 томах.* Vol. 1. Moscow 2002, 123.

Tveritina, Alena. "Soviet Children's Literature: The Struggle Between Ideology and Creativity," in *Russia Beyond the Headlines* ⟨http://rbth.com/literature/2014/06/27/soviet_childrens_literature_the_struggle_between_ideology_and_creativity_3776⟩ (Accessed November 1, 2017).

Tynjanov, Ju. N. "О литературной эволюции," in *Поэтика. История литературы. Кино.* Moscow 1977, 270-281.

Tynjanov, Ju. N. "Вопрос о литературной эволюции," in *На литературном посту* 10 (1927), 42-48.

Weld, Sara Pankenier. *An Ecology of the Russian Avant-Garde Picturebook.* Amsterdam: John Benjamins, 2018.

Weld, Sara Pankenier. "Delad läsekrets och dubbelt seende: Aisopiska djup i Osip Mandelstams *Två sparvagnar*," in *Tidskrift för litteraturvetenskap (Journal of Comparative Literature)* 2, trans. Maria Andersson. Stockholm 2014, 49-67.

Weld, Sara Pankenier. "The Obliteration of the Avant-Garde Aesthetic: Comparative Study of 1930s Picturebooks by Samuil Marshak," in *Детские чтения* 2: 6 (2014), 187-198.

Weld, Sara Pankenier. "Удвоенная аудитория и двойное видение: Эзоповские глубины *Двух трамваев* Осипа Мандельштама," in M. Gronas and B. Scherr, eds., *Лифшиц/Лосев/Loseff: Сборник памяти Льва Владимировича Лосева,* trans. Vladimir Kucherjavkin. Moscow 2017, 183-209.

CHAPTER 2

The Junctures of Child Psychology and Soviet Avant-Garde Film: Representations, Influences, Applications

Ana Hedberg Olenina

1   Introduction

The discipline of pedology (from the Greek *pais*, "child," and *logos*, "science") emerged in the late 19th century as a holistic study of childhood, which sought to integrate the achievements of neurophysiology, developmental psychology, sociology, pedagogy, and other related fields for the sake of understanding the specificity of the young mind and devising more wholesome strategies of upbringing. Originating in the United States, this interdisciplinary inquiry into the issues of childhood found enthusiastic supporters in pre-revolutionary Russia.[1] After 1917, pedology received further impetus thanks to the state's utopian aspiration to raise the "New Soviet Man" – the first generation of builders of socialism. Due to the government's ideological alliance with materialist directions in science, enlisted to legitimize the Bolsheviks' endeavors in restructuring society, new institutes of psychology received official endorsement and financial support. As a rule, they were chaired by psychologists who openly embraced communist ideology, vocalized the need for a Marxist platform in their field, and stressed the utopian promise of laboratory findings for pedagogical practice. In the words of one such leader, Aron Zalkind, pedology was to "provide the most valuable means for educating and reeducating man in a way that is most advantageous for the proletarian revolution."[2] At the First Pedological Conference in 1927, the Commissar of Enlightenment Anatolij Lunacharskij prophesized that "pedology, having studied what a child is, what laws govern his development [...] will illuminate for us the most important [...] process of creating the new man in tandem with the production of new equipment in the industrial sphere."[3] With political stakes being so

---

1   E. M. Balashov, Педология в России в первой трети XX века, St. Petersburg 2012, 7, 43-44.
2   Cited in Balashov, 17. All translations in this chapter are mine, unless otherwise noted – AO.
3   Cited in Aleksandr Etkind, "Общественная атмосфера и индивидуальный путь ученого: опыт прикладной психологии 20-х годов," in Вопросы психологии 5 (1990), 15.

high, multiple psychology laboratories competed with each other to articulate a convincing and all-encompassing materialist approach to the mind of a child. Among the leading trends were reflexology and its offshoot, "reactology," both of which emphasized neurophysiological functions, Freudian psychoanalysis, Pavel Blonskij's "bio-genetic" and Aleksandr Zaluzhnyj's "socio-genetic" approaches, which blended reflexology and sociology, and Lev Vygockij's cultural-historical theory of personality development, which argued that child's consciousness is shaped by her interaction with tools and concepts available in her cultural environment.[4] The diversity of perspectives came to an abrupt end in 1936, when pedology was banned under tightening Stalinism.

The pursuits of this discipline prior to the crackdown provide an invaluable source for mapping the diverse constructions of childhood articulated in early Soviet art. Perspectives on childhood negotiated in scientific research institutes responded to the ideological atmosphere of the time and, in turn, were assimilated by politicians and officials in charge of education. Psychologists' ideas reverberated in the cultural sphere, which in itself provided scientists with topical research questions and avenues of inquiry.

This chapter considers the echoes of pedology in films and the broader cinematic discourse of the 1920s and early 1930s. A rapidly developing young art form, cinema served as a mirror that reflected novel approaches to childhood. Early Soviet filmmakers, eagerly attuned to the cultural-political innovations of their epoch, represented research laboratories and pedagogical trends in documentaries and fictional narratives. Film theorists and critics absorbed ideas stemming from research in psychology of children and adults, particularly in areas pertaining to sensory perception, emotions, and aesthetic experience. Finally, cinema's influence on the young audience became an object of study for psychologists, educators, and film industry officials (Fig. 2.1).[5]

---

4 Balashov, 20-21; Jaan Valsiner, *Developmental Psychology in the Soviet Union*. Bloomington 1988; Etkind, *Эрос невозможного: история психоанализа в России*, St. Petersburg 1993; Petteri Pietikäinen, "The New Soviet Man: Psychoanalysis and the Conquest of the Unconscious in the Early Days of the Soviet Union," in *Alchemists of Human Nature: Psychological Utopianism in Gross, Jung, Reich, and Fromm*, New York 2016, 31-45.
5 See A.M. Gel'mont, "Изучение влияния кино на детей," in *Кино и культура* 4 (1929), 38-46. A recent anthology reprinted several pedological studies of children's audiences from the 1920s-1930s, including N.I. Zhinkin's "Изучение детского отношения к кинематографической картине," A.M. Gel'mont's "Изучение детского кинозрителя," and V.A. Pravdoljubov's "Кино и наша молодёжь: на основе данных педологии" (see Ju. U. Focht-Babushkin, ed., *Публика кино в России: социологические свидетельства 1910-1930х гг.* Moscow 2013). For a sustained analysis of approaches to audience studies, see Toropova, Anna, "Probing the Heart and Mind of the Viewer: Scientific Studies of Film and Theatre Spectators in the Soviet Union, 1917-1936," *Slavic Review* 76.4 (2017).

FIGURE 2.1 Pedologist Abram Gel'mont conducting a psycho-physiological study of children spectators' perception of films in 1929. A pheumograph is recording the girl's breathing patterns, while her finger's rhythmical oscillation is being registered by a kymograph.
IMAGE SOURCE: A.M. GEL'MONT, "ИЗУЧЕНИЕ ВЛИЯНИЯ КИНО НА ДЕТЕЙ," 43

Historically, the development of the early Soviet film industry paralleled that of pedology: in the 1920s, both fields experienced a peak of innovative theoretical activity, which waned by the mid 1930s, when individual intellectual pursuits were suppressed in favor of dogmas dictated by the Stalinist Party line. Soon after the Revolution, the utopian dream of raising the New Soviet Man brought the government's attention to the film industry. As early as in 1922, Lenin proclaimed cinema "the most important of all arts" in recognition of its potential for propaganda.[6] An emergent generation of Avant-Garde artists took up the call to revolutionize "bourgeois" forms and instill new ideals in the minds of the audience. Interpreting political slogans from an artistic perspective, early Soviet filmmakers embraced the utopian promise of science, heralded by ideologues. In the words of Sergej Eisenstein, a "synthesis of arts and science" was to become "the watchword for our epoch in the field of art."[7]

---

6 Anatolij Lunacharskij, "A Conversation with Lenin," in Richard Taylor, Ian Christie, eds., *The Film Factory: Russian and Soviet Cinema in Documents*, Cambridge, MA 1988, 57.

7 Sergei Eisenstein, "The Dramaturgy of the Film Form," in Richard Taylor, ed., *Sergei Eisenstein: Selected Works*, Vol. 1, London and New York 2010, 180.

Yet, in borrowing concepts from various trends in psychology and pedology, the film artists transformed and inverted scientific research, as well as its ideologically charged, popular version created by politicians. In what follows, I will consider some tensions, aporias, and gaps that occurred between the Bolshevik leaders' vision of pedology as a scientific program for raising the future collectives of workers, and the complex reality of the actual psychological research at its juncture with cinema.

2   The Soulless State: Child Reflexology in Pudovkin's *Mechanics of the Human Brain*

Vsevolod Pudovkin's documentary Механика головного мозга, или поведение человека (*The Mechanics of the Human Brain, or the Behavior of Man*, 1926) was conceived as a *kulturfilm* to educate the public about Ivan Pavlov's reflexology – a doctrine that the Party officials saw as the single most promising materialist direction in psychology.[8] Contemporary critics regarded Pudovkin's documentary as an illustration to Bucharin's pronouncement that "the teaching on the conditioned reflexes [... is an] instrument in the iron arsenal of materialist ideology."[9] Pudovkin's project seems to have been inspired by the romantic vision of reflexology as a neurophysiological key to the secrets of the psyche and a pathway towards harnessing mankind's inner resources for the sake of the new future. The film ends with a triumphant quotation by Pavlov, suggesting that the human civilization is a product of reflexological networks accumulated in mankind's brains: "Reflexes are linked together by a special reflex of the goal, or a drive towards possessing a certain stimulating object. Our entire culture is built by the goal reflex, built by people striving to attain the goal they had set for themselves in their lives."[10]

Peculiarly, this passage is illustrated not by an image of proletarians on some grand mission, but rather by a scene from a nursery, where small kids ingenuously construct a furniture pyramid to reach a high-hanging quoit – a metal ring suspended from the ceiling (Fig. 2.2). Thus, symbolically, the children stand in for the builders of socialist future. Judging from their identical

---

8   Механика головного мозга, или поведение человека, 1926, directed by Vsevolod Pudovkin. The film is preserved at the Gosfil'mofond Archive, Moscow (File P-1062); Amy Sargeant, "Pudovkin and Pavlov's Dog," Ph.D. Dissertation, University of Bristol, Bristol 1997, 58-59.
9   Vitalij Zhemchuzhnyj, "Поведение человека," in *Кино* 14 (September 1926), 3.
10 From Механика головного мозга, или поведение человека, 1926.

FIGURE 2.2 Young children in an orphanage supervised by Dr. Durnovo are demonstrating a Pavlovian "goal reflex" (a frame from Механика головного мозга [*The Mechanics of the Human Brain*]).

buzzed haircuts and minimalist room décor, these little construction workers are at a state institution, presumably an orphanage (according to the intertitles, they are in the care of Dr. Aleksandr Durnovo). The scene is preceded by images of two, four, and six-year olds engaged in other purposeful activities, such as inspecting a new toy, washing up, and setting the table for dinner. The sequence implies that civilized manners are acquired through establishing and reinforcing appropriate conditioned reflexes from an early age onward. The older children perform with increased sophistication, indicating, as the intertitles point out, a greater development of their brain.

Going back in time, the film presents the argument that complex habits are based on a foundation of elemental, inborn reflex functions, such as a newborn's instinctive grasping at an adult finger, or salivation in response to food. The latter reaction is given the greatest screen time due to its importance in Pavlov's original method. The film offers a glimpse into a laboratory of children's reflexology led by Nikolaj Krasnogorskij, a close associate of Pavlov. There, a preschooler tethered to a cookie dispenser is being conditioned to salivate and chew in response to random stimuli, such as the beat of the metronome or the tapping on his hand. We are led to infer that subconscious adaptations like these serve as the building blocks for larger behavioral tendencies, which may appear to laymen as conscious and purposeful acts. Yet, despite Pudovkin's logical exposition of his material, the film leaves many open questions and ultimately fails to affirm reflexology's power to rationalize behavior of children. Moreover, its unethical representation of human beings and animals creates a grave impression instead of affirming the utopian hopes associated with Pavlov's ideas taught by Soviet ideologues. The roots of these controversies lie in the history of the Soviet film Avant-Garde's engagement with reflexology.

Механика головного мозга was the debut work of Pudovkin, who would go on to become one of the most celebrated Soviet directors of the 1920s. His choice of reflexology as a subject had been influenced by Lev Kuleshov's workshop, where he had studied. Kuleshov, a pioneer of montage theory and a one-time ally of Constructivist designers, engaged his students in a quest for the "laws of expressivity" onscreen: they experimented with shot combinations, drafted striking screen compositions, and attempted to optimize actors' movements. Of particular interest to the group was the idea of couching performers to structure their actions in order to maximize visual impact. To that end, Kuleshov introduced acting etudes aimed at ingraining effective habits of movement in the performers' brain. In presenting his approach, Kuleshov stressed his reliance on the latest trends in physiological psychology, stating that "the training of the actor-model's exterior techniques should be complemented by the study of reflexes in human behavior."[11] Reflexology was thus mobilized as a theoretical justification for the workshop's acting experiments, along with other fashionable trends revolutionizing body techniques, such as those specific to Taylorism, and the Scientific Organization of Labor. When the Mezhrabprom-Rus' film studio approved young Pudovkin as the director a *kulturfilm* popularizing reflexology, Kuleshov accompanied his former student to Pavlov's laboratory near Leningrad and assisted him in conducting negotiations with the institute's staff.[12]

Kuleshov's reverence for reflexology was similar to that of many other leftist theorists and practitioners in the sphere of performance arts. One of the most

---

11   Lev Kuleshov, "Искусство кино: мой опыт," in *Собрание сочинений*, Vol. 1, Moscow 1987, 219.
12   Kuleshov and Aleksandra Chochlova, *50 лет в кино*, Moscow 1975, 76.

famous enthusiasts of Pavlov among the Avant-Garde was Vsevolod Mejerhol'd, whose theater temporarily hosted Kuleshov's workshop in 1922.[13] For Mejerhold, as for Kuleshov, reflexology appeared to offer a rationalist, deterministic alternative to the actor's intuitive work guided by inspiration. An anecdote from Mejerhol'd's memoirs dealing with the 1920s reflects the popular view that reflexology shattered the bourgeois notion of spirituality:

> On the occasion of Pavlov's birthday [юбилей], I sent him a telegram, in which I wrote, somewhat frivolously, that I was greeting the man who had finally put an end to an entity as mysterious and murky as the 'soul.' In response, I received a letter from Pavlov, in which he politely thanked me, yet remarked, 'With regards to the soul, let us not rush and wait before we can state anything definite.'[14]

The exchange is symbolic of the Avant-Garde radicalism and hasty misappropriation of reflexology, as well as of Pavlov's own guarded view of his research. In fact, Pavlov refused to cooperate with Pudovkin's film crew, fearing the disruption of his experiments and the vulgarization of his ideas.[15] The script of the film was penned by Pavlov's more adventurous junior colleague, Leonid Voskresenskij. At the time, popular publications on reflexology were scarce, and Pudovkin entrusted the issue of the film's scientific rectitude to Voskresenskij and two other consultants, and Pavlov's followers, Dmitrij Fursikov and Nikolaj Krasnogorskij.[16] The latter's research on children became a highlight of the film, since it demonstrated that Pavlov's experimental discoveries were pertinent to humans. Krasnogorskij's method was conceived, as one Russian historian put it, "in the same language as Pavlov's:" it involved registering the secretion of saliva and related motor reactions of suction, swallowing, and chewing.[17] The film shows a little boy wearing special headgear that records his jaw movements on a kymograph tape. Isolated in a narrow dimly lit room, the child is laying on a bed with a metal cookie feeder hovering above his mouth. Next door, Krasnogorskij and his assistant are manipulating a complex

---

13   Ibid., 75.
14   Cited in Aleksandr Gladkov, *Пять лет с Мейерхольдом. Встречи с Пастернаком*, Moscow 1990, 269.
15   Sargeant, 70.
16   Pudovkin, "The Mechanics of the Human Brain," in Richard Taylor, ed. *Vsevolod Pudovkin: Selected Essays*, London 2006, 21.
17   A. I. Kliorin, "Учение о высшей нервной деятельности ребенка в творчестве Н. И. Красногорского," in *Российский педиатрический журнал* 6 (2007), 36.

THE JUNCTURES OF CHILD PSYCHOLOGY & SOVIET AVANT-GARDE FILM

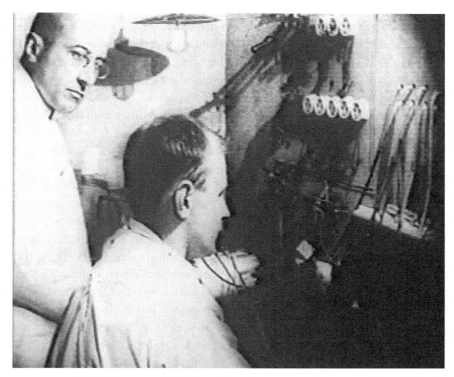

FIGURE 2.3 Nikolaj Krasnogorskij (left) and his assistant, operating a control board that administers cookies to the child and taps him on his hand. Their booth is isolated from the child to insure the purity of the experiment (a frame from *Механика головного мозга*).

control board that regulates the boy's feeding, as well as the random signals to which he is being conditioned (Fig. 2.3). The child exhibits a reaction of chewing in response to a particular beat of the metronome. Another beat frequency evokes no such reaction – this is a phenomenon known as "inhibition," whereby the brain's cortical "analyzer" recognizes the new acoustic stimulus as different and brakes the excitation of neural networks responsible for chewing.[18]

Although not discussed in the film in great detail, reflex inhibition was a crucial area of Krasnogorskij's research. In the 1910's, his experiments convinced Pavlov that inhibition was equivalent to sleep,[19] an idea that would go on to justify the ubiquitous use of hypnosis-induced sleep in Soviet psychiatry

---

18   N. I. Krasnogorskij, *Высшая нервная деятельность ребенка*, Leningrad 1958, 116.
19   Ibid., 160.

in the 1930s.[20] Krasnogorskij's laboratory investigated the formation of conditioned reflexes in relation to multiple variables: the type of the sensory stimulus, time of the day, child's age, various disorders, fatigue, etc. The intensity of reaction was measured by the number of saliva drops captured in a silver capsule placed inside the mouth. Like Pavlov, Krasnogorskij believed that humans have the same basic brain mechanisms as animals but differ from them in that they are capable of speech and abstract thought. He set out to describe these higher functions from a reflexological perspective.[21] One step towards attaining this goal was his experiment in which the child was conditioned to salivate in response to the word "ten." The child would then be ordered "to add five and five," while Krasnogorskij's instrument measured salivation as the right "verbal stimulant appeared in the child's inner speech [внутренняя речь]."[22] What this study proved, according to the researcher, was that an abstract stimulus had "a direct access" to the feeding center in the brain, activating the organism's primitive inborn reactions.[23] This cautious description, typical of Krasnogorskij's publications, could hardly explain how reflexology could serve in the utopian program of building a new society. But Bolshevik politicians thought otherwise. The First Conference on Pedology in 1927, presided over by Nadezhda Krupskaja, Bucharin, Lunacharskij, and the Commissar of Public Health, Nikolaj Semashko, singled out reflexology as the most promising direction in the study of children.[24]

When *Механика головного мозга* was released in theaters, a common thread in its reviews was a litany of Marxist-Leninist clichés pertaining to reflexology. *Pravda* wrote that the film "destroys the myth of the human soul. [...T]he life of the soul, its creation, its inspiration – all this is nothing more than the higher level of reflex."[25] *Kino-front* joined in:

> Pavlov's doctrine leaves no room for the notion of the 'soul.' Pavlov's doctrine is a crushing blow to idealistic beliefs. Pavlov's doctrine [...] is a scientific basis for the materialist understanding of the behavior of man and animals.[26]

---

20 Konstantin Bogdanov, "Право на сон и условные рефлексы: колыбельные песни в советской культуре, 1930е-50е гг.," in *Новое литературное обозрение* 86 (2007), ⟨http://magazines.russ.ru/nlo/2007/86/bo1.html⟩ (Accessed November 22, 2017).
21 Krasnogorskij, 9.
22 Ibid., 19.
23 Ibid.
24 A. Zalkind, "Педология в СССР: краткое изложение пленума съезда," in *На путях к новой школе* 1 (1928), 15.
25 *Правда*, December 14, 1926, translated and cited in Sargeant, 84.
26 E. Vilenskij, "Поведение человека," in *Кино-фронт* 1 (1927), 13.

It is worthwhile to meditate on this notion of "soullessness" and probe the ethics of the film's representation of its subjects. Indeed, *Механика головного мозга* is a token of the Soviet film Avant-Garde's romance with Pavlovian reflexology – a testimony to its utopian fascination with science, marred by violent, authoritarian undertones. The film's plot structure is that of a chain: it begins with a demonstration of elemental defensive reflexes in dissected frogs and then introduces the behavior of increasingly sophisticated kinds of animals, such as dogs and monkeys. In each new case, the mise-en-scène and the intertitles symbolically underscore the scientists' control over the neurophysiological processes and their authoritative invasion into the body of a living being: a canine is given acid and salivates into a calibrated flask implanted into a fistula in its muzzle; a simian undergoes brain surgery and loses the ability to recognize its toy. The logic of these experiments follows the so-called "destruction" principle of nineteenth century physiologist Claude Bernard, an early influence on Pavlov:[27] "it is only through the stopping of a "normal" activity – its suppression or damage – that the function of an activity can be known."[28] According to film historian Lisa Cartwright, early scientific documentaries often espoused Bernard's principle, thanks to its dramatic demonstrative power and its affirmation of the observer's ability to regulate and discipline the living body.[29] When *Механика головного мозга* introduces human subjects, the same focus on destruction is preserved. No "normal" adults are featured. Instead, Pudovkin shows the debilitating effects of brain injury: a bed-ridden syphilitic woman is too feeble to hold a bowl of soup, a mentally handicapped man investigates a flower bouquet by chewing on it, an adolescent with a gunshot wound demonstrates a palsied limb. Children – as if they too are somehow short of the adult norm – are shown within the same sequence. In a harrowing way, the film draws a parallel between their undeveloped motor skills and the loss of dexterity by the disabled. The film's presentation of children implies that they are more manageable, more revealing subjects for scientific inquiry. Indeed, this perspective is confirmed in Krasnogorskij's writings. He writes that, like Pavlov, he believed that the "higher nervous functions" of adults were too complex, while a study of young children and children with neurological disorders provided a more "realistic" direction in the development of human reflexology.[30]

---

27 Daniel P. Todes, *Ivan Pavlov: A Russian Life in Science*, Oxford 2014, 36.
28 Lisa Cartwright, *Screening the Body: Tracing Medicine's Visual Culture*, Minneapolis 1995, 26.
29 Cartwright, 29.
30 Krasnogorskij, 7.

FIGURE 2.4 Krasnogorskij's assistant peeks out of his booth to check upon the child (a frame from *Механика головного мозга*).

Nominally, the film celebrates neurophysiologists' conquest of the psychic processes. The image of Krasnogorskij's assistant peering down through the window of his booth at the child undergoing conditioning symbolizes the reflexologists' authoritative supervision of experiments involving human subjects (Fig. 2.4). The research center and the orphanage, where all employees wear white robes, are represented as methodical caretakers of the young. This vision, however, is undermined by multiple details that inadvertently throw the film's main message into question. One such image is that of a pitiful toddler gazing into the camera as he clings to the arm of a white-robbed research assistant, as he is being laid onto the laboratory bed (Fig. 2.5). Instead of validating the procedure, the image makes one ponder the child's deprivation from familial warmth and his isolation in the sterile and artificial institutional environment. An even more disturbing sight, that of an older child with a

THE JUNCTURES OF CHILD PSYCHOLOGY & SOVIET AVANT-GARDE FILM 83

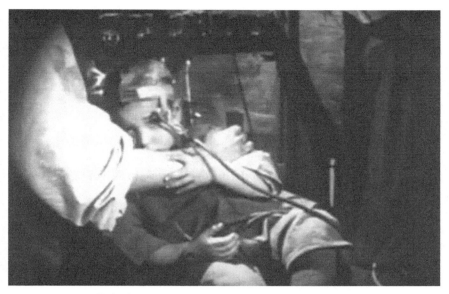

FIGURE 2.5 A small child in Krasnogorskij's experiment looks into the camera (a frame from *The Mechanics of the Human Brain*).

FIGURE 2.6 A child with a calibrated saliva collector inserted into a fistula on his cheek (a frame from *Механика головного мозга*).

saliva collector inserted into a wound on the side of his cheek, raises the issue of medical ethics: if the child had developed a fistula "because of a disease," as the intertitles announce, why is the perforation being widened instead of surgically repaired? (Fig. 2.6). Images like these constitute what may be called, after Walter Benjamin, the film's "optical unconscious"– the details that complicate Pudovkin's intended message and invite critical reflection on the utopian promise of reflexology.[31]

3 Distorted Echoes: Ideas Relating to Pedology in Sergej Eisenstein's Film Theory

Among the Soviet Avant-Garde filmmakers, Sergej Eisenstein stands out as a figure whose interest in psychology at large, and children's psychology in particular, reached a nearly professional level. It is not accidental that in 1929, a famous German psychologist of the Gestalt school, Kurt Lewin, invited Eisenstein to lecture at The Berlin Psychological Society – in the words of Aleksandr Lurija, "an unprecedented honor for a Russian scholar."[32] Lewin had been impressed by Eisenstein's insightful analysis of one of his case studies, in which the filmmaker applied the principles of Mejerhold's biomechanics to describe conflicting movements of a one-and-a-half-year-old girl, resulting from her efforts to achieve two opposing goals at once.[33] Throughout his career, Eisenstein voraciously studied psychological texts as a way of enriching his own thinking about cinema's engagement of sensory perception, emotions, cognition, speech, and expressive movement. Incorporating these ideas into his theoretical writings, he re-enforced them with concepts stemming from performance theory, art history, anthropology, Marxist philosophy and multiple other sources. Like many Modernist intellectuals, Eisenstein looked for the origins of mankind's deep-seated psychological tendencies in the accounts of myths, rituals, and customs of ancient cultures.

Eisenstein turned to children's psychology in order to gain insights into the early stages of developing consciousness, which he saw in terms of formation

---

31 Walter Benjamin, "The Work of Art in the Age of Its Technological Reproducibility (Second Version)," in Michael Jennings, Brigid Doherty, and Thomas Levin, eds., *The Work of Art in the Age of Its Technological Reproducibility and Other Writings on Media*, Cambridge, MA 2008, 37.

32 Oksana Bulgakowa, "From Expressive Movement to the 'Basic Problem,'" in Anton Yasnitsky, René Veer, and Michel Ferrari, eds., *The Cambridge Handbook of Cultural-Historical Psychology*, Cambridge, UK 2014, 431.

33 Ibid.

of archaic, universal layers under the influence of biological and socio-cultural factors. He believed that these strata of consciousness are gradually pushed back as the child matures and interiorizes complex cultural conventions and behavioral patterns, yet they still lay at the core of his mind, constituting a universal platform to which art can appeal. In the late 1920s, his quest for such fundamentals drew him, among many other sources, to two prominent trends in Soviet pedology: the children's reflexology produced by Vladimir Bechterev's school and the cultural-historical approach of Vygockij and Lurija.[34]

Eisenstein's 1929 extensive study "Как делается пафос?" ("How Is Pathos Created?") draws on *Рефлексологический подход в педагогике* (*Reflexological Approach in Pedagogy* 1925), written by Bechterev's follower Avgusta Dernova-Jarmolenko.[35] The basic premise of Dernova-Jarmolenko's treatise is that "the reflex, as a psychoneurological unit, allows us to consider the behavior of animals and men without dividing it into specific processes of varying value, such as the will, feeling, mind, etc."[36] The merit of reflexology, she writes, is that it builds

> a foundation ... of the notions of will, memory, and feeling: these concepts are being deciphered in a simple and clear way; they are described from a physiological-mechanical viewpoint; they can be compared to each other as something of the same nature – as reflexes.[37]

What this neurophysiological homogenizing of the old categories meant for her own project was the possibility to recount her experience as an orphanage psychologist in reflexological terms. In the passage below, cited by Eisenstein, Dernova-Jarmolenko discusses the trauma of bereavement as a sudden breakage of habitual "associative reflexes" established in the person's brain in relation to the deceased: "Every nascent activity in your nervous system gets inhibited by the void [...]. Nobody to work for. Nobody to share anything with.

---

34 On Eisenstein's engagement with Vygockij's and Lurija's ideas see Julia Vassilieva, "Eisenstein/Vygotsky/Luria's Project: Cinematic Thinking and the Integrative Science of Mind and Brain," in *Screening the Past* 38 (2013): 1-16; Vassilieva, "Eisenstein and Cultural-Historical Theory," in *Flying Carpet, Studies on Eisenstein and Russian Cinema in Honor of Naum Kleiman*, Joan Neuberger and Antonio Somaini, eds., Paris and Milan 2017, pp. 421-442.

35 Sergej Eisenstein, "Как делается пафос?" 1929, Box 1923, Folder 2, Item 793 (1), The Russian State Archive of Literature and the Arts (RGALI).

36 A. Dernova-Jarmolenko, *Рефлексологический подход в педагогике*, Leningrad 1925, 6. On Bechterev's school of children psychology see Andy Byford, "V. M. Bekhterev in Russian Child Science, 1900s–1920s: 'Objective Psychology'/"Reflexology' As a Scientific Movement," in *Journal of the History of the Behavioral Sciences*, 52.2 (2016): 99–123.

37 Ibid., 7.

Nobody to live for."³⁸ In this somewhat simplistic, commonsensical account of mourning, Bechterev's terminology appears to be almost superfluous. The reflexological description of mourning prefaces Dernova-Jarmolenko's recommendation that children should not be subjected to transfers from one orphanage to another and seems to belabor an obvious point.³⁹

Yet, in reading this simplified reflexological account, Eisenstein finds something fascinating for his own theory of pathos and catharsis: an insight into the psychological mechanisms underlying a strong emotional reaction. In his manuscript, he underlines Dernova-Jarmolenko's conclusion that "displeasure, suffering, and sorrow are but a rupture of habitual links" and argues that a relief from such negative effects – a discharge culminating in cathartic ecstasy – must similarly occur through a rupture.⁴⁰ As an artist, he literalizes the metaphor of fissure, contemplating the shape of movement appropriate for the expression of this extreme psychological state. Ecstasy for him is "ex-stasis," a leap out of the equilibrium:

> Mainly, we are interested in the fact that the motor-dynamic character of pathos coincides with the general dynamic of ecstasy: the quality of breakage, dispersal (разрядность), or falling "out of line" ("выход из ряда"). This breakage defines ecstasy as an exit from a certain state, that is, the rupture of habitual and predetermined form.⁴¹

This formula of explosion, radical transformation, and transcendence has consequences for structuring climactic scenes and visualizing actors' performances at the peak of dramatic action, as well as for understanding what is happening in the spectator's psyche as it becomes enraptured by the drama. Eisenstein compares the audience's entrancement to religious compassion during sacrificial rituals.⁴² Contemplating the radical physical and psychological transformations that accompany extreme suffering and subsequent elation, he examines Aristotle's writings on catharsis as well as interpretations of this notion by Bechterev, Freud, and philologists Nikolaj Novosadskij and Jakob Bernays.⁴³ Thus, through multiple recontextualizations, a specific example from children's reflexology explicated by Dernova-Jarmolenko leads Eisenstein towards a universal theory of art's impact on the emotional experience of viewers.

---

38   Cited in Eisenstein, "Как делается пафос?", 35.
39   Dernova-Jarmolenko, 134.
40   Eisenstein, "Как делается пафос?", 36.
41   Ibid., 34.
42   Ibid., 41.
43   Eisenstein, "Как делается пафос?", 37-51.

From 1928 to 1929, around the same time as he was researching the physical and psychological underpinning of pathos, Eisenstein began to work on his theory of cinema as a language, inquiring into its logic of signification and communication.[44] He planned to collaborate with Lurija and Vygockij, creators of the cultural-historical model in developmental psychology renowned for their research on children's cognition and speech. One more potential collaborator invited to join the team was the linguist Nikolaj Marr, who studied the origins of speech, protolanguages, and nonverbal communication.[45] Marr had authored a preface to a Russian edition of Lucien Lévi-Bruhl's anthropological treatise *Primitive Mentality*, which influenced Eisenstein's belief that the experience of ecstasy involves a plunge into "pre-logical," sensual thinking, which operates according to its own special laws.[46] With the help of this team, the director hoped to discover the foundational mechanisms of perception and cognition, which could be used in structuring maximally effective film scenes.[47] The collaborative project never materialized: it was interrupted by Eisenstein's trip abroad which lasted nearly three years, and, upon his return, by the deaths of Vygockij and Marr in 1934. Stalinist repression of pedology, which followed two years later, made Lurija abandon psychology and start a new career in neuroscience.[48]

However, some traces of Eisenstein's theoretical dialogue with Lurija and Vygockij's notion of pedology may be found in the filmmaker's contemplation of children's drawings, which served as key objects of study in the psychologists' cultural-historical approach to developmental psychology. One such instance appears in Eisenstein's essay "Кинематографический принцип и идеограмма" ("The Cinematographic Principle and the Ideogram," 1929):

> Professor Lurija, of the Moscow Institute of Psychology, has shown me a drawing by a child depicting 'the lighting of a stove.' Everything is represented in a reasonably accurate relationship and with great care. Firewood. A stove. A chimney. But what are those zigzags seen in that huge

---

44   Bulgakowa, *Sergei Eisenstein: A Biography*, Berlin 2001, 86.
45   Bulgakowa, *Sergei Eisenstein*, 168. Marr's controversial theory of language postulated similarities between the so-called "japhetic" languages, supposedly used by the culturally oppressed ethnic minorities, such as the Basques, and lower social classes, such as the Roman plebs. "Marrism" was officially endorsed by the Communist Party, and, similarly to Pavlov's reflexology, became a dogma, the criticism of which resulted in prosecution. In the 1950s, Marrism was discredited as pseudoscience (V. M. Alpatov, *История одного мифа: Марр и Марризм*, Moscow 1991).
46   Bulgakowa, *Sergei Eisenstein*, 170.
47   Ibid.
48   Bulgakowa, "From Expressive Movement," 426.

rectangle in the center? They turn out to be – matches. Taking into account the crucial importance of these matches in terms of the process depicted, the child provides a proper scale for them.[49]

For Eisenstein, the child's disregard for proportions demonstrates a representational logic untarnished by the dictate of realistic mimesis as taught, for instance, in Western schools of classical art. The magnification of the key object reflects the child's understanding of the situation. "It is possible to trace this particular tendency from its ancient, almost prehistoric source," Eisenstein writes, suggesting that the child naturally discovers the hierarchical principle governing the structure of icons and religious drawings in ancient China.[50] In the same way, Eisenstein argues, a cinematic close-up singles out and magnifies a detail that the director wants to be at the forefront of the audience's attention. According to this theory, a child's drawing serves a dual function: it both denotes the objects and expresses the artist's perspective.

Eisenstein's discussion of the thought process encoded in the child's drawing was inspired by Lurija and Vygockij's argument that drawing is a precursor to writing and should be construed as a mode of thinking, or an instrument that shapes mental development.[51] The evolving ability to convey thoughts by means of graphic art changes the child's consciousness as does her ongoing mastery of the spoken language. Through drawing, the young mind gains command of concepts, relations, and categories, articulating an active, transformative approach to the world.[52] For Vygockij, a drawing child does not strive for verisimilitude: he is a symbolist rather than realist, and depicts "not what he sees but what he knows."[53] The process of drawing thus resembles the creative act of giving a name rather than simply copying an object.[54]

To prove the relationship between drawing and writing as forms of speech, Lurija conducted experiments aimed at making children discover the mnemonic function of note-taking. Very young children, not yet able to write,

---

49   Eisenstein, "The Cinematographic Principle and the Ideogram," in Sergei Eisenstein, *Film Form: Essays in Film Theory*. Ed. and trans. Jay Leyda, New York 1949, 34. Vjacheslav Ivanov has discussed Eisenstein's interpretation of disproportionate objects in this child's drawing in reference to theories of the "reversed perspective." See Vjacheslav Ivanov, *Избранные труды по семиотике и истории культуры*, Vol. 1, Moscow 1998, 212.
50   Ibid.
51   Lev Vygockij, *Собрание сочинений*, Vol. 3: *История развития высших психических функций*, Moscow 1983, 186.
52   Ibid., 187.
53   Ibid., 186.
54   Ibid., 186.

were asked to memorize several sentences dictated to them verbally and given a pencil and a blank page. Over a series of such sessions, they began to use lines and squiggles to mark the words they wanted to recall. At first, they used identical lines for different words; then they learned to create unique shapes, which were further replaced by images and figurines (what Lurija and Vygockij called "pictograms"). At this stage, children were able to write down the whole phrase, combining pictograms into a kind of a rebus. Finally, pictograms were replaced by more advanced "ideograms," i.e. more abstract, abbreviated symbols.[55]

An "ideogram" as Lurija and Vygockij understood it becomes a key term in Eisenstein's article. He suggests that ideograms are used in Chinese writing, in which abstract elements, hardly reminiscent of pictograms, are combined to create new concepts. In contrast, realism, favored in Western art, hinders the artist's expressive evolution on the level of pictograms, a conceptually less sophisticated stage. The implication is that filmmakers should strive to move beyond realistic depiction and use film footage to form new conceptual structures, as the inventors of the Chinese writing system once did when they abandoned the initial figurative dimension of characters. Further, Eisenstein compares cinematic montage to a child's effort to convey a phrase by means of discrete pictures, or, at a later stage of development, by abstract symbols which originated from pictograms. Thus, it is possible to draw a parallel between ideogrammatic communication and Eisenstein's notion of "intellectual montage." He pioneered this experimental principle of combining shots in his film *Октябрь* (*October*, 1928), which contains a sequence of images detached from their situational context. This sequence starts with a recapulation of Catholic, Orthodox, Hindu and Buddhist religious attributes, and then depicts aboriginal idols and masks. The director's goal is to pose a rhetorical question: "What is religion?" at a moment in the film when a revolutionary Kronstadt sailor discovers his own anticlericalism and antimonarchism.

For Eisenstein, children's drawings mirror cinema not only because of their combination of elements, but also because they incorporate the principle of unfolding, or gradual disclosure. In his essay "Монтаж и архитектура" ("Montage and Architecture, 1935), Eisenstein uses a child's drawing to introduce the idea of a visual path as a compositional principle:

> This is a typical child's drawing. We cannot see it as a representation of a pond with trees along the bank until we understand its internal dynamics. The trees are not depicted from one viewpoint, as adults would show

---

55   Ibid., 188, 190.

them in a picture or in a single frame of film. Here the drawing depicts a series of trees as they are revealed along the path between them that the observer follows.[56]

For Eisenstein, the child's picture incorporates physical movement along the path and reflects the functioning of imagination, shifting from one lake scene to another. This interpretation is close to Vygockij's assertion that children's drawings "tell stories" – they do not represent objects as much as they narrate.[57] The link between the child's drawing and speech, writes Vygockij, can be observed in the young artists' tendency to utter a word before drawing what it represents. Eisenstein follows this principle when he uses the child's picture of a lake to contemplate the structure of the path around the Greek Acropolis and other architectural examples, in which different – and sometimes clashing – views open up along the walk. He compares these architectural juxtapositions to the way cinema guides the viewers' thought process through deliberately organized image sequences.

What model of child psychology emerges from Eisenstein's writings? The film director's quest for psychological universals makes him leap effortlessly from children's drawings to archaic and non-Western art. Add to this his interest in the reflexological inquiry into chimpanzees' "proto-language" by the zoologist Sergej Dobrogaev, and this combination begins to raise red flags in terms of its focus on specimens that are somehow not the norm or do not qualify as "sophisticated" Western adults.[58] But accusations of racism would be unjust in the case of Eisenstein. Similarly to Vygockij and Lurija, who wrote a book entitled *Этюды по истории поведения: обезьяна, примитив, ребенок* (*Essays on the History of Behavior: Ape. Primitive Man. Child*, 1930), in which they actually celebrated the creativity and sophistication of children and illiterate adults in Central Asia, he did not believe in the superiority of West over East, civilized over archaic cultures, adults over children, or humans over animals.[59] Although a certain amount of exoticism and cultural essentialism was undoubtedly present in his thinking (as in the thinking of many other Modernist artists of the early 20th century), Eisenstein was far from endorsing

---

56 Eisenstein, "Montage and Architecture," in Michael Glenny and Richard Taylor, eds., *Selected Works*, Vol. 2, London 2010, 59-82, 59.
57 Vygockij, *История развития*, 186.
58 Eisenstein and S.M. Dobrogaev, "Переписка" ("Correspondence"), 1928, Box 829, Folder 2, Item 41, The Archive of the Russian Academy of Sciences (ARAN), the St. Petersburg Branch.
59 Vygockij and A. R. Lurija, *Этюды по истории поведения: обезьяна, примитив, ребенок*, Moscow 1993.

bigotry. As the film theorist Homay King points out, Eisenstein's veneration of Chinese and Japanese calligraphy in his essay on the ideograms actually reverses the Orientalist binary oppositions, which traditionally equate the West with reason and language, and the East with senses and pictures.[60]

Replete with erudite comparisons and unexpected recontextualizations, Eisenstein's ideas on child psychology did not fit the Bolshevik ideologues' utopian hopes for a clear-cut manipulative schema. A testimony to this discrepancy was the official banning of his *Бежин луг* (*Bezhin Meadow*, 1935), an adaptation of the Pavlik Morozov story, starring an eleven-year-old boy.[61] In the Stalinist culture, the young Morozov was a martyr-hero: he had denounced his father, a "kulak collaborator," and died at the hand of his relatives. The event, which happened in the Urals in 1932 at the height of collectivization, was picked up by the press and acquired the status of a legend, as it resonated with the party slogans summoning the citizens to relinquish filial piety and join in the ranks of a new, statewide Socialist family.[62] The image of Morozov's brutal father, a kulak, fed into the fear-mongering campaign against saboteurs and enemies of the Revolution presumably entrenched in the countryside. Film historian Natalija Noussinova points out that the media representation of Morozov was foreshadowed by the popular film *Танька-трактирщица* (*Tan'ka the Innkeeper*, 1929), in which a battered teenage heroine rises up against her abusive kulak stepfather and, in the end becomes a young pioneer.[63] Other pioneer hero narratives, including newspaper accounts of children's exploits as well as works of poetry and fiction, which began to emerge in the mid-1920s, also contributed to the formation of the Morozov myth.[64]

The idea of a child's symbolic revolt against the old regime stood at the core of the film script for *Бежин луг* by the playwright Aleksandr Rzheshevskij. He borrowed the title of his screenplay from Ivan Turgenev's short story, in which

---

60   Homay King, *Lost in Translation: Orientalism, Cinema, and the Enigmatic Signifier*, Durham, NC 2010, 37.
61   Marie Seton, *Sergei M. Eisenstein: A Biography*, New York 1952, 353.
62   Naum Klejman, "Эйзенштейн, 'Бежин луг' (Первый вариант): Культурно-мифологические аспекты," in *Киноведческие записки* 41 (1999), 84-105, 93.
63   Natalija Noussinova, "'Теперь ты наша': Ребенок в советском кино 1920х-30х годов," in *Искусство кино* 12 (2003). ⟨http://kinoart.ru/archive/2003/12/n12-article12⟩ (Accessed October 22, 2017). Noussinova points out that the theme of children's rebellion against parents informed numerous productions in this period, notably *В город входить нельзя* (*No Entry into the City*, 1929) and *Дочь партизана* (*Partisan's Daughter*, 1934).
64   For a discussion of the evolution of the pioneer hero trope in Soviet children's literature, see Svetlana Maslinskaya's chapter "'Be Always Ready!': Hero Narratives in Soviet Children's Literature" in this volume.

poor village boys gather around a bonfire at night to share reflections on their daily hardships and the fear of the occult. In Turgenev's work, teenager Stepok emerges as a bright and resourceful leader, but at the end of the story, readers learn that he will die in an accident in a few years' time. Rzheshevskij transplants Turgenev's hero into the contemporary world, so as to channel Stepok's resolute, free spirit into the post-revolutionary rebellion against the oppressive and backward social order still lingering in the Soviet provinces.[65] Eisenstein was expected to create a tribute to the boy's emerging revolutionary consciousness. At one point during the production, Boris Shumjackij, the head of the State Directorate for the Film and Photo Industry, urged the director to make two film versions, one for adults and one for children.[66] Yet, instead of a straightforward piece of Stalinist hagiography, Бежин луг became a tour-de-force examination of a traumatic period in Soviet history. According to Eisenstein, the old village social order was clearly rotten, but the utopian Communist future was nowhere in sight either. Further complicating the Morozov myth, Eisenstein presented the murdered boy not as a sacrificial offering in the name of Socialism, but as a meaningless victim of the peasantry's delusional religiosity and chthonic beastliness. Moreover, he saturated the cinematic version of the story with allusions to literary and mythological narratives of tragic father-and-son confrontations – Laius and Oedipus, Isaac and Abraham, Rostam and Sohrab from the 10th century epic *Shahnameh* by Ferdowsi, and others.[67] Evoking these motifs, the director put Morozov's case into cultural perspective, turning his film into a reflection on archetypes which had haunted mankind's imagination for centuries, frequently resurfacing during events such as civil wars.[68]

Eisenstein's incursion into ancient myths of the parent-child conflict in Бежин луг was his way of reaching down into the deep recesses of the collective unconscious, the seat of universal complexes and archetypes. Curiously, this film was conceived in the wake of his preoccupation with pedology and Levi-Bruhl's anthropology, and his plans for elaborating on a theory of film as a non-verbal language with Vygockij and Marr. Eisenstein stated: "The method of my 'intellectual' cinema involves moving backwards from the expressions of a more advanced consciousness to the forms of a more primeval consciousness,"

---

65   Seton, 353.
66   Vladimir Zabrodin, "К истории постановки *Бежина луга*: Монтаж документов," *in Киноведческие записки* 87 (2008), 270. According to a different account, Eisenstein himself decided to make an additional "second version on a simpler, less tragic and complex level specially designed for children." Seton, 358.
67   Klejman, 96; Bulgakowa, "From Expressive Movement," 445.
68   Klejman, 99.

adding that the regression may proceed "along the path of either the mental evolution of peoples or the development of child psychology (I have read quite a few books on the subject!)."⁶⁹ Thus modeling his implied spectator's response, Eisenstein placed his bets on retelling the most dramatic moments of present-day history in a way that would target primeval, universally shared forms of perception exhibited by children and archaic cultures. It would not be a stretch to surmise that the experimental style of *Бежин луг* reflected his understanding of the internal dynamic of a child's sensory and emotional processing of reality. There is evidence that the director planned to apply the principle of reverse perspective he associated with children's drawings in a daring mise-en-scène, in which Stepok was going to be filmed against a rear-projection screen showing a giant figure of his father, in order to give the impression that the kulak was looming over the child despite standing far behind him.⁷⁰ Judging from the surviving fragments of the film in Naum Klejman's reconstruction (the authorities confiscated and destroyed Eisenstein's original print in 1937), *Бежин луг* had a slightly distorted, Mannerist visual atmosphere, produced by a predominantly low camera angle and unmotivated, sporadic illumination of objects within an overall chiaroscuro lighting scheme.⁷¹ Special lens filters increased the image contrast, filling Stepok's world with mystery and wonder. Stylized visuals amplified the emotional saturation of scenes. Staying true to the principle of montage, Eisenstein conveyed the ambiance of vast spaces and eerie events by walking the viewer through significant, and often clashing details – just as in children's drawings analyzed by Lurija.

This preference for step-by-step disclosure, proceeding through shifts of consciousness, can be seen in the director's tendency to present a mosaic of the character's emotional reactions to events – one shot of the face after another – at every important turn of the plot. The American Avant-Garde filmmaker Jay Leyda, who witnessed Eisenstein's work on the film set, recalled that he singled out individual elements of the mise-en-scène as an homage to Japanese ukiyo-e art, focusing "on isolation, on the rounded perfection of apparently chance selection."⁷² This "Impressionist" aesthetic principle, according to Eisenstein, resonated with Turgenev's poetics.⁷³ Above all, *Бежин луг*

---

69   Eisenstein, *Метод*, Vol. 1, Moscow 2002, 88.
70   Ivanov, 212.
71   Klejman, 88.
72   Cited in Seton, 354. For Eisenstein's reflections on the French Impressionists and Japanese ukiyo-e artists' use of detail for a "laconic transmission" of atmosphere, see Sergei Eisenstein, "On Imagery," *Eisenstein 2: A Premature Celebration of Eisenstein's Centenary*, ed. Jay Leyda, Calcutta 1985, 12-20, 15.
73   Ibid.

was a study of pathos and catharsis, and as such, it could not but incorporate Eisenstein's research in psychology when dealing with these topics, including the insights he gleaned from pedology. The story's climactic moments, whether light or dark, are all structured to foreground rupture. In one such scene, the destruction of a church altar by a village strongman, reminiscent of the Biblical Samson, inaugurates an ecstatic fraternization of peasants liberated from oppressive religious dogmas.[74] In another scene, when Stepok is shot by his father, the crazed parent presses the bleeding child to his heart and then pushes him away, disappearing into the dark landscape.[75] Stepok manages to rise up and walk a few steps behind him – in a loose white shirt, his arms extended like those of Christ. Unsurprisingly, the Party officials found Eisenstein's work overburdened with mysticism and incapable of providing ideological guidance to the Soviet youth.[76]

4 Conclusion

In 1927, pedology was hailed by Bolshevik cultural officials as an all-encompassing scientific program for fostering the future builders of society:

> It is precisely in the USSR, where a new, socialist man is being created within a growing socialist environment, pedology has for the first time ever been consolidated as a materialist-dialectical Marxist discipline, which incorporates and synthesizes the most valuable scientific findings concerning the relationship between the developing human being and the environment. Pedology extrapolates its material from sociology, general biology, physiology, reflexology, Marxist psychology, clinical research, hygiene, and pedagogy.[77]

This grandiose pronouncement had little to do with the actual situation on the ground, where the struggle between diverse schools of psychology, their methodological deficiencies, and the incompatibility of various disciplines destroyed any possibility of a common platform that could bring meaningful

---

74 This comparison belongs to Viktor Shklovskij who saw the original first version of the film. Shklovskij, *Эйзенштейн*, Moscow 1976, 107.
75 In Eisenstein's film, Trofim Morozov shoots his son, although the official version of Pavlik's murder was his dying of cut wounds inflicted by his grandfather and cousin. See Catriona Kelly, *Comrade Pavlik: The Rise and Fall of a Soviet Boy Hero*, London 2005.
76 Zabrodin, 243.
77 Zalkind, 14.

results for real-life pedagogy. The responses of Soviet Avant-Garde filmmakers to various trends in children's psychology serve as a litmus test for psychology schools' inherent problems. Consciously embracing the scientific research, the artists inadvertently revealed how inadequate the current state of this research was for the practical role of guiding young minds. Pudovkin's documentary, *Механика головного мозга*, demonstrating the laboratory practices of the child reflexologist Krasnogorskij, unintentionally exposed the underbelly of the biologically-oriented approach to the psyche, cherished by Bolshevik ideologues. Eisenstein's efforts to apply the insights of child psychology to his film theory and practice resulted in a creative appropriation and repurposing of reflexology, as well as in Lurija and Vygockij's historical-cultural approach to the development of personality. His film *Бежин луг*, devoted to the ur-myth of Soviet pioneer morality, frustrated the Bolshevik authorities precisely because the director chose to explore the ways in which film form engaged elemental structures of perception and cognition, something Eisenstein learned about from child psychologists, instead of creating a straightforward propaganda piece.

Works Cited

Primary Sources

Бежин луг Сергея Эйзенштейна: эпизоды незавершенного фильма 1935-1937, 1967, directed by Naum Klejman and Sergej Jutkevich, VHS tape. [London]: Hendring Glenbuck Films, [c. 1993].

Benjamin, Walter. "The Work of Art in the Age of Its Technological Reproducibility (Second Version)," in Michael Jennings, Brigid Doherty, and Thomas Levin, eds., *The Work of Art in the Age of Its Technological Reproducibility and Other Writings on Media*. Cambridge, MA 2008, 19-55.

Dernova-Jarmolenko, A. *Рефлексологический подход в педагогике*. Leningrad 1925.

Eisenstein, Sergej. "The Dramaturgy of the Film Form," in Richard Taylor, ed., *Sergei Eisenstein: Selected Works*. London and New York 2010, 161-180.

Eisenstein, Sergej. "Как делается пафос?", 1929, box 1923, folder 2, item 793 (1), The Russian State Archive of Literature and the Arts (RGALI).

Eisenstein, Sergej. "The Cinematographic Principle and the Ideogram," in Sergei Eisenstein, *Film Form: Essays in Film Theory*. ed. and trans. Jay Leyda. New York 1949, 28-44.

Eisenstein, Sergej. "Montage and Architecture," in Michael Glenny and Richard Taylor, eds., *Selected Works*, Vol. 2. London 2010, 59-82, 59.

Eisenstein, Sergej. "On Imagery," *Eisenstein 2: A Premature Celebration of Eisenstein's Centenary*, ed. Jay Leyda. Calcutta 1985, 12-20, 15.

Ejzenshtein, Sergej. *Метод*, Vol. 1. Moscow 2002, 88.

Ejzenshtein, S., and S.M. Dobrogaev. "Переписка," 1928, Box 829, Folder 2, Item 41, The Archive of the Russian Academy of Sciences (ARAN), St. Petersburg. Gel'mont A.M. "Изучение влияния кино на детей," in *Кино и культура* 4 (1929), 38-46.

Gladkov, Aleksandr. *Пять лет с Мейерхольдом. Встречи с Пастернаком*. Moscow 1990.

Krasnogorskij, N.I. *Высшая нервная деятельность ребенка*. Leningrad 1958.

Kuleshov, Lev. "Искусство кино: мой опыт," in *Собрание сочинений*, Vol. 1. Moscow 1987, 161-226.

Kuleshov, Lev, and Aleksandra Chochlova. *50 лет в кино*. Moscow 1975.

Lunacharskij, Anatolij. "A Conversation with Lenin," in Richard Taylor and Ian Christie, eds., *The Film Factory: Russian and Soviet Cinema in Documents*. Cambridge, MA 1988, 56-57.

Механика головного мозга, или поведение человека. 1926, directed by Vsevolod Pudovkin, film print, File R-1062, Gosfil'mofond Archive, Moscow.

Pudovkin, Vsevolod. "The Mechanics of the Human Brain," in Richard Taylor, ed. *Vsevolod Pudovkin: Selected Essays*. London 2006, 19-21.

Vilenskij, E. "Поведение человека," in *Кино-фронт* 1 (1927), 13.

Vygockij, L. S. *Педагогическая психология*. Moscow 1996.

Vygockij, L. S. *Собрание сочинений*, Vol. 3: *История развития высших психических функций*. Moscow 1983.

Vygockij L. S., and A. R. Lurija. *Этюды по истории поведения: обезьяна, примитив, ребенок*. Moscow 1993.

Zalkind, A. "Педология в СССР: краткое изложение пленума съезда," in *На путях к новой школе* 1 (1928), 14-22.

Zhemchuzhnyj, Vitalij. "Поведение человека," in *Кино*, 14 (September 1926), 3.

Secondary Sources

Alpatov, V. M. *История одного мифа: Марр и Марризм*. Moscow 1991.

Balashov, E. M. *Педология в России в первой трети XX века*. St. Petersburg 2012.

Bogdanov, Konstantin. "Право на сон и условные рефлексы: колыбельные песни в советской культуре (1930-50-е гг.)," *Новое литературное обозрение* 86 (2007). ⟨http://magazines.russ.ru/nlo/2007/86/bo1.html⟩ (Accessed November 22, 2017).

Bulgakowa, Oksana. *Sergei Eisenstein: A Biography*. Berlin 2001.

Bulgakowa, Oksana. "From Expressive Movement to the 'Basic Problem,'" in *The Cambridge Handbook of Cultural-Historical Psychology*, eds. Anton Yasnitsky, René Veer, and Michel Ferrari. Cambridge, UK 2014, 423-448.

Byford, Andy, "V. M. Bekhterev in Russian Child Science, 1900s–1920s: 'Objective Psychology'/'Reflexology' As a Scientific Movement," in *Journal of the History of the Behavioral Sciences*, 52.2 (2016): 99–123.

Cartwright, Lisa. *Screening the Body: Tracing Medicine's Visual Culture*. Minneapolis 1995.

Churakov, D.O. "У истоков новой педагогики: создание и деятельность 2-го МГУ в 1917-1930 гг., in *Образовательный портал «Слово»* ⟨http://www.portal-slovo.ru/history/35412.php⟩ (Accessed November 22, 2017).

Etkind, Aleksandr. "Общественная атмосфера и индивидуальный путь ученого: опыт прикладной психологии 20-х годов," in *Вопросы психологии* 5 (1990), 13-21.

Etkind, Aleksandr. *Эрос невозможного: история психоанализа в России*. St. Petersburg 1993.

Focht-Babushkin, Ju. U., ed. *Публика кино в России: социологические свидетельства 1910-30-х гг.* Moscow 2013.

Joravsky, David. *Russian Psychology: A Critical History*. Oxford 1989.

Kelly, Catriona. *Comrade Pavlik: The Rise and Fall of a Soviet Boy Hero*. London 2005.

King, Homay. *Lost in Translation: Orientalism, Cinema, and the Enigmatic Signifier*. Durham, NC 2010.

Klejman, Naum. "Эйзенштейн, 'Бежин луг' (Первый вариант): Культурно-мифологические аспекты," in *Киноведческие записки* 41 (1999), 84-105.

Kliorin, A.I. "Учение о высшей нервной деятельности ребенка в творчестве Н. И. Красногорского," in *Российский педиатрический журнал* 6 (2007), 36-40.

Noussinova, Natalija. "'Теперь ты наша': ребенок в советском кино 1920-30-х гг.," in *Искусство кино* 12 (2003). ⟨http://kinoart.ru/archive/2003/12/n12-article12⟩ (Accessed November 22, 2017).

Pietikäinen, Petteri. "The New Soviet Man: Psychoanalysis and the Conquest of the Unconscious in the Early Days of the Soviet Union," in *Alchemists of Human Nature: Psychological Utopianism in Gross, Jung, Reich, and Fromm*. New York 2016, 31-45.

Sargeant, Amy. "Pudovkin and Pavlov's Dog," Ph.D. Dissertation, University of Bristol. Bristol 1997.

Seton, Marie. *Sergei M. Eisenstein: A Biography*. New York 1952.

Shklovskij, Viktor. *Эйзенштейн*. Moscow 1976.

Todes, Daniel Philip. *Ivan Pavlov: A Russian Life in Science*. Oxford 2004.

Toropova, Anna. "Probing the Heart and Mind of the Viewer: Scientific Studies of Film and Theatre Spectators in the Soviet Union, 1917-1936," *Slavic Review* 76.4 (2017).

Valsiner, Jaan. *Developmental Psychology in the Soviet Union*. Bloomington, IN 1988.

Vassilieva, Julia. "Eisenstein/Vygotsky/Luria's Project: Cinematic Thinking and the Integrative Science of Mind and Brain," in *Screening the Past* 38 (2013): 1-16.

Vassilieva, Julia. "Eisenstein and Cultural-Historical Theory," in *Flying Carpet, Studies on Eisenstein and Russian Cinema in Honor of Naum Kleiman*, Joan Neuberger and Antonio Somaini, eds. Paris and Milan 2017, pp. 421-442.

Zabrodin, Vladimir. "К истории постановки *Бежина луга*: монтаж документов," in *Киноведческие записки* 87 (2008), 242-282.

CHAPTER 3

The Dictionary as a Toy Collection: Interactions between Avant-Garde Aesthetics and Soviet Children's Literature

Ainsley Morse

1   Introduction

This chapter[1] surveys the productive relationship between pre-revolutionary and early Soviet Avant-Garde practice and poetics and Soviet children's literature in the decades from the onset of Futurism (beginning about 1910) through the 1934 adoption of Socialist Realism as the official state policy in literature and the arts.[2] A key point of interest is the relationship between the childlike aesthetic favored by many Avant-Garde artists and how it was (and was not) applied in the production of literature for children. The importance of Avant-Garde models for many Soviet children's authors, from Daniil Charms to Genrich Sapgir and from Junna Moric to Michail Jasnov, is undeniable. That said, the aesthetic of fantasy, absurdity and unconventional logic proved in many instances to be incompatible with the goals and standards of Soviet children's literature, especially as the latter became more regulated. My goal is to demonstrate that the two phenomena nevertheless remained intertwined throughout the entire Soviet period, in part because of the disproportionate number of experimental authors writing for children and young adults.

Like most early twentieth-century modernisms, the pre-revolutionary Russian Avant-Garde was fascinated by the artistic and philosophical prospects of

---

1   The title refers to the statement Chlebnikov made in his essay "Наша основа" ("Our Foundation," 1919): "[...] слово — звуковая кукла, словарь — собрание игрушек" ("[...] a word is a sound puppet, a dictionary is a toy collection.") V. Chlebnikov, *Творения*, Moscow 1986, 627. Here and subsequently all translations are mine unless otherwise noted – AM.

2   The rich topic of early Soviet children's literature has been explored in previous scholarship including Marina Balina and Larissa Rudova, eds., *Russian Children's Literature and Culture*, New York and London 2008; Marina Balina and Valerij Vjugin, eds., *'Убить Чарскую ...': парадоксы советской детской литературы для детей (1920-е – 1930-е гг.): сборник статей*, St. Petersburg 2015; Ben Hellman, *Fairy Tales and True Stories: The History of Russian Literature for Children and Young People (1574-2010)*, Boston and Leiden 2013; Evgenija Putilova, *Очерки по истории критики советской детской литературы, 1917-1941*, Moscow 1982; Elena Sokol, *Russian Poetry For Children*, Knoxville 1984, and others.

the child's viewpoint.[3] For some artists, the childlike was essentially a synonym for the primitive, while others were expressly interested in specifically infantile modes of visual expression and language. Used as an umbrella term, childlike aesthetics, therefore, refers to formal and semantic manifestations of the naïve or primitive, preverbal, and absurd, alogical or nonsensical in literature and the arts. In Russia, most of the major representatives of the literary and artistic Avant-Garde experimented with some of its form in their work, either documenting or emulating it – and sometimes doing both. A short list of such practitioners would include Velimir Chlebnikov, Aleksej Kruchenych, Elena Guro, Vasilij Kamenskij and the Burljuk brothers in literature; Natalija Goncharova, Vasilij Kandinskij, Michail Larionov, Kazimir Malevich and others in visual art.[4] Although in the years before the revolution these figures were not involved in the production of actual children's literature, their work was to influence several generations of Soviet children's authors.

Calls for a brand-new Soviet children's literature began immediately after the revolution and elicited a wide, enthusiastic response, particularly among those representatives of the Avant-Garde who had actively supported the Bolsheviks or considered themselves "fellow travelers." The 1920s saw many of these experimental modernist writers trying their hand at children's literature, among them Konstantin Bal'mont, Osip Mandel'shtam, Boris Pasternak, Ilja Ehrenburg, Aleksej Remizov and Jurij Olesha. To many, the initial political support for experimental art and literature in all areas of public life seemed like a long-awaited recognition and confirmation of the contemporary relevance of the Avant-Garde moment, both at home and abroad. In the same decade, the increased interest in child psychology and cognitive development – including the major linguistic and psychological achievements of Lev Vygockij – also impacted developments in children's literature.[5] In another example, the

---

3   See Sara Pankenier Weld, *Voiceless Vanguard*, Evanston 2014.
4   This chapter focuses on Avant-Garde aesthetics in literature, primarily poetry, but many of its observations apply to visual art as well; as is known, Avant-Garde explicitly involves the mixing of genres, and the visual aspect of Avant-Garde literary experiment was very important. A seminal study of this mixing is Gerald Janecek, *The Look of Russian Literature: Avant-garde Visual Experiments, 1900-1930*, Princeton 1984. For more on Avant-Garde art and visual culture of this period in general, see the classic text by Camilla Gray, *The Russian Experiment in Art, 1863-1922*, New York 1986; Margaret Rowell and Deborah Wye, eds., *The Russian Avant-Garde Book*, New York 2002; Denis Ioffe and Frederick White, eds., *The Russian Avant-Garde and Radical Modernism. An Introductory Reader*, Boston 2012; John E. Bowlt, ed., *Russian Art of the Avant-Garde: Theory and Criticism*, New York 1976.
5   For more on early Soviet child development and educational theory, see Ana Hedberg Olenina's chapter in this volume, "The Junctures of Child Psychology and Soviet Film Avant-Garde: Representations, Influences, Applications."

poet and literary scholar Kornej Chukovskij – also one of the first critics to accept and analyze Futurist aesthetics[6] – published an influential book on the child's inventive, experimental relationship to language and the world, in which he pointed to the fundamental kinship between the child's viewpoint and folklore ("the people's literature") and encouraged Soviet children's writers to learn from both examples.[7] Chukovskij's book reflects the heightened interest in children's literature on the part of the still-forming Soviet state: the 1920s saw influential literary-political figures such as Maxim Gor'kij decrying the deplorable state of pre-revolutionary children's literature and calling for new, exciting and educational works for young Soviet citizens.[8]

These scholarly and artistic forays into children's language and psyche coincided with the realized metaphor of the Soviet state's "infancy," and the society's need to indoctrinate its youngest members in a completely new ideology and world order. Children's literature as a genre took on an unprecedented political significance. At the same time, it sought to be not just dynamic, progressive and educational, but also genuinely appealing and helpful to children. Pre-revolutionary Russian production and Western literature for children, by contrast, were derided as saccharine and dull, as well as ideologically doubtful (if not entirely inimical to Soviet values).

The popularity of the new children's literature – in its own time and subsequently – owed just as much to the Avant-Garde visual artists involved in illustrating children's books as to the writers who conceived and composed them.[9] As the first of Chukovskij's "commandments for children's writers" in

---

6 Kornej Chukovskij, "Эго-футуристы и кубо-футуристы," *Шиповник* XXII, Petrograd 1914, 95-154. Reproduced as "Футуристы" in *Собрание сочинений в 15-и томах*, Vol. 8, Moscow 2001, 202-239.
7 Chukovskij, *Маленькие дети*, Leningrad 1928-1929. The book was republished as the popular and influential *От двух до пяти* (*From Two to Five*) in a sequence of expanded versions between 1933-1955. See Chukovskij, *От двух до пяти*, in *Собрание сочинений*, Vol. 2. In what follows, I refer to the 1928 edition because of the shifts, evidently politically motivated, in the later publications.
8 See M. Gor'kij, "О безответственных людях и о детской книге наших дней," in A.V. Lunacharskij, ed., *Детская литература. Критический сборник*, Moscow and Leningrad 1931.
9 There were a number of fruitful collaborations between writers and artists in children's literature, such as those between Vladimir Lebedev, Samuil Marshak and Vladimir Majakovskij; Vladimir Konashevich and Chukovskij; Nikolaj Radlov and multiple writers; and many more. For a detailed discussion of Avant-Garde visual effects in Soviet children's literature, see Evgeny Steiner, *Stories for Little Comrades: Revolutionary Artists and the Making of Early Soviet Children's Books*, trans. Jane Ann Miller. Seattle 1999. For a fine selection of early Soviet children's book art, see Julian Rothenstein and Olga Budashevskaya, eds., *Inside the Rainbow: Russian Children's Literature 1920-1935: Beautiful Books, Terrible Times*, London 2013.

Маленькие дети (*Little Children*, 1928) declares, "poems for children must be graphic [...] every given part of a poem must be perceived by children as a visible phenomenon."[10] Children's books produced in the years immediately following the revolution, illustrated by major artists like Ljubov' Popova, El Lissitskij and Vladimir Lebedev, are revered today for their gorgeous and cutting-edge appearance.[11] The artists and writers often worked closely with one another, and the resulting books often demonstrate a syncretic unity typical of earlier Avant-Garde book art, such as the collaborations between Goncharova, Larionov, Kruchenych and Chlebnikov on books like *Игра в аду* (*A Game in Hell*, 1912) and *Мирсконца* (*Worldbackwards*, 1912). In this, as in other respects, early Soviet children's literature demonstrates its ongoing ties with such Avant-Garde aesthetic positions as the blurring of boundaries between different areas of artistic production.

Despite these important intersections, the heyday of direct alliance between the Avant-Garde and the new children's literature was brief. By the late 1920s – early 1930s, the latter had become an institution dominated by the state, and thus had acquired a political agenda. Although Avant-Garde-leaning artists and writers were still a notable (even sought-after) presence in official children's literature, the cultural and political debates around ideological correctness in artistic production had become increasingly virulent. Books written for children were not exempt from the scrutiny of ideological hardliners, which included prominent figures in the Russian Association of Proletarian Writers (RAPP), child education specialists known as "pedologists," and Lenin's widow Nadezhda Krupskaja, one of the founders of Soviet pedagogy and Deputy Comissar of Enlighenment (1929-1939). Having launched a pitched battle against Avant-Garde formal and semantic features in children's literature, they claimed that such elements were at best distracting from important ideological messages and at worst, downright deviant. As a result of this campaign, a number of arrests beginning in the early 1930s targeted specifically at children's authors, who were accused of promoting anti-Soviet sentiment through their Avant-Garde literary practice.[12]

---

10   Chukovskij, *Маленькие дети*, 178.
11   See, for instance, *Inside the Rainbow*, and many international exhibits devoted to early Soviet picture books.
12   Among the persecuted figures were Chukovskij, authors and editors of the Leningrad branch of Detgiz headed by Samuil Marshak, and the children's poets of the OBERIU, such as Aleksandr Vvedenskij, Nikolaj Olejnikov, Nikolaj Zabolockij, and Daniil Charms, to be discussed presently. For further discussion of the ideological scrutiny and subsequent subjugation of children's literature in 1920-30s Russia, see Putilova, *Очерки*, 44-65; Hellman, *Fairy Tales*, 354-362, and Oleg Minin's chapter, "Literary Avant-Garde and Soviet Literature for Children: OBERIU in the Leningrad Periodicals *Еж* and *Чиж*," in this volume.

FIGURE 3.1 Cover of *О том как старушка чернила покупала* (*How an Old Woman Went Shopping for Ink*), by Daniil Charms with illustrations by Eduard Krimmer (1929)

Defenders of creativity and invention in literature for younger audiences included such giants as Maksim Gor'kij and Anatolij Lunacharskij, alongside children's literature bigwigs like Chukovskij and Marshak. Partially thanks to these figures' involvement, the hardliners' efforts were not always successful: the skirmish over the genre of fairytale (*сказка*), for instance, was ultimately decided in favor of the creative imagination. And yet, many children's writers

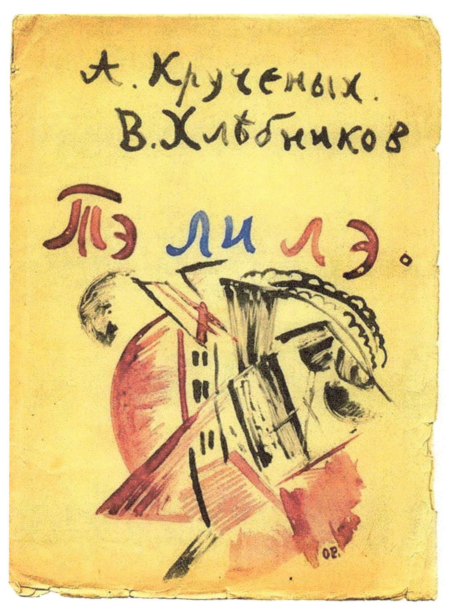

FIGURE 3.2 Olga Rozanova's cover of *Тэ ли лэ* (*Te Li Le*) by Aleksej Kruchenych and Velimir Chlebnikov (1914)

and artists fell afoul of the law throughout the Stalinist Terror of the mid- to late-1930s. The overall effect of state persecution of Avant-Garde followers was a distinct narrowing and flattening of the naïve and playful aesthetics of children's production. By the time Socialist Realism was officially adopted as state artistic policy in 1934, the traces of Avant-Garde experiment in children's literature had been whittled down to an acceptable minimum. Soviet children's authors would return to their Avant-Garde roots only during the "Thaw" of the 1950s-1960s.

2   The Prerevolutionary Avant-Garde and the Childlike Aesthetic

Many aspects of the childlike aesthetic as it appears in literature and art of the Soviet era can be traced to practices of the pre-revolutionary Avant-Garde, particularly the various subsets of Russian Futurism like Hylaea and Cubo-Futurism, but also the work of Symbolists (particularly Andrej Belyj), the Acmeist Osip Mandel'shtam, and other modernists.[13] With the exception of Majakovskij's highly didactic post-revolutionary work for young readers, the Futurists did not produce children's literature.[14] As Sara Pankenier Weld demonstrates in her discussion of the work of Michail Larionov, many visual artists of the Avant-Garde found their inspiration in the drawings of children; likewise, Futurist poets like Chlebnikov and Kruchenych were particularly drawn to the possibilities for new sounds and perspectives presented by children's use of language.[15] For forward-thinking artists, the unprejudiced and idiosyncratic perspective of the child would be part of a new aesthetic model, replacing that of the outdated themes and poetics of Alexander Pushkin or Lev Tolstoj. (Though it was Tolstoj, of course, who had early on advocated that writers learn from the unspoiled minds and imaginations of peasant children;[16] and Pushkin is famous for asserting that "poetry has to be a little bit

---

13   The Russian Futurist poets were certainly aware of their western counterparts' interest in primitivism and of modernist European writers' experiments with language. For more on Futurism generally, see V. Al'fonsov and S. Krasickij, eds., Поэзия русского футуризма, St. Petersburg 1999, and V. Markov, *Russian Futurism: A History*, Berkeley, CA 1968.
14   See Sokol's discussion of Majakovskij's children's poetry in *Russian Poetry for Children*, 152-166.
15   Weld, *Voiceless Vanguard*, 65. Also see Gerald Janecek's discussion of "children's babble, language learning and folklore" among the sources for заумь in *ZAUM: The Transrational Poetry of Russian Futurism*, San Diego 1994, 21-26.
16   A decade after the revolution, both Tolstoj and Pushkin would be back on the required-reading lists for all Soviet children (see Catriona Kelly, *Children's World: Growing Up in Russia, 1890-1991*, New Haven, CT 2007: 456, 531, etc.).

foolish.")[17] The authenticity of the child's work, meanwhile, was secondary to its aesthetic force: some of the Futurist "collaborations" with children probably did not involve any actual children. Meanwhile, the relationship between the Avant-Garde's exploitation of the childlike aesthetic and the application of this aesthetic in Soviet children's literature is not straightforward. The following examples show specific manifestations of the childlike aesthetic in the work of pre-revolutionary Futurist writers, some of which would subsequently be pointed to as good techniques or devices to be applied in the new Soviet children's literature.[18]

Among the Hylaea Futurists, Elena Guro had perhaps the most straightforwardly modernist version of the childlike aesthetic; her attempts to recreate an authentically child- or infant-like perspective in poetry sometimes recall Andrej Belyj's methodical efforts to depict even pre- and neonatal consciousness in *Котик Летаев* (*Kotik Letaev*, 1914-15). The most complete collection of Guro's work, *Небесные верблюжата* (*Baby Camels of the Sky*, published posthumously in 1914) contains a whole cycle called "Детская болтовня" ("children's jabber"). Many of the other poems and prose pieces in the collection likewise are voiced by childlike narrators or present childlike situations, like imaginary games, outdoor play and interactions with animals. Much of Guro's writing recalls nursery rhymes and fairytales and is marked by "domestic" coloring and unobtrusive neologisms, as is illustrated by her poem, "Words of Love and Warmth":

СЛОВА ЛЮБВИ И ТЕПЛА (1913)

У кота от лени и тепла разошлись ушки.
    Разъехались бархатные ушки.
    А кот раски-ис...
На болоте качались беловатики.
    Жил-был
    Ботик-животик:
      Воркотик
        Дуратик
    Котик-пушатик.
      Пушончик,

---

17   From a letter to Prince Vjazemskij, in A. S. Pushkin, *Собрание сочинений*, Vol. 10, Moscow 1961, 232.

18   For instance, Chukovskij refers to the verbal inventiveness of Igor' Severjanin, Chlebnikov, Majakovskij, and Charms in his *Маленькие дети*, 55, 202-203.

FIGURE 3.3 The cover of *Трое* (*The Three*) by Velimir Chlebnikov, Aleksej Kruchenych and Elena Guro, illustrated by Kazimir Malevich (1913)

Беловатик,

Кошуратик —

Потасик...[19]

The aptly-named poem is essentially a succession of gently mocking neologistic endearments, though framed by a realistic introduction (the cat being

---

19   "The cat's little ears have gone wonky from laze and warmth. / The velvet ears have slid apart. / The cat's gone lii-iimp...// The cattails are waving in the bog. / Once upon a time there was / A little bootie-belly: // A cooing little / Fooling little / Fuzzy little kitty. // A fluff-ball, // A cattail, // A cat-duster – // *A scuffler.*" Elena Guro, "Слова любви и тепла," in *Небесные верблюжата*, Rostov-on-Don 1993, 133-134.

stroked) and a fairytale-like setting of the scene ("[in the bog] once upon a time...").[20] It reminds the reader of a child's prattle, while retaining the inventive, morphologically-driven complexity of a linguistic experiment. For example, the diminutive "ик" suffix in "котик" and "животик" (as well as the made-up words "пушатик," "беловатик," "кошуратик"), which proliferates in Guro's poem, is echoed in the words containing the "ки" syllable ("ушки," "раскис," "беловатики"). This phonetic reversal imbibes the text with an elaborate "spiky" rhythm.

Guro's sense of the childlike has a curious dualism. Through the repeating motif of a (fictitious) deceased son, she simultaneously casts herself as a universal mother-figure ("Иногда мне кажется, что я мать всему") and takes on the perspective of that son (and his many doubles), an otherworldly, awkward and pointedly childlike figure affiliated explicitly with Don Quixote. For instance, the fragments featuring one of these figures, the Рыцарь Печального Образа (Knight of the Mournful Face, also known as Alonso Quixano the Good), have strong folkloric and childlike coloring: the final episode is a dialogue between a mother and child, which ends with the ironic line: "Леля, смотри, я тебя накажу, я не терплю бессвязную болтовню."[21] In this way, Guro's lyric subject embodies the child up to a point, but occasionally asserts an aesthetic distance from that perspective.

Unlike most of the other Futurists, there was no hint of the abrasive or hooliganish in Guro's artistic persona: in a disapproving 1914 review of the other Hylaea Futurists' 'obnoxious' experiments, Chukovskij refers to Guro as a near-saint, asking, disbelievingly, "What use did she have for drums, slaps and slurs?"[22] Still, Guro's poetic experiments could be just as radical as those of her colleagues, although her use of abstract sound-language (заумь) is conditioned by specific contexts like children's and foreign languages (the classic example is her poем "Финляндия").[23] In general, she draws on the capacity of the childlike aesthetic to 'make strange' and to convey liminal or supernatural experience, situations in which children's (or childlike) perceptions are misunderstood.

---

20   Leonid Usenko calls this poem the "apotheosis of [Guro's] 'childlike theme'." See Usenko, "Русский импрессионизм и Елена Гуро," in *Небесные верблюжата*, 26.
21   "Ljolja, look out, I will punish you, I can't stand nonsensical prattle." *Небесные верблюжата*, 68.
22   Chukovskij, "Эго-футуристы и кубо-футуристы," 100.
23   In V. Chlebnikov, E. Guro, A. Kruchenych, *Трое*, St. Petersburg 1913, 73-74. "Beyonsense" is Paul Schmidt's excellent translation of "заумь." See Velimir Khlebnikov, *The King of Time. Selected Writings of the Russian Futurian*, trans. Paul Schmidt, ed. Charlotte Douglas. Cambridge, MA 1985, 113.

Most of the Futurists and many other verbal artists experimented in different ways with some version of the idea of *заумь*, a "transrational" or "beyonsensical" language of made-up words or phonetic segments meant variously to clarify the muddle of existing natural languages or render it indeterminate (if not entirely anti-sensical). The term was coined by Chlebnikov and Kruchenych, though there were fundamental differences between their respective understandings of the concept. For Chlebnikov, *заумь* was connected to his infinitely precise *Ur*-language (alphabet), in which each letter (sound) had a range of specific associations.

> If you take a single word, let's say, *чашка* (teacup), we don't know what the meaning of each individual sound is for the whole word. But if you gather together all the words that begin with *Ch* (*чаша* [goblet], *череп* [skull], *чан* [vat], *чулок* [stocking], etc.), then all the other sounds cancel each other out, and the general meaning that these words have will be the meaning of *Ch*. When we compare these *Ch*-words, we see that they all mean 'one body encased by another'; *Ch* means casing. And thus *заумный* [beyonsense] language ceases to be beyonsensical.[24]

This passage comes from the essay, "Наша основа" ("Our Foundation," 1919). Chlebnikov explains that ordinary words with their conventional connection between signifier and signified are like toys, rag dolls made of arbitrary scraps of sound – and that using ordinary language is like playing with these dolls. The language of *заумь*, meanwhile, allows for a meaningful connection between signifier and signified, which in turn renders communication more accurate and harmonious.

For Kruchenych, meanwhile, the point of *заумь* was to make *less* sense, to complicate and break down existing systems of logic and meaning: Jurij Lotman noted that Kruchenych was interested in creating "subjective, fluid, individualized meanings in opposition to the 'frozen' ordinary language meanings of words."[25] Kruchenych places more theoretical and practical emphasis on this moment of destruction, rather than describing the utopian language expected to emerge on the far side of sense, like Chlebnikov. Thus the formal innovations of *заумь* are linked directly to the audacious behavioral positioning of manifestos like "Пощечина общественному вкусу" ("A Slap in the Face of Public Taste," 1912), which demanded that poets not only expand the dictionary with random and invented words, but also express "insurmountable

---

24   Chlebnikov, *Творения*, 694. Emphasis in the original.
25   Jurij Lotman, *Анализ поэтического текста: Структура стиха*, Leningrad 1972, 67, also quoted in Janecek, *The Look of Russian Literature*, 344.

hatred toward language as it has existed until now" and do their part to stamp out the concepts of "common sense" and "good taste."[26]

Children's language is implicitly favored in this system because of children's natural tendency to neologism and nonsense, and their ignorance of socially-conditioned concepts like taste. "Детский лепет" (children's babble) is included in Kruchenych's "Декларация заумного языка" ("Declaration of Zaum Language," 1921) as one of the areas of the application of *заумь*, "which has no need for reason."[27] Although Kruchenych did not attempt to write for children, his early publications included a collaboration with an eleven-year-old, identified as "Zina V," on a book of poetry and prose, *Поросята* (*Piglets*, 1913).[28] Zina's stories and poems take up most of *Поросята* and contrast favorably with Kruchenych's own contributions to the volume, most of which come across as polemical and heavy-handed in comparison with the light absurdity of pieces like the following: "В кармане у меня были 4 свиньи. Я очень гордилась. Визжат – есть хотят. Сбежались люди. Что такое? Какой крик? Свиньи! отвечаю я."[29] Zina's *pièce de résistance* is a tragicomic short story about a bear and a catfish that, plant-like, live happily rooted in an extraordinary garden until the cruel hand of fate ends their bliss. In addition to nonstandard punctuation, freely nonsensical descriptions and plot elements, the story also features a cheerfully unreliable narrator and an abrupt, open-ended conclusion.

> Когда медведь очнулся он увидел, что лежит в объятиях своего друга. Он несказанно стал благодарить его. И в то же время решил во что бы то ни стало отблагодарить Сома на деле.
> Но ему к сожалению не удалось этого сделать, так как автор сегодня очень устал и ему было лень придумывать для этого случай...[30]

---

26 Markov, *History*, 46.
27 Aleksej Kruchenych, *К истории русского футуризма: Воспоминания и документы*, Moscow 2006, 296. Also see Weld's chapter on Kruchenych's engagement with 'infantilist aesthetics' in *Voiceless Vanguard*, 62-101.
28 Aleksej Kruchenych and Zina V., *Поросята*, St. Petersburg 1913. The book came out again in 1914.
29 "I had 4 pigs in my pocket. I was very proud. Squealing – they're hungry. People came running. What is that? What's that yelling? Pigs! I answer." Kruchenych, *Поросята*, 4. Markov notes the possibility that Kruchenych may be the real author of all works in the volume, given his and Zina's shared fondness for both toilet humor and pigs.
30 "When the bear came to he saw that he was lying in the embrace of his friend. He began thanking him unspeakably. And at the same time decided that whatever it took he would find a way to thank Catfish for real. But, unfortunately, he didn't manage to do that since the author is very tired today and he was too lazy to think of how that would happen..." Ibid., 5.

THE DICTIONARY AS A TOY COLLECTION

FIGURE 3.4 A "drawing by 7 year-old M. E." from Kruchenych's *Собственные рассказы [и рисунки] детей* (*Children's Own Stories and Drawings*), 1914
PHOTOGRAPH BY MARIA VASSILEVA, COURTESY OF THE HOUGHTON LIBRARY, HARVARD UNIVERSITY

In this excerpt, the author presents an awkward reshuffling of partially-digested narration techniques borrowed from fairytales and more adult literary forms, as well as slightly garbled conversational phrasings ("He began thanking him unspeakably"). This is a slightly more sophisticated example of the child's ignorance of previous tradition and ultimately fresh perspective.

But the childlike aesthetic could take more linguistically radical forms as well. The year after *Поросята*, Kruchenych published a collection of children's poems and drawings (also, incidentally, featuring work by Zina). Again, this book was not written for children, although one of the poems is subtitled "Imitation of the Futurists," suggesting that some children were reading and being inspired by the Futurist movement.[31] The book opens with the following poem by two-year-old Muscovite Lilja-Elena, "publishing under the name Ii":

---

31   Aleksej Kruchenych, ed., *Собственные рассказы и рисунки детей, собрал А. Крученых*, Moscow 1914. Also reissued in 1923. For more on contemporary children's interactions with the Futurists, see the accounts in Weld, *Voiceless Vanguard*, 76.

> Ноча черная поди,
> Юна поди сюда,
> Часы динь-динь,
> Поя ба-бай...
> День поди – поя тавать.[32]

Kruchenych supplies the poem with clarifying commentary, noting that the stressed vowels have been printed in bold and explaining that "юна" means moon (луна), "поя" means "it's time" (пора) and "тавать" means "to get up" (вставать). In other words, the poem's apparent neologisms are actually loose phonetic renderings of childlike pronunciation, which render the poem's meaning very clear and prosaic: "Come black night / Come here moon / The clock bongs / It's time for beddy-bye... / Come day – it's time to get up." Kruchenych then suggests a more radical phonetic rendering for the poem (explaining that the existing version was written down by the little girl's mother), presumably one that more accurately still reproduces the distortions of lisping toddler-speak, with the first line reading: "Ноч(ц)я ч(ц)ейная пади." Kruchenych's recommendation that the poem's orthographic representation be moved further away from normative seems mostly motivated by his desire to obscure its banal content and create a cipher.[33] This tendency seems to justify detailed analysis of some of Kruchenych's own *заумь* poems, such as the notorious "дыр бул щыл," as containing the skeleton of some fixed meaning rather than being "completely beyonsensical" as advertised.[34]

Like Kruchenych, Chlebnikov also placed a high premium on actual children's writing: he begged publisher Michail Matjushin to include two pastoral poems by "thirteen-year-old Milica from Ukraine" in the 1914 collection *Садок судей (A Trap for Judges)*.[35] Chukovskij wrote that in the course of his research on children's language, he wrote down a great deal of "children's beyonsensical poems" for Chlebnikov, "who regarded them with great respect."[36] Chlebnikov's veneration of playful and rhythmically experimental children's poetry should not be surprising: he himself sought the roots of his universal language

---

32 Kruchenych, *Собственные рассказы и рисунки детей*, 5.
33 Although the interest in primitivism meant that some Avant-Garde artists appreciated precisely banality, as in the texts accompanying some of Michail Larionov's paintings (for a discussion of the latter, see Weld, 41-50).
34 See Janecek's chapter on "дыр бул щыл" in his *ZAUM: The Transrational Poetry of Russian Futurism*, 49-69.
35 Account reproduced, among other places, in A. Kobrinskij, *Поэтика ОБЭРИУ в контексте русского литературного авангарда*, Vol. 1, Moscow 2000, 121.
36 Chukovskij, *Маленькие дети*, 106.

in the speech patterns of child and primitive speakers. Jurij Tynjanov wrote that:

> The child's viewpoint [призма] and infantilism of the poetic word proclaimed themselves in Chlebnikov's poetry not through "psychology" but in its very elements, in the smallest phrasal and verbal segments. The child and the primitive were a new face for poetry, one that suddenly brought the fixed "norms" of word and meter into collision. The childlike syntax, the infantile "*вот*," the pinning-down of fleeting and non-obligatory successions of verbal series – all these devices struggled with the uttermost naked honesty against that dishonest literary phrase that had grown distant from people and the present moment.[37]

The huge influence of Chlebnikov on subsequent experimental poets, but also the ambiguity and confusion that still plague scholarship on his work have much to do with its seemingly childlike, even inept features. For example, Markov identifies as a weak point the poet's frequent elevation of "pariahs of literature" like the palindrome and the children's riddle to pathos-filled heights, as well as his fondness for rhymes, "precise to the point of banality," and abrupt conclusions.[38] But these elements are exactly what Tynjanov has in mind when he talks about a "new face for poetry," a new set of aesthetic priorities.

The following excerpt from *Зангези* (*Zangezi*, 1922) exemplifies Markov's concerns:

> Эр, Ка, Эль и Гэ —
> Воины азбуки —
> Были действующими лицами этих лет,
> Богатырями дней.
> [...]
> И тщетно Ка несло оковы, во время драки Гэ и Эр,
> Гэ пало, срубленное Эр,
> И Эр в ногах у Эля![39]

---

[37] Jurij Tynjanov, "О Хлебникове," *Собрание сочинений В. Хлебникова*, Vol. 1, Leningrad 1928, 23.

[38] Vladimir Markov, "О Хлебникове (попытка апологии и сопротивления)," in V. Chlebnikov, *Собрание сочинений в трех томах*, Vol. 1, St. Petersburg 2001, 25-32.

[39] "Er, Ka, El' and Ge - / Warriors of the alphabet / Were the actors of those years, / The bogatyrs of days. / [...] And it was in vain that Ka wore chains, during the fight of Ge and Er, / Ge fell, cut down by Er, / And Er was at the feet of El'!" Chlebnikov, *Творения*, 479-480.

The heroic vein of Chlebnikov's description of battle scenes is undercut by the somewhat silly associations evoked by, in the first example, the symbolically named alphabet-warriors; similar problems arise, for instance, in his poem "Пытка" ("Torture"), composed entirely of palindromes.[40] Aleksandr Zholkovskij also has in mind stylistic collisions when he refers to Chlebnikov's "графомания" ("graphomania") as a primary device used in challenging and breaking down traditional literary techniques and canons.[41] Even as Zholkovskij joins Markov in accusing Chlebnikov of performing ineptitude, he basically concurs with Tynjanov: Chlebnikov's poetry uses the childlike aesthetic – "childlike syntax, the infantile *вот*" and seemingly unmotivated diction – to find a new way for poetry to do its work.

Kruchenych's interest in the work of children often seems indelibly linked to his own consciously performed, capricious "little-boy" persona (which provided a certain behavioral motivation for his provocations in aesthetics). The portrait of Chlebnikov conveyed in the poet's particularly vivid biographical legend also contributes to a certain fusion of the childlike features of his poetry and his personage. Indeed, Vladimir Al'fonsov suggests it as a psychological-biographical explanation for his overall poetic tendency to contradiction: "'Eurasia' (as a literal junction, border, joining-point) was his childhood home, and Chlebnikov, in his own way a wholly undivided person, had no need to 'abandon' or repudiate his childhood."[42] The childlike aesthetic in poetry has often been explained with reference to the personality of the poet – another bid for authenticity, but one that subsumes the aesthetic function of childlike elements. For Chlebnikov, children's language was a source of primeval wisdom; this attitude of the earnest pupil should explain why he never thought of writing *for* children. Meanwhile, his beloved banal or "poor" rhymes, abrupt endings and seeming nonsense would resurface a generation later in the adult and children's work of the OBERIU poets.[43]

---

40 Palindromes, word games and archaisms in Chlebnikov's work are certainly tied to (fully adult) eighteenth-century poetic models as well. However, in the poetic system of Chlebnikov's time, these features stood out as strange and childlike.

41 Aleksandr Zholkovskij, "Графоманство как прием," in *Блуждающие сны и другие работы*, Moscow 1994, 54-68.

42 Vladimir Al'fonsov, "Поэзия русского футуризма," in Al'fonsov and Krasickij, eds., *Поэзия русского футуризма*, 39.

43 "Poor" or overtly forced rhymes would become a crucial device, for example, in Vvedenskij's poetry; consider the poet's dictum "уважай бедность языка" ("respect the poverty of language") made in "Некоторое количество разговоров." Aleksandr Vvedenskij, *Собрание сочинений в двух томах*, Vol. 1, Moscow 1993, 196.

Markov asserts that the interest in infantilism and primitivism is most characteristic of the early Hylaea stage of Futurism, to be subsequently overshadowed by the louder, more aggressively "modern" urbanist orientation of the Cubo-Futurists.[44] Although essentially contemporaneous with Guro, Chlebnikov and Kruchenych, the Burljuk brothers and Vladimir Majakovskij indeed demonstrated something closer to the juvenile-delinquent brand of the childlike aesthetic (though it should be mentioned that Kruchenych was also known for his obnoxious and provocative behavior). When around 1914 the Futurists became a public and to some extent nationwide sensation, it was largely due to the Burljuks and Majakovskij placing as much emphasis on public scandal and buffoonery as on innovative developments in poetry. Some of their verses, particularly the Burljuks', are hard to appreciate outside of the lively circumstances of their clowning around with costumes, face-paint, props, and assaults on the audience. At the same time, these escapades were calculated to have approximately the same effect on societal mores as Chlebnikov and Kruchenych's language experiments were to have on the norms of poetry-writing: the emphasis in both was on coarseness, anti-aestheticism and a shaking-up of the old order. The rude and youthful viewpoint, genuinely or demonstratively ignorant of social convention, proved just as useful behaviorally as formally. What is more, the two aspects were linked: lay audiences came for the circus but listened to the poems of both brash Majakovskij and shy, ill-spoken Chlebnikov.

The pre-revolutionary Futurists were not the only literary-minded actors interested in the child's viewpoint at this time. In "Искусство как прием" ("Art as Device," 1916), their contemporary Formalist critic Viktor Shklovskij was arguing for "остранение" ("defamiliarization" or "making strange") as the foremost literary device – itself a sort of formalized aesthetic naïveté.[45] For the Formalists, "making strange" meant up-ending the depiction of something, such that the familiar and predictable object or concept be perceived as if for the first time, cut loose from its conventional contexts. Referring to this concept in his *Маленькие дети*, Chukovskij writes that "The child has no templates. For her, all words are 'estranged' [остранены] to begin with."[46] There was always an ideological edge to "остранение" – seeing things anew or without a preconceived framework could imply seeing them the right or true way,

---

44 Markov, *History*, 36-37. Markov also mentions the Futurists' interest in the work of actual children and uneducated adults.
45 Viktor Shklovskij, "Искусство как прием," in *Гамбургский счет*, Moscow 1990, 60-62.
46 Chukovskij, *Маленькие дети*, 27.

as in the classic shout of the child in Andersen's tale: "The emperor has no clothes!" Although Shklovskij did not specify the child's gaze as primary in his concept of "остранение," several of his examples point obliquely in that direction: thus, he cites the scene of Natasha Rostova's (childlike) first impression of the theater in Tolstoj's *Война и мир* (*War and Peace*).[47] The child's perspective was prominent among many new ways of looking, embraced for its capacity to make perception more striking and profound or, alternatively, to emphasize the hidden absurdity of everyday life invisible to the habitual adult gaze.

Thus, the pre-revolutionary literary and artistic experimenters found a host of ways to use the child, but children did not yet have much use for them – even when Avant-Garde exhibitions displayed children's drawings or writers published children's poems, the children themselves were never an intended audience. The idea of the usefulness of Avant-Garde aesthetics for children's production would be put into practice only after the 1917 Revolution, with its ambitious program of erasing the pre-revolutionary "bourgeois" artistic heritage and of refashioning an entirely new kind of citizen, if not human being. The radical and utopian aesthetics of the Avant-Garde appeared ripe for deployment in helping the revolution achieve these ends by providing unprecedented and effective visual and verbal tools for teaching children the ways of the brave new world.

3 Early Post-revolutionary Children's Literature: Seeking a Common Language

In the rosy light of hindsight, early Soviet children's literature appears, like other areas of artistic production, to reflect the heady convergence of the building of a brand-new state and the experimental energy of the pre-revolutionary artistic and literary Avant-Garde: there were obvious parallels between the "infancy" of the new Soviet state and the educational and entertainment needs of its youngest citizens. However, this junction occurred variously over the course of the years following the revolution, and took many different forms before settling into an established institution by the mid-1930s. Despite their undeniable enthusiasm, Avant-Garde and modernist writers and

---

47 Perhaps even more childlike are the long quotations from Tolstoj's "Холстомер" ("Strider"). Cf. Guro's frequent conflation of children and animals as weak, innocent and limited in their ability to communicate in *Небесные верблюжата*. Shklovskij, "Искусство как прием," 60-62.

artists ultimately played a limited role in the actual institutional establishment and ongoing development of the Soviet children's literature.

Theoretical discussions of books for young readers at this time went hand in hand with discussions of the new Soviet culture overall. While the larger project of creating Soviet literature involved an exhaustive reassessment of the existing Russian and international literary canon, it was believed that children's literature had to start from scratch: the existing selection – Russian and foreign alike – was considered almost completely unacceptable. It was excoriated mostly for promoting "bourgeois" values and failing to represent the experience of the proletariat, along with other aspects of the new reality, as well as its aesthetic shortcomings.[48] The new Soviet children's literature was to be more entertaining, aesthetically valid and politically responsible than that which had come before. In this sense, the new theoreticians of children's literature co-opted wholeheartedly the Avant-Garde's total rejection of past tradition: every significant statement on the topic made between 1918 and 1934, culminating in speeches by Marshak and Chukovskij at the First All-Union Soviet Writers' Congress, necessarily included a repudiation of deplorable pre-revolutionary children's letters.[49] Thus the boom in children's literature was partly due to practical factors like the real shortage of books for young readers that resulted when most existing literature was declared unacceptable; but it also reflected the overall artistic ferment and broad support for innovation of the NEP period.[50]

The very first examples of early Soviet children's literature are the most immediately related to Avant-Garde and modernist experimentation. Accordingly, they may have been less successful with actual child audiences. The collection *Ёлка* (*The Christmas Tree*, 1918), which featured an impressive roster

---

48   It should be said that repackaged pre-revolutionary literature was sold quite successfully during the NEP period – see Balina and Rudova, "Preface," *Russian Children's Literature and Culture*, New York and London 2008, 6-7. And even at the ideological level, Lunacharskij, Gor'kij and Marshak all argued at various points that not all pre-revolutionary children's literature should be abandoned. See, for instance, A.V. Lunacharskij, "Пути детской книги," in *Книги детям* 1 (1930), 4-15.

49   "Содоклад С. Я. Маршака о детской литературе" and "Речь К. И. Чуковского," in *Первый всесоюзный съезд советских писателей*, Moscow 1934, 29, 180.

50   On the post-revolutionary influx of new children's books, and the pre-1929 relative openness to experiment in these books, see Marina Balina, "Creativity through Restraint: The Beginnings of Soviet Children's Literature," in *Russian Children's Literature and Culture*, 6-9; Putilova, "О наследстве и наследственности в детской литературе," 5-12. For a fascinating overview of interactions between state institutions and experimental artists in the NEP period, see Pamela Kachurin, *Making Modernism Soviet: The Russian Avant-Garde in the Early Soviet Era*, 1918-1928, Evanston, IL 2013.

FIGURE 3.5   Vladimir Majakovskij, *Советская азбука*, 1919

of well-known pre-revolutionary writers and artists (a mere smattering includes Gor'kij, Chukovskij, Aleksej Tolstoj, Valerij Brjusov, Aleksandr Benua [Benois], Ilja Repin, Mstislav Dobuzhinskij), provided an impossibly eclectic mix of rather adult compositions and inside-jokes, visual and verbal alike (consider Dobuzhinskij's visual riddle of "сто рож," consisting of one hundred caricatures of contemporary artists and writers).[51] In another vein, much of the other early children's fare was highly and rather bluntly politicized, often violent, coarsely humorous, and not especially child-oriented. Majakovskij's *Советская азбука* (*Soviet Alphabet*, 1919) featured threatening, violent and crudely abstract images of Soviet enemies like the banker, priest and bourgeois, with the letter "E" illustrated by two figures in suits holding bags of coins and the words "Европой правит лига наций / Есть где воришкам разогнаться."[52]

Later, critics issuing recommendations on children's literature would condemn excessive visual and verbal abstraction (e.g. that found in *Елка*) for ob-

---

51   Aleksandr Benua and Kornej Chukovskij, eds., *Елка. Сборник. Книжка для маленьких детей*. Petrograd 1918.
52   "Europe is run by the League of Nations / Petty thieves have plenty of room for action." Vladimir Majakovskij, *Советская азбука*, Moscow 1919, 8. Digital facsimile ⟨http://arks.princeton.edu/ark:/88435/44558f67b⟩ (Accessed December 3, 2017).

scuring important ideological and didactic content, such as "how cotton is grown" or "how Soviet citizens should behave" (see Majakovskij's *Что такое хорошо и что такое плохо* [*What is Good and What is Bad*], 1925).[53] The crude and violent images (some of them evocative of Futurist book art, such as Goncharova's illustrations for *Игра в аду*) and "adult" content of *Советская азбука* were also criticized and put aside in favor of an aesthetically tamer, "child-specific" approach.[54]

In keeping with the relevance and sanctity of the nation's new political project, children's literature also needed to become serious and deeply rooted in the real world. A particularly vicious debate over fairytales dragged on through the 1920s, with participants ranging from rural schoolteachers and Krupskaja to the influential linguist-psychologist Lev Vygockij and prominent modernist writers – eventually even Gor'kij weighed in.[55] The defenders of the fantastical and imaginary – predictably, writers and artists at the more experimental end of the spectrum – were essentially arguing for artistic freedom, which was coming under pressure in all areas of Soviet artistic production. The conflicts over children's literature thus reflected the larger and thornier question of the place of a non-utilitarian and non-ideological art in a society growing ever more ideologically didactic.

Majakovskij was the only one of the pre-revolutionary Futurists to achieve any success as a children's writer, and it was relatively short-lived: with the exception of the aforementioned *Советская азбука*, he only produced work specifically for children between 1925 and his death in 1930. Majakovskij's poetry for children is a mixed bag. The fast-paced youthful energy of his verse for children is the same force that dominates Majakovskij's poetic art as a whole. The folkoric *Сказка о Пете, толстом ребенке, и о Симе который тонкий* (*The Tale of Petja, a Fat Child, and of Sima Who Was Thin*, 1925) recalls the blunt political message of *Советская азбука* while embodying some of the appeal of Looney Tunes cartoons – the fat bourgeois Petja, for instance, explodes upon devouring half a city. Meanwhile, many of Majakovskij's

---

53 Putilova offers an overview of mid-1920s criticism of children's literature in the press: the emphasis is consistently on factual information, educational clarity and ideological soundness. Of particular interest are Krupskaja's articles, in which she condemns excessively 'tendentious' books (*Советская азбука* would certainly be one) but insists that children's literature be "extremely realistic," presenting "life as it is." Putilova, *Очерки*, 31.

54 Consider Chukovskij's condemnation of pre-revolutionary Russian children's literature in his 1934 speech. "Речь К. И. Чуковского," *Первый съезд*, 179-180.

55 For a summary of the fairytale debates, see Putilova, *Очерки*, 13-23, and Hellman, *Fairy Tales*, 354-362. Also note Gor'kij's defense of fantasy as it appears in myths and legends in his speech at the 1934 Writers' Congress: *Первый съезд*, 6-9.

"topical" children's poems are overtly didactic and notably weaker and duller than his pre-revolutionary work. *Что такое хорошо и что такое плохо* seems to prioritize plainspoken moralizing over lexical fireworks, wordplay or humor:

> Этот
>   в грязь полез
>   и рад.
> что грязна рубаха.
> Про такого
>   говорят:
> он плохой,
>   неряха.
> Этот
>   чистит валенки,
> моет
>   сам
>   галоши.
> Он
>   хотя и маленький,
> но вполне хороший.[56]

In this context, the familiar "лесенка" ("ladder") layout certainly works to "make sure that the naïve reader puts the pauses in the right places and thus interprets the words correctly," as Majakovskij had explained in his 1926 manifesto "Как делать стихи" ("How Verses Are Made").[57] But it seems like an unnecessary effort, given the exaggeratedly simple and predictable content and relatively pedestrian rhymes. Despite its apparently total devotion to the Soviet cause, Majakovskij's work for children was effectively banned following his suicide in 1930; it was criticized for "coarseness, poor quality and outdated ideological content."[58] It was not until Stalin himself reinstated Majakovskij as State Poet No. 1 in 1935, that his children's poetry was republished in enormous press-runs, but the poet's enduring popularity with young and older

---

56 "This one / crawled in mud / and is glad / that his shirt's all dirty. / Kids like that / they say / are bad / even slovenly. / This one / cleans his boots, / washes / his galoshes / all by himself. / Even though he's small / he's / certainly a good one." V.V. Majakovskij, *Полное собрание сочинений в тринадцати томах*, Vol. 10, Moscow 1958, 235.

57 Janecek, *The Look of Russian Literature*, 228.

58 Putilova, *Очерки*, 58.

readers alike rests more on his ingenious pre-revolutionary and early-1920s work.[59]

In addition to representatives of the Avant-Garde who had actively supported the revolution, like Majakovskij, many "fellow travelers" tried their hand at children's literature in the early 1920s: these experimenters included a surprisingly broad range of writers, from Osip Mandel'shtam, Boris Pasternak and Aleksej Remizov to Ilja Ehrenburg, Jurij Olesha and many others. For many of them, children's books – short and usually published in large press-runs – represented a way to earn money in a publishing market rendered less certain by the upheaval around the revolution.[60] But writing for young audiences also entailed a freedom for playful creative experimentation that dovetailed with the unbounded, primitivist-leaning principles of the Avant-Garde.

Children's poetry was one of the few things Osip Mandel'shtam managed to publish during 1924-26: he released four books of poems for little readers during this time. Contemporary and subsequent accounts attest to the poet's lack of emotional commitment to this form of self-expression.[61] The children's poems are notably less complex and nuanced than Mandel'shtam's adult work, although not entirely without imagination and pleasing sound-play, as in "Шары" ("Balloons," 1926):

Дутые-надутые шары-пустомели
Разноцветным облаком на ниточке висели,
Баловали-плавали, друг друга толкали,
Своего меньшого брата затирали.

– Беда мне, зеленому, от шара-буяна,
От страшного красного шара-голована.
Я шар-недоумок, я шар-несмышленыш,
Приемыш зеленый, глупый найденыш.[62]

---

59 For instance, a 1963 "Школьная библиотека" ("School Library") edition for younger readers put out in 100 000 copies by the State Children's Literature Publishing House does not include any of Majakovskij's poems for children. See Majakovskij, *Избранные произведения*, Moscow 1963.
60 See Steiner, *Stories for Little Comrades*, 14.
61 Sokol, *Russian Poetry for Children*, 170.
62 "All blown-up, full of hot air, the windbag-balloons / Hung like a multi-colored cloud on a string / Floating and frolicking, shoving each other, / Blocking in their littlest brother. // Poor green me, bullied by the ruffian balloon, / By the terrible big-headed red balloon. / I'm a little half-wit balloon, a silly little balloon, / A little green foster-child, a foolish foundling." O. E. Mandel'shtam, "Шары," in *Собрание сочинений в четырёх томах*, Vol. 2, Moscow 1993, 65.

In her memoirs, Nadezhda Mandel'shtam confirmed that her husband was frustrated in his efforts to write children's poetry, and that his more successful pieces were written rather in the genre of lighthearted "humorous" or "occasional" poems, not specifically child-oriented: "Short little poems, like sayings or proverbs. You fry an egg – write a poem about it. Forgot to turn off the kitchen sink – write a poem..."[63] Although "Шары" may be just such an improvisation, Mandel'shtam nods to the standards of the time by including folkloric standbys like doubled noun and verb expressions ("шары-пустомели," "баловали-плавали") and inversions ("Приемыш зеленый, глупый найденыш"). Meanwhile, at the level of plot, the poet presents a pathos-filled hymn to the underdog (perspicacious readers of Aesopian language might raise their eyebrows at the image of the "terrible big-headed red balloon").

In an interesting twist, it seems that Mandel'shtam's foray into children's literature, which in his case foregrounded humor and simplicity, may inform the ongoing presence of a childlike aesthetic in his "adult" poems of the early 1930s. A poem like "Куда как страшно нам с тобой..." ("You and I, we are so scared to death," 1930) presents an ominous, entirely adult "plot" through childlike lexicon and references (the first line's phrase "Куда как страшно," and the trio "Шелкунчик, дружок, дурак!"), folkloric or proverbial-seeming logic ("А мог бы жизнь просвистать скворцом / Заесть ореховым пирогом...") and an overall rollicking rhythm punctuated by explanation points.[64] We have already seen an example of the childlike aesthetic being equally or more applicable to non-children's literature in the case of the pre-revolutionary Avant-Garde; this situation resurfaces further in the work of experimental 1930s poets such as Charms and Vvedenskij.

In a 1931 essay extolling the new Soviet children's books (and scandalizing her fellow émigrés in Prague), Marina Cvetaeva wrote:

> An abundance of incontestable qualities. First and foremost, this is almost exclusively poetry, that is, these books are given in a language not only beloved by children but created by them – their native tongue. [...] The second quality (without which the first one, that is, the poems themselves, are a sin) is the extraordinary quality of the poetry itself. [...] *This is the high culture of verse at work.*[65]

---

63   N. Ja. Mandel'shtam, *Третья книга*, Moscow 2006, 469-470.
64   Mandel'shtam, *Собрание сочинений*, Vol. 3, 35.
65   Marina Cvetaeva, "О новой русской детской книге," in *Избранная проза в двух томах*, Vol. 2, New York 1979, 310-312. Cvetaeva's emphasis – *AM*.

THE DICTIONARY AS A TOY COLLECTION 123

While expressing admiration for the anonymity of most of the children's book producers, Cvetaeva gives special praise to her friend, the onetime Futurist Boris Pasternak, who published two book-length children's poems in 1924 ("Карусель" ["The Carousel"] and "Зверинец" ["The Menagerie"]). Without going into detail, she says that, in comparison to Marshak's zoo-themed poem, "Детки в клетке" ("Babies in Cages"), Pasternak's "Зверинец" is "genius" and "out of the ordinary."[66]

In his seminal 1924 essay "Промежуток" ("Interlude"), Jurij Tynjanov noted Pasternak's reliance on the "domestic efficiency" of children's language in his poetry: "Childhood – not canonical 'childhood,' but childhood as a changed course of vision – mixes up the object and verse, and the object comes to stand right next to us, while the verse can be probed with one's fingers."[67] Yet, Cvetaeva's observation that Pasternak's poetry for children does not fall into the category of ordinary (рядовая) children's literature is apt. Pasternak seems to have made little effort to adapt his poetic voice to the genre of children's poetry, such that the vocabulary and syntax in these poems tend to be as grandiose and complex as in the poet's adult work of the same time period. Consider the following excerpt from "Карусель":

Погружая в день бездонный
Кудри, гривы, кружева,
Тонут кони, и фестоны,
И колясок кузова.[68]

In the same spirit as Mandel'shtam nodding to folkloric models, Pasternak adheres to the notion that trochees, with their galloping and energetic rhythm, make the best meter for children's poetry.[69] But the convoluted syntax, abstract images like "unfathomable day" and improbable phrases like "bodies of the carriages" require multiple readings to unravel and thus seem to work

---

66   Ibid., 312.
67   Jurij Tynjanov, "Промежуток," in *Поэтика. История литературы. Кино*, Moscow 1977, 84.
68   "Plunging into the unfathomable day / Curls, manes and lace, / Sink the steeds and the festoons, /and the bodies of the carriages." "Карусель," in Boris Pasternak, *Собрание сочинений в пяти томах*, Moscow 1989, 495.
69   "But what is the rhythm of all these children's improvisations that are called into being by dancing and jumping? No matter how many of these poems I have listened to, they always have one and the same meter: the trochee [...]. And the overwhelming majority of the best children's folk songs formed over years of adaptation to children have that same rhythm – not just Russian, but foreign ones too." Chukovskij, *Маленькие дети*, 113-114.

counter to the straightforward, marching meter.⁷⁰ Like some of the other poets discussed here, Pasternak was applying modernist principles to children's poetry, but these were not the principles recommended by Chukovskij or Marshak.

Attempts at children's writing by modernist poets like Mandel'shtam and Pasternak show the extent to which the tenets for writing for children were open to interpretation during the early to mid-1920s. Mandel'shtam wrote humorous improvisations with the hope they might pass muster and bring in some income, while Pasternak basically wrote adult poems that appealed to his friends and fellow-poets. While their children's writing is symptomatic of the cultural moment and interesting in the larger context of the poets' work, the continuation of Avant-Garde aesthetics in children's literature would be forged by a slightly younger generation of poets in the following decade.

4   Ripe Socialism: Harnessing the Avant-Garde Aesthetic

Prominent among the defenders of imaginative literature were Marshak and Chukovskij, the two founding figures of the early Soviet children's literature. They had both begun writing children's poetry in the years before the revolution, and both were known for their translations of foreign work for children, particularly English nursery rhymes, such as the Mother Goose Tales, and the nonsense verse of Edward Lear.⁷¹ Complementing this esteem for foreign-produced nonsense, Chukovskij was also an early (though not unequivocal) advocate of the Futurists, attending their public performances and writing one of the first monographs on the phenomenon.⁷² His study of children's language and literary impulses, *Маленькие дети*, pointed out the apparent parallels between child language acquisition and early usage, and Avant-Garde practice, particularly заумь (the book included direct references to Chlebnikov, Majakovskij, Igor' Severjanin and Charms).⁷³

---

70   For a more detailed account of Pasternak's and Mandel'stam's forays into children's poetry, see Sokol, *Russian Poetry for Children*, 167-173.
71   See Chukovskij, *Собрание сочинений в пятнадцати томах*, Vol.1, Moscow 2001 (Kipling, English and Scottish folktales and songs); Marshak, *Собрание сочинений в восьми томах*, Vol. 2 (English folk songs and nursery rhymes, 79-195) and Vol. 3 (Lear, Carroll, Milne, 705-746).
72   Chukovskij, "Эго-футуристы и кубо-футуристы," 95-154.
73   In the republished and expanded version of *От двух до пяти*, Chukovskij removed many of the references to Avant-Garde writers.

The book provides a wealth of examples of children's innate fondness for *заумь*-like, nonsensical language and soundplay. At the same time, Chukovskij paints the child as a strictly prescriptive linguist, driven by nature to correct the arbitrariness of natural language. In his view, the child's language and speech errors reflected an iron-clad logic recalling Chlebnikov's conception of *заумь* as a complex linguistic and cosmogonic system. "The child rebels against [random combinations] of sounds with the same energy with which people had been rebelling for centuries and continue to rebel today. The child unconsciously demands that sounds have meaning, that words have a living, palpable image, and when it is absent the child himself gives the incomprehensible word the desired image and meaning. This pull toward meaning is not at odds with children's attraction to zaum language in the slightest [...]. These are two parallel processes that mutually complement one another."[74] Note Chukovskij's overtly political references to "the people" (народ), with the implication that they are constantly itching for a righteous rebellion. Elsewhere, Chukovskij posits a "logical" explanation for the emergence of *заумь* that evinces an impulse to chaos more reminiscent of Kruchenych:

> One time an unfamiliar child appeared beneath the balcony at my dacha, yelling ecstatically and showing me some kind of thin stick: "Эку пику дядя дал / Эку пику дядя дал!" [Unky gimme this stik! Unky gimme this stik!] But his rapture evidently carried him beyond the bounds of human language, because after a few minutes this song of his already sounded quite different: "Экикики диди да / Экикики диди да!" [Unky-gumky-disty-tik! Unky-gumky-disty-tik!] The poet had freed his song from sense, as if sloughing off an unnecessary weight, and found that afterwards he liked it even better.[75]

Chukovskij goes on to extend this explanation to cover English nonsense-rhymes, citing a study that traces rhymes like "Eenie-meenie-miny-moe" to entirely sense-filled ancient Celtic roots. There is, of course, a strong political dimension to Chukovskij's book: in keeping with the populist spirit of the new regime, he praises the practical reason and simplicity of folk genres and dialect-speech and condemns the "philosophizing" tendency instilled in children of the intelligentsia. But he also defends the free-

---

74   Chukovskij, *Маленькие дети*, 42.
75   Ibid., 107.

standing validity of nonsense: "But the Celts have disappeared, their language has been forgotten, and if a few of the old sounds have been preserved in children's songs, it is precisely because these sounds have *lost their meaning* and become dear to children only in their free-standing melody."[76] Chukovskij's book was published in 1928, ironically the year in which the pedologists' campaign against him reached its highest pitch.[77] The desirability of Avant-Garde elements in children's writing would not be presented in such a straightforward manner again until the post-Stalin "Thaw" period.

The end of the 1920s was also when Samuil Marshak took over as director of the Leningrad-based State Children's Publishing House (known variously as "ДетГиз," "Детиздат," and "Детская литература"), housed in the famous Singer building on the corner of Nevskij Prospekt and the Gribojedov Canal. Marshak had begun working with "Raduga" and other privately-funded children's publishing outfits in the early 1920s; he also founded several journals for children during this period (one of them, *Новый Робинзон* [*New Robinson*], was where Mandel'shtam published his efforts).[78] Detgiz would be officially instituted in 1933 as the sole state children's literature publishing house and was also responsible for publishing the magazines *Чиж* (*The Finch*) and *Ёж* (*The Hedgehog*), for small children and older "pioneers."[79]

Toward achieving his vision for the new children's literature, Marshak recruited a number of young poets and artists. He sought out youth partly in the interest of molding young talent, and partly because he was attracted to the technical abilities of the post-Futurist generation. Many of the young writers hired by Marshak – including Nikolaj Olejnikov, Jurij Vladimirov and Evgenij Shvarc – were experimentally-inclined; most of them were involved in various loose Avant-Garde groupings.[80] Years later, Marshak recalled hiring three young poets (Charms, Vvedenskij and Zabolockij), who as members of the OBERIU group had earned a certain reputation in Leningrad for their raucous

---

76 Ibid., 108-110. Emphasis in the original.
77 See Sokol, *Russian Poetry for Children*, 9-11. She includes a translation of Krupskaja's notorious article, "О 'Крокодиле' К. Чуковского," in *Правда*, 1 Feb 1928, 5 (207-209).
78 See Ben Hellman, "Samuil Marshak: Yesterday and Today," in Balina and Rudova, eds., *Russian Children's Literature and Culture*, 218-226.
79 For more on these journals and the OBERIU poets' contributions to them, see Oleg Minin's chapter in this volume, "Literary Avant-Garde and Soviet Literature for Children: OBERIU in the Leningrad Periodicals *Ёж* and *Чиж*."
80 The artists too, including Tatjana Glebova, Alisa Poret and others, had been students of Avant-Garde giants like Pavel Filonov, Kuz'ma Petrov-Vodkin and Kazimir Malevich.

and openly absurdist public performances:[81] "At one time I enlisted this group of poets who had made their mark in formal – really more like ironic-parodic – explorations." Marshak figured they would be good at churning out "the palindromes, tongue-twisters and little ditties so necessary for children's poetry"; in retrospect, he was impressed to see their talents exceeding his expectations.[82]

Still, many of the artists and writers of the OBERIU poets' generation came to children's literature not because of any passion for children or education, but because by the late 1920s it was clear that other literary means of employment were closed to them.[83] Lev Losev claims that "in the 30s and 40s [...] children's things were relegated to the very bottom [of the genre pyramid]. The vigilance of censorship was also allotted in strict accordance with these hierarchies."[84] It could be relatively easier to "stay out of trouble" through employment as a children's writer.[85] Paradoxically, one and the same writer could be barred from "adult" publications while being allowed to write and officially publish (sometimes aesthetically innovative) literature for children.[86]

---

81 OBERIU was an acronym standing for "Объединение реального искусства" ("Association of Real Art"). Under this name, the group existed for no more than three years, although the poets here discussed continued to associate with one another throughout most of the 1930s. Many scholars have opted to use "OBERIU" as an umbrella term encompassing the literary work of Vvedenskij and Charms; the longer-lived Zabolockij is more typically considered to have had an "OBERIU period." For more on the OBERIU, see Jaccard, *Даниил Хармс и конец русского авангарда* (1995), Roberts, *The Last Soviet Avant-Garde: OBERIU – Fact, Fiction, Metafiction* (1997), Kobrinskij, *Поэтика ОБЭРИУ в контексте русского литературного авангарда* (2000), Sazhin, *"Сборище друзей, оставленных судьбою"* (1998), and Ostashevsky, *OBERIU: An Anthology of Russian Absurdism* (2006).

82 Samuil Marshak, *Собрание сочинений в восьми томах*, Vol. 8, Moscow 1971, 509.

83 Nikolaj Chardzhiev discussed Vvedenskij and Charms as children's writers: "Vvedenskij produced reams of awful hack-work [...]. Charms was unable to write badly." He also described Charms refusing an offer to adapt *Don Quixote* for children, saying "I couldn't do it to Cervantes." Chardzhiev, *Статьи об авангарде*, Vol. 1, Moscow 1997, 364.

84 Lev Losev, "Предисловие," in Evgenij Shvarc, *Мемуары*, Paris 1982, 16.

85 Among the "gray areas" of official literary production in which writers were able to work, literary translation was the most prominent; later, in the 1960s-70s, a number of unofficial writers and artists worked in the film industry making cartoons and educational documentaries. For more on Soviet-era translations of work for children, see Maria Khotimsky's chapter in this volume, "Children's Poetry and Translation in the Soviet Era: Strategies of Rewriting, Transformation and Adaptation."

86 In the 1930s, however, even the bottom of the pyramid was occasionally subject to serious scrutiny, as evidenced by the arrests, imprisonments and executions of many of the writers here discussed. A dramatic example of this was the routing of the Leningrad Detgiz office in 1937. See Lidija Chukovskaja's account in *В лаборатории редактора*, Moscow 1963, 321-23.

The OBERIU group was the Russian Avant-Garde formation most directly involved in children's literature. But the relationship was not one of straightforward service: the OBERIU poets all exhibited a fairly cynical attitude toward children's literature as a day job, and the childlike aesthetic is arguably more evident in their unpublished "adult" work than in the poetry they wrote for children.[87] The work of these poets for children and adults demonstrates a kind of strange symbiosis between the forms and norms of Soviet children's literature and the Avant-Garde legacy. In the interest of brevity, the following examples will treat work by Charms and Vvedenskij only, though similarities run through both the poetics and the personal circumstances of the other OBERIU-affiliated poets as well.

At the time of their first contact with Marshak, the OBERIU poets were consciously following an explicitly leftist Avant-Garde line. The question of *заумь* and of their Futurist forbears in general was, however, a fraught one. Despite Vvedenskij's early affiliation with the *заумник* (*beyonsenser*) Alexander Tufanov, for instance, by the time of the OBERIU manifesto (1928) Vvedenskij had renounced any association with *заумь*.[88] His poetry is described as working with "...the *appearance* of nonsense [бессмыслица]. Why the *appearance*? Because obvious nonsense is what zaum is, and there is no zaum in Vvedenskij's work."[89] Wordplay approaching *заумь* or nearly-*заумь* language is also fairly common in Charms's work, and the childlike aesthetic is ubiquitous, ranging from transparent devices, such as repetition and counting rhymes, to more subtle elements of form and voice akin to those of Vvedenskij. Quite a few of Charms' poems from the mid-1920s to early 1930s end with the eminently childlike "ВСЁ" ["THAT'S IT"].

Charms and Vvedenskij both demonstrated an ongoing interest in applications of the childlike aesthetic toward experimental ends. There is Nikolaj Chardzhiev's famous story about taking Vvedenskij to meet Kruchenych in 1936. Upon hearing Vvedenskij read one of his poems, Kruchenych read a poem written by a "five or six-year-old girl" and asserted that her work was much better. When they left, Vvedenskij, ordinarily known for a total lack of personal and professional modesty, sighed sadly to Chardzhiev: "Her poem re-

---

87 See my *World Play: Experimental Poetry and Soviet Children's Literature* (forthcoming from Northwestern UP).

88 Tufanov did not think Vvedenskij's poetry demonstrated "real" *заумь*. See A. Tufanov, "О стихах А. Введенского," in Aleksandr Vvedenskij, *Все*, Moscow 2010, 732.

89 A. Aleksandrov, ed., *Ванна Архимеда*, Leningrad 1991, 485. See also Zabolockij's open letter "Мои возражения А.И. Введенскому, авторитету бессмыслицы" (1926), reproduced in *Все*, 393-395.

ally is better than mine..."⁹⁰ Leaving aside the intervening developments and changes in Futurism and Avant-Garde poetics, Kruchenych's challenge and Vvedenskij's reaction in the mid-1930s indicate that interest in the childlike aesthetic was unabated from the pre-revolutionary Avant-Garde through the "last" Avant-Garde of the OBERIU.⁹¹

For example, Vvedenskij's poem-story "Солдат Аз Буки Веди" ("The Soldier Ay Bee See," 1937-38) is a sort of fairytale about a soldier who, wandering along the seashore by evening, encounters some fishermen:

> Их рыбаков было пять человек. Они пристально ели суп с рыбой. Их звали: Андрей, Бандрей, Бендрей, Гандрей, и Кудедрей. У них у всех были дочери. Их звали: Ляля, Таля, Баля, Каля и Саля. Они все вышли замуж. Был вечер. Солдат Аз Буки Веди не зашел в дом к этим огородникам. Он не постучал к ним в дом. Он шел погруженный в свою мысль, основную им руководящую мысль об орехах.⁹²

In addition to the fairytale set-up (the fishermen and their daughters even have fantastical and childlike rhyming names), the piece also features songs evocative of children's nonsense rhymes and lullabies, a tendency to long lists and a kind of stilted, simplified syntax. The syntax, diction and character names all strongly evoke the childlike, and even more specifically, the bureaucratized language and space of Soviet school. At the same time, the mood of this late poem is one of melancholy philosophical inquiry. As Anna Gerasimova asserts, "The childlike quality of Vvedenskij's 'adult' work is in no way connected to his poems for children. It is not a reconstruction of the 'child's' worldview, but rather the straightforwardness of questions that according to the grown-up rules of the game cannot be asked,

---

90 See Chardzhiev, *Статьи об авангарде*, Vol. 1, 380.

91 That OBERIU group was Russia's last Avant-Garde formation is stated, for example, in the title of Graham Roberts's monograph, *The Last Soviet Avant-Garde: OBERIU – Fact, Fiction, Metafiction*, Cambridge 1997. Another OBERIU scholar, Jean-Philippe Jaccard, refers to the group in connection with the "end of the Russian Avant-Garde": *Daniïl Harms et la fin de l'avant-garde russe*, Wien 1991 (in Russian translation: *Даниил Хармс и конец русского авангарда*, St. Petersburg 1995).

92 "They the fishermen were five in number. They intently ate soup with fish. Their names were Andrej, Bandrej, Bendrej, Gandrej, and Kudedrej. They all had daughters. Their names were Ljalja, Talja, Balja, Kalja, and Salja. The daughters had all gotten married. It was evening. The soldier Aj Bee See did not stop by the home of these garden-patch minders. He did not knock on their home door. He walked deep in his thought, the main thought about nuts directing him." Translated by Eugene Ostashevsky in Alexander Vvedensky, *An Invitation for Me to Think*, New York 2013, 121.

FIGURE 3.6 *Конная Буденного* (*Budennyj's Cavalry*) by Aleksandr Vvedenskij
ILLUSTRATIONS BY V. KURDOV (1931)

because they have no answers [...]."[93] Although the OBERIU poets did not as a rule attempt to realistically emulate children's language or the child's viewpoint in their adult work, child-figures (and speaking animals) often appear as lyric personae, alongside language and forms typical of children's poetry.

---

93 Anna Gerasimova, "Проблема смешного в творчестве обэриутов." Ph.D. Dissertation, A. M. Gor'kij Institute of Literature, Moscow 1986, 212.

THE DICTIONARY AS A TOY COLLECTION 131

Comparing the aesthetics of OBERIU work for children and adults is complicated by the fact that their children's work was always subject to substantial editing, often conducted by Marshak personally and at all stages of production.[94] Despite this quality control, the crime for which Vvedenskij and Charms were arrested and temporarily exiled in 1931-32 was "putting *заумь* in children's literature."[95] Their sometime mentor Tufanov, a self-professed *заумь* poet who in 1922 had declared himself Velimir II, President of the Globe of Заумь (a variation on one of Chlebnikov's titles), was arrested with them and accused of encouraging the younger poets' subversive corruption of Soviet youth.[96] While taking into account the problematic nature of police records as historical documents, a general sense of condescension toward children's literature on the part of Charms and Vvedenskij is indeed evident in their interrogation reports (even when these are read as 'co-productions' with the interrogators).[97] Of his own work, Charms confesses: "In those instances when I for the sake of material gain tried to adapt to the declared societal requirements for children's literature, I produced obviously shoddy work," but he also affirms the ongoing significance of *заумь* in his work:

> I am very pleased with my most senseless poems, such as "О Топорышкине," which given their extreme senselessness were ridiculed in even the Soviet humorist press; I considered them to be poems of extraordinarily high quality, and the knowledge that they were indissolubly connected to my unpublished *заумь* work brought me greater inner satisfaction.[98]

While many of Vvedenskij's children's poems directly addressed Soviet themes in a loyal tone, revealing little of the fractured syntax and often bleak absurdity of his adult verse,[99] Charms's work demonstrates far less of a disconnect

---

94 See Chukovskaja, "Маршак-редактор," *В лаборатории редактора*, 219-334; in his diaries, Charms also writes about frequent editing visits to Marshak.
95 Valerij Shubinskij, *Даниил Хармс: Жизнь человека на ветру*, Moscow 2015, 323-339.
96 Ibid., 328-332.
97 For a thoughtful discussion of the usefulness of police documentation to literary scholarship, see Valerij Shubinskij and Gleb Morev, "Пусть меня расстреляют; но форму я не одену: Валерий Шубинский и Глеб Морев о том, можно ли верить следственным делам Хармса и Введенского," in *Colta.ru*, 4 February 2014 (http://www.colta.ru/articles/literature/1918) (Accessed December 5, 2017).
98 I. Mal'skij, ed., "Разгром ОБЭРИУ: материалы следственного дела," in *Октябрь* 11 (1992), 175.
99 Lidija Chukovskaja rightly praises some of Vvedenskij's lyric poetry for children. Chukovskaja, *В лаборатории редактора*, 271-275.

between the "adult line" and the poems published in *Чиж* and *Ёж*. The text Charms refers to in the interrogation records, "Иван Топорышкин" ("Ivan Littleaxe," 1928), demonstrates many devices found ubiquitously in the poet's work for children and not:

> Иван Топорышкин пошел на охоту,
> с ним пудель пошел, перепрыгнув забор.
> Иван как бревно провалился в болото,
> а пудель в реке утонул, как топор.
>
> Иван Топорышкин пошел на охоту,
> с ним пудель вприпрыжку пошел, как топор.
> Иван повалился бревном на болото,
> а пудель в реке перепрыгнул забор.
>
> Иван Топорышкин пошел на охоту,
> с ним пудель в реке провалился в забор.
> Иван как бревно перепрыгнул болото,
> а пудель вприпрыжку попал на топор.[100]

The poem plays a simple substitution game that nevertheless creates a series of recognizable situations like many of the short prose pieces in Charms's cycle "Случаи" ("Incidences," 1934-38).[101] Although the poem is demonstratively "senseless," it manages to convey a certain menace evocative of Charms's often violent adult work: it is full of wayward axes and its apparently random assortment of verbs tend to send its two protagonists toward various kinds of doom. This poem is an example of childlike silliness and absurdity smoothing the way to publication rather than hampering it (even though it eventually came under attack). It is certainly a "nonsense" rather than a *заумь* poem, since the

---

100 "Ivan Littleaxe went out on a hunt, / his poodle came along, jumping over the fence. / Ivan fell into the swamp like a log, / and the poodle drowned in the river like an axe. // Ivan Littleaxe went out on a hunt / his poodle came along, hopping like an axe. / Ivan toppled over the swamp like a log, / and the poodle jumped over the fence in the river. // Ivan Littleaxe went out on a hunt, / his poodle fell into the fence in the river. / Ivan like a log jumped over the swamp, / and the poodle hopping along fell onto an axe." Charms, *Полное собрание сочинений*, Vol. 3, 10.

101 For "Случаи," see Charms, *Полное собрание сочинений*, Vol. 2, 330-364. Around the mid-1930s Charms largely switched to writing prose, although he continued to write and publish poems for children until 1940.

words and syntax all conform to standard Russian, but it is easy to see how critics might conflate the two concepts.

Despite causing them serious trouble, the Avant-Garde-informed childlike aesthetic remained present in Charms and Vvedenskij's writing for children following their return from internal exile. Charms published a children's play, "Цирк Шардам" ("Shardam Circus") in 1935 that features a Filipino juggler named Am gam glam Kaba laba Saba laba Samba gib chip lib Chiki kiki Kiuki liuki Chukh shukh Sdugr pugr Of of Prr, who speaks in *заумь* poetry, at one point even offering the lines "Дыр дыр дыр/ Буль буль буль."[102] And as late as 1940, Vvedenskij was publishing lyric poems like the hypnotic, sleepy "О рыбаке и судаке" ("About the Fisherman and the Walleye"):

[...]
Вот рыбак сидел, сидел
И на удочку глядел,
Вот рыбак терпел, терпел,
Не стерпел и сам запел.

По реке плывет челнок,
На корме поет рыбак,
На носу поет щенок,
Песню слушает судак.

Слышит дудочки звучанье,
Слышит пенье петушка,
Стада громкое мычанье
И плесканье челнока.
И завидует он всем:
Он, судак, как рыба нем.[103]

The hypnotic quality comes from the simple grammatical rhymes and multiple repetitions, which mimic the near-absence of movement of the fisherman's

---

102 Charms, *Полное собрание сочинений*, Vol. 3, 213.
103 And so the fisherman sat and sat / And gazed at his pole, / And so the fisherman waited and waited, / Lost his patience and burst out singing. / The canoe floats down the river / The fisherman sings at the stern, /The pup sings at the prow, / The walleye listens to their song. / It hears the sounding of the pipes, / It hears the rooster's crow, / The loud lowing of the herd / And the plashing of canoe. / And it envies everything: / The walleye is mute as a fish. In Vvedenskij, *Стихи*, Moscow and Leningrad 1940.

boat quietly rocking. Although the fisherman bursts into song despite himself, the noises that follow are somehow muted, a fact which calls into question the meaning of the poem's striking last line (the tautological comparison, extremely common in Vvedenskij's adult work, appears only rarely in his poems for children). The poem is also implicitly connected to Vvedenskij's poems for older readers through the figure of the fisherman, recalling the fishermen in "Солдат Аз Буки Веди."[104] In this way, these experimental poets perpetuated certain aspects of the Avant-Garde childlike aesthetic (so abundantly represented in their work for adults) in Soviet children's literature of the 1930s, ensuring the legacy – albeit muted – of their radical predecessors.

5   Conclusion

Marshak's speech at the First Congress of Soviet Writers in 1934 marked a watershed moment in the life of Soviet children's literature: although Detgiz continued to publish the work of the young Leningrad Avant-Garde writers for a few more years, in 1937 the entire operation was purged.[105] Nearly everyone was fired and a number of its employees were arrested; Marshak fled Leningrad for Moscow. The following years saw the untimely deaths of many Detgiz writers and artists.[106] Still, the political status of children's literature established in the early 1930s remained in force for most of the rest of the Soviet period. After the Terror of the 1930s and the dark years of World War II, children's publishers in the post-war "Thaw" period once again employed many writers otherwise considered politically unsound.[107]

During the "Thaw" period, the rehabilitation and revival of Avant-Garde aesthetics was reflected in children's literature as elsewhere in contemporary Soviet culture. The fact that experimental poets were still limited to working in this area meant that children's literature often demonstrated more examples of Avant-Garde and experimental aesthetics than other officially-published liter-

---

104   Cf. also the earlier children's poem "Рыбаки," in *Еж* 4 (1929), 11.
105   Chukovskaja, *В лаборатории редактора*, 321-323.
106   See Shubinskij, *Жизнь человека на ветру*, 457-9; 465; 526, and Oleg Minin's chapter in this volume.
107   Unofficial writers employed in children's literature included Igor' Cholin, Oleg Grigorjev, Iurij Koval', Genrich Sapgir, Jan Satunovskij and many more. See Sokol on the legacy of the 1920s, 176-206; Morse, *Word Play*, forthcoming. For studies of the translation work of some of these writers, including Sapgir, see Maria Khotimsky's chapter in this volume: "Children's Poetry and Translation in the Soviet Era: Strategies of Rewriting, Transformation and Adaptation."

ature. A number of unofficial writers and artists of this period, whose work circulated only through clandestine channels, worked and were even well known as official children's writers and illustrators: Erik Bulatov, Oleg Grigorjev, Igor' Cholin, Ilja Kabakov, Viktor Pivovarov, Genrich Sapgir and many others. The attitude to this kind of work remained the same as for previous generations – it was first and foremost a source of income for individuals barred from publishing or showing work in official venues. At the same time, the revival of the early Soviet Avant-Garde and the republication of children's poetry by OBERIU poets around this time were hugely influential stimuli, and contributed to a sense of both aesthetic and institutional solidarity on the part of the new generation vis-à-vis their predecessors. The status of children's writer thus acquired a certain underdog flair, which happily resulted in the production of some excellent, inspiring children's books even in the plodding years of cultural "stagnation."

Works Cited

Primary Sources

Aleksandrov, A., ed. *Ванна Архимеда*. Leningrad 1991.

Al'fonsov, Vladimir and Simon Krasickij, eds. *Поэзия русского футуризма*. St. Petersburg 1999.

Benua, Aleksandr and Kornej Chukovskij, eds. *Елка. Сборник. Книжка для маленьких детей*. Petrograd 1918.

Charms, Daniil. *Полное собрание сочинений: В 4-х томах*, ed. V. N. Sazhin. St. Petersburg 1997–2001.

Chlebnikov, Velimir. *Творения*. Moscow 1986.

Chlebnikov, Velimir. *Собрание сочинений В. Хлебникова*. Leningrad 1928.

Chlebnikov, Velimir. *Собрание сочинений в трех томах*. St. Petersburg 2001.

Chukovskij, Kornej. *Собрание сочинений в пятнадцати томах*, Moscow 2001-2010.

Chukovskij, Kornej. "Речь К.И. Чуковского," in *Первый всесоюзный съезд советских писателей*. Moscow 1934, 179-182.

Chukovskij, Kornej. *Маленькие дети: детские слова и разговоры – экики – лепые нелепицы – читатели о детях*. Leningrad 1929.

Cvetaeva, Marina. *Избранная проза в двух томах*, Vol. 2 (1917-1937). New York 1979.

Guro, Elena. *Небесные верблюжата*. Rostov-on-Don 1993.

Khlebnikov, Velimir. *The King of Time: Selected Writings of the Russian Futurian*, trans. Paul Schmidt, ed. Charlotte Douglas. Cambridge, MA 1985.

Kruchenych, Aleksej. *К истории русского футуризма: Воспоминания и документы*, Moscow 2006.

Kruchenych, Aleksej. *Собственные рассказы и рисунки детей*. [St. Petersburg] 1914.
Kruchenych, Aleksej, and Zina V. *Поросята*. [St. Petersburg] 1913.
Majakovskij, Vladimir. *Полное собрание сочинений в 13-х томах*. Moscow 1955-1961.
Majakovskij, Vladimir. *Избранные произведения: Стихи, поэмы, проза*. Moscow 1963.
Majakovskij, Vladimir. *Советская азбука*. Moscow 1919.
Mandel'shtam, Osip. *Собрание сочинений в четырех томах*. Moscow 1993.
Marshak, Samuil. "Содоклад С.Я. Маршака о детской литературе," in *Первый всесоюзный съезд советских писателей*. Moscow 1934, 20-37.
Marshak, Samuil. *Собрание сочинений в восьми томах*. Moscow 1971.
Ostashevsky, Eugene, ed. *OBERIU: An Anthology of Russian Absurdism*. Evanston, IL 2006.
Pasternak, Boris. *Собрание сочинений в пяти томах*. Moscow 1989.
Pushkin, A.S. *Собрание сочинений в десяти томах*. Moscow 1959-1962.
Rothenstein, Julian and Olga Budashevskaya, eds. *Inside the Rainbow: Russian Children's Literature 1920-1935: Beautiful Books, Terrible Times*. London 2013.
Sazhin, Valerij, ed. *"Сборище друзей, оставленных судьбою": А. Введенский, Л. Липавский, Д. Хармс, Н. Олейников: 'Чинари' в текстах, документах и исследованиях: в двух томах*. Moscow 1998.
Vvedenskij, Aleksandr. *Стихи*. Moscow and Leningrad 1940.
Vvedenskij, Aleksandr. *Собрание сочинений в двух томах*, Vladimir Erl and Michail Mejlach, eds. Moscow 1993.
Vvedenskij, Aleksandr. *Все*, Anna Gerasimova, ed. Moscow 2010.
Vvedensky, Alexander. *An Invitation for Me to Think*, ed. and trans. Eugene Ostashevsky and Matvei Yankelevich. New York 2013.

Secondary Sources

Balina, Marina and Valerij Vjugin, eds. *"Убить Чарскую": парадоксы советской детской литературы для детей (1920-е – 1930-е гг.): сборник статей*. St. Petersburg 2015.
Balina, Marina and Larissa Rudova, eds. *Russian Children's Literature and Culture*. New York 2008.
Chardzhiev, Nikolaj. *Статьи об авангарде: в двух томах*. Moscow 1997.
Chukovskaja, Lidija. *В лаборатории редактора*. Moscow 1960.
Chukovskij, Kornej. *Собрание сочинений в шести томах*. Moscow 1969.
Chukovskij, Kornej. *От двух до пяти*. Leningrad 1933.
Gerasimova, A. "Проблема смешного в творчестве обэриутов." Ph.D. Dissertation, A. M. Gor'kij Institute of Literature, Moscow 1986.
Gray, Camilla. *The Russian Experiment in Art, 1863-1922*. New York 1986.

Hellman, Ben. *Fairy Tales and True Stories: The History of Russian Literature for Children and Young People (1574-2010)*. Boston and Leiden 2013.

Ioffe, Dennis and Frederick White, eds. *The Russian Avant-Garde and Radical Modernism. An Introductory Reader*. Boston 2012.

Jaccard, Jean-Phillipe. *Даниил Хармс и конец русского авангарда*. St. Petersburg 1995.

Janecek, Gerald. *The Look of Russian Literature: Avant-Garde Visual Experiments, 1900-1930*. Princeton, NJ 1984.

Janecek, Gerald. *ZAUM: The Transrational Poetry of Russian Futurism*. San Diego, CA 1996.

Kachurin, Pamela. *Making Modernism Soviet: The Russian Avant-Garde in the Early Soviet Era, 1918-1928*. Evanston, IL 2013.

Kelly, Catriona. *Children's World: Growing Up in Russia, 1890-1991*. New Haven, CT 2007.

Kobrinskij, Aleksandr. *Поэтика ОБЭРИУ в контексте русского литературного авангарда*. Moscow 2000.

Losev, Lev. "Предисловие," in Shvarc, Evgenij, *Мемуары*. Paris 1982.

Lotman, Jurij. *Анализ поэтического текста: Структура стиха*. Leningrad 1972.

Lunacharskij, Anatolij, ed. *Детская литература. Критический сборник*. Moscow and Leningrad 1931.

Malskij, I., ed. "Разгром ОБЭРИУ: Материалы следственного дела," in *Октябрь* 11 (1992), 166-191.

Mandel'shtam, Nadezhda. *Третья книга*. Moscow 2006.

Markov, Vladimir. *Russian Futurism: A History*. Berkeley, CA 1968.

Morse, Ainsley. *Word Play: Experimental Poetry and Soviet Children's Literature*. Evanston, IL. Forthcoming.

Putilova, Evgenija. *Очерки по истории критики советской детской литературы, 1917-1941*. Moscow 1982.

Roberts, Graham. *The Last Soviet Avant-garde: OBERIU – Fact, Fiction, Metafiction*. Cambridge and New York 1997.

Rowell, Margaret and Deborah Wye, eds. *The Russian Avant-Garde Book*. New York 2002.

Shubinskij, Valerij. *Даниил Хармс: Жизнь человека на ветру*. Moscow 2015.

Shubinskij, Valerij, and Gleb Morev. "'Пусть меня расстреляют; но форму я не одену: Валерий Шубинский и Глеб Морев о том, можно ли верить следственным делам Хармса и Введенского," in *Colta.ru*, 4 February 2014 ⟨http://www.colta.ru/articles/literature/1918⟩ (Accessed December 5, 2017).

Sokol, Elena. *Russian Poetry for Children*. Knoxville, TN 1984.

Steiner, Evgeny. *Stories for Little Comrades: Revolutionary Artists and the Making of Early Soviet Children's Books*, trans. Jane Ann Miller. Seattle 1999.

Tynjanov, Jurij. "Промежуток," in *Поэтика. История литературы. Кино*. Moscow 1977.

Tynjanov, Jurij. "О Хлебникове," in *Собрание сочинений В. Хлебникова*, Vol. 1. Leningrad 1928.

Weld, Sara Pankenier. *Voiceless Vanguard: The Infantilist Aesthetic of the Russian Avant-Garde*. Evanston, IL 2014.

Zholkovskij, Aleksandr. *Блуждающие сны и другие работы*. Moscow 1994.

CHAPTER 4

The Literary Avant-Garde and Soviet Literature for Children: OBERIU in the Leningrad Periodicals *Еж* and *Чиж*

Oleg Minin

1   Introduction

The field of cultural production which emerged in Soviet Russia in the years following the revolution and the Civil War was marked not only by an ongoing battle for cultural supremacy among a variety of literary and artistic groups, but also by an unprecedented incursion of experimental visual and literary arts into the domain of literature for children. The factors at play ran the gamut from the absence of a viable artistic marketplace, to increasing political pressure which prompted cultural producers seek new ways of adapting and remaining relevant to the new socialist project.[1] For many experimental writers and artists, political control over cultural production made the domain of children's literature particularly suitable for engagement. Relatively free from ideological and aesthetic oversight and censorship (although this situation would change in the second half of the 1920s and especially toward the end of the decade), it also promised a relative ease of the artistic task and a reasonably good compensation.[2] A plethora of major modernist and Avant-Garde writers and artists, as well as their students and adepts, contributed to the creation of new Soviet literature for children. Osip Mandel'shtam, Vladimir Majakovskij, and Boris Pasternak, all wrote poems for children, while artists such as Vera Ermolaeva, Tatjana Glebova, Vladimir Lebedev, El Lissitskij, Alisa Poret, and Vladimir Tatlin were active in the field of book illustration and design.

A group of Leningrad poets loosely united under the title of "Объединение реального искусства" ("The Association of Real Art" or OBERIU) was arguably the last experimental poetic alliance in Soviet Russia whose princi-

---

[1]   Evgenij Shtejner, *Авангард и построение нового человека. Искусство советской детской книги 1920-х годов*, Moscow 2002, 20; Arkady Ippolitov, "Imaginationland, USSR," in Julian Rothenstein and Olga Budashevskaia, eds., *Inside the Rainbow. Russian Children's Literature 1920-1935: Beautiful Books, Terrible Times*, London 2013, 19.
[2]   Valerij Shubinskij, *Жизнь человека на ветру*, St. Petersburg 2008, 240-241, 260-261.

pal member-writers – Daniil Charms, Jurij Vladimirov, Aleksandr Vvedenskij, Nikolaj Zabolockij, and the affiliated Nikolaj Olejnikov – were also actively involved in writing for children.[3] Throughout the late 1920s and 1930s, they produced many children's books which were illustrated by the likes of Ermolaeva, Glebova, Lebedev, Poret, Tatlin and Lev Judin – artists who at various points in their early careers belonged to the Avant-Garde. Often prior to appearing in book form, OBERIU's writings for young readers were featured on the pages of children's periodicals, two of which, *Еж* (*The Hedgehog*, 1928-1935) and *Чиж* (*The Finch*, 1930-1941) are especially noteworthy in this context. Both titles were acronyms: *Еж* stood for "ежемесячный журнал" or "monthly magazine," and *Чиж*, for "чрезвычайно интересный журнал" or an "extremely interesting journal." Having evolved from *Новый Робинзон* (*New Robinson*, formerly *Воробей* [*Sparrow*, 1923-1924]), *Еж* was geared toward ten to fourteen-year-olds. It was published monthly from 1928 to 1935 with the print run fluctuating between 30,000 and 120,000 copies. From 1928 to 1930, its circulation grew from 35,000 to 100,000 copies. From 1930 to 1932, the journal was published twice a month, though in 1932 its production was halted for several months due to a paper shortage. Starting in 1930, *Еж* came out with *Чиж* – a supplement for younger children (i.e. five to seven-year-old preschoolers [дошкольники, нулевики]) and the so-called "октябрята" ("Octobrists"). Ultimately, *Чиж* became an autonomous periodical; it continued to come out until 1941. Published in Leningrad by the children's section (Detgiz) of the Leningrad State Publishing House (Lengiz), these journals became the principal venues for the creative work of the OBERIU for children.[4]

---

3 The origins, history, evolution and "membership" of OBERIU are well documented in primary sources and critical literature. For all intents and purposes, this essay operates within Michail Mejlach's introduction of OBERIU as the last link in a chain of evolving artistic associations of the "left," experimental, art (i.e. Левый фланг [Left Flank], Радикс, Фланг левых [Leftists' Flank], and Академия левых классиков [The Academy of Left Classics]). See Mejlach, "Дверь в поэзию открыта...," in *Александр Введенский. Полное собрание сочинений в двух томах*, ed. M. Mejlach, Vol. 1, Moscow 1993, 25. According to Igor' Bachterev, one of the OBERIU founder-members, ca. 1928-1929, the group consisted of mostly poets. In addition to Bachterev himself, it included Charms, Olejnikov, Vladimirov, Vvedenskij and Zabolockij. Also affiliated with this diverse group of writers were Dojvber (Boris) Levin, and Konstantin Vaginov. See Bachterev, "Тот месяц в Ташкенте," in *Об Анне Ахматовой. Стихи, эссе, воспоминания, письма*, ed. M. M. Kralin, Leningrad 1990, 218.

4 While writing for *Еж* and *Чиж*, Charms, Vvedenskij and Zabolockij contributed to other children's journals as well. Charms and Vvedenskij, for instance, wrote for the journal-textbook *Большевистская смена* (*The New Bolshevik Generation*, 1931-1932), the journal *Маленькие ударники* (*Little Shock-Workers*, 1931-1932) and the journals *Октябрята* (*Octobrists*, 1931-1932), *Юные ударники* (*Young Shock-Workers*, 1930-1932),

Seeking to provide a general overview of the OBERIU poets' collaboration with the two journals, this essay looks at their *Ёж* and *Чиж* texts in an attempt to gauge how and what they contributed to the creation of new literature for the new Soviet child – the literature that would extol the accomplishments of the revolution, valorize its heroes and leaders, promote positive Soviet values, and help to bring up Soviet children in the spirit of internationalism and class consciousness.[5] In as much as it concerned the political conditions of literary production for children that emerged in Soviet Russia in the second half of the 1920s, the committed or uncommitted nature of the OBERIU texts vis-à-vis the ideological priorities of the day will in turn help explain the turbulent history of this experimental literary group. It will also shed light on the conflicts between OBERIU artistic practices and Soviet literary policies, the objectives of which were informed by the nascent proletarian agenda on the one hand, and the economic exigencies of the first Five-Year plans on the other. Some of OBERIU's most imaginative, popular and enduring works for children were published in *Ёж* and *Чиж*. Discussion of the intrinsic artistic and educational worth of these texts will complement the overall objective of evaluating their ideological suitability.

Ванька-Встанька (*Roly-Poly*, 1936), and others. In his autobiography, Zabolockij indicates that he published a series of poems and stories in the journals *Пионер* (*Pioneer*) and *Костер* (*Campfire*). Nikolaj Zabolockij, "Автобиография," in *Стихотворения*, Washington 1965, 2. In 1937, shortly prior to his arrest, Olejnikov edited the Moscow-published journal *Сверчок* (*Cricket*). Charms, Vvedenskij and Leonid Lipavskij (L. Savel'ev) were among this journal's contributors. Aleksandr Olejnikov, "Последние дни Николая Олейникова," in "*...Сборище друзей, оставленных судьбою,*" *А. Введенский, Л. Липавский, Я. Друскин, Д. Хармс, Н. Олейников. "Чинари" в текстах, документах и исследованиях в двух томах*, Vol. 2, *Д. Хармс, Н. Олейников*, ed. Valerij Sazhin, Moscow 2000, 574.

5 The essay is concerned principally with Charms, Olejnikov, Vladimirov, Vvedenskij and Zabolockij as they were the most active *Ёж* and *Чиж* contributors. Bachterev's contributions to these journals were sparse and amounted only to one riddle (загадка) in the 9th issue of *Ёж* for 1928 and the retelling of two былины (oral epic narrative poems) published in issues 6 and 7 of *Чиж* for 1937. Co-written with Charms and illustrated by Vera Ermolaeva, Dojvber Levin's innocuous and only story, "Друг за другом" ("One After the Other") was published in the May issue of *Ёж* for 1930. Vaginov, who, unlike other OBERIU writers, succeeded in publishing three novels before his untimely death in 1934, did not contribute to either *Ёж* or *Чиж*. His only work for children is an adaption of Alphonse Daudet's story *Le secret de maître Cornille* published as a book in 1927 under the Russian title *Тайна дедушки Корнилия* (*The Secret of Grandfather Kornilij*).

FIGURE 4.1 Back cover ad for *Ёж* 2 (1930)

2 From Irony to Tragedy: The Trajectory of the OBERIU Poets' Work for *Еж* and *Чиж*

Overall, the OBERIU poets' work at Detgiz may be characterized as fraught with irony and tragedy. For instance, Charms, who claimed to dislike children, succeeded in becoming a popular children's writer: young Soviet readers knew his works by heart and his public readings in schools and kindergartens were popular and well-attended.[6] It was tragically ironic that despite their popularity, talent and an apparent affinity with the young readers, the OBERIU poets were nonetheless persecuted by the Soviet state for their writings for children. Yet, the abysmal reception in the press and public condemnations at professional meetings, the resultant arrests, humiliating interrogations, harsh sentences and exile did not stop Charms and Vvedenskij from contributing to *Еж* and *Чиж*. The latter journal was the more enduring of the two periodicals; its publication was halted only by the Nazi invasion of the Soviet Union. The sixth and last issue of *Чиж* came out in June of 1941 and featured Charms's clever rhymes "Девять картин" ("Nine Pictures") accompanied by Lev Judin's signature illustrations. Printed on the edition's very last page, Charms's short and playful lines may be seen as a symbolic closure that signaled not only the end of the journal, but also the end of the era of the OBERIU poets' writing for children. Only a few months later, the end of *Чиж* was tragically mirrored by the ultimate physical demise of Charms and Vvedenskij, two of its longest and most talented OBERIU contributors: arrested preventively in Charkov, where the poet had lived since 1936, Vvedenskij died in December of 1941 en route to a prison camp. Charms perished in February of 1942 in his native Leningrad in the psychiatric ward of the Kresty prison. He had been arrested several months prior for the alleged "counter-revolutionary disposition, [for] spreading libelous and defeatist attitudes and attempting to cause panic and dissatisfaction with the Soviet government."[7]

---

6 This phenomenon is aptly described in Shubinskij, *Жизнь человека на ветру*, 235-236, 263, and in Aleksandr Kobrinskij, *Даниил Хармс*, Moscow 2009, 156-157; 287-296.

7 See "Дело № 2196-41 г.," in "…*Сборище друзей, оставленных судьбою*." Vol. 2, 592. Charms and Vvedenskij's friends and colleagues were painfully aware of the poets' tragic fates. In the extant 1942 letters from evacuation in Kazakhstan to the *Еж* and *Чиж* artist and Charms and Vvedenskij's fellow-Kursk exile Elena Safonova, who at the time was residing in Leningrad, Tatjana Glebova and Vladimir Sterligov first thank her for the good news about Charms: "What joy that Daniil Ivanovich is alive. This news shocked us." Several weeks later, after Safonova had informed Glebova and Sterligov about Charms's demise, Sterligov responded: "Your news about Daniil Ivanovich pains my heart and soul. I can't believe it! I do not agree! And I protest wrathfully. The same way [I protest the news] about Aleksandr Ivanovich

All in all, the poets of OBERIU worked for *Еж* and *Чиж* for thirteen years, a long stretch which can be divided into two distinct periods.⁸ The first period opens with the inaugural publication of *Еж* in January of 1928, likely as a link in a chain of responses to the Bolshevik Party's call for the creation of more literature for members of the fledgling pioneer organization.⁹ This period corresponded almost exactly to the Soviet Union's First Five-Year Plan and to what Sheila Fitzpatrick has called the first "false" proletarian Cultural Revolution (1928-1932) – factors that influenced the editorial and thematic direction of both *Еж* and *Чиж* (especially concerning the close attention the journals paid to urgent political themes such as socialist construction), and, as a consequence, the fates of their OBERIU contributors.¹⁰ It may be argued

[Vvedenskij]." Глебова Татьяна Николаевна. Стерлигов Владимир Васильевич. *Письма Сафоновой Елене Васильевне*, ca. Feb. – March, 1942, in Manuscript Section, State Russian Museum, St. Petersburg, Fund 212, File 256, 1-3. The fates of Charms and Vvedenskij's OBERIU colleagues varied: Vladimirov and Vaginov died of consumption in 1931 and 1934 respectively; Olejnikov was arrested in July of 1937 and shot five months later for his alleged involvement with a counter-revolutionary Trotskyite organization; Zabolockij was arrested and sentenced in 1938 for "anti-Soviet propaganda." At the time of Charms and Vvedenskij's deaths, he was serving time in the camps in the Far East and the Altai regions. Dojvber Levin perished at the front at the beginning of World War II. Bachterev was the only surviving OBERIU member: during the war, he lived in Tashkent and, apart from his 1931 arrest that resulted in a short exile, by and large avoided persecution and died in St. Petersburg in 1996.

8   This division is based principally on the break in the continuity of work as regards Charms and Vvedenskij (due to their arrest and exile) and is less applicable to Olejnikov and Zabolockij.

9   *Еж* commenced its publication four years after the XIII Bolshevik Party Congress (May 23-31, 1924), which, in its resolution, called for the creation of literature for children under rigorous party control and guidance with the objective of emphasizing the aspects of class, international, and labor upbringing. Specifically, the resolution stressed the need to create literature for pioneers. "О печати. Из резолюции Тринадцатого съезда РКП(б)," Section 12, in *Советская печать в документах*, Moscow 1961, 65-66. Prior to *Еж*, several pioneer journals were published both in Moscow and Petrograd (Leningrad) shortly before and immediately after the XIII Party Congress. Among these were the journals *Юные товарищи* (*Young Comrades*, Moscow, April-September 1922), *Барабан* (*Drum*, Moscow 1923-1926) and *Воробей* (*Sparrow*, Petrograd, 1923). In 1924, *Воробей* was renamed *Новый Робинзон* (*The New Robinson*, Leningrad 1924-1925); it became a direct precursor to *Еж*. Two years later, *Новый Робинзон* was superseded by *Красный галстук* (*The Red Tie*, Leningrad, 1926). The journal *Пионер* (*Pioneer*) commenced its publication in Moscow in 1924. In 1925, *Пионер* absorbed *Юные товарищи* and in 1926, *Барабан*. N. Iljina, "Из истории детских журналов 20-30-х годов," in *Вопросы детской литературы*, Moscow 1958, 24-61.

10 Sheila Fitzpatrick, "Cultural Revolution in Russia, 1928-1932," in *Journal for Contemporary History* 9 (1), January 1974, 33-52.

in this connection that the first arrest of Bachterev, Charms and Vvedenskij in the winter of 1931 could be in part explained by the poets' lingering reluctance to address in their *Еж* and *Чиж* contributions themes of social significance as mandated by the state. The situation, of course, was far more complex and many other "valid" reasons contributing to the arrests can be identified. The negative reception to the OBERIU texts for adult readers and public appearances prior to 1928, as well as to those that coincided with the first year of their work in Detgiz, no doubt also led to the persecution.[11] At the same time, the young poets' unwillingness to conform may be explained, as suggested by Michail Mejlach, by their probable lack of sympathy for the new regime.[12] Be that as it may, the first, shorter, but, perhaps more prolific and fruitful period of the OBERIU writing for *Еж* and *Чиж* culminated in 1931 with the poets' arrests in December and their subsequent exile. This period was followed by a several months' hiatus from January through October of 1932, during which time no texts by Charms or Vvedenskij (or even by Olejnikov and Zabolockij, who were not arrested) appeared in *Еж*, and only four of Zabolockij's poems were published in *Чиж*.[13]

The second, longer period of writing for *Еж* and *Чиж* ensued after Charms and Vvedenskij returned from exile in Kursk and Borisoglebsk in October, 1932, and January, 1933, respectively. This period continued with various degrees of success for another eight years until the ultimate closure of *Чиж*. Vvedenskij's brief visit to Leningrad during his transition from Kursk to Vologda, in October of 1932, resulted in two poetic contributions to *Чиж* – the ideologically potent poem "Что это вы строите?" ("What Are You Building?") and the politically neutral "Умный Петя" ("Clever Petja").[14] The first poem describes little children decorating their kindergarten to celebrate the fifteenth anniversary of the October Revolution, while "Умный Петя" employs one of OBERIU's favorite

---

11   For a detailed description of the negative critical reception to OBERIU public appearances and readings ca. 1928-1930, see, for instance, Mejlach, "Дверь в поэзию открыта…," 27-31.

12   See Michail Mejlach, "Я испытывал слово на огне и на стуже," in *Поэты группы ОБЕРИУ*, St. Petersburg 1994, 55.

13   These were the tendentious "Восемь лет без Ленина" ("Eight Years Without Lenin," in *Чиж* 1, 1932) and "За окном" ("Out the Window," in *Чиж* 4/5, 1932) – each respectively devoted to the veneration of Lenin as the great proletarian hero and to the theme of collective labor – as well as the less politicized poems "На площадку" ("To the Playground," in *Чиж* 6, 1932) and "У моря" ("By the Sea," in *Чиж* 7/8, 1931).

14   *Чиж* 9/10, and 11/12, 1932. Vvedenskij left Kursk for Vologda on Oct. 1 to accompany Elena Safonova, who was ordered to relocate. En route, the poet made a brief stop in Leningrad, arriving there on Oct. 3. See Mejlakh, "Дверь в поэзию открыта…," 33; Shubinskij, *Жизнь человека*, 341.

devices, prevarication, to tell a humorous story about a boy with a penchant for explaining natural phenomena in the most imaginative, but utterly erroneous way.[15] After permanently returning to Leningrad, Vvedenskij resumed his work at Detgiz and actively contributed to both journals. Charms came back to the city two months before Vvedenskij's return, but did not resume writing for Чиж until the summer of 1933, when two of his entertaining, albeit politically unassuming stories about a certain professor Trubochkin appeared in the 7 (July) and 8 (August) issues.[16] Charms's first and last contribution to Еж – a topical poem about socialist construction, "Новый город" ("A New City") – came out only in the May issue of the journal for 1935, which was also the last year of its publication.

As an organized entity, OBERIU had effectively dissolved by 1930, in some part due to the negative critical reception of its public readings and performances, and the mounting political pressure. During the second, post-exile period of writing for Еж and Чиж (1932/33-1941), the OBERIU legacy continued to survive at the level of personal interactions between the former fellow-*chinary* friends.[17] However, the group sustained further losses with the arrest in July, and execution in November, 1937, of Olejnikov and the arrest and imprisonment of Zabolockij in March of the following year. Overall, OBERIU Еж and Чиж contributions of the second period amounted to over a hundred texts, with Vvedenskij being the most often published OBERIU author.[18]

---

15   Charms, Vvedenskij and Zabolockij used this device in many of their Еж texts. See, for instance, Charms's poem "Врун" ("Liar," in Еж 24, 1930), Vvedenskij's poem "4 хвастуна" ("4 Boasters," in Еж 2/3, 1933), Zabolockij's short story "Приключения врунов" ("Liars' Adventures," in Еж 4, 1929) and his variant of a somewhat politicized Kalmyk fairytale "Два обманщика" ("Two Tricksters," in Еж 12, 1935).

16   Charms and Vvedenskij's relocations and travels during this period are also described in A.V. Ustinov, "Дело детского сектора Госиздата 1932 года: Предварительная справка," in *Михаил Кузмин и русская культура XX века: тезисы и материалы конференции 15-17 мая 1990 г.*, ed. G. A. Morev, Moscow 1990, 125-136, and in Kobrinskij, *Даниил Хармс*, 246-300.

17   Kobrinskij, *Даниил Хармс*, 277-288. The term "chinari" refers to an unofficial circle of friends comprising at various times during the mid-1920s through the late 1930s Charms, Vvedenskij, Jakov Druskin, Leonid Lipavskij, Olejnikov, Zabolockij, and Tamara Meyer-Lipavskaja. See, Graham Roberts, *The Last Soviet Avant-Garde: OBERIU – Fact, Fiction, Metafiction*, Cambridge UP 1997, 125. Charms and Vvedenskij also used the singular form of this mysterious term (i.e. "chinar'") to sign their texts ca. 1925-1927. See, Druskin, J. S. "Chinari," *Аврора* 6 (1989): 103-115.

18   Between 1934 and 1941, OBERIU poets contributed one hundred and thirty-seven works to the journals Еж and Чиж, while earlier, between 1928 and 1931, they published there only ninety-one texts. During the second period, Vvedenskij's works appeared in print

OBERIU poets' encounter with children's literature began in earnest in 1927. The initial suggestion that the experimental poets "write something for children" belonged to Olejnikov and Evgenij Shvarc, the two friends and writer-editors already in the employ of Detgiz. Nikita Zabolotsky writes that Olejnikov and Shvarc persuaded his father Nikolaj and his OBERIU co-conspirators, Charms and Vvedenskij, "that their novel poetic devices, their immediacy of perception and the amusing unpredictability of their bold 'collisions of meaning' would bring brilliant new color into publications for children."[19] This proposal was supported by Samuil Marshak – then one of the leading figures in the field of children's literature and a Detgiz literary consultant, who subsequently also became an avid contributor to both *Еж* and *Чиж*.[20] By inviting the "trans-sense poets" ("поэты-заумники") to write for children, the farsighted Marshak had hoped they would add to children's literature something novel, interesting and refreshing. "It seemed to me," Marshak recalled, "that these people may bring whimsy (причуду) into children's poetry in rhymes, repetitions and choruses, which are abundantly present in

---

fifty-four times, Charms's – thirty-nine, Zabolockij's (prior to his arrest) – thirty-nine, and Olejnikov's (also prior to his arrest), four times. This count includes a reprint, in the July issue of *Чиж* for 1936, of Vladimirov's playful poem "Самолет" ("Airplane"): it was originally published in the May issue of *Еж* for 1930. This original publication was devoid of ideological undertones, but in the re-print, the political twist was added by new illustrations depicting the poem's airplane against the backdrop of an imposing building reminiscent of the unrealized Palace of the Soviets.

19 Nikita Zabolotsky, *The Life of Zabolotsky*, ed. R.R. Milner-Gulland, trans. R.R. Milner-Gulland and C.G. Bearne, Cardiff 1994, 70. A member of OBERIU since its inception, Igor' Bachterev recalled some thirty years later that the initial invitation came in the early spring of 1927 during the intermission of the OBERIU poetry and prose reading by himself, Charms, Levin, Vaginov, Vvedenskij and Zabolockij at the Chamber Music Circle of Friends in Leningrad. I. Bachterev and A. Razumovskij, "О Николае Олейникове," in *День поэзии*, Leningrad 1964, 154. At the time of this encounter, both Shvarc and Olejnikov, who technically was not a member of the group and with whom Charms and his OBERIU colleagues had close ties, were already writing for the children's magazines *Новый Робинзон* and *Красный галстук*. Subsequently, both Olejnikov and Shvarc became *Еж* and *Чиж* contributors and the de facto editors. For more on the genesis of OBERIU collaboration in these journals, see Ch. 6 ("The Oberiu poets") of Elena Sokol, *Russian Poetry for Children*, Knoxville 1984, 122-151.

20 Initiated by Kornej Chukovskij, in the late 1920s, the children's section of the State Publishing House was labeled "Marshak's Academy" due to the key role Marshak played in it. Originally it was located on the fifth floor of the House of Books (Дом книги) on Nevsky Prospect. For more on the goings-on and creative environment at the children's section, see I. Rachtanov, *Рассказы по памяти*, Moscow 1971, 137-182; "Nikolaj Chukovskij," in *Мы знали Евгения Шварца*, ed. Z.A. Nikitina, L.N. Rachmanov, and S.L. Cimbal, Leningrad, Moscow 1966, 24-41; E. M. Raush-Gernet, *Нина Гернет – Человек и Сказочник*, St. Petersburg 2007, 54-61.

children's folklore all over the world."²¹ Chukovskij's daughter Lidija, who at the time served as a Detgiz secretary, perceived that in OBERIU poets' "youthful and flamboyant experimentation" Marshak recognized "talent and an acute feeling of the word. In their 'trans-sense-ness' (заумничанье), he saw something quite precious for children's literature – their penchant for word play."²² Recalling this episode much later, Marshak himself admitted that the OBERIU poets in fact exceeded his expectations and managed to do much more than just create palindromes (перевертыши), tongue twisters (скороговорки), and refrains (припевы).²³ Indeed, quite paradoxically, Charms and Vvedenskij succeeded in becoming popular Soviet children's writers and were known almost exclusively as such until the rediscovery of their adult writings in the 1960s.

3 OBERIU in *Еж* and *Чиж*: The First Period (1928-1931)

During the first period of writing for *Еж* and *Чиж*, the poets of OBERIU actively contributed to these journals in a variety of genres, which, in addition to short works based on wordplay and repetition, included poems, humorous, fantastical and realistic short and serialized stories, riddles, feature essays (очерки) and articles (статьи). In many instances, these texts displayed elements of what has been described as the poetics of the OBERIU's works for children, namely the element of play, a variety of metric combinations and deformations, repetitions, fantastical elements, comic and anecdotal situations and ironic portrayals.²⁴ In spite of their poetic homogeneity, OBERIU's *Еж* and *Чиж* contributions differed from poet to poet in terms of their ideolog-

---

21 Lidija Chukovskaja, *В лаборатории редактора*, Archangelsk 2005, 304.
22 Ibid., 304.
23 Adrian Makedonov, *Николай Заболоцкий. Жизнь. Творчество. Метаморфозы*, Leningrad 1968, 161.
24 For a detailed discussion of the OBERIU's children's poetics, see V. A. Rogachev, "Своеобразие поэтики 'обериутов,'" in *Проблемы детской литературы*, Petrozavodsk 1979, 38-46. In his recollections, Rachtanov also touches upon certain elements of OBERIU's children poetics, including those of the little-studied works by Vladimirov (Rachtanov, *Рассказы по памяти*, 137-182). Among the reviews contemporary to OBERIU, of note is B. Ja. Buchshtab's perceptive article "Стихи для детей" ("Poems for Children"), in which the Formalist critic, addressing Charms's writing for children in particular, identifies such elements as repetitions, parallelisms and alternation of rhythmic, syntactic and formal-sound schemes. Buchshtab's essay, which appeared in *Детская литература. Критический сборник*, ed. A. Lunacharskij (Moscow and Leningrad 1931), was one of several OBERIU-friendly reviews published in the same collection. For more on this seminal volume, see Shubinskij, *Жизнь человека*, 302-305. For an insightful discussion of the formal elements of OBERIU stories for children (and their juxtaposition

ical commitment and, therefore, ultimate suitability for the new proletarian project. For instance, Olejnikov and Zabolockij treated the desired political and topical themes and subject matter diligently and frequently. These poets' willingness to comply with the party line contrasted with a nearly complete disregard for such themes in Charms and Vladimirov's texts, whereas Vvedenskij may be positioned somewhere in-between. In the first two years of the publication of Еж (1928-1929), Olejnikov and Zabolockij penned most of the ideologically appropriate material. In such texts as "Праздник" ("Celebration"), "Отто Браун" ("Otto Braun"), "Сколько тебе лет?" ("How Old are You?"), "Пионеры шведские и пионеры советские" ("Swedish and Soviet Pioneers"), the writers celebrated Soviet holidays, featured Soviet and foreign pioneers, told stories about international communists and the victorious Red Army, and addressed the anti-colonial theme.[25]

Along with his OBERIU friends, Olejnikov lived in two parallel universes. In his private world, he wrote poetry for adults, which, like that of Charms and Vvedenskij, was published only sparsely during his lifetime.[26] In the other, public sphere, Olejnikov edited children's journals and, between 1928 and 1931, actively wrote for them. Overall, during this period, Olejnikov published twenty-six different texts in both Еж and Чиж – more than any other OBERIU author.[27] Olejnikov's contributions to the journals differed substantially from his unpublished, clandestine writings in terms of their genre, thematic orientation and didactic qualities. Written predominately in prose, his Еж and Чиж texts were in line with the journals' general editorial policy: they strove to educate Soviet children in the new ways of thinking and appreciating Soviet values. This, of course, could hardly have been otherwise: an early and ardent supporter of the new regime, Olejnikov fought for the Red Army in

---

with the OBERIU works for adult readers), see *The Man with the Black Coat. Russia's Literature of the Absurd*, ed. George Gibian, Evanston 1987.

25 In *Еж*: 3, 1928; 5, 1928; 2, 1928; 8, 1928.
26 Copied by hand, committed to memory and passed around, Olejnikov's adult texts were nonetheless known and held in great esteem by his contemporaries. They continued to be remembered after his untimely and tragic demise. In their recollections, Bachterev and Razumovskij briefly examine some of Olejnikov's works for grown-ups and, establishing their proximity to the writings of "Koz'ma Prutkov," a fictional author of fables, aphorisms, and nonsense verses invented by the Zhemchuzhnikov brothers, cite some of the rare publications (appearing, in particular, in the mid-1930s). Bachterev and Razumovskij, "О Николае Олейникове," 154-160. In his monograph on Zabolockij, Makedonov provides a list of Olejnikov's published adult poetry. The critic also examines the satirical aspects of Olejnikov's works for adult audiences (165). See also recollections of Olejnikov, his adult poetry and his work at Detgiz in Rachtanov, *Рассказы по памяти*, 137-142.
27 By comparison, Zabolockij published twenty-one texts, Vvedenskij, nineteen, Charms, seventeen, and Vladimirov, seven.

FIGURE 4.2   Nikolaj Olejnikov's photograph from *Ёж* 5 (1929), 36

the Civil War and joined the Communist Party in 1920.[28] Even though ultimately he had arrived at a somewhat ironic understanding of the Soviet way of life, which was manifested in his adult works, his public authorial persona was that of a diligent transmitter of the Bolshevik ethos into the field of children's literature.[29] In his stories for children, Olejnikov paid tribute to the new Soviet holidays, praised Communist leaders, and depicted heroic episodes in the history of the young Soviet republic. He also told adventure stories, the principal hero of many of which was his literary *alter ego*, Макар Свирепый (Makar the Fierce) – a daring and adventurous member of the Det-

---

28 Zabolotsky, *The Life of Zabolotsky*, 70. As noted by Mejlach, Olejnikov's party affiliation at times effectively precluded him from full-scale participation in OBERIU public appearances and readings. "Дверь в поэзию открыта…," 23.

29 In his essay, Mejlach points to S. Poljakova's analysis of Olejnikov's adult works. The critic detected in them the poet's ironic perception of Soviet realities as well as traces of mockery. "'Я испытывал слово на огне…,'"47. For a recent discussion of Olejnikov's reaction to everyday life (быт) in Soviet Russia of the late 1920s and early 1930s, see Oleg Lekmanov and Michail Sverdlov, "Жизнь и стихи Николая Олейникова," in *Николай Олейников. Число неизреченного*, Moscow 2015, 105-106.

giz editorial team who, pictorially resembling Olejnikov, travelled the world as far as Africa and America to promote *Еж* and rescue his comrades-in-arms from the hostile capitalist and fascist adversaries. Especially noteworthy in this connection are "Удивительные приключения Макара Свирепого" ("Incredible Adventures of Makar the Fierce"), "Новые приключения Макара Свирепого" ("New Adventures of Makar the Fierce"), and "Макар Свирепый в Америке" ("Makar the Fierce in America").[30] These stories were serialized in the form of comic strips in which Boris Antonovskij's illustrations accompanied Olejnikov's captions.[31] On other occasions, the artist depicted Makar the Fierce (Olejnikov) in the company of his other *Еж* colleagues, one of whom was often Charms's *Еж doppelganger* Иван Хармсович Топорышкин (Ivan Charmsovich Toporyshkin [Littleaxe]) – a member of the journal's editorial team. Toporyshkin happened to be Makar the Fierce's best friend, an inventor, and a woodworker. He also appeared in one of Charms's most playful, absurd, and popular *Еж* poems.[32]

From the very beginning, Zabolockij welcomed the opportunity to write for children, which, among other advantages, secured him "a regular income."[33] In 1928-1931, he contributed to *Еж* and *Чиж* more often than Charms, Vvedenskij and Vladimirov.[34] Zabolockij's writings often appeared under the pen-

---

30   *Еж* 5-7, 1929; *Еж* 13, 15/16, 17/18, 22/23, 1930; *Еж* 4, 6, 10, 14, 19/20, 21, 22, 1931.

31   Some of Olejnikov's stories were also published in book form. For a list of Olejnikov's books for children, see "Книги Николая Олейникова" in Nikolaj Olejnikov, *Вулкан и Венера. Стихотворения*, St. Petersburg 2004, 170-171.

32   "Иван Топорышкин" ("Ivan Littleaxe"), in *Еж* 2, 1928. For more on Toporyshkin-Charms, see Shubinskij, *Жизнь человека*, 265-273.

33   Zabolotsky, *The Life of Zabolotsky*, 70. Although other factors may have been at play, the extant evidence suggests that financial considerations played a major role in the OBERIU poets' writing for children in general and for *Еж* and *Чиж* in particular. This was their principal, if not the only, source of income. Remuneration from writing for children and for *Еж* and *Чиж* was vital for Charms. This was something that the poet stressed, for example, in his correspondence with colleagues. See, for instance, drafts of Charms's letters to Boris Zhitkov of October 1936, in which the poet delineates his dire monetary situation and asks his older colleague for advice on how to secure the most advantageous contractual and financial conditions for the publication of his translation of Wilhelm Busch's writings. Daniil Charms, "Письма Борису Степановичу Житкову," October 9, 1936, and n/d, Russian National Library, Manuscript Division, The Archive of Ja. S. Druskin, Fund 1232, File 389. And yet, in her recollections, Charms's wife and widow Marina Malich (Durnovo) suggested that Charms took his writing for children seriously and argued against the prevalent critical assumption that her husband wrote for children only to secure an income. Vladimir Glocer, *Марина Дурново. Мой муж Даниил Хармс*, Moscow 2015, 71.

34   In addition to the twenty-one texts Zabolockij published in *Еж* and *Чиж* between 1928 and 1931, ten of his other pieces appeared in the journals during the interim period, i.e. in 1931-1932.

FIGURE 4.3   Nikolaj Olejnikov as Makar the Fierce
ILLUSTRATION FROM *ЕЖ* 11 (1928), 8

name "Яков Миллер" ("Jakov Miller") and included both poetry and short prose pieces with many of the texts expressing what a later Soviet critic called the "pathos of the heroic traditions of the revolution."[35] Often published as

---

35   Makedonov, *Николай Заболоцкий*, 168.

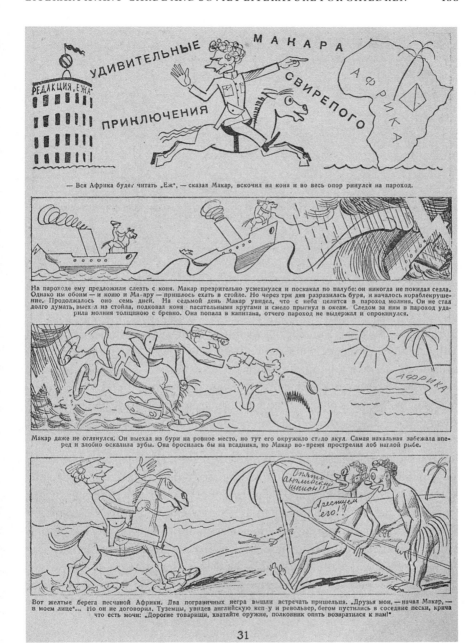

FIGURE 4.4 "Incredible Adventures of Makar the Fierce," in *Еж* 5 (1929), 31

FIGURE 4.5 "Makar the Fierce (Olejnikov) and Ivan Charmsovich Toporyshkin (Charms)"
ILLUSTRATION BY BORIS ANTONOVSKIJ FROM *ЕЖ* 6 (1929), 23

autonomous booklets, Zabolockij's *Еж* and *Чиж* texts told stories about Red Army soldiers, pioneers, world revolutions, shock workers (ударники), the struggle of German communists with the local Fascists and capitalists, and the Soviet elections.³⁶ Zabolockij's penchant for "political and literary conformism," as Mejlach puts it, resulted in an array of ideologically acceptable imagery (i.e. collective farmers, laborers, the October Revolution, hammer and sickle, etc.) seen frequently in the texts addressing the socialist construction and the proletarian class warfare.³⁷ Like Olejnikov, Zabolockij also partook in the establishment of the tradition of venerating deceased Soviet leaders. Illustrative of this tendency are his poems "Восемь лет без Ленина" ("Eight Years without Lenin") and "Прощание" ("Farewell").³⁸ Lavishly illustrated by Nikolaj Travin and featuring an enormous statue of Lenin who is pointing with his right hand to Soviet Russia's bright future and industrial success, "Восемь лет..." extols the dead Bolshevik leader as a proletarian hero, while "Прощание" is devoted to the memory of the Leningrad party boss, Sergej

---

36 See, for instance, Zabolockij's stories "Красные и синие" ("The Reds and the Blues," in *Еж* 3, 1928) and "Песня ударников" ("Shock Workers' Song," in *Чиж* 9/10, 1930).

37 See, for instance, Zabolockij's poem about a Soviet collective farm, "Маслозавод" ("A Butter Factory," in *Чиж* 11, 1930), and his anti-kulak poem "Кулацкий маневр" ("A Kulak Maneuver," in *Еж* 18, 1931).

38 *Чиж* 1, 1932; *Еж*, Special issue, December 1934.

Kirov.³⁹ Although Zabolockij also published many texts which shunned the political themes and often reflected the OBERIU poets' proclivity for playfulness, (i.e. "Приключения врунов" ["Liars' Adventures"]), the ideologically oriented works nonetheless dominated his contributions to *Еж* and *Чиж* in those years as well as during the second period of his writing for the journals.

By contrast to Olejnikov and Zabolockij, Charms and Vladimirov by and large stayed within the purview of imaginative and playful, but politically neutral and noncommittal texts. Between 1928 and 1931, Charms contributed to *Еж* and *Чиж* many of the poems and short stories which established his reputation as an inventive and popular children's writer. These texts included the poem "Иван Иваныч Самовар" ("Ivan Ivanych Samovar"), which was both jocular and didactic; the adventure story "Рассказ о том, как Панкин Колька ездил в Бразилию, а Ершов Петька ничему не верил" ("The Story of Kol'ka Pankin's Travel to Brazil and Pet'ka Ershov not Believing Anything"), the absurd tongue-twister "Иван Топорышкин," a mathematical riddle "17 лошадей" ("17 Horses"), the adventure story "Во-первых и во-вторых" ("Firstly and Secondly"), the strange, meta-literary narrative "О том, как старушка чернила покупала," ("How an Old Woman Went Shopping for Ink"), and a hyper realistic poetic riddle "Почему" ("Why").⁴⁰ "Иван Иваныч Самовар" is one of Charms's better-known poems. It is a bouncy verse which employs many typically Charmsian devices (i.e. multiple repetitions, internal rhyme, and assonance) to deliver a gentle moral message about the disadvantages of laziness:

> Иван Иваныч Самовар
> был пузатый самовар,
> трехведерный самовар.
> В нем качался кипяток,
> пыхал паром кипяток,
> разъяренный кипяток;
> [...]
> Самовар Иван Иваныч!
> На столе Иван Иваныч!
> Золотой Иван Иваныч!
> Кипяточку не дает,

---

39   In the same December issue of *Еж* for 1934, Zabolockij's "Прощание" was complemented by Olejnikov's short story "Портрет" ("Portrait"), also a tribute to Kirov.
40   *Еж* 1, 1928; *Еж* 2, 1928; *Еж* 2, 1928; *Еж* 8, 1928; *Еж* 11, 1928; *Еж* 12, 1928; *Еж* 12, 1928.

опоздавшим не дает,
лежебокам не дает.⁴¹

Praised by contemporary critics as an outstanding example of Charms's mastery of "verbal play, where the whole narrative is given such a laughably single-minded (and very child-like) quality," this iconic poem exemplifies the apolitical lightheartedness which dominated Charms's contributions to *Еж* and *Чиж* in the early stages of his writing for the two journals.⁴²

Like Charms, the young Vladimirov, the great-grandson of the famous Russian romantic artist Karl Brjullov and a lover of yachts and sea travel, supplied *Еж* with poems and short stories in which word play and curious, anecdotal situations superseded the topical social themes. In the poem "Барабан" ("The Drum"), a tour de force tongue-twister "based entirely on incantatory verbal play," Vladimirov conveys a simple anecdote about a punctured drum taken by the drummer to Leningrad for repairs; in "Самолет" ("The Airplane"), he muses about the wonders of flying; while in "На яхте" ("On a Yacht"), he describes children's dreams of sea travel.⁴³ Illustrative of Vladimirov's playful but politically disinterested approach is perhaps one of his better-known poems, "Чудаки" ("The Eccentrics"). Published in the 6th issue of *Еж* for 1930, it features three absent-minded eccentrics who are given money and sent to the market to purchase various household items:

Я послал на базар чудаков,
Дал чудакам пятаков,
Один пятак
на кушак,
Другой пятак
на колпак,
А третий пятак
так.⁴⁴

---

41 "Ivan Ivanych Samovar / [He] was a big-bellied samovar, / A three-bucket samovar. / Boiling water was rolling in him, / Boiling water was puffing out steam, / Furious boiling water; [...] Samovar Ivan Ivanych! / On the table Ivan Ivanych! / Made of gold Ivan Ivanych! / [He] does not give any boiling water, / [He] does not give it to late-comers, / [He] does not give it to lazybones." Charms, "Иван Иваныч Самовар," in *Еж* 1, 1928, 28-29.
42 Kornej Chukovskij, *От двух до пяти*. Cited in Sokol, 133.
43 *Еж* 10, 1929. See Sokol, *Russian Poetry for Children*, 141-142; *Еж* 10, 1930; *Еж* 19/20, 1930.
44 "I sent the eccentrics to the market, / I gave them five-kopeck coins, / One five-kopeck coin / to buy a sash, / the other / to buy a bonnet, / and the third one / just because." Vladimirov, "Чудаки," in *Еж* 6, 1930, 20.

Along the way, the eccentrics forget which coin is meant to buy which item or serve which purpose, thus laying bare the absurdity of the situation, since all coins are of equal five-kopeck denomination. The eccentrics return when it is already dark and report, apologetically, the terrible confusion which prevented them from using the money.

> Только ночью пришли
> чудаки,
> Принесли мне назад пятаки.
> – Извините,
> но с нами беда:
> Мы забыли –
> который куда.
> Который пятак
> на кушак,
> Который пятак
> на колпак,
> А который пятак
> так.[45]

Vladimirov published only two short stories in *Чиж*: "Синяя точка" ("Blue Dot") and "На улице" ("On the Street").[46] Instructive at best, like his *Еж* texts, these stories were also ideologically neutral. Although almost none of Vladimirov's adult texts have survived, his *Еж* and *Чиж* poems and stories are vivid testimonies to the common ground he shared with his OBERIU colleagues in the use of linguistic and thematic playfulness and the absurd, as well as to his manifest prowess as a gifted writer for children.

Unique in their own way, Charms and Vladimirov's 1928-1929 *Еж* and *Чиж* texts have two characteristics in common. On the one hand, they are largely devoid of ideologically required themes and topics, and thus openly refuse to promote revolutionary pathos and Soviet values and contribute to the communist upbringing of the Soviet child; this feature, with regard to Charms in particular, did not go unnoticed by the proletarian critics and punitive or-

---

45 "Only at night did the eccentrics come back. / Our apologies, but a disaster had occurred: / we forgot – / which [coin] was meant to be used for which purpose. / Which five-kopeck coin was meant / to buy a sash, / which one was meant / to buy a bonnet, / and which one was meant / for no specific purpose." Ibid.
46 *Чиж* 7/8, 1930, and *Чиж* 10, 1931.

gans.⁴⁷ On the other hand, Charms and Vladimirov's *Еж* and *Чиж* contributions endure due to their verbal originality and lightheartedness. Wordplay, and tongue-in-cheek humor permeates these texts on so many different levels making them, as Isaj Rachtanov and Elena Sokol aptly demonstrated, both appealing and educational for children.⁴⁸

Vvedenskij also wrote for *Еж* and *Чиж* in the late 1920s and early 1930s, but the ideological suitability of his contributions varied. In 1928-29, his texts were akin to those of Charms and Vladimirov: they included many lighthearted poems and short stories in which ideology as such was largely absent. In "Фонарь" ("Lantern"), "Железная дорога" ("Railroad"), "Кто?" ("Who?"), "Рыбаки" ("Fishermen"), and "Лошадка" ("A Little Horse"), Vvedenskij described comic situations, often adding to them an element of a detective narrative, and touched upon a variety of themes, from railway travel and childhood fears to the difficult lot of fishermen and fantastical horses.⁴⁹ Even several of Vvedenskij's moralizing poems of this period were devoid of ideological overtones. In "Коля Кочин" ("Kolja Kochin"), for instance, the poet instructs children to help one another, but does not promote the Soviet collective spirit or address the socially significant theme of socialist construction.⁵⁰ A noticeable change in the treatment of politically-themed subject matter in Vvedenskij's *Еж* and *Чиж* contributions occurs in 1930-1931. This change was likely to have been informed by his sense of the shifting socio-political climate in the country in general, and in the field of literary production in particular. For *Еж*, Vvedenskij now writes texts that project a positive image of Soviet pioneers. He favorably compares Soviet accomplishments to those of pre-revolutionary Russia, and, like Olejnikov, produces verses which celebrate Soviet holidays.⁵¹ The journal reached its peak of ideological conformity in the second half of 1930. That year, Vvedenskij wrote for *Еж* "Туристы" ("Tourists"), "Подвиг пионера

---

47   Vladimirov's untimely death spared him from this criticism and the resultant repercussions. See Sokol, *Russian Poetry for Children*, 128.
48   Rachtanov, *Рассказы по памяти*, 137-182. Sokol's insightful exposition is especially noteworthy. The critic posits that play in Charms's texts for children "falls into two categories: linguistic play, which helps build and exercise children's developing language skills, and intellectual play, which [...] facilitates their mental development. In these works, he succeeded in channeling his own seemingly boundless capacity for play toward children." Sokol, *Russian Poetry for Children*, 133.
49   *Еж* 6, 1929; *Еж* 3, 1928; *Еж* 3, 1929; *Еж* 4, 1929; *Еж* 8, 1929.
50   *Еж* 9, 1929.
51   See, for instance, Vvedenskij's poems "Зима кругом" ("Winter All Around," in *Еж* 5, 1930); "Турксиб" ("The Turkestan–Siberian Railway," in *Еж* 7, 1930); and "1-е мая" ("May the First," in *Еж* 8, 1930).

Мочина" ("Pioneer Mochin's Exploit") and "Октябрь" ("October") – poems in which he addressed the theme of socialist construction, heralded the establishment of Soviet control in Central Asia, and rationalized the revolutionary events of 1917.[52] The same year, similar poems by Vvedenskij appeared in *Чиж*, along with a plethora of his texts devoid of ideology. A curious case in point, which additionally illustrates Vvedenskij's effort to comply with the social demand of the day, is a short poem entitled "Не позволим" ("We will not Allow"). Published in December 1931 issue of *Чиж*, it upheld the banning of the Christmas tree and the Soviet policy of denigrating Christmas:

Не позволим мы рубить
молодую елку,
не дадим леса губить
вырубать без толку.
Только тот, кто друг попов,
елку праздновать готов.
Мы с тобой – враги попам,
рождества не надо нам![53]

Pedestrian in its poetics and militant in tone, the poem is best understood as part and parcel of the period's country-wide anti-religious propaganda.[54] The books Vvedenskij wrote and published in 1931 mirrored the politically correct nature of his *Еж* and *Чиж* texts, such as "Не позволим." For instance, in his *Конная Буденного* (*Budennyi's Cavalry*), Vvedenskij valorizes the valiant army of workers, sailors, peasants and partisan warriors, calls on the proletarians of Moscow, Petrograd and the Urals to wage a war on the bankers, merchants and

---

52 "Туристы" (in *Еж* 12, 1930); "Подвиг пионера Мочина" (in *Еж* 14, 1930), and "Октябрь" (in *Еж* 19/20, 1930).

53 "We will not allow to cut / a young fir tree, / we will not permit the ruination of the forests / which are logged pointlessly. / Only he, who is a friend of the clergy, / is prepared to celebrate Christmas. / You and I – we are enemies of the clergy, / And we have no use for christmas!" Vvedenskij, "Не позволим," *Чиж* 12, 1931, 6. Note that "Рождество" ("Christmas") was spelled in the poem with the lower-case "р[r]" to demonstrate the holiday's by then diminished status.

54 In this issue of the journal, Vvedenskij's short poem complemented Anatolij Finogenov's propagandistic story "Без елки" ("Without a Christmas Tree"). Illustrated with anti-religious children's drawings, it delineated the Bolsheviks' efforts to eradicate persisting pre-revolutionary traditions of celebrating Christmas. Another example of Vvedenskij's politically correct contributions to *Чиж* during this period is the poem entitled "Мы на слет" ("We are off to a Congress," in *Чиж* 7/8, 1930). It tells of Soviet pioneers heading off to a pioneer congress in the German city of Halle.

generals of the *ancien régime*, and rallies against the enemies of the Red Army: Baron Wrangel, Nestor Machno and an unnamed Polish "mister (pan)."[55]

Soviet Russia's changing socio-political climate affected not only Vvedenskij, but also Charms, who, toward the end of 1931, made a rather insincere effort to become a topical poet. In the 19/20th issue of *Еж* for that year, Charms published a short poem entitled "Что мы заготовляем на зиму" ("What We Preserve for the Winter"), in which he described young pioneers working at collective farms to gather berries, fruits, vegetables and mushrooms for the winter and then turning their preserves over to a state farm for future redistribution to workers' and children's cafeterias.[56] Speaking of this poem, critic Mal'skij suggested that Charms wrote it on a "social demand" ("социальный заказ") articulated by Marshak himself.[57] Despite containing some of the necessary topical vocabulary and the acceptable imagery and ideas (i.e. laborer, kolkhoz, pioneers busy with socially useful work), this poem in prose subverts the seriousness of the socialist intent by including typically Charmsian absurd elements. The latter are especially noticeable in the poem's advice to collect, along with fruits and vegetables, cockroaches as chicken feed for the winter. Equally amusing is the last stanza's vision of a new Soviet child-artist, who is urged to find green clay by the river and make out of it little men (человечков), and possibly himself, a pioneer at work in the summer. Charms concludes the poem by telling his readers that this clay pioneer would then be cast in iron or bronze and put on prominent display in a museum. The poem's playful absurdity led to it being singled out during Charms's interrogations after his December 1931 arrest. Pressed by the OGPU, the poet condemned it as "anti-Soviet" and "harmful," and confessed to a ridiculous charge that he had

---

55 Aleksandr Vvedenskij, *Конная Буденного*, Leningrad 1931.
56 This was not the only early text in which Charms, uncharacteristically, used tendentious but topical vocabulary and imagery. As Sokol points out, the text of Charms' book *Театр (Theater)* published with Marshak's help in 1929, contained stanzas worthy of Majakovskij's propagandistic ROSTA Windows: "Распроклятого буржуя в три минуты уложу я / Девочка-комсомолка не боится волка" ("I will topple down the accursed bourgeois in three minutes / A Young Communist girl is not afraid of a wolf"). Sokol, *Russian Poetry for Children*, 133. M. Nechaeva also discusses three poems by Charms which were published in 1931 in the journal *Октябрята* (*Octobrists*): "Влас и Мишка" ("Vlas and Mishka"), "Сдали в срок" ("They Turned It in on Time"), and "Миша Гришу вызывает" ("Misha is Challenging Grisha"). As the critic explains, these texts presented "typical sketches from Soviet life, with its obligations to the state, the competitive spirit, and the fight for supremacy in everything." M. N. Nechaeva, "'Где голы короли – опасны дети,' или В чем виноват Хармс?" in M.R. Balina and V.I. Vjugin, eds., *"Убить Чарскую..." Парадоксы советской литературы для детей, 1920-е – 1930-е гг.*, St. Petersburg 2013, 284-285.
57 I. Mal'skij, "Разгром ОБЕРИУ: материалы следственного дела," in *Октябрь* 11 (1992), 169.

intentionally replaced the valid socio-political theme of a pioneer camp with a theme that pertained more to the natural sciences. Charms further acknowledged that this substitution shifted the Soviet child's attention away from the "active-social elements of Soviet life" ("активно-общественных элементов советской жизни") presumably toward the contemplation of fun but pointless issues.[58]

Charms and Vvedenskij's effort to write on relevant topics did not help them avoid political persecution. In 1931 both poets, as well as their seemingly conformist *Еж* and *Чиж* colleague and fellow-*oberiut*, Zabolockij, came under attack from the militant critics whose rhetoric was unleashed by the iconoclastic Cultural Revolution. As Fitzpatrick explains, it was a spontaneous, aggressive and violent movement of young proletarian and communist activists against the conservative cultural alliance between Narkompros (the state Commissariat of Enlightenment led by Anatolij Lunacharskij) and the "bourgeois" intelligentsia who dominated the cultural landscape of the NEP era. Also known as "the class war on the cultural front," the Cultural Revolution was not instigated at the highest levels of party leadership. Its vanguard was made up of lesser authorities and grass-roots groups, with the agitprop department of the Party Central Committee, the Komsomol, the Communist Academy and the Revolutionary Association of Proletarian Writers (RAPP) taking the lead.[59] The radical character of the Soviet class war on the cultural front was reflected in the period's *Правда* (*Truth*) editorials, and, inasmuch as it concerned literature in general and writing for children in particular, in the Bolshevik Party resolution of August 15, 1931.[60] Entitled "Об издательской работе" ("On Publishing"), this directive demanded that publishing in Soviet Russia [ought to]

---

58 "Протоколы допросов Д. И. Хармса," in"...*Сборище друзей, оставленных судьбою*," Vol. 2, 524-532.

59 Fitzpatrick, "Cultural Revolution," 35-36. At the same time, it may be argued that class war on the cultural front was, in fact, inspired by the Soviet leadership; with Stalin in charge, the government declared 1929 to be the year of the "great break with the past," which saw, on the one hand, the reversal of the New Economic Policy (NEP) instituted under Lenin, as well as the ruthless enforcement of urban-style industrialization and compulsory collectivization in the countryside, and, on the other hand, the promulgation of the rhetoric of heightened class struggle. The latter resulted in the drive toward the liquidation of the *kulaks* "as a class" and in the excesses of the Cultural Revolution.

60 Two *Правда* editorials are especially noteworthy. The May 18, 1928, editorial urged the Soviet people "to forge the armor of socialist culture which [...] must be an impenetrable wall protecting us [...] from alien class influences, bourgeois degeneration, petty-bourgeois wavering and the blunting of revolutionary vigilance in the face of the more cultured class enemy." Intensifying this rhetoric, the second editorial, of September 2, 1928, urged the populace "to drive out all traces of liberal culture-mongering from cultural work and conduct it as *proletarian struggle* for the real creation of a new culture." Cited in Fitzpatrick, 42.

support the state agenda in every possible way: for instance, by creating works that depicted more deeply and comprehensively the "heroism of [...] class struggle" and "the growth of the new people – the heroes of socialist construction."[61] The resolution also called for the mobilization of the masses for socialism and, reiterating the dictums of *Правда* editorials, emphasized the need to expose and fight petty-bourgeois ideologies and other deviations from the Leninist line.[62]

In the four years of the Cultural Revolution "the proletarian organizations exercised great administrative and coercive power," and encouraged every kind of harassment of conservative intellectuals, non-party specialists and Soviet bureaucrats. At the same time, Party ideologues began to see signs of political deviation in artists' uncritical attitudes toward "bourgeois culture" and apoliticism.[63] A product of this turbulent time, the resolution "Об издательской работе" signaled a new campaign to rid Soviet literature of undesirable, "petty-bourgeois," elements.[64] In their fourth year of writing for *Еж* and *Чиж* and now on the payroll of the state publishing house, a factor which undoubtedly made OBERIU more susceptible to public scrutiny, Charms, Vvedenskij and Zabolockij (as well as their mentors, Marshak and Chukovskij) found themselves targets of proletarian criticism. Its new defining characteristic was attacks against specific personalities. Critics publicly identified names of deviant men-of-letters and supplied them with such worrisome labels as "a counter-revolutionary" and "an anti-Soviet writer." In their comprehensive accounts of Charms's life and work, critics Kobrinskij and Shubinskij investigated rhetorical clichés and ideological criteria of such criticism. Two of the hostile articles, penned by the OBERIU poets' Detgiz colleagues Ol'ga Berggolc and Abram Serebrjannikov, are especially noteworthy as they put forth accusations which were almost immediately replicated in the OGPU charges leveled against Charms and Vvedenskij. Serebrjannikov attacked Charms's poem "Миллион" ("Million") as well as Vvedenskij and Zabolockij's rather acquiescent *Еж* poems "Письмо Густава Мейера" ("Gustav Meier's Letter") and

---

61   See the section "О задачах издательской работы" ("On the Tasks of the Publishing Work") of the decree "Об издательской работе. Постановление ЦК ВКП(б) от 15 августа 1931 г.," in *Советская печать в документах*, Moscow 1961, 332-334.

62   Ibid. This rhetoric, put to practice in the course of the Cultural Revolution, was also conveyed in the Bolshevik Party's earlier pronouncements. See, for instance, "О политике партии в области художественной литературы. Резолюция ЦК ВКП(б) от 18 июля 1925 г.," and "О мероприятиях по улучшению юношеской и детской печати. Постановление ЦК ВКП(б) от 23 июля 1928 г.," in *Советская печать в документах*, 73-77; 244-246.

63   Fitzpatrick, "Cultural Revolution," 37, 42.

64   Shubinskij, *Жизнь человека*, 305.

"Восток в огне" ("The East in Flames") as hackwork in his article entitled "Золотые зайчики на полях детской литературы" ("Golden Bunnies on the Fields of Children's Literature"), published on November 15, 1931 in the journal *Смена* (*Shift*).[65] Despite these texts' compliant nature (Vvedenskij and Zabolockij's poems, for instance, expressed distinct anti-bourgeois and anti-imperialist sentiments), the critic nonetheless found their writing to be of "low quality," presumably due to the poets' treatment of sacrosanct Soviet themes in a haphazard, ironic and playful manner. Similarly, in her article "Книга, которую не разоблачили" ("The Book That Was Not Exposed"), published in the newspaper *Наступление* (*Attack*), an organ of the Leningrad Association of Proletarian Writers, Berggolc pronounced the poets' choice of themes unacceptable. In particular, she parsed and attacked Charms's "Во-первых и во-вторых," "О том, как старушка чернила покупала," "Га-ра-рар," "Почему," "Рассказ моего папы" ("My Father's Story") and Vvedenskij's "Мяу" ("Meow"), "Поездка в Сухум" ("A Trip to Sukhum") and "Кто." Berggolc asserted that these texts were quite absurd: divorced from any kind of life experience, they took the child away from the realities of the day and put his class consciousness to sleep. Like Serebrjannikov, Berggolc also condemned Charms and Vvedenskij's treatment of the "pioneer theme," especially in such texts as Vvedenskij's "Подвиг пионера Мочина," and, again, Charms's "Миллион," works that, in her opinion, discredited worthy subject matter. Berggolc concluded her invective by stating that under the "current conditions of heightened class struggle," Charms and Vvedenskij's approach was nothing less than hostile and counter-revolutionary propaganda.[66] Although Serebrjannikov's and Berggolc's articles were just two of several such evaluations of OBERIU writings for children, they present classic examples of the thinking and power of young proletarian critics, who, as Fitzpatrick aptly put it, "shot words not bullets at the fleeing bureaucrat and wavering intellectual [...] which carried a real threat of deprivation of livelihood, loss of employment and employability."[67] In the case of Bachterev, Charms, Vvedenskij, and later Olejnikov and Zabolockij, public denigration in the mass media also meant incarceration and, in some instances, death. Facilitated by the criticism that aimed to annihilate dissent, the arrests of Bachterev, Charms and Vvedenskij in December

---

65   Illustrated by Vladimir Konashevich, "Миллион" was originally published as a book (Leningrad 1931). The poem appeared in *Чиж* only in 1935. "Письмо Густава Мейера," in *Еж* 15/16, 1931. "Восток в огне," in *Еж* 15/16, 1930. It was Zabolockij's poem, "Восток в огне," the line from which, "Солнышко, солнышко, золотые зайчики" ("Sun, sun, golden bunnies"), supplied Serebrjannikov with the title of his diatribe.

66   Kobrinskij, *Даниил Хармс*, 337.

67   Fitzpatrick, "Cultural Revolution," 36.

of 1931 concluded the first period of the OBERIU poets' collaboration with *Еж* and *Чиж*.⁶⁸

4   After Arrest and Exile: The Second Period of OBERIU's Collaboration with *Еж* and *Чиж* (1932-1941)

Charms and Vvedenskij survived their first imprisonment and resumed their work for Detgiz upon their return from exile in the fall and winter of 1932/33. However, in the three remaining years of *Еж* (1933-1935), the majority of OBERIU contributions to the journal came from Zabolockij, who published in it twenty-four pieces in total. Vvedenskij, in comparison, contributed nine works, while Charms and Olejnikov were published only once each.⁶⁹ A similar dynamic is observed with regards to their writing for *Чиж*. Taking the lead, Vvedenskij contributed twenty-seven texts to the journal, followed by Zabolockij, whose work was published there fourteen times. Charms and Olejnikov, again, were less prolific: the latter contributed only twice, while the former, seven times. Olejnikov was now increasingly preoccupied with editorial work, while Charms, as diagnosed by Kobrinskij, appeared to have been in the throes of a creative crisis exacerbated by his exile.⁷⁰ Conversely, the frequency of Zabolockij's contributions may be explained by his adaptation for children of François Rabelais' *The Life of Gargantua and of Pantagruel* and Jonathan Swift's *Gulliver's Travels*. *Еж* and *Чиж* serialized both translations throughout 1934 and 1935.⁷¹ It is only in the last six years of the publication of *Чиж* (1936-1941) that the ratio was reversed: after Olejnikov's demise

---

68   The history of Bachterev, Charms and Vvedenskij's arrests and the ensuing interrogations in the House of Preliminary Detention, during which Charms and Vvedenskij admitted to the charges closely resembling the accusations of Serebrjannikov and Berggolc, is well documented in critical literature and first and foremost in "...*Сборище друзей, оставленных судьбою,*" Vols. 1 and 2.

69   To the special December, 1934, issue of *Еж*, Olejnikov contributed the aforementioned imaginative and sympathetic short story "Портрет" about a little boy, Vanja, who had a fortuitous chance to draw a portrait of Kirov when the latter spoke at a meeting of factory workers. In 1935, Charms published the politically correct poem "Новый город" ("A New City"), which glorified socialist construction.

70   Kobrinskij, *Даниил Хармс*, 269-270.

71   "Повесть об удивительной жизни Великого Гаргантюа отца Пантагрюэля" ("A Novella about the Incredible Life of the Great Gargantua, Pantagruel's Father," in *Еж* 3-7, 9-12, 1934; 1-10, 1935) and "Гулливер у великанов" ("Gulliver in the Land of the Giants," in *Чиж* 5-12, 1935).

and Zabolockij's arrest, most OBERIU contributions came, predictably, from Charms and Vvedenskij.[72]

In the 1930s, the Soviet government continued its drive for economic development through the implementation of its Second and Third Five-Year-Plans. The cultural policy of this period was dominated by the introduction of Socialist Realism – the artistic doctrine which superseded the dubious accomplishments of the Cultural Revolution and put forth new thematic and formal parameters that would also determine the editorial direction of Soviet children's magazines. The ideological suitability of OBERIU *Еж* and *Чиж* texts of the 1930s retained elements of the dynamic of the pre-exile phase: ironically, prior to their arrests, Olejnikov and Zabolockij authored the greatest number of tendentious and politically correct material. In his rare contributions, Olejnikov told stories about brave Soviet parachutists, described heroic feats of children in the service of the revolution and extolled the fearless leadership of Red Army commanders in the Civil War.[73] Zabolockij, in turn, narrated ethnic fairy stories, which celebrated the intellectual superiority of "simple people" and laughed at the stupidity of the rich, and composed inspirational poems and didactic fairytales.[74] His adaptations of *Gargantua and Pantagruel* transmitted the rhetoric of anti-religious propaganda befitting Rabelais' own pronounced anti-clerical stance.[75] In addition, both Olejnikov and Zabolockij partook in the eulogizing of Kirov, following the latter's assassination in December of 1934. Many of the texts and images in the special, December, issue of *Еж* were devoted to the remembrance of the maverick Soviet leader. Olejnikov contributed to this effort with the short story "Портрет" ("Portrait"),

---

72 During this period, Charms published thirty-one pieces in *Chizh*, and Vvedenskij published eighteen.

73 See Olejnikov's short stories "Полет парашютиста Евсеева" ("Parachutist Evseev's Flight," in *Чиж* 1, 1934), "В октябрьскую ночь" ("On an October Night," in *Чиж* 11, 1935), and a longer story "Красный бант" ("The Red Bow," in *Чиж* 5, 1936).

74 See Zabolockij's adaptation of the Armenian fairytale "Хозяин и работник" ("Master and Man," in *Чиж* 4/5, 1934), his poem "Картонный город" ("Cardboard City," in *Чиж* 11, 1933) and the didactic "Сказка о кривом человеке" ("A Fairy-Tale about a Crooked Person," in *Чиж* 8, 1933).

75 The prologue, which preceded Zabolockij's adaptation of Rabelais's narrative, explicitly explained that the story was selected for its adamant and all-pervasive anti-religious satire ("Пролог," in *Еж* 3, 1934). Zabolockij was aware of this ethical predicament, confessing once to Leonid Lipavskij: "I signed the contract to rework *Gargantua and Pantagruel*. It seems that this work is even pleasant. Besides, I feel an affinity to Rabelais. Despite not being a believer, he [...] nonetheless kissed the Pope's hand. And I too, when it is necessary, kiss the hand of some Pope." Cited in Lipavskij, *Исследование ужаса*, Moscow 2005, 420.

while Zabolockij penned an impressionistic and sorrowful poem "Прощание" ("A Farewell"), which was also published in *Известия* (*News*). In addition, for *Чиж*, Zabolockij wrote a prose piece in verse entitled "Ночь в степи" ("Night in the Steppe"), in which he dramatized an episode from Kirov's propagandistic campaign in the Northern Caucasus during the Civil War. According to Zabolockij, the eloquence, simplicity, and conviction with which Kirov spoke about the fight waged by the Bolshevik workers and peasants against generals and princes captivated the attention of the indigenous people as they listened throughout the night.[76]

Vvedenskij continued to write on politically urgent subjects and themes, often incorporating ideologically charged imagery (i.e. pioneers, red flags) into his otherwise unbiased poetic texts. Among his most agenda-driven works for *Еж* were poems on such subjects as the importance of being familiar with the basics of military training and the value of growing healthy crops. These were the themes of his poems "4 хвастуна," ("4 Boasters"), and "Не отдавай сорняку урожай," ("Do Not Let the Weed Take the Crop").[77] For *Чиж*, Vvedenskij wrote about the Red Army, especially emphasizing its ability to resist the enemy and secure a peaceful life for Soviet children. He also published verses that promoted friendship among Soviet children of all nationalities, described festive May Day celebrations, and extolled the happiness of Soviet children in the summer camps and Soviet Russia in general.[78] In addition to these original texts, Vvedenskij also adapted several of the Grimm Brothers' fairytales for young readers. Appearing in *Еж* and *Чиж* throughout 1935, some of his adaptations expressed a tendentious, predominately anti-imperialist, sentiment.[79]

---

76   *Чиж* 12, 1934.
77   *Еж* 2/3, 1933; *Еж* 4, 1933.
78   See, for example, the poems "Пограничник" ("Boarder Guard," in *Чиж* 2/3, 1933), "Ивасик-танкист" ("Ivasik-the Tank Driver," in *Чиж* 4, 1938), "Приезжайте к нам!" ("Come and Visit Us," in *Чиж* 4, 1933), "Маша на паровозе" ("Masha is on the Locomotive," in *Чиж* 5, 1935), "Первое мая и девочка Мая" ("May First and a Girl Named Maja," in *Чиж* 4, 1939), "Маша в гостях у пионеров" ("Masha Visits Pioneers," in *Чиж* 7, 1935), and "Письмо бабушке" ("Letter to Grandma," in *Чиж* 4, 1940).
79   See, for instance, Vvedenskij's re-narration of the Grimm Brothers' "The Valiant Little Tailor." Published in the August, 1934, issue of *Чиж* under the title "Храбрый портной," it is mildly tendentious (for example, there is an episode in which a king flees his kingdom). Vvedenskij also adapted Grimm's "Волк и семеро козлят" ("The Wolf and the Seven Young Kids," in *Еж* 5, 1935), "Вшестером всю землю обойдем" ("How Six Made Their Way in the World," in *Еж* 7, 1935), "Муж и жена [Husband and Wife]" ("Frederick and Catherine," in *Еж* 10, 1935), "Соломинка, уголь и боб" ("The Straw, the Coal, and the Bean," in *Чиж* 3, 1935), "Семеро храбрецов [Seven Brave Men]" ("The Seven Swabians," in *Чиж* 4, 1935), and "Горшок каши [A Pot of Porridge]" ("Sweet Porridge," in Чиж 7, 1935).

It must be noted that Vvedenskij also wrote many less political – or not at all politicized – poems and short stories. These included his interpretation of Wilhelm Busch's slightly absurd poem about Max and Moritz that glorified disobedience, "Два класса учителя Басса" ("Two Classes of a Teacher Named Bass"), the whimsical "Что кому?" ("What to Whom?") and "Триста семьдесят ребят" ("Three Hundred and Seventy Children"), the light-hearted "Лагерная песня" ("A Camp Song"), the fantastical "Силач" ("Strongman") and "Стихи про орла, про лису, про медведя" ("A Poem About the Eagle, the Fox and the Bear").[80] In these and other playful and fantastic works, which numerically surpassed Vvedenskij's earlier output, the poet truly shone as an inventive and talented writer for children.

Unlike Vvedenskij who flourished in the 1930s, Charms reacted to the increased ideological control by withdrawing from direct political commentary. Between 1933 and 1938, he avoided any straightforward ideological content in his works for children; the only exception to this general tendency was his poem "Новый город" ("A New City," 1935), already mentioned in this essay. Published in *Еж*, the poem opens with a Lermontovesque but topical phrase "Скажи, товарищ" ("Tell Me, Comrade") and continues with a vivacious monologue of a narrator describing a rapid – in four years only! – transformation of a wooded hill and an empty field into a new Soviet metropolis. This miracle of urban design features bridges, tram cars, lavish gardens, and electrical turbines. The Soviet flag crowns all of these remarkable accomplishments:

Смотри! Прошло четыре года,
Зажегся новый день, и вот:
Преображенная природа
Над миром заново встает.
Бежит с холма трамвай шумливый,
Сады раскинуты кругом,

---

[80] Some of these texts were later published in book form. See Grimm Brothers, *Сказки*, Archangelsk 1939.
Еж 1, 1933; *Чиж* 1, 1933; *Еж* 2, 1934; *Еж* 8, 1934; *Еж* 1, 1935; *Чиж* 9, 1940. The opening lines of "Два класса учителя Басса," which tell of the resolve of the authorities in the city of Frankfurt to cut the number of school teachers to balance the city budget, may be read as a jab at a deleterious way of dealing with the working people in a capitalist society. The solution to the resultant shortage of teachers – to create an opening in the ceiling so that one teacher could instruct classes on both levels – is absurd and therefore laughable. See discussions of other renderings of Busch's eulogy to mischief in Maria Khotimsky's chapter on Soviet translations of poetry for children in this volume.

> И над толпою торопливой
> Советский флаг шумит крылом.[81]

Еж folded in 1935. Shortly prior and after its closure, Charms contributed mostly to *Чиж*. Between 1933 and 1938, he wrote fantastical adventure tales, erudite stories about "Умная Маша" ("Smart Masha"), and many inventive bits of prose and poetry, including ads urging *Чиж* subscribers to buy the journal. Among these were stories about "Профессор Трубочкин" ("Professor Pipekin"), amusing captions to "Как Маша заставила осла везти ее в город" ("How Masha Made the Donkey Take Her to the City"), the poem "Что это значит?" ("What Does This Mean?"),[82] and "Миллион," already attacked by the critics.[83] In the March issue of *Чиж* for 1937, Charms published a short limerick, "Из дома вышел человек" ("A Man Had Left His Home One Day"). It told a story of a man who once left his home on foot, walked for some time without eating, drinking or sleeping, then entered a dark forest and vanished. The concluding lines of the poem implored young readers to let it be known if the man were ever seen again:

> Но если как-нибудь его
> Случится встретить вам,
> Тогда скорей,
> Тогда скорей,
> Скорей скажите нам.[84]

The publication of this seemingly innocent poem had grave repercussions for Charms's position at Detgiz, and, as a consequence, his financial stability. In the context of Soviet Russia of the mid-1930s, at the height of Stalinist terror, the inexplicable disappearance of characters could easily be understood as an

---

81 "Look! Four years have passed, / A new day kindled, and behold: / Transformed nature / Rises above the world again. / A noisy tram is running down the hill, / The gardens spread all around, / And the wing of the Soviet flag is flapping / Over the hurried crowd." Charms, "Новый город," in *Еж* 5, 1935, 21.

82 *Чиж* 7, 8, 12, 1933; *Чиж* 2, 1934; *Чиж* 12, 1935. Curiously, in the latter poem, in addition to the message meant to promote the journal, Charms included many protagonists from his and Vvedenskij's works published in *Чиж* throughout the year.

83 *Чиж* 9, 1935. During his second interrogation on December 18, 1931, Charms identified "Миллион," along with "Что мы заготовляем на зиму" (in *Еж* 19/20, 1935), as "politically harmful" and "hostile," admitting to his substitution of the socially significant themes with those pertinent to natural sciences in both poems. See "Протоколы допросов Д. И. Хармса" in "*...Сборище друзей, оставленных судьбою,*" Vol. 2, 526-527.

84 "But if somehow you happen / to meet him, / Then quickly, / Then quickly, / Quickly tell us." Charms, "Из дома вышел человек," in *Чиж* 3, 1937, 18.

allusion to mass arrests and, thus, "disappearances" of people. As Kobrinskij suggests, when published, the poem was likely to have been interpreted as a political blunder, the outcome of which was Detgiz's refusal to publish Charms or pay him for the texts that had already appeared in print.[85] Charms's difficult relationship with Detgiz and his precarious financial situation took on a troublesome new dimension three months later, when the secret police arrested his colleague and editor, Nikolaj Olejnikov.

Although conditions at Detgiz seemed to have ultimately improved, Charms's noncommittal attitude toward writing for children changed in the wake of the publication of "Из дома вышел человек" and Olejnikov's demise. Between 1938 and 1940, he often wrote pro-Soviet, patriotic texts. For example, in "Это резвый конь ребенок" ("This is a High-Spirited Horse Child"), Charms told his *Чиж* readers how fine horses for the Red Army were raised; in his translation of Lev Kvitko's poems "Танкист" ("Tank Driver") and "Песня про пограничника" ("A Song about Boarder Guard"), he described little children desirous of becoming tank drivers and fighting the Fascists, and extolled the well-trained and valiant Soviet border guards always ready to keep the enemy away.[86] Charms's most conformist text for children of this period was, perhaps, "Первомайская песня" ("The First of May Song"). Published in the April 1939 issue of *Чиж*, it urged boys and girls to rise early in order to get a place near the podium at the May Day rally so that they could be the first to greet Stalin with a resounding "Hurray." Although it is difficult to ascertain, the writing of such tendentious texts was perhaps a desperate measure on Charms's part: he needed to secure a much-needed income. It may also be argued that, to some extent, Charms's transition to writing politically engaged texts affected his poetics. The predominance of ideological content made his lively and playful verses more somber and straightforward; the element of the absurd was reduced considerably, if not completely eradicated. Even then, every so often, as in the translation of Kvitko's "Танкист," young readers were treated to vintage Charms. Replete with syntactic repetitions and bouncy rhymes, this poem, one of his last published in *Чиж*, retained the recognizable hallmarks of his writings for children.

5   Conclusion

The OBERIU poets contributed to *Еж* and *Чиж* throughout these journals' runs. Their collective oeuvre was comprised of both topical and ideologically

---

85   Kobrinskij, *Даниил Хармс*, 381-387.
86   *Чиж* 3, 1938; *Чиж* 11, 12, 1938.

suitable texts, as well as those that claimed a degree of autonomy from matters of "proletarian" and "socialist" significance. The tendency towards more politicized output was more pronounced in Olejnikov, Zabolockij, and to some extent, Vvedenskij's writings, while the noncommittal approach was more characteristic of Charms and Vladimirov. Overall, the OBERIU poets' contributions did not substantially differ from the general content of these journals. Both *Еж* and *Чиж* contained texts and illustrations, which were predominantly propagandistic, aiming at molding a new Soviet individual.[87] But the journals also offered plenty of other works for children, which had little to do with the socialist agenda or propaganda purposes. Many of their authors, including the OBERIU detractor Berggolc, published ideologically neutral texts.[88] The irony and the tragedy that characterized OBERIU poets' work at Detgiz throughout their careers as children's writers (especially during the initial period of their writing for *Еж* and *Чиж*, before Charms and Vvedenskij were arrested and exiled) was grounded in the critics' negative reaction to their unsuspecting, yet at the same time outlandish and often shocking, public appearances and readings of their no less unorthodox adult works in 1928-1930, and earlier, before they even considered becoming children's authors. This initial hostile public reception was accentuated by the heightened ideological zeal of the Cultural Revolution. By the end of the first Five-Year Plan, the deleterious image of OBERIU acquired a purely negative connotation in the articles of young proletarian critics. Coupled with some of the member-poets' reluctance to fully embrace the spirit and the ideals of the first socialist state, this destructive response resulted in the ultimate rejection and persecution of OBERIU by the nascent Soviet establishment. Fortuitously, the trials and tribulations did not prevent them from writing for children. Although the legacy of some of Olejnikov, Vvedenskij, Zabolockij and even Charms's politically tendentious texts

---

87   In a recent study, Elvira Suzdorf remarks that *Ёж* made the editorial decision to include more propagandistic material in mid-1929, after the press criticized the journal for its lack of ideological content. Replicated in *Чиж*, this editorial policy was sustained, with various degrees of intensity, from the beginning of the 1930s onward. Both journals started to publish a significantly larger amount of material devoted to the Five-Year Plan, agricultural accomplishments, and the pioneer movement, as well as works on anti-clerical themes. Suzdorf surmised that generally *Еж* and *Чиж* differed favorably from other children's journals of the period, because their presentation of the ideological material was often artistically and creatively more attractive. Suzdorf, *Журналы "Еж" и "Чиж" в контексте советской детской печати 1920-1930-х гг. Автореферат диссертации*, Moscow 2011, 21, 26.

88   See, for instance, Berggolc's ideologically unassuming short story "Зима-лето попугай" ("Winter-summer Parrot," in *Чиж* 2, 1930).

is questionable, the artistic, educational and entertainment value of such poems as Charms's "Иван Иваныч Самовар," Vladimirov's "Чудаки," and Vvedenskij's "Коля Кочин" far outweighs the compromises that the authors had to make along the way. Arguably, neither *Еж* nor *Чиж* would have been able to acquire popularity and artistic excellence, appreciated by subsequent generations of publishers,[89] if it were not for the poems, short stories, and sketches written for them by the OBERIU poets.

Works Cited

Primary Sources

Bachterev, Igor'. "Тот месяц в Ташкенте," in *Об Анее Ахматовой. Стихи, эссе, воспоминания, письма*, ed. M. M. Kralin. Leningrad 1990, 216-223.

Bachterev, I., and A. Razumovskij. "О Николае Олейникове," in *День поэзии*. Leningrad 1964, 154-160.

Berggolc, Ol'ga. "Зима-лето попугай," in *Чиж* 2 (1930), 1-4.

Berggolc, Ol'ga. "Книга, которую не разоблачили," in *Наступление* 2 (1932), 2.

Bush, D. (Daniil Charms). "Озорная пробка," in *Еж* 1 (1928), 1-4.

Charms, Daniil. "17 лошадей," in *Еж* 8 (1928), 28.

Charms, Daniil. "Влас и Мишка," in *Октябрята* (1931).

Charms, Daniil. "Во-первых и во-вторых," in *Еж* 11 (1928), 16-19.

Charms, Daniil. "Врун," in *Еж* 24 (1930), 10-11.

Charms, Daniil. "Га-ра-рар," in *Еж* 12 (1929), 5-7.

Charms, Daniil. "Девять картин," in *Чиж* 6 (1941), 22.

Charms, Daniil. "Иван Иваныч Самовар," in *Еж* 1 (1928), 28-29.

Charms, Daniil. "Иван Топорышкин," in *Еж* 2 (1928), 21.

Charms, Daniil. "Из дома вышел человек," in *Чиж* 3 (1937), 18.

Charms, Daniil. "Как Маша заставила осла везти ее в город," in *Чиж* 2 (1934), 20.

Charms, Daniil. *Миллион*. Leningrad 1931.

Charms, Daniil. "Миллион," in *Чиж* 9 (1935), 11.

Charms, Daniil. "Миша Гришу вызывает," in *Октябрята* (1931).

Charms, Daniil. "Новый город," in *Еж* 5 (1935), 21.

Charms, Daniil. "О том, как старушка чернила покупала," in *Еж* 12 (1928), 11-16.

Charms, Daniil. "Песня про пограничника," in *Чиж* 12 (1938), 6-7.

Charms, Daniil. "Первомайская песня," in *Чиж* 4 (1939), 9.

---

89 As Suzdorf points out, the creators of the St. Petersburg-published children's journal *Еж и Чиж* (*The Hedgehog and the Finch*, since 2002) consider themselves to be the heirs to the traditions of the original Leningrad periodicals. Suzdorf, *Журналы "Еж" и "Чиж,"* 4.

Charms, Daniil. "Письма Борису Степановичу Житкову," October 9, 1936.
Charms, Daniil. *Полное собрание сочинений: В четырех томах*, ed.V. N. Sazhin. St. Petersburg 1997–2001.
Charms, Daniil. "Почему," in *Еж* 12 (1928), 28.
Charms, Daniil. "Профессор Трубочкин," in *Чиж* 7, 8, 12, (1933), 5-7 (7), 16-17 (8), 20 (12).
Charms, Daniil. "Рассказ о том, как Панкин Колька ездил в Бразилию, а Ершов Петька ничему не верил," in *Еж* 2 (1928), 1-12.
Charms, Daniil. "Сдали в срок," in *Октябрята* (1931).
Charms, Daniil. "Танкист," in *Чиж* 11 (1938), 18-19.
Charms, Daniil. *Театр*. Leningrad 1929.
Charms, Daniil. "Что мы заготовляем на зиму," in *Еж* 19/20 (1931), 12-13.
Charms, Daniil. "Что это значит?" in *Чиж* 12 (1935), 11.
Charms, Daniil. "Это резвый конь ребенок," in *Чиж* 3 (1938), 7.
Chukovskaja, Lidija. *В лаборатории редактора*. Archangelsk 2005.
Daudet, Alphonse. *Тайна дедушки Корнилия*, adapted by Konstantin Vaginov. Moscow, Leningrad 1927.
Finogenov, Anatolij. "Без елки," in *Чиж* 12 (1931), 4-6.
Glebova, Tatjana Nikolajevna and Vladimir Vasiljevich Sterligov. *Письма Сафоновой Елене Васильевне, ca. Feb. - March, 1942*, in Manuscript Section, State Russian Museum, St. Petersburg, Fund 212, File 256, 1-3.
Grimm Brothers. *Сказки*, narrated by Aleksandr Vvedenskij. Archangelsk 1939.
Levin, Dojvber, and Daniil Charms. "Друг за другом," in *Еж* 9 (1930), 21-25.
Miller, Jakov (Nikolaj Zabolockij). "Восемь лет без Ленина," in *Чиж* 1 (1932), 4.
Miller, Jakov (Nikolaj Zabolockij). "Восток в огне," in *Еж* 15/16 (1930), 1-4.
Miller, Jakov (Nikolaj Zabolockij). "За окном," in *Чиж* 4/5 (1932), 6.
Miller, Jakov (Nikolaj Zabolockij). "На площадку," in *Чиж* 6 (1932), 2.
Miller, Jakov (Nikolaj Zabolockij). "Песня ударников," in *Чиж* 9/10 (1930), 6.
Miller, Jakov (Nikolaj Zabolockij). "У моря," in *Чиж* 7/8 (1931), 3.
Olejnikov, Nikolaj. "В октябрьскую ночь," in *Чиж* 11 (1935), 1-4.
Olejnikov, Nikolaj. "Красный бант," in *Чиж* 5 (1936), 4-12.
Olejnikov, Nikolaj. "Макар Свирепый в Америке," in *Еж* 4, 6, 10, 14, 19/20, 21, 22 (1931), 8-9, 20-21, 18-19, 20-21, 24-25, 31-31, 17.
Olejnikov, Nikolaj. "Новые приключения Макара Свирепого," in *Еж* 13, 15/16, 17/18, 22/23, (1930), 22, 16, 10, 28.
Olejnikov, Nikolaj. "Отто Браун," in *Еж* 5 (1928), 15.
Olejnikov, Nikolaj. "Полет парашютиста Евсеева," in *Чиж* 1 (1934), 8-10.
Olejnikov, Nikolaj. "Портрет," in *Еж* (Dec., 1934), 22-25.
Olejnikov, Nikolaj. "Праздник," in *Еж* 3 (1928), 15-19.
Olejnikov, Nikolaj. "Сколько тебе лет?" in *Еж* 2 (1928), 22-29.

Olejnikov, Nikolaj. "Удивительные приключения Макара Свирепого," in *Еж* 5-7 (1929), 31-33, 34-36, 30.
Rachtanov, Isaj. *Рассказы по памяти*. Moscow 1971.
Serebrjannikov, Abram. "Солнышко, солнышко, золотые зайчики," in *Смена* (Nov. 15, 1931).
Vladimirov, Jurij. "Барабан," in *Еж* 10 (1929), 28-29.
Vladimirov, Jurij. "На улице," in *Чиж* 10 (1931), 14-15.
Vladimirov, Jurij. "На яхте," in *Еж* 19/20 (1930), 22-28.
Vladimirov, Jurij. "Самолет," in *Еж* 10 (1930), 14-15.
Vladimirov, Jurij. "Самолет," in *Чиж* 6 (1936), 12-13.
Vladimirov, Jurij. "Синяя точка," in *Чиж* 7/8 (1930), 12-13.
Vladimirov, Jurij. "Чудаки," in *Еж* 6 (1930), 20.
Vvedenskij, Aleksandr. "1-е мая," in *Еж* 8 (1930), 15-17.
Vvedenskij, Aleksandr. "4 хвастуна," in *Еж* 2/3 (1933), 41-43.
Vvedenskij, Aleksandr. *Конная Буденного*. Leningrad 1931.
Vvedenskij, Aleksandr. "Волк и семеро козлят," in *Чиж* 5 (1935), 23-27.
Vvedenskij, Aleksandr. "Вшестером всю землю обойдем," in *Еж* 7 (1935), 23-27.
Vvedenskij, Aleksandr. "Горшок каши," in *Чиж* 7 (1935), 6-9.
Vvedenskij, Aleksandr. "Два класса учителя Басса," in *Еж* 1 (1933), 46-47.
Vvedenskij, Aleksandr. "Железная дорога," in *Еж* 3 (1928), 12-13.
Vvedenskij, Aleksandr. "Зима кругом," in *Еж* 5 (1930), 18.
Vvedenskij, Aleksandr. "Ивасик-танкист," in *Чиж* 4 (1938), 2-3.
Vvedenskij, Aleksandr. "Коля Кочин," in *Еж* 9 (1929), 29-31.
Vvedenskij, Aleksandr. "Кто?" in *Еж* 3 (1929), 30-33.
Vvedenskij, Aleksandr. "Лагерная песня," in *Еж* 8 (1934), 8.
Vvedenskij, Aleksandr. "Лошадка," in *Еж* 8 (1929), 30-31.
Vvedenskij, Aleksandr. "Маша в гостях у пионеров," in *Чиж* 7 (1935), 1-6.
Vvedenskij, Aleksandr. "Маша на паровозе," in *Чиж* 5 (1935), 1-6.
Vvedenskij, Aleksandr. "Муж и жена," in *Еж* 10 (1935), 26-29.
Vvedenskij, Aleksandr. "Не отдавай сорняку урожай," in *Еж* 4 (1933), 13.
Vvedenskij, Aleksandr. "Не позволим," in *Чиж* 12 (1931), 6.
Vvedenskij, Aleksandr. "Октябрь," in *Еж* 19/20 (1930), 8-10.
Vvedenskij, Aleksandr. "Первое мая и девочка Мая," in *Чиж* 4 (1939), 10-13.
Vvedenskij, Aleksandr. "Письмо бабушке," in *Чиж* 4 (1940), 5.
Vvedenskij, Aleksandr. "Письмо Густава Мейера," in *Еж* 15/16 (1931), 5-6.
Svedenskij, Aleksandr. "Пограничник," in *Чиж* 2/3 (1933), 4.
Vvedenskij, Aleksandr. "Подвиг пионера Мочина," in *Еж* 14 (1930), 7-11.
Vvedenskij, Aleksandr. *Подвиг пионера Мочина*. Moscow 1931.
Vvedenskij, Aleksandr. "Приезжайте к нам!" in *Чиж* 4 (1933), 1-2.
Vvedenskij, Aleksandr. "Рыбаки," in *Еж* 4 (1929), 11.

Vvedenskij, Aleksandr. "Семеро храбрецов," in *Чиж* 4 (1935), 14-17.
Vvedenskij, Aleksandr. "Силач," in *Еж* 1 (1935), 28-31.
Vvedenskij, Aleksandr. "Соломинка, уголь и боб," in *Чиж* 3 (1935), 1-4.
Vvedenskij, Aleksandr. "Стихи про орла, про лису, про медведя," in *Чиж* 9 (1940), 16-17.
Vvedenskij, Aleksandr. "Триста семьдесят ребят," in *Еж* 2 (1934), 27.
Vvedenskij, Aleksandr. "Туристы," in *Еж* 12 (1930), 1-3.
Vvedenskij, Aleksandr. "Турксиб," in *Еж* 7 (1930), 23.
Vvedenskij, Aleksandr. "Умный Петя," in *Чиж* 11/12 (1932), 1.
Vvedenskij, Aleksandr. "Фонарь," in *Еж* 6 (1929), 6-9.
Vvedenskij, Aleksandr. "Храбрый портной," in *Чиж* 8 (1934), 1-7.
Vvedenskij, Aleksandr. "Что кому?" in *Чиж* 1 (1933), 5-7.
Vvedenskij, Aleksandr. "Что это вы строите?" in *Чиж* 9/10 (1932), 1.
Zabolockij, Nikolaj. "Автобиография," in *Стихотворения*, Washington 1965.
Zabolockij, Nikolaj. "Гулливер у великанов," in *Чиж* 5 (1935), 7-11; 6 (1935), 1-5; 7 (1935) 9-13; 8 (1935), 9-13; 9 (1935), 16-20; 10 (1935), 20-24; 11 (1935), 8-10; 12 (1935), 7-9.
Zabolockij, Nikolaj. "Два обманщика," in *Еж* 12 (1935), 24-26.
Zabolockij, Nikolaj. "Картонный город," in *Чиж* 11 (1933), 1.
Zabolockij, Nikolaj. "Красные и синие," in *Еж* 3 (1928), 1-7.
Zabolockij, Nikolaj. "Кулацкий маневр," in *Еж* 18 (1931), 9.
Zabolockij, Nikolaj. "Маслозавод," in *Чиж* 11 (1930), 3-5.
Zabolockij, Nikolaj. "Ночь в степи," in *Чиж* 12 (1934), 2-3.
Zabolockij, Nikolaj. "Пионеры шведские и пионеры советские," in *Еж* 8 (1928), 22.
Zabolockij, Nikolaj. "Повесть об удивительной жизни Великого Гаргантюа отца Пантагрюэля," in *Еж* 3-7, 9-12 (1934); 1-10 (1935).
Zabolockij, Nikolaj. "Приключения врунов," in *Еж* 4 (1929), 22-26.
Zabolockij, Nikolaj. "Прощание," in *Еж* (Dec., 1934), 27.
Zabolockij, Nikolaj. "Сказка о кривом человеке," in *Чиж* 8 (1933), 10-13.
Zabolockij, Nikolaj. "Хозяин и работник," in *Чиж* 4/5 (1934), 14.
Барабан. Moscow 1923-1926.
Большевистская смена. Leningrad 1931-1932.
Ванька-Встанька. Leningrad 1936.
Воробей. Petrograd 1923.
Еж. Leningrad 1928-1935.
Костер. Leningrad 1936-1946, 1956.
Красный галстук. Leningrad 1926.
Маленькие ударники. Leningrad 1931-1932.
Новый Робинзон. Leningrad 1924-1925.
Октябрята. Leningrad 1931-1932.
Пионер. Moscow 1924-1925.
Сверчок. Leningrad 1937.

Чиж. Leningrad 1930-1941.

Юные товарищи. Moscow 1922.

Юные ударники. Leningrad 1930-1932.

"Дело № 2196-41 г.," in Valerij Sazhin, ed., *"...Сборище друзей, оставленных судьбою," А. Введенский, Л. Липавский, Я. Друскин, Д. Хармс, Н. Олейников. "Чинари" в текстах, документах и исследованиях в двух томах*, Vol. 2, *Д. Хармс, Н. Олейников*. Moscow 2000, 592-607.

"Об издательской работе. Постановление ЦК ВКП(б) от 15 августа 1931 г.," in *Советская печать в документах*. Moscow 1961, 332-334.

"О печати. Из резолюции Тринадцатого съезда РКП(б)," Section 12, in *Советская печать в документах*. Moscow 1961, 65-66.

"О политике партии в области художественной литературы. Резолюция ЦК ВКП(б) от 18 июля 1925 г.," in *Советская печать в документах*. Moscow 1961, 73-77.

"О мероприятиях по улучшению юношеской и детской печати. Постановление ЦК ВКП(б) от 23 июля 1928 г.," in *Советская печать в документах*. Moscow 1961, 244-246.

"Протоколы допросов Д. И. Хармса," in Valerij Sazhin, ed., *"...Сборище друзей, оставленных судьбою," А. Введенский, Л. Липавский, Я. Друскин, Д. Хармс, Н. Олейников. "Чинари"в текстах, документах и исследованиях в двух томах*, Vol. 2, *Д. Хармс, Н. Олейников*. Moscow 2000, 524-532.

Secondary Sources

Buchshtab, Boris. "Стихи для детей," in Anatolij Lunacharskij, ed., *Детская литература. Критический сборник*. Moscow, Leningrad 1931, 103-130.

Chukovskij, Kornej. *От двух до пяти*, in *Собрание сочинений в восьми томах*. Moscow 1968-1972.

Druskin, J. S. "Chinari," in *Аврора* 6 (1989): 103-115.

Fitzpatrick, Sheila. "Cultural Revolution in Russia, 1928-1932," in *Journal for Contemporary History* 9:1, (January 1974), 33-52.

Gibian, George, ed. *The Man with the Black Coat. Russia's Literature of the Absurd*. Evanston, IL 1987.

Glocer, Vladimir. *Марина Дурново. Мой муж Даниил Хармс*. Moscow 2015.

Iljina, N. "Из истории детских журналов 20-30-х годов," in *Вопросы детской литературы*. Moscow 1958, 24-61.

Ippolitov, Arkadij. "Imaginationland, USSR," in Julian Rothenstein and Olga Budashevskaia, eds., *Inside the Rainbow. Russian Children's Literature 1920-1935: Beautiful Books, Terrible Times*. London 2013, 17-21.

Kobrinskij, Aleksandr. *Даниил Хармс*. Moscow 2009.

Lekmanov, Oleg, and Michail Sverdlov. "Жизнь и стихи Николая Олейникова," in *Николай Олейников. Число неизреченного*. Moscow 2015, 11-211.

Lipavskij, Leonid. *Исследование ужаса*. Moscow 2005.

Makedonov, Adrian. *Николай Заболоцкий. Жизнь. Творчество. Метаморфозы*. Leningrad 1968.

Mal'skij, I. "Разгром ОБЕРИУ: материалы следственного дела," in *Октябрь* 11 (1992), 166-191.

Mejlach, Michail. "Дверь в поэзию открыта...," in M. Mejlach, ed., *Александр Введенский. Полное собрание сочинений в двух томах*, Vol. 1. Moscow 1993, 10-39.

Mejlach, Michail. "Я испытывал слово на огне и на стуже," in *Поэты группы ОБЕРИУ*. St. Petersburg 1994, 5-58.

Nechaeva, M. N. "'Где голы короли – опасны дети,' или В чем виноват Хармс?" in M.R. Balina and V.I. Vjugin, eds., *"Убить Чарскую..." Парадоксы советской литературы для детей, 1920-е – 1930-е гг*. St. Petersburg 2013, 272-287.

"Nikolaj Chukovskij," in Z.A. Nikitina, L.N. Rachmanov, and S.L. Cimbal, eds., *Мы знали Евгения Шварца*. Leningrad, Moscow 1966, 24-41.

Olejnikov, Aleksandr. "Последние дни Николая Олейникова," in Valerij Sazhin, ed., *"...Сборище друзей, оставленных судьбою," А. Введенский, Л. Липавский, Я. Друскин, Д. Хармс, Н. Олейников. "Чинари"в текстах, документах и исследованиях в двух томах*, Vol. 2, *Д. Хармс, Н. Олейников*. Moscow 2000, 573-580.

Olejnikov, Aleksandr. "Книги Николая Олейникова" in Nikolaj Olejnikov, *Вулкан и Венера. Стихотворения*. St. Petersburg 2004, 170-171.

Raush-Gernet, E. M. *Нина Гернет – Человек и Сказочник*. St. Petersburg 2007.

Roberts, Graham, *The Last Soviet Avant-Garde: OBERIU – Fact, Fiction, Metafiction*. Cambridge UP 1997.

Rogachev, V. A. "Своеобразие поэтики 'обериутов,'" in *Проблемы детской литературы*. Petrozavodsk 1979, 38-46.

Shtejner, Evgenij. *Авангард и построение нового человека. Искусство советской детской книги 1920-х годов*. Moscow 2002.

Shubinskij, Valerij. *Даниил Хармс. Жизнь человека на ветру*. St. Petersburg 2008.

Sokol, Elena. *Russian Poetry for Children*. Knoxville, TN 1984.

Suzdorf, Elvira. *Журналы "Еж" и "Чиж" в контексте советской детской печати 1920-1930-х гг. Автореферат диссертации*. Moscow 2011.

Ustinov, A.V. "Дело детского сектора Госиздата 1932 года: Предварительная справка," in G. A. Morev, ed., *Михаил Кузмин и русская культура XX века: тезисы и материалы конференции 15-17 мая 1990 г*. Moscow 1990, 125-136.

Zabolotsky, Nikita. *The Life of Zabolotsky*, ed. R.R. Milner-Gulland, trans. R.R. Milner-Gulland and C.G. Bearne. Cardiff 1994.

PART 2

*Constructing Socialism, Building the Self:
History, Ideology, Narrative*

∴

CHAPTER 5

Re-imagining the Past for Future Generations: History as Fiction in Soviet Children's Literature

Marina Balina

> *At the core of culture is a continuous dialogue between myth and history, 'plain invention' and 'the core of historical fact.'*
> RICHARD SLOTKIN, "Fiction for the Purpose of History"[1]

∴

1   Introduction

In 1979, the cultural historian Jakov Gordin, who has contributed much to our understanding of the role of history in the human experience, wrote:

> We are all subject to the historical nostalgia that comes from a temporal rupture. Only high-level historical prose is capable of psychologically removing the sensation of such a break. Its mission is to restore the connection between times, to create a spiritual-emotional unified field. For it is only under these conditions that an exchange of spiritual experience takes place.[2]

How applicable would such a comment be to Soviet children's historical prose? Would we be justified in speaking of the creation of a "unified emotional field" vis-à-vis a young reader whose historical knowledge was formed under the influence of the history textbooks that Soviet authorities were constantly rewriting? In the 1920s, Osip Mandel'shtam commented that recent historical cataclysms had "cast people out of their own biographies like balls out of pool-table pockets."[3] What, then, was supposed to become of historical prose, a

---

1   Richard Slotkin, "Fiction for the Purpose of History," in *Rethinking History*, 9:2 (2005), 221-36.
2   Jakov Gordin, "Связь времен," in *Детская литература* 11 (1979), 42-45.
3   Osip Mandel'shtam, *Конец романа*, Moscow 1990, 203-4.

genre called upon to "restore the connection between times," at the time when that connection was being consciously severed?

According to Boris Dubin, historical prose in Soviet Russia arose "already at the very initial stage of the formation of the 'new literature'"; specifically, it was "to sum up the revolutionary takeover and the Civil War."[4] In this, Dubin notes, the new historical narrative was being created during a period in which Soviet power "was proclaiming a demonstrative ideological 'break with the past.'" He elaborates: "Essentially, proclaiming such a 'break' meant one thing: the victorious power and its adherents were claiming exclusive ownership of the interpretation of social life, both of people's pre-revolutionary history and of the post-revolutionary present."[5] It was this worldview that shaped the new historical prose for children, wherein the "voice of power" determined which historical material and historical personages were suitable for the post-revolutionary generation of readers.

Soviet-era historical prose for children, like, indeed, most children's literature of the period, is most frequently examined in terms of ideological dogma.[6] This approach is entirely understandable, as it was precisely historical knowledge that was called upon to incarnate such crucial Soviet postulates as, for instance, patriotism and proletarian internationalism, and to render a Marxist understanding of the "formational approach" to history – i.e., the alternation of economic formations amid class struggle – and thus reduce to a minimum the role of culture and the individual in a given historical process. Still, as I would like to show in this chapter, the Soviet-era children's historical tale was a contradictory phenomenon. In fact, I intend to demonstrate that it was precisely in this genre that historical knowledge, which Gordin saw as necessary to restore temporal connection, fulfilled its (however ambiguous) formative

---

4   Boris Dubin, "Семантика, риторика и социальные функции прошлого: к социологии советского и постсоветского исторического романа," Moscow 2003, 30-31.
5   Ibid.
6   See A. V. Fateev, *Сталинизм и детская литература в политике номенклатуры СССР (1930-е-1950-е гг.)*, Moscow 2007; Julie K. deGraffenried, *Sacrificing Childhood: Children and the Soviet State in the Great Patriotic War*, Lawrence, KS 2014; Ben Hellman, *Fairy Tales and True Stories: The History of Russian Literature for Children and Young People (1574-2010)*, Leiden and Boston 2013; Jacqueline Olich, *Competing Ideologies and Children's Literature in Russia, 1918-1935*, Saarbruecken 2009; Felicity Ann O'Dell, *Socialization through Children's Literature: The Soviet Example*, Cambridge 1978; and some chapters in Catriona Kelly, *Children's World: Growing Up in Russia, 1890-1991*, New Haven and London 2007. An interesting and original view on early Soviet children's literature may be found in Sara Pankenier Weld, *Voiceless Vanguard: The Infantilist Aesthetic of the Russian Avant-Garde*, Evanston 2014. Comparative aspects of Soviet-era children's literature and children's literature of the American Left are presented in Julia L. Mickenberg, *Learning from the Left: Children's Literature, the Cold War, and Radical Politics in the United States*, Oxford, UK 2006.

role. In my opinion, historical narrative allows us to observe various trends in children's literature discourse, from blatant propaganda to the no less blatant dissent-stance of *fronda* – the complex phenomenon that Gordin terms an act of "oppositionist enlightenment."[7] In some of my other works, I have expressed the hypothesis that the processes that led Soviet literature as a whole to "petrify" – the *Verstaatlichung* of which the German scholar Hans Günther has written – generally began in literature for children, spreading thence to its adult counterpart.[8] The onset of this calcification may be traced to the 1920s, nearly a decade before the Socialist Realist canon took final hold in Soviet literature.[9]

Commentary on the infantilism of Soviet literature is not new (Evgenij Dobrenko has written in great detail on this subject),[10] but such childishness has its place in children's literature, and it was precisely therein that ideological devices were developed in draft form, so as then to be transferred into literature for adults. By its very nature, children's literature allowed opposing discourses to exist in parallel, even though they overlapped only for a time. For instance, both ecological prose and "playful poetry" ("игровая поэзия") served as testing grounds for ideological discourses later adapted for grown-up readers.[11] Observing the process by which the "new literature" took shape, Marietta Chudakova writes of the rise of the "social demand" ("социальный заказ"), which she asserts was not at all synonymous with administrative pressure: "This was more a matter of sensing whether the orientation of one's work was 'necessary' or 'not necessary' – a feeling one got from the event that was the revolution."[12] The "usefulness" principle had been in use already

---

7 Jakov Gordin, "Занятия историей как оппозиционный акт," in *Знамя* 3 (2001), 180-84.
8 Hans Günther, *Die Verstaatlichung der Literatur: Entstehung und Funktionsweise des sozialistisch-realistischen Kanons in der sowjetischen Literatur der 30er Jahre*, Stuttgart 1984.
9 See Marina Balina, "Литературная репрезентация детства в советской и постсоветской России," in N. B. Barannikova and V. G. Bezrogov, eds., *И спросила кроха: Образ ребенка и семьи в педагогике постсоветской России*, Moscow and Tver 2010, 20-38; see also Balina, "Советская детская литература как культурная институция," in N. L. Lejderman, M. N. Lipoveckij, and M. A. Litovskaja, eds., *Русская литература XX века (1930-е – середина 1950-х годов)*, Vol. 1, Moscow 2014, 331-50.
10 See Evgenij Dobrenko, "Соцреализм и мир детства," in Hans Günther and Evgenii Dobrenko, eds., *Соцреалистический канон*, St. Petersburg 2000, 31-41; as well as his *Формовка советского читателя: социальные и эстетические рецепции советской литературы*, St. Petersburg 1997.
11 On "playful poetry" see Elena Sokol, *Russian Poetry for Children*, Knoxville 1984; Larissa Rudova, "Invitation to a Subversion: The Playful Literature of Grigorii Oster," in Marina Balina and Larissa Rudova, eds., *Russian Children's Literature and Culture*, New York and London 2008, 325-43.
12 M. O. Chudakova, *Избранные работы в двух томах*, Vol. 1, Moscow 2001, 310.

among nineteenth-century populist producers and critics of children's literature; among revolutionary democrats, such theoreticians as Nikolaj Chernyshevskij and Nikolaj Dobroljubov discussed the categories of "usefulness" and "necessity," while Konstantin Ushinskij followed the imperative of "useful and consequential reading" in compiling his Детский мир (*Children's World*) anthology (1861).[13] Analyzing the career of Sergej Auslender,[14] the author of children's historical tales who was fairly popular in the 1920s, Chudakova quotes from Boris Peres's 1928 foreword to his collected works that outlines, she argues, the fundamental aspects of the "necessary" *adult* literature of the Socialist Realist future: "an entertaining plot that makes you read the book continuously through to the end; heroism on the part of the main character that elicits the reader's sympathy; [...] and finally, the lightness, simplicity, and harmoniousness of language and construction."[15] Describing Auslender's tales in his foreward, Peres particularly highlighted their "educational function," of which Chudakova writes:

> First conceived in the works of those writing for children or for Red Army personnel, the 'educational function' had not yet made the qualitative and quantitative leap; was not yet a necessary feature of a work of the new literature. This could only be brought about through the efforts of a writer whose caliber differed from Auslender's; but those in his set did their part to lay the groundwork for the reconfiguration of the literary corpus.[16]

At its very beginning, children's literature already responded to all the demands that would soon begin to be made of literature for adults: thus, for instance, an important merit of the children's writer (in this case, Auslender) is that he "makes readers put themselves in a character's shoes and experience along with them the sensation of heroic uplift, of self-sacrifice in battle, a fervid togetherness with one's own, and a potent hatred toward one's enemies."[17]

---

13   F. I. Setin, ed., *Русская детская литература*, Moscow 1972, 6-8.
14   Sergej Auslender was arrested in 1937 and perished in the Gulag in 1943. His historical tales for children dealt with the history of Russia ("Пугаченок" ["The Pugachev Cub"], 1925; "Пугачевщина" ["The Pugachev Uprising"], 1928) as well as other countries ("Ли Сяо" ["Li Tsao"], 1927; "Маленький Хо" ["Little Ho"], 1929).
15   Chudakova, *Избранные работы в двух томах*, Vol. 1, 315. See also: Auslender, *Собрание сочинений*, Vol. 1, Moscow 1928.
16   Chudakova, 316.
17   Ibid.

Also to this writer's credit is the "vigorous mood" he inculcates, which the author of the foreword describes as particularly valuable for "our kids, needful as they are not just of certain prospects to discover, but of the creation of a mood that would help them understand and perceive these prospects."[18] Thus, even before the rise of the Socialist Realist canon, children's literature forms its future foundations, such as polarization (a clear opposition between *us* and *them*) and the demand that the work be accessible, since the new literature is aimed not at the reader schooled by the previous epoch, but at *"those who so far have not been readers at all."*[19] In particular, this latter requirement manifests a kind of switch: adult discourse is being saddled with the demands of children's literature, and is invariably infantilized.[20] It would be fair to suggest, then, that it was precisely children's literature that was turned into a laboratory – of poetics, of structure, of genre mutation – for its "elder comrade," literature for adults. However, by the time the postulates of accessibility, vigor, and the "us and them" binary became integral to Socialist Realist discourse, children's literature had already accumulated definite practices in dealing with these demands. Children's discourse, including the historical variety, handled these readymade formulae with considerably more freedom and inventiveness than what literature for adults could afford. In this chapter, my goal is to analyze various practices of children's historical writing that demonstrate the genre's eclecticism, with a special emphasis on the authors of historical tales who managed to create, alongside purely propagandistic pieces, works that went far beyond any political dictate.

2   Historical Prose for Children: Toward a History of the Genre's Emergence

The historical tale as a standalone genre took shape in Russian children's literature over the course of several centuries. Natalja Zhitomirova, the genre's Soviet researcher, pinpoints three types of historical works for children: the historical-biographical, historical-everyday, and historical-revolutionary.[21] The

---

18   Ibid.
19   Ibid., 317; emphasis mine – MB.
20   For more detail on the literature of Socialist Realism, see Dobrenko, "Соцреализм и мир детства"; and Omri Ronen, "Детская литература и социалистический реализм," in Hans Günther and Evgenii Dobrenko, eds., *Соцреалистический канон*, St. Petersburg 2000, 969-80.
21   N. N. Zhitomirova, *Советская историко-художественная книга для детей и ее воспитательное значение*, Leningrad 1975, 16-17.

latter variant took shape mainly during the Soviet period, but the former two emerged in Russia as early as in the latter half of the eighteenth century. Thus, a key contribution to the genre was *Vorbereitung zur Weltgeschichte für Kinder* by August Ludwig von Schlözer, a German historian who was a member of the Academy of Sciences in St. Petersburg and taught at the boarding school run thereby. By the standards of children's books of the time, this work, prepared by Schlözer specifically for his pupils, was remarkable in that it used simple language and presented historical events in an engaging manner.[22] Historical sketches also appear in Nikolaj Novikov's *Детское чтение для сердца и разума* (*Children's Reading for Heart and Mind*, 1785-89). In particular, historical prose aimed at young Russian readers featured translated foreign works, for instance, Pierre Blanchard's *Плутарх для юношества* (*Plutarch for Young Men*, 1809) and Catherine-Joseph-Ferdinand Girard de Propiac's *Плутарх для молодых девиц* (*Plutarch for Young Ladies*, 1816-1820).[23] A significant contribution to the development of the "story about history" was made by Sergej Glinka who produced a ten-volume *Русская история* (*Russian History*) for children, as well as a collection of *Русские исторические и нравоучительные повести* (*Russian Historical and Edifying Tales*).[24] From 1819 to 1824, Glinka published the journal *Новое детское чтение* (*New Reading for Children*), which ran many of his own writings devoted specifically to Russian history. First and foremost, this veteran of the Franco-Russian War commonly known as the Patriotic War of 1812 (Отечественная война 1812 года), was keen to teach children how to be patriotic.[25]

Other Russian authors who contributed to the formation of children's historical prose included, first and foremost, Aleksandr Vel'tman, Anna Zontag, Aleksandra Annenskaja, Vasilij Avenarius, and Vasilij Nemirovich-Danchenko. Especially prominent in the development of nineteenth-century historical prose style was Aleksandra Ishimova who undertook the daunting task of retelling Nikolaj Karamzin's *История Государства Российского* (*History of the Russian State*, 1816-1829) for children. Her *История России в рассказах для детей* (*History of Russia in Stories for Children*, 1837) opens with the following message to the little readers:

---

22   Ibid., 16.
23   Pjer Blanshar, *Плутарх для юношества, или Жития славных мужей всех народов, от древнейших времен доныне*, Moscow 1809; Zhirar de Propiak, *Плутарх для молодых девиц, или Краткия жизнеописания славных жен*, Moscow 1816-1820 (Parts 1 through 4).
24   S. N. Glinka, *Русская история*, St. Petersburg 1817; Glinka, *Русские исторические и нравоучительные повести*, Moscow 1810.
25   I. N. Arzamasceva and S. A. Nikolaeva, eds., *Детская литература*, Moscow 2005, 167.

Dear children: You like to hear stories of brave heroes and beautiful princesses; you like tales of kind and wicked sorceresses. But wouldn't you like it even more if you could hear not a fairytale, but [a tale of] reality, that is, the honest-to-goodness truth? Listen then, and I shall tell you about the deeds of your ancestors.[26]

A key advantage of Ishimova's *История* was not so much its adherence to fact as its ability to convey historical material to a child-reader. She frequently interrupts her story to address her audience; maintaining an atmosphere of constant dialogue, she asks her readers' opinion and makes reference to the knowledge they have already acquired: "You recall that, almost at the very outset of the Russian state, the Novgorodians were disobedient to their princes."[27] The emotional force of her narrative and the constant "immersion" of the reader in the historical process ("You can scarcely imagine how happy the inhabitants of Smolensk were to rejoin their ancient fatherland!"[28]) lends a tone of authenticity to the historical past and, at the same time, encourages one to trust the narrator. Through Ishimova's artful storytelling, history does not just come alive in pictures of the past, but becomes an integral part of the present. The author helps children get their bearings in history, which is no longer a collection of dead dates and figures, but, rather, a compendium of lively images of people and events. Interestingly, although Ishimova's treatment includes both the everyday and biographical variants of the genre, both forms of the historical narrative she employs are based in actuality. What she relates is first and foremost a *historical fact* enriched with details from everyday life and from the lives of particular individuals.

Petr Furman was particularly prominent among nineteenth-century historical novelists for children. He produced historical-biographical tales about Menshikov (*Александр Данилович Меньщиков*, 1847) and Peter the Great (*Саардамский плотник* [*The Carpenter of Saardam*], 1849). His heroes also included Generalissimo Aleksandr Suvorov (1848) and Grigorij Potemkin (1848). Strictly segregating his readers by gender, Furman also wrote a three-part historical "tale for young ladies" about Princess Nataljia Dolgorukova (1856). Predominant in his interpretation of history is not the fact but personality; he revives thereby the idea of the "плутарх" ("plutarch") – a term that

---

26   Aleksandra Ishimova, *История России в рассказах для детей. От древних славян до Петра I*, St. Petersburg 2013, 7.
27   Ibid., 61.
28   Ibid., 199.

had been used in Russia for collections of edifyingly heroic examples from history.

From the very beginning of its existence, the nineteenth-century children's historical tale was developing as an utterly free, even eclectic, genre, combining historical with biographical narratives, historical tales with narratives of everyday life, and history with adventure narratives. We see "mutations" of this sort not only in the early years of the genre, but also in the works that appeared later, for example, *Впереди веков: историческая повесть из жизни Леонардо да Винчи* (*Ahead of the Centuries: A Historical Tale from the Life of Leonardo da Vinci*, 1910) or *Король и инфант: историческая повесть времен Филиппа Второго* (*King and the Infante: A Historical Tale from the Time of Phillip II*, 1915) by Al. Altaev (Margarita Jamshchikova, 1872-1959). This eclecticism would survive and be preserved in the Soviet period. It enabled the conjoining of two key aspects of historical narrative identified by Gabriele von Glasenapp as *Historie* (that which is narrated in fictional form) and *Geschichte* (a particular historical event, most frequently perceived in the historical narrative as a decorative background).[29] As von Glasenapp describes, authors of historical tales may preserve the specificity of a historical event (*Geschichte*) while allowing themselves considerable latitude in inventing characters – dramatis personae of the *Historie* who serve to disseminate historical knowledge, even as the truly historical personages are locked within specific historical bounds.

Skillfully combining historical knowledge and didacticism (children were to take their cue from great men) with an entertaining adventure element, historical prose became one of children's literature's favorite genres. At different periods in Russia's development, interest in national history competed with the demand for works on world history, but both were quite broadly represented in children's reading matter. The primacy of works about Russian history was always a considerable part of children's experience with history as a concept; in particular, as Lomonosov put it, Russian history was to teach the young how to take pride in "the glorious name of the Russian people."[30]

When it came to antiquity as a part of world history, the situation was somewhat more complex. Beginning with the first Russian гимназии (secondary schools) of the eighteenth century, such as Pastor Johann Ernst Glück's Moscow school (1702-08), the knowledge of ancient languages was a require-

---

29   Gabriele Glasenapp, "'Was ist Historie? Mit Historie will man was.' Geschichtsdarstellungen in der neueren Kinder- und Jugendliteratur," in Glasenapp and Gisela Wilkending, *Geschichte und Geschichten: die Kinder- und Jugendliteratur und das kulturelle und politische Gedächtnis*, Frankfurt am. Main 2005, 15-40.

30   Michail Lomonosov, *О воспитании и образовании*, Moscow 1991, 24.

ment for academic success and career advancement. Their students studied ancient history during Greek and Latin lessons, mostly when reading texts in the original. Broadly promoted during the reign of Aleksandr I, the knowledge of Greek, however, was substantially curtailed in the subsequent period, when Nicholas I was tsar. According to his contemporaries' reminiscences, the Decembrists' revolt of 1825 and the Revolution of 1848 instilled in Nicholas I "an antipathy toward the Greek," since he believed that ideas of the republic as a form of governance spread through that language. Therefore, ancient history was removed from secondary-school curricula in 1848, "lest there be any discussion as to the advantage of a republic over a monarchy."[31] Interestingly, the Russian statesmen whom Soviet historiography presented as notorious "conservatives," such as ministers of education Sergej Uvarov and Dmitrij Tolstoj, consistently espoused the need for a classical education. They believed that language study provided deep knowledge of history and life, and that historical tales "from ancient life," typically of the historical-biographical variety, would focus the students' attention on "noble examples of the behavior of the ancients."

The model of classical education was renounced immediately after the October revolution. One of the first Bolshevik decrees of 1918 established "единые трудовые школы" ("unified labor schools"), in which instruction was to focus on information about productive work, with historical knowledge centered first and foremost on the history of labor – the prism through which the history of society was to be conceptualized generally. Classical languages were brushed aside as "dead" knowledge. Speaking at the Third Congress of the Komsomol (1920), Lenin insisted on "purging" education of the "unnecessary carrion."[32] Thus, the post-revolutionary development of children's historical prose called for new rules and new priorities. The dependence of children's literature on the political situation in the country and a rapidly forming political correctness led to the creation of a particular *metatext* of the historical tale for the young. Now it had to include the following mandatory components: class struggle portrayed as the engine of historical progress; emphasis on the leadership role of the masses; an elevated revolutionary pathos serving as a key emotional mode and enlivening historical didacticism; and the framing of the historical space by means of the "us and them" binarity. Not surprisingly, predominant among historical tales for children were texts directly touching on

---

31   V. V. Davydov, A. M. Prochorov, and E. D. Dneprov, eds., *Российская педагогическая энциклопедия*, Moscow 1993, Vol. 1, 211-213.
32   Ibid., 392.

Russian revolutionary history. Both the historical-biographical and historical-everyday tales became superimposed over this historical-revolutionary text, which, in its turn, began to appear as the defining component of children's historical prose.

Russian history would now be read according to the interpretation of the Marxist scholar Michail Pokrovskij, about whom his contemporary Aleksandr Kiezewetter, a historian forced to emigrate in 1922, would subsequently write: "His striving to fit Russian history into the Procrustean bed of the class struggle led to departures from the strictly scholarly method."[33] In children's literature, it was no longer a matter of scholarly integrity, but the outright falsification of historical knowledge. In an essay on children's historical prose for a critical volume published in 1931, Lidija Ginzburg characterized the situation as follows: "a good old historical conception is taken and subjected to a corresponding 'sympathy shift,' for which at times there is not even any need, as in our country practically since time immemorial it has been the norm to generally sympathize with the poor and oppressed, and to condemn cruel landowners."[34] A mere listing of historical tales of the 1920s-30s gives a fairly clear picture of the ideological predilections involved: Aleksandr Slonimskij, "Черниговцы" ("Chernigovians"), on the 1825-26 mutiny in the Chernigov military regiment that followed the Decembrists' revolt; Leonid Saveljev, "Штурм Зимнего" ("Storming the Winter Palace"); Sergej Grigorjev, "Берко-кантонист" ("Berko the Cantonist"), on the difficult life of a Jewish boy before the revolution; Tatjana Bogdanovich, "Ученик наборного художества" ("The Typesetting Student") and especially its sequel, "Горный завод Петра Третьего" ("The Mining Plant of Peter III"), on the Pugachev rebellion; Stepan Zlobin, "Салават Юлаев" ("Salavat Julaev"); Al. Altaev, "Декабрята" ("Little Decembrists"), "Когда рушатся дворцы" ("When Palaces Fall"), and "Под знаменем Башмака" ("Under the Banner of the Boot").[35] By way of underscoring Ginzburg's point, I would clarify that this latter work on the Reformation-era peasant uprising led by Thomas Müntzer was first published in the children's press in 1906, so we could hardly insist on a shortage of revolutionary subjects in pre-October children's historical prose.[36] In the article cited above, Ginzburg proposed that the historical tales for children were viewed "not just as a means of affirming ideology, but also as a school for historical thinking,"

---

33   Anatolij Chernobaev, *Историки России. Биографии*, Moscow 2001, 266.
34   Lidija Ginzburg, "Пути детской исторической повести," in A. V. Lunacharskij, ed., *Детская литература*, Moscow and Leningrad 1931, 169.
35   The boot in the title is a reference to Bundschuh (a peasant shoe) hoisted during town uprisings in Southwestern Germany in the late fifteenth and sixteenth centuries.
36   Al. Altaev, *Под знаменем Башмака*, Petrograd 1920.

that is, for perceiving the historical process as a unified field in which the critic offers to teach young readers how to detect "signs of the times," be they linguistic (such as the archaic language used in period texts) or those of everyday life.[37]

In the 1930s, government dictate also conditioned both writers' and readers' interest in historical prose: in 1931, the Central Committee of the Communist Party issued the decree "О начальной и средней школе" ("On Elementary and Middle Schools"), which restored history as a school subject. Now it could be studied again, and thematically, for example, with the Ancient World History allotted its place in the fifth and sixth grade curriculum. In 1934, the Council of People's Commissars and the Central Committee adopted the decree "О преподавании гражданской истории в школах СССР" ("On the Teaching of Civilian History in the Schools of the USSR").[38] At the First Congress of Soviet Writers, which took place that year, Samuil Marshak, ever sensitive to political clashes of his time and mindful of what could and had to be done, subjected historical fiction for children to fairly sharp criticism for its schematic and sketchy approach to the past: "In the child's consciousness, world history is arranged approximately thus: Spartacus – Ivan the Terrible – Peter the Great – the Pugachev rebellion – the period of Nicholas I (the Decembrists) – Nicholas II, 1905 and 1917."[39] Following Marshak's lead, critics and educators called upon children's authors to fill in the gaps and blind spots in historical knowledge post-haste, but in particular they demanded that "children's literature concentrate first and foremost on those key moments of history that underscore the oppressed classes' resentment."[40]

It would take two more post-Congress years for a children's history-tale canon to emerge. In 1936, the leading critical journal *Детская литература* (*Children's Literature*), began a discussion on history books for children. The joint (3-4) issue of this publication opens with an editorial statement by the critic and Children's Literature Publishing House (Детиздат) editor Genrich Ejchler with the promising title "Детиздат работает над историческими книгами" ("Detizdat Is Working on History Books").[41] "Schools," Ejchler writes,

---

37   Ginzburg, "Пути детской исторической повести," 180.
38   Davydov, Prochorov, and Dneprov, eds., *Российская педагогическая энциклопедия*, Vol. 1, 314.
39   *Первый Всесоюзный съезд советских писателей. Стенографический отчет*, Moscow 1934, 54-55.
40   P. Lysjakov, "За историческую повесть для детей," in *Детская литература* 4 (1935), 10-13.
41   Genrich Ejchler, "Детиздат работает над историческими книгами," in *Детская литература* 3-4 (1936): 2-12.

"do not just need good history textbooks. They also need a big library of history books for extracurricular reading."[42] Among the indubitable breakthroughs on the "history front" the critic names Aleksej Tolstoj's adaptation of his own *Петр Первый* (*Peter the First*) and Zlobin's rendering of "Салават Юлаев" for young audiences, as well as two books aimed directly at children: Elena Danko's *Китайский секрет* (*The Chinese Secret*) and Tatjana Bogdanovich's "Ученик наборного художества." Lamenting the scarcity of children's books on history, Ejchler encourages children's authors to begin "working from scratch," pointing out that a fairly concrete plan has already been put forward to create the missing historical library for young readers within the next two or three years.[43] The 1936 Detizdat plan he refers to called for the creation or adaptation of books on ancient and medieval history and the history of the French "bourgeois" revolution, as well as books on the Russian revolutions of 1905 and 1917 – both February and October. Interestingly, Detizdat's arrangement for books on Russian history, mostly fixed on *Geschichte*, i.e., the historical specifics, presupposed literary works written to order by contemporary authors. For adventure narrative (*Historie*), however, with all its entertainment and excitement, the publishing house planned to turn to foreign authors who were already well known to the pre-revolutionary Russian public. Thus its 1936 booklist included translations from Walter Scott (*Quentin Durward* and *Ivanhoe*), Victor Hugo (*Notre-Dame of Paris*), and Charles de Coster (*The Legend of Thyl Ulenspiegel and Lamme Goedzak*). At first glance, such a broadening of the framework of historical space beyond Russian national history seemed encouraging. It must be noted, though, that literary critics promoting the party agenda immediately imposed on the publishing house a new condition for adding foreign authors to its catalogue of children's texts: the works of Western European authors now had to be processed ("пройти обработку"), or, rather, get scrupulously edited so that the texts would end up featuring a "Marxist viewpoint." In a later issue of *Детская литература*, critics Arkadij Gornfel'd and Aron Epshtejn summarized this imperative by saying that "in the interest of children's education, we are within our rights to rework, adapt, and retell an artistic work. This is necessary and justified."[44]

---

42   Ibid., 2.
43   Ibid., 10.
44   *Детская литература* 15 (1937), 7. Such a "processing" of classic texts had existed before the revolution as well, but authors thereof had typically been guided by the need to adapt a given work to a child's reading level. Gornfel'd and Epshtejn are referring rather to adjustments at the level of ideology, i.e., the Marxist principles of the revolutionary development of history and the class struggle.

Another important landmark in the development of the Soviet historical tale for children was also established on February 22, 1936, in Leningrad, when a "roundtable of writers, historians, and publishing personnel at a narrowly focused and strictly businesslike conference discussed measures regarding the prompt production of historical texts."[45] This gathering took place exactly one year before the wipeout of Marshak's editorship at Detizdat in Leningrad, when his main assistants, editors Tamara Gabbe and Aleksandra Ljubarskaja had been jailed, and Vera Zadunajskaja dismissed, while Lidija Chukovskaja had barely managed to escape her arrest.[46] But even under such conditions and the constantly worsening political pressure, these people remained steadfast in their devotion to children's books and sought to defend their views on how children's literature was to develop. In particular, the February conference ushered back the idea of producing Soviet-style *"plutarch"* collections, albeit on the condition that they would include biographies of people "of great passion, enormous will, and intense tenacity who gave their lives to the struggle against a disordered world, against rulers and oppressors, ignorance and superstition."[47] Rejecting children's historical prose by Avenarius and Salias, the Leningrad editors nevertheless chose not to forsake the literary tradition they espoused, proposing that the new booklist included works of such classic authors as Ivan Lazhechnikov, Michail Zagoskin, Victor Hugo, and Joseph Henri Honoré Boex (Rosny the Elder). Participants of the conference also discussed at length the collaboration between children's authors and historians and the importance of shaping children's historical knowledge. Although the meeting ended with a statement to the effect that historical books for children should be "retrospective" (i.e., employing a Soviet variant of "Whig historiography"), their primary task was still to "inculcate a correct understanding of historical struggle."[48]

Thus, in 1936, the delicate balance between *Historie* and *Geschichte* was violated. It was precisely historical specifics that ended up being supplanted, leaving a path for invention relatively clear. Children's authors were now expected to concentrate their efforts on filling this space. They were to educate their young readers through the noble examples of their fictional characters, while choosing actual historical figures for their protagonists according to the

---

45   I. Bachterev, "Совещание по вопросу об исторической книге в Ленинграде," in *Детская литература* 8 (1936), 39-40.
46   On the attack on Marshak's Detizdat, see Lidija Chukovskaja, *Записки об Анне Ахматовой*, Vol. 1, Moscow 2001, 94-104.
47   Ibid., 13.
48   Ibid., 12.

vaunted criterion of class provenance. In this context, the specifics of Soviet historical fiction become more "true-to-life" than the crux of the constantly re-evaluated revolutionary history, wherein yesterday's heroes keep turning into today's "enemies of the people."[49] As the prominent scholar of Soviet censorship Arlen Bljum remarks: "The children's reading list was subjected to perhaps the most radical deformation of all."[50]

In his analysis of the historical novels of American writer Karen Cushman, Joseph Zornado comments on the unique connection between the status of historian and fiction writer, as both "share the will to invent, to order, and to discriminate among [...] countless historical moments."[51] In its Soviet context, the children's historical narrative was subjected not only to ideological pressure of the censorship, but also to that of the author's own self-censoring. The state's constant rewriting of history ultimately led to one's loss of political bearings. The desire to invent, then, was most often dictated by the politics of the moment, not just by the author's wish to select historical events and arrange them into a narrative according to a chosen order. In other words, the "discrimination" vis-à-vis particular moments of history was rarely the result of an authorial decision; rather, it was dictated by the set of events and a roster of heroes determined by the party's interpretation of Grand History. Moreover, the closer history in question was to the contemporary moment, the more difficult it was for a children's author to write about it.

The historical tales and stories produced during World War II provide a telling example of party censorship and authorial self-censoring coming together to shape historical narratives for children. In those stories, two moments of Russia's heroic past became enshrined along with the more recent historical events: The Patriotic War of 1812, and the defense of Sebastopol (1854-55) during the Crimean War.[52] Zhitomirova notes that the war years saw

49 Thus, for instance, during the Great Terror, biographies of the Civil War heroes Vasilij Bljukher, Semen Kostovskij, and Nikolaj Shchors were removed from libraries. Sergej Grigorjev's stories about Aleksandr Suvorov were censured for the author's failure to see that the main character was a "serf-owning landlord." See Natalja Zhitomirova, *Советская историко-художественная книга для детей и ее воспитательное значение*, 81.

50 Arlen Bljum, *Советская цензура в эпоху тотального террора: 1929-1953*, St. Petersburg 2000, 211.

51 Joseph Zornado, "A Poetics of History: Karen Cushman's Medieval World," in *Lion and Unicorn* 21:2 (April 1997), 251.

52 Among authors superimposing different historical contexts during World War II, we note V. Jurjev, M. Bragin, N. Kal'ma, and A. Barmin. In 1941 M. Ezerskij's historical tale "Дмитрий Донской" ("Dmitrij Donskoj") came out; and in 1942 E. Andreeva published the story "Иван Рябов" ("Ivan Rjabov"), about the heroic feats of a Pomeranian helmsman on the White Sea at the outset of Peter the Great's Northern War against Sweden.

a "marked expansion of the military and patriotic theme in historical books for children."[53] Although she writes in the Aesopian language typical of a Soviet critic, her message is fairly easy to decode. What Zhitomirova really suggests is that at the moment of national crisis, the embargo on previously taboo historical subjects and names was lifted, since inculcating patriotism had become literature's most crucial agenda. At that point, heroes of every social background sufficed as long as their behavior was patriotic. An example of such shifting priorities was Marshak's statement from 1943. He describes the sort of children's book called for in wartime as one that "teaches a sense of civic and personal honor," and as "imbued with love for the motherland and consciousness of one's responsibility toward it."[54]

The War of 1812 and the Crimean War – the two historical moments previously unpopular in Soviet children's literature – now dominated narratives for children because they lent themselves to a direct juxtaposition of World War II with Russia's military past. They also allowed authors to validate heroism worthy of imitation by presenting it in a historical context. And here again we see the eclectic nature of the historical tale for children. Its historical-biographical theme is interwoven with the historical-everyday one, for the Soviet children's authors writing about World War II are bringing together the moralizing qualities of traditional biographies of great men and the setting and everyday details of the more recent historical period.

Sergej Grigorjev was one of the authors working within this permitted temporal framework. Citing the interaction of *Geschichte* and *Historie* in one of his works, I will demonstrate how Grigorjev both selected his historical events and constructed his fictional plot within a framework of literary borrowing, performing a skillful recycling of preexisting historical prose. His example proves that the events of *Geschichte* and the main character of the *Historie* may, both, remain beyond the reach of the almost inevitable ideological pressure.

Grigorjev's "Малахов курган" ("The Malachov Mound," 1941) presents a curious intertextual synthesis of Lev Tolstoj's cycle "Севастопольские рассказы" ("The Sebastopol Tales," 1855) and Konstantin Stanjukovich's short novella *Севастопольский мальчик: повесть из времен Крымской войны* (*The Boy from Sebastopol: A Novella from the Time of the Crimean War*, 1902) – two prerevolutionary works the Soviet censorship considered acceptable for adults

---

[53] Zhitomirova, *Советская историко-художественная книга для детей и ее воспитательное значение*, 90.
[54] Samuil Marshak, "Мир в картинках," in *Литература и искусство*, 2 October 1943, 40:92, 8.

and children. Taking the events Tolstoj described in "Севастополь в декабре" ("Sebastopol' in December"), "Севастополь в мае" ("Sebastopol' in May"), and "Севастополь в августе 1855 года" ("Sebastopol' in August 1855") as his tale's chronological background, Grigorjev also borrows the main character from Stanjukovich's novella, the sailor's son Markushka, and turns him into Venja Moguchenko, the youngest child in a family of sailors, all of whom take part in the defense of their native city. Whereas Stanjukovich's main character is an orphan, Venja is well cared for, especially by his older sisters. While Markushka is filled with blind hatred toward the French and English who killed first his father and then his uncle who had cared for him in the former's stead, Venja is rational and level-headed. Moreover, the adults around him ensure that he has a childhood, even in the time of war. To Grigorjev's credit, he makes no attempt to turn Venja into a prototypical "moriturus" ("смертник"), a pioneer-hero ready to die for the defense of his country. The youngest Moguchenko is a conscientious helper to grownups, who, in their turn, guard and protect him despite all the hardships. Although Venja joins adults in reconstructing military fortifications that had been destroyed, all his military feats take place *with* Sebastopol's heroic sailors – and never in their stead. Using this fictional adolescent hero, and thus, using *Historie*, Grigorjev constructs a role model to be imitated. His character remains an adolescent caught up in the turmoil of *Geschichte*.

The constant interweaving of *Geschichte* and *Historie* lends "Малахов курган" a curious compositional polyphony. Grigorjev's fictional characters seem to enter into immediate contact with such historical figures as Admirals Pavel Nachimov and Vladimir Kornilov; the engineer Eduard Totleben who constructed Sebastopol's original fortifications; and Nikolaj Pirogov, the Crimean War's "wonder-doctor." That said, the level of *Geschichte* is strictly censored: all of these historical personages belong to the roster approved by the Soviet historiography. Besides, no matter what their political views really were and their aristocratic origins notwithstanding, they unanimously oppose "autocracy" and denounce Russia's "autocratic regime." They understand and love the simple people of the *Historie*, the tale's fictional characters, and the commoners, in turn, respond to them with devotion and committed service. It is precisely this entwinement of history and fiction that allows Grigorjev to turn "Малахов курган," its ideological "message" notwithstanding, into an emblem of patriotic unity – a wartime alliance of figures real and invented, aristocratic and plebeian, bonded in the face of danger. As one of the country's leading children's authors, Grigorjev was making an appeal for this sort of unity, which was so necessary at the moment of global disaster. Buttressing himself with the texts by Tolstoj and Stanjukovich enabled him to emphasize the emotional context while avoiding political clichés and Stalinist slogans. The tale's intertextuality and its connection to the nineteenth-century literary models testify to the eternal postulates of historical narrative that gave rise to the genre of children's historical prose in the first place. Most importantly, they pay tribute to the people's patriotic love of their country, resulting in their readiness to defend it. Literary allusions render this sentiment intact despite the political cataclysms of the period.

In other children's historical tales that, although written during World War II, encapsulated the Russian people's experience in the Franco-Russian War of 1812, the historical-biographical stratum also predominates. V. Jurjev's (Jurij Veber's) tale "Гренадер Леонтий Коренной" ("Grenadier Leontij Korennoj," 1945) is devoted to a prisoner of war, a hero who would not otherwise be lionized in Stalinist political culture. Jurjev had studied archival documents to produce his story of the captive grenadier who managed to amaze no one other than Napoleon with his bravery and devotion to Russia. It is hard to say whether the author of this brief work was attempting to shed light on the fate of war prisoners at the time, but the tale became a canonical work of children's literature. Published in the "Малая историческая библиотека" series ("Little Historical Library"), it would remain this period's only work for children featuring a main character whose "failure" to avoid captivity led to a victory on the spiritual and even political front.[55] Typically, "education via noble examples" came down to describing lives of victors. But, as Jurjev's narrative demonstrates, children's literature written during the war permitted a deviation from this norm, with the non-class approach to the question of whose life was "worthy of imitation" temporarily prevailing. Other heroes of historical-biographical tales about the War of 1812 included not only the peasant partisan Gerasim Kurin, but also Prince Petr Bagration as well as Generals Ermolov, Raevskij, and Platov. The slackening of ideological criteria in choosing heroic prototypes for children's historical fiction allowed novelist Sergej Golubov, who during this time produced an entire series of stories for children about the Fatherland War of 1812, to transform his book *Генерал Багратион* (*General Bagration*) into a historical tale for young adults.[56]

Recreating a character's aristocratic childhood was a fairly complex task for an author working on a Socialist Realist text: the gentry childhood was a controversial topic throughout the whole existence of Soviet literature and was

---

55 V. Jurjev, *Гренадер Леонтий Коренной*, Moscow 1945.
56 Sergej Golubov, *Генерал Багратион*, Moscow and Leningrad 1943.

typically portrayed in a negative light.⁵⁷ With good reason does Chudakova note that Soviet literature's last gentry-childhood work was Aleksej Tolstoj's quasi-fictional *Повесть о многих превосходных вещах: детство Никиты* (*A Novella about Many Excellent Things: Nikita's Childhood*, 1922).⁵⁸ In order to downplay this fraught theme, Golubov concentrates his narrative specifically on the events of war, introducing his hero as an adult, a colonel cast in a Suvorov mold. His Bagration is energetic, temperamental, and always defying authority: he would defer to Kutuzov only, but never to the tsar.⁵⁹ He also presents Kutuzov as a Suvorov disciple. These two decisive warriors are contrasted with the army commander Barclaj de Tolly, an indolent foreigner incapable of understanding the patriotic impulses of the Russian soul. A key moment in Golubov's narrative is the description of Bagration's demise, whereby a chronological description of a "life worthy of imitation" is broken up by a coordinate shift, from childhood to "dying in the name of the fatherland." Thus *Geschichte*, which is necessary for the historical-biographical description, turns out to be truncated: in Bagration's case, there appears to be no childhood, no gentry upbringing, and even no previous battle experience. Golubov's *Historie*, too, is not fully developed. His main character is universally beloved by the soldiers, while all the fictional characters merely fulfill their prearranged function of confirming Bagration's preeminence. Golubov endows not even one of them, including rank-and-file soldiers, partisans, and officers, with any conceptual or functional importance.⁶⁰ The narrative's main focus is the protagonist's heroic death, an act of self-sacrifice for the good of his fatherland. And yet, as far as the genre is concerned, this tale does demonstrate a certain movement within an already entrenched canon: it shows how the unfilled lacunae in the history of a life can paralyze the author's historical imagination.

---

57   See Marina Balina, "Crafting the Self: Narratives of Prerevolutionary Childhood in Soviet Literature," in Balina and Larissa Rudova, eds., *Russian Children's Literature and Culture*, 91-113; see also Balina, "Воспоминания о детстве в советской детской литературе: к вопросу о специфике жанра," in N. Barkovskaja and M. Litovskaja, eds., *Семантическая поэтика русской литературы*, Ekaterinburg 2008, 322-33.

58   M. O. Chudakova, "Без гнева и пристрастия: Формы и деформации в литературном процессе 20-30-х гг.," in M. O. Chudakova, *Избранные работы*, Vol. 1, 327.

59   The Suvorov theme was quite popular during the "Great Patriotic War." On July 29, 1942, the three classes of the Order of Suvorov were established; in 1943, Suvorov military academies were organized throughout the country; and 1944 saw the publication of Valentin Kataev's novella *Сын полка* (*The Son of the Regiment*), whose main character has a dream that he is being escorted on his path to military glory by Suvorov himself.

60   Golubov was much criticized for downplaying the role of the masses in this war, and for a non-Marxist approach to history, which, in 1943, was a fairly dangerous accusation. See A. Derman, "Генерал Багратион," in *Новый мир* 9 (1943), 117-118.

3   Ancient History as Children's Fiction: A Case Study

History is what it is, but it is also what we make of it. What we call "history" is not a thing, an object of study, but a story we choose to tell about things.
RICHARD SLOTKIN[61]

Irina Arzamasceva notes that under the Soviet regime, "the classical world fared rather better" in literature than Christianity did:

> Of course, the whole strata bearing the stamp of reactionary names (e.g. Gippius and Merezhkovskij) were consigned to oblivion. [But] thanks to certain old-school intellectuals who took part in the creation of 'socialist' culture, the ideas of 'Russian antiquity' were carried over, albeit with some losses, to the generations born after the October [Revolution]. A 'Roman' stratum of literature quickly accumulated in children's publications of the 1920s and 30s, as well as in fiction and educational works and textbooks. All manner of knowledge of Rome was passed on to Soviet children. And in this, free Hellas remains in the shadow of imperial Rome.[62]

This assertion is incontrovertible. Here one could speculate that its verity had to do with the controversies of Soviet imperial consciousness, but to me it seems that the issue is far simpler: Rome and Roman history were "in demand" because of the existence of a universally accepted *metatext* – the history of the Spartacus uprising, albeit not at all in its Italian version. Soviet critics, and especially those specializing in children's literature, rejected Raffaello Giovagnoli's novel, *Spartacus*, which in their view took "the sole hero in Roman history that could be truly close to our hearts" and reduced him to the status of "a passionate lover."[63] In 1933, as a sort of do-over of this theme, Vasilij Jan produced a historical tale *Спартак* (*Spartacus*) for children and young adults. This new composition opened with a quote by Lenin: the leader of the Bolshevik revolution extolled the impact of the uprising on the destruction of

---

61   Slotkin, "Fiction for the Purpose of History," 222.
62   I. N. Arzamasceva, *"Век ребенка" в русской литературе 1900-1930 годов*, Moscow 2003, 299.
63   I. Zhelobovskij, "Рассказывание на историческую тему," in *Детская литература* 4 (1935), 37.

the slave system.[64] The introduction not only validated Jan's choice of a historical subject matter but also suggested that his plot, written from scratch, fitted in perfectly with the Soviet historiography's approach to historical fiction as a "formational" ("воспитательное") reading matter. Although novels and stories that deviated from the uprising-centered metatext continued to be published, for instance, Milij Ezerskij's *Марий и Сулла* (*Marius and Sulla*, 1937) and "Аристоник" ("Aristonicus," 1937), they were now subjected to harsh criticism frequently bordering on political denunciation: "Ezerskij's novel is a lamentable departure from Bolshevik vigilance on the part of our publishers and critics [...]. The revolutionary motivation for events has 'gone missing' from the novel [...] [which] contains only a few words on the Sicilian uprising," one of the vigilant critics wrote.[65] Stamped "not recommended for school reading," Ezerskij's and other such works typically did not reach their intended audience.

Strange as it may seem, the late 1940s and early 1950s saw a revival of classical philology and antiquity as school subjects. Along with the school uniform and instruction segregated by gender, Latin studies made a comeback in Soviet secondary schools. The Latin textbook bore a dedication, as was wont, to Stalin, with his portrait on the title page.[66] This return of classical studies did not last long, but it did justify creation and publication of antiquity-themed fiction for young readers. Therefore, in the late 1950s and 1960s Soviet readers "discovered" ancient history as opposed to classical antiquity – the history long preceding Spartacus. Not only tales of the ancient world now appeared in children's literature, but they were also incorporated in the widely-circulated volumes for "extracurricular reading." Among the new historical fiction of this kind were Klara Moiseeva's *Дочь Эхнатона* (*Akhenaten's Daughter*, 1967) and *В древнем царстве Урарту* (*In the Ancient Kingdom of Urartu*, 1953); Revekka Rubinshtejn's *Глиняный конверт* (*The Clay Envelope*, 1962) and *За что Ксеркс высек море* (*Why Xerxes Whipped the Sea*, 1967) – an adaptation of Herodotus's *History* for children. Historians specializing in various eras and cultures now began to write for children: for instance, the eminent Egyptologist Milica Matje produced *День египетского мальчика* (*An Egyptian Boy's Day*, 1954), followed by *Кари, ученик художника* (*Kari, the Artist's Apprentice*, 1963); in

---

64 Vasilij Jan, *Спартак: историческая повесть для детей младшего и среднего возраста*, Moscow 1933.

65 A. Knjazev, "Рецензия на роман Милия Езерского, 'Марий и Сулла'," in *Детская литература* 1 (1938), 38-43.

66 S. P. Kondratjev, *Учебник латинского языка для 8-10-го классов средней школы*, Moscow 1950.

both cases, she had the official imprimatur to publish the books. And while all these authors tended to preserve the Marxist postulates in their works – in their tales of antiquity, class struggle remained the driving force of historical development – they seasoned this politicized scheme with adventures of their child protagonists, fascinating enough for the standoff between the oppressor and the oppressed to take a back seat. The living and breathing hero of history, typically a coeval of the young reader, came to the fore of their narratives, which now centered on the characters' everyday life, on historical events affecting them, and, most important of all, on the historical meaning of their actions – a semantic shift that ushered in a new kind of historical thinking, gradually liberated from ideology.

The phenomenon of tales of antiquity in children's literature did not entirely fit within the customary framework of the post-Stalin "Thaw," with its return to playfulness, childlike aesthetics and Avant-Garde-style experimentation. More likely, it was a return to the principles of Detgiz as headed by Marshak in the late 1920s. An experienced editor, he, too, recruited first and foremost professionals from a variety of fields, such as travelers, scientists, engineers, as well as experts in nature and art, to write for children.[67] The 1950s historians that tried their hand at children's literature were like those "old hands" and scholars Marshak sought out and encouraged to engage in literary work. They infused historical fiction with a sense of the world's multidimensionality, thereby breaking down the ideological binarity predominant in children's literature of World War II and the immediate postwar years. Most crucially, they replaced a pioneer-hero with a peer-hero, a boy or a girl whose story was not only and not so much of "class struggle," but of the fascinating world of the past accessible only through knowledge.[68]

Matje's historical tales serve as some of the more interesting examples of the Spartacus metatext's influence on the children's historical narrative temporally and geographically disconnected from the Roman history. The daugh-

---

67   See Marina Balina, "Creativity through Restraint: The Beginning of Soviet Children's Literature," in Balina and Larissa Rudova, eds., *Russian Children's Literature and Culture*, 1-19. See also Balina, "Die sowjetische Kinderliteratur zwischen ästhetischem Experiment und ideologischer Normierung," in Yuri Murashev and Tomas Liptac, eds., *Schrift und Macht*, Vienna, Cologne and Weimar 2013, 119-35.

68   In 1936, the historian of antiquity Solomon Lurje produced the educational children's tale, "Письмо греческого мальчика" ("A Greek Boy's Letter"). In this text, history and contemporaneity are interwoven: the reader follows the lead of a scholar decoding an ancient manuscript. The new historical children's prose would be constructed on a different principle, namely, that of combining history-as-knowledge with adventure as the transmitter of this knowledge.

ter of a Russianized Englishman, Matje (1899-1966) was a historian specializing in the religion and art of Ancient Egypt. Her first attempt to write a children's book was *День египетского мальчика*. From its very first pages, even in a foreword she also wrote, the author appealed to the imagination of her young readers. To begin with, Matje frankly admitted that, having devoted her entire life to the study of ancient Egypt, she had ("of course") never been there. Sadly, neither had she visited modern Egypt, for researchers of her time, and especially of her family background, were denied any opportunity to travel abroad. Therefore, when Matje invited her audience on a journey through history, she began the invitation with an indication that she had reconstructed the Egyptians' everyday life at a remove of three millennia.

In the first of her two children's tales, Matje combines two key functions of historical prose for children: the book aims to saturate readers with appropriate information, but it also contributes to their moral education (воспитание).[69] The narrative is full of colorful details related to just one day in the life of the Egyptian boy Setu. The author describes his parents' home as well as his school, with its kindly teacher Amenchotep and the mean-spirited instructor, Shedsu, who is quick to strictly punish his pupils. The dense informational layer of Matje's *Geschichte*, rich in historical knowledge, is constantly diluted by *Historie* – the particulars of the fictional world in which Setu and his friend, Ini, live. Thus, even as the function of moral education in *День египетского мальчика* remains ideologically programmed, predicated on the inevitable portrayal of "class struggle," the story of everyday life, even, more specifically, the story of the objects surrounding the boy, becomes more important and interesting. Nevertheless, upsetting the balance between historical "evidence" and adventure is the usual ideological binarity – Matje's "documentation" of the conflict between the oppressor and the oppressed. Thus, while wandering around the city, the well-off Setu becomes acquainted with the life of poor people, and it is these encounters that cause him to see anew the world of the ancient city and ponder the need to change this reality.[70]

Eventually, Setu goes from being a reader's guide through history's labyrinth to, potentially, becoming a revolutionary. But the pressure of the Socialist Realist canon eases up at the end of the tale, for there Matje, turning from the purely informational component of her storytelling to the historical narrative, devotes her full attention to fairytales and stories of ancient Egypt, which Setu and his friends diligently copy in hieroglyphs on clay tablets during school

---

69   For more detail on these functions, see V. A. Judin, *Человек. История. Память*, Moscow 1990, 3.
70   Milica Matje, *День египетского мальчика*, Moscow 1954.

lessons. But if in this first tale, Matje was able to at least reduce the pressure of the meta-canon, concentrating predominantly on *Historie*, in her second tale, *Кари, ученик художника*, she got so carried away with informational side of *Geschichte* that she almost abandoned the ideologically correct model of history predicated on revolt against injustice and the exploiters behind it. While also present in *Кари, ученик художника*, the political agenda merely influences the *Historie*'s development.

Unlike Setu, Kari is a simple boy from a village of "call-heeders" – the term used in ancient Egypt for servants, including workers engaged in the construction of royal tombs. Everyone in Kari's family is employed in this industry, and the boy's entire life proves subject to class struggle between the poor and honest people of the village and the corrupt city elite. In accordance with the state-endorsed requirement of a heavily ideologized narrative model, the adventure plot concerning three different boys from Thebes turns into a story of the unmasking of dishonest and two-faced aristocrats, against whom the artist Chevi, the teacher and patron to whom the talented Kari is apprenticed, raises the rebellion of "call-heeders." Like Spartacus (in his Soviet rendition), Chevi seeks to gain nothing for himself: his goal is to aid the disadvantaged. He is unselfish, noble, and honest; his ideology and leadership is above reproach; and he has no fear of the power, which he must still serve with his art. Thus, does the brave Chevi refuse to ornament the pharaoh's tomb until the innocently condemned are set free.[71] Still, this "leader" of the disadvantaged lingers outside the revolutionary roster of trailblazers' Soviet readers were accustomed to. By the standards of Matje's contemporaries, he is an intellectual, an artist, and he fights for the rights of the downtrodden not with a weapon in hand, but through his creativity, which he refuses to subjugate to the dictates of those in power.

It may still be true, however, that amid the gallery of heroes of children's historical literature, Chevi is an ancient Egyptian equivalent of Spartacus, although his leadership example is influenced by the culture of the 1960s. The book came out right after the Cuban Missile Crisis and followed the appearance in print of Aleksandr Solzhenitsyn's *Один день Ивана Денисовича* (*One Day in the Life of Ivan Denisovich*, in *Новый мир*, in November of 1962).[72] This was a frightful time in the lives of Soviet intellectuals and artists: although greatly relieved by Stalin's death in 1953, in December, 1962, they saw Chrushchev's infamous attack on the works of abstract art at the Manezh exhibition hall, which shattered everyone's illusions about the possibility of an

---

71 Milica Matje, *Кари, ученик художника*, Moscow 1963.
72 See Aleksandr Tvardovskij, *Новомирский дневник, 1961-1966*, Vol. 1, Moscow 2009, 68.

alliance between the authorities and the "thawed out" intelligentsia.[73] In this context, Matje's choice of a member of the intelligentsia vested with privileges and yet able to maintain his sense of social justice for a hero of a children's book was fairly unusual, especially as her Chevi is not alone in resisting the social evil. In the tale, he is joined by Bekenmut, a doctor willing to treat Kari's paralyzed sister free of charge and serve as a surrogate father to the lonely, albeit rich, grandson of a high priest of Amon-Ra's temple. Bekenmut hides Kari when the latter seeks escape from pursuers who have beaten him. It is worth noting that, in such instances, Matje's fiction (*Historie*) controls the events of Grand History; that is, her invented characters change the course of history according to the laws of justice. Of particular importance in this regard is the episode in which Amon-Ra presides over a "fair trial" during the year's main holiday, the Festival of the Valley.

Matje unfolds all the stages of preparing for the holiday before her readers, describing in detail, for instance, the selection of flowers and weaving of garlands with which officials would deck their homes; she also depicts the masks of gods considered to be part of the procession and notes their places in the complex system of the ancient Egyptian religion. Masterfully, with such enthusiasm that there would hardly seem to be room for any revolutionary subtext, she guides her readers through a dense layer of historical knowledge, recreating the minutest aspects of the procession. Then, as if suddenly catching herself, Matje rather precipitously redirects her story towards antireligious propaganda. The festival's "fair trial," her narrator explains, is carried out not by the chief god of the Egyptian pantheon, Ra, but by the high priests themselves: they have beforehand decided upon the verdicts. One of the unjustly accused turns out to be Kari's father, the carpenter Onachtu; his boss Paneb, a man in charge of pyramid construction, had been trying to get him steal the gold meant for a sarcophagus. Onachtu is saved by Kari's friend, Rames, who has long been employed by his high priest grandfather to carry out Ra's "will"; that is, during the procession, Rames hides inside the god's statue and, following the priest's secret sign, pulls a strap guiding the "hand of god" toward either the pottery shard that indicates the defendant's condemnation, or the one stating that he should go free. Risking his life, Rames refuses to pronounce his friend's father guilty, and instead has the god touch the shard of acquittal.[74] Justice triumphs, but it comes not from a deity, but from a faithful friend.

---

73   I am far from attempting to discern dissident activism in Matje's tale; but it is curious to observe how texts aimed at children reflect the changing political accents of the contemporary moment, which seems to call for new kinds of heroes.

74   Matje, *Кари, ученик художника*, 64.

And yet, even amid such politically "useful" aspects of narrated history, it is the informational material *not* corresponding to preset ideology that proves far more solid. The "call-heeders" collectively revolt against injustice and thereby triumph: the high priests who had overseen the whole life of ancient Thebes quickly give up their positions, and the thieving boss Paneb is replaced with a new construction chief. What seems more important for the tale's young readers, however, is not so much the (wholly fictitious) revolutionary situation foisted on the plot from without by the Socialist Realist canon, but, rather, the actual story of three boys: Kari; Rames, who dreams of becoming a doctor and treating the poor; and Titu, the son of the city's chief landscaper. *Historie* and *Geschichte* seem to balance each other out, relegating revolutionary propaganda to the back burner.

Due to the structure of a children's book, and especially because of the educational function children's literature was supposed to perform, historical commentary was an indispensable part of historical narratives for the young. It also became an important method of disseminating knowledge that released historical text from its ideological "captivity." An explanatory footnote began to fulfill an educational function in the children's historical tale. Among the books that relied on footnotes to "enlighten" young readers were *Приключения мальчика с собакой* (*The Adventures of a Boy and His Dog*, 1959) by Nadezhda Ostromenckaja and Nataljia Bromlej, both of whom had previously taught history in schools. To supplement their knowledge, they recruited a Hermitage Museum expert in Roman History, Marija Sergeenko. The narrative centers on Cleo, a Sicilian boy captured (along with his dog Leo) by pirates and sold into slavery. Included here is the requisite description of the boy's suffering as he becomes a plaything for the patrician's spoiled son; but this politically correct twist does not preclude the work's turning into a sort of "short course" on everyday life in Ancient Rome. Violating the ideological parameters of the metatext, the authors focus on historical knowledge not directly related to the binarity of the oppressor and the oppressed. Unlike Matje, however, they present their information in footnotes, which form, to use Gerard Genette's term, a paratext – here, the one full of ordinary Roman realities like atrium, lararium, toga, bulla, Senate, pantheon, assemblies, as well as of the complex relationship between patricians and clients. Ostromenckaja and Bromlej present all this "everydayness" of ancient Roman life as clearly connected with the events taking place in the life of their main character. Their paratext becomes a background for Cleo's adventure-journey, but it in no way hinders the unfolding of the narrative.

Indeed, Cleo's story is constructed as a travelogue: he is always moving about the ancient Roman territory. The reader follows him first to the slave market, then to latifundia and the urban villas of Roman patricians. Together, they "visit" the Circus Maximus, the Forum and the Coliseum. The reader even accompanies Cleo to the camp of ... Spartacus, so there could be no ideological complaints regarding this boy and his dog's adventures! Surprisingly, however, Spartacus does not let the young hero stay in his camp, sending him instead back home to his family. Thus, Cleo does not become a young avenger – and Ancient Roman analogue of the pioneer hero. What's more, the clairvoyant Spartacus tells this young would-be follower that his cause is doomed; he says that Cleo must live as he is still very young.[75] In a way, this episode illustrates that the seeds Grigorjev had sown at the outset of World War II in "Малахов курган," have finally sprouted – but in the soil of antiquity: both of these historical texts suggest to children that they should remain within the domain of childhood, instead of turning into a weapon of grownups' vengeance. Remarkably, the authors completely violate the heroic principle of Soviet children's literature when they explain that many slaves were dissatisfied by the severe discipline Spartacus enforced in his army. Some of them had signed on for the sake of bloody vengeance, for which their leader had no appetite; while others came in search of easy plunder, and were thus looting not just noble manors, but the property of poor peasants as well.[76] Such coverage of the Spartacus uprising clearly contradicted every postulate of the historical dialectics that the Soviet educational system aimed to establish. Even so, this tale did become required extracurricular reading, and was very popular not just among schoolchildren, but among history teachers as well.

4 Conclusion

The works of children's historical prose analyzed in this article show how complex and contradictory was the rise and development of this genre in Soviet children's literature as well as how frequently the delicate balance between *Geschichte* and *Historie* was upset. It is possible that the historical tale for children preserved the pre-revolutionary edificatory tradition like perhaps no other genre of Soviet children's literature. Significant, too, is that it was precisely in children's historical prose that such pre-revolutionary authors as Al. Altaev (Margarita Jamshchikova) wrote the bulk of their works; and that a

---

75 N. Ostromenckaja and N. Bromlej, *Приключения мальчика с собакой*, Moscow and Leningrad 1959.
76 Ibid., 92.

key figure in the creation of Detizdat's "Little Historical Library" series was Milij Ezerskij, a writer steeped in the history of the ancient world, whose fusion of *Geschichte* and *Historie* in such books as Аристоник (*Aristonicus*, 1937), acquainted a new generation of Soviet readers with historical facts that ranged well beyond the limits of the post-revolutionary class binary. It was specifically the "enlightenment" mission of children's historical prose that distinguished it from children's works on revolutionary history, as well as from the historical-biographical propaganda texts on Lenin and other leaders of the "workers' movement" ("рабочее движение") that constituted their own block of required school-age reading.[77]

Broadening the reader's worldview through immediate contact with history of the ancient world and antiquity, as well as through facts and dates packaged into an exciting journey to the world of the past, would remain a primary goal of the "education through words" ("воспитание словом") practiced by Soviet writer-historians (and not just those writing for children).[78] It was works by such authors as Matje, Ostromenckaja, and Bromlej that preserved the traditions and experiments of the 1920s and early 1930s, that "golden" period in Soviet children's literature, the time of Marshak's Leningrad Detizdat which welcomed the seasoned professionals, the "old hands," to create literary works for the young. The people Detgiz encouraged were of the most varied life experience, and it was Marshak who taught them how to address children.[79] The professionals involved in children's historical prose were scholars and historians, individuals with knowledge of *Geschichte*. Facing them was the complex task of conveying their experience in the climate of constantly shifting historical authorities, of the varying interpretations of historical events filtered through the prism of Marxism. Fortunately for their readers, *Historie* came to the rescue; a fictional hero at the center of the narrative became one's guide through historical reality. The reader's peer as well as the fanciful product of the author's imagination, this main character seemed free to avoid the evaluations and re-evaluations of history required by Soviet ideology. He led readers

---

77 Particularly popular were Anna Grinberg's book on the Uljianov family and Zoja Voskresenskaja's *Сердце матери* (*A Mother's Heart*); stories by Lenin's widow N. K. Krupskaja and Central Committee secretary E. D. Stasova; and reminiscences of Lenin by V. D. Bonch-Bruevich and G. M. Krzhizhanovskij. These books were constantly reprinted right up to the late 1980s as part of the "Historical-Revolutionary Library" series, which had been revived by Detgiz in 1960.

78 *Education through Words* was the title of a foundational book by Samuil Marshak on literature, including the children's variety. Marshak, *Воспитание словом*, Moscow 1961.

79 See Lidija Chukovskaja, *Прочерк*, Moscow 2009, 66-87.

into an exciting world where the past came alive through images and thematically organized subjects; where it became familiar and understandable thanks to the enthralling adventures unfolding in the readers' imagination. It was precisely thus, through a mixture of invention and historical fact, that the "connection between times" mentioned by Gordin was restored in the consciousness of Soviet children.

Notably, it was the children's historical tale that laid the foundations for the future historical-fiction genre Gordin defines as the literature of "oppositionist enlightenment." Such novels as Natan Ejdelman's *Лунин* (*Lunin*, 1970) and Aleksandr Lebedev's *Чаадаев* (*Chaadaev*, 1965) emerged specifically from a blending of *Geschichte* and *Historie* – a technique that had been developed in children's prose – with the main "oppositionist" role assigned to the hero of *Historie*, a fictional character. Writers of the "oppositionist enlightenment" thus "saved" the factology of *Geschichte* from Soviet censors, successfully deploying a tactic adopted from children's works. Even at the most "stagnant" moments of the Soviet period, fiction gave more freedom than perennially revised historical facts. And the fictional heroes of historical narratives – invented, in the case of Soviet children's prose, so as to hold the attention of the child-reader and maintain the story's spirit of adventure – began, in literature for adults, to serve the new mission of educating the *adult* reader. Emphasizing the special role of popular historiography in the 1970s, Gordin remarks that this literature's contribution to "the erosion of Soviet ideology was enormous."[80] The combination of the concreteness of *Geschichte* and the freedom of *Historie* contributed to a new understanding of historical fact as a contradictory phenomenon ranging well beyond the conceptions of historical "truth" imposed by the Soviet state system.

The children's historical tale has not attained the intellectual intensity and depth of historical analysis characteristic of oppositional novels by Ejdelman or Bulat Okudzhava, but common to the most varied authors working in this genre was their aspiration to *enlighten* as a prerequisite for education, and their understanding of the role of *enlightenment* as the transmission of knowledge. This viewpoint united a broad array of authors, from the "diehards" who preserved the legacy of pre-revolutionary classicist scholarship through all the years of tribulation, to writers and historians eminently loyal to Soviet power. This advent of ancient history in children's literature may to some extent be associated with an observation by Shimon Markish, a philologist and scholar of antiquity, regarding the "unparalleled atmosphere of the ancient classics" that

---

80   Gordin, "Занятия историей как оппозиционный акт," 181.

reigned in hearts and minds during the most desolate periods of Soviet history, "when people imbibed the words, phrases, ideas, and images of the ancients – imbibed them as an antidote to Soviet savagery and boorishness, imbibed civilization as an alternative to barbarism."[81]

Works Cited

Primary Sources

Altaev, Al. (Margarita Jamshchikova). *Впереди веков: историческая повесть из жизни Леонардо да Винчи*. St. Petersburg 1910.

Altaev, Al. (Margarita Jamshchikova). *Король и инфант: историческая повесть времен Филиппа Второго*. Moscow 1915.

Altaev, Al. (Margarita Jamshchikova). *Декабрята*. Moscow and Leningrad 1926.

Altaev, Al. (Margarita Jamshchikova). *Когда рушатся дворцы*. Moscow and Leningrad 1929.

Altaev, Al. (Margarita Jamshchikova). *Под знаменем Башмака*. Petrograd 1920.

Andreeva, Ekaterina. *Иван Рябов*. Moscow 1942.

Auslender, Sergej. *Ли Сяо*. Moscow and Leningrad 1927.

Auslender, Sergej. *Маленький Хо*. Moscow 1926.

Auslender, Sergej. *Пугаченок*. Moscow and Leningrad 1926.

Auslender, Sergej. *Пугачевщина*. Moscow 1928.

Blanshar, Pjer. *Плутарх для юношества, или Жития славных мужей всех народов, от древнейших времен доныне*. Moscow 1809.

Bogdanovich, Tatjana. *Ученик наборного художества*. Moscow and Leningrad 1933.

Bogdanovich, Tatjana. *Горный завод Петра Третьего*. Moscow and Leningrad 1936.

Dan'ko, Elena. *Китайский секрет*. Moscow and Leningrad 1929.

Eidelman, Natan. *Лунин*. Moscow 1970.

Ezerskij, Milij. *Димитрий Донской*. Moscow and Leningrad 1941.

Ezerskij, Milij. *Власть и народ. Часть 2: Марий и Сулла*. Moscow 1936.

Ezerskij, Milij. *Аристоник*. Moscow 1937.

Furman, Petr. *Александр Васильевич Суворов-Рымникский*. St. Petersburg 1848.

Furman, Petr. *Григорий Александрович Потемкин*. St. Petersburg 1848.

Furman, Petr. *Наталья Борисовна Долгорукова*. St. Petersburg 1856.

Furman, Petr. *Саардамский плотник*. St. Petersburg 1849.

Furman, Petr. *Александр Данилович Меньщиков*. St. Petersburg 1847.

---

[81] Shimon Markish, "Советская античность. Из опыта участника," in *Знамя*, no. 4 (2001), ⟨http://magazines.russ.ru/znamia/2001/4/itogi.html⟩ (Accessed January 15, 2017).

Glinka, S. N. *Русские исторические и нравоучительные повести*. Moscow 1810.

Glinka, S. N. *Русская история*. St. Petersburg 1817.

Golubov, Sergej. *Генерал Багратион*. Moscow and Leningrad 1943.

Grigorjev, Sergej. *Берко-кантонист*. Moscow and Leningrad 1927.

Grigorjev, Sergej. "Малахов курган," in *Пионер* 3 (1941), 2-18; 4 (1941), 35-53.

Ishimova, Aleksandra. *История России в рассказах для детей*. St. Petersburg 1837.

Ishimova, Aleksandra. *История России в рассказах для детей. От древних славян до Петра I*. St. Petersburg 2013.

Jan (Janchivetskij), Vasilij. *Спартак*. Moscow and Leningrad 1933.

Jurjev, V. *Гренадер Леонтий Коренной*. Moscow 1945.

Kondratjev, S. P. *Учебник латинского языка для 8-10-го классов средней школы*, Moscow 1950.

Kuznecov, A. (A. I. Kuzmin). *Крепостные мастера*. Moscow and Leningrad 1953.

Lebedev, Aleksandr. *Чаадаев*. Moscow 1965.

Lomonosov, Michail. *О воспитании и образовании*. Moscow 1994.

Lurje, Solomon. *Письмо греческого мальчика*. Moscow and Leningrad 1930.

Marshak, Samuil. *Воспитание словом*. Moscow 1961.

Matje, Milica. *День египетского мальчика*. Moscow 1954.

Matje, Milica. *Кари, ученик художника*. Moscow 1963.

Moiseeva, Klara. *В древнем царстве Урарту*. Moscow and Leningrad 1953.

Moiseeva, Klara. *Дочь Эхнатона*. Moscow 1967.

Ostromenckaja, Nadezhda, and Natalija Bromlej. *Приключения мальчика с собакой*. Moscow 1959.

Propiak, Zhirar de. *Плутарх для молодых девиц, или Краткия жизнеописания славных жен*. Moscow 1816.

Rubinshtejn, Revekka. *Глиняный конверт*. Moscow 1962.

Rubinshtejn, Revekka. *За что Ксеркс высек море*. Moscow 1967.

Saveljev, L. (Leonid Lipavskij). *Штурм Зимнего. Ленин идет в Смольный*. Moscow 1938.

Shklovskij, Viktor. *О мастерах старинных*. Moscow and Leningrad 1951.

Slonimskij, Aleksandr. *Черниговцы. Повесть о восстании Черниговского полка в 1826 году*. Moscow and Leningrad 1928.

Stanjukovich, Konstantin. *Севастопольский мальчик: повесть из времен Крымской войны*. St. Petersburg and Moscow 1902.

Tolstoj, Aleksej. *Повесть о многих превосходных вещах: детство Никиты*. Moscow and Berlin 1922.

Tolstoj, Lev. *Севастопольские рассказы*. Moscow 1943.

Zlobin, Stepan. *Салават Юлаев*. Moscow and Leningrad 1929.

Secondary Sources

Arzamasceva, Irina. *"Век ребенка" в русской литературе 1900-1930 годов*. Moscow 2003.

Arzamasceva, I. N. and S. A. Nikolaeva, eds. *Детская литература*. Moscow 2005.

Bachterev, Igor'. "Совещание по вопросу об исторической книге в Ленинграде," in *Детская литература* 8 (1936), 39-40.

Balina, Marina. "Воспоминания о детстве в советской детской литературе: к вопросу о специфике жанра," in N. Barkovskaja and M. Litovskaja, eds., *Семантическая поэтика русской литературы*. Ekaterinburg 2008, 322-33.

Balina, Marina. "Литературная репрезентация детства в советской и постсоветской России," in N. B. Barannikova and V. G. Bezrogov, eds., *И спросила кроха: Образ ребенка и семьи в педагогике постсоветской России*. Moscow and Tver' 2010, 20-38.

Balina, Marina. "Советская детская литература как культурная институция," in N. L. Lejderman, M. N. Lipoveckij, and M. A. Litovskaja, eds., *Русская литература XX века (1930-е – середина 1950-х годов)*, Vol. 1. Moscow 2014, 331-50.

Balina, Marina. "Crafting the Self: Narratives of Prerevolutionary Childhood in Soviet Literature," in Marina Balina and Larissa Rudova, eds., *Russian Children's Literature and Culture*. New York and London 2008, 91-113.

Balina, Marina. "Creativity through Restraint: The Beginning of Soviet Children's Literature," in Marina Balina and Larissa Rudova, eds., *Russian Children's Literature and Culture*. New York and London 2008, 1-19.

Balina, Marina. "Die sowjetische Kinderliteratur zwischen ästhetischem Experiment und ideologischer Normierung," in Yuri Murashev and Tomas Liptac, eds., *Schrift und Macht*. Vienna, Cologne and Weimar 2013, 119-35.

Bljum, Arlen. *Советская цензура в эпоху тотального террора: 1929-1953*. St. Petersburg 2000.

Chernobaev, Anatolij. *Историки России. Биографии*. Moscow 2001.

Chudakova, Marietta. *Избранные работы в двух томах*. Moscow 2001.

Chukovskaja, Lidija. *Прочерк*. Moscow 2009.

Chukovskaja, Lidija. *Записки об Анне Ахматовой*, Vol. 1. Moscow 2001.

Davydov, V. V., A. M. Prochorov, and E. D. Dneprov, eds. *Российская педагогическая энциклопедия*. Moscow 1993.

deGraffenried, Julie K. *Sacrificing Childhood: Children and the Soviet State in the Great Patriotic War*. Lawrence, KS 2014.

Derman, A. "Генерал Багратион," in *Новый мир* 9 (1943), 117-118.

Dobrenko, Evgenij. "Соцреализм и мир детства," in Hans Günther and Evgenij Dobrenko, eds., *Соцреалистический канон*. St. Petersburg 2000, 31-41.

Dobrenko, Evgenij. *Формовка советского читателя: социальные и эстетические рецепции советской литературы*. St. Petersburg 1997.

Dubin, Boris. *Семантика, риторика и социальные функции 'прошлого': к социологии советского и постсоветского исторического романа*. Moscow 2003.

Fateev, Andrej. *Сталинизм и детская литература в политике номенклатуры СССР (1930-е-1950-е гг.)*. Moscow 2007.

Ginzburg, Lidija. "Пути детской исторической повести," in A. V. Lunacharskij, ed., *Детская литература*. Moscow and Leningrad 1931, 159-81.

Gordin, Jakov. "Занятия историей как оппозиционный акт," in *Знамя* 3 (2001), 180-84.

Gordin, Jakov. "Связь времен," in *Детская литература* 11 (1979), 42-45.

Günther, Hans. *Die Verstaatlichung der Literatur: Entstehung und Funktionsweise des sozialistisch-realistischen Kanons in der sowjetischen Literatur der 30er Jahre*. Stuttgart 1984.

Hellman, Ben. *Fairy Tales and True Stories: The History of Russian Literature for Children and Young People (1574-2010)*. Leiden and Boston 2013.

Judin, Vladimir. *Человек. История. Память*. Moscow 1990.

Kelly, Catriona. *Children's World: Growing Up in Russia, 1890-1991*. New Haven 2007.

Knjazev, A. "Рецензия на роман Милия Езерского, 'Марий и Сулла'," in *Детская литература* 1 (1938), 38-43.

Lysjakov, P. "За историческую повесть для детей," in *Детская литература* 4 (1935), 10-13.

Mandel'shtam, Osip. *Конец романа*. Moscow 1990.

Markish, Shimon. "Советская античность. Из опыта участника," in *Знамя* 4 (2001), 188-191.

Marshak, Samuil. "Мир в картинках," in *Литература и искусство*, 2 October 1943.

Mickenberg, Julia L. *Learning from the Left: Children's Literature, the Cold War, and Radical Politics in the United States*. Oxford 2006.

O'Dell, Felicity Ann. *Socialization through Children's Literature: The Soviet Example*. Cambridge 1978.

Olich, Jacqueline. *Competing Ideologies and Children's Literature in Russia, 1918-1935*. Saarbruecken 2009.

Ronen, Omri. "Детская литература и социалистический реализм," in Hans Günther and Evgenij Dobrenko, eds., *Соцреалистический канон*. St. Petersburg 2000, 969-80.

Rudova, Larissa. "Invitation to a Subversion: The Playful Literature of Grigorii Oster," in Marina Balina and Larissa Rudova, eds., *Russian Children's Literature and Culture*. New York and London 2008, 325-43.

Setin, F. I. *Русская детская литература*. Moscow 1972.

Slotkin, Richard. "Fiction for the Purpose of History," in *Rethinking History*, 9:2 (2005), 221-36.

Sokol, Elena. *Russian Poetry for Children*. Knoxville 1984.

Tvardovskij, Aleksandr. *Новомирский дневник*, Vols. 1 and 2, *1961-1966*. Moscow 2009.
von Glasenapp, Gabriele. "'Was ist Historie? Mit Historie will man was': Geschichtsdarstellungen in der neuren Kinder-und Jugendliteratur," in Gabriele von Glasenapp and Gisela Wilkending, eds., *Geschichte und Geschichten: die Kinder-und Jugendliteratur und das kulturelle und politische Gedächtnis*. Frankfurt am Main 2005, 15-40.
Weld, Sara Pankenier. *Voiceless Vanguard: The Infantilist Aesthetic of the Russian Avant-Garde*. Evanston 2014.
Zhelobovskij, I. "Рассказывание на историческую тему," in *Детская литература* 4 (1935), 10-13.
Zhitomirova, Nataljia. *Советская историко-художественная книга для детей и ее воспитательное значение*. Leningrad 1975.
Zornado, Joseph. "A Poetics of History: Karen Cushman's Medieval World," in *Lion and Unicorn* 21:2 (April 1997), 251-66.

CHAPTER 6

Education of the Soul, Bolshevik Style: Pedagogy in Soviet Children's Literature from the 1920s to the Early 1930s

Olga Voronina

1   Introduction

In Gleb Pushkarev's short story for children, "Яшка Таежник" ("Jashka the Taiga Dweller"), written in 1925, four teenagers deliberate what to do with Jashka's dad, Semjon, who had given his son a flogging after hearing about the boy's wish to join the pioneers. Hurt and indignant, Jashka bit his father's hand and ran away, but now he wants to return home and, somehow, avoid a more severe beating.

> "We will have to reconcile you with your dad," Keshka said.
> "Sure, your dad needs to be reformed, Jashka," the youngest of them, Sanka, suggested.
> "Re-educated," Keshka added.
> "It's him who will re-educate you," Fedka chuckled. "By flogging."
> "We will do it, though," Sanka assured them confidently. "If all of us pioneers will keep on him, we will prevail."[1]

This dialogue provides an edifying insight into the post-revolutionary literature's portrayal of children's power to "re-educate" ("перевоспитывать") the older generation. Jashka's fervor to join the Soviet youth organization finds its match in the vicious reaction of his "retrograde" father. But while Semjon is stronger and has bread, milk and potatoes, without which the boy cannot survive in the taiga, he and other young people are not flustered. They have confidence in their ability to eventually reform their parents. At the end of the story, Jashka wins his father's support by reading him news from a national newspaper, thus enabling the illiterate peasant to participate in local self-government.

Pushkarev portrays Jashka and his friends as both beneficiaries and agents of the Soviet anti-illiteracy campaign. The children prevail, because access to

---

[1] "Яшка-таежник," in Gleb Pushkarev, *Два Петра Ивановича*, Novosibirsk 1949, 9.

FIGURE 6.1 Cover of Gleb Pushkarev's "Яшка Таежник" ("Jashka the Taiga Dweller," Moscow 1927)
ILLUSTRATION BY R. CHERUMJAN

FIGURE 6.2 Illustration by G. G. Likman to "Яшка Таежник" ("Jashka the Taiga Dweller") in Pushkarev's collection *Два Петра Ивановича* (*Two Peter Ivanoviches*, Novosibirsk 1949)

learning endows them with political authority, the right to promote the case of mass education and, thus, the Soviet agenda, to the people who, like Semjon, previously had no hope of knowing what the newspapers said. As pioneers and "reformers" of uneducated adults, the story's protagonists embody the expectations of the party for the newly launched children's communist movement, with one of its key missions being "constantly shaking up their backward parents (отсталые родители), brothers and sisters, influencing them and thus, performing the revolutionary task" of strengthening the new regime.[2]

The fact that a conflict between an ignorant parent and a well-read son forms the plot of a whole array of literary works for children testifies to the importance of the role played by the young Soviet citizens in the Cultural Revolution.[3] It also reveals the critical social function adopted by children's literature in the 1920s and the early 1930s – namely, the imperative to represent children as catalysts of the Soviet-style enlightenment capable of reforming the older, apolitical or aggressively anti-communist, population. Works by such children's authors as Nikolaj Bogdanov, Lidija Budogoskaja, Anatolij Finogenov, Innokentij Grjaznov, Aleksej Kozhevnikov, Larisa Larina, Grigorij Medynskij, Ivan Shorin, and Boris Vinnikov, demonstrate that the real heroes of children's novellas and short stories of that time were the fledgling *kulturträgers*, eager to coach their mothers and fathers and willing to instruct teachers how to convey knowledge, run schools, and improve students' morals. Often depicted as mature beyond their years, intellectually independent, and free from emotional attachment to their families, the children preferred to claim direct descent from the state or its leaders. Poems and holiday chants, often printed alongside works of fiction, underscored this lineage: "I am alone, no father and no mother, / I am only your son, my republic. / [...] Neither father nor mother I have. / I am your son, Revolution!"[4] Or: "Pioneers! / Lenin is no more! / Send a call to the world! / To battle! / Our grandfather summoned us so – / Our dear Iljich!"[5]

---

2 Ja. A. Pregel' and A. A. Ljubimova, eds., *Детское коммунистическое движение*, Moscow, Leningrad 1932, 40.

3 Young people's agency in Cultural Revolution is explicated in Sheila Fitzpatrick, *The Cultural Front: Power and Culture in Revolutionary Russia*, Ithaca 1992.

4 Sergej Malachov, "В детском доме" ("In the Orphanage," 1920), in *Муза в красной косынке: Комсомольская поэзия 1980-1950 гг.*, Moscow 1970, 51; V. Andreeva, "Пионерский песенник. Молодые побеги," ⟨https://litlife.club/br/?b=272297&p=2⟩ (Accessed December 31, 2017). The story of pioneers' reciting this poem at a meeting is recorded in T. N. Bagratjan, ed., *Юность комсомольская: Воспоминания первых кубанских комсомольцев*, Krasnodar 1956, 223.

5 Andrej Irkutov, "На смерть Ильича" ("On the Death of Il'ich"), in *Барабан* 2 (1924), 24. Iljich is Lenin's patronymic.

The reversal of the adult-child relationship made Jashka's literary siblings and friends, protagonists of the early Soviet children's literature, appear as direct opposites of the curious and playful, but generally humble and obedient little heroes of Russian fiction for young readers.[6] Similarly, the contemporaneous depiction of Soviet parents and educators often emphasized their ignorance, ethical and ideological flaws, lack of discipline, passivity, and disorientation, thus turning the fictional adults into a pathetic parody of strict, controlling, but also dependable, God-loving and affectionate mothers, fathers, nannies, governesses and a few chosen teachers from Lev Tolstoj's reading primers (1871, 1875), Nikolaj Garin-Michajlovskij's *Детство Темы* (*Tema's Childhood*, 1892), works by Aleksandra Annenskaja, Lidija Charskaja, Aleksandr Kruglov, Lidija Lidanova, Nikolaj Poznjakov, Vera Zhelichovskaja, and other writers of the pre-revolutionary era. The difference is striking and requires an explication. Why was the early Soviet children's literature so vested in presenting children as agents of the revolutionary enlightenment? How could a literary work for young readers maintain its didactic potency while portraying incompetent, illiterate, and morally depraved adults? Moreover, how did early Soviet children's authors, intent on violating the causal hierarchy of a traditional children's story (a child learns a lesson from an adult or acquires a valuable experience by interacting with an older and wiser person), preserve the narrative integrity of their fiction?

Recent literary scholarship has provided perceptive assessments of the idiosyncratic deviations of the post-revolutionary children's narratives from the pedagogical and discursive traditions of the preceding and following decades. Igor' Kondakov, for example, commented on the reversal of parent-child roles by comparing the image of childhood created by authors from the 1920s to the early 1930s to their representation of the young Soviet state either as a gigantic "kindergarten" or an insecure "adolescent." Since the majority of the adult population of the former Russian empire participated in such dramatic historic processes as the three Russian revolutions passively, Kondakov suggested, they had to be represented as inert people feeling childish "excitement and bewilderment, hope and despair, exultation and protest" in the face of the new and ruthless power.[7] Orlando Figes, who studied the 1930s phenomenon of chil-

---

6 Marina Kostjuchina suggests that the obedience discourse in Russian pre-revolutionary children's literature was sometimes taken to an extreme, to the point of young protagonists' complete loss of willpower. M. S. Kostjuchina, *Золотое зеркало. Русская литература для детей XVIII-XIX веков*, Moscow 2008, 22.

7 Igor' Kondakov, "'Убежище-2': 'Детский дискурс' советской литературы в 1930-е годы," in *Ребенок в истории и культуре, Библиотека журнала* Исследователь / Researcher, Vol. 4, Moscow 2010, 72-73.

dren renouncing their parents, illuminated a different side of this relationship. In his opinion, films, books, and songs that young people encountered in their daily lives taught them to believe that they could emulate achievements of Soviet heroes only if they broke up with their families or revealed their political digressions to the authorities.[8]

Irina Arzamasceva presented the anti-pedagogical enthusiasm of the era as a struggle – first, for the "discreditation of family values and the curtailment of the family theme in early Soviet books for children," and later, for the literary reappearance of loving and controlling parents.[9] Evgenij Dobrenko, in his turn, analyzed the evolution of the Soviet school novella by comparing its vicissitudes to the transformation of the Soviet education system, from the destruction of the "traditional scheme of 'pedagogical influence'" to the disciplinary strategies and pedagogical violence of the Stalin era. Dobrenko expertly documented the genre's transition from such literary works about children's "self-organization," free will, and insubordination as Leonid Panteleev and Grigorij Belych's *Республика Шкид* (*The Republic of Shkid*, 1926) to the "internalization" of Soviet pedagogy in Arkadij Gajdar's novels and its "institutionalization" in the Socialist Realist prose of the postwar period.[10] In Dobrenko's opinion, the consolidation of the genre in the 1940s and the following decade coincided with the return of the authoritarian educator as well as with the elimination of such themes from children's literature that might have reminded young readers of the post-revolutionary "new school (новая школа)" – an institution in which children were given the right to mastermind the academic process and organise political engagement of faculty and students.[11]

And yet, it was the new school and its dynamic new students that reigned supreme in the literary imagination of the 1920s and early 1930s. Accordingly, such key features of Soviet pedagogy as the replacement of moral education (воспитание) with the development of class consciousness (сознательность), the emphasis on collective learning, and the requirement that young people actively engage in teaching adults how to read, lead a "cultured" life, and participate in the construction of Socialism, became central in Soviet works for children of that time. In contrast, the image of a strict and demanding teacher lost its relevance in fiction for a while, just as it

---

8   Orlando Figes, *The Whisperers: Private Life in Stalin's Russia*, New York 2008, 131.
9   Irina Arzamasceva, "'Век ребенка' в русской литературе 1900-1930 годов, Moscow 2003, 97-98.
10 E. A. Dobrenko, "'Весь реальный детский мир' (школьная повесть и 'наше счастливое детство')," in M. R. Balina, V. Vjugin, eds., *'Убить Чарскую ...': Парадоксы советской литературы для детей (1920-е – 1930-е гг.)*. St. Petersburg 2013.
11 Ibid., 201.

did in real life.[12] Reduced to the ranks of "old specialists," if not "counter-revolutionary elements," experienced educators and their theories were suppressed. Konstantin Ushinskij, a luminary of pre-revolutionary Russian pedagogy, insisted that teachers focus intensely on "the needs of the human soul" and praised their desire to study the student "whole, as he is in reality, with all his weaknesses, in all his glory" so that educators could better direct their students' development.[13] Vladimir Shul'gin, who in 1922-1932 led the Soviet Research Institute for School Methodology, on the contrary, demanded that children be "liberated from the teacher's domination" and introduced to the idea of socialist construction directly, through productive labor or political work.[14]

This essay traces the evolution of the concept of "the education of the soul" ("воспитание души") in early Soviet children's books. It draws parallels between the portrayal of "воспитание" ("moral education") in novels and short stories for young readers written in the 1920s and early 1930s and in pre-revolutionary Russian children's literature. Analyzing the child-parent and child-state relationship in texts written during these two periods, it juxtaposes pedagogical models propagated by Soviet children's writers and those espoused before the Revolution. To begin with, the traditional image of children obedient to the point of losing their will and creativity is compared to a new type of protagonist that emerged in early Soviet children's books: a young person who is an educator, judge, and moral guide for her parents and teachers. Secondly, the model of education for the collective and through the collective is featured here as a distorted incarnation of the Enlightenment paradigm of "closed schooling," namely, of bringing up children in state-run educational establishments where they were isolated from the influence of their families. Al-

---

[12] "Student independence was a characteristic feature of Soviet schools in the 1920s, especially of advanced level city schools [...]. Organizers of children's self-governance had almost unlimited authority in some schools. Students regulated not only their own daily lives, but often spread their influence to pedagogues and staff." A. Ju. Rozhkov, "Неформальные сообщества школьников и типичное в обретении коллективной идентичности в 1920-е годы," in *Ребенок в истории и культуре*, 344. Valerij Shubinskij writes about the authority of student self-governance committees in early Soviet schools in his biography of Daniil Charms. See, *Даниил Хармс: Жизнь человека на ветру*, Moscow 2015, 68-69.

[13] "О нравственном элементе воспитания," in K. D. Ushinskij, *Собрание сочинений*, Vol. 5, Moscow 1949, 282; Ushinskij, "Человек как предмет воспитания. Педагогическая антропология," in S. V. Jakimec, ed., *История педагогики и образования в России. Хрестоматия*, Orsk 2011, 87-88.

[14] V. N. Shul'gin, "О целях школы," in *Советская производственно-трудовая школа. Книга для чтения и работы по основам советской системы воспитания*, Moscow 1928, 71-72.

though by the mid-1930s, political, pedagogical, and literary attempts to erect a wall between the family and the child growing up in a collective environment had failed, these efforts inspired a variety of fictional communities in which child protagonists were endowed with unprecedented agency. The essay ends with a discussion of the return of the authoritarian parent to Soviet children's literature during the country's transition to totalitarianism.

2 New Times, New Virtues: Learning from Life and from Each Other

Lev Tolstoj's story "Птичка" ("Birdie"), written for his reading primer *Новая азбука* (*New Azbooka*, 1875), features a dialogue between Serezha, who has caught a bird and wants to keep it as a pet, and his mother, who disapproves of the little boy's desire to hold a wild creature in captivity. Tolstoj's narrative focuses on Serezha's actions and feelings (he boasts of his ability to care for the finch but is shamed and grieves sincerely when the bird dies), but it also allows the adult to be heard. Although the mother does not force the child to follow her will, she voices her concern, gives advice, and reminds Serezha of his duties. Serezha's decision to "never catch birds again," which ends the story, is presented to the young reader as a lesson well-learned.[15]

Still read by Russian children in textbooks and anthologies, Tolstoij's "Птичка" exemplifies a traditional didactic tale, with its narrative climax reduced to a child's internalization of a virtue or a parent's will. Other, less anthologized, works of pre-revolutionary children's literature replicated this model. For example, *Колокольчики* (*Bluebells*), an 1890 reader for preschoolers by V. P. Andreevskaja, is almost entirely made up of stories which culminate in children's learning a moral lesson from upright and intelligent adults.[16] Not surprisingly, eighteenth-century moralistic fiction was even more committed to asserting the authority of honorable and enlightened grown-ups. In Evgenija Putilova's summation, it mostly comprised "sententious conversations between fathers and children, educators and students, teachers and well-mannered tutees."[17]

The configuring of the eighteenth and nineteenth century children's story around a child's interaction with adults reflected pedagogical goals of the

---

15 Lev Tolstoj, *Новая азбука* (*New Azbooka*), Moscow 1875, 76-77.
16 V. P. Andreevskaja, *Колокольчики* (*Bluebells*), St. Petersburg 1890.
17 E. O. Putilova, *Детское чтение для сердца и разума. Очерки по истории детской литературы*, St. Petersburg 2005, 257.

time. Pre-revolutionary "воспитание," or "moral education," focused on fostering such virtues as "intense concentration," "intellectual agency," and "wholesomeness," along with respectfulness, charity, and patriotism.[18] With Christian morality at its core, Russian pedagogy directed teachers' efforts towards investigating the "deepest recesses" of children's psyche in the belief that, expertly guided towards goodness, children would eventually reproduce "supreme ideas and the noblest actions" of their virtuous role models.[19] This approach differed greatly from the teaching style required of a Soviet pedagogue who, following Anton Makarenko's lead, was expected to "get as close as possible to the children's collective, to form a close friendship with it [...], to encourage the activity of the brigade and stimulate the demands of the collective towards each individual."[20] Even the youngest Soviet citizens were meant to learn and acquire virtue independently of adults. In the words of a preschool education theoretician Raisa Charitonova-Ostrovskaja, "from an early age they could investigate and untangle the problems of nature and society on their own," while the goal of educators was to "teach children causal logic, connection, the dynamics of real-life experiences and thus foster the foundations of the Marxist, dialectical worldview."[21]

Soviet Children's literature, and especially its politically zealous vanguard, readily adopted the new educational agenda. Like Marxist pedagogues, children's writers who identified with the party program assumed the task of bringing up "a proletarian child capable of participating in class struggle" and "a strong individual endowed with tools of dominating nature and subjecting it to the needs of humankind."[22] As a consequence, in the first post-revolutionary decades, hundreds of robust, vociferous, self-aware child protagonists emerged, pushing meek Serezhas and their respectable mothers out of literature for young readers. Dimka and Zhigan, in Gajdar's novella *P.B.C.*

18   Jakimec, *История педагогики*, 42.
19   Ushinskij, *Собрание сочинений*, Vol. 5, 282.
20   A. S. Makarenko, *Собрание сочинений*, Vol. 5, Moscow 1971, 185.
21   R. Charitonova-Ostrovskaja, *Детское коммунистическое движение и дошкольное воспитание*, Moscow, Leningrad 1926, 10. Theoreticians of Soviet education believed that even four-year-olds would benefit from political indoctrination, since the earlier they started, the more active supporters of Bolshevik ideology they would become. M. Sventickaja, *Наш детский сад*, Moscow 1924, 204.
22   *Советская производственно-трудовая школа*, 73, 77. In the words of he editor-in-chief of the central State Publishing House (Госиздат), "Literature needs to create ideological weapons for all areas of socialist construction. It must attain objectives of proletarian ideology not only by forming a common proletarian worldview, but also by endorsing methods of applying it to all areas of activity and cognition." M. B. Vol'fson, *Пути советской книги*, Moscow 1929, 34.

(*The R[evolutionary]. M[ilitary]. C[ouncil].*, 1925), overcome an anarchist bully Goloven', help Dimka's family to withstand Goloven's threats, and rescue a wounded soldier. Zhigan, who repeatedly risks his life to help the Red Army, obtains from it a document stating that he is "not a hoodlum or hooligan, but someone who has proven his revolutionary worth."[23] A peasant lad from Lev Ostroumov's Макар-следопыт (*Makar the Scout*, 1925) turns out to be smarter and more resourceful than many adults when he helps red partisans during the Civil War.[24] In a less known novella in verse, Vol'f Erlich's *О ленивом Ваньке и его щенке* (*On Lazy Van'ka and His Pup*, 1926), an idle and obtuse youth learns not from his parents, but from a sensible, diligent pioneer. Mit'ka teaches Van'ka how to work hard and thus emulate Lenin, who "spared no effort to the day he died / And gave his life up for the people."[25] Even children portrayed as weak from hunger and disease, such as tuberculosis patients in Kornej Chukovskij's Солнечная (*Sunny Place*, 1933), defy adults who treat them as sufferers. They want to contribute "if only a brick, or a tiny screw" to the gigantic socialist construction project, so that "sooner, not the day after tomorrow, but tomorrow, happiness for the entire world would ensue – against the will of the blood-sucking bourgeois."[26]

The author of imaginative and playful poetic tales, Chukovskij, unlike the majority of his colleagues, was aware of the "phony" spirit of his novella, of its sham doctrinal undertones.[27] He himself was a victim of political attacks and harsh criticism. In 1928, the magazine Красная печать (*Red Press*) called the writer an advocate of "the ideology of the disappearing philistinism, the cult of the dying-away family, and the bourgeois childhood."[28] But in spite of this and other attacks, Chukovskij tried to fight direct censorial interference in his works. He once pointedly refused to make the protagonist of Крокодил (*Crocodile*), the "valiant Vanja Vasil'chikov," a Komsomol member and always affirmed a child's right to experience, through reading, the only true kind of "moral satisfaction" – that of "good overcoming evil."[29] Like educators of the past, Chukovskij insisted on the children's writers' need to study not political doctrine, but young people's "psychology, thinking, and literary demands."[30]

---

23   Arkadij Gajdar, Сочинения, Vol. 1, Moscow, Leningrad 1949, 59.
24   Lev Ostroumov, Макар-следопыт (*Makar the Scout*), Vols. 1 and 2, Moscow 1925.
25   Vol'f Erlich, О ленивом Ваньке и его щенке (*On Lazy Van'ka and His Pup*), Moscow, Leningrad 1926, 13.
26   Kornej Chukovskij, Солнечная (*Sunny Place*), Moscow 1933, 34.
27   Chukovskij, Дневник, 1901-1969, Vol. 2, Moscow 2003, 22.
28   K. Sverdlova, "О чуковщине," in Красная печать 9-10 (1928), 92.
29   Chukovskij, Дневник, 1901-1969, Moscow 2003. Vol. 1 , 299; Vol. 2, 210.
30   Chukovskij, От двух до пяти, Moscow 1990, 364.

Nevertheless, several times throughout his life he was forced to acknowledge the importance of ideological content in his own work and that of others.[31] *Солнечная* serves as an edifying example of the survival tactics of Soviet children's literature. Dependent on support from the new regime, the author of the novella had to endorse the Soviet model of moral development by emphasizing children's individual and collective agency in learning, advancing the country's economy, and fighting counter-revolution, even though the book's central story was the struggle of his youngest daughter against tuberculosis in a Crimean therapeutic facility, where she died in 1931.

Soviet children's writers' depiction of Boshevik-style moral education differed from the representation of Russian "воспитание" by their predecessors. A child's "soul" – one's ability to think, feel and behave ethically – was no longer on the dramatically altered educational agenda of the state. The objective Soviet pedagogy had in mind was much bolder – instead of focusing on one specific boy or girl and their spiritual needs, it targeted a group of children, the so-called "коллектив," a social class, or the country's entire population. The ambitiousness of this approach is one of the reasons why Aleksandr Zaluzhnyj, the 1920s authority on collective education, spurned the long-standing pedagogical system of John Locke on the grounds of its "anachronistic" concentration on an individual child.[32] While Locke maintained that children's "souls" were a unique psychological phenomenon that required teachers' unremitting care, Zaluzhnyj believed that the "spirit of collectivism" was the main goal of any educational project. He insisted on teaching children in peer groups engaged in organized activities and physical work. According to Zaluzhnyj, social skills could be shaped by means of fostering leadership, encouraging competition, and facilitating imitation of more "conscientious" individuals. His methods were similar to the pedagogical techniques applied to adults who were "reformed" through collective labor.[33]

In Soviet pedagogy, spiritual maturity became synonymous with the appropriation of the communist worldview, an amalgamation that allowed Anatolij Lunacharskij to equate the soul of a young adult with his or her political integrity. Explicating the party's ideas on education in a speech given to students

---

31   For a detailed analysis of the 1928-29 campaign against "Chukovshchina" and Chukovskij's "repentance" under pressure, see I. V. Lukjanova, *Корней Чуковский*, Moscow 1997, 496-541.

32   Aleksandr Zaluzhnyj, "Задачи изучения детского коллектива," in *Детский коллектив и ребенок*, A. Zaluzhnyj, S. Lozinskij, eds., Charkov 1926, 11-12.

33   Aleksandr Zaluzhnyj, *Учение о коллективе. Методология. Детский коллектив*, Moscow, Leningrad 1930, 291.

of the Sverdlov Communist University in Moscow on January 25, 1924, three days after Lenin's death, the first People's Commissar of the Enlightenment urged his audience to obtain general and specialized knowledge by enduring the torturous struggle "for your own soul and for the soul of your roommate, your desk-mate – the struggle to attain the [...] complete communist consciousness, which should infiltrate your flesh and blood to the bone, and to your very bone marrow."[34] Lunacharskij placed communist consciousness above learning. He also devised an eloquent, albeit mixed, metaphor, which presented the acquisition of the required ideological outlook as a spiritual as well as physiological process, violent at its core. By suggesting that ideology was appropriated through struggle and by urging others to adopt this strategy, he expected students to have communist ideals penetrate their souls, flesh, and blood and thus take over their entire being. Moreover, education, for Lunacharskij, was a "collective" project and therefore presupposed mutual control and encouragement of the less politically conscious students by their more enthusiastic comrades. And last but not least, Lunacharskij's presentation of ideologized learning as a struggle rendered teachers' participation in the educational process unnecessary: from his standpoint, students did not receive knowledge from educators, but absorbed it directly from a collective experience, as some kind of potent substance that facilitated their cognitive transformation.

Just as Soviet children were losing their individuality and becoming dispensable elements in a gigantic social machine, their moral selves were also deemed unnecessary and dissolved in group activities. Pedagogy was becoming more prone to abstraction, and so were its charges. The nineteenth-century critic Vissarion Belinskij envisioned an ideal child reader who enjoyed books which explained that happiness "consisted not in superficial and spectral chance, but in the depth of one's soul."[35] Conversely, little bookworms begot by communist schooling turned out to be lovers of conjectural, ideologically pointed narratives and action-packed violent stories.[36] In the words of one school principal, early Soviet fourth-graders named novellas "about children assisting adults in the Civil War" and "helping adults in building a new life" among their favorite reading.[37]

---

34 Anatolij Lunacharskij, "Ленин и молодежь," in A. Lunacharskij, *Ленин*, Moscow 1924, 40-41.
35 Cited in N. V. Chechov, *Детская литература*, Moscow 1909, 5.
36 For a convincing study of violence in Avant-Garde Soviet children's literature and the young readers' reaction to it, see Evgeny Steiner, *Stories for Little Comrades: Revolutionary Artists in the Early Soviet Children's Book*, Seattle 1999.
37 M. M. Lychina, *Внеклассное детское чтение в нашей школе*, Moscow 1936, 8-9.

Children's literature of the 1920s and 30s fed this need by churning out novels and short stories dominated by little slogan carriers – or diminutive bearers of *Zeitgeist*. Take the example of Ivan Shorin's story "Одногодки" ("Born the Same Year," 1934). Lidija Chukovskaja, a perceptive scholar and Kornej Chukovskij's elder daughter, praised its protagonist, Shurka Grachev, as the "master of his land and his destiny – a true hero of his time."[38] Chukovskaja's praise notwithstanding, Shurka seems to be an embodiment of a political concept, rather than a lifelike little child. The boy baffles his interlocutor, the story's narrator, when he says that, unlike a character in H. G. Wells' *The Time Machine* (1895), he would be happy to travel ahead in time and stay there. Not only is Shurka unaware of the pessimistic epilogue of Wells' novella, but his dream is also as pragmatic as it is opportunistic. He wants to grow up fast so that he can drain swamps, uproot tree stumps, and become chairman of the local collective farm (председатель колхоза).[39]

Child heroes of Innokentij Grjaznov's *Искатели мозолей* (*Callus Seekers*, 1931) also emblematize political conformity. The boys form a collective and start a summer camp so that they can build an unprecedented monument to socialist society – an enormous public park, which, when seen from above, will outline the portrait of Lenin. Their loyalty to communist ideas manifests itself in the heroes' actions and dialogues, some of which offer direct paraphrases of the party leaders' speeches and propaganda pamphlets:

> Archipelashka put his saw down and straightened himself up: "[…] We have to be ready for anything. This is our duty!"
> "Not for anything. For struggle!" we corrected him.
> Archipelashka began to argue: "For what kind of struggle?"
> "For communism, of course."
> "And what did Lenin say about communism?"
> "Communism is Soviet power plus electrification."
> "And on top of that?"
> "Do you know yourself?"
> "So you give up? Then I will teach you!" And Archipelashka solemnly articulated every word: "'Communism can be built by the hands of millions of people after they have learned to do everything on their own.' Do you get it? Now, shouldn't we learn how to do everything?"[40]

---

38 Lidija Chukovskaja, "О книгах забытых или незамеченных," in *Вопросы литературы* 2 (1958) ⟨http://www.chukfamily.ru/lidia/prosa-lidia/stati-prosa-lidia/o-knigax-zabytyx-ili-nezamechennyx⟩ (Accessed December 29, 2017).

39 Ivan Shorin, "Одногодки" ("Born the Same Year"), in T. Gabe, L. Zheldin, and Z. Zadunajskaja, eds., *Костер*, Moscow 1934, 53-54.

40 I. Grjaznov, *Искатели мозолей* (*Callus Seekers*), Moscow 1931, 22.

FIGURE 6.3   Cover of Innokentij Grjaznov's *Искатели мозолей* (*Callus Seekers*, Moscow 1931)
ILLUSTRATION BY M. RAJSKAJA

Archipelashka and his buddy Shurka Grachev are stick figures, rather than portrayals of real children. Their speeches are full of party slogans, while their actions are too purposefull and politically motivated to be convincing. All the same, these mouthpieces of party propaganda ruled supreme in children's fiction of the first two post-revolutionary decades, along with other, somewhat more believable, child characters, such as Mishka Dodonov in Aleksandr Neverov's *Ташкент – город хлебный* (*Tashkent, the City of Bread*, 1923) or Garas'ka Ershov in Vladimir Jurezanskij's *Клад* (*The Treasure*, 1927).[41] What sustained their appeal and made young readers ask for more books with artificially constructed, bombastic protagonists? In all probability, the heroes' popularity lied in their unintentional but audacious autonomy. Homeless or uncared for, gaining knowledge from their daily experiences or already too mature for teachers to endow them with any useful knowledge, they claimed verisimilitude on two levels. On the one level, they belonged to the time-honored type of an adventure story protagonist who, like Jim Hawkins in *Treasure Island* by Robert Louis Stevenson (1883) or Mary and Robert Grant in *In Search of the Castaways* by Jules Verne (1867-68), rescued adults as many times as they were rescued by them and learned from their elders while teaching them important moral lessons in return. On the other level, Archipelashka and Garas'ka's independence and resourcefulness were not entirely fibs of their authors' imagination. These characters reminded young Soviet readers of the recent tragedy of children's "liberation" from the grown-ups, when, in the wake of the Civil War and the Red Terror, entire provinces were left depopulated, demoralized, and incapable of caring for their young.[42]

---

41 Child protagonists also delivered party slogans in such books as Aleksandr German's *Слушали-постановили* (*We Have Listened and Decided*, Orel 1925), Petr Zamojskij's *Озорник шатущий* (*A Wagabond Scoundrel*, Moscow 1926), *Вместе веселей* (*It Is Merrier Together*, Moscow 1928), *Деревенская быль* (*A True Story from the Countryside*, Moscow 1924), and *Смутьян* (*Mischief-Maker*, Moscow 1926), Konstantin Minaev's *Школьники* (*Schoolchildren*, Moscow 1926) and *Назарка-атаман* (*Nazarka the Ring Leader*, Moscow, Leningrad 1925), Georgij Nikiforov's *Наши ребята* (*Our Lads*, Moscow, Leningrad 1925), and Andrej Irkutov's *Все за одного* (*All for One*, Charkov 1926).

42 In 1920, more than two million people in Central Russia had typhus; many of them died of the disease. The two subsequent years were the years of the famine; hundreds of thousands starved to death in the Middle Volga district, in the Ukraine, in the Ural region, and in Kazakhstan. In 1922, the number of orphans populating the new Soviet State reached seven million. The Children's Emergency Committee (*Детская чрезвычайная комиссия*) established in 1921 and run initially by Feliks Dzerzhinskij could not find placement for all the homeless children; in 1922-23, it managed to institutionalize only 350,000 orphans. Jörg Baberowski, *Красный террор: история сталинизма*, Moscow 2007, 50-51; A. N. Krivonosov, "Исторический опыт борьбы с беспризорностью," in *Государство и право* 7 (2003), 92-98.

The tragic history of the young Soviet state, along with the post-revolutionary shift in pedagogical discourse from the teacher-driven education to that where students were learning in an unmediated way, either collectively or from experience, help explain why the unsupervised life of strong-willed, resourceful youngsters became one of the master plots of the early Soviet fiction for children. Novels and memoirs about homeless childhood and the transformation of former vagabond boys and girls (беспризорники) into dependable Soviet citizens formed a genre of great interest.[43] Children's authors, however, did not stop at the portrayal of quick-witted orphans. In such works as Nina Lipina's *Бабушка Андрюша* (*Grandmother Andrjusha*, 1926) or Sergej Rozanov's *Приключения Травки* (*The Adventures of Travka*, 1928), even the offspring of relatively privileged families had to struggle with vagrancy or a temporary sense of abandonment and disorientation so that they could overcome these temporary difficulties by getting help from a collective of strangers.[44] In a word, the pedagogical goal of cultivating the politically determined class consciousness in Soviet youth ushered in narratives about single-minded little protagonists who were relinquishing their families for the sake of a more desirable parent – the Soviet state itself.

3 Upside-Down Education: How Soviet Children "Reformed" Adults

Intent on schooling its youth in the spirit of communism, Soviet pedagogues embraced the idea of the state as the sole educator of the country's younger generation. The upbringing of a child "for the society and through the soci-

---

43   In addition to Belych and Panteleev's *Республика Шкид*, first published in 1926, and Anton Makarenko's *Педагогическая поэма* (*The Pedagogical Poem*, 1931), Soviet publishing houses issued such works about homeless children as Aleksej Kozhevnikov's *Шпана. Из жизни беспризорных* (*Hoodlums. From the Life of the Homeless*, Moscow, Leningrad 1925), Vjacheslav Shishkov's *Странники* (*Wanderers*, Leningrad 1931), Lidija Sejfullina's *Правонарушители* (*Lawbreakers*, Novonikolaevsk 1922), Viktor Savin's *Шаромыжники* (*Tearaways*, Moscow 1925), and Ivan Mikitenko's *Уркаганы* (*Delinquents*, Charkov 1929 and Moscow 1931). Not all of these authors expressed the pedagogical optimism characteristic of Belych, Panteleev, and Makarenko's narratives.

44   When Andrjusha's grandmother ends up in a hospital with a broken leg, the fourteen-year-old has to learn how to nurse his two younger siblings, cook for his hard-working dad, and take care of the cow (Lipina, *Бабушка Андрюша* [*Grandmother Andrjusha*], Moscow 1926). Travka is a Moscow preschooler who gets separated from his father at a Moscow railroad station. His odyssey through the capital's suburbs back to his parents allows the author to portray Soviet people as one caring family, kind to one another and especially to children (Rozanov, *Приключения Травки* [*The Adventures of Travka*], Moscow 1928).

ety" meant, first and foremost, a separation of children from their families.⁴⁵ Wife of Grigorij Zinovjev, Zlata Lilina, an early proponent of communist education and the head of the children's section of the State Publishing House (Госиздат), insisted that "to educate a child correctly meant to turn him into a designer of new life not only for himself but for all the workers [...] to bring up the child as a healthy fighter-constructor (борец-строитель)."⁴⁶ In Lilina's opinion, children were to be "nationalized" – taken away from the "rough influence" of their families.⁴⁷ Having observed the anti-sanitary, crowded, drunken lifestyle of workers at industrial enterprises in the vicinity of Moscow, where children lived in barracks, drank alcohol and suffered from sexually transmitted diseases, she articulated ten "commandments" of the communist education that aimed to improve the life of this generation. If the children were not isolated, Lilina stated, they would be lost to the Soviet cause.⁴⁸ In her "fifth commandment," the party pedagogue demanded:

> Not every parent, not every family is capable of bringing up a child. Children need to be brought up in a collective, with the help of the Soviet public [общественность], with entrusting the education of children to people who are specially trained for that.⁴⁹

Lenin's widow Nadezhda Krupskaja, Lunacharskij, Lev Trockij, and other prominent Bolsheviks reiterated this idea. Krupskaja became one of the founders of the Soviet industrial-labor school (производственно-трудовая школа). Its goals matched "those of the working class" and included the eradication of class oppression, the expansion of "intellectual horizons" of the future builders of communism, and inculcation of children in how to be useful and self-reliant.⁵⁰ Krupskaja's other project was the Children's Movement (детдвижение), which acquired a formal political status and became known as the Pioneer Organization or Young Pioneers in 1922. According to Krupskaja, the children's movement "had a huge pedagogical significance," because

---

45 S. Lozinskij, "Социальные уклоны в современной педагогике," in *Детский коллектив и ребенок*, A. Zaluzhnij and S. Lozinskij, eds., Charkov 1926, 3.

46 Z. I. Lilina, *Родители, учитесь воспитывать своих детей*, Moscow 1929, 3.

47 Cited in V. M. Zenzinov, *Беспризорные*, Paris 1929, 36.

48 Out of six hundred and ten children polled in Moscow's Zamoskvoretskij district alone, 79% of boys and 60% of girls drank alcohol regularly. Lilina, *Родители*, 10.

49 Ibid., 11.

50 N. K. Krupskaja, "К вопросу о целях школы," in *Советская производственная трудовая школа. Педагогическая хрестоматия*, A. G. Kalashnikov, ed., Moscow 1925, 73.

it "taught children how to connect their interests to those of the collective" and "helped them form collectivist psychology," which was supposed to "regulate instincts and eliminate the sense of helplessness and loneliness."[51] Krupskaja welcomed pioneers' participation in academic self-governance, encouraged their involvement in every aspect of school management, and insisted on their right to prevent "maltreatment" of students by teachers.[52] Additionally, Krupskaja kept stressing the failure of the family to bring up a successful Soviet man or woman. In her opinion, the pioneer movement could replace the father, who was always busy earning the daily bread and engaging in political activism, and the mother, buried in housework. Unlike the negligent parents, the child collective provided young people with "food for thought" and "many happy experiences," she wrote.[53]

Early Soviet children's authors embraced the educational agenda promulgated by Lilina and Krupskaja, turning it into the central conflict of their school and pioneer novellas. Short stories, poems, and plays written for young readers in the 1920s and early 1930s featured school not only as "the main lever of proletarian dictatorship in the field of education and moral upbringing," but also as a socialist haven for youngsters who would otherwise suffer from parental neglect.[54] Likewise, children's books of the period frequently showcased the aberrant, politically incorrect, or criminal behavior of parents, relatives, and elder siblings of child heroes. Adults' misdemeanors served as an explicit counterpoint to the activities of precocious children aspiring for leadership and academic success. This is why heroes of books for young readers often had to fight for the right to abandon their families' ways before they could begin their quest for socialist morality. Their pursuit of righteousness emblematized the weaning of the politically aggressive, socially active young generation of Soviet people – those who accepted the state as their progenitor – from their retrograde families and traditionally-minded teachers.

In Anatolij Finogenov's novella *Кто впереди* (*Who Is Ahead*, 1932), two brigades of "октябрята" ("little Octobrists") compete for academic excellence and political engagement; they also have a punctuality contest – the students who are repeatedly late to school bring their "collectives" down on the competition scale.[55] When a new student, Manja, starts to miss morning classes regularly, her classmate Len'ka Leshtykov pays her a visit and discovers that Manja's

---

51   Krupskaja, *Детское коммунистическое движение*, Moscow 1925, 41.
52   Ibid., 45.
53   Ibid., 22.
54   Ibid., 57.
55   "Октябрята" were a junior league of the Pioneer movement.

FIGURE 6.4 Cover of Anatolij Finogenov's *Кто впереди* (*Who Is Ahead*, Leningrad 1932)
ILLUSTRATION BY M. GEREC

grandmother refuses to discipline the child. The conversation between the seven-year-old boy and the old woman clearly establishes on whose side the author of the book is. Finogenov juxtaposes irresponsible behavior of adults with the integrity of the younger generation:

> "Is Manja at home?" Len'ka asked, panting.
> The old woman replied: "Manja is asleep."
> "How come she is asleep? And her school?"
> "Let her sleep," the old woman said. "The school won't disappear. Manja was out late last night."[56]

---

56   Anatolij Finogenov, *Кто впереди* (Leningrad 1932), 19.

Stigma had a powerful, dramatic potential in Soviet literature as well as in Soviet politics. Finogenov takes advantage of it to represent the shaming of an adult by a conscientious child. Len'ka's dialogue with Manja's grandmother demonstrates that her affection is misplaced: it deprives the girl of her education, the benefit of which is more important than sleep. According to Finogenov and other children's authors of the first post-revolutionary years, not only parents misunderstand the needs of their children, but they also misjudge their enthusiasm for group activities offered by the school. They also underestimate the redemptive power of political children's movements. This confusion affords children's writers a chance to deepen the generational conflict and thus make narratives about children's political and moral righteousness more captivating. By turning families into battlefields where the younger generation successfully fights the older, children's authors are able to conceive compelling fictional adversaries against whom child protagonists could struggle and win. In Finogenov's novella, for example, Len'ka overcomes the doting old woman, gets Manja to earn points for avoiding tardiness, and helps his brigade get the first place in the "socialist competition."

Fictional parents in the Soviet children's books from the 1920s and early 1930s are often portrayed as anti-heroes – they are either confused about politics or criminally unable to adopt the Bolshevik way of life. In *Кто впереди*, Len'ka's actions can propel the plot towards a happy ending, because the boy is endowed with the gift of leadership. It is he who forces his brigade to earn better grades as well as escort Manja to school every morning. And yet, Len'ka himself is an academic underachiever. Because of his poor school record, he cannot overcome his mother's resistance to the activities of "октябрята." The poor overworked woman is afraid that the Soviet youth movement will distract her son from improving his grades. Other children must help Len'ka with his studies before "citizen Leshtykova" could agree to his joining the "октябрята."[57] Ultimately, Len'ka rises to prominence as the best student in his class, while his mother has to admit her defeat and let him become a member of the children's political organization.

Parents cast in the role of their children's adversaries proliferated in stories and plays published in the journal *Барабан* (*The Drum*, 1923-1926), the early periodical of the Soviet Pioneer Organization. In the play "Две мамы" ("Two Moms") that appeared in its April 1924 issue, one of the mothers is reluctant to let her daughter go to school and participate in pioneer activities. She is constantly tired, but, nevertheless, advises the girl to be true to a woman's

---

57 Ibid., 28.

only mission in life – to "placate her husband" with hard domestic work. Soon, however, not only the woman's own child confronts her, but also the mother of another girl, Olja. Olja's mother convinces the fatalist to start going to workers' meetings, resist her husband's abuse, and respect school work and political activities of girls as their only means of achieving happiness. None of this changes the mind of the ignorant adult. Trapped in her old ways of thinking, she remains the play's key antagonist, while other "progressive" parents and their offspring join Olja's mother in celebrating their togetherness by chanting: "A girl who is a pioneer. / A young woman who is a member of the Young Communist League. / A woman who is a Communist. / Our road is straight. / Walk directly towards your goal."[58]

The generational conflict definitely helped children's authors make their stories more exciting. Such ideology-driven narratives as *Кто впереди* and "Две мамы" were faulty in many ways: unimaginative and stylistically stilted, they lacked psychologically convincing characters and were short of devices that could sustain suspense. This is why even such a relatively conservative storyteller as Lidija Budogoskaja would create stories in which children confront their parents or encourage them to become more politically engaged. In *Нулевки* (*Zero-Graders*, 1933), Budogoskaja describes preparatory school students who are just beginning the process of indoctrination by the Soviet state. "Нулевки" decorate their class for the celebration of March 8th, the Day of Women Workers and Peasants, with slogans that summon their mothers to action: "Mother, take your children to nursery schools and kindergartens!"; "Mother, start attending nursing classes!"; "Mother, learn how to shoot!"[59] These proclamations alone make readers imagine children longing for a parent who is very different from the ones they have: she is politically active, energetic, and, if necessary, ready to wield a gun. Contemplating the mothers that "нулевки" dream of and the mothers who come to visit them at school creates dramatic tension within the otherwise bland and actionless story.

In Budogoskaja's other book, "Как Саньку в очаг привели" ("How San'ka Started Preschool," 1933), San'ka's life at home appears to be full of peril: since all adults work in the fields, there is no one to look after him, food is scarce, and the family's dog pounces on the little boy repeatedly, rolling him around the room like a rag doll. Reluctant to leave the familiar place at first, San'ka eventually understands that the only alternative to his meager domestic existence is the comfort and security of a state-run institution for preschoolers,

---

58   Andrej Irkutov, "Две мамы," in *Барабан* 4 (1924), 5-8.
59   Lidija Budogoskaja, *Нулевки*, Moscow, Leningrad 1933, 33.

FIGURE 6.5 Cover of Lidija Budogoskaja's *Нулевки*
ILLUSTRATION BY EDUARD BUDOGOSKIJ

"очаг."[60] The preschool provides children with food and offers them regularly scheduled activities: playing outdoors, reading, even drumming.[61] San'ka's journey from a neglectful home to a Soviet daycare reads as an adventure story, because its contrast between the boy's life before and after "очаг" is so vivid and dramatic, but also because the Bolshevik state as a benevolent parent figure looms large in it, overshadowing San'ka's inept and ignorant mother.

The opposition of home, often run by irresponsible parents, and school, governed by conscientious children, is the main theme of Boris Vinnikov's *Победа* (*Victory*, 1932). A novel for teenagers, it features many politically confused, undisciplined, and morally flawed adults. Following a class of fourteen-year-olds through a school year, Vinnikov's narrative portrays not only dysfunctional families, but also parents who are saboteurs – they stall socialist competition at a local factory. One of dramatic highlights of *Победа* is a description of a meeting of the school administration and its self-governance committee chaired by students. At that gathering, a ninth-grader Nina Zlatova tries to explain to skeptical teachers how the school system that incorporates industrial labor classes in the curriculum – as promoted by Krupskaja – would be beneficial for the student body as well as for the faculty. Nina is the central protagonist of the novel and an obvious advocate of young people's right to be in charge of the school collective. Unlike Ivan Iljich, the class tutor whom students do not heed because of his indecisiveness, and the German teacher Gennadij Adol'fovich who is forcefully opposed to their combining academic pursuits and "производственный труд" ("productive labor"), Nina is indoctrinated in Bolshevist ideas and endowed with a gift of persuasion. It is she, and not the novel's adults, who is a true "leader, able to organize children, provide them with a solution to this or that question [...], conduct a meeting, keep students within proper limits, and restore discipline," Vinnikov writes.[62] Thanks to her leadership qualities, Nina is capable of steering her school towards higher academic results and greater achievements in productive labor. She is also the one who confronts parents of other children, most of whom look positively seedy when compared to her and several other teenagers, champions of the political agenda of the Soviet state.

The delinquency of adults who are supposed to instruct and morally educate children, but cannot do so properly, is the defining feature of Vinnikov's

---

60   The name of the nursery school literally meant "hearth," but, most likely, it alluded to "очаг культуры," a term frequently used in Soviet propaganda work to denote a source of communist-style cultural education.
61   Budogoskaja, *Как Саньку в очаг привели*, Moscow, Leningrad 1933, 3-15.
62   Boris Vinnikov, *Победа*, Leningrad 1932, 16, 48, 67.

FIGURE 6.6 Nina Zlatova addresses a group of students and teachers. K. Rudakov's illustration to Boris Vinnikov's *Победа* (*Victory*, Leningrad 1932)

novel. Even the title of the book refers to the adolescents' victory over the older generation. Some parents, such as Kol'ka Morozov's abusive father, drink heavily. Others work irresponsibly or assist saboteurs. But Vinnikov also depicts grown-ups who are not cruel or depraved. Those mothers and fathers care for their offspring by doing things which pedagogues of the past considered part of a virtuous upbringing: they insist on their own authority, for example, or go to church. Nevertheless, children who are trained according to the Soviet code of ethics, perceive such behavior as aberrant and resist it. To highlight this conflict, Vinnikov adds several dramatic episodes to his otherwise lackluster narrative. In one of his more intense chapters, the author describes a theatrical production in which students act and by means of which they lampoon their parents. The event brings together all young protagonists as well as their adult nemeses and serves as a moment of catharsis for the older generation. Parents recognize themselves in the wrongdoers ridiculed on stage. They repent. Eventually, they change their ways.

It is important to note that Vinnikov's child actors portray a father who beats his son and a grandmother who advocates prayer and fasting as similarly wicked. For them, both adults are guilty, because they hinder the children's main agenda: to become true Soviet citizens unencumbered by the ideological, psychological, or emotional burdens of the past. Remarkably, the author sees no difference between an attack on a religious grandparent and that on a violent adult who harms his son physically. Neither does this inconsistency baffle one of Vinnikov's main heroes, the principal of the school, Grabar'. Stepping out onto the stage to summarize the message of the satirical performance, Grabar' sides with the young people. Similarly to them, the principal envisions a "good family" as a byproduct of the new regime with its mandatory atheism, everyone's obligation to study, and an insistence on moral and physical purity. In fact, Grabar' suggests that being an authoritarian parent of a Soviet child is going to be problematic for all adults, unless they agree to reform their ways according to the new ethical standards promoted by the Soviet state and upheld by the students. Model your behavior on the behavior of your children, Grabar' demands of his audience, or you may no longer be able to partake of the fruits of the Revolution:

> You have gathered today to laugh at the kids' shenanigans. But it has turned out not as you have expected. [...] Your sons and daughters have taught you a good lesson. [...] These days, we are masters of our country. But we are still standing up to our knees in the dirt and debris of the past. [...] We still wish to teach our children how to pray, we tell them holy tales, we send them out to fetch vodka, we box their ears, we don't let them go to the club or to the movies, we are too cheap to buy them an extra textbook. So, have we endured three revolutions [...] to live like this? If it is not a big deal to you, then let us go back to the bourgeoisie

and ask them to return and rule us! [...] Without the right kind of family our case would be lost.⁶³

Grabar's oration is addressed to grown-ups, but it is included in a novel for young people. By portraying a character who teaches parents how to be better citizens in front of their offspring, Vinnikov sends the readers of *Победа* a message that they are more morally upright than most adults in their lives. Because of this statement and many similar affirmations of children's political agency and pedagogical potential, Vinnikov's novel perceptibly deviates from didactic narratives of the past, which paid respect to the older generation by celebrating the virtuousness and integrity of fathers and mothers, teachers and those who merely happened to be part of the children's familial circle.

Grabar's understanding that grown-ups need to be "re-educated" is typical of early Soviet children's literature, committed to turning upside down the hierarchy of relationships between fathers and sons. In Vinnikov's novel, the moral superiority of children results from their accepting ideological dogmas of the Soviet regime, such as atheism, as uncontestable facts. In 1932, when *Победа* came out, its protagonists were coevals of the revolution of 1917. Their adolescence presupposed their inherent acceptance of the party line: they knew no other. The age of Vinnikov's protagonists also reflected the overall youthfulness of their country. In 1926, thirty-nine percent of Soviet urban dwellers were fifteen years and younger, and fifty percent were twenty and younger.⁶⁴ Children's authors and theoreticians of public education considered these energetic and politically engaged individuals to be most competent conveyors of moral and ideological values of the new Bolshevik state. Among those who pointed out children's right to "reform" their parents was E. D. Kantor (Davydov), a party educator who, in one of his pamphlets for teachers, insisted on channeling the pedagogical fervor of young people towards re-educating "отсталые" ("backward-looking") adults. According to Kantor, due to children's involvement in "reforming" grown-ups, "the Soviet school [...] has become a political and cultural nucleus for the adult population as well, [...] a cultural oasis in the dark and ignorant desert."⁶⁵

No wonder that moral lessons contained in children's books written in the 1920s and early 1930s simultaneously targeted the younger and the older generations. Some stories, like Pushkarev's "Яшка таежник" or Larissa Lar-

---

63   Vinnikov, *Победа*, 111.
64   Matthias Neumann, *The Communist Youth League and the Transformation of the Soviet Union, 1917-1932*, London and New York 2011, 7.
65   E. D. Kantor (Davydov), *Советская школа и учитель*, Moscow 1924, 44.

ina's "Помогла" ("She Has Helped," 1925), were dedicated to pioneers' defying their illiterate mothers and fathers; other children's books featured heroes who shamed parental cruelty or took petty criminals to task.[66] In Nikolaj Bogdanov's *Пропавший лагерь* (*The Camp That Disappeared*, 1929), pioneers set out to expose moonshine brewers.[67] In Petr Zamojskij's story, little Vas'ka denigrates a village priest for his refusal to work in the fields along with peasants.[68] Nikolaj Dorofeev's protagonists are city pioneers who denounce bearded country men for wasting village lumber. The children produce a handwritten "newspaper," in which they insist that the logs should be used to build a local club where the youth organization can hold its regular meetings.[69] As it often happens in works of fiction where young people confront or "re-educate" the older generation, the class origin of adult antagonists may be the only attribute of their "delinquency." In *Пятеро на одних коньках* (*Five on One Pair of Skates*, 1927), Lev Ovalov's poetic account of children's skating adventures, teenage Misha trips up and snubs a well-dressed lady who also came out for a spin around the rink. "Just try, you, bourgeois woman, / To beat up us little kids!" Misha shouts at her, triumphantly.[70]

A popular narrative closure of an early Soviet school and pioneer novella is a detailed account of children's "show trial" ("показательный суд"). Fictional precursors of the notorious Moscow Trials of the late 1930s, these politicized theatricals allowed children to judge and "convict" irresponsible, neglectful, or politically unengaged adults. Andrej Irkutov's "Суд над дедом Архипом" ("Grandfather Archip's Trial," 1925) tells the story of peasant boys and girls hauling a family patriarch over the coals for his abusive behavior (the grandfather used to flog his grandchildren). In Irkutov's story, Archip publicly repents: he promises to stop the abuse and says that he will let his young charges join the local pioneer cell and go to meetings, instead of forcing them to attend Sunday church services.[71] In Elena Bobinskaja's *Пионерский суд* (*The Pioneer Trial*, 1926), a group of city pioneers arrive in a village to publicly condemn peasant Ermolaev for his thrashing Petja Gorshunov, a shepherd boy. Ermolaev apologizes, while Petja, in what seems to be a typical outcome of such interventions, joins the local pioneer organization.[72]

---

66 Larisa Larina, "Помогла," in *Барабан* 4 (1925), 2-4.
67 Nikolaj Bogdanov, *Пропавший лагерь. Подлинные приключения пионерского отряда* (*The Camp That Disappeared: Real Adventures of a Pioneer Camp*), Moscow, Leningrad 1929, 47-50.
68 Petr Zamojskij, "Буржуй" ("A Bourgeois"), in *В деревне*, Moscow 1928, 14-16.
69 Nikolaj Dorofeev, *Зажили по-другому* (*They Started a New Life*), Moscow 1927, 42-44.
70 Lev Ovalov, *Пятеро на одних коньках*, Moscow 1927, 10.
71 Andrej Irkutov, "Суд над дедом Архипом," in *Барабан* 10 (1925), 5-6.
72 Elena Bobinskaja, *Пионерский суд*, Leningrad 1926.

The authority of Soviet children in exposing adults' idleness, lack of political fervor, and moral turpitude was tremendous. Reporting to the Sixth Congress of the Soviets in 1931, the Central Bureau of the Pioneer Organization outlined dozens of cases of young people's interference in disciplinary work among grown-ups. Children stood outside factories with megaphones, directing workers to meetings. They submitted lists of men shirking work ("прогульщики") to administrators of industrial enterprises, recorded and posted names of production underachievers and shamed alcohol addicts.[73] Books for young readers highlighted these accomplishments and emphasized children's ability to transform adults into laborers yielding higher results as well as into more honorable people. In Grigorij Zamchalov's short story "Харитон" ("Chariton," 1930) children defend the irresolute "председатель колхоза" from accusations by wealthy peasants. It is the peasants themselves who repeatedly make the party-appointed farm leader drunk, children assert, thus finalizing the decision of the village council not to fire the collective farm chair.[74] E. Bykov's *Пионеры и прогульщики* (*Pioneers and Shirkers*, 1931) describes a campaign of young activists against lazy employees at a machine-building plant. When several men fail to show up for work, children put up disgracing posters over their workstations.[75]

In the late 1920s and early 1930s, the central conflict of the school and pioneer novella begins to shift from children's discrediting irresponsible behavior of adults to their exposing parents and teachers as "enemies of the people." According to Catriona Kelly, most of these narratives, with their focus on the martyrdom of young heroes, owed their popularity to the broadly publicized case of Pavlik Morozov, a teenager from a village in the Ural region who was killed after turning his kulak father over to the authorities.[76] Kelly's observation is correct, but it may benefit from an elaboration. While stories of pioneer martyrs did become widespread after 1933 (Pavlik died in September of 1932), episodes of children confronting adults for their breaking the Soviet law began to appear in children's fiction much earlier. For example, in Konstantin Minaev's *Против отца* (*Against Father*, 1927), little Tan'ka saves a village teacher whom her father prepares to assassinate, thus exposing her parent's criminality.[77] Similarly, Kostja Zajcev, a hero of Vinnikov's *Победа*, publicly condemns

---

73   Pregel' and Ljubimova, *Детское коммунистическое движение*, 72-74.
74   G. E. Zamchalov, "Харитон," in *Наши дела*, Moscow 1930.
75   E. Bykov, *Пионеры и прогульщики*, Moscow 1931.
76   Catriona Kelly, *Comrade Pavlik: The Rise and Fall of a Soviet Boy Hero*, London 2005, 161-164.
77   K. Minaev, *Против отца*, Moscow, Leningrad 1927. Under the direction of Boris Svetozarov, the novel was quickly turned into a film: *Танька-трактирщица*, Sovkino, 1928.

his father as a kulak.[78] With the publication of Gajdar's *Военная тайна* (*Military Secret*, 1935), the novel in which the slaying of a six-year-old boy, Al'ka, by saboteurs is uncovered by his older camp-mates, children's heroic struggle against enemies of the people begins to acquire centrality in fiction for young readers.[79]

The transition made by children's authors from portraying children as teachers of adults to representing them as assistants to the government in eradicating political dissent mirrored the transformation of the Soviet public sphere. In the mid-1930s, the Stalinist state restructured its relationship with Soviet citizens along the lines of political conspiracies, enemy-seeking and spy mania. In her work on the political upbringing of children in the 1920s, Julija Salova points out that, at the end of the decade, the Soviet pedagogical agenda also became modified: ideological indoctrination and moral upbringing switched from cultivating class consciousness in children to fostering their "классовая ненависть" ("class hatred").[80] Maturing in twisted and frightening ways, the regime itself was moving towards the cult of personality. The totalitarian reincarnation of Stalin as the father of the nation coincided with a dramatic increase in the number of orphanages for "young criminals," among whom there were many children of Gulag inmates and other victims of the Great Purge.[81]

It is not surprising, then, that after a decade of representing parents as feeble, anti-social, politically disengaged, or criminally minded, Soviet books for young readers began to embrace traditional didacticism based on the portrayal

---

78   Vinnikov, *Победа*, 165-169.
79   See Anatolij Rybakov's *Кортик* (*Cutlass*, 1948); Arkadij Gajdar's *На графских развалинах* (*On the Ruins of the Count's Estate*, 1929) and *Дальние страны* (*Far-Away Lands*, 1932); Venjamin Kaverin's *Два капитана* (*Two Captains*, 1938-1944); Valentina Oseeva's *Динка* (*Dinka*, 1959); Elena Verejskaja's *В те годы* (*In Those Years*, 1956). See Svetlana Maslinskaya's chapter "'Be Always Ready!': Hero Narratives in Soviet Children's Literature'" in this volume for a discussion of a proliferation of child hero narratives in the 1930s children's literature, with a special focus on children and young adults fighting enemies of the state.
80   Ju. G. Salova, *Политическое воспитание детей в Советской России в 1920-е годы*, Jaroslavl 2001, 120.
81   Figes documents the steady increase in the number of adolescent inmates of the Gulag that began in 1934-5 (329,663 inmates in 1934; over 100,000 children between the ages of 12 and 15, in 1935-1940). See Figes, *The Whisperers*, 99. Karl Schlögel who also provides some terrifying statistics, draws a parallel between the new surge in orphancy and the veneration of Stalin: "It is not hard to see that there is a direct connection between the actual loss of fathers and the formation of the cult of Stalin as the father of nations." Schlögel, *Террор и мечта: Москва, 1937*, Moscow 2011, 626.

of adults as repositories of virtue and knowledge. The mid-1930s to early 1940s generated narratives in which authoritarian parents or teachers with a party mandate directed the learning and social activities of children.[82] One example of such teacher-centric fiction is Georgij Medynskij's *Девятый А* (*Nine A*, 1940). In the novel, educators guide teenagers towards sensible decisions, while parents vocalize their desire to reclaim control over children's lives. When one of the students, Valerij, strays away, his mother vows to become "a mistress (хозяйка) of [her] son's moral upbringing and direct him towards a different course."[83] Another mother brings her son's poems to a teacher of literature who, in her turn, sends the adolescent poet to a "literary consultant" and then to a school creative writing club.[84] The number of adult protagonists who appear to be talented educators increases in children's fiction written in the 1950s, when many teachers – Valentina Oseeva, Marija Prilezhaeva, Nikolaj Nosov, and Frida Vigdorova among them – become children's authors themselves.[85]

Pre-war children's literature underscores the association between fictional adults as the embodiment of the patriarchal totalitarian state and fictional youngsters as the personification of the Soviet nation. In the late 1930s, not only protagonists of children's books continue to claim the Union of Soviet Socialist Republics and its leader as their parent, but the state itself – "this huge happy land which is called the Soviet country" – begins to assert its parental rights over the young people.[86] In Konstantin Paustovskij's short story "Доблесть" ("Valor," 1935), citizens of a city district try to stay quiet for several days to help a little boy with a concussion recuperate in silence. Paustovskij, who calls the recovered patient "everybody's child" ("общий ребенок"), echoes statements about the commonality and affinity of Soviet children made by other writers.[87] This idea is especially pronounced in Gajdar's novels and short stories. Gajdar's heroic Al'ka proclaims that the power

---

82   See Lev Kassil''s *Черемыш, брат героя* (*Cheremysh, the Brother of a Hero* 1938); German Matveev's *Семнадцатилетние* (*Seventeen-Year-Olds*, 1954); Evgenij Shvarc's *Первоклассница* (*A First-Grader*, 1949); Ljubov Voronkova's *Старшая сестра* (*The Elder Sister*, 1955); Natalija Zabila's *Катруся уже большая* (*Katrusja Has Grown Up*, 1957); Frida Vigdorova's *Мой класс* (*My Class*, 1949).
83   Georgij Medynskij, *Девятый А*, Moscow 1940, 254.
84   Ibid., 257.
85   See Dobrenko's analysis of this phenomenon in "'Весь реальный детский мир,'" 201.
86   The phrase ends Gajdar's 1939 novella "Чук и Гек" ("Chuk and Gek"), in which the journey of two little boys from Moscow to Siberia reunites them with their father as well as connects them to their vast, "happy" land. Gajdar, *Сочинения*, Vol. 2, 325.
87   Konstantin Paustovskij, "Доблесть," in *Рассказы*, Moscow 1935, 12.

of the Soviet country lies in its children's commitment to the state as their common progenitor – and in "even us little kids knowing the Military Secret and keeping our word of honor so firmly."[88]

The myth of children as bearers of national strength had its visible downside: the nation itself was in danger of becoming infantilized. The risk of an adult growing young again transpires in Gajdar's "Горячий камень" ("The Hot Stone,"1941). In this parable, little Ivashka discovers a rock that, if broken, can magically rejuvenate its holder. A Bolshevik veteran Ivashka encounters nearby teaches the boy a moral lesson. According to the old man, eternal youthfullness is not what people should strive for, because the greatest virtue is making one's country "powerful and magnificent."[89] Impressed by this idea, Ivashka refuses to partake of the stone's magic. He rolls the heavy boulder up the mountain and leaves it there for everyone to ponder. The open-endedness of "Горячий камень" is atypical of Gajdar's other narratives for children and thus points out a certain ambiguity of the message delivered by the parable. Its protagonist is supposed to mature, acquiring his knowledge by means of hard work similar to the labor of pushing a heavy stone up the hill. But Ivashka's virtue will never result from a specific quest, since his moral education has to follow a communal goal – his people's pursuit of learning. Unlike the old Bolshevik whose life was full of personal accomplishments, Ivashka will perform a collective task, acting as a Sisyphus endlessly rolling uphill the "rock" of moral ineptitude. Moreover, with the stone within close reach, he and his fellow countrymen may always be in peril of getting young and inexperienced again – ideal subjects of the country that is both ready to learn from and dominate its youth.

4 Conclusion: The Thrill of Disobedience

In a 1967 review of Maks Bremener's novella *Чур, не игра!* (*Keep Away, It's Not a Game!* 1963), critic Ivan Motjashov praises as "believable" the character of Vovka who repeatedly disobeys his parents. Alternatively, Motjashov sees no didactic potential in the off-putting Jurik, a boy whom he regards as too deferential to his "bourgeois" mother:

> [Jurik] is told: respect adults. But under such circumstances the difference between respect and fear is almost erased. And a pioneer, as

---

88 Gajdar, "*Военная тайна*," in *Сочинения*, Vol. 2, 59.
89 Gajdar, "Горячий камень," in *Сочинения*, Vol. 2, 421.

Vovka correctly notices, should not be afraid. He should be conscientious [сознательным]. Jurik is being brought up as a child incapable of Pavlik Morozov's feat. Fear and true civic conscientiousness, a sense of dependence and a sense of freedom are incompatible [qualities in a child].[90]

Motjashov's review demonstrates that decades after the first Soviet children's books had presented children's contempt for their parents as a useful step towards becoming a better man and a worthy citizen, writers and critics continued to exploit the topos of disobedience in their works. In the 1920s and early 1930s, generational conflict possessed the robustness and originality that helped politically motivated children's literature sustain its narrative vigor. In the subsequent decades, however, the disobedience topos lost some of its didactic potential, if not its capacity to thrill. While stories about children standing in opposition to "untrustworthy" adults remained widespread, children's authors removed their protagonists' struggle against grown-ups from a school setting or domestic sphere and relocated it to more distant domains. In the late 1940s to 1970s, novels about pioneer "martyrs" and fictional accounts of the revolutionary past portrayed child heroes who confronted adults by emulating the battle of their elder comrades – communists and members of the Komsomol – against real or imaginary enemies. Likewise, the paradigm of a virtuous child teaching adults a moral lesson, which early Soviet children's fiction helped to create, reemerged in literary and cinematic works about children's valor and self-reliance during World War II. Protagonists of such works as Valentin Kataev's *Сын полка* (*Son of the Regiment*, 1946), Valentina Oseeva's *Васек Трубачев и его товарищи* (*Vasek Trubachev and His Comrades*, 1947-1952), Elena Iljina's *Четвертая высота* (*The Fourth Summit*, 1946), and Jurij Slepuchin's *Перекресток* (*At the Cross-Roads*, 1962) learn collectively and from real-life experience, rather than from adults. They also teach grown-ups how to be moraly staunch individuals.

Postwar narratives about children happily building a new utopia became another variation on the school and pioneer novellas of the 1920s and early 1930s. Literary works about orphans building a new collective life together in a government facility or pioneers whose bodies and characters grow stronger after a summer spent in a sports-and-health camp (спортивно-оздоровительный лагерь) elaborated the earlier paradigm of children as moral educators, capable of teaching adults an ethical lesson. Because of the

---

90 Ivan Motjashov, *Воспитание гражданина. О новых книгах для детей*, Moscow 1967, 30.

persistence, discipline, collective spirit, and virtue of the young literary heroes, their school, orphanage or pioneer camp gained the luster of an ideal socialist institution, a blueprint of the future communist paradise. Since publishing fictional accounts of the lives of destitute war orphans and child victims of political violence was still unfeasible in the first decades after World War II, some children's authors chose to incorporate the early post-revolutionary motifs of home lost and gained, of children's unity and kinship, and of the happy, welcoming spirit of children's collectives in their works. Svetlana Mogilevskaja's *Дом в Цибикнуре* (*The House in Cibiknur*, 1949), Prilezhaeva's *Над Волгой* (*Above the Volga*, 1952), Vigdorova's *Дорога в жизнь* (*Road to Life*, 1954), and Galina Karpenko's *Как мы росли* (*How We Grew Up*, 1959) are among the works that feature child protagonists who live collectively, teach one another moral lessons, and improve lives of others as well. Later, such children's writers as Kassil', Vladislav Krapivin, Anatolij Aleksin, Vitalij Gubarev, Michail Korshunov, Viljam Kozlov, and Oleg Korjakov further re-interpreted the utopian motif of children's growing, learning, and exploring the world untarnished by the interference of adults, including unscrupulous and depraved individuals.[91]

Young protagonists of Sovieth children's books from the 1920s and early 1930s appear to be capable of teaching grown-ups how to act in accordance with the Soviet code of ethics because of an inherent virtue – their morality stems from their being "untainted" by the "bourgeois ideology." Their fictional "descendants," heroes of the 1950s, 60s, and 70s works for young readers, seem to have the right to morally educate others not because they are better disciplined or more "conscientious" than adults, but because they have been able to gain independence – and thus avoid the harmful influence of the society – at an early age. The thrill of disobedience is taken to the extreme in Nikolaj Nosov's tales *Приключения Незнайки и его друзей* (*Adventures of Dunno and His Friends*, 1953-54), *Незнайка в Солнечном городе* (*Dunno in the City of the Sun*, 1958), and *Незнайка на Луне* (*Dunno on the Moon*, 1964-65), which portray a community of children unguarded and unguided by grown-ups. Even more bizarre from the traditional pedagogical standpoint is the fictional realm populated by Eduard Uspenskij's charismatic characters. In *Дядя Федор, кот и пес* (*Uncle Fedor, Cat, and Dog*, 1973), a pre-adolescent boy decides to abandon his absent-minded, careless, infantile parents to start a new life in the

---

91 See Krapivin's *Мальчик со шпагой* (*A Boy with a Sword*, 1972-74); Kassil''s *Будьте готовы, Ваше Высочество* (*Be Prepared, Your Highness*, 1965); Kozlov's *Президент Каменного Острова* (*The President of Stone Island*, 1964); and Korjakov's *Формула счастья* (*The Formula of Happiness*, 1965).

country with only a cat and a dog for his protectors and moral guardians. Uspenskij's work may be considered an ironic response to Sergej Michalkov's fantasy *Праздник непослушания* (*The Disobedience Fest*, 1971), in which all adults leave the city so that their lazy, selfish, and obnoxious children could learn virtue and become self-reliant. But it may also be interpreted as a response to Pushkarev's "Яшка Таежник" and other early works of Soviet children's fiction. While Michalkov's child protagonists fail to improve without their parents and teachers at hand, Uncle Fedor ends up being successful, like Jashka. He discovers how to milk a cow and grow potatoes, keep his house clean and take care of his friends. Having learned his lessons, the boy teaches his mother and father what it means to be responsible and respectful. Moreover, Uncle Fedor does something that his literary predecessors have not been able to do. Facing the big world in the company of just his cat and his dog, he survives and matures as an individual, rather than as part of a Communist collective. Because of that, his pedagogical authority seems more tangible than that of Jashka or Archipelashka. It is hard-earned, but it also carries more weight.

Works Cited

Primary Sources

Andreevskaja, V. P. *Колокольчики*. St. Petersburg 1890.

Bagratjan, T. N., ed. *Юность комсомольская: Воспоминания первых кубанских комсомольцев*. Krasnodar 1956, 223.

Belych, Grigorij and Leonid Panteleev. *Республика Шкид*. Moscow, Leningrad 1927.

Bobinskaja, Elena. *Пионерский суд*. Leningrad 1926.

Bogdanov, Nikolaj. *Пропавший лагерь. Подлинные приключения пионерского отряда*. Moscow, Leningrad 1929.

Budogoskaja, Lidija. *Как Саньку в очаг привели*. Moscow, Leningrad 1933.

Budogoskaja, Lidija. *Нулевки*. Moscow, Leningrad 1933.

Bykov, E. *Пионеры и прогульщики*. Moscow 1931.

Chukovskij, Kornej. *Дневник 1901-1969*, Vols. 1 and 2. Moscow 2003.

Chukovskij, Kornej. *Собрание сочинений*, Vol. 2. Moscow 2001.

Chukovskij, Kornej. *Солнечная*. Moscow 1933.

Dorofeev, Nikolaj. *Зажили по-другому*. Moscow 1927.

Ekaterina II. *О царевиче Хлоре*. St. Petersburg 1790.

Erlich, Vol'f. *О ленивом Ваньке и его щенке*. Moscow, Leningrad 1926.

Finogenov, Anatolij. *Кто впереди*. Leningrad 1932.

Gajdar, Arkadij. "*Военная тайна*," in Gajdar, *Сочинения*, Vol. 2. Moscow, Leningrad 1949.

Gajdar, Arkadij. "Горячий камень," in Gajdar, *Сочинения*, Vol. 2. Moscow, Leningrad 1949.

Gajdar, Arkadij. *Дальние страны*. Moscow 1932.

Gajdar, Arkadij. *На графских развалинах*. Moscow 1929.

Gajdar, Arkadij. "Чук и Гек," in Gajdar, *Сочинения*, Vol. 2. Moscow, Leningrad 1949.

German, Aleksandr. *Слушали-постановили*. Orel 1925.

Grjaznov, Innokentij. *Искатели мозолей*. Moscow 1931.

Irkutov, Andrej. "Две мамы," in *Барабан* 4 (1924), 5-8.

Irkutov, Andrej. "На смерть Ильича," in *Барабан* 2 (1924), 24.

Irkutov, Andrej. "Суд над дедом Архипом," in *Барабан* 10 (1925), 5-6.

Kassil', Lev. *Будьте готовы, Ваше Высочество!* Moscow 1965.

Kassil', Lev. *Черемыш, брат героя*. Moscow, Leningrad 1938.

Kataev, Valentin, *Сын полка*. Leningrad 1946.

Kaverin, Veniamin. *Два капитана*. Moscow and Leningrad 1945.

Kozlov, Viljam. *Президент Каменного Острова*. Leningrad 1964.

Krapivin, Vladislav. *Мальчик со шпагой*. Moscow 1976.

Larina, Larisa. "Помогла," in *Барабан* 4 (1925), 2-4.

Lipina, Nina. *Бабушка Андрюша*. Moscow 1926.

Makarenko, Anton. *Собрание сочинений*, Vol. 5. Moscow 1971.

Makarenko, Anton. *Педагогическая поэма*. Moscow 1935.

Malachov, Sergej. "В детском доме," in *Муза в красной косынке: Комсомольская поэзия 1980-1950 гг.* Moscow 1970, 51.

Matveev, German. *Семнадцатилетние*. Leningrad 1954.

Medynskij, Georgij. *Девятый А*. Moscow 1940.

Mikitenko, Ivan. *Уркаганы*. Charkov 1929.

Minaev, Konstantin. *Назарка-атаман*. Moscow and Leningrad 1925.

Minaev, Konstantin. *Против отца*. Moscow and Leningrad 1927.

Minaev, Konstantin. *Школьники*. Moscow 1926.

Oseeva, Valentina. *Динка*. Moscow 1959.

Oseeva, Valentina. *Васек Трубачев и его товарищи*. Moscow 1947.

Ostroumov, Lev. *Макар-следопыт*, Vols. 1 and 2. Moscow 1925.

Ovalov, Lev. *Пятеро на одних коньках*. Moscow 1927.

Paustovskij, Konstantin. *Рассказы*. Moscow 1935.

Pushkarev, Gleb. "Яшка-таежник," in Pushkarev, *Два Петра Ивановича*. Novosibirsk 1949.

Rozanov, Sergej. *Приключения Травки*. Moscow 1928.

Rybakov, Anatolij. *Кортик*. Moscow and Leningrad 1948.

Shorin, Ivan. "Одногодки," in T. Gabe, L. Zheldin, and Z. Zadunajskaja, eds., *Костер*. Moscow 1934, 53-54.

Shvarc, Evgenij. *Первоклассница*. Moscow and Leningrad 1949.

Sventickaja, M. *Наш детский сад*. Moscow 1924.
Tolstoj, Lev. *Новая азбука*. Moscow 1875.
Ushinskij, Konstantin. *Собрание сочинений*, Vol. 5. Moscow 1949.
Vinnikov, Boris. *Победа*. Leningrad 1932.
Voronkova, Ljubov. *Старшая сестра*. Moscow 1955.
Zabila, Natalija. *Катруся уже большая*. Moscow 1957.
Zamchalov, Grigorij. "Харитон," in *Наши дела*. Moscow 1930.
Zamojskij, Petr. "Буржуй," in *В деревне*. Moscow 1928, 14-16.
Zamojskij, Petr. *Вместе веселей*. Moscow 1928.
Zamojskij, Petr. *Деревенская быль*. Moscow 1924.
Zamojskij, Petr. *Озорник шатущий*. Moscow 1926.
Zamojskij, Petr. *Смутьян*. Moscow 1926.

Secondary Sources

Arzamasceva, Irina. "*'Век ребенка' в русской литературе 1900-1930 годов*." Moscow 2003.
Baberowski, Jörg. *Красный террор: история сталинизма*. Moscow 2007.
Charitonova-Ostrovskaja, Raisa. *Детское коммунистическое движение и дошкольное воспитание*. Moscow and Leningrad 1926.
Chechov, Nikolaj. *Детская литература*. Moscow 1909.
Chukovskaja, Lidija. "О книгах забытых или незамеченных," in *Вопросы литературы* 2 (1958) ⟨http://www.chukfamily.ru/Lidia/Publ/zabytie.htm⟩ (Accessed December 29, 2017).
Dobrenko, E. A. "'Весь реальный детский мир' (школьная повесть и 'наше счастливое детство')," in M. R. Balina, V. Ju. Vjugin, eds., *'Убить Чарскую ...': парадоксы советской литературы для детей (1920-е – 1930-е гг.)*. St. Petersburg 2015, 189-230.
Epp, George K. *The Educational Policies of Catherine II: The Era of Enlightenment in Russia*. Frankfurt am Main 1984.
Figes, Orlando. *The Whisperers: Private Life in Stalin's Russia*. New York 2008.
Fitzpatrick, Sheila. *The Cultural Front: Power and Culture in Revolutionary Russia*. Ithaca, NY 1992.
Iljina, Elena. *Четвертая высота. О комсомолке Гуле Королевой, участнице Великой Отечественной войны*. Moscow and Leningrad 1946.
Irkutov, Andrej. *Все за одного*. Charkov 1926.
Jakimec, S. V., ed. *История педагогики и образования в России. Хрестоматия*. Orsk 2011.
Kantor (Davydov), E. D. *Советская школа и учитель*. Moscow 1924.
Kelly, Catriona. *Comrade Pavlik: The Rise and Fall of a Soviet Boy Hero*. London 2005.

Kondakov, V. "'Убежище-2': 'Детский дискурс' советской литературы в 1930-е годы," in *Ребенок в истории и культуре. Библиотека журнала* Исследователь / Researcher, Vol. 4. Moscow 2010, 72-73.

Korjakov, Oleg. *Формула счастья*. Moscow 1965.

Kostjuchina, M. S. *Золотое зеркало. Русская литература для детей XVIII-XIX веков*. Moscow 2008.

Kozhevnikov, Aleksej. *Шпана. Из жизни беспризорных*. Leningrad 1925.

Krivonosov, A. N. "Исторический опыт борьбы с беспризорностью," in *Государство и право* 7 (2003), 92-98.

Krupskaja, Nadezhda. *Детское коммунистическое движение*. Moscow 1925.

Krupskaja, Nadezhda. "К вопросу о целях школы," in A. G. Kalashnikov, ed., *Советская производственная трудовая школа. Педагогическая хрестоматия*. Moscow 1925, 73-76.

Lilina, Zlata. *Родители, учитесь воспитывать своих детей*. Moscow 1929.

Lozinskij, S. "Социальные уклоны в современной педагогике," in A. Zaluzhnyj and S. Lozinskij, eds. *Детский коллектив и ребенок*. Charkov 1926.

Lukjanova, Irina. *Корней Чуковский*. Moscow 1997.

Lunacharskij, Anatolij. *Ленин*. Moscow 1924.

Lychina, M. M. *Внеклассное детское чтение в нашей школе*. Moscow 1936.

Motjashov, Ivan. *Воспитание гражданина. О новых книгах для детей*. Moscow 1967.

Neumann, Matthias. *The Communist Youth League and the Transformation of the Soviet Union, 1917-1932*. London and New York 2011.

Nikiforov, Georgij. *Наши ребята*. Moscow and Leningrad 1925.

Pregel', Ja. A. and A. A. Ljubimova, eds. *Детское коммунистическое движение*. Moscow and Leningrad 1932.

Putilova, Evgenija. *Детское чтение для сердца и разума. Очерки по истории детской литературы*. St. Petersburg 2005.

Rozhkov, A. Ju. "Неформальные сообщества школьников и типичное в обретении коллективной идентичности в 1920-е годы," in *Ребенок в истории и культуре. Библиотека журнала* Исследователь / Researcher, Vol. 4. Moscow 2010, 72-73.

Salova, Julija. *Политическое воспитание детей в Советской России в 1920-е годы*, Jaroslavl 2001.

Savin, Viktor. *Шаромыжники*. Moscow 1925.

Schlögel, Karl. *Террор и мечта: Москва, 1937*. Moscow 2011.

Sejfullina, Lidija. *Правонарушители*. Novonikolaevsk 1922.

Shishkov, Vjacheslav. *Странники*. Leningrad 1931.

Shubinskij, Valerij. *Даниил Хармс: Жизнь человека на ветру*. Moscow 2015.

Shul'gin, V. N. "О целях школы," in *Советская производственно-трудовая школа. Книга для чтения и работы по основам советской системы воспитания*. Moscow 1928.

Slepuchin, Jurij. *Перекресток*. Leningrad 1962.

Steiner, Evgeny. *Stories for Little Comrades: Revolutionary Artists in the Early Soviet Children's Book*. Seattle 1999.

Sverdlova, K. "О чуковщине," in *Красная печать* 9-10 (1928).

Verejskaja, Elena. *В те годы. Рассказы о революционных событиях 1905-1917 годов*. Leningrad 1956.

Vigdorova, Frida. *Мой класс: записки учительницы*. Moscow and Leningrad 1949.

Vol'fson, M. B. *Пути советской книги*. Moscow 1929.

Zaluzhnyj, Aleksandr. "Задачи изучения детского коллектива," in A. Zaluzhnyj, S. Lozinskij, eds., *Детский коллектив и ребенок*. Charkov 1926, 11-12.

Zaluzhnyj, Aleksandr. *Учение о коллективе. Методология. Детский коллектив*. Moscow, Leningrad 1930.

Zenzinov, Vladimir. *Беспризорные*. Paris 1929.

CHAPTER 7

"Be Always Ready!": Hero Narratives in Soviet Children's Literature

Svetlana Maslinskaya

1 Introduction

The figure of the heroic child in Soviet culture is an obvious, but little-studied phenomenon. Those Russians who were born in the early 1980s or before that, know at least ten names of "pioneer heroes" that younger generations may not be aware of. Today's forty-year olds, their parents and grandparents had to learn about Pavlik Morozov and Lenja Golikov, Zoja Kosmodemjanskaja and Volodja Dubinin in the classroom, since their biographies were part of the school curriculum and an essential foundation of many extracurricular activities. That said, contemporary theoretical and detail-oriented scholarly works on the Soviet representation of heroism in literature and the arts pay much attention to the figure of the adult hero, while neglecting the question of the depiction, invention and propagation of the child hero trope.[1] Moreover, only a few scholars addressed the representation of child heroes in Soviet children's literature. Like Catriona Kelly, they investigate the myth of most remarkable figures in the Soviet pantheon of national heroes, such as Morozov, analyzing its history and textual representations; or, like Marija Litovskaja, they study child warriors as powerful archetypes of Soviet interwar culture.[2] There are also works, such as an essay by Ann Livschiz, dedicated to the cultural and psychological impact of the postwar child hero on the contemporary reader and on Post-Soviet Russian culture.[3]

---

1 See, for example, Hans Günther, "Education and Conversion: The Road to the New Man in the Totalitarian Bildungsroman," in Hans Günther, ed., *The Culture of the Stalin Period*, London 1990; Evgenij Dobrenko, *Метафора власти: Литература сталинской эпохи в историческом освещении*, Munich 1993; Catriona Kelly, *Comrade Pavlik: The Rise and Fall of a Soviet Boy Hero*, London 2005.
2 Marija Litovskaja, "Воюющие дети в русской литературе первой половины XX века," in Igor' Kargashin, ed., *"Homo Militaris": Литература войны и о войне. История, мифология, поэтика*, Kaluga 2010, 93-99.
3 Ann Livschiz, "Children's Lives after Zoia's Death: Order, Emotions and Heroism in Children's Lives and Literature in the Post-War Soviet Union," in Juliane Furst, ed., *Late Stalinist Russia: Society between Reconstruction and Reinvention*, London and New York 2006, 192-208.

And yet, a comprehensive picture of the Soviet child-hero narrative is still lacking.

This chapter attempts to fill in the gap by tracing the evolution of child-hero narratives in Soviet children's literature of the 1920s to 1980s. I aim to demonstrate how the notion of a heroic child was formed by evoking the political contexts which begot and shaped such protagonists. I am also interested in the development of the evolution of genres that constitute the tradition of Soviet children's literary portrayals of heroic children. This is why I investigate the entire continuum of Soviet works about them – from the representation of Soviet children's heroism in the 1920s-40s, during the formation of this particular canon, all the way through its consequent flourishing and eventual ossification in the 1950s-80s. In summary, my approach to fictionalized biographies of child heroes includes both surveying them as an evolving literary phenomenon ingrained in complex historical context and their study as a literary convention which, at its most advanced stage, integrated a rigid plot structure and a number of well-established and, therefore, categorizable poetic devices.

2   What Is a Pioneer Hero?

Let us begin with a definition. Child heroes are ten- to sixteen-year-olds who have performed a feat – a socially meaningful act which involved risking one's life for the people or the regime. Feats may include such deeds as saving someone from fire, preventing a train crash, or a combat-style encounter with an enemy of the state. After the Pioneer Organization was founded in 1922, child-heroes began to also be called pioneer-heroes. The term reflected the frame of mind of the Soviet government: if all Soviet children were to become pioneers, all of them could and should be heroes ready for self-sacrifice.[4]

At the turn of the nineteenth century, literary representations of children's heroism did not refer to acts of real individuals, except for the early chapters in the biographies of great men written for the young. This impersonal heroism acquired factual biographic features only by the beginning of the 1930s, when stories about heroic Soviet children became both politically indispensable and popular. It must be noted that the number of texts about child heroes

---

4 Vladimir Sulemov, ed., *История ВЛКСМ и Всесоюзной пионерской организации имени В.И. Ленина*, Moscow 1983; Andrej Gusev, *Год за годом...: Из пионерской летописи*, Moscow 1964.

endowed with real names grew exponentially in the beginning of World War I,[5] but it was the Russian revolutions of 1905 and 1917 and the Civil War of 1917-1923 that turned an anonymous child hero into a particularized protagonist with a more or less "authentic" biography. This new version of life narratives about child heroes was politically conditioned; in the following decades, it would become more and more closely connected to the ideological realities and dogmatic imperatives of the day. In the 1920s, stories about children fighting the *kulaks* (peasants who resisted forced collectivization) and "plunderers of socialist property" appeared, to be followed by the spy-tracking narratives of the mid-1930s and the war-time and postwar combat-centered novels and novellas. In most of them, little heroes were named and described as "real" individuals.

With the Great Patriotic War drawing to a conclusion, the innovations of children's authors in storytelling and characterization of child heroes petered out: there would be neither new plot twists, nor new types of enemies. By May, 1945, writers covering the war in their works for young audiences had managed to form a unified set of fabulaic patterns for depicting pioneers' feats, including skirmishes with the enemy, fire rescue episodes, portrayals of children participating in resistance movements in the rearward, and other such vignettes. Those writers working within this genre in subsequent decades would uniformly adhere to the already established canon of representing pioneer heroes. They continued to develop fictionalized biographies of valiant young fighters, embellishing them in a retrospective manner, for example, by discovering prototypes of Soviet children's heroic behavior in the state's recent "revolutionary past." By the early 1980s, Soviet bibliographers and literary scholars were able to synopsize existing documentary and literary material in *Пионеры-герои: Учебное пособие* (*Pioneer-Heroes: A Study Manual for Students and Teachers*). It was a bio-bibliographic reference manual, containing carefully selected excerpts from the fictional and non-fictional "lives" of courageous, conscientious, and loyal children from 1905-1945.[6] This collection accumulated storyline patterns and formulaic clichés typical of child-hero narratives, thus providing both descriptive and prescriptive formulas for a new

---

5 An increase in the number of such texts, from an essay or a photo caption in a newspaper to works of fiction, could be noticed in a special issue of the journal *Война: Дети-герои на войне* 22 (1915). See also Lidija Charskaja's novella, *Игорь и Милица (Соколята): повесть для юношества из великой европейской войны* (*Igor' and Milica (Young Falcons): Children's Novella from the Times of the Great European War*), Petrograd 1915, which exemplifies this trend.

6 Dmitrij Gunin, ed., *Пионеры-герои: Учебное пособие*, Moscow 1982.

generation of children's authors who were expected to continue the tradition.[7]

3   "They Were the First": *En Route* to the Child-Hero Canon

The breakneck speed with which the tradition of fictionalized narratives about child heroes developed in the early twentieth century can be explained by the readjustment of the society's perceptions of childhood, as well as by the actual emancipation of the child in the pre-revolutionary Russian culture.[8] Both the general public and those who supervised and directed the course of children's literature, such as educators and critics, participated in this process. As soon as children's literature emerged (in Russia, this happened in the eighteenth century), they approached it as a means for providing young readers with fictional and non-fictional role models. From the second half of the nineteenth century on, life stories of great men of the past and present were considered ideal pedagogical tools, no matter whether their subjects were actual paragons of virtue or not. According to the educator Nikolaj Poznjakov, children's authors were obliged to depict holy martyrs, national and military leaders, accomplished writers and self-taught scholars – "the people of industry, intellect, strong will and inspiration" – as examples for Russian children to follow. "[H]ow could one fail to desire that the object of his teaching would not be given illustrations of such life that, to a degree, bordered on the ideal?" Poznjakov asked rhetorically.[9]

In the 1870s, Russian authors and their critics began to accept the idea that the childhood of a future hero could, in itself, serve as a suitable didactic material. Such publications as *Детство великих полководцев* (*Childhoods of Great Military Leaders*, 1875) and *Жизнь замечательных детей. Черты детства великих детей* (*The Life of Great Children. Features of Childhood of Great Children*, 1871) appeared in print and were readily consumed. Their authors accompanied descriptions of the early years of future great men with admonitions pertaining to readers' obligation to emulate ideal child heroes. For instance,

---

7 This does not mean that the tradition of the genre is petering out. Several children's books about pioneer-heroes have recently appeared in print. Their authors attempt to re-animate Soviet pioneer hero narratives while overcoming the formulaic constraints of the genre. See, for example, Valerij Voskobojnikov's *Рассказы о юных героях* (*Stories about Young Heroes*, 2015) and Eduard Verkin's *Облачный полк* (*The Cloud Regiment*, 2012).
8 Catriona Kelly, *Children's World: Growing Up in Russia, 1890-1991*, New Haven and London 2007, 3.
9 Nikolaj Poznjakov, "Критика и библиография," in *Женское образование* 8 (1884), 521-522.

one such early collection of biographies for young readers, a chronicle of Giovanni Pico della Mirandola's life, is prefaced with a moral, which is explicitly stated as: "Having read this story, you will see, children, how much happiness one's love for learning can elicit and what glorious fame it can bring about."[10] Teachers, in their turn, welcomed the publication of moralistic works which featured biographies "not of the entire life [of great men], but only of their adolescence and youth and only to such a degree that their talents revealed themselves."[11] In the opinion of those who compiled biographical compendiums and of their critics, a model childhood would already make one's talents and virtues come forth.

By the beginning of the twentieth century, Russian society had accepted childhood as a self-sufficient, meaningful period in an individual's life. Now it was not just the childhoods of great men that were universally seen as suitable didactic material for educating the young. The emerging children's literature of the new era was a great step towards replacing the old moralistic model with a new one. Instead of featuring a nun's virtuous adolescence or the early years of a military commander spent hard at work and in self-disciplinary exercises, the "age of the child" preferred books about feats that an ordinary child could commit.[12] Among the typical story-lines of that time, two in particular stand out. In one, a child would fall through the ice when skating, while a second child – often a mere passer-by – would rescue her without a moment's hesitation. Another paradigmatic plot pivoted around a "common" young hero who saved a little girl or a very small boy from death by fire. In other words, childhood now became an autonomous source of heroic behavior, for children's authors were finally able to construct heroic narratives with child protagonists at their core.[13] Their little "good guys" did not have to grow into saints or victorious army commanders; they could be celebrated for what they had accomplished as children.

---

10   Luiza Kole, *Детство и юность великих людей*, St. Petersburg 1894, 5.
11   Michail Sobolev, "Обзор детских книг за 1875 год," in *Педагогический сборник* 4 (1881), 1002.
12   In 1900-1918, a prolific man of letters Sigizmund Librovich, often working under pen-names (such as Rysakov), produced several collections of model biographies, including biographic narratives for young readers. See, for example, Viktor Rysakov, *Юные русские герои: Очерки и рассказы о военных и довоенных подвигах русских мальчиков* (*Young Russian Heroes: Sketches and Short Stories about Wartime and Prewar Feats of Russian Boys*), Petrograd and Moscow 1914.
13   Lev Tolstoj's "Пожар" ("Fire"), Konstantin Stanjukovich's "Севастопольский мальчик" ("A Boy from Sebastopol"), Aleksandr Kuprin's "В недрах земли" ("In the Depths of the Earth") and Aleksandr Serafimovich's "В бурю" ("In the Storm") are exemplary of such stories.

Soviet mass media and children's literature adopted and embellished this paradigm. In 1938, the newspaper *Ленинские искры* (*Lenin's Sparks*) published an article, "Геройский поступок Саши Плетцова и Жени Спирина" ("The Heroic Feat of Sasha Pletcov and Zhenja Spirin"), which encapsulated several features of the up-and-coming genre:

> The other day, a sawmill worker M. Lisicyn fell through the ice on the Severnaja Dvina [river], a kilometer away from its shore (near Archangelsk, Severnaja Dvina is still fully covered [with ice]). Having heard the man's cries, activists of the water post [водная станция] – tenth-graders Sasha Pletcov and Zhenja Spirin – rushed to his rescue.
>
> Risking their lives, they reached the place where the worker was drowning and pulled him out of the water. The boys were issued a commendation.[14]

This and other such texts represent the plot which may be termed as "resisting nature." Its structure is limited to the heroes' struggle with the elements or against a technology-related catastrophe. Here and elsewhere, heroic children make an immediate decision to subjugate nature and then manage to conquer it. Their actions, focused on overcoming danger, may result in a rescued toddler, an extinguished fire, or a train stopped in its tracks right before it crashed. Obviously, the truthfulness of such heroic accounts varied significantly. It ranged from the compressed clichés of newspaper reports with their claims of evidentiary support, to fictionalized biographic vignettes and further, to fully fictional texts. There was even a fixed trajectory of heroic child narratives transitioning from mass media into belles-lettres. At first, a newspaper for young readers would publish such an account, then a similar story would appear in a collection of abridged or, more often, embellished hero narratives for children. Soon thereafter, a fully fictional version of the same story would come out.

Needless to say, not every heroic case deserved a full cycle of fictionalization; many of them reached only as far as a short didactic fragment in a reading primer or a Russian language textbook. See, for example, two such stories, "Героический поступок Насти Кузнецовой" ("The Heroic Deed of Nastja Kuznecova") and "Школьник-герой" ("Schoolboy Hero").[15] Having first

---

14 "Геройский поступок Саши Плетцова и Жени Спирина," in *Ленинские искры* 58 (2052), April 28, 1938.

15 "Героический поступок Насти Кузнецовой" and "Школьник-герой," in Petr Afanasjev, I. N. Shaposhnikov, E. E. Solovjeva, eds., *Сборник статей для изложения. Пособие для учителей начальной школы*, Moscow 1948, 48, 44.

appeared in a leading Soviet periodical for children, they were later included in a collection of essays for writing from memory in the classroom, which was published in 1937 and then re-issued many times. In comparison to how many accounts of children's heroic behavior were propagated this way before the war, the number of hero narratives that bloomed into expanded fictionalized versions appear to be small.[16] In order to make the cut, they had to be not simply "resisting nature" stories, but also politicized narratives especially propitious for propaganda, such as the cases of Pavlik Morozov, who informed the authorities about the wrongdoings of his family members, or the World War II-era guerilla fighter, Lenja Golikov.

In the 1920s, children's authors tried to emphasize the particular aptitude of Soviet young people, such as Komsomol members or the Red Army servicemen, for decisive actions in the face of danger. Thus, Pavel Egorov, in his short story "Праздник труда" ("The Festival of Labor," 1924) describes an accomplishment of a boy named Grishutka who, risking his life, rescued a ferry-boat full of passengers, while the adults who were also present, including his father, the ferryman, did not demonstrate any capacity for heroism. Grishutka nearly drowned, but the young men who picked him up on the shore were able to bring him back to life. Egorov underscores the fact that the rescuers were members of the Young Communist League (Komsomol), all the while indicating that the politically uncommitted onlookers had no first-aid skills and, moreover, did not want to take upon themselves any responsibility for the unfolding drama.[17]

"Праздник труда" may serve as a paradigmatic snapshot of characterization principles that began to dominate literary representations of Soviet child heroes. Responsibility and quick thinking at the moment of crisis became their most distinctive features. We can see many examples of these two virtues celebrated by the leading Soviet children's authors. One of them is Samuil Marshak's famous poem "Рассказ о неизвестном герое" ("The Story of an Unknown Hero," 1937), in which a young man, possibly a Komsomol member, saved a little girl from fire "without wasting a single minute" ("даром минуты одной не теряя") in sight of many people who were watching the catastrophe from the sidewalk.

In the 1930s, literature for the young was busy constructing a notion of ordinariness of an act of valor. Among other things, it declared that heroic be-

---

16   One such example is a story "Коноплюшки" ("Little Hemp Girls") by Jakov Tajtc, in which a little girl Shurka saves a train from crashing by waving her red Pioneer tie to warn the engineer of danger. Ja. Tajtc, *Рассказы*, Moscow 1940, 3-7.

17   Pavel Egorov, "Праздник труда," ("A Celebration of Labor") in *Юные строители* 9 (1924), 3-4.

havior was attainable by every child or adolescent because Soviet reality was so full of situations demanding one's immediate involvement in heroic action, be it some kind of struggle or crisis management. Not only did children's authors now accept the view of contemporary history as the socialist state's epic march towards its glorious future, but they also began to represent risky, potentially self-destructive feats as commonplace events – history's very fabric. Every Soviet man or woman was expected to act heroically, hence the underscored absence of protagonist's name in Marshak's poem. A young man delivers a rescued child to her mother and disappears in the crowd, so that firemen, policemen, and photographers "in our capital" have to look for him in vain (Evgeny Dobrenko calls this approach the "depersonification of heroism").[18] It is not surprising, then, that the heroes of the "resisting nature" narratives did not even have to rely on real prototypes. Most of them emerged within a work of fiction and remained there, for stories about saving drowning men and preventing train crashes merely expanded a literary tradition which had formed in children's literature before the revolution and became ideologically propitious in the 1920s. The authors of the 1930s copiously elaborated an already molded paradigm.

Throughout its history, Soviet children's literature embraced the "resisting nature" plot and exploited it with gusto. Its prevalence decreased only in the 1980s, when pioneer newspapers became less popular and eventually dwindled out. And yet, fiction's dependence on the disappearing periodicals, in which reports on real children saving their drowning peers had been published, can only partially explain the genre's deterioration. In fact, it began to fade when the collapsing Soviet ideological apparatus stopped producing not just newspapers, but also a whole variety of other media that multiplied and circulated heroic stories for children. Those books included school primers, collections of texts for readings in public spaces, and numerous brochures used in pioneer activities (such as aids for teachers for "conversing around a campfire"). Before the Soviet state ran its course, the Ministry of Education and its subsidiaries had also promoted a variety of semi-fictional publications that infused young readers with a healthy dose of heroism while addressing other behavior issues. One such example is a collection of short works of fiction entitled Пожар (*The Fire*, 1940). It included several sketches about children's carelessness that led to fires and two stories about young people's heroic actions inside burning buildings. In one of them, Evgenij Ruzhanskij's "Молоко" ("Milk"), little Jashka helps to put out the fire when a house goes up in flames, so that "when firemen arrived, there was nothing else to extinguish – the house

---

18   Evgeny Dobrenko, *Political Economy of Socialist Realism*, New Haven, CT 2007, 217.

had been saved." Mit'ka, the protagonist of "Удочка" ("A Fishing Rod"), another story by the same author, saves his blind grandfather accidentally locked up in a burning house.[19] Many other such books, published in hundreds of thousands of copies, disappeared from sight in the beginning of Perestrojka.

No matter how much the Soviet pedagogues and ideologues were willing to celebrate children's decisive actions at the moments of extreme danger, the "resisting nature" narratives belonged to the least historically and politically motivated storylines. Although many of these stories mentioned or implied child heroes' membership in the Pioneer organization (their behavior was often labeled "an act of a real pioneer" ["он поступил как настоящий пионер"]), their genre features and principles of characterization were not nearly as ideologically motivated as other types of hero narratives described below. The stories of a child hero's fight against this or that enemy of the state were much more ingrained in the historical context and the state's ideological priorities. When young heroes faced the raging elements and conquered them, they nevertheless remained their child-like selves. In contrast, while facing a human adversary – the politically defined "other" – they appeared to represent not just their heroic selves, but also the nation's future, won either in real military combat or by means of courageous class struggle.

4 "Red Adventure" Narratives of the 1920s

The portrayal of a child at war, and especially of his or her direct encounter with the enemy, became the first type of plot that authors of ideologically motivated Soviet hero narratives for children explored and exploited. These stories' protagonists are either child soldiers or child guerilla fighters (партизаны). The literary tradition of representing children at war, however, is not entirely of Soviet origin. It emerged during World War I, in 1914-16, when the figure of the child warrior became prominent both in Russian and European children's literature.[20] Kimberly Reynolds traces the tradition of diminutive "*homo militaris*" in British fiction even further back – to children's books written in the 1850-1900s.[21]

---

19   Evgenij Ruzhanskij, "Молоко"; "Удочка," in *Пожар*, Moscow 1940, 32-39; 55-56.
20   Marija Litovskaja, "Воюющие дети…," 93-99.
21   Kimberley Reynolds, "Words about War for Boys: Representations of Soldiers and Conflict in Writing for Children before World War I," in *Children's Literature Association Quarterly* 34:3 (Fall 2009), 255-271.

World War I-era periodicals for children and adults were full of reports about children who volunteered to serve in the army, including accounts of their feats and the awards they received for valor in battle. As a rule, these editorials began with a short introductory passage listing the child's name, age or grade, the academic institution where he used to study, and his birth place. Then the boys' heroic actions would either be enumerated or briefly outlined, with a passage about the quantity and denomination of earned awards concluding the story. At that time, child soldiers still did not merit full-fledged biographies, for journalists did not find it necessary to describe the stages of young heroes' maturation. One recurrent biographical motif, however, did emerge in stories about youngsters fighting in World War I – the motif of leaving home and clandestinely making it to the frontline. It appeared both in newspaper reports about the number of children who escaped to the front and in sketches about individual heroes. Ten years later, this trope became a staple of Soviet children's war narratives. In Arkadij Gajdar's novella *Школа* (*School*, 1930), for example, it both reflects the realities of the war and serves as a psychologically loaded component of a coming-of-age story. In a way, the motif of escape to the front is part of a broader paradigm related to children's ever-increasing lack of dependence on adults. Events of the first World War had provoked this autonomy, while war-time media campaigns had made it public.

An anonymous narrative with a verbose title *Геройский подвиг 3 русских добровольцев, которые взорвали 42-сантиметровую пушку, склады пороха, улетели на неприятельском аэроплане и еще масса приключений* (*The Heroic Exploits of Three Russian Volunteers Who Exploded a 42-cm Cannon, Blew Up Gun Powder Warehouses, and Flew Away on an Enemy Airplane, Along with Many Other Exploits*, 1914), follows the storytelling patterns typical of adventure literature for children. The book describes heedless undertakings of three youngsters, fourteen-year-old Alesha Sitnikov, sixteen-year-old Vasilij Kirsanov, and fifteen-year-old Fedor Korovin. They "hacked up everyone who happened to be nearby," hijacked an airplane, and embarked on many other reckless missions. Introduced as army volunteers (добровольцы), they actually fought at the front, but their story is more reminiscent of popular literary accounts of young heroes' journeys and escapes, such as *Treasure Island* by Robert Louis Stevenson (1883) and *Dick Sand, A Captain at Fifteen* by Jules Verne (1878).[22]

22　*Геройский подвиг 3 русских добровольцев, которые взорвали 42-сантиметровую пушку, склады пороха, улетели на неприятельском аэроплане и еще масса приключений*, Moscow 1914, 9.

In a few years, the type of narrative that may be termed a "war adventure story" would become predominant in the children's authors' portrayal of the Russian Revolution and the Civil War. Unlike the exploits of children during World War I, similar events related to that period did not immediately enter the children's media discourse. This does not mean that the post-revolutionary Russian society lacked interest in the historical events that had ravaged the country and disrupted the lives of its young people. Rather, the new government was short of means for subsidizing a mass artistic response to the social upheaval directed towards children's audiences. Having published Leonard Kormchij's famous manifesto about the need of the state to monopolize literature for children (his article, 'Забытое оружие' ['A Forgotten Weapon'], appeared on February 17, 1918, in *Правда*), it still could not afford sponsoring ideologically conditioned and yet entertaining works for young readers.[23] Children's authors began to portray child participants in the revolutionary events and their aftermath retrospectively, starting in 1923, after the pioneer movement had emerged and several pioneer newspapers and journals had been launched. Around that time, book publishing for children was also reestablished, with new print-runs of children's books significantly surpassing those of pre-revolutionary editions for children.[24]

Hero and adventure narratives published between 1923 and 1926 include dozens of works dedicated to the everyday life as well as battles of the revolutionary and Civil War-era Russia. An upsurge in the publishing of such works was caused by a direct party commission for serialized pioneer "Nate Pinkerton"-style literature, which was similar to a requirement for revolutionary adventure literature for adults announced by Nikolaj Bucharin in October, 1922, at the Fifth All-Russian Komsomol Congress.[25] Bucharin suggested that children's authors and other writers of adventure stories use material based on "war battles, exploits, our [i.e. the Bolsheviks'] underground work, [...] the Civil War, the All-Soviet Emergency Committee's activities, various adventures of our workers, when workers used to rush from one front to the other, the activities of the Red Army and the Red Guards."[26] Pavel Bljachin's novella *Красные*

---

23 Leonard Kormchij, "Забытое оружие," in *Правда*, February 17, 1918, 3.
24 In 1912, Russian publishers issued 1,318 titles of children's books (see Svetlana Kara-jchenceva, *Книговедение: Литературно-художественная и детская книга*, Moscow 2004, 227). In 1918-1932, 10,7878 editions for children were published, as documented in Ivan Starcev, *Детская литература (1918-1931)*, Moscow 1933.
25 "Adult" literature also responded to this requirement. See Marija Malikova, "'Скетч по кошмару Честертона' и культурная ситуация нэпа," in *Новое литературное обозрение*, 78:2 (2006), 31-59.
26 Nikolaj Bucharin, "Доклад на V Всероссийском съезде РКСМ. Коммунистическое воспитание молодежи в условиях НЭПа," in *Правда*, February 14, 1922, 2.

дьяволята (*The Little Red Devils*), published in Charkov in 1923, became the writers' first response to Bucharin's appeal. It features the fantastic adventures of three adolescents who survived and conquered the enemy during Semen Budennyj's First Cavalry campaign against the anarchistic detachments led by Nestor Machno. Bljachin's young heroes tricked and overcame their adult adversaries with unbelievable ease.

New heroes of Soviet children's "red adventure" literature performed tasks that surpassed the limits of the possible. According to Evgenij Balashov, most of them were "'red partisans' who, having encountered a class enemy face to face, for example, when captured by the White Guards, escaped dangerous situations and overcame all obstacles competently, quickly, and with a minimum of resources. Their adversaries, on the contrary, were far from being nimble or smart. They appeared to be scoundrels, gluttons, drunkards, lazy-bones and idiots, so that to cheat and conquer them was not especially difficult."[27] There are plenty of fictional examples of such an opposition. In 1924, the journal *Юные строители* (*Young Construction Workers*) published an essay under the title "Юный герой" ("A Young Hero"), which, by then, had already become a typical headline for a child hero narrative. Its author, Aleksandr Ushagin, reported on the exploits of one Vanjushka who, when fighting with the Reds against the Whites, exhibited unchild-like ingenuity and adult-like agility.[28] Kol'ka Osipov, protagonist of Aleksandr Ryzhov's story "Теплушка № 36084" ("Freight Car No. 36084"), is similarly heroic.[29] He helped the Red Army men to disarm the bandits who had attacked a train sponsored by the party's Cental Executive Committee. Adults took the charred corpse of a bandit for Kol'ka's remains and buried it with great fanfare. But the young hero re-appeared at the most dramatic moment of the burial ceremony, unscathed and in good spirits.[30] Girl heroes were also smart and skillful, much more so than the adults against whom they struggled. In Petr Zamojskij's story "A She-Hero" ("Еройка"), little Man'ka helps to incapacitate a gang of White Guards.[31] She also exposes

---

27   Evgenij Balashov, *Школа в российском обществе 1917-1927 гг. Становление нового человека*, St. Petersburg 2003, 38.
28   Aleksandr Ushagin, "Юный герой", in *Юные строители* 5 (1924), 1-3.
29   Aleksandr Ryzhov, "Теплушка № 36084," in *Барабан* 12 (17) (1924), 3-11.
30   The storyline about civic funeral ceremonies dedicated to child heroes was very popular in 1923-25. It is likely that the farcical plot inversion in this story not only paid tribute to the traditional trickster narrative (dead man coming back to life), but also responded to newspaper publications about children burying other youngsters without adults' help. See Svetlana Maslinskaya (Leontjeva), "По-пионерски жил, по-пионерски похоронен: материалы к истории гражданских похорон 1920-х годов," in *Живая старина* 3, 2012, 49-52.
31   Petr Zamojskij, "Еройка," *Юные строители* 11-12 (1924), 5-8.

the misdeeds of the kulak Gordeev who keeps a surplus of rye and a bootleg moonshine-making gadget away from the Bolshevik requisitioning committee.

The fabulaic elements of early Soviet adventure storytelling for children included cross-dressing, near escapes, chases, and last-minute liberations, as well as heroes' exhibiting remarkable strength and acting with uncommon self-control and efficiency. All these lucky traits come from the toolkit of traditional literary tricksters – those happy-go-lucky characters who could solve any kind of problem and fool any adversary, no matter how strong he or she was. A typical trickster is Fed'ka from M. Michajlov's novella *Федька Апчхи* (*Fed'ka the Sneeze*, 1925).[32] This young boy runs away from home to the front, encounters a revolutionary armored railroad train, and talks Red Army soldiers into taking him along on a mission. Single-handedly, Fed'ka liberates Red Scouts from arrest by White Guards, steals a briefcase with documents, and saves his armored train from destruction. His adventures are as endless as his energy and wit.

Pavel Dorochov's short story, "Сын большевика" ("Son of a Bolshevik," 1925), contains a similar array of adventures. First published in 1925 and reissued eight times by 1930, it portrays Misha whose father is a Bolshevik gone into hiding because the Whites have been hunting him, and whose mother needs to leave their hometown with the boy in tow. They wander around until the father sends them a note, indicating the place where the family could be reunited. Having reached that little town, Misha writes his dad a letter, but the messenger by whom it should be delivered dies of severe frostbite in the steppe. The old Bolshevik finds the letter by accident. After many hardships and smart escapes, in which Misha plays the leading role, the parents and the child finally meet, but their happiness is short-lived. The father will have to go away again, while Misha, inspired by his example, is beginning to plan a Bolshevik life full of adventures and hardships for himself. The elements of danger (escapes, accidental meetings, chases, and such) and the hero's constant wandering, typical of a traditional adventure narrative, here, however, begin to be closely connected to the new ideological system and the new social practice. Misha's family, for example, no longer appears to be a stable and reliable institution. It changes its shape in accordance with the new historical and political demands.[33]

Child-heroes of the 1920s "red adventure" narratives were still lacking a biography, however fictional it was. Those that emerged in the books written be-

---

32   M. Michajlov, *Федька Апчхи*, Charkov 1925.
33   Pavel Dorochov, *Сын большевика*, Moscow 1925.

tween 1923 and 1926 were especially schematic: their age was not particularly defined, their social profile was roughly hewn, and the psychological motivation for their actions was not always clear. Their feats belonged to the universal cloak-and-dagger literary repertoire typical of Fenimore Cooper's and Louis Boussenard's works, which were actively emulated and reproduced in the turn-of-the-century Russian literature without presupposing deep insights into protagonists' behavior. The revolutionary and Civil War settings in which these little fighters operated were rather provisional as well. Gajdar's portrayal of heroic young citizens is especially illustrative of the development of these rough features and the refinement of artistic devices that subsequently led to fully evolved hero narratives in Soviet children's literature. His early works for children, such as *P. B. C. (The R[evolutionary]. M[ilitary]. C[ouncil].*, 1925) and *На графских развалинах (On the Count's Estate's Ruins,* 1928) were markedly impersonal adventure stories, but *Обыкновенная биография (An Ordinary Biography,* 1929), reissued, in 1930, as *Школа (School),* already contained socially and psychologically detailed images of children coming of age in the years of the revolutionary turmoil. It is not accidental that the first title of the novella about Boris Gorikov, a near namesake of the author, Arkadij Golikov (1904-1941), writing under the pen-name Gajdar, evoked an autobiography. This work was one of the first to introduce a self-analytical dimension in the previously depersonalized reality of young adult adventure stories.[34]

Children's authors who wrote about the revolution between 1923 and 1926 portrayed the historical events just as factitiously as they wrote about the Civil War. In 1922, an excerpt about Gavroche from Victor Hugo's *The Dispossessed* (1862) was first issued as a separate edition by the Central Committee of the Komsomol within its "Library of a Young Commune Member" series.[35] Immediately after that, Soviet children's periodicals published stories about other French children – members of the Paris Commune who perished on the barricades defending the revolutionary regime. The publications were supposed to establish a continuity of children's heroic behavior by drawing a parallel between little Russian revolutionaries and their French predecessors. For ex-

---

34 For a more detailed analysis of the change in narrative structure in Gajdar's *Школа* as well as the author's portrayal "of the existential life experience in the constant presence of death," see Marija Litovskaja, "Аркадий Гайдар. 1904-1941," in *Детские чтения,* 2012, 2 (002), 87-104.

35 Viktor Gjugo, *Гаврош,* Moscow 1922. More on subsequent re-editions of *Гаврош* and the ideological editing of Hugo's work can be found in Myriam Truel, "Гаврош и Козетта – советские рассказы? (К проблеме освоения французского романа на русской почве)" in *Детские чтения,* 2 (005) (2014), 366-380.

ample, Aleksandr Ryzhov tells of four valorous French boys slaughtered at Porte Maillot in "Заговор барабанщиков" ("The Conspiracy of Drummers," 1926), establishing a continuity between the young heroes of the Paris Commune and Soviet pioneers.[36] In his short story, the old witness of the revolutionary events, Uncle Gavot, arrives in Soviet Russia bearing a drumstick that formerly belonged to the French "Gavroches." He gives it to the Pioneer detachment in Moscow's Krasnaja Presnja district, one of the first formed in the city.

Fed'ka Vichr' from Larisa Larina's story "Федька вихрь" ("Fed'ka the Hurricane," 1925) begins his life in revolution from a children's game imitating one of the protest demonstrations of 1905.[37] But soon thereafter, the boy starts participating in real fighting at the Moscow barricades, getting his hand cut off in a skirmish with the Cossacks. The story ends in 1925, when Fed'ka, already an adult, tells about his war experience to the new revolutionary generation, the pioneers. In Fedor Kiselev's story "Знамя спасли" ("They Saved the Banner"), young heroes rescue a red flag from the Cossacks who tried to disperse the first May Day demonstration of 1907.[38] Valentina Kordes, in "Мишкин Первомай" ("Mishka's First of May") also elaborates on a barricade plot with its, by then already established, motif of child heroism. Characteristically, Kordes juxtaposes her young protagonist's goodness with the brutality of class struggle (the boy hero witnesses the death of an older comrade in her story). "Nearly smothered by the heavy corpses, shocked by the ferocious slaughter," Mishka "was barely able to stand; horrified, he looked around, trying to understand what had just happened." Having come to his senses, the young revolutionary shakes his fist at "the silent mansions," certain that it is their inhabitants who bear responsibility for the murders.[39] The cited children's authors' and others writings about the revolution around that time only approximated the past, incorporating quasi-historical events into their fiction. When their child protagonists died, which happened often, they depicted their deaths as martyrly.

---

36 Aleksandr Ryzhov, "Заговор барабанщиков," in *Барабан* 5, 1926, 4-8.

37 Larisa Larina, "Федька вихрь" in *По разному*, Charkov 1925, 18-32.

38 Fedor Kiselev, "Знамя спасли," in *Юные строители* 8 (1925), 3-4. Typographic font was another typical attribute of revolutionary activities: it was used for setting and printing proclamations. In Elena Verejskaja's story "Таня-революционерка" ("Tanja the Revolutionary") first published in 1928, a smart little daughter of an underground printer-typographer hides the lead fonts in a jug of milk during the police search. Thus she saves her father from arrest and, possibly, death. *Таня-революционерка*, Moscow and Leningrad 1928.

39 Valentina Kordes, "Мишкин Первомай" in Dmitrij Bedrinskij and Valentina Kordes, *Из прошлого: рассказы*, Moscow 1925, 18.

This was a necessary element of the plot, for it allowed adult protagonists to commit to avenging the young sufferers and to fighting on for their "just cause."[40]

In the second half of the 1920s, some Soviet pedagogues and literary critics attacked the "red adventure" literature for children, proclaiming it subversive.[41] Not only new, inexperienced, writers, but also those who were well-known, such as Lev Ostroumov, author of "Макар-следопыт" ("Makar-the-Sleuth"), Sergej Grigorjev ("Мальчий бунт" ["Boys' Revolt"] and "Красный бакен" ["The Red Buoy"]) and Pavel Bljachin, were severely reprimanded. Critical attacks came both from the State Academic Council Committee (GUS) led by Krupskaja and from the allies of Anna Pokrovskaja and Nikolaj Chechov who represented the old pre-revolutionary school of children's literary criticism.[42] Both groups demanded that children's writers portray real events and investigate non-fictional conflicts in everyday Soviet life. Even child readers were prompted to express the same position in their critical responses to literary texts. One of them, a junior journalist ("деткор") writing for a children's periodical, asserted that authors "had to turn literature into a mirror reflecting the contemporary life in its entirety, reflecting the socialist construction which is now going on in our country."[43] Those expected to hold that mirror

---

40 The same type of barricade narrative was used in Germany in National Socialist propagandistic books for the young. Karl Aloys Schenzinger used it in his *Hitlerjunge Quex* (1932), while other authors imitated his work in theirs. For example, in Jozef Viera's (Jozef Sebastian Vierasegerer's), *Utz kämpft für Hitler* (1933), children die a heroic, martyrly, death at the hands of the Communists, while their comrades swear to avenge them. See Karsten Leutheuser, *Freie, geführte und verführte Jugend: Politisch motivierte Jugendliteratur in Deutschland 1919-1989*, Paderborn 1995, 100.

41 The term "красное приключенчество" ("red adventure") was coined by Anna Grinberg. She was among the educators who actively criticized the genre and its authors and promoters. Grinberg, "О новой детской книге и ее читателе," in *Народный учитель* 9, 1926, 98. Later versions of "red adventure" stories had to acquire new genre connotations in order to assert their legitimacy. Gajdar's "Сказка о военной тайне, Мальчише-Кибальчише и его твёрдом слове" ("The Tale about a Military Secret, Mal'chish-Kibal'chish, and his Firm Word," 1933) is a typical example of such an apology (it functioned first as a story within a story in Gajdar's *Военная тайна* and later frequently appeared on its own).

42 Nadezhda Krupskaja, "Об учебнике и детской книге для I ступени. Речь на I Всероссийской конференции по учебной и детской книге 8-15 мая 1926 г.," in *На путях к новой школе* 7-8 (1926), 3-13; Anna Pokrovskaja, "Приключения в современной детской литературе. Обзор 19-ти книг," in *Новые детские книги* 4 (1926), 17-92; Stepan Molozhavyj, "По вопросу о реализме в детской литературе," in *Новые детские книги* 4 (1926), 6-7; Ignatij Zhelobovskij, "Против снижения жанра. По поводу статьи Остроумова," in *Книга детям* 1 (1930), 24-25.

43 Detkor S. Selektor, "Хорошие и плохие книги," in *Товарищ* 9 (1931), 39.

could not avoid catching an image of an always prepared, observant, loyal, and selfless child in it.

5 Mirroring Contemporary Life: Soviet Children and Their Enemies

Life as it was depicted after 1923 – the moment when Soviet children's literature was born – meant a child's constant struggle with the nation's enemies. As Hans Günther famously wrote, the Soviet culture of the 1920s-40s was the culture of a confrontational type: "Just as a totalitarian society cannot do without a hero, it cannot do without an enemy, either. An enemy and a hero are the phenomena that precipitate one another."[44] In children's literature, a plot in particular modeled this conflict. Children's authors elaborated on the fictional constructs in which all Soviet young people emulated adults in their constant seeking out and confronting the enemy. The confrontation, in its turn, gave life to the protagonists' heroic behavior.

The militaristic literary discourse incorporated a broad network of foes whose names were always defined politically. Marija Litovskaja suggests that "there were kulaks, spies, deserters, imperialists, the White Guard, 'басмачи' [members of the anti-Soviet resistance in Central Asia – SM], and saboteurs, – and this is not even a complete list of active enemies of the new regime."[45] In Soviet children's literature these bad guys appeared under different, more or less schematic, masks. White Guardsmen were the earliest antagonists in fictional works for young readers, but in the mid-1920s they began to transform into bandits, kulaks, and spies.[46] These historically determined enemy types easily coexisted in fictional space, because the way they functioned in the text was pretty much the same. All of them could sabotage the socialist construction work by mining industrial sites, setting warehouses on fire, malnourishing kolkhoz horses or killing communists, Komsomol members and pioneers. Their appearance in the text, however, was frequently determined

---

44 Günther, "Архетипы советской культуры," in Hans Günther, Evgenij Dobrenko, eds., *Соцреалистический канон*, St. Petersburg 2000, 743-784.
45 Litovskaja, "Воюющие дети...," 93-99.
46 An example of such a narrative is E. Kochetkova's story "Миша" ("Misha"), which appears to be autobiographical. Its narrator recalls the events of 1920, when Siberian railroad workers, now guerrilla fighters, challenged the gang of Ataman Semenov. Kochetkova clearly substitutes bandits for white guardsmen. They murder the narrator's parents, torch his house, and accidentally kill the hero's younger sister in the fire. Misha's heroic feat – his attempt to save his sister from the burning house – acquires additional ideological connotations. He is not simply rescuing his sibling from the flames, but also asserting his political credo. E. Kochetkova, "Миша," in *Сибирский детский журнал* 2 (1928), 8-9.

by the stories' chronotopes. Thus, from the time of collectivization on, kulaks had operated within the rural social landscape, while spies were more typical of urban settings of the industrialization era and, since they were frequently engaged in industrial espionage and sabotage, more often than not they appeared to be engineers and other "specialists" ("спецы"). It also happened that depictions of some hostile social types were confusingly blurry. For example, children's authors of the 1920s and early 1930s could portray clergy both as wealthy landowners and as spies assisting "bourgeoisie" or "imperialists."

The spy discourse was popular in pre-revolutionary Russian literature for children. In the 1920s, Soviet children's literature picked it up again and made it serve ideological purposes of the new regime. In earlier Soviet works, however, the motif of children discovering a spy was embedded in an adventure narrative.[47] In a short story published in 1924, Larisa Larina, for instance, portrayed two boys, Vanja and Janek, "adopted" by a military detachment. Vanja, who had suspected the other youngster of spying for the White Poles, managed to trace down and disarm "the enemy," only to discover that Janek had been delivering fake documents to Polish commanders in order to fool them. Larina made no attempt to provide a socio-psychological portrait of her protagonists or characterize their class consciousness and political affiliation. The main narrative device that makes her story, as well as many other such narratives, shuffle forward is the trope of "accidental encounter." The narrative itself is characterized not by the "evolution of class struggle" – the theme later works for children would have to amplify – but by a chain of accidents connected neither to Vanja and Janek's political maturity, nor to their revolutionary conscientiousness. Michail Leonov's play *Радио-Май. Первомайское зрелище* (*Radio-May. May Day Spectacle*, 1925) appears to be a rare attempt to provide a class-based interpretation of events within an early spy story for children.[48] Its main characters, young pioneers, are supposed to meet and greet the guests arriving for the May Day gathering of international children's communist collectives. Instead, they discover a British spy, who is an adult, and two children also doing the spy work: one of them is a boy-scout and another, a "little *kadet.*"[49] But even Leonov's play is not yet fully politicized, because it is a work of literature created outside of the emerging Socialist Realist tradition.

---

47 Larisa Larina, "Шпион" ("A Spy"), in *Барабан* 7-8 (1924), 3-8.
48 Michail Leonov, *Радио-Май. Первомайское зрелище*, Moscow 1925.
49 "Kadet" is a member of Russia's Constitutional Democratic Party. The party was instrumental in bringing about the February revolution of 1917 but was later banned and ostracized by the Bolsheviks. Since most prominent Kadets (such as Pavel Miljukov, Maksim Vinaver, Vasilij Maklakov, Vladimir Nabokov Sr. and others) emigrated to Berlin and Paris, the young Kadet from Leonov's play could be one of their offspring, a child of the emigration that resisted the Soviet regime.

From the mid 1920s, Soviet works for children begin to incorporate storylines about spies penetrating the Soviet territory in the era of peaceful socialist construction. Thus, in Vasilij Korenkov's story "Всегда готов!" ("Always Ready!" 1925), with its not-so-subtle subtitle "Геройский подвиг пионера" ("A Pioneer's Heroic Feat"), the main character Pet'ka Bojkov notices a suspicious car, decides that it must belong to a spy, and tracks it down. Having followed the people in the car and heard their speaking a foreign language, Pet'ka draws the following conclusion: "It is obvious that a conspiracy is taking place. The non-Russian conversation convinced Pet'ka of this. Miners [шахтеры] should not expect anything fair from such educated people."[50] Korenkov's protagonist ends up putting his inventiveness and bravery to good use. He crawls into a mine and cuts off the wires leading to an explosive device, thus preventing a catastrophe. After that, Pet'ka goes to a police office and reports on the enemies of the Soviet state. Thanks to his early developed "political conscientiousness," he is able to act independently of adults. This autonomy is not accidental: it is a result of the protagonist's espousal of Soviet education, with its prerequisite of loyalty, and of his adherence to the pledge of the Soviet pioneer.

Apart from the motif of Soviet children's reporting on a spy to the authorities, catching the enemy with their own hands also becomes a popular narrative device. Authors begin to include it in their works for young readers in the second half of the 1930s – a development obviously determined by the political climate. Around that time, the Soviet government began to actively fight not only the "inner enemy," but also the enemies beyond the Soviet borders, constantly mentioning their ability to penetrate the confines of the state in the press as well as commenting on it in public discourse. In children's literature, the motif of border-crossing became an essential component of many a plot, which led to the formation of a separate category of protagonists – the so-called "children of the borderlands" ("ребята пограничной полосы"). Without the help of adults, these heroes were usually capable of recognizing and detaining foreign agents who attempted to cross the border. Their vigilance and self-sufficiency were remarkable. Although the strength of these children would not equal that of adult antagonists, they would enter into a challenging physical combat and usually come out triumphant. For example, Valja Vitushko in a 1938 story entitled "Пионеры-герои" ("Pioneer Heroes"), detained a female spy at the border by biting the woman's ankle.[51] "Children of the borderlands" also appeared in Agnija Barto's poem "На заставе" ("At the

---

50 Vasilij Korenkov, *Всегда готов! (Геройский подвиг пионера)*, Moscow 1925, 19.
51 Elizar Smirnov, "Пионеры-герои," in *Вожатый* 10 (1938), 47-51.

Outpost," 1936). Ekaterina Boronina introduced the same motif in her short story "В дупле" ("Inside a Tree Hollow," 1938), in which she described an encounter between a stranger and two village boys whose "collective farm was not far from the border." One of the children ran to the border check point to report the incident, while the other, when the spy discovered and began to smother him, shouted for help. At the last minute, the "border patrol got there right in time."[52]

Identifying adult protagonists as "good guys" in such narratives was accentuated not only by their being part of the Soviet nomenclature (a policeman, an employee of OGPU or NKVD, a communist), but also by their single-minded attention to every child's report and the proactive swiftness of their reactions. Leva, a child hero of a 1938 story "Незнакомец с пакетом" ("A Stranger with a Package") discovered that his neighbor wanted to blow up an industrial plant while eavesdropping on a conversation between adults. The boy ran to a street-corner policeman to report: "The policeman realized that it was serious business. He sprinted to a telephone booth and dialed the right number. In a few minutes, two men in military uniforms with red insignia were listening attentively to Leva's story. He was telling them about everything in detail."[53]

From 1936 to 1939, the spy theme became more widespread than ever.[54] In part, the discourse owed its popularity to Gajdar's elaborating on the subject of spies and saboteurs in his 1938 novella *Судьба барабанщика* (*The Fate of a Drummer*). Children's poets, especially those already well-established like Gajdar, were also prone to explore the time's signature trope. In addition to the already mentioned poem "На заставе" by Agnija Barto, Sergej Michalkov included it in his 1937 poems "Шпион" ("A Spy") and "Оборона" ("Defense"), while Elena Blaginina tackled the theme in her "Баллада о часах" ("The Ballad of the Watch," 1936). Such experienced *Правда* columnists as Grigorij Ryklin also wrote about children of the borderlands ("Дело было на чердаке" ["It Happened in the Attic"], "Исчезновение Алеши" ["Alesha Disappeared"], and "Всегда готов" ["Always Ready"]). Critics who responded to Ryklin's 1937 collection, *Рассказы о пограничниках* (*Stories about Border Guards*), were especially taken by his shunning typical tactics of adventure narratives, his adhering to "realism" and even by the naturalism of his descriptions:

52   Ekaterina Boronina, "В дупле," in Boronina, *Обвал*, Moscow 1938, 14-17.
53   Lev Zil'ver, *Быть на-чеку! Рассказы о коварных методах агентов фашистских разведок и работе славной совразведки по их разоблачению* ("To Stay Alert! Stories about the Treacherous Methods of Fascist Intelligence Agents and the Work of Valiant Soviet Intelligence on Their Exposure"), Moscow 1938, 53.
54   Spymania of the 1930s is well-documented in Sheila Fitzpatrick, *Everyday Stalinism: Ordinary Life in Extraordinary Time: Soviet Russia in the 1930s*, New York and Oxford 1999.

Ryklin's stories have nothing fantastic in them, they are completely lacking in adventure [авантюра]. Nonetheless, it is a fascinating read for children, because it tells of self-sacrifice and heroism. And what could engage children more than a story about an individual with such qualities?[55]

Works for young readers that appeared during World War II had very few storylines based on children detaining a spy. Igor' Vsevolozhskij's "Собака полковника" ("The Colonel's Dog," 1945) stands out as an exception.[56] The most prominent spy narrative of the war time is German Matveev's *Зеленые цепочки* (*Little Green Chains*, 1945).[57] This novella about young Leningraders who helped to neutralize and detain enemy infiltrators came out immediately after the war. It was followed by two sequels, *Тайная схватка* (*Secret Combat* 1948) and *Тарантул* (*Tarantula*, 1957).

Between the 1950s and 1980s, the setting of spy stories and novellas shifted from the socialist construction sites to the state border, predominantly in the South-Eastern part of Russia. Children's authors now focused not as much on the direct encounters between "children of the borderlands" and the country's enemies as on the young people's everyday lifestyles modified by their living in a perpetual danger zone. Jurij Jakovlev's short story, "Кепка-невидимка" ("An Invisibility Cap") is a typical example of such a narrative.[58] Jakovlev subtitled his work "a fairytale," thus making it clear that at the end of the Soviet era, the exceptionally heroic experiences of Soviet children, especially those having taken place at the state border, should be transferred from the realistic narrative style into the realm of fantasy and myth-making.

Post-"Thaw" children's literature reincarnated the "tightly locked border" ("граница на замке") formula that appeared in 1930s literary discourse.[59] Propagandistic concepts of the Cold War helped to reinforce the trope. Most

---

55 Grigorij Ryklin, *Рассказы о пограничниках*, Moscow 1937; I. Dvorkin, "Книга о героизме, находчивости, отваге," in *Детская литература* 10 (1938), 19.
56 Igor' Vsevolozhskij, "Собака полковника," in *Три поединка*, Majkop 1946.
57 German Matveev, *Зеленые цепочки*, Moscow 1945.
58 Jurij Jakovlev, *Кепка-невидимка*, Moscow 1987.
59 See, for example, Pavel Klubkov, "На посту пограничник стоит," in Evgenij Kuleshov, Inna Antipova, eds., *Детский сборник. Статьи по детской литературе и антропологии детства*, Moscow 2003, 405-411. For a study of the borderlands theme in academic texts addressed to children, including stories for writing from memory (изложения), see Ol'ga Iljucha, "Советские границы в учебно-воспитательных текстах сталинского времени" in Iljucha, and Irma Mullonen, eds., *Границы и контактные зоны в истории и культуре Карелии и сопредельных регионов. Гуманитарные исследования*, Vol. 1, Petrozavodsk 2008, 205-214.

authors of later Soviet children's fiction about border-crossing, however, endowed adult border guards with greater agency than child protagonists had enjoyed previously.[60] Their child heroes became secondary, albeit attentive and helpful, participants in heroic events. The active role they were able to play in catching spies during the time of peace was reduced to their participation in the training of service dogs, who, in their turn, would assist border patrols in their dangerous work.[61]

6 Kill the *Kulak*!

The *kulak* becomes the predominant antagonist in children's fiction written from the mid-1920s until the end of the Stalin era. The figure of a vile, exploitative rich peasant appeared in the writings of Turgenev and Chekov, as well as in the works of lesser known writers (Ivan Nikitin, Nikolaj Karonin-Petropavlovskij) even before the revolution, although it became more clearly defined and brought back to literary life with greater force during the 1930s collectivization. Now the *kulak* stood out as someone totally averse to the Soviet power – a man willing to destroy it. As expected, the height of interest in the portrayal of *kulaks* by children's authors coincided with a state-orchestrated campaign against Russian peasantry, marked by violence, famine, and displacement. Later it would peter out, so that only a small number of stories of heroic children fighting the *kulaks* would survive in children's literature of the post-war years. Among those were the narratives about Pavlik Morozov, Kolja Mjakotin, and a few other pioneers who participated in collectivization or perished during the campaign.

As a rule, stories about fighting the *kulaks* would revolve around episodes of direct encounters between children and adult enemies. Only rarely would young protagonists win by physically destroying their adversaries. Although the motif of armed resistance against the enemies of the state by children, inherited from the stories about the Civil War and the red youth's struggle against the "White bandits," did exist, in the 1930s, Soviet authors chose not to depict children as aggressors supplied with weapons. When, in A. Taezhnyj's novella "Ростки" ("Young Shoots"), published in the Novosibirsk children's magazine *Товарищ* (*Comrade*) in 1931, a child protagonist shot at a kulak, other villagers

---

60 Lev Lin'kov, *Рассказы о пограничниках*, Moscow 1954; Vladimir Druzhinin, *Кто сказал, что я убит?* Moscow 1969.
61 Arvid Grigulis, *Пограничники, два мальчика и собака Марс*, Moscow and Leningrad, 1952.

interpreted this attack as something out of the ordinary: "It's no laughing matter for a child to shoot at a living being ..."[62]

Revealing the enemy's "wicked plans" ("подлые замыслы") through publication in a newspaper or a report to the authorities, often submitted clandestinely, was a more acceptable type of behavior for protagonists in children's books. Denouncement was the first method of confronting the enemy typical of the 1930s representations of pioneer heroism. In fictional and non-fictional works about pioneer heroes, the denunciation plot harkened back to the story of Pavlik Morozov and the myth that formed around the boy's personality and actions.[63] The "advertising campaign" that propagated Pavlik's feat started in September, 1932, when newspapers first reported on the Pioneer's denouncement of his *kulak* father, and lasted until 1941, when World War II began on Soviet territory. Actions of those children who imitated Pavlik were also reflected in media publications and literary texts. Pioneer newspapers published in major cities such as *Пионерская правда* (*Pioneers' Truth*, Moscow) and *Ленинские искры* (*Lenin's Sparks*, Leningrad) were especially keen to contribute to this discourse. In almost every issue, they published articles about "new Pavliks," describing their actions by means of a laconic formula: "His (or her) exploit was analogous to that of Pavlik Morozov." It is important to note that the ideological import of Morozov's feat was grounded in the fact that the boy informed on his very father, who was a *kulak*. The numerous media publications about the young people who emulated Pavlik's act of valor were especially emphatic about the significance of children denouncing their family members.

Men-of-letters used "local reports" to create short biographical works of fiction about certain child-denouncers. Newspapers and magazines reprinted these stories after they had been reworked this way. In the late 1930s and early 1940s, some of them were published as separate editions for mass consumption.[64] The texts themselves contained remarkable moments of reflection on the reader reception and mechanics of narrative continuity. For example, six years after Pavlik's death, the magazine *Вожатый* (*Camp Counselor*) published an essay that incorporated such illuminating insights:

---

62 A. Taezhnyj, "Ростки," in *Товарищ* 7-8 (1931), 42.

63 Catriona Kelly investigated the literary embodiment of "товарищ Павлик" and the emergence of his cult of personality in the Soviet Union in her monograph, *Comrade Pavlik: The Rise and Fall of a Soviet Boy Hero*, London 2005.

64 Elizar Smirnov, *Славный пионер Гена Щукин. Эпизоды из жизни пионера, разоблачившего планы врагов народа и убитого ими*, Moscow 1938; Gleb Pushkarev, *Пионер Павлик Гнездилов*, Novosibirsk 1940.

> Who in our country would not know Pavlik Morozov's glorious name? At school or in a Pioneer brigade, that name has become [synonymous to] a banner of heroism, of valor, of courage, [serving as] a great Bolshevik example.
>
> When boys or girls put on their red [Pioneer] ties for the first time, they remember Pavlik. Each and every one of them wants to become as loyal a child to their Motherland as Pavlik was. When Pioneer Olja Balykina from the Tatar Republic, in spite of enemy threats, exposed her father as a traitor, she also *remembered* Pavlik Morozov. Vanja Becherikov from the Northern Territory, while being beaten up by a gang of kulaks and persecuted by them, also *recalled* the fearless Pavlik at such a horrifying moment; he bravely exposed the enemies who were destroying his kolkhoz. Later, when the enemies went on trial, Vanja Becherikov said in court: 'I was scared. I was afraid of them. But I *read* about Pavlik Morozov, and I felt better. Daddy and I sat down and wrote a letter to the editor about the kulaks.' Pavlik's image fortified Gena Shchukin from the Shira railroad station who, at the cost of his own life, revealed a despicable gang of Trotskyists, saboteurs and spies who had been wreaking havoc at the gold mines of Chakassia: it gave him strength, confidence, it made him a real Pioneer. 'Let us be like Pavlik!' is the slogan which the third generation of Bolsheviks has raised as a banner.[65]

Elizar Smirnov, Pavlik Morozov's first hagiographer, utilized increasing narrative tension and the rhetoric of emotional dynamism. In this particular text, he painted an epic picture of a pioneer-hero network consisting of those who emulated Pavlik's feat. The motif of following Pavlik's example was essential for the integrity of the story-line not only in media panegyrics, but also in fictionalized biographies of heroic children. For instance, according to Gleb Pushkarev's account, Pioneer Pavlik Gnezdilov, having listened to his brigade leader's report under the provocative title "What Pioneers Should Be Like," began to ponder whether he should disclose an underground leather-tanning enterprise. As a result of this reflection, Gnezdilov wrote an essay on "*kulak* holdovers" ("кулацкие недобитки"), in which he targeted his stepmother.[66]

Authors of stories about Pioneers who denounced *kulaks* endowed their child protagonists with the right to control and punish adults, while presenting their capacity for keen observation as a skill serving the socialist state.

---

65   Elizar Smirnov, "Пионеры-герои" ("Pioneer Heroes"), in *Вожатый* 10 (1938), 47-51. Italics are mine – SM.
66   Gleb Pushkarev, *Пионер Павлик Гнездилов*, Novosibirsk 1940.

In the 1930s, watching over peasants' efforts to preserve every bit of harvested crops for state expropriators became one of the Pioneers' main projects. The children engaged in this activity called themselves "harvest watchmen" ("дозорные урожая"), while those who were especially vigilant earned such honorifics as "heroes of harvest preservation," "young heroes of socialist fields," and the "vigilant guard." In 1934, in particular, the government embarked on a campaign to expose the individuals who pilfered or sheltered kolkhoz-grown grains as "anti-Soviet elements." Children were given a leading role in this crusade: newspapers and Pioneer leaders urged them to report on every instance of "enemy behavior," including their relatives' actions.

Pioneers who took active part in this movement were rewarded with trips to the Pioneer camp Artek in the Crimea. They could also attend regional gatherings of the "harvest watchmen" and receive valuable or memorable gifts from the government. In the summer of 1934, newspapers announced that "two hundred of the best [activists] would go to Artek." Пионерская правда published a list of those two hundred heroes, allocating a short paragraph to the outline of each child's feat:

> 1. Olja Balykina is a Pioneer from Tataria who has exposed her father and, along with him, a group of thieves of the kolkhoz grain.
> 2. Vanja Becherikov is a Pioneer from the Northern Territories (Северный край) and a young correspondent of Пионерская правда. He has exposed a gang of thieves of kolkhoz property in his village. [...]
> 17. Pronja Kolybin is a Pioneer from the Northern Territories who has exposed his mother who pilfered the kolkhoz grain. [...]
> 37. Mitja Ljubcev is a Pioneer from the Moscow Region who exposed his stableman father: he was regularly drunk and would often not feed kolkhoz horses.[67]

Most active children – Pavlik Morozov, Kolja Mjagotin, Kolja Jakovlev, Kychan Dzakypov, Gena Shchukin, and Pavlik Gnezdilov – were also "rewarded" with first personal fictionalized biographies for fighting the *kulaks*. Appearing as early as the 1930s, these narratives were reworked and republished many times in the following decades. All of them were forged according to the same template. First, all subjects of these hagiographic portrayals were given unofficial (often diminutive) names, such as Pavlik (from Pavel), Volodja (Vladimir), Grisha (Grigorij), Lida (Lydia), and so on. The anthropometric diminutiveness accentuated the protagonists' childlike nature and thus emphasized

---

67   Пионерская правда, June 18, 1934, 76; July 4, 1934, 84.

the significance of their heroic acts. There were no exceptions to this rule, which is why Pioneer heroes were known by nicknames rarely encountered in state-controlled publications: Kirja (Kirill), Njura (Anna), Lusha (Glafira), and Pronja (Prochor). When identically named Pioneer heroes appeared, their hagiographers would choose different diminutives for their names, thus excluding the possibility of the readers' confusing them. Therefore, a less famous child, Pavlusha Morozov, was added to the Pantheon of Pavlik Morozov heroes.

Secondly, when authors described the appearance of valiant Pioneers, they did not attempt to make them look heroic. In fact, the noted features of child heroes never gave the impression of anything extraordinary. Quite to the contrary, they were to look "average," indistinguishable from other children. By underlining the heroes' unexceptional appearance, writers and journalists supported the ideologically potent idea that every Soviet child, no matter what he or she looked like, was capable of carrying out heroic exploits.

Thirdly, when the narrative included episodes related to the Pioneers' childhoods, the rule of ordinariness was forfeited. A protagonist's childhood always featured foreshadowing of future heroism, including signs marking his or her birth as special (for example, that it occurred on the day of the "Great October Revolution"), and an enumeration of skills and talents that spelled out the hero's future uncommon fate – for example, early political conscientiousness, athletic abilities, and so on.[68] Clearly, this emphasis on the special circumstances of the protagonist's birth had referenced a specific literary prototype – namely, the hagiographic canon of portraying saints' childhoods. There are several intersections between the two genres. Not only does the characterization in Pioneer hero narratives owe its structure to hagiography, but the configuration of their plots also overlaps (in both types of text, there would be a trial by torture or a moment of recovering the body). Tracing similarities between the Soviet pioneer-hero stories and saints' lives, however, is not a completely new pursuit. Other scholars, Katerina Clark included, have noted the influence of hagiographic literature on a variety of Soviet literary genres, from novels to allegorical fairytales.[69]

Many detailed narratives about Pioneer heroes dwell on the period in the child's life that served as a preparation for the feat. Authors of such stories stress that their protagonists were endowed with virtues which the Soviet code of conduct considered essential for a citizen of the new utopia. The genesis of the moral qualities, however, was far from being homogeneous. For the

---

68 Kelly records hagiographers' attempts to make Pavlik Morozov a peer of the October Revolution, thus falsifying the boy's actual date of birth. Kelly, *Comrade Pavlik*, 164.
69 Katerina Clark, *The Soviet Novel. History as Ritual*, Chicago 1981, 46-48.

most part, such features as children's respect for their parents, industriousness, love for reading, and excellent academic achievements did not differ much from the virtues listed in the eighteenth-century etiquette primer, Юности честное зерцало (*The Honest Mirror of Youth*, 1717). There were other virtues, however, that belonged entirely to the Soviet moral catechesis. Among them were atheism and militant anti-religiosity, active participation in politically charged social activities, and devotion to the communist dogma.

Virtuousness makes the future heroes stand out among other children, marking them as extraordinary individuals:

> In the spring, classes were over at school, so his father sent Pavlik to the fields where other students were working as well.
>
> The days were intense. Everyone was busy to the utmost, so in their free time they tried to lie down on the grass, to rest, even to nap for an hour. Pavlik, however, would pull a book out of his bag, sit down somewhere in a corner so that others would not bother him, and give himself entirely to the book.[70]

The hero's circle – "other students" – were usually portrayed as children guided by the protagonist. They often possessed vices which the protagonist exposed and criticized. For example, Gena Shchukin gave the wallet he had found to the village literacy teacher. By doing that, he went against the flawed opinion of his peers: other students wanted to spend the money on gingerbread.[71]

The Pioneer heroes' loyalty to Soviet ideals, their political activism and desire to enlighten their peers as well as adults were ranked most highly among their moral achievements.

> The brigade's chairman now had many new things to do. 'A Pioneer is an example for all other fellows,' he used to say to his comrades while tirelessly fighting for each red tie-clad young man to become a true young Bolshevik. 'We should study to earn "good" and "excellent" grades only,' Pavlik told them at a meeting, and all the pioneers in a shock-worker fashion, as they used to say then, began to tackle their learning.[72]

---

70 Gleb Pushkarev, *Тайга расскажет*, Tomsk 1958, 8. Morozov was reading Michail Sholochov's *Поднятая целина* (*Virgin Soil Upturned*, 1932).

71 Elizar Smirnov, *Славный пионер Гена Щукин. Эпизоды из жизни пионера, разоблачившего планы врагов народа и убитого ими* (*Valiant Pioneer Gena Shchukin. Episodes from the Life of a Pioneer Who Revealed Plans of Enemies of the People and Was Killed by Them*), Moscow 1938.

72 Elizar Smirnov, "Павлик Морозов," in *Дети-герои*, Moscow 1961, 65.

Some stories included a "written oath" subplot: a child hero revealed his or her willingness to perform a feat by committing to an exploit in writing and then sending that pledge by post to a newspaper, to the Kremlin, to comrade Stalin, or merely to Moscow. Pavlik Gnezdilov, for example, avowed the following in his letter to Stalin:

> ... and when I grow up, I will without fail become a pilot just as courageous as Vodopjanov and other heroes of the Soviet Union. I will carry out with honor any assignment that comrade Stalin will give me.
> November 1, 1937
> Village "Zarja," Gnezdilov Pasha.[73]

Often before children became heroes, they had demonstrated their willingness to perform a feat by participating in propaganda work and serving as informants. Such Pioneers worked as correspondents of a local or central newspaper and wrote denunciatory letters to the authorities.

The descriptions of children getting ready for heroic activity were followed by episodes of their trial by action. The goal of this test was to confirm that the boys and girls were real Pioneers, i.e. that their reactions to danger or hardship corresponded to the ideal model of behavior already articulated in other similar literary works and media discourse. Usually, there was one trial episode per story, but in some rare cases, narratives included a number of the protagonists' preliminary feats crowned by the main exploit. Thus, Gena Shchukin, besides his main act of heroism, repeatedly behaved in a virtuous manner by protecting little children and returning the lost money-purse; he also demonstrated magnanimity towards his ideological enemy Vasja (not a Pioneer) and rescued him from drowning.[74]

Quite often, the culmination of child-hero narratives was the protagonist's death: the texts that included this dramatic episode were centrifugally drawn towards its description. In the 1930s, a hero's death was always torturous; the martyrdom demonstrated protagonist's readiness for self-sacrifice for the Soviet state. As a rule, authors of such narratives lingered on and even delighted in providing details of the martyr-child's torture. Ivan Antonov's "Багровый снег" ("Scarlet Snow"), Elizar Smirnov's "Славный пионер Гена Щукин," Gleb Pushkarev's "Пионер Павлик Гнездилов" ("Pioneer Pavlik Gnezdilov") and

---

73   Pushkarev, *Тайга расскажет*, 8. "Паша" is another, somewhat more masculine, diminutive of Pavel. Apparently, the protagonist himself prefers to be called by that name.
74   Smirnov, *Славный пионер Гена Щукин* (*Valiant Pioneer Gena Shchukin*).

many other similar stories included such gory elements. Even when pioneer-hero narratives crossed the boundary of children's fiction into other genres or literary forms – textbooks, for example, or academic-style readers – the books' editors chose episodes of the Pioneer or Komsomol heroes' deaths for inclusion in these volumes, focusing their attention on the protagonists' physical torture. In a broader context, the Soviet culture as a whole is characterized by a visual and textual portrayal of a hero's pre-mortem agony. Physical suffering exemplifies the Soviet idea of self-sacrifice as the only type of attitude possible in the conditions of the nation's perpetual struggle against its enemies.

In children's fiction of the 1930s, an enemy's revenge was always furtive, and Gothic settings were required to underline its cloak-and-dagger nature. Antagonists of child-hero narratives killed their young victims in the dark, most frequently in late autumn, waiting till they were already asleep. Or they could lure children to a desolate location, such as the outskirts of a city or a village, a dark forest, or a bog, and execute them there – single-mindedly and maliciously. Pavlik Gnezdilov's death, for instance, abounds in oppressive details: the enemies strangled him with a piece of rope, then they hacked him up with an axe, then threw him in a cellar, dragged him out later and buried him in a bog. This obvious tribute to the aesthetics of horror is not accidental. As it has been previously mentioned, a pioneer-hero narrative almost always began on the pages of *Пионерская правда* or in a local newspaper. The language of the early Soviet periodicals had an obvious influence on printed propaganda, of which brochures about Pioneer heroes were an integral part. Writers who hammered away at those fictionalized biographies borrowed their rhetorical devices from reporters contributing to "crime news" columns. For example, in a scene depicting the murder of Grisha Akopjan whose 1929 exploit was similar to Pavlik Morozov's, there are such elements as the enemy threats against the child, the hero's defiance of the enemy, and an ominous description of his last moments:

> 'Stop babbling, you, red devil! Or I will smash your head with this [rock])!' He grabbed the boy by his red tie.
> 'Or we will string you up on a tree. Got it?'
> Grisha was not a coward. He responded quietly:
> 'I am not the only one who wears a tie. Millions of Pioneers do. You won't be able to hang us all up. Off my road, you bandit!' And he pushed the kulak's son away.
> Grisha kicked Armenak with his foot, but the bandits, like *feral beasts*, seized his body. *A sharp Finnish knife slid across his neck*, and a muted cry escaped Grisha's throat. *The earth turned scarlet with his blood.* Misha

> Nersesjan, a little shepherd who was taking his goats out to the cemetery, saw how the bandits killed Grisha. Misha rushed to tell others how the pioneer had been slaughtered. The murderers ran after him to destroy the boy and thus conceal every trace of their crime. Only the little Octobrist's swift legs could save him from sure death.[75]

The "freezing" of narrative time (what Viktor Shklovskij called "торможение"), is another important element of the Pioneer hero sacrificial murder scenes. In the episode of Grisha Akopjan's death cited above, the son of the *kulak* enumerated the ways in which the boy could be killed to serve exactly this purpose. Overall, the fragment's style consists of lexical bits borrowed from a variety of sources: the official newspaper rhetoric ("how the Pioneer had been slaughtered"; the figure of "*kulak*'s son" ["кулацкий сынок"]); the terminology used by criminal news columnists ("every trace of their crime," "murderers"); and the references to urban folklore and other folk genres containing "horror" elements. The topoi that bring them together range from fixed epithets ("a sharp Finnish knife," "feral beasts," "sure death") to extended metaphors ("the earth turned scarlet with his blood").

A story of Kolja Jakovlev, a Pioneer killed by the *kulaks* in 1934, shortly after the murder of Kirov, culminated in a similar description of the hero's death.

> Ivan Bojkov, who stood nearby, sent Kolja tumbling into a snowdrift with a stroke of his cutlass.
> Blood gushed out of the wound. And yet, Kolja gathered all of his strength, jumped to his feet, and, having pushed Bojkov off with his ski poles, began to move forward, swaying slowly. Bojkov followed him. Drunk and heavy, he stumbled through the loose snow. But as soon as he managed to reach the escaping boy, he would push him down to the ground with another blow.
> Kolja was losing his strength. He could not walk anymore – so he crawled, trailing a crimson stripe on the snow behind him. The bandit continued to strike him again and again. Kolja Jakovlev collapsed to the ground sprinkled with the snow and stopped dead…
> This is how the pioneer from Luga, Kolja Jakovlev, died, but his name will forever live in people's hearts and memory. Heroes do not die.[76]

---

75   Sarkis Mnacakanjan, "Герой пионер Гриша Акопян," in *Пионеры-герои: Альбом-выставка*, Moscow 1967-1969, 24.
76   Ivan Antonov, "Багровый снег" ("The Scarlet Snow"), in *Всегда готов! Рассказы о ленинградских пионерах*, Anna Mojzhes, ed., Leningrad 1962, 145.

The many inconsistencies in this text testify to its spur-of-the-moment, political agenda-driven nature. Kolja Jakovlev skis across the field at the moment when his murderers reach him. There are snowdrifts which slow down the culprit Bojkov's movements. But at the end of the story, Kolja falls down to the "ground sprinkled with snow." It is also unclear how he fell if, after trying to walk laboriously, he had already started to crawl across the field. The author is obviously striving for emblematic expressiveness here – and these attempts to sound entertaining eclipse the logical consistency of his narrative. Ivan Antonov, who wrote this story, adheres to the folkloric stereotype of "a beautiful death." One of its most important motifs is the discomfort of the hero's demise. Another inevitable element of this topos is the barrage of deadly blows that the hero receives from his attackers, along with the torments and tortures he or she endures. In the 1960s, Antonov went back to the life story of the same pioneer, adding a detail that previously did not appear in his text. When the enemy strikes Kolja with a knife, the boy has two rabbits hid in his bosom (he carries the animals to a pioneer farm so that the children could breed them).[77] The blade hits one of the rabbits, thus putting off the final deadly blows to the boy himself. Such "freezing" or "stretching" of narrative time leads to the postponement of the hero's death and, subsequently, fulfills the task that brings together this and other heroic narratives: to attract the readers' attention to the protagonists' courageous behavior at the moment of their martyrdom.

The types of heroes' reactions to the attempts on their lives vary, but are not determined by the personalities of protagonists. No matter what the Pioneer was like in life, when facing death, he or she either demonstrates a stern scorn of death – similarly to how Grisha Akopian and Kolia Jakovlev appear to behave – or acts as a "sacrificial lamb." The latter model is exemplified by Kolja Mjagotin, who, in Stepan Suchachevskij's rendering of his life, asks his tormentors why they attacked him:

> Before his very eyes, Kolja saw the gun's black muzzle.
> 'Uncle Fotej!.. But why?'
> 'You, pioneer activist, know it yourself!'[78]

A much rarer case would be works in which authors chose to replace the murder scene with pregnant silence.

---

77   Ivan Antonov, "Багровый снег," in *Гремите, барабаны!* I. Smol'nikov, ed., Leningrad 1982, 22-30.
78   Stepan Suchachevskij, *Коля Мяготин (Kolja Mjagotin)*, Moscow 1967, 29.

> Gena returned home anxious and tired.
>
> It was dark and cheerless inside. Without turning on the lamp, Gena undressed quickly and got into bed. [His stepfather, kulak] Akimov was not home. 'But where is he?' Gena thought. He became afraid.
>
> It was the middle of the night, the fearless pioneer's last night. Gena fell asleep...
>
> In the morning, they found his corpse, already stiff.[79]

In this episode, it is the setting that suggests the inevitability of death encroaching upon the sleeping child.

Authors of pioneer-hero fiction also supplied descriptions of recovery of the protagonist's body, or of his secret burial with gory details typical of horror narratives.

> The militiaman rushed there. The dog yelped and ran away. A boy's disfigured corpse was lying on the ground. Fragments of a sack and a scrap of a red shirt were scattered around. At twenty paces to the side, an unfinished burial hole was gaping darkly.[80]

To sum up, by the end of the 1930s, the canon of a pioneer-hero's life had already been formed. The opening part of the canonical narrative would describe the protagonist's preparation for a heroic exploit; it could also include the hero's portrait or psychological profile. As a rule, this opening was shorter and less obligatory than the second part of the story, which was dedicated to the pioneer's confrontation with the enemy and his or her imminent death. After the war, children's authors would start fitting fresh content to this canonical template, creating stories of heroic adolescents fighting the enemy at the front. Although a new type of protagonist – the warrior child – would now proliferate in postwar Soviet children's hero narratives, the earlier structure of heroic fiction remained fairly intact. For a short story about a valiant child written for a magazine or a newspaper, the "artistic" description of the heroic exploit itself would be sufficient. But when full versions of pioneer life stories appeared in book form, they followed the model already developed during the actual and ideological campaigns against the *kulaks*.

It should be noted, however, that as the genre evolved, the next generation of heroic protagonists of children's fiction emerged. They were heroes who no

---

79   Smirnov, *Славный пионер Гена Щукин*, 45.
80   Pushkarev, *Тайга расскажет*, 47.

longer had to fight against saboteurs and spies. A new era ushered in a different array of standardized exploits and heroic behaviors. It was determined by the historical realities of World War II and the experience of the Soviet people fighting in it.[81]

7   All Is Fair in … War

A child at war became the last and most prolific heroic type in Soviet literature for children. It evolved in the 1940s, during the Soviet fight against the Nazi Germany and its allies on the USSR's territory and abroad. The evolution of war narratives for children went hand-in-hand with authors' experimenting with two subtypes of this trope: usually a male child as an adopted "son of the regiment" or a child stuck in an occupied territory. Similar to other varieties of heroic narratives, this particular paradigm in all its complexity was initially formed during World War I. As I have already established, the Russian Civil War, which could have given it a new push, ended up being represented by only one plot type, the "war adventure" story of the 1920s. Thus, by 1941, two literary traditions emerged in the Soviet portrayal of a heroic child: the so-called "adventure model" and the "realist model." During the four years when the war wreaked havoc on the Soviet territory, their varied structures merged into a single pattern for all writers to follow. Namely, children's authors had to sequence their war-time pioneer-hero narratives by starting with the protagonists' early childhoods, then describing their preparation for an exploit, and, finally, outlining the exploit itself. A variety of genres, such as ballads, songs,

---

81   Ann Livschiz notes rightly: "While there must have been children of traitors who turned on their fathers and proved their loyalty and dedication to the state, none of them made it into the heroic pantheon." Livschiz, "Children's Lives after Zoia's Death," 195. And yet, there are some cases of admiring children's denunciations of their family members. For example, Aleksandr Ivich begins his essay about Valentin Kataev's Сын полка (*Son of the Regiment*) with describing an incident that took place in a town recently liberated from the German occupation. A twelve-year-old boy approached an officer and, demonstrating "an aptitude for moral selectivity and an extraordinary willpower," reported that "his mom was hiding a German man." Ivich explains this by saying that "the child had to sacrifice his love for his mother for the properly understood [civic] duty," while also suggesting that the informant's deep sense of loyalty to Motherland appeared to be the result of Soviet education. "The entire system of Soviet upbringing and the influence of our social environment appeared to be more powerful than the malicious influence of the child's family and stronger than the two-year-long impact of the German occupation on the child-like soul." Aleksandr Ivich, "Подросток и книга," in *Советская книга* 3-4 (1946), 28.

documentary essays, short stories, plays, and novels, attempted to replicate this model. Although some of the Pioneer heroes ended up as main characters of several such works (for example, of a song, a newspaper editorial, a ballad or a novella), there were also many lives of war hero children that appeared only in short newspaper reports, never to be mentioned again in the public discourse.

An essay written on the road became the main war-time genre during the first two years of the "Great Patriotic War" ("Великая Отечественная война"). Solomon Garbuzov was the first author to accumulate pioneer hero narratives in his collection *Фронтовые ребята* (*Little Guys from the Front*, 1942). The stories he published did not have authentic prototypes. To explain this drawback, the author made his narrator refer to the need to protect the protagonists' real identities: "It is still too early to call my heroes by their real names. They are still at the front or close to the front. Anything could happen at war."[82] This conspiratorial attitude – echoing Gajdar's works – was quickly overcome a few months later, however. The collection *В огне Отечественной войны* (*In the Fire of the Patriotic War*) featured representations of individualized heroic behavior. Thus, V. Fin, in his essay "Наташенька" ("Natashen'ka"), spoke of a fifteen-year-old girl who managed to drive a train with supplies to the Soviet army while injured. Natasha's peer, a girl protagonist of Agnija Barto's story "Галя" ("Galja"), provided fascists with kerosene instead of water – a brave act that led to a fire and thus aided the attack of the approaching Soviet troops. Meanwhile, Aleksandr Isbach in "Сын" ("Son") and Anton Prishelec in the poem "Володя" (about Volodja Kozyrev) elaborated on the idea of the continuity of military valor: their boy protagonists took over from their fathers in fighting the enemy.[83] Around the same time, Ruvim Fraerman published his "Маленький герой" ("Little Hero"), an essay about a twelve-year-old Vanja Dlusskij who was adopted by a military unit as "the son of the regiment" ("сын полка").[84] All these works, along with Sofija Zarechnaja's novella "Орленок" ("The Little Eagle," 1942), demonstrate that in the war's early days, children's authors developed realist approaches to portraying children at war. All of their storylines had evolved within the preceding adventure hero narrative model, while their typical stylistic devices – such as the heroes' diminutive first names and their physical and psychological characterization – had been

---

82 Solomon Garbuzov, *Фронтовые ребята*, Moscow 1941, 3.
83 *В огне Отечественной войны: Сборник стихов, очерков, рассказов*, G. N. Petnikov, ed., Nalchik 1942.
84 Ruvim Fraerman, "Маленький герой," in *Пионер* 6 (1942), 15.

polished during the preceding era. Nevertheless, the structure and tone of war fiction about valiant pioneers changed dramatically. First of all, children's exploits no longer appeared to be full-fledged adventures, because the authors shifted toward plausibility in describing children's participation in war activities. Secondly, they represented the behavior of their heroic protagonists in accordance with the pioneers' developmental age. Finally, the little heroes' actions were motivated by their Soviet upbringing and their membership in the Pioneer organization.

This period is also characterized by the children's authors' embracing the ballad – the genre that had been actively used for propaganda purposes in "adult" Soviet literature by Nikolaj Tichonov, Michail Svetlov, Eduard Bagrickij, Aleksandr Prokofjev, Aleksej Surkov, and others. Stories and poems about Pioneer heroes could reveal their epic, song-like properties in their titles, such as Ol'ga Berggolc's "Баллада о младшем брате" ("The Ballad of a Younger Brother," 1941), Pavel Antokolskij's "Баллада о мальчике, оставшемся неизвестным" ("The Ballad of the Boy Who Remained Unknown," 1942), and Nikolaj Rylenkov's "Баллада о маленьком разведчике" ("The Ballad of a Young Scout," 1943). Other works for children, such as Konstantin Simonov's "Сын артиллериста" ("The Son of an Artillery Man," 1942) and "Рассказ танкиста" ("A Tank Commander Story," 1942) were given less ambitious titles, although they still adhered to the narrative principles of the ballad genre formed in Russian literature by the beginning of the twentieth century and later modified by Avant-Garde innovations. Thus, the mid-century ballad-like children's narratives included such motifs as a nameless protagonist (the child hero is one of many and, therefore, he or she is 'unknown'), continuity (for example, a younger brother takes the place of the elder in battle), self-sacrifice, choosing martyrdom consciously and firmly, enduring torture staunchly, and being valiant in the face of death. The recycling of thematic elements notwithstanding, war ballads for children had a new feature as well: their focus shifted towards a more lyrical representation of child heroism. In the previous two decades, children's authors had avoided exposing their protagonists' emotions; their enemies and comrades-in-arms appeared similarly unfeeling. The new emotionality in war ballads was not only apparent, but also nuanced: it ranged from the stoicism in the spirit of Marshak's translation of Robert Louis Stevenson's "Heather Ale" (1880; "Вересковый мед," 1941) to the melodramatic outbursts reminiscent of urban lyrical sentimental songs ("городской романс") which were prominent, for example, in Rylenkov's "Баллада о маленьком разведчике."

In 1943, literary critics who had initially welcomed the lyrical principle in war narratives began to ostracize the ballad-style mawkishness for its "non-historicity."⁸⁵ Apparently, the heroic romanticism of the 1920s, already made popular through many trivial literary forms, had accomplished its propaganda purposes and no longer seemed necessary to party ideologues. After the turning point of the war, the Agitation and Propaganda Bureau did not encourage writers to elicit the excitement of emotional communion with the heroes in their readers. Instead, critics and censors demanded a new artistic angle, namely, the epic distancing from war heroism.⁸⁶ Since military action itself was now moving away from the Soviet mainland, Soviet literature was given permission to start monumentalizing the war as an elapsed historical experience.⁸⁷

Yet another problem arose to affect the literary processes and modify ideologues' attitude towards the romantic or lyrical coloration of heroic children's narratives. The Soviet children's unbridled commitment to assist the war effort in the beginning of the war, and especially their unsanctioned departures to the front, began to worry the authorities and the pedagogical community, let alone the parents. The German army's rapid advancement into the Soviet territory, the increasing number of orphans that led to a new wave of homelessness among the young, and, to no less a degree, the success of patriotic propaganda during the war's first year and a half, led to the large-scale participation of children in military action at the front as well as in the occupied hinterland. Consequently, young fighters died on a massive scale.⁸⁸ As a result, in the second half of 1942 and in the beginning of 1943, the Department of Propaganda and Agitation of the Komsomol Central Committee (КСС) and the Narkompros Collegium articulated a new agenda for Soviet children's writers.⁸⁹ Now

---

85   Lidija Poljak, "О лирическом эпизоде Великой Отечественной войны," in *Знамя* 9-10 (1943), 295-297.

86   Similar processes were taking place in literature for adults. See Dobrenko, "Литературная критика и институт литературы эпохи войны и позднего сталинизма," in *История русской литературной критики: Советская и постсоветская эпоха*, Evgenij Dobrenko, Galin Tikhanov, eds., Moscow 2011, 368-379.

87   This is one of the reasons why Kornej Chukovskij could not publish his new tale, "Одолеем Бармалея!" ("We Will Overcome Barmalej!"), the psychotherapeutic effects of which had been directed towards children traumatized by the war. Chukovskij had made a great effort to get the book out in print, but when this did happen, in 1943, critics, such as Pavel Judin, completely destroyed it by calling it "politically harmful nonsense." (Judin, 'Пошлая и вредная стряпня К. Чуковского,' in *Правда*, March 1, 1944). For more on this skirmish, see Maslinskaya, "Корней Чуковский (1882-1969)," in *Детские чтения* 2 (002) (2012), 65-68.

88   See, for example, the well-known collection of propaganda essays *Советским детям*, Moscow 1941. It brought together many high-ranking children's and "adult" authors, such as Gajdar, Ilja Erenburg, Marshak, and Aleksej Tolstoj.

89   Andrej Fateev, *Сталинизм и детская литература в политике номенклатуры СССР. 1930-1950-е гг.*, Moscow 2007, 97-112.

they had to stop summoning Soviet youth by reiterating feats of child heroes. Instead, authors were invited to portray select exploits which could not be replicated in actuality. Leonid Panteleev's short story "Маринка" ("Marinka," 1943) is a typical example of a children's author carrying out this assignment. Panteleev presented Marinka's heroic resistance to death in Leningrad under siege as an unattainable ideal not only because the girl's heroism was exceptional, but also because one could not repeat it after the siege had been lifted.

The purpose of the new state order was not to diminish the value of children's participation in military action, but to limit the onslaught of young people trying to make it to the battlefield. This is why Gajdar's Timur, the protagonist of *Тимур и его команда* (*Timur and His Team*, 1940) was proclaimed the new hero of children's war literature. Kelly's assertion that Timur had replaced Pavlik Morozov is only partially true, and it is true only for the actual time of war, because Timur's team's social engagement embodied the legitimate form of children's participation in the war effort: it was taking place in the hinterland, and not at the front.[90]

There were several reasons for children's authors to embrace the trope of a warrior child specifically when the war was coming to an end. One of them is the gradual accumulation of documentary and oral narratives about heroic behavior of real children during the war. Secondly, public demand for realistic heroic narratives for children was still strong. Finally, the national cultural memory had shifted towards monumentalizing the war. The subsequent fictionalization of factual children's exploits corresponded to the already existing literary tradition (biographies of heroic children), while contributing to the new epic canon glorifying the Soviet participation in World War II.

If, in the 1920s-30s, children's authors profiled young fighters against the *kulaks*, saboteurs, and spies so that they could serve as role-models for Soviet youth, now they were creating a new "passionary" of children who died at the hands of German invaders or resisted them successfully and valiantly. Writing life stories of those little heroes allowed them to fulfill several ideological tasks: to produce new examples of patriotic self-sacrifice; to create an updated Soviet version of "a novella about the virtuous childhood" (events depicted in Gajdar's *Школа*, for example, by then had already become history); and to continue to expand the body of literature about contemporary children, which, in spite of its still being meager, was nevertheless backed by the regime. Because neither contemporaneity nor heroic narratives in Soviet children's literature could be allowed to peter out, biographies of real Pioneers who fought

---

90   Kelly, *Comrade Pavlik*, 177-183.

in World War II were supposed to replace the already dated prewar texts about heroic children.[91]

Valentin Kataev created the precedent in treating the theme of children fighting in World War II when he released his *Сын полка* in 1944. It is important to note that the novella, which received the Stalin Prize of the second degree in 1945, was a fictionalized "biography" of a little soldier. In spite of the fact that its protagonist Vanja Solncev did have several prototypes, he was a literary personage and not an actual child combatant.[92] Kataev's character was an orphan: his entire family had been exterminated by the fascists. At first, his joining the artillery brigade that would replace his family was accidental, but later Vanja proved that he truly deserved becoming a little soldier and an artillerist. Although in the end, his artillerist friends sent the boy to the Suvorov Military School for adolescents, Vanja participated in scouting and military action, saving lives and helping the Red Army to win.[93] Some of the novel's episodes bordered on fantasy, and yet, Kataev's character proved to be not only convincing, but also very influential.

Before *Сын полка*, there were no such nuanced, large-scale works about a warrior child in Soviet children's literature. The age of Kataev's hero had a special significance: Vanja was only ten years old when he joined the artillery brigade. Previously, young readers had encountered Gajdar's Boris Gorikov, who was fifteen at the time when he started to be involved in military action, or followed exploits of seven- to twelve-year-old accosters and victims of "enemies of the state." Since a pre-adolescent warrior was a novelty, critics immediately pounced on Vanja's age and reproached Kataev for his novella's lack of veracity. In spite of the Stalin Prize, they doubted that the image of all of *Сын полка* characters, but especially that of Vanja, was valid and genuine. Especially militant in this respect were the reviewers who grounded their responses in the aesthetic theory of Socialist Realism (many of them had trouble with its dichotomy "real" / "artful" anyway).[94] Therefore, unable to decide whether

---

91   For a discussion of socio-psychological effects of narratives about heroic children in World War II on postwar generations, see Livschiz, "Children's Lives after Zoia's Death," 192-208.

92   The latter type appeared in Lev Kassil' and Maks Poljanovskij's *Улица младшего сына* (*The Street of the Younger Son*, 1949), which documented exploits of Volodja Dubinin who, indeed, fought in the war in the city of Kerch on the Black Sea coast.

93   Valentin Kataev, *Сын полка*, Moscow 1945.

94   Among other critical works that address this topic, see: N. Pavlovich, "Книги для детей," in *Октябрь* 7, 1945, 146-151; E. Kuprijanova, "Детская тема в творчестве В. Катаева," in *Звезда* 12 (1945), 131-135; Samuil Marshak, "О жизни и литературе," in *Литературная газета*, July 2, 1945; Osip Chernyj, "Сын полка В. Катаева," in *Знамя* 7, 1945, 155-161; Aleksandr Ivich, "Подросток и книга," in *Советская книга* 3-4 (1946), 28-38; Aleksandra Brushtein, "Любимый герой," in *Литературная газета*, June 29, 1946.

Vanja was a real boy who ended up in the pages of a children's book, or simply his author's invention, they found the same drawbacks in Kataev's work as their predecessors did in the Civil War narratives of the 1920s: for instance, they denigrated the novella's excessive "adventurousness."[95] Even when critics did compliment Kataev for the positive portrayal of his hero ("The artlessness of Vanja's heroism is touching"), they could not avoid pointing out certain "schematic quality" in Kataev's characterization. Some of them dismissed the author's attempts to psychologize his hero, seeing only run-of-the-mill sentimental devices in his emphasis on Vanja's vulnerability.[96]

It is likely that the 1945-46 critical campaign resulting from the publication of Сын полка shaped future expectations regarding the portrayal of children at war. According to one of the critics, E. Kuprijanova, "many children's writers would benefit from learning from Kataev how to make the childish consciousness of their protagonists embrace the most essential phenomena of our reality."[97] Other reviewers, representing the normative Socialist Realist poetics, were just as keen to see the psychological portrayal of children and adult characters in war fiction while showing contempt for the genre's previous penchant for adventure. Thus, this first postwar attempt to analyze the future development of the heroic narrative as a genre of Soviet children's literature encouraged authors to overcome the tradition of depicting child heroes merely as reckless fortune hunters or loyal political trailblazers.

Subsequent works about children at war, however, did not fully adhere to the required balance of the "genuine" representation of reality and the engaging storytelling embedded in the fantastic brand of heroism. The decades of profiling heroic children in mass media and works of fiction continued to affect children's authors' approaches and literary techniques. This effect is particularly noticeable in fictionalized biographies of real pioneer heroes which proliferated after the war.

8 The Immortal Regiment

In postwar Soviet literature, the right of children who fought in World War II for fictionalized biographies was prioritized, while boys and girls who had previously confronted *kulaks* and spies were relegated to the second tier on the

---

95 Among the adventure features of Сын полка, there were Vanja Solncsev's running away from Bidenko, an experienced scout, and his lucky escape during the last battle described in the novella.

96 E. Kuprijanova, "Детская тема в творчестве В. Катаева," in *Звезда* 12 (1945), 134.

97 Ibid., 135.

hierarchical ladder of children's heroism. Currently, one can count no more than a dozen fictionalized lives of pre-war heroic narratives about valiant children. At the same time, there are scores of biographies celebrating pioneer heroes who sacrificed themselves during the Great Patriotic War.

Sofja Zarechnaja's *Орленок* (*A Little Eagle*) forcefully advanced the tradition of a fictionalized biography of a warrior child based on a real prototype (in Zarechnaja's case, it was Aleksandr Chekalin).[98] Lev Kassil' and Maks Poljanovskij's *Улица младшего сына* (*The Street of the Younger Son*, 1949) became the first full-fledged literary version of the life and death of a pioneer hero (Volodja Dubinin) which went through several editions.[99] *Партизан Леня Голиков* (*Partisan Lenja Golikov*, 1953) by Jurij Korol'kov was also reissued time after time, along with Nadezhda Nadezhdina's *Партизанка Лара* (*Lara the Partisan*, 1963). In the early 1950s in particular, many authors approached heroic children's narratives with enthusiasm, producing numerous "рассказы о пионерах-героях" ("stories about pioneer heroes") for the thirtieth anniversary of the Soviet Pioneer Organization and the tenth anniversary of victory over fascism.

Around that time, several collections of fictionalized lives of pioneer heroes came out. They included abridged or, conversely, expanded versions of previously published accounts of children's exploits. For example, in 1956, the Moscow City House of Pioneers published a brochure with ten such stories.[100] In 1958, a volume with the same table of contents came out in Sverdlovsk; a year later, it appeared in Voronezh.[101] The second edition included one new paragraph. It was a citation from the directive issued by the Plenary Session of the Komsomol Central Committee that had taken place before the first book came out and before the second book went into print ("To know about the Pioneer-heroes' exploits is a requirement for one of the Pioneer advancement ranks established by the Second Plenary Session of the KCC of July 30, 1958").[102] The Voronezh edition featured protagonists' portraits. None of such collections about children who fought *kulaks* had previously appeared.

Lives of four adolescents – Lenja Golikov, Zina Portnova, Marat Kazej and Valja Kotik – inspired the most mass-produced biographies. Their cult spread

---

98 Sofja Zarechnaja, *Орленок*, Moscow 1942.
99 Later, Kassil' and Poljanovskij reworked this novella, incorporating into its new versions their responses to literary critics' comments. Several revised editions of *Улица младшего сына* came out in 1950, 1952, 1960, etc.
100 *Пионеры-герои*, Moscow 1956.
101 *Пионеры-герои*, Sverdlovsk 1958; *Пионеры-герои*, Voronezh 1959.
102 *Пионеры-герои*, Sverdlovsk 1958, 3.

around the entire country, for only they had been awarded – posthumously – the illustrious status of Heroes of the Soviet Union.[103] Dozens of other courageous children whose feats had been recognized with a variety of medals and other military decorations, however, also earned fictionalized life histories, ranging from very short stories or songs to rather long novellas.[104] Plots of those narratives usually belonged to one of the two types of representation heroic children at war. They could tell about a "son of a regiment" serving in an infantry unit or in the navy or they portrayed a child making himself useful to a guerilla detachment either as a scout or as a demolitionist.

Due to the large volume of such publications, children's military valor became the leading type of juvenile heroism celebrated by the Soviet ideological apparatus as a self-sacrifice worthy of a personalized biographical narrative. According to Ann Livschiz, heroic children's biographies appeared and became canonized because "the youthful heroes of the Great Patriotic War who had died in the fulfillment of their patriotic duty, could be safely frozen in their moment of triumph, with either real of manufactured life-stories of near perfection leading to the heroic deed, which was presented for other children's emulation."[105] In my opinion, Livschiz's position should be clarified. In fact, the opposition between the real and the fantastical does not work well in heroic narratives. The real foundation of every child's exploit (if it, indeed, took place) had no initial orientation towards the superhuman or the fantastic: it was the genre that had corroded it. Not only would Soviet children's authors falsify history by diminishing their protagonists' real age, for example, by making up behavior traits that did not correspond to their real age, they would also recreate the hero's life path, making the child seem more righteous. Thus Korol'kov portrayed Lenja Golikov as a boy who loved horses and cared about nature, while Nadezhdina wrote about Lara Micheenko as a girl "who treated everything alive with kindness" (she felt sorry for a stray dog and took it home) and who cherished her red pioneer tie the most.[106] These and

---

103 Children were awarded the title of the Hero of the Soviet Union at different times: Lenja Golikov on April 2, 1944; Zina Portnova, on July 1, 1958; Valja Kotik, on June 27, 1958; and Marat Kazej on May 8, 1965. Monuments in their honor also did not appear simultaneously. The busts of pioneer heroes Golikov and Kotik were erected on the grounds of the All-Soviet Exhibition of Achievements of National Economy (ВДНХ) in 1960; two more busts, of Kazej and Portnova, were erected at the same site in 1982. Two future Heroes of the Soviet Union, Kazej and Kotik, were featured together in the film *Орленок* (*A Little Eagle*, 1957), directed by Eduard Bocharov.

104 The child-hero trope is explored from the historical and sociological perspective in Olga Kucherenko, *Little Soldiers: How Soviet Children Went to War, 1941–1945*, Oxford 2011.

105 Livschiz, "Children's Lives after Zoia's Death," 196.

106 Nadezhda Nadezhdina, "Лара Михеенко," in *Пионеры-герои*, Moscow 1967-1969, 4.

other future heroes did not act out and they were never silly. From a very early age, they demonstrated a conscientious, ever-alert attitude while constantly preparing themselves for physical hardships and psychological stress. Before the war, of course, they could indulge in carefree activities, such as fishing and horseback riding, but under graver circumstances, wartime concerns began to fully govern their behavior. Since pioneer hero narratives turned out to be such an ideologically valuable commemorative resource, their authors could not ignore the canon of portraying an ideal child their readers had already embraced.[107]

This is why, in war narratives, just as in the stories of children fighting *kulaks*, authors' attention was drawn predominantly to the portrayal of the hero's exemplary death. It was either a quick heroic death in battle (the child could blow himself and the fascists up with his last grenade; he could also fight to his last bullet and get killed at the end) or a ritual murder in a Gestapo prison. The torture of Nadja Bogdanova, for instance, exemplifies the suffering and martyrdom of the Pioneer heroes:

> She was captured for the first time on November 7, 1941, when posting, along with Vanja Zvoncov, a red flag in the occupied Vitebsk. They beat her with a whipping-rod, tortured her, but when they brought her to the ditch to be executed by shooting, she had no strength left and thus fell into the ditch a moment before the bullet hit. Vanja died, but the partisans found Valja in the ditch, still alive… Next time, she was captured closer to the end of 1943. And again, there was torture: they drenched her in ice-cold water outside in freezing temperatures, they branded a five-cornered red star on her back. Thinking that the scout was dead, the German invaders abandoned her when the partisans were attacking Karasevo. Local people eventually brought the paralyzed and nearly blind girl back to life.[108]

At the early stages of hero narrative's formation, children's authors still emphasized that their protagonists were not ready to die: Grisha Akopjan, Kolja Mjagotin, Pavlik Morozov did not want to die and even begged their murderers to spare them. But when the canon was finally formed, the Great Patriotic War

---

107 Contemporaneous depictions of adult heroes of World War II differ from the depictions of child-heroes. See, for example, the image of Sergej Tjulenin in Aleksandr Fadeev's *Молодая гвардия* (*The Young Guard*, 1946, 1951). Livschiz refers to him as an alternative model of a hooligan hero ("He was definitely the least 'perfect' and most human male protagonist"). See, "Children's Lives after Zoia's Death," 196.
108 Z. Kolesnikova, ed., *Юные герои Великой Отечественной войны*, Alma-Ata 1985, 5.

child heroes would behave staunchly in the face of death, demonstrating to the enemy their absolute composure and fearlessness.

There are numerous examples of literary biographies of real child heroes, although what matters is not their number, but their lack of individualization and psychological nuancing, contrary to Kataev's critics' requirements and expectations. In these narratives protagonists appear as strong-willed, imperturbable warriors who overcome the momentary fear of death by recalling their duty to the fatherland as well as by thinking of future Soviet generations who would remember them with gratitude. They often mentally compose their own epitaphs. At least, this is what Volja, a character from "Гвардии мальчик" ("A Boy of the Guards," 1948), does:

> Every man is born for something. One man is born to do some useful work all his life, even if it were only gluing stamps onto envelopes. Another man is born, perhaps, just to raise himself, once his life, and [urge others to attack with an exclamation] 'Forward!' That he did not live long does not mean anything. What is important is that he would remain in the entire book of mankind as a single comma or a period or a little letter… And I am thinking now that to the history-book chapter, where it tells how the Soviet people fought their enemies, I, too, have added my comma. I can see the entire book: it is thick, it is beautiful. Our chapter in it is the longest and most important.[109]

9   The Commemorative Potential of Child Hero Narratives

Although the fact that after the war children's authors received the assignment to shift their narratives to a peaceful track is well-known, it is clear now that for decades, they had continued to work on fictionalized biographies of Pioneer heroes retrospectively, evoking and enhancing the past.[110] There was a great

---

109 A. Kepler, "Гвардии мальчик" in *Гвардии мальчик: сборник рассказов*, Stalingrad 1948, 3-9.

110 One such well-articulated order stipulated a requirement to create literary works about post-war Soviet schools: *Стенограмма заседания коллегии Министерства просвещения РСФСР от 10 февраля 1949 года о работе Государственного издательства детской литературы Детгиз и материалы к стенограмме*, in: Государственный Архив Российской Федерации, Fund 2306, File 71, Folder 303. For more information on how this order was implemented, see: Ilja Kukulin, Marija Majofis, Petr Safronov, *Острова утопии. Педагогическое и социальное проектирование послевоенной школы (1940-1980-е)*, Moscow 2015, 84-100. When Detgiz publishing plans were discussed in 1949, other themes, such as socialist labor, school, and life abroad were approved. Andrej Fateev, *Сталинизм и детская литература*, 141.

political demand for war-time children's heroism, for it gradually became an essential component of national commemorative practices. It was the narrative's potential for ritualized commemoration, rather than the ethical problems or traumatic experiences it might address, that the party apparatus – as the primary procurer of this type of literature – considered most important.

The stigmatization of Ruvim Fraerman's *Дальнее плавание* (*Sailing Long-Distance*, 1946) exemplifies that trend.[111] Fraerman was criticized for "getting carried away by a make-believe plot" ("увлечение надуманным сюжетом"), and, in particular, for his suggestion that a tenth-grader, such as Galja Strazheva, could not accept her formerly beloved history teacher, Ivan Sergeevich, because he had come back from the war with a disfigured face. In general, Soviet critics refused to reflect upon the psychological trauma and the post-traumatic stress disorder with which the youngest generation of war survivors had to deal. Instead, they insisted on the main character's "believability," saying that Galja was unlike "our highschoolers – [for] they are more insightful, intelligent, and interesting, they are even more complex than this 'extraordinary' Galja the writer has concocted."[112]

For such "analysts" and the writers who were willing to heed them, only Pioneer-heroes of World War II and their predecessors were "extraordinary" and truly believable. In the 1950s-70s, they added heroic children whose exploits dated back to the foundational years of the Soviet Pioneer Organization as well as to the pre-revolutionary and early revolutionary years to the pantheon of valiant young people fighting in World War II. Consequently, those earlier prototypes also began to play a commemorative role in culture.[113] A typical example of how children's authors fabricated or fictionalized real facts of revolutionary history is the series of novelized biographies of Kotja Mgebrov-Chekan – a young actor and propagandist from Petrograd who died in 1922 under unclear circumstances. Following the boy's death, the Petrograd Soviet decreed that Kotja be proclaimed a hero of the revolution and buried

---

111 See Livschiz, "Children's Lives," 201-202.
112 Elena Kononenko, "Драма без почвы," in *Литературная газета*, August 3, 1946, 2.
113 Compare this to David Brandenberger's thoughts on the commemorative potential of prototypical literary heroes in the 1930s: "Proletarian Internationalism, 'Soviet Patriotism' and the Rise of Russocentric Etatism during the Stalinist 1930s" in *Left History* 6:5 (1999), 80-100. Brandenberger, however, does not discuss the fact that children's literature did not have to confront the difficulties with re-writing history. Children's authors did not need to erase recently coined "enemies of the people" from historical works they wrote and published, because the few child heroes of the first revolutionary years were absolutely legitimate at the time of their biographies' creation – and remained legitimate thereafter.

in the Field of Mars, where other notable Petrograd revolutionaries had been laid to rest. In 1958, A. Orljanskij published a short story about him, "Сердце коммунара должно быть чистым!" ("The Heart of the Communard Must Be Pure!"). It was followed, in 1971, by a novella about Kotja: *Был настоящим трубачом* (*He Was a Real Trumpeter*). The author of the second work, Jurij Jakovlev, had by then become famous thanks to his innovative young adult fiction as well as because he had written a screen-play for *Умка* (*Umka*, 1969), a popular animated film about a polar bear cub, directed by Vladimir Pekar and Vladimir Popov. In spite of Jakovlev's eminent reputation and the two works about the heroic child already in print, yet another version of Kotja's life came out in 1976. It was *Легенда о маленьком коммунаре* (*The Legend of a Little Communard*) – a novella by Konstanting Kurbatov.[114] Kurbatov called Kotja "Gavroche" and a "Communard" because, according to his spin on the boy's story, the young actor was initially assigned the role of Gavroche in a propagandist play. Kurbatov's hero ended up embodying his prototype in real life by perishing in the streets of Petrograd when confronting the enemies of the revolution.

The fictionalization of Kotija Mgebrov-Chekan's life in several consecutive, regularly reprinted works for children exemplifies the model of Pioneer-heroes' canonization and reveals how the tradition of child-hero narratives evolved over decades after the Great Patriotic War. From studying lives of Pavlik Morozov, Zina Portnova and other young fighters for the Soviet state, it becomes clear that at the most advanced stage in their evolution, pioneer-hero narratives encompassed hundreds of multi-genre works of fiction and non-fiction which recorded lives of heroic children acting in defense of their fatherland during the revolution, the Civil War, the collectivization and industrialization campaigns, and World War II.[115] This vast and varied body of literature also includes fictional, semi-fictional, or non-fictional stories about

---

114 There were several editions of the book. It was last re-printed in 1982.
115 Among works on pioneer heroes, some require special mention. On Pavlik Morozov: Pavel Solomein, *В кулацком гнезде* (*In the Kulaks' Nest*, 1933); Elizar Smirnov, *Павлик Морозов* (*Pavlik Morozov*, 1938); Sergej Michalkov, *Песня о Павлике Морозове* (*Song about Pavlik Morozov*); Stepan Shchipachev, "Павлик Морозов" ("Pavlik Morozov," an epic poem, 1949-1950); Vitalij Gubarev, *Павлик Морозов* (*Pavlik Morozov*, 1947); on Lara Micheenko: Nadezhda Nadezhdina, *Лара Михеенко* (*Lara Micheenko*, 1967) and *Партизанка Лара* (*Partisan Lara*, 1968); Viktor Viktorov, "Не только мальчишки" ("Not Just Boys," a song, 1969); on Zina Portnova: Grigorij Nabatov, *Юность, огнем опаленная* (*Youth Charred by the War*, 1960) and *Зина Портнова* (*Zina Portnova*, 1980); Anatolij Solodov *Девочка с косичками* (*A Girl with Little Plaits*, 1975); Vasilij Smirnov, *Зина Портнова* (*Zina Portnova*, 1980), etc.

children rescuing other youngsters or adults from fire or saving drowning people.[116]

In spite of the seeming diversity of literary works created within this tradition, by the 1950s-60s, when it had fully matured, children's authors bent on producing short stories and novellas about pioneer heroes were able to wield only a limited number of standardized structural and poetic devices. The lack of development within the tradition becomes noticeable when we look at the child-hero narratives written after the "Thaw" and continuing into the 1980s. During those last two or three decades, the canon continued to be replicated, but it did not change, just as its heroes remained the same. The only part of the child-hero narratives that would occasionally undergo a transformation was the image of the enemy, although even the courageous protagonists' nemeses – a storm, an invader, or a saboteur – did not really evolve. Rather, children's authors re-created them within the taxonomy already used by their predecessors.

This is why scholars who attempt to trace the evolution of little heroes in Soviet children's literature err when suggesting that their succession paradigm is linear, evolving "from a hero to a hero." Thus, Catriona Kelly and Olga Kucherenko both agree that Gajdar's Timur had superseded Pavlik Morozov because, in their opinion, in the early 1940s helpful young adults, rather than tattletales, were proclaimed ideal role models for Soviet children. As we have seen, though, Pavlik and Timur cannot be compared this way because they belong to different genres of child-hero narratives. Pavlik, along with Alka from *Военная тайна* and Serezha from *Судьба барабанщика*, Vanja Solncev from *Сын полка*, and the Pioneer heroes Lenja Golikov, Lara Micheenko and Kotja Mgebrov-Chekan belong to the rank of fighter-heroes – those who sacrifice themselves or get sacrificed for the Soviet cause. Timur, however, is part of a group of protagonists who demonstrate perpetual readiness to serve the Soviet fatherland by helping others or performing tedious daily work. Katja, who rescues a drowning goat in Ekaterina Boronina's short story "Веревка" ("The Rope")[117] and "commandoes" and knights of the Blue Mountains in Kassil''s novella *Дорогие мои мальчишки* (*My Dear Boys*, 1944), belong to the second category as well.

It is not accidental that only children from the first group were chosen to become protagonists of fictionalized biographies, while not a single child from

---

116 A typical compendium of child hero biographies that span the entire history of the Soviet state, from 1917 to what the volume calls "the present day," is I. K. Goncharenko and N. B. Machlin, eds., *Дети-герои*, Kiev 1984.
117 Ekaterina Boronina, "Веревка," in *Обвал* (*An Avalanche*), Leningrad 1938.

the group of protagonists who saved people from fire or drowning merited such an honor. The reason for that is not the extreme form of Pavlik Morozov's or Lenja Golikov's heroism, namely, a self-sacrifice leading to death. (In fact, some of the young heroes whose exploits during the war children's literature celebrated were still alive when their biographies appeared in print: for example, Nadja Bogdanova, Volodja Kaznacheev and Nadja Zenkina did not perish). Children whose biographies were, indeed, written, happened to commit acts of inimitable heroism – feats that others would be unable to replicate. This "matchless," mythological quality of some types of exploits allowed children's authors to create multiple versions of lives of young vigilantes who turned their parents in or of children who perished heroically during the Great Patriotic War. Their biographies were often published together between the covers of a single collection.

Kassil' is one of the Soviet children's authors who followed this principle to a tee, creating one model work in each genre and thematic canon. His *Дорогие мои мальчишки* continued Gajdar's tradition of fiction about children whose play was no laughing matter.[118] According to Andrej Fateev, it "facilitated the continuation of the Timur tradition, namely, the proliferation of unofficial social organizations among children and adolescents."[119] Kassil''s *Улица младшего сына*, on the contrary, adhered to the tradition of heroic war narratives. Its protagonist was a teenager who fearlessly fought against the German invaders for the Kerch underground.

In the late Soviet and early Post-Soviet era, the literary conveyer belt continued to manufacture heroes according to the two templates outlined above. But since only child heroes of the revolutionary barricades, those fighting *kulaks* and wartime warriors merited personalized biographies, their exploits seem to be the only kind chosen for individualized recognition and preservation. Moreover, biographies of Pioneer heroes reissued or newly written demonstrate that Post-Soviet keepers of Russia's past deem only the memory of the Great Patriotic War heroes sacred and unassailable. There are exceptions to this rule, of course: for example, Eduard Verkin's *Облачный полк* (*Cloud Brigade*, 2012), a novella about Lenja Golikov, became the first response to the Soviet critics who blamed such authors as Kataev for the sentimentality

---

118 Critics would upbraid him for "adventurousness" as well: "Here Kassil' has also submitted to the power of a standart adventure plot, which would make even experienced writers turn the thorny path of life-likeness and artistic truth into a comfortable, smoothly paved, highway-like road of impressive exploits and unthinkable victories." Ivich, "Подросток и книга," 34.
119 Fateev, *Сталинизм и детская литература*, 176, also 111.

and adventurousness of their prose. Verkin made his character older (in his novella, Lenja is called Sanych, as an older man would be called), de-glorified his death, and discredited his military valor. That said, he also managed to rewrite Lenja Golikov's heroic biography without straying too far away from the Soviet realist tradition: stylistically, his novel is reminiscent of the so-called "lieutenants' prose" ushered in the 1950s-70s by such authors as Vasyl' Bykov, Grigorij Baklanov, Jurij Bondarev and others. In *Облачный полк*, Verkin replicated these writers' lyrical accounts by adhering to a first-person narrative, embracing their naturalist way of depicting war and death, bringing in additional angles at which the war is seen by imitating epistolary discourse (for example, through citing children's letters found in a bag of a German photojournalist), and by including a melodramatic episode of the death of Alja, the young woman for whom Sanych is longing.

As I have tried to show above, in spite of post-war Soviet literature's proclivity for more insightful psychological characterization, it seldom implemented devices typical of the genre of "lieutenants' prose." In war narratives for children, in particular, Pioneer heroes never seemed to be afraid. Moreover, they seldom experienced any kind of psychological shock after killing a man, be it a "Fascist invader" ("фашистский захватчик") or a local hired by the Germans to serve as a village policeman. Children's authors revealed neither the weaknesses nor the desires of their young protagonists. Although there are exceptions to this rule, it would not be an exaggeration to say that in most works of Soviet fiction for children, little soldiers neither removed dirt from under their fingernails in public (as Verkin's Sanych does) nor picked their noses. In the Soviet era, writers were able to afford very few digressions from this norm of behavior. Among the tolerable deviations, there could be the removal of the Pioneer tie – as Volodja Dubinin does, when displeased with himself, in Kassil' and Poljanovskij's *Улица младшего сына*. In short, the heroic paradigm in children's literature appears to be more restrictive and uncompromising than the hero canon developed in adult fiction, because children's authors could not allow any kind of "human factor" to affect their readers' perception of the heroic.

Contrary to Soviet historical narratives for children, which, as Marina Balina suggests in this volume, often formed a genre prototype for literature for adults to follow, in novels and short stories about the war, children's authors seem to have lagged, and not only stylistically, behind their colleagues. Although Verkin did enter into a dialogue with the Soviet child warrior canon, he was still using an already established artistic method, namely, the tradition of a more psychologically nuanced depiction of an individual at war. Here, we can see not only Verkin's predilection for "lieutenants'" discourse in fiction, but also the tendency of children's literature to lag behind when appropriating new literary devices.

This tardiness is not always the fault of the children's authors themselves, but rather, of the forced obstruction of the evolution of literature in Soviet Russia. Among those who stymied it after the war were party ideologues and politically-minded pedagogues – the main commissioners of literary works that were supposed to inspire patriotic feelings and educate young readers according to the example set by Pioneer heroes. But there were other keepers of the canon as well: the editors who made decisions about publishing this or that book, and critics who could easily kill a remarkable work of fiction or praise a worthless piece of propaganda to the skies. Safeguarding works for children, they effected greater severity than editors and critics working with authors writing for adult audiences. After all, among the latter there eventually appeared extraordinary writers, such as Bykov, Baklanov, and Bondarev, who managed to get their talented fiction published in journals and later, in separate editions, while children's periodicals and books for young readers continued to feature staunch and unwavering pioneer heroes – matchstick creations of ideologically conditioned and firmly guarded children's authors.

Works Cited

Primary Sources

Afanasjev, Petr et al, eds. *Сборник статей для изложения. Пособие для учителей начальной школы*. Moscow 1937.

Anon. "Геройский поступок Саши Плетцова и Жени Спирина," in *Ленинские искры* 58 (2052), April 28, 1938.

Anon. *Геройский подвиг 3 русских добровольцев, которые взорвали 42-сантиметровую пушку, склады пороха, улетели на неприятельском аэроплане и еще масса приключений*. Moscow 1914.

Antonov, Ivan. "Багровый снег," in Anna Mojzhes, ed., *Всегда готов! Рассказы о ленинградских пионерах*. Leningrad 1962, 137-145.

Antonov, Ivan. "Багровый снег," in I. Smol'nikov, ed., *Гремите, барабаны!* Leningrad 1982, 22-30.

Boronina, Ekaterina. "В дупле," in Boronina, *Обвал*. Moscow 1938, 14-17.

Boronina, Ekaterina. *Обвал*. Leningrad 1938.

Bucharin, Nikolaj. "Доклад на V Всероссийском съезде РКСМ. Коммунистическое воспитание молодежи в условиях НЭПа," in *Правда*, February 14, 1922, 2.

Charskaja, Lidija. *Игорь и Милица (Соколята): повесть для юношества из великой европейской войны*. Petrograd 1915.

Detkor Selektor, S. "Хорошие и плохие книги," in *Товарищ* 9 (1931), 39.

Dorochov, Pavel. *Сын большевика*. Moscow 1925.

Druzhinin, Vladimir. *Кто сказал, что я убит?* Moscow 1969.

Egorov, Pavel. "Праздник труда," in *Юные строители* 9 (1924), 3-4.

Fraerman, Ruvim. "Маленький герой," in *Пионер* 6 (1942), 15.

Garbuzov, Solomon. *Фронтовые ребята*. Moscow 1941.

Gjugo, Viktor. *Гаврош*. Moscow 1922.

Grigulis, Arvid. *Пограничники, два мальчика и собака Марс*. Moscow and Leningrad, 1952.

Gunin, Dmitrij, ed. *Пионеры-герои: Учебное пособие*. Moscow 1982.

Gusev, Andrej. *Год за годом... Из пионерской летописи*. Moscow 1964.

Jakovlev, Jurij. *Кепка-невидимка*. Moscow 1987.

Kataev, Valentin. *Сын полка*. Moscow 1945.

Kepler, A. "Гвардии мальчик," in *Гвардии мальчик: сборник рассказов*. Stalingrad 1948, 3-9.

Kiselev, Fedor. "Знамя спасли," in *Юные строители* 8 (1925), 3-4.

Kochetkova, E. "Миша," in *Сибирский детский журнал* 2 (1928), 8-9.

Kole, Luiza. *Детство и юность великих людей*. St. Petersburg 1894.

Kolesnikova, Z., ed. *Юные герои Великой Отечественной войны*. Alma-Ata 1985.

Kordes, Valentina. "Мишкин Первомай," in Dmitrij Bedrinskij, and Valentina Kordes, *Из прошлого: рассказы*. Moscow 1925, 18.

Korenkov, Vasilij. *Всегда готов! (Геройский подвиг пионера)*. Moscow 1925.

Kormchij, Leonard. "Забытое оружие," in *Правда*, February 17, 1918, 3.

Larina, Larisa. "Шпион," in *Барабан* 7-8 (1924), 3-8.

Larina, Larisa. *По-разному*. Charkov 1925.

Leonov, Michail. *Радио-Май. Первомайское зрелище*. Moscow 1925.

Lin'kov, Lev. *Рассказы о пограничниках*. Moscow 1954.

Matveev, German. *Зеленые цепочки*. Moscow 1945.

Michajlov, M. *Федька Апчхи*. Charkov 1925.

Nadezhdina, Nadezhda. "Лара Михеенко," in *Пионеры-герои*. Moscow 1967-1969.

Petnikov, G. N., ed. *В огне Отечественной войны: Сборник стихов, очерков, рассказов*. Nalchik 1942.

Pushkarev, Gleb. *Пионер Павлик Гнездилов*. Novosibirsk 1940.

Ruzhanskij, Evgenij. "Молоко," in *Пожар*. Moscow 1940, 55-56.

Ruzhanskij, Evgenij. "Удочка," in *Пожар*. Moscow 1940, 32-39.

Ryklin, Grigorij. *Рассказы о пограничниках*. Moscow 1937.

Rysakov, Viktor. *Юные русские герои: Очерки и рассказы о военных и довоенных подвигах русских мальчиков*. Petrograd and Moscow 1914.

Ryzhov, Aleksandr. "Заговор барабанщиков," in *Барабан* 5, 1926, 4-8.

Ryzhov, Aleksandr. "Теплушка № 36084," in *Барабан* 12(17) (1924), 3-11.

Smirnov, Elizar. "Павлик Морозов," in *Дети-герои*. Moscow 1961.

Smirnov, Elizar. "Пионеры-герои," in *Вожатый* 10 (1938), 47-51.

Smirnov, Elizar. *Славный пионер Гена Щукин. Эпизоды из жизни пионера, разоблачившего планы врагов народа и убитого ими*. Moscow 1938.

Suchachevskij, Stepan. *Коля Мяготин*. Moscow 1967.

Sulemov, Vladimir, ed. *История ВЛКСМ и Всесоюзной пионерской организации имени В.И.Ленина*. Moscow 1983.

Taezhnyj, A. "Ростки," in *Товарищ* 7-8 (1931), 42.

Tajtc, Jakov. *Рассказы*. Moscow 1940.

Ushagin, Aleksandr. "Юный герой," in *Юные строители* 5 (1924), 1-3.

Verejskaja, Elena. *Таня-революционерка*. Moscow and Leningrad 1928.

Verkin, Eduard. *Облачный полк*. Moscow 2012.

Voskobojnikov, Valerij. *Рассказы о юных героях*. Moscow 2015.

Zamojskij, Petr. "Еройка," in *Юные строители* 11-12 (1924), 5-8.

Zil'ver, Lev. *Быть на-чеку! Рассказы о коварных методах агентов фашистских разведок и работе славной совразведки по их разоблачению*. Moscow 1938.

Пионеры-герои: Альбом-выставка. Moscow 1967-1969.

Пионеры-герои. Moscow 1956.

Пионеры-герои. Sverdlovsk 1958.

Пионеры-герои. Voronezh 1959.

Пожар. Moscow 1940.

Советским детям. Moscow 1941.

Стенограмма заседания коллегии Министерства просвещения РСФСР от 10 февраля 1949 года о работе Государственного издательства детской литературы Детгиз и материалы к стенограмме, in Государственный Архив Российской Федерации, Fund 2306, File 71, Folder 303.

Secondary Sources

Balashov, Evgenij. *Школа в российском обществе 1917-1927 гг. Становление нового человека*. St. Petersburg 2003.

Brandenberger, David. "Proletarian Internationalism, 'Soviet Patriotism' and the Rise of Russocentric Etatism during the Stalinist 1930s," in *Left History* 6:5 (1999), 80-100.

Brushtein, Aleksandra. "Любимый герой," in *Литературная газета*, June 29, 1946.

Chernyj, Osip. "Сын полка В. Катаева," in *Знамя* 7, 1945, 155-161.

Clark, Katerina. *The Soviet Novel. History as Ritual*. Chicago 1981.

Dobrenko, Evgenij, and Galin Tikhanov, eds. *История русской литературной критики: Советская и постсоветская эпоха*. Moscow 2011.

Dobrenko, Evgeny. *Political Economy of Socialist Realism*. New Haven, CT 2007.

Dobrenko, Evgeny. *Метафора власти: Литература сталинской эпохи в историческом освещении*. Munich 1993.

Dvorkin, I. "Книга о героизме, находчивости, отваге," in *Детская литература*, 10 (1938), 19.

Fateev, Andrej. *Сталинизм и детская литература в политике номенклатуры СССР. 1930-1950-е гг.* Moscow 2007.

Fitzpatrick, Sheila. *Everyday Stalinism: Ordinary Life in Extraordinary Time: Soviet Russia in the 1930s.* New York and Oxford, 1999.

Grinberg, Anna. "О новой детской книге и ее читателе," in *Народный учитель* 9, 1926, 96-99.

Günther, Hans. "Архетипы советской культуры," in Günther, Hans, and Evgenij Dobrenko, eds., *Соцреалистический канон.* St. Petersburg 2000, 743-784.

Günther, Hans. "Education and Conversion: The Road to the New Man in the Totalitarian Bildungsroman," in Günther, Hans, ed., *The Culture of the Stalin Period.* London 1990.

Iljucha, Ol'ga. "Советские границы в учебно-воспитательных текстах сталинского времени," in Iljucha, Ol'ga, and Irma Mullonen, eds., *Границы и контактные зоны в истории и культуре Карелии и сопредельных регионов. Гуманитарные исследования*, Vol. 1. Petrozavodsk 2008, 205-214.

Ivich, Aleksandr. "Подросток и книга," in *Советская книга* 3-4 (1946), 28-38.

Judin, Pavel. "Пошлая и вредная стряпня К. Чуковского," in *Правда*, March 1, 1944.

Karajchenceva, Svetlana. *Книговедение: Литературно-художественная и детская книга.* Moscow 2004.

Kargashin, Igor', ed. *"Homo Militaris": Литература войны и о войне. История, мифология, поэтика.* Kaluga 2010, 93-99.

Kelly, Catriona. *Children's World: Growing Up in Russia, 1890-1991.* New Haven and London 2007.

Kelly, Catriona. *Comrade Pavlik: The Rise and Fall of a Soviet Boy Hero.* London 2005.

Klubkov, Pavel. "На посту пограничник стоит," in Kuleshov, Evgenij, and Inna Antipova, eds., *Детский сборник. Статьи по детской литературе и антропологии детства.* Moscow 2003, 405-411.

Kononenko, Elena. "Драма без почвы," in *Литературная газета*, August 3, 1946, 2.

Krupskaja, Nadezhda. "Об учебнике и детской книге для I ступени. Речь на I Всероссийской конференции по учебной и детской книге 8-15 мая 1926 г.," in *На путях к новой школе* 7-8 (1926), 3-13.

Kucherenko, Olga. *Little Soldiers: How Soviet Children Went to War, 1941–1945.* Oxford 2011.

Kukulin, Ilja, Marija Majofis, and Petr Safronov, eds. *Острова утопии. Педагогическое и социальное проектирование послевоенной школы (1940-1980-е).* Moscow 2015, 84-100.

Kuprijanova, E. "Детская тема в творчестве В. Катаева," in *Звезда* 12 (1945), 131-135.

Leutheuser, Karsten. *Freie, geführte und verführte Jugend: Politisch motivierte Jugendliteratur in Deutschland 1919-1989.* Paderborn 1995.

Litovskaja, Marija. "Аркадий Гайдар. 1904-1941," in *Детские чтения*, 2012, 2 (002), 87-104.

Litovskaja, Marija. "Воюющие дети в русской литературе первой половины XX века," in Kargashin, Igor, ed. *"Homo Militaris": Литература войны и о войне. История, мифология, поэтика*. Kaluga 2010, 93-99.

Livschiz, Ann. "Children's Lives after Zoia's Death: Order, Emotions and Heroism in Children's Lives and Literature in the Post-War Soviet Union," in Furst, Juliane, ed., *Late Stalinist Russia: Society between Reconstruction and Reinvention*. London and New York 2006, 192-208.

Malikova, Marija. "'Скетч по кошмару Честертона' и культурная ситуация нэпа," in *Новое литературное обозрение*, 78:2 (2006), 31-59.

Marshak, Samuil. "О жизни и литературе," in *Литературная газета*, July 2, 1945.

Maslinskaya (Leontjeva), Svetlana. "По-пионерски жил, по-пионерски похоронен: материалы к истории гражданских похорон 1920-х годов," in *Живая старина* 3, 2012, 49-52.

Maslinskaya (Leontjeva), Svetlana. "Корней Чуковский (1882-1969)," in *Детские чтения* 2 (002) (2012), 65-68.

Molozhavyj, Stepan, "По вопросу о реализме в детской литературе," in *Новые детские книги* 4 (1926), 6-7.

Pavlovich, N. "Книги для детей," in *Октябрь* 7, 1945, 146-151.

Pokrovskaja, Anna. "Приключения в современной детской литературе. Обзор 19-ти книг," in *Новые детские книги* 4 (1926), 17-92.

Poljak, Lidija. "О лирическом эпизоде Великой Отечественной войны," in *Знамя* 9-10 (1943), 295-297.

Poznjakov, Nikolaj. "Критика и библиография," in *Женское образование* 8 (1884), 521-522.

Reynolds, Kimberley. "Words about War for Boys: Representations of Soldiers and Conflict in Writing for Children before World War 1," in *Children's Literature Association Quarterly*, 34:3 (Fall 2009), 255-271.

Sobolev, Michail. "Обзор детских книг за 1875 год," in *Педагогический сборник* 4 (1881), 1002.

Starcev, Ivan. *Детская литература (1918-1931)*. Moscow 1933.

Tajtc, Jakov. *Рассказы*. Moscow 1940.

Trjuel', Miriam. "Гаврош и Козетта – советские рассказы? (К проблеме освоения французского романа на русской почве)," in *Детские чтения*, 2 (005) (2014), 366-380.

Zhelobovskij, Ignatij. "Против снижения жанра. По поводу статьи Остроумова," in *Книга детям* 1 (1930), 24-25.

CHAPTER 8

Unspeakable Truths: Children of the Siege in Soviet Literature

Tatiana Voronina and Polina Barskova

1   Introduction

Within the voluminous and rather rigid Soviet literature about war childhood, works about children of the Siege of Leningrad stand out. In the society tightly controlled by ideology, writing about the urban humanitarian disaster exacerbated by starvation was a risky task. The Siege with its thousands of victims did not allow writers to fully adhere to the Soviet narrative template of war literature, reliant on structural and thematic principles of Socialist Realism. As a whole, essays, short stories and novels about young survivors of World War II were supposed to construct a heroic behavioral model for post-war generations to follow and thus serve as a tool for moral education and ideological indoctrination designed by the regime. The experience of young Leningraders, however, did not fit into that mold. Children of the Siege suffered from intolerable hunger and cold; watched their parents, siblings, classmates, and teachers die from brutal deprivations, bombardments, or disease; and were too weak to commit acts of valor. In literature of the Siege that emerged in the decades after the war's end, the image of a child performed several metapoetic functions, but none of them corresponded to the incendiary, propagandistic role played by most works of Soviet war poetry and prose.

Between the late 1940s and 1990s, documenting and fictionalizing the Siege, and especially investigating the tragic destinies of its youngest victims became a serious challenge for Soviet writers. The post-war proliferation of war literature for young audiences did not allow children's authors and their political controllers to ignore the Siege completely. As a known historical fact, it belonged to the history of Leningrad, the city named a "hero" ("город-герой") by the Supreme Commander himself as early as on May 1, 1945. But to describe the Siege meant to tell some truth about the atrocities of the war, including the government's initial, nearly total, abandonment of Leningrad, surrounded by the enemy on September 8, 1941, making it rely on its own resources. This is why, when narratives about the Siege began to appear in print, they differed greatly from children's books about heroic youth serving their Motherland on the front lines or behind them. They dealt with the tragedy of war more directly, offering a truer perspective on victims' experiences. Consequently, books that shed light on the Siege by portraying it through its children eventually turned into a cultural, historical, and even social phenomenon, while writing about the Siege presented new, paradoxical possibilities for the authors who were ready to eschew the monolithic discourse of Soviet war heroism.

This chapter explores works for children about the Siege as a dissenting genre and, possibly, the first more or less factual documentation of the Soviet war experience. We provide an analytical introduction to the canon of Siege literature for young readers and introduce some of its notable authors: Jurij German, Vera Panova, Leonid Panteleev, Aleksandr Krestinskij, Jurii Pomozov, and Ilja Mikson. By reading some of these works closely, however, we aim to prove that by portraying children as innocent victims who needed to be avenged, the Siege narratives exploited the figure of the Siege child as a symbol of weakness and vulnerability. While exploring these contradictions, we furthermore juxtapose images of Siege children and their "mentors," adults who worked and survived in the isolated, starved, and shelled city. Finally, our analysis of literature of the Siege not directly aimed at young audiences allows us to pose a question about the significance of the Siege child image in shaping the collective cultural memory about the war among Soviet and Post-Soviet readers. Writing about the Siege childhood forced Soviet children's authors into a discursive area of paradox, while the traumatic complexity of their subject matter allowed them to investigate subjectivity on a more nuanced level and thus particularize and complicate a traditional child hero trope.

2 (Re)imagining Trauma: The Place of Siege Narratives in the Soviet Literary War Canon

The Soviet authors and artists' depiction of the Leningrad Siege was part of a larger paradigm, that of literary and artistic representations of the Soviet participation in World War II. Driven by the political agenda of the Soviet State, constructed in accordance with poetic, structural, and figurative clichés already adopted as a literary norm, and easily lending themselves to propaganda, Soviet texts about the military conflict were mostly concerned with the events that unfolded in 1941-1945 on the Soviet territory and, only marginally, beyond its borders. Understandably, they played an integral part in the postwar re-configuration of the Soviet ideology and artistic practices.[1] For decades,

1 Anatolij Bocharov, *Человек и война. Идеи социалистического реализма в послевоенной прозе о войне*, Moscow 1973; Viktor Chalmaev, *На войне остаться человеком. Фронтовые*

hundreds of literary works about the war recycled the same, albeit vastly heterogeneous, themes, such as fighting the enemy behind the front lines; the defense of a military outpost "to the last drop of blood"; acts of heroic self-sacrifice; and love that survived through all the trials and tribulations. They also produced a unified set of protagonists, such as seasoned, wise, and merciful commanders; inexperienced, quickly maturing, and valiant young fighters; loyal, strong, and gentle women waiting for their beloved on the home front; and quick-witted, dexterous, but also emotionally vulnerable orphans.

In spite of this consistency of topoi and types, however, the body of war literature that emerged in the wake of World War II did not offer an entirely realistic account of the traumatic national experience. Every literary work written for publication was created within a rigid censorial framework, which forced authors to adhere to a very specific historical vision, limited, for example, by the imperative to glorify the Soviet war effort. Soviet writers were also expected to downplay the suffering of individuals that resulted from the regime's ruthlessness – the totalitarian disregard for personal suffering. Anybody who dared to challenge this imperative was severely punished: such was the case of Vasilij Grossman, the author of Жизнь и судьба (*Life and Fate*, 1959), and the historian Aleksandr Nekrich, whose monograph, *1941. 22 июня* (*June 22, 1941*, 1965), documented the Sovied state's unpreparedness for war and thus placed blame on the government for the human sacrifice that could have been avoided. Nekrich's book was removed from all the libraries which did not have "special security" ("спецхран") vaults for banned books, while the author himself was expelled from the Communist Party.[2] Since the war was a crucial component in the Soviet power's self-legitimization, literature about it could never truly become a means of collective therapy and healing: its purpose was to achieve urgent political goals and justify the old ones. And yet, as the Soviet critic Anatolij Bocharov suggested, this objective was not always one-dimensional; it shifted with time. Whereas in the 1940s-50s, war literature was supposed to venerate the Soviet victory and monumentalize the people's war effort, it refocused its aims in the following decades in an attempt to un-

---

страницы русской прозы *1960-1990 годов*, Moscow 1998; Katherine Hodgson, "The Soviet War," in *The Cambridge Companion to the Literature of World War II*, ed. Marina Mackay, Cambridge and London 2009, 111-123; Don Piper, "Soviet Union" in *The Second World War in Fiction*, ed. Holger Klein, John Flower and Eric Homberger, London 1984, 144; Angela Brintlinger, *Chapaev and His Comrades: War and the Russian Literary Hero Across the Twentieth Century*, Boston 2012.

2 Aleksandr Nekrich, *1941. 22 июня*, Moscow 1995. The volume includes a transcript of the vicious discussion of Nekrich's book at the Institute for Marxism and Leninism in Moscow (February 16, 1966).

derstand the philosophical significance of the military conflict and come to grips with its dramatic consequences.[3]

War literature was a corpus of texts unified by the commonality of themes and purposes, and Soviet critics frequently perceived it is such.[4] That said, the body of works about the national tragedy was more diverse than what the regime wanted it to be. It varied in perspective and genre, encompassing a range of approaches to the historical experience, from grandiose epic novels to the more personalized accounts of World War II in "lieutenants' prose." It also showed a discrepancy in the veracity of literary representations of actual events, which depended on the authors' engagement with censorship: some of it was minimal (resulting in works written for the "desk drawer [в стол]," i.e. with no hope of being published), other – unquestionable and, even, self-imposed. Pompous war literature produced in the years immediately following the war was replaced by the lyricism and nuanced psychologism of the works written during the "Thaw." In the 1980s-90s, these trends were further complicated by revelatory naturalism and a certain political apathy of Soviet authors writing about World War II from the perspective of the second generation of trauma survivors.

Known as the "Nine Hundred Days" ("900 дней") of starvation, cold, and other brutal deprivations which claimed lives of more than a million people, the Siege of Leningrad remains one of the war's most tragic chapters. An integral part of the Soviet post-war literary canon, novels, stories, memoirs, essays and poetry about the Siege are now firmly ingrained in the national imagination. They abided by the same poetic and ideological principles as the rest of the war literature and followed its evolutionary trajectory. On the one hand, works about the Siege always carried a heavy ideological load, for example, justifying the suffering of Leningraders by always citing the greater military goal – the Soviet Union's collective victory over Germany and its allies. On the other hand, they, too, went through a series of transformations, transitioning from the more or less straightforward, albeit censored, documentation of the Siege experience to the psychological, philosophical and poetic elucidation of its catastrophic outcome. Socialist Realism remained the main narrative mode of the official Soviet literature in the first three post-war decades, which means that the Soviet Siege writing mostly evolved within its confines. Like other war narratives, it remained exceedingly didactic in its depictions and interpretations of the tragedy of Leningrad and its citizens.

---

3   Bocharov, *Человек и война*, 18.
4   Chalmaev, *На войне остаться человеком*, 5.

And yet, deviations from the Socialist Realist norm appeared in literature about the Siege as early as the 1940s. This could be explained by the statement by Aileen G. Rambow who noticed that a "limited area of freedom," including new themes and forms of literary expression, was allowed during the war itself so that authors could reach their audiences more directly.[5] Both Ol'ga Berggolc' *Февральский дневник* (*The February Diary*, 1942) and Vera Inber's *Пулковский меридиан* (*The Pulkovo Meridian*, 1942) exemplified this tendency. Their subject itself – the suffering of individuals who faced the inhuman, beastly conditions of hunger, cold, and isolation – did not allow these authors, as well as some others writing about the Siege, to follow the Soviet narrative template of war writing in a direct, uncritical way. Because they had to digress from the Socialist Realist template with its heroic narrative tone, the body of literature they produced clearly demonstrated the impossibility of transposing the Siege experience into canonical Soviet war fiction. To begin with, it was hard for Siege writers to generate narratives centering around epic battles and action-driven combat scenes usually associated with master plots of war literature. Such heroism was simply not possible in a besieged city, where the internal enemy was absent and the external enemy remained detached and often invisible. Enduring malnutrition, grieving over the loss of loved ones, and leading, in Lidija Ginzburg's words, a "life cleared of substitution and hoaxes," Siege heroes never confronted their foes face to face.[6] Unlike soldiers attacking the enemy on the Ukranian Front or defenders of Stalingrad, they could neither throw themselves in front of oncoming machine gun fire nor urge others to rush into battle by personal example. Therefore, authors who dared to explore the Siege in their works had to readjust the Soviet approaches to writing about the war by looking for patterns of heroism that would reflect the ideologically acceptable norm while portraying the traumatic experiences remembered by the Siege survivors in a psychologically truthful and artistically plausible way.

Since Socialist Realist war literature required a great measure of forced optimism, the uniquely traumatic aspect of the Siege and its memory appears to have been the main problem for writers attempting to transform historical events into heroic tales. In fact, from the early post-war days, those authors who survived, witnessed, or recognized the tragedy undergone by Leningrad's population began to interpret the mere act of living in the besieged city as its own brand of heroism. In 1946, Berggolc, who by then had already responded

---

5   Aileen G. Rambow, "The Siege of Leningrad: Wartime Literature and Ideological Change," in Robert W. Thurston, ed., *The People's War: Responses to World War II in the Soviet Union*, Bernd Bonwetsch, Urbana 2000, 155.
6   Lydia Ginzburg, *Blockade Diary*, London 1996, 10.

to this challenge in her poetry, championed the notion of Leningraders' heroic endurance in her essays written for Soviet periodicals. An early proponent of the realist, ardently pro-Socialist approach to Soviet poetry for children and a tragically effective critic of such OBERIU writers as Daniil Charms and Aleksandr Vvedenskij, she now had to counterattack the criticism by Nikolaj Tichonov who had accused her of the writing that evoked "a strange trace of sadness."[7] In her response, Berggolc insisted that suffering in Leningrad under Siege was unavoidable. For her, it was a valiant act of superhuman misery that required recognition and remembrance:

> If a poet depicts how a human being has overcome the most horrific suffering, how he came out of it without being broken, but rather becoming enriched, maturing into someone who is, perhaps, less joyous and light-minded than he was before – who can accuse this author of "celebrating suffering"? How can one who attempts to depict the courage of the victorious Soviet individual neglect depicting his suffering, through which this very courage expressed itself?[8]

According to Berggolc, suffering was an essential narrative component in the literary portrayal of traumatic Siege experiences, as well as the most insightful way of highlighting the Leningraders' heroic behavior. She and her fellow poet Zinaida Shishova upheld this position when writing about their own lives during the Siege and the lives of others, especially in the long narrative poems produced in the winter of 1941-42, the notorious "death season" which carried hundreds of thousands to their graves. Altough Berggolc and Shishova could not portray soldiers in the midst of battle, they did include intensely graphic descriptions of the Siege victims' plight. Shishova's poem "Блокада" ("The Siege," 1941) is structured as a monologue of a woman addressing those who are so debilitated by hunger that they can no longer bring water from the Neva or get out of bed to light up the stove. Her narrator compares her own journey to the ice-hole for water to a sojourn in Dante's Tenth Circle. She mentions the water's being "poisoned by the cadaveric alkaloid" and lists the corpse awaiting its funeral on the balcony among the inhabitants of her apart-

---

7 Cited in Ljudmila Chashchina, "Высказывания погибших. Литературная хроника послевоенных лет с комментариями," in *Нева* 10 (1990), 182. For a discussion of Berggolc's role in the proletarian critics' attack on Charms and Vvedenskij, see Oleg Minin's chapter "Literary Avant-Garde and Soviet Literature for Children: OBERIU in the Leningrad Periodicals *Еж* and *Чиж*" in this volume.
8 Ol'ga Berggolc, "Путь к зрелости," in *Литературная газета*, May 26, 1946, 2.

ment.⁹ Berggolc focuses on a similar array of tragic, but seemingly trivial states and actions. In her "Второй разговор с соседкой" ("The Second Conversation with a Neighbor," 1944), she contrasts the army heroes' experience with her own and that of other survivors:

> Мы с тобою танков не взрывали.
> Мы в чаду обыденных забот
> безымянные высоты брали, –
> но на карте нет таких высот.
>
> Где помечена твоя крутая
> лестница, ведущая домой,
> по которой, с голоду шатаясь,
> ты ходила с ведрами зимой?¹⁰

Documenting the Siege from its victims' perspective, the two poets negated the idea of heroism as purely associated with combat, all the while making Leningraders' survival appear not only epic, but also laudable and comparable to military feats at the front. Although still portraying the Siege through the lens of the official Soviet teleology to make their work publishable, Berggolc and Shishova managed to describe the agony and endurance of the civilian population with rare honesty – as a tragedy that deserved not only a recognition, but also the right to be engrained in the nation's cultural memory.

Berggolc's and Shishova's narrators and protagonists – as well as the unseen "chorus" of their tragedies in verse – were women: they were strong, but vulnerable, capable of great compassion, but also pitilessly exposed to the brutalities of the Siege winter. Soon, as other narratives about Leningraders' suffering appeared after the lifting of the Siege, the figure of an impaired adult dealing with pain and deprivations began to be juxtaposed with or even overshadowed by the figure of a starving, agonizing, and grieving child. From the perspective of authors who wanted to highlight the Siege experience, the portrayal of children in distress was another effective way of bringing the whole

---

9   Zinaida Shishova, "Блокада," in *Блокада*, Leningrad 1943, 6.
10 "You and I, we have not set tanks on fire, / But, in the mire of everyday chores, / We conquered such heights – / There are no such heights on the map. / Where can you find a mark / Of your steep staircase leading home, / Which you climbed, staggering from hunger, / Carrying water in buckets, in the winter?" Berggolc, "Второй разговор с соседкой," in *Избранное*, Leningrad 1973, 67. Here and below, translations from the Russian are mine – PB.

city's suffering into relief. They were relying on the existing literary tradition, in which the image of a miserable child contributed to conveniently black-and-white, morally economical storytelling. In a variety of literary works, from the Romantics to Dickens and from Dostoevskij to Charskaja, the magnitude of children's suffering manifested the powerfulness and relentlessness of forces of evil. Those writers also often capitalized on the fact that a child's cognitive and emotional reactions to suffering were more acute than those of adult protagonists. Authors of the Soviet Siege literature seemed to recognize that the earlier portrayals of abused, neglected, or malnourished children resulted in gripping narratives, in which the emphatic presentation of evil – as seen or experienced by a young protagonist – led to an ethically charged finale. This is why, while shunning many conventional patterns of heroic representation, they frequently focused on the figure of a suffering child in order to demonstrate the dreadful magnitude of Leningraders' war-time torment. Juxtaposed with adult protagonists, child heroes of Siege literature also allowed their creators to generate a didactic attitude to war and victory required by the Soviet literary and ideological practices.

3 Child Protagonists of War-Time Siege Narratives

Leafing through the old issues of the children's monthly *Костер* (*The Campfire*), which, even in the besieged Leningrad, came out without an interruption, one finds it lacking in specific Siege material. The magazine features Leningrad as a "front-city," one of the many Soviet urban centers that struggle against the enemy due to their proximity to the front line. *Костер* pointedly does not mention the Nazi military ring that isolated the city from the rest of the country, cutting off its food and medical supplies and making the evacuation of civilians virtually impossible. Neither is there any discussion of starvation. When the periodical's authors dare to approach such touchy subjects, they either treat the situation in Leningrad favorably in comparison with the unfortunate circumstances of other besieged cities, or write, as Samuil Marshak does in his poem "Ленинграду – в день Красной Армии" ("To Leningrad on the Red Army's Day," 1943) about a putative, semi-illusory Siege as an event that happened in a remote past but will, paradoxically, end in the near future:[11]

---

11 Ekaterina Boronina referenced other besieged cities by comparing Leningrad under Siege to the Siege of Paris (1870). Carrier pigeons were a central element of her story. Boronina, "Вестник осажденного города" ("The Herald of the Besieged City"), in *Костер* 7-8 (1942), 20.

Ребенка не кормила мать
Мороз входил в дома,
Но не могла тебя сломить
Голодная зима.
И вот из вражьего кольца
Мы выбили звено,
И знаем – скоро до конца
Рассыплется оно.¹²

Костер was a children's periodical, and it was produced in Leningrad. Nevertheless, just as the magazine failed to feature truthful accounts of the Siege itself, it also almost completely avoided portraying its readers' war experience. Neither the little victims of the first Siege winter's famine nor brave elementary and middle-school students attempting to study in spite of the cold were profiled on its pages. In addition, the magazine did not keep a record of the city's monumental loss of life. *Костер*'s refraining from documenting the Siege is representative of the general Soviet politics of silencing the Siege experience – a political strategy that lasted at least until the end of the war. Since the ideological priority during those years was to conceal the tragic historical reality from the majority of the Soviet population, the shocking fatalities of the Siege – including its young victims – were hidden from sight. The consequences of such a policy were dire. Not only did this ban on historical truth deprive the actual survivors of literary self-reflection, but it also influenced how the image of the Siege child was constructed in the post-war years. Initially appearing in fiction and non-fiction for adult readers and only later making its way into children's literature, the figure of the Siege child followed a strictly defined ideological model. Depicted in a tragic light and yet represented in a much mitigated, not fully accurate way, the suffering young Leningraders were there only to ignite empathy and desire for revenge in adult readers of the Siege fiction.

When *Костер* did publish works about children of the Siege, its authors aimed to create images of brave young boys and girls who, like other heroes of pre-war and war-time children's literature, including works by Gajdar, Panteleev, Voskresenskaja, Kataev, and Kassil', were not only capable of overcom-

---

12 "Mother could not feed her child, / Frost entered houses, / But the winter of starvation / Was not able to break you. / So we broke the chain / In the enemy's ring, / And we know that soon / This ring will fall apart." Samuil Marshak, "Ленинграду – в день Красной Армии," in *Костер* 2 (1943), 1. The poem also appeared in *Правда* (*Truth*, February 22, 1943) and *Ленинградская правда* (*Leningrad Truth*, February 23, 1943).

ing the "circumstances," but also acted heroically. This is why war-time stories published in *Костер* featured Leningrad boys and girls, predominantly in their teens, assisting those in need or helping adults to fight the enemy. Since it was impossible to correlate most of those feats with the reality of the Siege without violating the Socialist Realist requirement of a believable setting, the heroic deeds of the fictionalized Siege children took place in unidentified locations. In other words, the setting of the stories published in *Костер* was not in the besieged city, but rather, on its outskirts, often in close proximity to the front. For example, in September 1941, when Leningrad was first overcome by the shelling and the threat of starvation, the magazine featured a short story by Lev Brandt about Kolja Bublikov. The schoolboy committed an act of heroism by helping adults to repair an electrical circuit. Another protagonist of the same story, a female student Valja Dergach, cared for the wounded transported to the hospital at a train station in the vicinity of the city.[13]

Child protagonists of the stories about the Siege were brave, and yet, unlike other valiant characters proliferating in the Soviet hero narratives for children, they were not portrayed as completely fearless, politically conscientious, and bearing full responsibility for the outcome of their actions.[14] On the contrary, in the case of *Костер*, the lives of others and the city's safety remained in the hands of adults, including professional military personnel. In earlier Soviet children's books, for example, those written in the 1930s during the collectivization campaigns as well as at the height of the Stalinist spymania, the unprecedented courage and conscientiousness of child-protagonists equaled if not surpassed that of grown-ups.[15] The Siege narratives were different. They portrayed children who, in spite of their loyalty to the Soviet state and their unquestionable patriotism, seemed less staunch than the pioneers following Pavlik Morozov's example or imitating the well-organized "Timur and his team" from Gajdar's eponymous novella. Sometimes, authors of fiction about the Siege even allowed their young protagonists to be unjust and intolerant towards each other or misbehave. Thus, in Aleksandr Krestinskij's story, Russian boys in a bomb shelter accuse their Estonian peers of taking bread

---

13 Lev Brandt, "Коля Бубликов" ("Kolja Bublikov"), in *Костер* 9 (1941), 34-36; Ekaterina Boronina, "Горячее сердце," in *Костер* 9 (1941), 36-38.
14 See Svetlana Maslinskaya's essay on child hero narratives in this volume.
15 Among the pre-war children's books that celebrate the valor and political loyalty of Soviet children are Veniamin Kaverin's *Два капитана* (*Two Captains*, 1940); Arkadij Gajdar's *Военная тайна* (*The Military Secret*, 1935) and *Судьба барабанщика* (*Fate of the Drummer*, 1939); and Valentin Kataev's *Белеет парус одинокий* (*The Lonely Sail is White Afar*, 1936).

from native Leningraders, later regretting their accusations.[16] Misha Alekseev, the protagonist of German Matveev's trilogy Зеленые цепочки (*Little Green Chains*, 1945), *Тайная схватка* (*Secret Combat*, 1948), and *Тарантул* (*Tarantula*, 1957), nearly becomes a thief. He manages to overcome his predilection for crime so that he can join the ranks of righteous Soviet citizens.[17]

To remain publishable, Soviet children's fiction had to introduce its young readers to positive role models and patterns of politically approved behavior. This is why, even in those works of fiction about the Siege in which children's acts of valor cannot be featured, child protagonists are still able to appear heroic. They overcome their weaknesses, endure hardships, and exercise self-control, while remaining symbolically subordinated to their adult mentors.[18] Nevertheless, children's lack of political and moral agency is rather apparent in Siege literature. One finds an interesting illustration of this deviation from the ideological norm in Ol'ga Kuznecova's "Страх" ("Fear," 1942). Although Kuznecova portrays a boy partisan fighter Serezha, her sketch of him represents a generic aberration of the Soviet war narratives for the young, especially the stories in which children avenge their parents killed at war.[19] Kuznecova starts "Страх" on a typical note, by telling her readers about the orphaned boy's act of valor – he joins a partisan regiment to take vengeance on the Germans for his mother's death. And yet, Serezha is different from other heroic children. Young protagonists of other works of fiction about runaway kids who become soldiers or partisans, such as Vanja Solncev in Kataev's *Сын полка* (*Son of the Regiment*, 1944), quickly mature emotionally and physically, undergo an initiation into the society of politicized peers and adult warriors, and, at the end, perform a heroic act of revenge against the Nazis, often at a cost of their own life. Serezha remains his vulnerable teenage self much longer. Although at the end of the story he does fulfill the task of vengeance he has set for himself, he makes many mistakes before accomplishing it. Some of them reveal his unpreparedness to be a combatant. For example, Serezha

---

16 Aleksandr Krestinskij, "А потом началась война" ("And Then, the War Began"), in *Мальчики из блокады: Рассказы и повесть*, Leningrad 1983, 88.

17 German Matveev, *Зеленые цепочки*, Moscow 1945; *Тайная схватка*, Moscow 1948; and *Тарантул*, Moscow 1957. It should be noted that children's predilection for theft was a narrative element already familiar to readers of Soviet narratives of repentance and pedagogical "reforging" ("перековка"). Take into account, for example, Leonid Panteleev and Grigorij Belych's novel *Республика Шкид* (*The Republic of Shkid*, 1927) or Anton Makarenko's *Педагогическая поэма* (*Pedagogical Poem*, 1931).

18 Katerina Clark, *The Soviet Novel: History as Ritual*, Bloomington and Indianapolis 2000, 193.

19 Ol'ga Kuznecova, "Страх," in *Костер* 5-6 (1942), 2.

is not afraid of killing the enemy, but he is scared of its bizarre "representative" – the harsh and alien voice coming from a loudspeaker. His distress and emotionality mark him as a vulnerable child, rather than a stereotypical war hero:

> – So, you were saying that even darkness won't scare you – but the loudspeaker did? – asked the Stutterer.
> – The loudspeaker? – Serezha repeated in amazement. He suddenly understood everything. He blushed: first his face, then his ears and neck. Even his back turned red, he felt it. "A loudspeaker!" the boy thought with bitterness.
> – Do not cry, or you'll make your gunpowder wet! — the Stutterer joked, patting Serezha on his shorn-off hair. "He treats me like a baby!" – Serezha thought, tears in his eyes.[20]

Having overcome his fears, Serezha successfully goes through his initiation by killing an enemy soldier and thus avenging his mother. But his fear, which Kuznecova does not hesitate to emphasize, takes his heroism down a notch. Even when Serezha's character appears to grow stronger and partisan fighters declare him a member of their regiment, his actions do not fully comply with the norms of a Socialist Realist. war story. Serezha's imperfection, his giving in to fear, prevents the possibility of young readers modeling themselves after him.

Ekaterina Boronina's "Мальчик из Севастополя" ("A Boy from Sebastopol," published in the July-August, 1942, issue of Костер), similarly deviates from the stereotypical Socialist Realist hero narrative for young readers. Boronina tells the story of a boy who, right before the war, moves from Sebastopol to Leningrad with his mother. As he is building a sand castle in the courtyard of his new house, a sailor approaches to convey the sad news: his father perished in combat when defending the Sebastopol fortress. The messenger hands the boy his father's cigarette case: it is filled with the soil from the city where the tragedy struck. Since Boronina's hero is too young to avenge his parent, Boronina translates his reaction to the tragic news into a symbolic gesture. She portrays him as putting a little red flag into the precious container, thus connecting Sebastopol to Leningrad, and himself, to his dead hero-father.[21] Just like Kuznecova's Serezha, Boronina's protagonist cannot replicate the attitudes and behaviors of a Soviet adult hero. The boy's age explains his lack

---

20   Ibid., 4.
21   Boronina, "Мальчик из Севастополя," in Костер 7-8 (1942), 2-4.

of more consequential agency, but it is not the only reason why he cannot act in a fully stereotypical way. Because he is isolated in the besieged Leningrad, he cannot take part in real war action, for example, by running away from his home to the front as Vanya Solncev does, or by doing courier work for a group of partisans as a boy in Vladimir Bogomolov's novella *Иван* (*Ivan*, 1958) would do.[22] And yet, Boronina's child hero still appears to be valiant. He takes care of his grandmother and dreams about acting heroically in the future. Having provided her character with the box of Sebastopol soil, which brings him closer to his father as well as to the land the father strove to defend before perishing in battle, Boronina encourages her readers to believe that her protagonist will be fully able to accomplish his heroic mission in the future: he understands the real and symbolic value of adults' war actions.

The Soviet war stories written in the 1960s-80s became more psychologically nuanced and acquired narrative features that deviated from the Socialist Realist canon of heroic war fiction. Similarly, the Thaw-era and late Soviet children's literary works about the Siege deviated even further from the stereotypically schematic – and ideologically dogmatic – form.[23] Thus, Mishka, the protagonist of *Вот как это было* (*This Is How It Was*, 1978), a story by Jurij German, is depicted in a much more nuanced way than the adult war heroes or even child protagonists of war fiction that emerged in the 1940s-50s and kept appearing thereafter.[24] Like Boronina's "boy from Sebastopol," Mishka is precociously conscientious. Although he is only seven years old, he is the story's first-person narrator who describes Leningrad during the Siege and documents the plight of his friends and neighbors in a coherent, unsentimental manner. Mishka's narrative position, and especially the contrast between the ideologically unclouded, innocent perspective of the child and the gruesome reality of the Siege allows German to create an effect of estrangement, and thus feature

---

22 In 1962, Andrej Tarkovskij reworked Bogomolov's plot into *Иваново детство* (*Ivan's Childhood*), a heartrending film about a child's traumatic war experience.
23 See, for example, *Солдатский подвиг. Рассказы* (*A Soldier's Feat. Short Stories*), Moscow 1968; Vladimir Vygovskij, *Огонь юного сердца* (*The Fire of a Young Heart*), Moscow 1960; Andrej Zharikov, *Подвиги юных: Рассказы и очерки* (*The Feats of Young People: Short Stories and Sketches*), Moscow 1960; Vjacheslav Morozov, *Им было по четырнадцать: О Марате Казее, Володе Щербачевиче* (*They Were Fourteen: About Marat Kazej and Volodja Shcherbachevich*), Minsk 1969; Grigorij Nabatov, *Юные подпольщики* (*Young Underground Fighters*), Moscow 1963.
24 Jurij German, *Вот как это было*, Moscow 1985. It is unclear when the novella was written. From the introduction to the 1978 edition, we learn that German probably composed it during the war or immediately after it. But it could not be published in the author's lifetime (German died in 1967).

the horrors of the war in a fresh and yet emotionally subdued way. For example, in an episode in which German bombs hit a city hospital, Mishka's perception of the tragedy is fragmented, and his emotional reactions are numb:

> I cannot even recall what happened. I remember some whistles blowing, some blue lamps swaying around, and some very loud shooting. And also — the awful thirst. Somebody is screaming: "Oh, my little leg is hurting, my little leg is hurting!" Then somebody lifted me up and carried me away. And then I fell asleep or forgot everything...[25]

The author's description of the bombing is an accurate rendering of a child's reaction to trauma: Mishka is thirsty, sleepy, and unable to fully register the impact of violence. As any child, he concentrates on his own feelings while being incapable of providing a panoramic description of the destruction; neither is he able to retell the sequence of events in a coherent manner. Just like the actions of the "boy from Sebastopol," Mishka's behavior during the Siege is not heroic – especially when viewed in the context of the struggles of the surrounding adults. To underline this fact, German also shows us such "real" heroes of the Siege as Mishka's parents who put out incendiary bombs and extinguish the fire; local militia men with their signal rockets who pursue alleged spies; and the wounded pilot and general whom Mishka meets at the hospital. And yet, Mishka is unquestionably the hero of German's story as well as of its every war episode. The author makes it obvious that the boy's acts are valiant by demonstrating that, even at a time of crisis, they are mundanely morally impeccable. In spite of his terrible living conditions, Mishka remains a noble, modest, respectful child who always does whatever good he can and maintains impeccable behavior: he crosses the street only at designated crosswalks, he never complains when he is in pain, and he does not accept an invitation from his friend, the general, for a horse ride at the parade, because he cannot share the adventure with his best friend.[26]

It is important that Boronina and German's child protagonists do not function as agents of Soviet victory or as fearless warriors. Rather, they perform the role of innocent victims who inspire adults to avenge their traumatized childhoods. Appearing to be the essential feature in the representation of children in the Siege literature, this rousing function adds a new dimension to the paradigmatic trope of a victimized child – be it Hugo's Cosette, Dickens' Oliver

---

25   German, *Вот как это было*, 44.
26   Ibid., 48-49, 78.

Twist, or Dostoevskij's Netochka Nezvanova. Virtuous casualties of the Great Patriotic War, children of the Siege dominate literary narratives because their plight helps authors to accentuate the Nazi atrocities. At the same time, authors of these stories assert that the Leningrad adults' ability to save the young is what constitutes actual acts of heroism, of courageousness that ensures the moral victory of good over evil. An example of such distribution of fictional roles may be found in Aleksandr Fadeev's "Дети осажденного Ленинграда" ("The Children of Besieged Leningrad," 1942), an essay which opens with a line that clearly juxtaposes adult characters and their underage protégées: "Citizens of Leningrad, and women most of all, can be proud that they were able to save the city's children."[27] In his essay, Fadeev not only shows children as the war's passive victims, but he also pronounces women's and the municipal government's attempts to save them heroic. Having visited Leningrad's orphanages in July of 1942, Fadeev reported that "the majority of children had a rather healthy appearance and, in their behavior, the type of games they played, their laughter and cheerfulness, they did not look any different than other normal children." He concluded that the children's survival "was the result of the great sacred labor of Leningrad women, most of whom volunteered their energy to save and bring up the children. A typical Leningrad woman invested so much motherly love and self-sacrifice into this that we should bow deeply to the greatness of her exploit."[28]

One of the most powerful examples of the symbolic role enacted by a victimized Siege child in the postwar Soviet literature is the celebrated figure of Tanja Savicheva (1930-1944). Although Tanja died shortly after her evacuation from the besieged city, her diary, which documented the daily Siege existence of the Savichev family as well as their gradual expiration from malnutrition, remained as a testimony of the tragic experience of all children who perished during those brutal "nine hundred days" of hunger and cold. The diary was made public by Lev Rakov, director of the first Museum of the Defense of Leningrad (Музей обороны Ленинграда), who not only publicized Tanja's text, but also made it a centerpiece of the museum's permanent exhibition. When, in 1953, the museum was demolished as a result of the "Leningrad Affair," a series of fabricated criminal cases aimed at destroying promising political leaders that emerged in the city after the war, the diary was given a prominent place at the Museum of Leningrad History (Музей

---

27 Aleksandr Fadeev, "Дети осажденного Ленинграда" ("The Children of Besieged Leningrad") in *От Советского Информбюро, 1941-1945*, Vol. 2, Moscow 1982, 7.
28 Ibid.

истории Ленинграда).²⁹ This document of a child's combat with hunger and death is so powerful that it inspired a monument to the children of the Siege, constructed in 1968-1975 near the town of Vsevolozhsk, from where the winter transport route began across Lake Ladoga.³⁰ A copy of Tanja's records of her family members' deaths was also included in a permanent exhibit at the Piskarevo Memorial Cemetery (Пискаревское мемориальное кладбище), where many Siege victims were buried.³¹

Tanja's tragic fate became the subject of a literary exploration and scholarly evaluation rather late, first with Ilja Mikson's documentary book for children published in 1991, and, almost two decades later, with the online publication of Lilija Markova's "Блокадная хроника Тани Савичевой" ("The Siege Chronicle of Tanja Savicheva," 2009).³² And yet, some Soviet authors decided to portray this suffering Siege child even before specific details of her plight had become known.³³ Thus, in a short story "Сергей Иванович и Таня" ("Sergej Ivanovich and Tanja," 1973), Vera Panova used some of the better-known facts about the Savichevs to create a consolidated – and rather formulaic – image of a young girl fighting for her life in the besieged city.³⁴ After she is orphaned by the Siege, Panova's Tanja finds a new home in a local orphanage. In the

---

29   Zoja Piven', *Навечно в памяти народной: Записки работника музея Истории Ленинграда*. Leningrad 1984.

30   That winter, Дорога жизни (The Road of Life) provided supplies of food and ammunition to citizens of Leningrad and the city's defenders. It also served as a means of evacuating the wounded as well as sick and malnourished individuals, mostly women and children. The total number of people evacuated from Leningrad during the twenty-nine months of the Siege amounted to 1.3 million. The monument marks the road's entry point, where trucks left the firm ground to cross the lake over ice. Its architects, A. D. Levenkov and G. G. Fetisov, conceived it as a concrete replica of Tanja's diary, with eight stelae representing the diary's eight pages.

31   For an account of Tanja's fate in English see Patricia Heberer, *Children during the Holocaust*, Lanham, MD 2011, 53-54.

32   Ilja Mikson, *Жила, была... Историческое повествование* (*Once Upon a Time There Lived... A Historical Narrative*), Leningrad 1991; Lilija Markova, "Блокадная хроника Тани Савичевой," in *Петербургская семья: еженедельная интернет газета* (2009) ⟨http://www.spb-family.ru/history/history_15.html⟩ (Accessed November 12, 2017).

33   Such literary explorations of Tanja's life include Jurij Jakovlev, *Девочки с Васильевского острова* (*Girls from Vasiljevsky Island*), Moscow 1978; "Мистерия. Страсти по четырем девочкам" ("Mystery Play. The Passion of the Four Little Girls"), in Jakovlev, *Избранное*, Moscow 1992; S. Smirnov, "Таня Савичева" ("Tanja Savicheva"), in *Венок славы. Антология художественных произведений о Великой Отечественной войне*, Vol. 3, *Подвиг Ленинграда*, Moscow 1983, 297-300.

34   Vera Panova, "Сергей Иванович и Таня," in *Наши дети. Рассказы, повести и пьеса*, Leningrad 1973.

same vein as other war narratives about children survivors of the war, which often documented the improvement of the child-protagonist's character and behavior under harsh war conditions in temporary schools or children's asylums away from home, Panova shows her protagonist as weak-willed before death claims her adult relatives. For instance, Tanja washes her hands and face only with warm water and avoids walking outside in the cold. However, under the capable tutelage of the principal of the orphanage, Sergej Ivanovich, the girl discovers her willpower and learns how to take care of herself: "Teachers and mentors from the orphanage revived her survival skills, fortifying her will so that she could get farther in life, one step at a time," Panova writes.[35] Unlike the real Tanja Savicheva who perished from tuberculosis or dysentery after being evacuated from Leningrad with a group of other orphans, Panova's protagonist regained her health and acquired self-sufficiency and valor – the character traits that helped her to become a real Soviet citizen.

The propagandistic aspect of the Soviet children's literature about the Siege can only partially explain why its authors did not avoid portraying children as physically weak and in need of moral guidance of the kind Sergej Ivanovich is able to provide for Tanja. Another reason children's writers who were writing about the Siege refused to focus on the "staunchness" and "valor" of children as heroes of World War II was their understanding that the compulsory optimism of the Socialist Realist method and its imperative to present the Soviet people as capable of overcoming every difficulty and emerging victorious did not correspond to the reality of Leningrad's war experience with its hundreds of thousands of victims. Even though the cheerful enthusiasm and confidence in the country's glorious future were the *de rigeur* features of Soviet children's literature in the 1930s-50s, literary works for young readers that appeared closer to the end of the Soviet regime began to lose this gloss of artificial buoyancy. Greater psychological nuancing and more accurate historical truth came to the fore. Thus, in short story "Гном" ("The Gnome," 1983), Aleksandr Krestinskij depicts a boy suffering from nutritional dystrophy, a disease caused by starvation. Just as Jurij German before him, Krestinskij constructs a first-person narrative that is impressionistic and somewhat melancholy. The tone of his storytelling is clearly imitating the mood and survivor behavior of the short story's protagonist, Dima, whom other children have called "the Gnome" for his solitary ways, lack of cheerfulness, and appearance of an old man. Krestinskij's narrator appears to us both as a child and an adult. It is his more mature self that feels guilty about not supporting Dima many years prior,

---

35 Panova, *Сергей Иванович и Таня*, Moscow 1973, 18.

when the malnourished child was in dire need of his peers' understanding and acceptance:

> Now I realize that it was the Siege that had caused all of this. It kept holding the boy firmly in its grip, not letting him go. I know such people. Even now, thirty years later, the Siege will not let go of them. All of us have found a way to return to our lives then, but he … he was still looking back at some horrific visions that only he was able to see.[36]

Krestinskij outlines a conflict between Dima, the famished victim of the Siege, and other, healthier, children at a summer camp for survivors. His narrator recalls how, as a teenager, he came to the camp immediately after the Siege had been lifted. When forced to live in the same room as Dima, he discovered that the boy's Siege habits lingered: he was slow, suffered from nightmares, and was obsessed with food. While the rest of the campers devoured their rations, "the Gnome" approached lunch as a sacred act:

> He ate slowly, as if unwillingly, making his pleasure last. He pinched off microscopic bits from his bread and chewed on them for a long time, as if listening to something inside himself. That alone was enough to annoy everyone. They teased him, but he pretended that he did not notice. And when plates with little chunks of butter and sugar in cups were brought in – we poured our tea ourselves – he would begin his sacral ritual. The Gnome would pull two plastic jars out of the hobo bag that he wore – even when working in the fields he wouldn't part with it. He would put butter in one of them and sugar in another. Then he would neatly wipe the trace of butter off his plate with a crust of bread. He would do it without a hurry, in a concentrated manner, without paying attention to anyone.[37]

At first, Dima's afflictions made him a stranger to other children: they laughed at and even bullied the Gnome. But then another outsider, a boyish-looking, aggressive and unkempt girl Galja decided to take care of him. Once the jars of sugar and butter which Dima had been collecting with the zeal of a post-dystrophic victim disappeared, forcing the boy to leave the camp, Galja followed him back to the city, where the two apparently survived to become a

---

36 Aleksandr Krestinskij, "Гном," in *Мальчики из блокады. Рассказы и повесть*, Leningrad 1983, 45.
37 Ibid., 46.

couple whom the narrator would later observe during a chance encounter in a restored, peaceful Leningrad. The story ends with the narrator's confessing his embarrassment about misunderstanding Dima's situation. "I pulled back and averted my eyes [from them]. I did it involuntarily, when passing by."[38] The narrator says that he "wouldn't approach the Gnome" because "he felt ashamed."[39]

Dima's failure to socialize with his peers, his illness, and his trauma represent the dark side of the Siege survivors' existence. A similarly sorrowful interpretation of the Siege experience may be found in other, post-Perestroika, fictional accounts of the tragedy written for children, such as Igor' Smirnov-Ochtin's story "Школа судей" ("The School for Judges," 1999), Lev Razumovskij's novella *Дети Блокады* (*Children of the Siege*, 1999), and Oleg Shestinskij's collection of short stories *Ангельское воинство* (*The Angelic Guard*, 1999).[40] In the 1960s-80s fiction, child protagonists of Siege narratives began to differ from their earlier literary predecessors in one important way: as soon as writers were able to describe starvation in the city, the Leningraders' malnourishment became the central focus of every story and novel. Thus, in short stories by Vera Karaseva, published in 1965, children's heroism consists of sharing bread with their hungry friends, while Denis Dragunskij's otherwise sanguine and often hilarious stories in the cycle, *Денискины рассказы* (*Deniska's Tales*, 1959-1966), include a heartrending account of the two boys' scavenging for food during the war.[41] Although this short story, "Арбузный переулок" ("The Watermelon Lane"), is set in Moscow, the tone of Dragunskij's depiction of children suffering from hunger corresponds to that of the more psychologically nuanced Siege narratives.

Soviet children's authors often idealized their characters when writing about the Siege. Even when they showed children as enfeebled or distressed, they rarely portrayed them as incapable of moral judgment or self-control. Like the majority of Soviet children's narratives written after Gajdar's *Тимур и его команда* (*Timur and His Team*, 1940), the Siege stories celebrated such virtues as productivity, conscientiousness, and leadership – the latter understood as an ability to organize others, especially one's friends and classmates, in well-structured, efficient collectives. Vladimir Druzhinin, for example, endowed with these laudable qualities the protagonist of his 1942

---

38   Ibid., 53
39   Ibid., 40.
40   Igor' Smirnov-Ochtin, "Школа судей," in *Нева* 1 (1999), 88-101; Lev Razumovskij, "Дети блокады. Документальная повесть," in *Нева* 1 (1999), 4-68; Oleg Shestinskij, *Ангельское воинство. Рассказы*, in *Нева* 1 (1999), 69-87.
41   Vera Karaseva, *Кирюшка* (*Kirjushka*), Kiev 1965.

short story "Мировой бригадир," ("A Terrific Leader of the Brigade"). Borja Levikov attends a trade school (техникум) that offers a work-study program for teenagers. He is young, but his aptitude for leadership allow him first to replace his mentor, a head of the brigade who succumbs to Siege dystrophy, and then mastermind the repair operations at the factory that contributes to the war effort.[42]

Overall, children's authors writing about the Siege tried to cut their protagonists out of the same cloth as that allocated to other Socialist Realist portrayals of loyal Soviet citizens. Even when dying, they appeared to be strong-willed, goal-oriented, and ready to help those in need. The older the literary heroes of children's books were, the closer was their affinity with saviors rather than victims. While the younger Siege children represented an ideal Soviet child due to their ability to inspire adults to protect them and thus fight the enemy, teenagers featured in children's books, especially Komsomol members, appeared to behave in accordance with the code of heroic conduct. That is why the main character of Lev Uspenskij's tale "Птичка в клетке" ("Bird in a Cage," 1984) is able to complete a difficult assignment usually given to adult workers.[43] Iurij Aljanskij, in his sketch "Танец в огне" ("A Dance in Fire," 1984), presents young performers of a children's dance collective in the same idealized light. Cold and starving, they give all their energy to the art that revives and inspires others.[44]

Although fiction about older survivors of the Siege more or less adheres to the conventional paradigms of the Soviet war narrative, the vulnerability and lack of heroic agency in younger protagonists of Siege literature appears to undermine the overwhelming sovereignty of Socialist Realism. Acceptable because of its potential to highlight other heroic aspects of the experience of war (such as adults' valor and self-sacrifice), it was the feature that allowed children's authors to portray certain "unspeakable" truths about the Siege, truths which could hardly be shared through narratives involving adult protagonists alone.

4   Mentors in Soviet Siege Literature for Children

As Katerina Clark explains, the "big family" trope prominent in Socialist Realist fiction led to a proliferation of literary protagonists who were young and

---

42   Vladimir Druzhinin, "Мировой бригадир," in *Костер* 11-12 (1942), 16-17.
43   Lev Uspenskij, "Птичка в клетке," in *Дети военной поры*, Moscow 1984, 93-147.
44   Jurij Aljanskij, "Танец в огне," in *Дети военной поры*, 148-152.

in need of adult guidance.[45] The figure of a mentor and his or her protégé was convenient for other reasons as well. When Soviet authors portrayed a dynamic relationship between a student and a teacher or focused on the evolution of the younger person's political views and personality, they were able to assert the universality and verity of Soviet ideology in a less didactic way, presenting it as a "truth" acquired by children or adolescents in the process of their maturation. Some children's authors chose to adhere to the model in Siege fiction as well. Their dependent, feeble young heroes managed to overcome their weakness under the guidance of a well-meaning, kindly, responsible adult. Even when children's writers introduced protagonists with flawed personalities in their narratives, they did so in order to document the transformation of debilitated and morally malleable young victims of the Siege into strong and virtuous Soviet individuals. In such texts, the Siege ended up serving as a dramatic setting for an orthodox Socialist Realist master plot with its prerequisite focus on the forging of an impeccable Soviet man or woman.

In most Soviet literary works about the Siege, children spend their time helping adults. Largely devoid of such child-like qualities as playfulness, disobedience, and inquisitiveness, they represent embryonic Soviet individuals on their way towards becoming full-fledged members of the socialist society. If children dare to be naughty – like Karaseva's Kirjushka does – it is only so that the author can add depth and drama to the plot by portraying children who overcome their shortcomings and thus become better prepared for productive life among adults. In the case of Siege fiction, the lack of child-like qualities characteristic of other Soviet children's war narratives corresponds to the children's physical fragility and emotional numbness. This is why Boronina's character, the "boy from Sebastopol," does not cry when he learns of his father's death, while her other protagonists, young factory workers, do not complain in spite of their being cold and hungry.

According to Soviet pedagogical and political theory, the evolution of a child or adolescent into a mature Soviet individual endowed with "communist consciousness" was a collective project. For this reason, children's authors frequently paired their young protagonists with an adult hero, a true role model. But while the Socialist Realist fiction for adults usually delegated the role of the mentor to an older, wiser, or more experienced colleague – a factory manager, an army officer, a chair of a kolkhoz, or a senior Party member – literature for children explored a broader variety of options. Theoretically, every loyal, articulate, politically "conscious" adult could guide the young and shape

---

45   Clark, *The Soviet Novel*, 114-135.

their souls. And yet, children's authors preferred to avoid ambiguity by appointing teachers with a party mandate, parents involved in propaganda work and socialist labor competitions at their workplaces, former or current officers of the Red Army, or the already "evolved" members of the Komsomol as mentors to the young. Arkadij Gajdar's Natka in *Военная Тайна* (*The Military Secret, 1935*) is mentored by her uncle, a high-ranking government official, as well as by Alka's father, Ganin, while the boy who promised to guard his "military post" in Leonid Panteleev's story "Честное слово" ("The Word of Honor," 1941) agrees to give up the game and go home only when released from duty by a Major. The Siege literature for children, however, narrowed this selection of mentor figures down to Militia officers or NKVD agents. In other words, it appears that the dramatic conditions of the besieged city, where scores of grown-ups perished and where survival and death were facts of even the youngest of Leningraders' lives, made children's authors choose their adult protagonists with special care. More often than not, they portrayed representatives of the most authoritative branches of the Soviet regime as the people who could advise and guide the young. This choice goes well with Clark's observation that the mentor figure in Soviet literature was connected to the authors' understanding – be it sincere or forced – of the central role played by the Communist Party and its institutions in shaping and directing the Soviet society.[46] The Siege was obviously a catastrophic event that exemplified the Party's loss of control over the lives of the whole city and compromised the well-being of hundreds of thousands of Soviet citizens. If fictional accounts of that experience failed to assert Soviet authority in Leningrad at the time of the war, they would have immediately appeared as politically subversive and, therefore, unfit for publication.

One of the examples of affirmation by children's authors of the authority of the Soviet regime in the besieged city comes from Jurij Pomozov's novella *Блокадная юность* (*Youth During the Siege*, 1989). Pomozov describes a Trade School for young adults which functioned in Leningrad during the war; the author allocates the role of adolescent students' mentor to the chief of its political department, Arkadij Prokofievich Skorochodov, a man who is "able to be both angry and cold-blooded, assertive and patient, joyous and serious, generous and miserly, wise and courageous."[47] In praising his hero, Pomozov emphasizes integrity as Skorochodov's most important characteristic: "In short," Pomozov writes, "he could be different, depending on the situation, but in his every quality he was wholesome."[48] Had Skorochodov been a protagonist

---

46   Ibid.,119.
47   Jurij Pomozov, *Блокадная юность*, Leningrad 1989, 101-102.
48   Ibid., 101.

of another war narrative or of an "industrial construction" novel for adults, his ambivalent nature could have been a reason to ban the book. But in this story about the Siege, where the Leningraders' everyday dealings with the state were determined by the isolated condition of the city and the overall powerlessness of the population, the mentor's ability to be different, to adjust his behavior according to the existing conditions, became an asset rather than a weakness. Pomozov shows how Skorochodov's influence over his charges fluctuated drastically, depending both on Soviet progress in the war and on the story's plot development. But no matter how authoritative or inconsequential Skorochodov appears to be, his main strength always lies in his power of observation and in his belief in the greatest of Soviet virtues – one's love of labor. For example, when studying how employees under his command were doing, Skorochodov noticed "that the former foreman became apathetic, spending a long time dimly gazing at the fireless little oven, drinking so much water that he became swollen, and then barely dragging his feet to the medical station to ask for more food." At that moment, Skorochodov decided not to take pity on the man, but to send him to a different shop to chop wood instead. "There he'd improve his health by working!" he thought.[49]

While mentors in Soviet children's war narratives were usually men, ranging from fathers to the Red Army officers and various educators, in Siege literature women often stepped in to play the traditionally masculine role. Their presence may be explained not only by the historical reality of the Siege, since many men were drafted during the first days of the war, but also by the association of female heroes with the symbolic figure of Motherland, or "Mother Russia," which was frequently featured in poetry and on propaganda posters as a powerful, mournful woman who incited Soviet men to protect and avenge their families as well as all women and children. This was, of course, an ambivalent role, for a protectress could also turn out to be a victim of enemy's violence herself in need of male protection. The ambivalence explains why German, in *Вот как это было*, portrays Mishka's mother, though a member of an anti-aircraft unit charged with the task of detecting and disabling incendiary bombs, as afraid of mice. In Panova's story, the mother figure appears not only to be weak but also morally flawed: it was she who enabled Tanja Savicheva's laziness and fear of cold.[50] But in Krestinskij's "Гном," Galja acts as a mentor to Dima, the boy suffering from nutritional dystrophy and Siege-induced trauma. She is obviously an unusual female protagonist, for the author highlights her unattractive looks, emphasizing that she is also much taller than her protégé.[51]

---

49   Ibid., 103.
50   Vera Panova, *Сергей Иванович и Таня*, 18.
51   Krestinskij, "Гном," 46.

Nevertherless, Galja's tomboyish appearance makes her an ideal mentor figure: although unquestioningly a female (at the end of the story, the narrator explains that she married Dima and continued to support him as an adult), she is not entirely feminine and not entirely weak – especially in comparison to the enfeebled male protagonist. By making Galja look somewhat masculine or at least gender-neutral, Krestinskij attempts to make acceptable the predominantly male roles that women were playing during the Siege. In his prose, women's mannishness appears constructive, if not romantically promising.

The gender imbalance typical of more conventional war narratives is likewise shifted towards women in Mikson's story about Tanja Savicheva. Here, the mentor figure is Tanja's grandmother, whom the author portrays in a consistently positive light: "She is older than everyone in the family, but full of energy and has time for everything: she is the family's main caretaker," Mikson writes.[52] Uncharacteristically, however, the mentor's skills do not get passed on to the younger generation. When the grandmother dies, other members of the Savichev family become helpless and more or less abandon Tanja, thus facilitating the death of the young protagonist.

Mikson's narrative, written in the 1990s, when the Socialist Realist canon in children's literature was on the wane, demonstrates that in children's fiction about the Siege, the figure of a mentor went through a series of dramatic transformations. If, during the war, authors mainly delegated this function to powerful representatives of the state, later on they began to imagine socially "powerless" individuals in the role of protectors and advisers of Siege children. In addition to Krestinskij's and Mikson's narratives, Jurij Jakovlev's "Балерина политотдела" ("Ballerina from the Political Department," 1979) exemplifies this trend. Its mentor figure is the dance teacher Boris Korbut, who is dismissed from the army to organize a ballet collective recruited from his former students, who are adolescents emaciated by the Siege. Although Korbut is a man, the role he plays has many maternal and feminine aspects. Not only does he call his little dancers "My children [мои чада]," but he also knows that he can bring them back to life by giving them a meaningful – and aesthetically valuable – occupation.[53] His despair, however, and sense of powerlessness arising from daily encounters with death and suffering are such that he keeps thinking how his always white hair may one day turn dark from grief.[54]

To summarize, the figure of a mentor in Siege narratives for children evolved to include outsiders who deviated from the Soviet archetype of an

---

52   Mikson, *Жила, была*, 7.
53   Jurij Jakovlev, "Балерина политотдела," in *Жить нам суждено*, Moscow 1979, 117-203.
54   Ibid., 120.

all-controlling, wise and unwavering adult. Although authors of the earlier stories about the Siege allocated the role of an educator to conscientious factory workers and demanding but courageous NKVD officers, those who chose to write about wartime Leningrad in the 1970s-90s portrayed the Siege protectors and caretakers of the young as caring and warm. Thus, children's literature about the Siege contributed to the recognition of one of the most tragic failures of the Soviet state – the failure to protect and control the city during the war. Krestinskij's, Jakovlev's, and Mikson's narratives are ambiguous in this respect. They give an impression of a reality in which this political situation is manageable. Their adult protagonists are physically weak and traumatized, but they take leadership in managing life in the besieged Leningrad as well as in sustaining the lives of their children.

5 Initiation by Siege: Children on Duty

The tragic toll of the Siege comprised deaths that were caused by many kinds of horrors, from starvation, disease and workplace injuries to cannibalism. Ideologically conditioned to focus on the heroic aspects of the Soviet war experience, Soviet writers could not fully describe the everyday activities of Leningrad's population, including family routines and social rituals leading to survival.[55] This is why Siege narratives often depicted Leningraders' existence during the war as a darker version of an ordinary Soviet man's daily life, albeit more difficult and unfolding under severe circumstances. Descriptions of Soviet children's mundane tasks, including such social duties as studying, assisting adults in their work, and participating in pioneer meetings was a necessary element of any Socialist Realist literary work for younger audiences; they remained an essential component of Siege fiction as well. According to many children's novellas and short stories, including those published in war-time *Костер*, Leningrad children were able to lead normal lives like their peers in other cities. Enrolled in schools, they seemed to strive to earn highest grades. They also helped their parents to grow vegetables in makeshift street gardens and built defense structures on the outskirts of the city. Readers were usually

---

55   There are many scholarly works that explore the issue of censorship during and after the Siege. See, for example, Sergej Jarov, *Блокадная этика. Представления о морали в Ленинграде в 1941-1942 годах*, St. Petersburg 2011; Jarov, *Повседневная жизнь блокадного Ленинграда*, Moscow 2013; Arlen Bljum, *Как это делалось в Ленинграде. Цензура в годы оттепели, застоя и перестройки, 1953-1991*, St. Petersburg 2005; Andrej Dzeniskevich, *Блокада и политика. Оборона Ленинграда в политической коньюнктуре*, St. Petersburg 1998.

spared details of the city's mortality rates; neither were they given accounts of depression, emotional numbness, and other mental conditions afflicting students who faced severe food deprivation. One example of a Siege teenager's more or less normal daily routine can be found in "На обороне города" ("Defending the City"), a sketch published in the July-August issue of *Костер* for 1942. Its author tells the story of Vasja Boldenkov, a Leningrad trade school student learning to be an engine driver. Not only does Vasja remain at the top of his class academically, but he also helps adults to organize a group of students – all of them highly capable factory workers – and engage them in productive activities. Two other adolescents featured in "На обороне города" are Nadja Solovjeva and Tamara Kireeva. The girls are awarded honorary diplomas for their arduous work on the construction projects related to the defense of the city. Tamara is particularly productive: her brigade manages to build twice as many shelters as it had been assigned – a feat almost unimaginable for starving women.[56]

Another essay in *Костер* tells of two sisters, one of whom is twelve and another fourteen years old. The girls lost their mother during the Siege, and their father is fighting at the front. In the spring of 1942, they join a camp where children grow vegetables for the city. Though their work is hard (the younger sister starts her summer with complaints and whining), the siblings manage to succeed in collective farming: eventually, their pictures are posted on a local billboard for honorable workers. In the fall of 1942, the two sisters return to school where they earn excellent grades, with the youngest becoming an independent and conscientious student. The author of the essay surmises that the girls' father, still on military duty, would be proud of his daughters: "These two sisters are real Leningrad girls. Not only because they live in Leningrad, attend a Leningrad school, and have a father who is fighting on the Leningrad front, but also because they behave as young pioneers from Leningrad really should."[57]

The author ignores the actual plight of young people in Leningrad during the Siege to construct a heroic narrative in which children lead exemplary lives and manage to be useful to adults. Although he does not compare the girls' activities to the exploits of war-time pioneer heroes (the latter will soon become part of a specific genre, with its own set of narrative strategies and ideological clichés), he nevertheless describes the children's routine as "heroic." Growing vegetables, for example, exemplifies their fulfillment of social duty. All other components of this Siege story, such as the sisters' overall virtuousness and

---

56 "На обороне города," in *Костер* 7-8 (1942), 26.
57 "Сестры из Ленинграда" ("Sisters from Leningrad"), in *Костер* 9-10 (1942), 3.

their ability to improve morally, are also in strict alignment with the Socialist Realist norms of a children's war narrative. The dehumanizing toll of hunger and cold notwithstanding, these intrinsically good Soviet girls are celebrated for their fulfilling a Soviet citizen's duty to the state and receiving approval from adults, in this case an exemplary father who is fighting the enemy at the front.

We see similar dynamics in Vsevolod Vishnevskij's "Комсомольцы Ленинграда" ("The Leningrad Komsomol"), a story written and published in 1943, the second year of the Siege. A celebrated playwright, Vishnevskij writes about Leningrad school students who are also members of the Young Communist League (Komsomol). His protagonists explore the city's roofs and attics searching for Nazi spies, chop and store wood to feed makeshift stoves during the winter, grow vegetables, stuff envelopes for the postal service, and break into empty apartments looking for abandoned children.[58] Although the majority of Siege children and youth were actually the most deprived and, therefore, most quickly incapacitated group of Leningrad citizens, literary works and media reports geared towards young readers portrayed them as energetically engaged in the physical activities which only a healthy, well-nourished person could accomplish.[59]

In general, children's literature about the Siege mythologized the Soviet youth's resilience and willpower. Although some of the Siege narratives from the mid-1940s, including the *Костер* stories quoted here, portrayed young Leningraders as vulnerable and in greater need of emotional and social support, children's fiction written after World War II notably intensified the pitch of the heroic. Portrayed in retrospect, child protagonists of Siege literature would become more and more capable and proactive. They helped adults not only by growing cabbages or performing postal duties, but also by actually committing acts of valor, thus turning from emaciated "goners" into full-blown Socialist Realist heroes. For example, in Matveev's novel *Зеленые цепочки* and its sequels, adolescents fight criminals and obstruct the enemy-initiated sabotage on par with their mentors from the Leningrad Secret Police. Similarly, Jurka, the protagonist of Pomozov's *Блокадная юность*, manages to put out the burning incendiary bombs while also working after hours at a local factory, rescuing his dying friends, and exposing an enemy secret agent.[60] This increased emphasis on productive labor and social duty in post-war Siege narratives for children can be explained by the gradual emergence of the war

---

58   Vsevolod Vishnevskij, "Комсомольцы Ленинграда," in *Костер* 7 (1943), 2-3.
59   See *Жизнь и смерть в блокадном Ленинграде. Историко-медицинский аспект*, St. Petersburg 2001.
60   Jurij Pomozov, *Блокадная юность*, Leningrad 1989.

fiction canon. As Svetlana Maslinskaya writes in this volume, the paradigm of heroic childhood evolved over the course of several decades. In war narratives, it included such protagonists' exploits as direct combat with the enemy and self-sacrifice for the sake of collective victory over fascism. By the beginning of the 1950s, Soviet children's agency in fighting the invaders and their brave attitude in the face of all kinds of hardship became the benchmark features of Soviet war fiction for young readers.[61]

It must be noted that authors of Siege narratives consistently allocated different social roles – and, therefore, implied different levels of agency in committing a heroic act – to boys and girls. More often than not, male protagonists would be portrayed as putting out bombs on the rooftops of the city's buildings or working at factories. Girls' duty was to take care of younger children, tidy up, and assist the weak and the ailing in shelters and hospitals. These gender-specific roles almost never changed. Even if a female protagonist appeared to have a somewhat "confused" gender identity – as it happened in *Кирюшка*, with its soccer-playing heroine Kira who, before the war started, had been the leader of an all-boys gang – the fictional tomboy was transformed during the Siege. Subdued and made "normal" by her dramatic experience in the dark, cold, and food-deprived city, she was now taking part in such exclusively "girlish" activities as cleaning bomb shelters and taking care of orphaned babies. For Kirjushka, the Siege became not only a test of her perseverance and survival skills, but also a way to reclaim her femininity. No longer a genderless and obnoxious child, she evolved into a well-rounded, conventional girl-hero.[62] Kira's example demonstrates that Soviet children's authors eventually chose to show the Siege as a rite of passage. Although very painful, it was an initiation which allowed young protagonists to transition from not being socially conscious, sometimes described as ambivalence towards one's identity or moral stance, to being a responsible, fully politically conscious individual and a loyal Soviet subject.

6   Just Like the Grown-Ups: Children's Experience of the Siege in Soviet Fiction for Adult Audiences

Alongside didactic depictions of Siege children as role models for young readers, Soviet war fiction written for adult audiences was also prone to peculiar

---

61   Vladimir Selivanov, *Стояли, как солдаты: блокада, дети, Ленинград*, St. Petersburg 2002; Spartak Chernik, *Советская школа в годы Великой отечественной войны*, Moscow 1975.
62   Karaseva, *Кирюшка*, 18.

aberrations in portraying young Leningraders during the war. More often than not, narratives about the Siege aimed to provide grown-ups with a neatly censored and thus ideologically acceptable version of the Soviet participation in World War II. That said, like works of children's literature, "adult" literature revolving around the figure of a suffering – or valiant and resilient – Siege child also deviated in important ways from the poetic norms and psychological clichés typical of the Socialist Realist canon.

Two examples of fictional texts for adults analyzed here were published two and three decades after the end of the war. In fact, they appeared in print well after the "Thaw," i.e. when many other works of Soviet Siege literature had already found a readership and even gained significant popularity. Leonid Panteleev's *Живые памятники* (*Living Monuments*, 1966) included a series of notebook entries and a cycle of short stories; *Блокадная книга* (*The Blockade Book*), which Ales' Adamovich wrote in collaboration with Daniil Granin, was published in instalments between 1977 and 1981. Both books offer refreshingly candid, edifying, and often graphic accounts of the Siege. And yet, their authors mitigated the candor and sincerity of their narratives by adding explanatory comments that guided their readers towards politically correct interpretations of the Siege trauma.

Panteleev depicted dystrophy, the starvation disease, in a graphic way, shattering whatever illusions his readers may have had previously about the severity of the Siege experience. He also discussed the "black market," an institution of great importance for Siege survivors, since it was there that food items could be traded illegally for rare objects such as artwork and antique books or services, and commented on the mainstream Soviet media's overwhelming silence about the plight of Leningraders. Similarly, Adamovich and Granin deliberated the horrific living conditions in the besieged city and the psychological and emotional toll they took on its citizens.

Emblematic of these authors' subversive narrative strategies are their depictions of two adolescents, Volodja in *Живые памятники* and Jura Rjabinkin in *Блокадная книга*. Since the border between Soviet children's and adult fiction was not clearly marked, one could imagine children and adolescents reading and emotionally reacting to Panteleev, Adamovich, and Granin's stories about their peers. Contemplating young readers' probable access to these narratives is especially significant in view of the books' lack of coherent didactic patterns, which, as has already been shown, proliferated in the Soviet Siege literature for children.

Leonid Panteleev was a celebrated Soviet children's writer and a bestselling author of *Республика Шкид* (1930), a semi-autobiographical novel about a school for juvenile delinquents "adopted" and "reformed" by the Bolshevik state after the revolution. In the 1930s, Panteleev wrote a variety of short stories for and about children. It is not surprising that when documenting his Siege experience, Panteleev continued to be singularly interested in the youngest of Leningraders – the readers of his work, but also its subjects: they constantly figure in his short stories, essays, and diary entries. In fact, to explain his emphasis on the Siege childhood, Panteleev makes a somewhat paradoxical assumption, drawing a parallel between the most famous work of classical Greek literature and the war stories that emerged from the besieged Leningrad:

> It is good that there are children in the besieged city! [...] By their very presence they highlight the great meaning of our struggle. It is akin to Homer's *Iliad*, where in the episode of Hector's farewell, the appearance of a child turns the fight against the Trojans near the city walls into a deep and troubling human tragedy.[63]

By candidly portraying children of the Siege and telling their stories, Panteleev aims to elucidate the dreadful suffering in Leningrad during the war and bring it closer to his reader. For example, in a diary entry entitled "Близнецы" ("The Twins"), he describes an impossible "Sophie's choice" of a Siege mother who has to decide which of her children is to be saved from starvation and which will perish.[64] In another sketch, "Кожаные перчатки" ("The Leather Gloves"), a father fighting at the front receives a letter from his children in which they apologize for boiling and eating his gloves when hunger became unbearable.[65]

In the short story "Живые памятники" ("Living Monuments"), Panteleev seems to follow the conventions of a Soviet war narrative when describing the transformation of Volodja, a teenager who turns from a desperate emaciated "блокадник" ("victim of the blockade") into an athlete ably serving his Motherland. As in his other work, here Panteleev ostensibly attempts to stay within the bounds of Socialist Realist fiction. Not only does his protagonist evolve into a dutiful Soviet citizen, but he does so thanks to a mentor who inspires Volodja's ideological "improvement." This reverence to the canon is illusory, however, for "Живые памятники" also contains graphic descriptions of the Siege, which one can barely find in other literary works about it written either for children or for adults. In one of the story's subchapters, "Человек умирает" ("Man is Dying"), Panteleev shows Volodja on the verge of agony: the boy is locked in an apartment full of dead people, all of whom are his family

---

63 Panteleev, "Дети" ("Children"), in *Живые памятники*, Leningrad 1966, 179.
64 Panteleev, "Близнецы," in *Живые памятники*, 186-187.
65 Panteleev, "Кожаные перчатки," in *Живые памятники*, 336-337.

members. Even more unusual is the open-endedness of this stirring short narrative. The author refuses to tell his readers what happened to Volodja, leaving open the possibility of his dying or getting sucked into the brutal war vortex.[66] Panteleev's focus on human suffering as well as the ambiguity of his story's ending makes "Живые памятники" stand apart from other war narratives for children. It is an ambiguous work that demonstrates its author's willingness to compromise the accepted literary approach, rather than his conscience. In "Живые памятники," Panteleev manages to shed light on the then littleknown reality of the Siege and to show Leningraders' tragic experience, while mostly remaining within the poetic and structural parameters expected of him as a Soviet author.

Jura Rjabinkin's diary in *Блокадная книга* is even more ambivalent. Authentic and heart-rending, it is one of the many texts and interviews that the author-editors accumulated during their work on preserving the memory of the Siege. Adamovich and Granin chose to accompany the publication of the diary, written by a Leningrad schoolboy and discovered only after the Siege, with voluminous and, in places, heavy-handed commentary. It is their writing, overlaid with Jura's horrific story of struggle for life and his ultimate failure to survive, which creates a stark dissonance between the conventions of a war narrative and a first-person account of the Siege. The purpose of the commentary is to guide readers, telling them what Jura "actually" felt and elucidating how others should react to his suffering. But while Adamovich and Granin pivot their interpretation around the word "борьба" ("struggle"), thus framing Jura's experience as a typical Socialist Realist masterplot – one's fight with deprivation and death – the doomed child speaking about his demise resists being turned into yet another Soviet hero. When Jura writes about his frostbitten hands and lists all the people he knew who died of starvation, his voice, the voice of a witness, undermines Adamovich and Granin's "anesthetic," teleological efforts.[67]

Both Panteleev and the authors of *Блокадная книга* chose adolescents as heroes and narrators of their Siege stories, thus creating a hybrid, in-between mode of presenting the history of the Siege to their readers. By making sure that their narrative's dominant voice belongs to a person oscillating between childhood and adulthood, and by interspersing their stories with Socialist Realist elements while also breaking the rules of the canon, they sought and

---

66 Panteleev, "Живые памятники," in *Живые памятники*, 133-134.
67 Ales' Adamovich, Daniil Granin, *Блокадная книга*, Leningrad 1984, 378-383, 390-393, 397, 431-439, 446-450, 453-460.

achieved a compromise between conventional – and thus publishable – war fiction and the work testifying to the actual experience of the Siege. The borderline figure of a "child-adult" allowed them to show the Siege from the perspective of its victim, rather than of its hero. While in Soviet war fiction, young individuals habitually perform a dual role of stoic heirs to the staunch, politically motivated adults, as well as that of the victims of Nazi atrocities, they could be allowed a deeper level of honesty in the Siege literature. Their testimonies were also more penetrating. Coming from children and adolescents, they jolted the audiences whose perception of the war had already been numbed by the carefully crafted, ideologically polished, heavily censored Soviet war literature. Therefore, the "Siege child," or, rather, "child-adult" trope functioned in the texts as a loophole: it allowed authors to widen the possibilities of accuracy and psychological verity of their Siege discourses. And while Panteleev, Adamovich, and Granin approached their tasks with a certain reserve, they still managed to challenge the heroic model of Siege behavior by depicting the reality of the Siege as unprecedented horror.[68] This, predictably, caused problems with publication: *Блокадная книга* was banned by the angered city government and its authors had to wait years before it could appear in an unabridged version.

7   Can Siege Narratives Have Happy Endings?

As many other traumatic events in twentieth-century Soviet history, such as the Civil War of the 1920s and the Great Terror of the late 1930s, the Siege left a scar on Russian cultural memory and historical imagination. Paradoxically, most Siege stories for children ended on a happy note. Not only did their protagonists survive the ordeal, but they also managed to accomplish difficult social tasks, as if undergoing a particularly dreadful initiation ritual. Having thus matured both psychologically and politically, these child-heroes were expected to become role models for their readers. On those rare occasions when protagonists died, children's authors implied their living on in posterity. Thus, in Panteleev's "На кладбище" ("At the Cemetery"), the handwritten epitaph to a thirteen-year-old boy who died during the Siege is cited alongside the inscription made on a gravestone of a hero of Sebastopol, Captain

---

68   *Блокадная книга* was initially published with significant cuts in the journal *Новый мир* (1977); its fuller version came out in 1984. See: Daniil Granin, "О блокаде" ("About the Siege"), in *Тайный знак Петербурга*, St. Petersburg 2000, 139-143.

of Cavalry Suchovcev. Both deserve commemoration, Panteleev suggests, for their exploits are compatible and their heroism incontestable.[69] Other authors of children's Siege narratives also insisted that their protagonists' contribution to the Soviet victory over fascism and thus, their names, images, habits, and aspirations continued to live on in the hearts of other youngsters – the young readers who were now enjoying their peaceful lives in the city.

In this context, it is important to bear in mind the tragic end of Tanja Savicheva, the Siege's most celebrated heroine. Paradoxically, her story, monumentalized in Siege children's literature, sounds optimistic. Every author writing about Tanja placed an emphasis on the girl's courage, rather than on her losses, suffering, and death. Moreover, Tanja's biographers did not elaborate on what her courage actually consisted of or how she carried out her "struggle." They either mythologized Tanja's experience or filled in the gaps in her biography with fantastic inventions. For example, Jakovlev wove together into a single narrative Tanja Savicheva's original story and a story about her post-Siege namesake he invented. The "other Tanja" continued the legacy of the Siege child by copying her diary on concrete, with her handwriting adding a personal touch to the new monument to all Siege children. The idea of child's scribbles on the monument was conceived by Siege veterans who insisted that the next-generation Tanja write the diary entries out by hand, thus symbolically replacing the perished girl.[70]

What mattered most for Soviet children's literature about the Siege was not the tragic interruption of people's lives, but the assertion of their continuation in the timeless realm of Soviet history. Ideologically biased, Soviet authors' representation of the Siege was two-sided. On the one hand, their stories and novels portrayed the Siege as a litmus test of children's ability to reveal and model Soviet virtues, such as resilience in the face of hardship and unwavering dedication to the Soviet case. On the other hand, literary works for young readers presented the Siege as a tragedy in which children played the role of holy innocents, or, rather, sacrificial victims whose very suffering called for vengeance and embodied the heavy "price" the Soviet people had to pay for their victory. This uneasy duality bestowed the Siege with a kind of sacredness which even young persons could understand. Reading about it in a time of peace, they could easily draw a parallel between themselves and the Siege children – those little citizens who may have not committed heroic acts, but of whom heroism, loyalty, and self-sacrifice were nevertheless expected.

---

69   Panteleev, "На кладбище" ("At the Cemetery"), in *Живые памятники*, 156.
70   Jakovlev, *Девочки с Васильевского острова*, Moscow 1978.

Works Cited

Primary Sources

Adamovich, Ales', and Daniil Granin. *Блокадная книга*. Leningrad 1984.

Aljanskij, Jurij. "Танец в огне," in *Дети военной поры*. Moscow 1984, 148-152.

Berggolc, Ol'ga. "Второй разговор с соседкой," in *Избранное*. Leningrad 1973, 67.

Berggolc, Ol'ga. "Путь к зрелости," in *Литературная газета*, May 26, 1946, 2.

Boronina, Ekaterina. "Вестник осажденного города," in *Костер* 7-8 (1942), 20.

Boronina, Ekaterina. "Горячее сердце," in *Костер* 9 (1941), 36-38.

Boronina, Ekaterina. "Мальчик из Севастополя," in *Костер* 7-8 (1942), 2-4.

Brandt, Lev. "Коля Бубликов," in *Костер* 9 (1941), 34-36.

Druzhinin, Vladimir. "Мировой бригадир," in *Костер* 11-12 (1942), 16-17.

Fadeev, Aleksandr. "Дети осажденного Ленинграда," in *От Советского Информбюро, 1941-1945*, Vol. 2. Moscow 1982, 7.

Gajdar, Arkadij. *Военная тайна*. Moscow 1935.

German, Jurij. *Вот как это было*. Moscow 1985.

Jakovlev, Jurij. "Мистерия. Страсти по четырем девочкам," in Jakovlev, *Избранное*. Moscow 1992.

Jakovlev, Jurij. *Девочки с Васильевского острова*. Moscow 1978.

Jakovlev, Jurij. "Балерина политотдела", in *Жить нам суждено*. Moscow 1979, 117-203.

Karaseva, Vera. *Кирюшка*. Kiev 1965.

Kataev, Valentin. *Белеет парус одинокий*. Moscow 1936.

Kaverin, Veniamin. *Два капитана*. Moscow 1940.

Krestinskij, Aleksandr. "А потом началась война," in *Мальчики из блокады. Рассказы и повесть*. Leningrad 1983, 70-142.

Krestinskij, Aleksandr. "Гном," in *Мальчики из блокады. Рассказы и повесть*. Leningrad 1983, 40-54.

Kuznetsova, Ol'ga. "Страх," in *Костер* 5-6 (1942), 2.

Markova, Lilija. "Блокадная хроника Тани Савичевой," in *Петербургская семья: еженедельная интернет газета* (2009) ⟨http://www.spb-family.ru/history/history_15.html⟩ (Accessed November 12, 2017).

Marshak, Samuil. "Ленинграду – в день Красной Армии," in *Костер* 2 (1943), 1.

Matveev, German. *Зеленые цепочки*. Moscow 1945.

Matveev, German. *Тайная схватка*. Moscow 1948.

Matveev, German. *Тарантул*. Moscow 1957.

Mikson, Ilja. *Жила, была… Историческое повествование*. Leningrad 1991.

Morozov, Vjacheslav. *Им было по четырнадцать: О Марате Казее, Володе Щербачевиче*. Minsk 1969.

Nabatov, Grigorij. *Юные подпольщики*. Moscow 1963.

Panova, Vera. *Наши дети. Рассказы, повести и пьеса*. Leningrad 1973.

Panova, Vera. "Сергей Иванович и Таня," in *Наши дети: Рассказы, повести и пьеса*. Moscow 1973.

Panteleev, Leonid. *Живые памятники*. Leningrad 1966.

Panteleev, Leonid. "Честное слово," in *Костер* 6 (1941), 1-3.

Piven', Zoja. *Навечно в памяти народной: Записки работника музея Истории Ленинграда*. Leningrad 1984.

Pomozov, Jurij. *Блокадная юность*. Leningrad 1989.

Razumovskij, Lev. "Дети блокады. Документальная повесть," in *Нева* 1 (1999), 4-68.

Shestinskij, Oleg. *Ангельское воинство. Рассказы*, in *Нева* 1 (1999), 69-87.

Shishova, Zinaida. "Блокада," in *Блокада*. Leningrad 1943, 6.

Smirnov, S. "Таня Савичева," in *Венок славы. Антология художественных произведений о Великой Отечественной войне*, Vol. 3, *Подвиг Ленинграда*. Moscow 1983, 297-300.

Smirnov-Ochtin, Igor'. "Школа судей," in *Нева* 1(1999), 88-101.

Uspenskij, Lev. "Птичка в клетке," in *Дети военной поры*. Moscow 1984, 93-147.

Vishnevskij, Vsevolod. "Комсомольцы Ленинграда," in *Костер* 7 (1943), 2-3.

Vygovskij, Vladimir. *Огонь юного сердца*. Moscow 1960.

Zharikov, Andrej. *Подвиги юных: Рассказы и очерки*. Moscow 1960.

"На обороне города," in *Костер* 7-8 (1942), 26.

"Сестры из Ленинграда," in *Костер* 9-10 (1942), 3.

Солдатский подвиг. Рассказы. Moscow 1968.

Secondary Sources

Bljum, Arlen. *Как это делалось в Ленинграде. Цензура в годы оттепели, застоя и перестройки, 1953-1991*. St. Petersburg 2005.

Bocharov, Anatolij. *Человек и война. Идеи социалистического реализма в послевоенной прозе о войне*. Moscow 1973.

Brintlinger, Angela. *Chapaev and His Comrades: War and the Russian Literary Hero Across the Twentieth Century*. Boston 2012.

Chalmaev, Viktor. *На войне остаться человеком. Фронтовые страницы русской прозы 1960-1990 годов*. Moscow 1998.

Chashchina, Ljudmila. "Высказывания погибших. Литературная хроника послевоенных лет с комментариями," in *Нева* 10 (1990), 182-188.

Chernik, Spartak. *Советская школа в годы Великой отечественной войны*. Moscow 1975.

Clark, Katerina. *The Soviet Novel: History as Ritual*. Bloomington and Indianapolis 2000.

Dzeniskevich, Andrej. *Блокада и политика. Оборона Ленинграда в политической коньюнктуре*. St. Petersburg 1998.

Ginzburg, Lydia. *Blockade Diary*. London 1996.

Granin, Daniil. "О блокаде," in *Тайный знак Петербурга*. St. Petersburg 2000, 139-143.

Heberer, Patricia. *Children during the Holocaust*. Lanham, MD 2011.

Hodgson, Katherine. "The Soviet War," in Marina Mackay, ed., *The Cambridge Companion to the Literature of World War II*. Cambridge and London 2009, 111-123.

Jarov, Sergej. *Блокадная этика. Представления о морали в Ленинграде в 1941-1942 годах*. St. Petersburg 2011.

Jarov, Sergej. *Повседневная жизнь блокадного Ленинграда*. Moscow 2013.

Nekrich, Aleksandr. *1941. 22 июня*. Moscow 1995.

Piper, Don. "Soviet Union" in *The Second World War in Fiction*. Eds., Holger Klein, John Flower and Eric Homberger. London 1984.

Rambow, Aileen G. "The Siege of Leningrad: Wartime Literature and Ideological Change," in Robert W. Thurston, Bernd Bonwetsch, eds. *The People's War: Responses to World War II in the Soviet Union*. Urbana 2000.

Selivanov, Vladimir. *Стояли, как солдаты: блокада, дети, Ленинград*. St. Petersburg 2002.

Жизнь и смерть в блокадном Ленинграде. Историко-медицинский аспект. St. Petersburg 2001.

PART 3

*New Approaches to the Avant-Garde:
Reconstructing the Canon*

∴

CHAPTER 9

Children's Poetry and Translation in the Soviet Era: Strategies of Rewriting, Transformation and Adaptation

Maria Khotimsky

1   Introduction

Nursery rhymes, lullabies, and poems one learns as a child shape our matrix of individual linguistic development. Their sounds and rhymes stay with us for years. Initially, they help us acquire speech skills and feel the poetry of our native language, especially because younger children hear, rather than read poems and stories.[1] Later, these texts become life-long sources of metaphors, a shared repository of memories and allusions. Such a combination of unique structural features and deep connections with cultural and generational contexts make children's poetry a particularly difficult challenge for translators. Contemporary researchers of children's literature point to several factors that influence its complexity. As Gillian Lathey observes, "one inescapable fact that governs the process of writing and translating for children is the unequal relationship between the adult writer or translator and the child audience. It is adults who decide the very extent and boundaries of childhood."[2] In the realm of poetry, it is also adult authors who determine the nature of the poetic and choose themes and styles appropriate for children. Such a special position of children's literature between artistic and pedagogical realms accounts for the phenomenon of "dual address," with texts being directed simultaneously at child and adult audiences.[3] This aspect of children's literature is particularly important during the times of social change when, to quote Emer O'Sullivan,

---

1 Gillian Lathey, "The Translation of Literature for Children," in Kirsten Malmkjaer and Kevin Winde, eds., *The Oxford Handbook of Translation Studies*, Oxford 2011, 206.
2 Gillian Lathey, "Introduction," in Gillian Lathey, ed., *The Translation of Children's Literature. A Reader*, Clevedon 2006, 4-5.
3 For more on "dual address" and ambivalent status of children's literature see Zohar Shavit, "Translation of Children's Literature as a Function of Its Position in the Literary Polysystem," in *Poetics Today* 2:4 (1981), 171-179; and Shavit, "The Ambivalent Status of Texts: The Case of Children's Literature," in *Poetics Today* 1:3 (1980), Special Issue: *Narratology I: Poetics of Fiction*, 75-86.

"there are new values to be conveyed or old ones to be defended."[4] It is the juncture of historical, ideological, and aesthetic questions that makes Soviet-era translations of children's literature, and poetry in particular, an important case study of the methodological boundary beween translation and children's literature, especially in the context of rapid social and cultural transition.

In the years following the 1917 Revolution, particular attention was given to pedagogical practices as instrumental for building a new society. Many recent studies explore the role of childhood in Soviet cultural history,[5] as well as significant changes in children's literature after the Revolution.[6] However, most authors writing about Soviet artistic production for children do not pay special attention to the area of literary translation. Indeed, poetry translation may appear small on the scale of other cultural phenomena, but, as I would like to argue, investigating this field provides a unique perspective on the complex processes that have shaped both translation and children's literature during the Soviet time.

Because this particular topic has not yet been treated in detail (apart from Michail Jasnov's 2004/2015 overview article on the history of translation in children's poetry), the primary goal of my chapter is to outline the most important names and developments in translation of poetry for children focusing on texts and authors that have made a lasting impact on the Soviet culture of childhood.[7] Drawing on the methodology of children's literature and translation studies, I will ponder creative choices made by Soviet children's authors and translators, and the expression of their artistic individuality in the context of such politically determined literary institutions as censorship, restrictive editorial policies, and state-controlled publishing. Marina Balina has deftly defined this paradox: "The contemporary researcher of Soviet children's

---

4   Emer O'Sullivan, *Comparative Children's Literature*, New York 2005, 62.
5   Lisa Kirschenbaum, *Small Comrades: Revolutionizing Childhood in Soviet Russia, 1917-1931*, New York 2001; Catriona Kelly, *Children's World: Growing up in Russia, 1890-1991*, New Haven and London 2007.
6   Elena Sokol, *Russian Poetry for Children*, Knoxville 1984; Ben Hellman, *Fairy Tales and True Stories: The History of Russian Literature for Children and Young People (1574-2010)*, Boston 2013; Marina Balina, and Valerij Vjugin, eds., *"Убить Чарскую..." Парадоксы советской литературы для детей, 1920-е – 1930-е гг*, St. Petersburg 2013; Judith Inggs, "Translation and Transformation: English Language Children's Literature in Soviet (Russian) Guise," in *International Research in Children's Literature* 8:1 (2015), 1-16.
7   Michail Jasnov, "От Робина-Бобина до малыша Русселя," in *Дружба народов* 12 (2004), ⟨http://magazines.russ.ru/druzhba/2004/12/ias12.html⟩ (Accessed October 20, 2017). The article is also included in Jasnov's monograph *Путешествие в Чудетство. Книга о детях, детской поэзии и детских поэтах*, St. Petersburg 2015.

literature unwittingly finds himself between Scylla and Charybdis, while trying to simultaneously explore the question of ideological dependence of children's literature and its notorious freedom."[8] In order to explain this peculiar dynamic relationship, I will follow Balina's lead in tracing the institutional and aesthetic changes that took place in the fields of literary translation and children's literature immediately following the Revolution. Both fields witnessed the simultaneous growth of ideological control as well as an influx of new artistic voices – mainly, authors who could not publish their own works due to censorship. These developments, in turn, created rich grounds for multiple address and hidden communication with readers. As I will try to show, the dynamic balance between ideological control and potential for self-expression via the translated text defined some of the key trends both in the area of literary translation and in writing for children.

While a detailed history of poetic translation within Soviet children's literature by far exceeds the scope of this chapter, I will focus on some key names and approaches to translating poetry for children that are characteristic of different time periods within the Soviet era and that represent distinct models of artistic adaptation of verse – both in content and form. The first section of this chapter addresses Kornej Chukovskij's and Samuil Marshak's translations as part of their foundational role in establishing new directions in poetry and works of translation for children in the 1920s. The second section turns to the 1930s through the 1950s, focusing on authors of both children's and adult literature (such as Daniil Charms) as well as on various modes of textual adaptation, particularly in translations by Charms and Sergej Michalkov. In the final section, I discuss developments in the translation of poetry of the "Thaw" era, with Boris Zachoder's and Genrich Sapgir's translations as the primary case studies.

2 Translating Children's Poetry in the 1920s

The cultural upheaval of the post-revolutionary years had an immediate effect on children's literature. Broader initiatives of the early Soviet literacy campaign encompassed significant investments in this sphere, so that several institutions, such as the World Literature publishing house, Raduga, Detskaja

---

8 Marina Balina, "Советская детская литература: несколько слов о предмете исследования," in M. Balina and V. Vjugin, eds., *"Убить Чарскую": Парадоксы советской литературы для детей. 1920-е–1930-е*, St. Petersburg 2013, 8. Unless indicated otherwise, translations from the Russian are mine – MK.

Literatura and Detgiz (a branch of the State Publishing House devoted to children's literature) were able to initiate and support editions of literature for children. Innovative book production flourished thanks to many Avant-Garde artists who found employment in illustrating children's books.[9] This time is often defined as a founding moment in children's poetry in general, and translations for younger audience in particular, with Marshak and Chukovskij pioneering this work. Efim Etkind suggests that "a tradition of poetic translation for children was created only by Soviet-era authors," – a statement that elucidates why, although translation had long nourished Russian poetic tradition, it didn't play a significant role in the realm of children's literature until after the Revolution.[10] Following Etkind, Michail Jasnov describes the pivotal changes that resulted in a more central position of translation and children's literature within the Soviet literary field:

> A social, aesthetic, and linguistic revolution was necessary in order to move translation from a marginal position in literature toward its center. One needed, unfortunately, the advent of Soviet power with all the ideological restrictions to push the best children's and adult poets toward translation and set its hidden forces in powerful motion.[11]

Jasnov offers a succinct summary of various socio-cultural processes that have shaped the fields of children's literature and translation. Such practices as professionalization of translation and the growing ideological control over its scope and methods determined new directions in theory and practice of literary translation and in children's literature.[12] Both fields benefitted from the significant state investment into developing new cultural policies and shaping new models of readership and authorship.[13] At the same time, the position

---

9   See Evgeny Steiner's analysis of this phenomenon in *Stories for Little Comrades: Revolutionary Artists and the Making of Early Soviet Children's Books*, trans. Jane Ann Miller. Seattle 1999.

10 Efim Etkind, "Для маленьких читателей," in *Поэзия и перевод*, Moscow 1963, 345.

11 Jasnov, "От Робина-Бобина."

12 On censorship in translation, see Samantha Sherry, *Discourses of Regulation and Resistance. Censoring Translation in the Stalin and Khrushchev Era Soviet Union*, Edinburgh 2015; Susanna Witt, "Arts of Accommodation: The First All-Union Conference of Translators, Moscow, 1936, and the Ideologization of Norms," in Leon Burnett and Emily Lygo, eds., *The Art of Accommodation: Literary Translation in Russia*, Bern 2013, 141-184. On the ideology's impact on translation, see Witt, "The Shorthand of Empire: Podstrochnik Practices and the Making of Soviet Literature," in *Ab Imperio* 3 (2013), 155-190.

13 Brian James Baer, *Translation and the Making of Russian Literature*, New York 2016.

of children's literature and translation as an intellectual "niche" that allowed politically "suspect" writers and poets to support a living at the time when they could no longer publish their own works, resulted in the proliferation of new artistic voices in children's literature and translation. In addition, both fields offered rich grounds for critical debates, as the notions of Soviet children's literature and a "Soviet school of literary translation" were developed and contested.[14]

Exemplary in both fields is the figure of Kornej Chukovskij (1882-1969). Numerous scholars have noted his importance in establishing Soviet children's literature; likewise, his analysis of translation has drawn broad critical attention.[15] As I would like to suggest, Chukovskij's creative legacy also embodies the cross-influences between literary translation and children's literature. Chukovskij's work at the editorial offices of World Literature positioned him among the early theoreticians of translation who contributed to *Принципы художественного перевода* (*Principles of Artistic Translation*, 1919), a theoretical pamphlet released by the publishing house. His contribution discussed various stylistic aspects of prose translation, focusing on translators' choices in rendering the syntax, the style, and the imagery of the original work. Chukovskij's goals were mainly practical, as he sought to "improve the qualifications of translators who had not received appropriate training."[16] Later, he published expanded versions of his contribution, titled *Искусство перевода* (*The Art of Translation*) or *Высокое искусство* (*A High Art*) in subsequent editions. Several chapters of his book were devoted to poetic translation, including Marshak's nursery rhymes, to which I will turn later. Among Chukovskij's own translations addressed to children were Oscar Wilde's *The Happy Prince* (1918), Rudyard Kipling's stories (various editions, some in collaboration with Marshak), and Hugh Lofting's *Doctor Dolittle* (1925). The latter served as an inspiration for his fairytale in verse *Доктор Айболит* (*Doctor Ajbolit*, 1929).

Chukovskij's poems and translations were directly linked to his innovative ideas about children's linguistic sensibility. The boundary between his multiple activities – writer, translator, literary critic, and theoretician of children's

---

14 Susanna Witt, "Byron's 'Don Juan' in Russian and the 'Soviet School of Translation'" in *Translation and Interpreting Studies* 11:1 (2016), 23-43; Witt, "Arts of Accommodation: The First All-Union Conference of Translators, Moscow, 1936, and the Ideologization of Norms," in Leon Burnett and Emily Lygo, eds., *The Art of Accommodation: Literary Translation in Russia*, Bern 2013, 141-184.
15 On Chukovskij as a translator of poetry, see Barry Scherr, "Chukovsky's Whitmans," in *Russian Literature* 66 (1), 2009, 65-98.
16 Kornej Chukovskij and Andrej Fedorov, *Искусство перевода*, Leningrad 1930, 3.

literature – was fluid. In his book on children's language *От двух до пяти* (*From Two to Five*, 1933), Chukovskij catalogued various examples of children's linguistic ingenuity. He admired such aspects of children's speech as attention to sound and rhythm, experimentation and play, use of nonsense rhymes and unsettling of traditional linguistic categories and idioms (which he labeled "flip-floppers" – "перевертыши"). As Chukovskij suggests in "Заповеди для детских поэтов" ("Tenets for Children's Poets"), the concluding chapter of *От двух до пяти*, poets should learn from their young audience and incorporate word play into the structure and style of their texts.[17] In addition to this keen in-depth linguistic study of children's speech, it was Chukovskij's experience of translating nursery rhymes that contributed to his understanding of children's poetry.

Referring to his trip to England in 1912-1913, Chukovskij notes: "During my sojourn in England I literally fell in love with the ancient folk songs for children, the so-called nursery-rhymes. [...] The opulent fantasy of their daring fancifulness entranced me forever, and I studied their poetics and their ancient and modern history assiduously."[18] Chukovskij's translations of nursery rhymes share many features with his poetry for children. These include use of play, humor, and paradox, as well as appreciation of Russian folk imagery and rhythms (including trochee and accent verse). Consider his translation of this popular ditty:

> There was a crooked man, and he walked a crooked mile.
> He found a crooked sixpence upon a crooked stile.
> He bought a crooked cat, which caught a crooked mouse,
> And they all lived together in a little crooked house.[19]

Below are several stanzas of the Russian text of the poem, and, although the interlinear prose translation cannot fully convey all the shifts and creative additions to the text, it is also offered:

> Жил на свете человек,
> Скрюченные ножки,
> И гулял он целый век
> По скрюченной дорожке.

---

17 "A poet who writes for preschool-age children should treat almost each of his topics as a game." Chukovskij, *От двух до пяти*, Moscow 1955, 226.
18 Chukovskij, quoted in Sokol, *Russian Poetry for Children*, 4.
19 *The Little Mother Goose*, New York 1912, 72.

А за скрюченной рекой,
В скрюченном домишке
Жили летом и зимой
Скрюченные мышки.

[...]

А за скрюченным мостом
Скрюченная баба
По болоту босиком
Прыгала, как жаба.

И была в руке у ней
Скрюченная палка,
И летела вслед за ней
Скрюченная галка.[20]

Similar to the source text, the repetition of the passive participle "скрюченные / скрюченная" ("crooked") sets the rhythm of Chukovskij's translation. In Russian, however, the recurrence of this four-syllable word sounds even more absurd, for it mostly modifies disyllabic words. While the original text is compositionally enclosed (it focuses on the strange inhabitants of a "crooked little house"), Chukovskij's translation opens up the narrative space and sets the story in motion. Only "crooked little mice" inhabit his "crooked little house," while the poem's main protagonist is depicted as a life-long wanderer. Added rhyming pairs, such as "волки – елки" ("wolves – fir trees" not quoted above) and "баба – жаба" ("woman – toad"), invoke Chukovskij's own fairytales and poems for kids. The truly bizarre image of a "crooked woman" (denoted by the colloquial "баба") hopping in a bog while swaying a "crooked stick" in her hand conveys the notion of freedom and play that Chukovskij admired both in nursery rhymes and in laudable poetry for children. Moreover, a similar folk-sounding rhyme ("баба-жаба") reappears in Chukovskij's own fairytale in verse, *Федорино горе* (*Fedora's Sorrow*, 1926), as well as in his poem "Головастики" ("Tadpoles," 1929).

---

20 "Once upon a time, / There lived a man / With crooked little legs, / And all his life he walked / Down a crooked little path. // And behind a crooked river, / In a crooked little house / Little crooked mice / Lived in the summer and in the winter. // [...] And behind a crooked bridge / A crooked woman, / Like a toad, / Jumped around the bog, barefoot. // And in her hand she had / A crooked stick / And a crooked jackdaw / Was flying after her." Kornej Chukovskij, *Собрание сочинений*, Vol. 1, Moscow 2001, 162-163.

On a deeper level, substitutions that take place in translation reflect the linguistic and cognitive structures of children's language, as perceived by Chukovskij. As he observes in *От двух до пяти*, "A poet writing for preschool-age children should treat each of his topics as a game. A person who is unable to participate in play should not attempt to write children's verse."[21] Chukovskij insists that all children are inventors in language, and when writing for them, one should try to reproduce their whimsical sense of language and their worldview filled with fun and wonder. Here, we may note that the phenomenon of "unequal address" or "double address" (which, according to contemporary scholars, often plays a didactic role in establishing the boundaries of children's literature) becomes a vehicle for aesthetic and theoretical innovation.

Predictably, Chukovskij's understanding of children's linguistic freedom inadvertently went against ideologically conservative pedagogical concepts of his era. Although Chukovskij established innovative approaches in writing and translating for children and through his poems, fairytales in verse, and translations became popular with the audience, his status as a children's classic was contested from the late 1920s on for a variety of reasons, not the least of which was the regime's well-documented distrust of playfulness in both content and form of children's literature. Several campaigns against Chukovskij's approach to writing for the young – most notably the 1929 attack on him as an author of "harmful" verse corrupting the new generation of Soviet citizens – resulted in a derogatory term "Чуковщина," which literally meant "drivel written by Chukovskij."[22] And yet, despite the criticism of his poems and translations, the author and critic continued to advocate the notions of humor and word play in children's literature: "It's no small task to foster humor in a child. It is a precious quality that, as the child grows up, will increase his resilience against any adverse circumstances and will help him stay above petty and insignificant things."[23] Eventually, his notions of linguistic play and humor as manifestations of personal and aesthetic freedom set important trends for the development of Soviet children's poetry of the following decades.

Chukovskij's opinions on literary translation were contested less and therefore appeared to become influential more quickly. Along with Marshak, he contributed to the development of the Soviet school of poetry translation as

---

21 Chukovskij, *От двух до пяти*, 226.
22 The term "Чуковщина" was coined in 1909 by Lukjan Sil'nyj who did not approve of the author's methods of literary criticism. See Lukjan Sil'nyj "Что такое чуковщина?" in *Вестник литературы* 3 (March 1909), 78-80.
23 Chukovskij, *От двух до пяти*, 196.

a translator of English and American literature, an editor of translation, and the head of the English literature section of the World Literature publishing house in the 1920s. His theoretical contributions to translation thought were mainly prescriptive: they included criticism of translation examples, advice on stylistic decisions regarding translation, and a general call for professionalism and higher quality of poetic renderings of foreign texts. In *Искусство перевода*, Chukovskij often referred to Marshak's translations for adult and children's audiences as exemplary. He praised their poetic and stylistic consistency and extolled Marshak's ability to "conquer" foreign verse by finding a uniquely Russian poetic sound for it: "Somehow, it seems strange to call Marshak a translator. He is more like a conquistador, a conqueror of foreign poets who makes loyal Russians of them by the sheer force of his poetic talent."[24] Marshak himself took pride in the variety of works he had translated specifically for the reason outlined by Chukovskij: "To me personally it was always important – above all – to feel the musical structure of Burns, Shakespeare, Wordsworth, Keats, Kipling, Blake, and English nursery rhymes."[25] The list here is representative of the mission embraced by the two poet-translators: it combines works addressed both to children and adults and emphasizes the breadth of the new Soviet translation canon.

Marshak shared Chukovskij's dedication to the high new standard for poetry translation and for children's literature. Echoing Chukovskij's thoughts about the translators' challenges, he observed: "…children's books may and should be a matter of high art, and that should not allow any compromises due to the reader's age."[26] His vision of children's literature, however, is more reflective of Soviet ideology. Unlike Chukovskij, who came under increasing criticism for the absence of ideological "tendency" in his fairytales and poems and who continued to advance his innovative views on playfulness in children's poetry and language, Marshak chose to remain "ideologically correct" and adhere to the poetic and thematic clichés of mainstream Soviet literature.

Characteristically, it was Marshak, not Chukovskij, who addressed the needs of young readers in his speech at the First All-Union Congress of Soviet Writers in 1934. He emphasized the importance of "heroic examples" from contemporary life and criticized the absence of good literature for children in Russia before 1917. However, in his critique of pre-revolutionary children's poetry Mar-

---

24 Ibid.
25 Marshak, quoted in B.E. Galanov, et al., eds., *Я думал, я чувствовал, я жил. Воспоминания о С. Я. Маршаке*, Moscow 1971, 106.
26 Marshak, *Вслух про себя. Воспоминания*, Moscow 1975, 181.

shak did recognize the value of some of Chukovskij's ideas. He also appealed to European sources, thus linking the evolution of the Russian literary tradition of writing for children to translation as a borrowing from other cultures in both content and form:

> And the children needed action, needed song and dance-like rhythms, they needed humor. They found all of it in quick translations of *Struwwelpeter*, in funny but at times cruel books about Maks and Moric [...] by Wilhelm Busch, and in sloppily executed translations of wonderful British folk songs (Mother Goose).[27]

Even on the brink of the new Soviet literature that came to be dominated by Socialist Realism and strict ideological control, it is the style and the subject matter of European poetry for children that Marshak quoted as desirable but lacking in Russian poetic production for young audiences. He also referred sympathetically to Chukovskij's children's works, praising them as a synthesis between traditions of play found in European poetry and the stylistic richness of Russian poetic and folk tradition.

Marshak's own poetics style, as Ben Hellman notes, pursued principles similar to Chukovskij's, for he was "using short, laconic lines and a simple vocabulary to create clear and cogent images and plots."[28] However, in comparison to Chukovskij's translations and verse for children, Marshak's poems displayed greater stylistic consistency (and sometimes simplification), as well as a higher level of semantic and ideological adaptation in content. Efim Etkind pointed out these features of Marshak's translations in his comparative analysis of "Robin Bobbin," an English nursery rhyme rendered in Russian both by Chukovskij and Marshak. Etkind notes that Marshak's translation was longer, more didactic in tone, and more subdued in the choice of imagery (e.g., it omitted a reference to the priest in the line "He ate the priest and all the people," which in Marshak's rendition became "пять церквей и колоколен" ["five churches and bell towers"]).[29] Other scholars observed similar trends in Marshak's translations for adults, especially in his versions of Shakespeare's sonnets, which were often quoted as high achievements of the Soviet school of

---

27 Samuil Marshak, "Содоклад С. Я. Маршака о детской литературе," in *Первый Всесоюзный Съезд Советских Писателей. 1934. Стенографический отчет*, Moscow 1934, 22.
28 Hellman, *Fairy Tales and True Stories*, 321.
29 Efim Etkind, "Для маленьких читателей," in *Поэзия и перевод*, Moscow 1969, 371-372.

poetic translation.³⁰ As Natalija Avtonomova and Boris Gasparov remarked in their early critique of Marshak's renderings of the sonnets, he "translated in accordance with the style of nineteenth-century Russian poetry," creating a rhetorical modus that would appeal to the mass reader as "poetic."³¹

We can extend this analogy and note that, with his mastery of style and expression, Marshak also set the precedent of a unified style in children's poetry and translations for children. Among its features were the use of simple and coherent syntax, regular rhythm and rhyme schemes, the avoidance of complex metaphors, and the use of didactic conclusions. As Marshak himself advised authors of children's literature, "each little poem and each short story for children should be crafted as carefully as a large novel," for works for children should preserve "pure and living language."³² Many famous Soviet-era authors, such as Agnija Barto, Elena Blaginina, Sergej Michalkov, and others followed these stylistic trends in their translations and in their poetry for children.

Marshak's rendition of Rudyard Kipling's poem "Rolling down to Rio" from the story "The Beginning of Armadillos" provides a telling example of his poetic and linguistic approaches to translation:³³

> I've never sailed the Amazon,
> And I've never reached Brazil;
> But the *Don* and *Magdalena*,
> They can go there when they will!
>
> Yes, weekly from Southampton,
> Great steamers, white and gold,
> Go rolling down to Rio
> (Roll down – roll down to Rio!)

---

30 For example, Andrej Fedorov, one of the theoreticians of literary translation, lists Marshak's translations, along with translations by Michail Lozinskij, and prose translations of Ivan Kashkin's group among the key achievements of the Soviet school of translation. Andrej Fedorov, "К вопросу о переводимости," in V. Ganiev et al., eds., *Актуальные проблемы художественного перевода. Материалы Всесоюзного Симпозиума (25 февраля – 2 марта 1966 г.)*, Moscow 1967, 34.

31 N. S. Avtonomova and M. L. Gasparov, "Сонеты Шекспира – переводы Маршака," in *Вопросы литературы* 2 (1969), 111.

32 Marshak, "О наследстве и наследственности в русской литературе," *Собрание сочинений в восьми томах*, Vol. 7, Moscow 1969, 294.

33 This was a collaborative project with Chukovskij, where Marshak provided translations of the poems. R. Kipling, *Сказки*, trans. K. Chukovskij, poems translated by S. Marshak. Moscow 1923.

And I'd like to roll to Rio
Some day before I'm old!

I've never seen a Jaguar,
Nor yet an Armadill
O dilloing in his armour,
And I s'pose I never will,

Unless I go to Rio
These wonders to behold –
Roll down – roll down to Rio –
Roll really down to Rio!
Oh, I'd love to roll to Rio
Some day before I'm old![34]

Below are the first two stanzas of Marshak's translation:

На далекой Амазонке
Не бывал я никогда.
Никогда туда не ходят
Иностранные суда.
Только "Дон" и "Магдалина" –
Быстроходные суда –
Только "Дон" и "Магдалина"
Ходят по морю туда.

Из Ливерпульской гавани
Всегда по четвергам
Суда уходят в плаванье
К далеким берегам.
Плывут они в Бразилию,
Бразилию,
Бразилию.
И я хочу в Бразилию –
К далеким берегам![35]

---

34 Rudyard Kipling, *The Kipling Reader*, New York, 1994, 42.
35 "I have never visited / The faraway Amazon. / Foreign vessels / Never sail there. / Only Don and Magdalena, / Fast-sailing ships, / Only Don and Magdalena / Sail there by the sea. // From the Liverpool haven / Always on Thursdays / The vessels depart on a voyage /

Marshak's translation contains several adaptations, which serve to convey the rhythm and the rich alliterations of the original and to develop its main themes. First of all, Marshak chooses to change the place name to "Бразилия" instead of "Rio" as a refrain of the poem. Such substitution extends the length of the poem and adjusts the meter of the refrain. Marshak also omits Kipling's world play on the theme of the story, "armadillos": "I've never seen a Jaguar/ Or yet an Armadill / o'dilloing in his armour/ And I s'pose I never will," – either because its Russian counterpart ("броненосец") is by far less sonorous or, perhaps, because the word has a military connotation, bringing to the reader's mind the naval destroyer ships deployed in World War I. On the other hand, the word "Бразилия" replicates some sounds in "armadillo," thus helping translation approximate the original phonetically, if not in every thematic detail. Marshak also adds a note of admiration for the faraway Brazil: "А в солнечной Бразилии, Бразилии моей / Такое изобилие невиданных зверей" ("In the sunny Brazil, my Brazil, / There is such an abundance of never-seen before animals"). Efim Etkind has observed that in this stanza, the rhyme "Бразилия – изобилие" highlights the image of a wonderful distant land, thus making the poem rich and memorable.[36] Other changes (e.g., Liverpool haven instead of Southampton) opt for more familiar place names and sounds.

As we may note, images of foreignness are carefully mediated for the sake of rhyme and reason. Marshak's translation allows the young readers to imagine a far-away, exotic, and joyful country; at the same time, it avoids foreign toponyms which children may find difficult to pronounce. The changes he makes to the poem's content emphasize the sense of longing for a remote land and even hint at the impossibility to travel: "Увижу ли Бразилию до старости моей?" ("Will I see Brazil before I'm old?"). It is not unlikely that the added layer of meaning made this poem extremely popular, especially after it was set to music by Viktor Berkovskij and Moris Sinel'nikov in 1968.

As it circulated as a song, Marshak's translation took a life of its own. It even acquired additional significance for adult listeners, although such ambivalence was, perhaps, intended neither in the original text nor in its Russian rendition. Thus Marshak's "На далекой Амазонке…" began to exemplify the trend of double address, with adults responding to children's literature as a

---

To the faraway shores. / They sail to Brazil, Brazil, Brazil, / And I want to go to Brazil, / To the faraway shores!" Marshak, *Собрание сочинений в восьми томах*, Vol. 1, Moscow 1969, 675.

36 Moreover, as Etkind notices, half of the fifty-eight syllables in this strophe, are comprised of the rhyming words "Бразилия" (repeated six times), and "изобилие." Etkind, "Для маленьких читателей," 356.

FIGURE 9.1 Cover page of Kipling's *Сказки* (*Fairytales*) in Marshak's and Chukovskij's translation. Moscow 1923

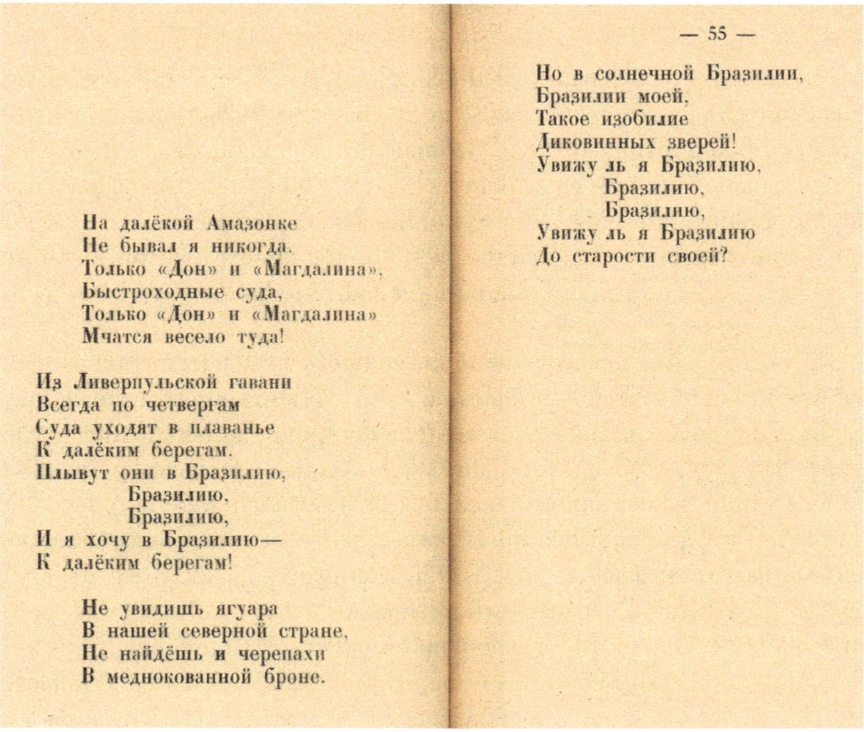

На далёкой Амазонке
Не бывал я никогда.
Только «Дон» и «Магдалина»,
Быстроходные суда,
Только «Дон» и «Магдалина»
Мчатся весело туда!

Из Ливерпульской гавани
Всегда по четвергам
Суда уходят в плаванье
К далёким берегам.
Плывут они в Бразилию,
Бразилию,
Бразилию,
И я хочу в Бразилию—
К далёким берегам!

Не увидишь ягуара
В нашей северной стране,
Не найдёшь и черепахи
В медникованной броне.

— 55 —

Но в солнечной Бразилии,
Бразилии моей,
Такое изобилие
Диковинных зверей!
Увижу ль я Бразилию,
Бразилию,
Бразилию,
Увижу ль я Бразилию
До старости своей?

FIGURE 9.2 Original publication of Marshak's translation of Kipling's poem which concludes the fairytale "Как появились броненосцы" ("The Beginning of Armadillos"). Moscow 1923

compendium of texts that may harbor an encoded seditious meaning. Initiated in the 1920s, when both Marshak and Chukovskij had to deal with the party ideologues' attacks on children's literature as a potentially subversive mode of expression, this tendency only intensified in the following decades marked by increased ideological pressure on literature in general and children's literature in particular.

3 1930s-1950s: Artistic Escapes and Creativity in Translation

From the 1930s to the 1950s, tensions between ideology and creativity in children's literature were part of broader sociocultural developments.[37] The establishment of Socialist Realism as a dominant aesthetic doctrine led to the

37 Hellman, *Fairy Tales and True Stories*, 364.

impoverishment of children's literature in subject and form. As Ol'ga Oktjabr'skaja suggests, with the new thematic priority given to party principles, dogmatic codes of behavior and thinking representative of the totalitarian state, and various aspects of class struggle, the formerly dazzling diversity of children's books dwindled.[38] Ben Hellman also comments on the increasing artistic isolation of the Soviet children's literature induced by the regime's isolationist politics. It resulted in the loss of ties with contemporaneous works for younger audiences produced in the West, "on the pretext that this literature was ideologically foreign or event harmful and, as such, incomprehensible to the Soviet readers."[39]

The change in the repertoire of approved books written by foreign authors led to translators' and editors' choosing fewer Western sources. Instead, they began to pay greater attention to the literary output of authors writing in the languages of Soviet republics and, after World War II, of ideologically "friendly" nations within the communist bloc. Thus, Soviet readers were introduced to translations of accomplished poets (e.g., Ukrainian authors Lesja Ukrainka and Marija Poznanskaja) as well as translated works of "invented" national bards (e.g., Dzhambul Dzhabaev, whose "Колыбельная" ("Lullaby") was popularized and recommended for school performances).[40] Consequently, the Soviet children's literary canon was reshaped to include epic tales and folklore of different nations brought together under the Soviet aegis. Thus, although the new political environment was not propitious to creativity, it did allow translation as a craft to flourish. After all, it offered poets and writers a rare opportunity to earn a living when they could no longer find a publisher because their own works were deemed either devoid of political context or outright subversive.[41] In this period, major Russian poets, Boris Pasternak, Anna Achmatova, Marija Petrovych, Arsenij Tarkovskij, and Nikolaj Zabolockij in-

---

38   O.S. Oktjabr'skaja, *Пути развития русской детской литературы XX века (1920-2000-е гг.)*, Moscow 2012, 103.
39   Hellman, *Fairy Tales and True Stories*, 364.
40   For more on the Dzhambul phenomenon, see Konstantin Bogdanov et al., eds. *Джамбул Джабаев: Приключения казахского акына в советской стране*, Moscow 2013. On the history of publication and popularization of Dzhambul's "Колыбельная" see Konstantin Bogdanov, "Право на сон и условные рефлексы: колыбельные песни в советской культуре 1930-1950х годов," in Natalja Borisova, et al., eds., *СССР: территория любви*, Moscow 2008, 79-127.
41   For the analysis of translation as a "cultural niche" for Soviet intellectuals and a space for communication and exchange of ideas, see Baer, *Translation and the Making of Russian Literature*, and Vsevolod Bagno, ed., *RES TRADUCTORICA. Перевод и сравнительное изучение литератур: к восьмидесятилетию Ю. Д. Левина*, St. Petersburg 2000.

cluded, translated on a daily basis. So did Michail Lozinskij, Pavel Antokol'skij, Georgij Shengeli, David Samojlov, Boris Slutskij, and other remarkable authors who, had there been no ideological barriers to their self-expression, would have appealed to their readers directly. Moreover, many of them also translated for children: Zabolockij, for instance, created an adaptation of Francois Rabelais's *Gargantua and Pantagruel* specifically for young audiences.[42]

The period of the 1930s-1950s is also characterized by a gap between the literary production for children and its theoretical validation. Scholars have noted "an apparent discrepancy between the literary texts for children produced in that era and their metatexts – the works of critics, teachers, and theoreticians."[43] Poems and translations for children created in this period presented new models of textual adaptation, but critics and censors either failed to notice or considered it safe to overlook many of the semantic innovations and rich allusions inherent in the texts whose authors had a double addressee in mind. The OBERIU poets' works for children serve as a notable example of stylistic and thematic freedom in the time of growing censorship. Aleksandr Vvedenskij, Daniil Charms, Nikolaj Olejnikov, and Zabolockij contributed to the tradition of poetic playfulness and embraced poetry as a writer's "игра с читателем" ("game with a reader") advocated by Chukovskij. Beloved for their ability to produce bits of "innocent" verse that children learned by heart, and adults often quoted in ironic, if not dissident, conversation, they also offered a model of "artistic survival or escape" by means of children's literature.[44]

In their chapters in this volume, Ainsley Morse and Oleg Minin discuss, respectively, the innovative nature of OBERIU writing for children and Charms, Olejnikov, Zabolockij and Vvedenskij's contributions to two very popular children's periodicals of their day, *Еж* (*The Hedgehog*) and *Чиж* (*The Finch*). Here it is important to measure the scope and estimate the value of OBERIU's impact on translation. It includes various levels of textual adaptation in content and imagery, hidden allusions and self-references, as well as innovative poetics. The latter would soon not be allowed, with the Soviet censorship becoming increasingly conservative and nitpicking. Discussing Daniil Charms's work as a poet and translator is especially pertinent here. In his biography of Charms, Valerij Shubinskij convincingly proves that the poet's greatest ambition was to

---

42 François Rabelais, *Гаргантюа и Пантагрюэль*, trans. Nikolaj Zabolockij, Moscow 1935.

43 E. V. Kuleshov, "Предисловие," in *Детский сборник. Статьи по детской литературе и антропологии детства*, Moscow 2004, 12.

44 Ilja Kukulin and Marija Majofis, "Детское чтение советской эпохи: несоветский взгляд. От редакторов," in *Новое Литературное Обозрение* 60 (2003), ⟨http://magazines.russ.ru/nlo/2003/60/ikmm.html⟩ (Accessed November 20, 2017).

write for adults. He allegedly "hated children," considered most of his *Еж* and *Чиж* assignments hackwork, and thought of the central children's publishing house, Detgiz, only as a source of income.[45] And yet, Charms's children's poetry was popular to the point of adulation. Moreover, he constantly evolved as a children's writer, and his actual survival – at least for ten years after his first arrest – partly depended on his ability to publish as a children's author.

Charms's rendition of Wilhelm Busch's *Plisch und Plum* (1882), an illustrated humorous poem about two mischievous puppies rescued by brothers Peter and Paul Fittig, bears the unique signature of the poet-translator. It also reveals two models of authors' dodging being censored: one of them concerns the translator's techniques of poetic adaptation, and another reflects his strategies of choosing foreign works which could be adapted to the Soviet cultural context. Soviet children's writers were not only aware of Busch's artistic heritage, but considered it worthy of their readers' attention. Thus Marshak, in his 1934 speech on children's literature, commended Busch's other illustrated poem, *Max und Moritz* (1865). Significantly more popular than *Plisch und Plum* not only in its native Germany, but also throughout Europe,[46] this action-packed saga about two obnoxious boys, however, did not fit the ideological and pedagogical bill of the new Soviet state, with its stilted didacticism and focus on political upbringing. As a result, pre-revolutionary translations of this book, by Konstantin L'dov, among others, were never published again in the Soviet Union. Instead, they were issued by émigré literary presses.[47] This is why Charms's translation of *Plisch und Plum* completed in the late 1930s, just a few years before the poet's second arrest and death in prison, is so remarkable as a deviation from the norms of literary production of the period and of this author's ability to overcome ideological barriers. Overall, Charms's own poems and notebooks are quite congenial with Busch's macabre humor emblematized by *Max und Moritz*. In its turn, his *Плюх и Плих* is a good example of

---

45   See Valerij Shubinskij, *Даниил Хармс. Жизнь человека на ветру*, St. Petersburg 2008, 244-293.

46   On the reception of Busch in Slavic context, see Brigitte Schultze, "Wilhelm Buschs Max und Moritz Slavisch: Variantenbildung im Zeichen Von Textverständnis, Intermedialität und Kultureller Differenz," in *Guttenberg Jahrbuch*, 2007, 211-238.

47   Konstantin L'dov's 1890 translation "Весёлые рассказы про шутки и проказы" ("Funny Stories about Jokes and Mischief") was republished several times in Moscow and St. Petersburg, and subsequently, in Berlin (e.g., Berlin 1929). Not until after the fall of the Soviet Union did new editions of *Max und Moritz* with a full set of Busch's illustrations appear in Russia in new translations by Vladimir Letuchij, *Макс и Мориц. Мальчишечья история в семи проделках*, Moscow 2003, and Andrej Usachev, *Макс и Мориц и другие истории для детей. Истории в стихах и картинках*, Moscow 2011.

mimetic behavior only a brilliant artist could indulge in without immediately getting punished. It reveals the veiled cultural and psychological assimilation that would have been absent from a direct translation of an ideologically tolerable text.

Daniil Juvachev (Charms), who wrote children's poetry since the late 1920s, had studied German at school and even kept a diary in the language. Unlike his pen-name, derived from the English "charm" or, perhaps, "harm," the handful of Charms's translations from the German demonstrate his great affinity not with English culture, but, rather, with heavy-handed German satire and Busch's anti-philistine aesthetics.[48] *Плюх и Плих* is a work of an accomplished author: by the time it was serialized in 1936 in volumes eight through twelve of *The Finch*, Charms had already contributed many poems and humorous sketches to that journal as well as to books and collections published by Detgiz and other companies.[49]

Oleg Lekmanov, who analyzed Busch's original and Charms's translation, noticed important differences between the two texts. The most important of them derived from the instances of authorial and editorial censorship, especially where Charms or his editor mollified Busch's depictions of violence, removed the poem's erotic overtones, or refused to replicate his portrayals of a cozy "bourgeois" lifestyle. For example, in Chapter Two, Busch depicts a homey scene where Papa Fittig and Mama Fittig await the return of the children before the evening meal:

Papa Fittig, treu und friedlich,
Mama Fittig, sehr gemütlich,
Sitzen, Arm in Arm geschmiegt,

Sorgenlos und stillvergnügt
Kurz vor ihrem Abendschmause
Noch ein wenig vor dem Hause,

---

48 Apart from *Plisch und Plum*, Charms's poem "Как Володя на саночках с горки катался" ("How Volodya Went Sledding on a Small Hill"), as scholars have determined later, is a translation of Busch's "Die Rutschpartie." For more on Charms's translations from the German, see Jean-Philippe Jaccard and T. Grob "Хармс – переводчик или поэт барокко?" in *Шестые тыняновские чтения. Материалы*, Moscow and Riga 1992, 31-44.

49 An updated version of *Плюх и Плих* appeared in a book format in 1937. On textual differences between the journal and the book publication see Oleg Lekmanov's article "О двух редакциях одного перевода Даниила Хармса," in E. Kiseleva, ed., *Лотмановский сборник* 4, Moscow 2014, 496-501.

Denn der Tag war ein gelinder,
Und erwarten ihre Kinder.[50]

In translation, this excerpt is significantly shorter, and all the evaluative adjectives that denote a cozy home space and convey a sense of comfort are omitted. Instead, we find a syntactic repetition typical of Charms's poetics. Rhythmical and poetically pleasing, it nevertheless transforms a domestic scene into a burlesque while depriving the two protagonists, the father and the mother, of their main "bourgeois" characteristics – friendliness and coziness. To add an even greater sting to this buffoonery, the last line of Charms's quatrain alludes to Pushkin's and Ershov's fairytales in verse:

Папа Фиттих рядом с мамой,
Мама Фиттих рядом с папой
На скамеечке сидят,
Вдаль задумчиво глядят.[51]

While the omitted details minimized the descriptions of the daily life that might have seemed too "foreign" or even "too German" to Charms's readers, the mirroring structure of the poem's first two lines also played up to the dogmatic ideological thinking by over-emphasizing unity. They can be read as ironic and fun, but also as subversive and critical, containing a hidden reference to the time of enforced togetherness during which many families were tragically torn apart.

In a similar way, Charms mitigates many references to death and violence in his translation. The original text, for example, describes Kaspar Schlich's plans for drowning the puppies, since his principle is "to get rid of everything that is of no use to him." While Charms neither gives much space to Schlich's detailed deliberation nor mentions the word "to drown," his succinct version nevertheless sounds sinister in a more abstract and thus, eerier way: "Шлих ушел, куря табак / Шлиха нет, и нет собак" ("Schlich left, smoking tobacco / There is no Schlich, and no dogs"). The evocations of violence and punishment, which

---

50   Wilhelm Busch, *Plisch und Plum*, ⟨http://gutenberg.spiegel.de/buch/plisch-und-plum-4189/4⟩ (Accessed on November 20, 2017).

51   "Papa Fittig, next to mama, / Mama Fittig, next to papa, / Are sitting together on a bench, / Looking thoughtfully into the distance." Charms, *Плюх и Плих*, in *Полное собрание сочинений*, Vol. 3, St. Petersburg 1997, 92. The line "вдаль задумчиво глядят" alludes to Pushkin's *Сказка о Царе Салтане* (*The Tale of Tsar Saltan*, 1832) and to Ershov's *Конек-горбунок* (*The Little Hunchbacked Horse*, 1834).

abound in the original poem, obviously acquired a different meaning in the Soviet context of the 1930s, when people disappeared without trace. Larisa Klein Tumanov applies Lev Loseff's notion of "Aesopian language" to analyze how children's writers circumvented censorial restraints in their original works.[52] Translations, and especially those by Charms, also partook in this trend. An example of Charms's "Aesopism" may be seen in his extending Pappa Fittig's promise of punishment to each chapter. His young protagonists receive threats from controlling adults on a regular basis – just as the terrorized Soviet population did, from the nation's dictatorial "father."

In its subversivity and by means of its deviations from the original, Charms's version of *Plisch und Plum* reflects broader trends in Soviet translation for children. The first one is translators' lack of concern for the integrity of the original work. In the 1936 journal version of the poem, Charms shortened Busch's text, but used most of his graphics. Later editions included an expanded text of the translation, but took great liberties with the original illustrations, rearranging Busch's pictures and thus re-distributing the correlation between text and image, which was crucial for this particular author.[53] Such omissions, as Ljudmila Iljicheva observes, shifted the emphasis from the visual to the textual elements of the poem and thus, to Charms's creative rendering of the original.[54] While in Busch's story graphics play an integral part in advancing the plot and generating suspense, the Soviet editions' focus on the text reduces illustrations to decorative elements that play no vital role in the narrative. Moreover, the discrepancy between image and text reveals an ideological motivation, such as in Charms's subdued interpretation of corporal punishment in the sixth chapter of the book. As Aleksandr Kobrinskij shows, Charms's lines "Потому что от битья/Умным сделаться нельзя" ("Since from beating / One can't become smart") contradict Busch's pedagogical message.[55] Whereas the German author portrays the insufferable brothers who appear transformed after regular beatings in Teacher Bokelmann's class, his Russian translator seems to be

---

[52] See Larissa Klein Tumanov, "Writing for a Dual Audience in the Former Soviet Union: The Aesopian Children's Literature of Korney Chukovsky, Mikhail Zoshchenko, and Daniil Kharms," in Sandra L. Beckett, ed., *Transcending Boundaries. Writing for a Dual Audience of Children and Adults*, New York 1999, 129-148.

[53] Some editions omit Wilhelm Busch's graphics altogether and use illustrations by Russian artists instead.

[54] L. V. Iljicheva, "Рисованные рассказы В. Буша в переводах Д. Хармса и С. Маршака," ⟨http://www.d-harms.ru/library/risovanniy-rasskazy-busha-v-perevodah-harmsa-i-marshaka.html⟩ (Accessed November 24, 2017).

[55] Charms, *Плюх и Плих*, 97.

obliquely pointing out the meaninglessness of terror as a country-wide "beating" of whole social classes or professional groups.[56]

In spite of Charms's disregard for exactitude in translation, his desire to preserve the word and sound play of the original poem is apparent. The stylistic changes that he makes to achieve this goal begin with the poem's title in Russian. In Busch's version, boys named puppies Plisch and Plium after saving them from getting drowned by their previous owner, Kaspar Schlich. Charms's choice of names Плюх and Плих not only conveys the sound of splashing, but also partially rhymes with the name of the dogs' former owner Shlich. The wordplay continues, when, having refused to Russianize Busch's characters or alter the poem's setting, Charms uses protagonists' German names as material for his own puns. For example, over the course of the poem, the name of the boys' father, "Papa Fittig" ("Фиттих") forms an imaginative and funny rhyme with "бить их," ("beat them") "получить их," ("get them") and "посмотрите" ("look at them").

Charms's creative advancement of Busch's poetic techniques points to another important aspect of this particular translation, and of Soviet translation in general, namely, its representation of foreignness in works for children. As Emer O'Sullivan observes:

> There is a paradox at the heart of the translation of children's literature: it is commonly held that books are translated in order to enrich the children's literature of the target language and to introduce children to foreign cultures, yet at the same time that foreign element itself is often eradicated from translations which are heavily adapted to their target culture, allegedly on the grounds that young readers will not understand it.[57]

In the Soviet cultural context, many ideological and political factors that have influenced reception of foreign cultures and societies complicated and exacerbated this problem.[58] Charms implemented a number of techniques to make his translation not only comprehensible to the children's audience of his day,

---

56 Aleksandr Kobrinskij, "О некоторых подтекстах одного хармсовского вольного перевода," in Ekaterina Ljamina et al., eds., *История литературы. Поэтика. Кино. Сборник в честь Мариэтты Омаровны Чудаковой*, Moscow 2012, 161-165.

57 O'Sullivan, *Comparative Children's Literature*, 76.

58 For more on representation of foreignness in children's books, see Yuri Leving's article on Marshak's satirical poem "Mister Twister" (Leving, "Mister Twister in the Land of Bolsheviks: Sketching Laughter in Marshak's Poem," in *Slavic Review* 70:2 (2011), 279-306) and Evgeny Steiner's chapter "Kids of Many Colors," in *Stories for Little Comrades*, 99-109).

but also more compatible with the Soviet nationalist and internationalist policies. Though he chose to keep the distinctly German setting of the poem, he omitted Chapter Five of the original text, which featured an ironic and derogatory image of a Jew, Schmulchen Schiefelbeiner.[59] Alternatively, Charms's version retained the image of an Englishman, "Mister Pief," whom Busch satirized in his last chapter. His translation did not convey Busch's ironic depiction of the English accent ("Mister Pief sprach: Weriwell! / Diese zwei gefallen mir"), but it did keep the irony intact by means of aligning the characters' names with other images. For example, in the original text, the name Mister Pief rhymes with the archaic word for spyglass ("das Perspektiv"). Charms created another rhyming pair: "Мистер Хопп" and "телескоп." The obvious foreignness of his "Misters" thus transpired not by way of their speech, but by means of their association with peculiar inanimate objects, which were often used by travelers and explorers.

In the German original, the text itself appears more succinct, while the illustrations convey the image of the unfortunate traveler:

> Ohne Perspektiv und Hut
> Steigt er ruhig aus der Flut.
>
> „Alleh, Plisch und Plum, apport!"
> Tönte das Kommandowort.
> Streng gewöhnt an das Parieren,
> Tauchen sie und apportieren
> Das Vermißte prompt und schnell.
>
> > Mister Pief sprach: „Weriwell!
> > Diese zwei gefallen mir!
> > Wollt ihr hundert Mark dafür?"[60]

As in the beginning of his translation of Busch's poem, Charms's use of names in rhyming position makes his lines sound redundantly repetitive – a device reminiscent of his own poems for children:

---

59 This clearly anti-Semitic image is omitted in some American publications as well. Aleksandr Kobrinskij's article explores cultural and ideological motivations for this omission, such as an implicit reference to the town Schivelbein (presently Świdwin in Poland), the birthplace of Rudolf Virchow whose works in medicine and anthropology contributed to the anti-Semitic discourse. Kobrinskij, "О некоторых подтекстах одного хармсовского вольного перевода," 161.

60 Busch, *Plisch und Plum*.

Плих и Плюх помчались сразу,	Plich and Pljuch raced at once,
Громко лая и визжа.	Barking and squealing loudly.
Видят – кто-то долговязый	They see – someone very tall
Лезет на берег дрожа.	Climbs up to the shore, shivering.
"Где мой шлем и телескоп?" –	"Where are my helmet and telescope?"
Восклицает мистер Хопп.	Exclaims Mr. Chopp.
И тотчас же Плих и Плюх	And all of a sudden Plich and Pljuch
По команде в воду – бух!	As if by command spring into the water – boom!
Не прошло и двух минут,	Barely two minutes have passed,
Оба к берегу плывут.	And they both swim to the shore.
"Вот мой шлем и телескоп!" –	"Here are my helmet and telescope!" –
Громко крикнул мистер Хопп.[61]	Loudly exclaimed Mr. Chopp.

Charms's phonetic and rhythmical inventiveness, however, does not stop at the level of names and rhymes. He also adds an ironic epithet "долговязый" ("lanky") and readjusts Busch's verbs: instead of the original "steigt er ruhig aus dem Flut," the Russian text has "лезет на берег, дрожа," where "лезет" and "дрожа" emphasize the misadventures of the unfortunate Englishman. Moreover, while the original text uses "Hut" to describe mister Pief's hat, in translation, we find "шлем" ("helmet, casque") – an accessory which highlights the foreign appearance of the traveler. Charms's repetitions and exclamations (a typical feature of his poetry for children) as well as the different verbs he uses to describe the protagonist's loud, emphatic manner of speaking ("восклицает," "громко крикнул") further emphasize the foreignness of Chopp's image. For such an outsider as Charms, the emphasis was well-placed. With his quirky humor, fascination with the horror of the mundane, and his mild political subversivity, he was a foreigner in Russian children's poetry. His affinity with Busch was predominantly poetic, as the likeness of their wordplay, humor, and redundancy of imagery and repetition clearly reflects. And yet, Charms's translation of *Plisch und Plum* and especially the reflection of Busch's techniques in his own original works demonstrates that he was choosing for translation not merely a foreign poet who was stylistically similar to him, but also an author of a comparable worldview and artistic sensibility. It is due to the propitiousness of this choice and other selections of text to be rendered by him into Russian that Charms enriched the children's literature of the 1930s not only in translation, but through many creative works that read as if they had been translated from the German and/or English.

---

61 Charms, *Плюх и Плих*, 92.

Charms's appropriation of Busch's artistic heritage took many forms and directions. In addition to changing descriptions of the characters and connecting their names to the poem's intricate tapestry of rhyming jokes, he supplied *Плюх и Плих* with humorous references to Russian poetry for children and to his own poems. Busch, for instance, makes the angry Papa Fittig smack Kaspar Shlich with a pancake pan, described humorously as "Pfannekuchenmütze" ("a pancake hat"):

> Lästig durch die große Hitze
> Ist die Pfannekuchenmütze.[62]

Charms's 1936 translation presented an abbreviated version of this episode. It preserved the picture, but omitted the colorful description of the fight, possibly to avoid a reference to one adult beating another in the presence of children (see Fig. 9.3).

In his 1937 version, however, Charms expanded the translation to include allusions to Marshak's famous 1930 poem "Человек рассеянный" ("The Absent-Minded Man"), the protagonist of which wears a frying pan on his head:[63]

> Вместо шапки на ходу
> Он надел сковороду.
> Вместо валенок – перчатки
> Натянул себе на пятки.
> Вот какой рассеянный
> С улицы Бассейной![64]

Moreover, the added phrasing in Charms's translation engages not just Marshak's poem, but a variety of different literary sources in a surprising way:

Папа Фиттих на ходу	Papa Fittig, as he ran,
Вдруг схватил сковороду	Grabbed at once a frying pan,
И на Шлиха блин горячий	And a hot pancake on Schlich's head
Нахлобучил на ходу.[65]	He smacked as he ran.

---

62 Busch, *Plisch und Plum*.
63 Noted by Iljicheva, "Рисованные рассказы В. Буша в переводах Д. Хармса и С. Маршака."
64 "Instead of a hat, he put on / A frying pan. / Instead of felt boots, / He pulled gloves on his heels. / Such an absent-minded fellow / From the Bassejnaja Street." Marshak, *Собрание сочинений*, Vol. 3, 240.
65 Charms, Ibid., 96.

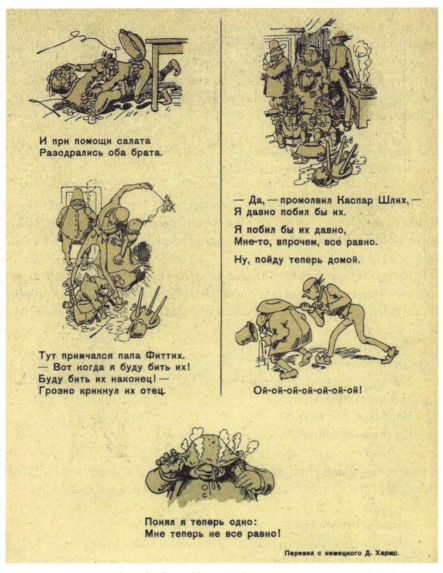

FIGURE 9.3 An excerpt from the first publication of "Плюх и Плих," in *Чиж* 11 (1936)

Here, we encounter a verse with three rhyming lines dominated by the tautological circular rhyme ("на ходу"), which emphasizes the hidden allusion to the quoted excerpt from "Вот какой рассеянный" ("The Absent-Minded Man"). One of Marshak's most popular poems, this text is somewhat similar to the chapter in *Plisch und Plum* that describes Mr. Pief (Мистер Хопп) – both portray an outsider, a person who does not fit in the everyday world, which, undoubtedly, is an image that has affinities with the poetic self in many of Charms's texts. Likewise, the tautological repetition of the stanza's first and the fourth referential lines is reminiscent of Charms's own poetics of the absurd.

Charms's translation of *Plisch und Plum* surpassed the Chukovskian tradition of poetry for children to include play with identities, allusions, and embedded cultural references that both children and adults could relate to. Recreating a foreign world in translation allowed Charms a certain degree of irrationality, and thus justified the translators' right to take liberty with the form as well as content. Following his lead, other translators of children's poetry strove to amplify their poetic freedom. One of the approaches favored by Soviet children's poets was to erase the indication of foreignness altogether, while adjusting plots and images of translated works to a home setting. Such is, for example, Sergej Michalkov's translation of Julian Tuwim's poem "Okulary" ("Eyeglasses").[66] Known as "Где очки?" ("Where are the Eyeglasses?"), the poem was frequently published without any reference to the source text. Russian readers, including the author of this chapter, were surprised to find out that one of their popular childhood texts was, in fact, a translation from the Polish.

The name of Tuwim's protagonist, Pan Hilary, rhymes with the word denoting the title object ("Okulary," with the stress on "a" in both words). Hastily searching for his eyeglasses, the clumsy man turns the entire house upside down before discovering the eyeglasses on his own nose upon looking in a mirror:

Biega, krzyczy pan Hilary:	Mr. Hilary runs and screams:
"Gdzie są moje okulary?"	"Where are my glasses?"
Szuka w spodniach i w surducie,	He searches in his pants and in his frock,
W prawym bucie, w lewym bucie.	In the right boot, in the left boot.
Wszystko w szafach poprzewracał,	He turned everything around in the closets,
Maca szlafrok, palto maca.	He pats his bathrobe, he pats his coat.

---

66   Julian Tuwim (1894-1953), one of the leading modernist poets in Poland, wrote several books of children's poetry. Many of his texts are widely popular in Poland and known in translation as well. Tuwim's poems were translated by a number of Russian children's authors, including Marshak, Michalkov, Blaginina, Eppel', and others.

"Skandal! – krzyczy – nie do wiary!	"[This is] scandalous! – he yells – it's beyond belief!
Ktoś mi ukradł okulary!"	Who has stolen my glasses!"
Pod kanapą, na kanapie,	Under the couch, on the couch,
Wszędzie szuka, parska, sapie!	He looks everywhere, snorts and wheezes!
Szuka w piecu i w kominie,	He searches in the oven and in the chimney,
W mysiej dziurze i w pianinie.	In the mouse hole and on the piano.
[...]	
Znalazł! Są! Okazało się,	Found! It turned out,
Że je ma na własnym nosie.[67]	That they were on his very own nose.

Michalkov's translation, which remains true to the original's plot (lost glasses) and poetic features (lists of nouns and verbs; repeated use of specific grammatical constructions; and the ultimate comic relief), nevertheless 'transplants' Tuwim's character to Russia. Not only is Michalkov's domestic setting deprived of any sign of foreignness, his protagonist is turned into a female, "тетя Валя," and also becomes thoroughly Russianized:

– Что стряслось у тети Вали?	– What has happened to Aunt Valja?
– У нее очки пропали!	– Her glasses got lost!
Ищет бедная старушка	The poor old lady searches
За подушкой, под подушкой,	Behind the pillow, under the pillow,
С головою залезала	Burying her head
Под матрац, под одеяло,	Under the mattress, under the blanket.
Заглянула в ведра, в крынки,	She has looked into buckets, into jugs,
В боты, в валенки, ботинки,	Into boots, into *valenki* and shoes,
Все вверх дном перевернула,	Having turned the entire house upside down,
Посидела, отдохнула,	She sat for a little, rested,
Повздыхала, поворчала	Sighed a bit, grumbled a bit,
И пошла искать сначала.	And went back to her search.

---

67 Julian Tuwim, *Wiersze wybrane*, Wrocław 1969, 258-259.

[...]	
Обыскала кладовую –	She has searched the entire closet –
Все напрасно! Все впустую!	Everything is in vain! Everything is to no avail!
Нет очков у тети Вали –	Aunt Valja has no glasses –
Очевидно, их украли!	Evidently, they have been stolen!
На сундук старушка села.	The old lady sat down on a chest.
Рядом зеркало висело.	A mirror hung nearby.
И старушка увидала,	And the old lady saw
Что не там очки искала,	That she was looking for glasses all in the wrong places,
Что они на самом деле	That they were, in reality,
У нее на лбу сидели.	Sitting above her very forehead.
Так чудесное стекло	That's how the wonderful glass
Тете Вале помогло.[68]	Has helped Aunt Valja.

Michalkov's "domestication" techniques in translation are noteworthy. The poet changes many details of Tuwim's original text to surround his little old lady with specifically Russian household objects (e. g. валенки; сундук); he also omits Pan Hilary's appeal to the police for help. Though Michalkov does employ pair rhymes, syntactically his text is not composed in couplets, and some sentences carry over several lines. This creates an effect of accumulation but destroys the laconic structure of the original. The most significant adaptation in this translation, though, concerns not the transformation of a Polish incident into a Russian anecdote, but the poem's added morale. Michalkov expands the final four lines of Tuwim's text to eight, adding an unnecessarily long explanation about the mirror. This choice slows down poetic action and makes the finale more moralistic. Such added didactic explanations were not uncommon in Soviet-era poems and translations for children, including works by Michalkov himself, as well as Barto, Blaginina, and Zinaida Aleksandrova.

Charms's *Плюх и Плих* and Michalkov's rendering of Tuwim's "Okulary" illustrate two contrasting attitudes to foreignness in Soviet translation for children. One of them is a willingness to appropriate another culture; another, a strong desire to reject and displace "the Other." Furthermore, their texts reveal two distinct paradigms in the Soviet-era children's poetry. While Charms's contribution exemplifies a strong presence of an adult in children's verse, in his case – the poet who is willing to amuse and entertain by making his oeuvre a vehicle for puns, allusions, and other playful means of covert communica-

---

68   Sergej Michalkov, *Собрание сочинений в шести томах*, Vol. 1, Moscow, 1981, 240.

tion with young and adult readers – Michalkov's work represents the model in which the poetic text communicates with the child directly, by dint of its being "simpler" and "more accessible" in terms of style and subject matter. This rhetorical and figurative artlessness however, does not mean that the authorial presence is completely missing in his poems and other didacticized verse. In fact, it points out that implied authors and narrators in the poetry of Michalkov, Barto et. al., are "too grown-up": they are not willing to reach down to the level of children. They not as much play with their readers as instruct them how to perceive the world, think about it, and behave.

That said, the notion of "poetic quality" on which both poets relied kept re-emerging in the discourse on literary translation for younger audiences well after Charms's era in Soviet children's poetry had ended. During the "Thaw," children's authors continued to look for balance between stylistic integrity and the genuineness of self-expression. Many of those who considered themselves heirs to OBERIU aspired to retain poetic playfulness of their translations while maintaining the notion of ease in understanding as central for literary production for children.

4 Translating Children's Poetry during the "Thaw"

Post-Stalinist era, characterized by gradual opening of cultural space, offered new artistic possibilities for writers and translators of children's literature. Prose translations played an increasingly important role during this period, since it was in the 1960s and 1970s that the works by Astrid Lindgren, Tove Jansson, C. S. Lewis, J. R. Tolkien, Antoine de Saint-Exupéry, and Ottfried Proissler finally broke through the Soviet censorial barriers and appeared in print. Although marketed as children's literature, these books were avidly read by children and adults alike. Grown-ups admired them for their philosophical content, mythological and existential depth, as well as heightened attention to questions of self-identity and personal liberty. Concurrently, the theme of childhood as a time of freedom acquired centrality in Soviet prose and poetry of the "Thaw" era. More and more frequently, Soviet authors began to return to the Modernist notion of childhood as a time of an individual's independence from social, ideological, and political conventions. This reoccurrence of an earlier paradigm allowed for poetic representation of "a child hidden within the adult, the one who takes pleasure in remembering his own childhood."[69] Many poems of that period, including those by Emma Moshkovskaja and Elena Blaginina, were thus written from the perspective of a child.

---

69 Oktjabr'skaja, *Пути развития русской детской литературы XX века*, 238.

Authors of the older generation, such as Zinaida Aleksandrova, Agnija Barto, Michalkov, and Elena Blaginina, continued to publish original poetry and translations. Simultaneously, poets who began to enter the literary scene from the late 1950s onwards rediscovered Russian and European poetry previously inaccessible to them and their readers. When Boris Zachoder, Genrich Sapgir, Roman Sef, Valentin Berestov, Jakov Akim, Grigorij Kruzhkov, Junna Moric, and others turned to translation, many of them chose to split their attention between "adult" and "children's" literature. Whimsical, inventive, and marked by acute emotionality, their works for children also embraced such new cultural currents as conceptualism and postmodernism.[70]

Boris Zachoder's translation of Alan Alexander Milne's *Winnie the Pooh* exemplifies the Thaw generation's openness to experimentation as well as its readiness to embrace childhood as a realm of artistic and individual freedom. This cultural project was successful for two reasons: it created a surprisingly different yet widely popular interpretation of a foreign literary character; and it demonstrated how Russian culture could appropriate and even enrich a classical work of Western European literature for children.[71] Vinni-Puch truly became a children's literary celebrity. The merits of Zachoder's translation, *Винни-Пух и Все-все-все* (*Vinni-Puch and Everyone Else*), as well as the sheer ingenuity of Fedor Chitruk's animated films it inspired contributed to the domestication of Milne's character.[72] The chubby, verse-sputtering toy bear became deeply entrenched in Soviet and Post-Soviet popular culture.

Zachoder describes his translation experience in an intensely personal way. He recalls his earliest encounter with Winnie the Pooh as if it were a first date followed by a happy and productive life-long relationship:

> Our meeting happened in a library where I was leafing through a children's encyclopedia. It was love at first sight. I saw an image of a cute bear, read several poetic quotations, and rushed to find the book. With that en-

---

70 For more on children's literature as a conduit for postmodernist aesthetics in children's literature and animation, see Ol'ga Pleshakova, *Теория литературы и практики читательской деятельности*, Moscow 2012, 162-163.

71 Zachoder's version of *Winnie the Pooh* is different from earlier Soviet "appropriative" projects, such as Aleksej Tolstoj's *Приключения Буратино* (*The Adventures of Buratino*, translation of Collodi's *Pinocchio*), or Aleksandr Volkov's *Волшебник Изумрудного города* (*The Wizard of Emerald City*, adaptation of Frank L. Baum's *The Wizard of Oz*), because he keeps the reference to the foreign work and emphasizes the aspect of co-creation.

72 Alan A. Miln, *Винни-Пух и все остальные: О плюшевом медвежонке и его друзьях*, trans. Boris Zachoder, Moscow 1960; a fuller version, more in accordance with Zachoder's vision, appeared five years later: *Винни-Пух и Все-все-все*, Moscow 1965.

sued some of the happiest days of my life – the days when I worked on Winnie the Pooh.[73]

Zachoder's confession brings to mind the pre-revolutionary Russian tradition of translating for love's sake, when the result was engendered not by a publisher's commission, but by an author's admiration for a foreign literary work. Zhukovskij, Gnedich, Pushkin, Lermontov, Tjutchev, and Annenskij, to name just a few, translated poetry from the German, Greek, English, and French because they were inspired by their great European predecessors and contemporaries and wanted their works to find a new readership in Russian. Zachoder follows in their footsteps when formulating his own translator's credo:

> To translate poetry means to write it anew in our language. To write it as the original author would have written it, had he been writing in Russian. Of course, this is an unachievable goal. But in poetry one can achieve a lot, especially if you pose such goals. […] it gives the translator a sense of freedom, the same freedom as the author possessed.[74]

Although Zachoder's reflections echo some of the ideas expressed in Marshak's articles on translation and children's literature and Chukovskij's *Искусство перевода*, he takes the conversation further by offering a critical assessment of the Soviet school of translation and some of its methods. Describing his work on Lewis Carroll and Milne, Zachoder confesses the need, felt deeply at that time, "to find an absolutely new approach, that would be very, very different from the dominant 'school.'"[75] Zachoder's belief in translator's poetic and interpretive liberties can explain his resistance to the established tradition and his desire to revolutionize it. While his Soviet forerunners in translation favored a domesticating approach and placed poetic qualities of the Russian text above those of the original, he refused to make Vinni-Puch a Russian bear and retained the truly Victorian character of the menagerie of Christopher Robin's friends as intended by Milne. In crafting the image of Vinni-Puch, Zachoder produced, to use Aleksandra Borisenko's apt expression, a "congenial translation," which, nevertheless, possessed an originality of form and spirit that it could call its own.[76]

---

73   Boris Zachoder, "Приключения Винни-Пуха. Из истории моих публикаций," *Вопросы литературы* 5 (2002), 197-225.
74   Boris Zachoder, *"Но есть один поэт": Неопубликованное наследие в двух томах*, Vol. 2, Moscow 2008, 274-275.
75   Ibid.
76   Aleksandra Borisenko, "Песня невинности, она же опыта. О новых переводах Винни-Пуха," in *Иностранная литература* 4 (2002), 257-265.

Some of the significant changes in Zachoder's version of *Winnie-the-Pooh* include the conflation of two books (*Winnie-the-Pooh* and *The House at Pooh Corner*) in one; the combination of several chapters to create a more coherent narrative; and the renaming and reconfiguring of Milne's characters so that the Owl, for example, becomes a female. The translator's other liberties – and perhaps his greatest achievement – pertain to his highlighting the poetic aspirations of the book's main protagonist. Unlike Milne's Pooh, Zachoder's Puch is a poet created by a poet. This starts with the image of a bear whose head is stuffed not only with sawdust, but also with poems, songs, rhymes and ditties. Contrary to the original's matter-of-factness in treating Pooh's poetry, Zachoder invents special names for the rhymes and songs that his protagonist composes: "кричалки, шумелки, сопелки..." ("yelling-songs, noise-making-songs, huffing-and-puffing-songs"). Any of these productions in Russian may serve as an example of Vinni's resourcefulness as well as attest to the playful spunk of Zachoder's poetic adaptation.

Milne's original unfolds the following way:

> ...Then he climbed a little further ... and a little further ... and then just a little further. By that time he had thought of another song.
>
> It's a very funny thought that, if Bears were Bees,
> They'd build their nests at the bottom of trees.
> And that being so (if the Bees were Bears),
> We shouldn't have to climb up all these stairs.
>
> He was getting rather tired by this time, so that is why he sang a Complaining Song.[77]

Zachoder's rendition of this episode is emotionally more diverse and contains a good deal of tongue-in-cheek humor which hints at the narrator's tacit admiration for the plucky poet:

> ... Вот он влез еще немножко повыше... и еще немножко... и еще совсем-совсем немножко повыше... И тут ему пришла на ум другая песенка-пыхтелка:
>
> Если б мишки были пчелами,
> То они бы нипочем

---

77 Alexander Milne, *Winnie the Pooh*, London 1994, 16.

> Никогда и не подумали
> Так высоко строить дом;
>
> И тогда (конечно, если бы
> Пчелы – это были мишки!)
> Нам бы, мишкам, было незачем
> Лазить на такие вышки!
>
> По правде говоря, Пух уже порядком устал, поэтому Пыхтелка получилась такая жалобная.[78]

The prosaic excerpts that accompany Puch's ditty in this passage help to clarify how Zachoder's translation pays equal attention to rhythm and sound in poetry as well as in prose. While the bouncy repetition of adverbs in the first sentence of the description of Puch's climb belongs to Milne and is simply reiterated by Zachoder, the alliterative sequence in the citation's last sentence ("По правде […] Пух […] порядком […] Пыхтелка получилась […]") is Zachoder's own. Overall, his translation never borders on literalism, for he always finds phrases and idioms that allow for a fun and light narrative flow in Russian even when the pace of the original may seem lackluster. In the example above, Zachoder uses such diminutive forms as "немножко" ("a little bit") and the emphatic repetition "совсем-совсем" ("totally-totally") that are typical of children's speech and of emotional conversation in general. Moreover, in rendering Vinni-Puch's songs and thoughts, Zachoder emphasizes the peculiar point of view of this philosophically disposed bear by expanding and enlivening Milne's similes and metaphors. Although he captures the syllogisms about bears and bees from the beginning of the second stanza quite precisely, he chooses to deviate from the original later, when naming Milne's "Complaining Song" "пыхтелка," or "a huffing-and-puffing song," which also contains a reference to Puch, the bear-poet himself.

Thanks to Zachoder's boldness and virtuosity, the signature feature of the Russian Vinni-Puch is his ability to compose short songs not only of various genres, but also of varying poetic modalities. Most tellingly, this quality evolved after the translation's publication. When collaborating with director Chitruk on his cartoon script in the early 1970s, Zachoder wrote several additional short songs. Frequently cited and often published separately, they are now perceived if not as Russian Vinni-Puch's "oeuvre," then as Zachoder's

---

[78] Alan A. Miln, *Винни-Пух и Все-все-все*, trans. Boris Zachoder, Moscow 1992, 17.

original productions. Here's one of these popular ditties that cannot really be traced back to Milne:

Если я чешу в затылке –	Even if I'm scratching the back of my head –
Не беда!	No worries!
В голове моей опилки,	My head is stuffed with sawdust,
Да, да, да.	Yes, yes, yes.
Но хотя там и опилки,	But even though there is sawdust there,
Но кричалки и вопилки,	I can sometimes compose yelling-songs, screaming-songs,
А также:	And also:
Шумелки, пыхтелки и сопелки,-	Noise-making-songs, huffing-and-puffing-songs, sniffle-and-snuffle-songs,
Сочиняю я неплохо иногда.	Which are not bad at all.
Да!!!![79]	Yes!!!

It is not surprising that many Russian readers and viewers see in Vinni-Puch a literary character who is more endearing and fascinating than Milne's reflective, comfort-loving bear. Zachoder's Puch is a poet who is both talented and daring; he is afraid neither to break the rules, nor to share his creativity with others. The Russian bear's lovability is also emphasized by his propensity for bragging and his willingness to take his role of Pjatachok's ('Piglet') mentor beyond the original Pooh's warm and co-dependent friendship. Zachoder's character knows very well who he is and what traits of his personality he is willing to pass on to his younger charge.[80]

Vinni-Puch also owed his popularity to his new visual image made popular not by the illustrations to Zachoder's translation, but by Chitruk's animated film. In the Russian cartoon, Vinni looked strikingly different from the original drawings by Ernest Howard Shepard as well as from the Walt Disney version: he was chubbier, wore a surprised expression on his seldom-changing face, and spoke in a husky voice of the enormously popular film actor Evgenij Leonov.

But even before the animated film appeared on Soviet screens, the originality of Vinni-Puch and his friends, Pjatachok, Ia-Ia (Eeyore), Krolik (Rabbit), and Tigra (Tigger), as well as others, had become quite apparent. Many

---

79 Miln, *Винни-Пух и Все-все-все*, 62.
80 Anna Fishzon describes Vinni-Puch's gender identity and mentor's role in her analysis of the Thaw-era Soviet animation in Chapter 12 of this volume.

Russian readers and viewers would agree with the poet's wife Galina Zachoder who claimed that "Boris gave these characters such features that Milne himself did not notice."[81] Her statement points to an important cultural trend in children's literature and animation of the 1960s-1970s, namely, their active use of postmodernist aesthetics that unofficial Soviet literature was simultaneously exploring. Like Andrej Bitov and Venedikt Erofeev in their novels, Zachoder indulged in authorial play with characters, subtexts, and identities in his translation. His ill-mannered but well-meaning Vinni-Puch – as well as Vinni's alter ego from Chitruk's animated films – became an iconic representation of a nerdy Russian litterateur, an amiable loser who could be likable despite his flaws. Readers saw in Zachoder's bear a poet-philosopher who broke conventions. They also perceived Vinni's friends, each of whom possessed unique individuality but lacked in virtue, as "apolitical characters that were free of class ideology and occupied themselves with meaningful trifles."[82] While other such heroes – for example, the always-drunk truth-teller Venichka from Erofeev's *Москва – Петушки* (*Moscow to the End of the Line*, 1973) – populated then-unpublishable works of "adult" authors that could only be distributed through Samizdat, Zachoder's children's books and the animated films they engendered had an immensely broad reach, becoming not only a pathway to the realm of the literary subversive, but also an integral part of the nation's collective memory, with many jokes and ironic quotations circulating in public discourse up to the present day.

Zachoder's work in translation for children provides a telling example of yet another cultural trend that was characteristic of the "Thaw." If, in the 1920s-30s, children's literature offered many Avant-Garde poets and artists an occupational niche and thus a chance to endure harsh socio-political conditions, during the 1960s, children's poetry and translation stopped being a vehicle for cultural survival. Though the censorship climate had softened, many authors were still not able to publish their original work. They could, however, carry over the "adult" side of their poetic personae into poetry and translations for children. Unlike Charms, who eventually suffered for his unbending commitment to his authorial self in everything he wrote or translated, Zachoder and some of his contemporaries in the end were celebrated for their originality and spunk. Genrich Sapgir (1928-1999), recognized now as one of the central figures of Russian conceptualism, belonged to the generation's few who were able to create a distinctive presence in children's poetry and translation.

---

81   Galina Zachoder, *Заходер и все-все-все: воспоминания*, Moscow 2003, 146.
82   Pleshakova, *Теория литературы...*, 99.

In spite of the fact that most of his original poems and prose could not be published until the 1990s, Sapgir worked extensively in children's literature and translation. In his own words, he was inspired to transfer his creative energies to children's poetry by a colleague, Boris Sluckij, who had once suggested that he "should be able to write good poetry for children" because he was "a formalist."[83] And so Sapgir did write, quite successfully, even though he never fully committed to his career of a children's author. The latter happened partly because of his dedication to the poetics of the Moscow Lianozovo group, of which he was a member, and partly because he was trying to distance himself from the ideologically conformist classics of Soviet children's literature: "[...] I had a bright future of becoming widely accepted and following in the footsteps of Michalkov the elder, but, thank God, the 'adult' verse saved me from it," Sapgir remarked in his memoirs.[84] The ironic self-comparison to Michalkov emphasizes Sapgir's resistance to writing stylistically bland and politically orthodox poetry for the young audience. In fact, as Maksim Shrayer notes, this poet drew a very clear line between his truly poetic output and the works he created due to financial considerations. The exception to this rule were his translations from the Yiddish of Ovsej Driz's poetry (those were the only translations Sapgir wanted to include in his collected works).[85] Translating Driz offered Sapgir the possibility of a double estrangement. By doing so, he distanced himself not only from composing the ideologically appropriate original verse that could merit a publication, but also from writing for adults who could be more willing than children to accept a politically sanctioned literary text.

Similarly to translations from the languages of other Soviet republics and national minorities, translations from the Yiddish could be read as attempts to spruce up Soviet literature with "local color." The preservation of peculiar national features in translation, however, often served poets as an excuse for introducing unusual form and delighting in strange, sometimes unorthodox content. The concise poems of Ovsej (Shike) Driz (1908-1971), who invariably wrote in Yiddish, were known for their intense lyricism and metaphorically rich, impressionistic imagery. Driz's colorful images would not fit in the prevalent poetic style of the Soviet era, but, by containing references to the Jewish folklore and customs, they certainly could pass censorship as markers of the author's national identity. Because in his renderings of Driz's poetry Sapgir

---

83 Sapgir, quoted in Maksim D. Shrayer and David Shrayer-Petrov, *Генрих Сапгир: Классик авангарда*, St. Petersburg 2004, 49.
84 Sapgir, quoted in Shraer, Ibid.
85 Shraer, 9.

capitalized on the translator's right to replicate strange stylistic qualities of the original, he was able to create highly individualized "variations" of the original text.

Sapgir's example demonstrates that the more relaxed ideological atmosphere of the "Thaw" actually allowed translation to become a performance – the shift in the authorial role that accentuated the poetic persona and emphasized a distinctive style of any given translator. During the same time, perhaps as a consequence of this new kind of literary role-playing, the practice of "invented authors" made a come-back. Translations from non-existent, imaginary authors representing small regions or ethnic minorities appeared, thus augmenting Soviet literature's colonial claims of subjugating and Russifying other national literatures. In Sapgir's case, characteristically, the nature of his authorship in translations from Ovsej Driz was performative and collaborative, rather than suppressing. As Viktor Pivovarov asserts, "Driz can be called Sapgir's 'personal author.' Sometimes there were no recorded authorial versions of the poems at all: Driz dictated the interlinear version, and Genrich created his poems based on it."[86]

Sapgir's rendition of Ovsej Driz's "Di grine shnayderlekh" ("Little Green Tailors"), known as "Зеленая карета" ("Green Carriage") in Russian, is one of the most telling examples of such collaborative practices. This poem-lullaby conjures an image of a green carriage rolling across the sky, in silence. Spring itself is the carriage's mysterious passenger: it is travelling to little woodland tailors to procure a beautiful new garment made to order. Here is an excerpt from the original poem, in transliteration and line-by-line translation to English:

Di grine shnayderlekh	The Green Little Tailors
Rutelen	*for Ruth*
Gendz un katshkes, shof un rinder,	Geese and ducks, sheep and cattle,
kats un moyz un kleyne kinder,	cat and mouse and little children,
lyalkes, hezelekh un bern	dolls, hares and bears
muzn bald antshlofn vern,	must soon fall asleep,
nit gerirt zikh funem ort,	not moving from the spot
vayl di sheyne vesne fort!	because beautiful spring is on the move!

---

86 Viktor Pivovarov, "Его голос," in T. Michajlovskaja, ed., *Великий Генрих. Сапгир и о Сапгире*, Moscow 2003, 324.

In a karete a viner,	In a carriage, a Viennese one,
in a karete a griner,	in a carriage, a green one,
mit di beste oyf der erd	with the best on earth
ayngeshpante zeks por ferd,	six pairs of harnessed horses,
mit tsilinders oyf di kep,	with top hats on their heads,
grine stenges oyf di tsep,	green ribbons in the braids,
mit kamashn oyf di fis,	with boots on their feet,
ufgeneyt fun vaysn plis,	sewn from white velvet,
fliyen zey, badekt mit pine,	they fly by covered in foam
tsu di shnayderlekh di grine,	to the green tailors,
vos mit smitshkelekh, mit nedelekh—	who with bows, with needles—
aher-ahin oyf fedemlekh—	back and forth over the threads—
fidlen oys dos grine kleyd	will fiddle out a green dress
in der finster shtilerheyt...	silently, in the dark...
Shloft zhe, shloft gezunterheyt!	Sleep, sleep in good health!
Vayl di vesne mest dos kleyd—	Because the spring is trying on the dress—
akurat a zeyger tsen	at exactly ten o'clock
vet ir zi in kholem zen.[87]	you will see her in your dream.

The text stitches together many of Ovsej Driz's characteristic lyric images dominated by the color green – one of the poet's favorite, symbolic, colors. Sapgir's translation preserves the melodious rhythm of the original and retains all of main metaphors (the carriage, the dress, the fast motion across the night sky), but it also shifts some of its accents. Having chosen "зеленая карета" for the poem's title, Sapgir deprives Driz's "green little tailors" of their importance and reassigns agency to the magic vehicle – and thus to Spring itself:

---

[87] Ovsej Driz, *Di ferte strune*, Moscow 1969, 215-216. I am grateful to Dr. Saul Noam Zarrit for his help with the translation of the Yiddish text.

Зелёная карета	Green Carriage
Спят мышата, спят ежата.	Asleep are little mice, asleep are little hedgehogs,
Медвежата и ребята.	Little bear cubs, and little kids.
Всё уснуло до рассвета.	Everything has fallen asleep until the sunrise.
Лишь зелёная карета	Only the green carriage
Мчится, мчится в вышине – В серебристой тишине.	Rushes, rushes up above – Along the silvery silence.
Шесть коней разгорячённых В шляпах алых и зелёных	Six fiery horses Wearing crimson and green hats
Над землёй несутся вскачь. На запятках – чёрный грач.	Gallop above the earth. On the footboard a black rook is standing.
Не угнаться за каретой – Ведь Весна в карете этой,	One can't catch up with this carriage – Because Spring is in this carriage,
И спешит она к лесным Удивительным портным...	And it hurries to the wonderful Woodland tailors...
Вот зелёные портные Взяли нитки травяные,	Now the green tailors Have taken their threads of grass,
Взяли острые иголки У густой зелёной ёлки,	[They] have borrowed their sharp needles From a thick green fir-tree,
На полянке сели в ряд, Шьют Весне они наряд.	And sat down in a row on a little meadow. They are sewing a garment for Spring.
Спите, спите, медвежата, И ежата, и ребята:	Sleep, sleep, baby bears, Little hedgehogs and little kids,

Ведь зелёная обнова	For the new green outfit
Не совсем ещё готова.	Is still not quite ready.
В самый тихий, ранний час	In the quietest, earliest of hours
Звон подков разбудит вас.	You will be awakened by the clinging of horse hoofs.
Только глянешь из окна –	And as soon as you peek out the window –
На дворе стоит Весна.[88]	There will be Spring standing in your courtyard.

Sapgir's translation is lyrical and melodious. He favors the music of the original text over its precise imagery. By using rhyming couplets of varying length, he not only conveys the overall rhythm of Driz's lullaby, but is also able, in some stanzas, to render the original's precise metrical structure. Having achieved this harmonious correspondence, he then deviates from Driz's choice of tropes and thus introduces his own ontological complexity to the fairytale world of the Yiddish lullaby. When, in the translation's opening stanza, the cozily snuggling world is getting overcome by slumber, Sapgir uses nouns that denote little children and baby animals who are falling asleep, rather than toys which Driz's poem features. Similarly, the main focus of the poem is Spring herself, and not the green little tailors who are supposed to make her a dress. Sapgir's world is no longer miniscule, reduced to the nursery with its stuffed inhabitants and bedtime stories. It expands to include the creatures of the woods as well as humans, minor folk characters and an allegory either of one's coming of age or of spiritual rejuvenation.

It is significant that Sapgir capitalizes the word "Spring," thus highlighting its anthropomorphic and magical attributes. While the tailors in Driz's text sew Spring's garment with "bows," an unlikely instrument which evokes another popular trope in Jewish culture, the trickster and mourner Fiddler, Sapgir chooses to ignore this folkloric reference. Instead, he emphasizes the forest imagery with its promise of regeneration and renewal: his little tailors sew with green needles borrowed from a fir tree; they also use threads made of blades of grass. The most substantial changes, however, occur in the concluding lines of this translation. If Driz, who dedicated the lullaby to his daughter, playfully outlined an evening curfew – "Sleep, sleep in good health! [...] / at exactly ten o'clock / you will see her in your dream," – the translator transformed the

---

88   Ovsej Driz, *Зеленая карета*, trans. Genrich Sapgir, Moscow 1972, 5.

melodious lullaby into a song of longing and hope. The translation's circular composition appeals to little animals and children, and its word "Spring" reiterated three times, saturates the evening family ritual with an air of eternity. Where Driz's original poem is playful and intent on keeping domestic bliss intact, Sapgir's variation on it evokes a similarly attractive and soothing world outside of one's home. He does seem to cherish tranquility, peace, and fragile beauty, but for him, they do not exist within enclosed or densely populated spaces.

Like many other translations for children from that era, Sapgir's "Зеленая карета" implied a dual addressee. In 1972, the poem became the title text of Driz's book for children published by "Detskaja literatura" in Sapgir's translation and with illustrations by Viktor Pivovarov. This short but widely available publication (it had a print run of 300,000 copies) appealed to many adult readers, due to both its intense lyricism and beautiful visual images. The latter were reminiscent of Mark Chagall's paintings – the "forbidden fruit" of Western European art then hidden from broader Soviet audiences but well-known to connoisseurs. Full-page color illustrations alternated with black and white graphic vignettes displayed side-by-side with poetic text.

Pivovarov's illustrations are consonant with the lyrical world of Driz as well as with Sapgir's poetic vision. Following in the translator's footsteps, the artist adds new characters and expands spatial horizons of the literary texts. For instance, he depicts a black rook on the carriage's footstep – a creature absent from the original text but added in Sapgir's rendering of "Зеленая Карета." Evoking rich colors and abound in whimsical imagery, both the poem and the drawings are steeped in the aura of Jewish folklore: they conjure a magical world filled with beauty, music, and metaphysical promise. This sense of strangeness as well as the intangible hope and the enthralled waiting for something wondrous to happen are representative not only of Sapgir's poetics of translation, but also of his era's general mood. Overall, such mood resonated with Russian readers and even listeners, who also learned "Зеленая Карета" as a song. Set to music by Aleksandr Sukhanov, it was frequently performed in the 1970s-80s, becoming a real favorite of several generations raised in the late Soviet singer-songwriter (i.e. "бардовская" ["bard"]) tradition. Needless to say, even when "bards" sang to large audiences, only a few people were aware of Shike Driz's authorship of the song's lyrics – or of Sapgir's translation from the Yiddish.

As Zachoder's and Sapgir's works show, the liberties these poets took in treating the original depended on their willingness to take creative risks while avoiding a strict adherence to the source text's imaginative and poetic structure. The 1960s witnessed a new freedom to experiment with imagery and mood in translation, which, in its turn, resulted in a unique mode of poetic interpretation – namely, a kind of appropriation of others' work that felt very personal and appeared "intrinsic" to the new cultural context. Both translators spoke of their affinity with their sources, and yet they preferred to remain true to their artistic individualities at the expense of deviating significantly from the form and content of the original texts. The success of their choice to forego veracity for the sake of innovative self-expression is obvious from the fact that these and other translations of the "Thaw" era quickly invaded the Russian cultural space and then began to permeate it in a variety of multimedia forms: as songs, graphic art, animated and even feature-length films. The afterlife of those "Thaw"-era Soviet translations continues well into the new millennium, thanks to their first grateful audience's eagerness to share them with their children and grandchildren.

To summarize, the resurgence of translation during the "Thaw" resulted in a dynamic experimentation with poetic voices and identities. Poets who then stepped out onto the literary scene had greater access to Western literature. Inventive and imaginative, talented and ideologically uninhibited, their translations contributed to the restoration of Soviet literature's previously interrupted ties with the European and American literary traditions. Many of the poets who began their work in the 1960s by translating for children have evolved into the leading authorities in children's literature and translation. Such authors as Michail Jasnov, Marina Boroditskaja, Grigorij Kruzhkov, and Andrej Usachev often blend the boundary between the two fields while continuing to offer their readers a chance to admire their work as well as that of their American, French, German, Italian, and British counterparts.

5 Conclusion

In the Soviet Union of the 1920s-60s, translation and children's literature intersected as zones of freedom – the two fields of literary production that allowed authors to retain their poetic identity while being creatively, if not happily, engaged. The connection between these two modes of literary work, however, would benefit from further detailed exploration. The Soviet paradox of concurrent ideological control and artistic freedom explored by Marina Balina points to a specific communicative situation inherent in translation, and in translating for children specifically. As I have tried to show, translations of poetry for children in the Soviet state reflect broader ideological and institutional changes that took place over decades, including the increasing censorship and editorial control over the selection of source texts, greater attention to the style and method of translation, and one-time preference for "domesticating approach." Then again, Soviet cultural reforms of the 1920s, 30s, and 60s as well as the sense Soviet authors seemed to share of creating a "new" literature for children allowed for a range of stylistic experiments and poetic innovations. None of these creative endeavors were possible on such a broad scale in literature addressed to adults.

In particular, complex notions of childhood creativity, children's language and play established by Chukovskij appealed to many "adult" authors who had turned to children's literature as a creative outlet, a source of income, or both. Their own poetics often influenced children's poems they produced, bringing them to the level of stylistic sophistication which grown-ups could detect and appreciate. This "maturation" of Soviet children's poetry accounted for the phenomenon of dual address. Although a common feature of writing for children in general, it acquired special significance even in the midst of totalitarian oppression precisely due to the juncture of political subversivity and aesthetic complexity. Moreover, translations of children's poetry created over decades reflect multiple scenarios of borrowing, adaptation and rewriting that also imply a second addressee, for their authors were able to imbue foreign texts with new and sometimes unexpected meaning. From Marshak's and Chukovskij's nursery rhymes and translations of Kipling to Michalkov's adaptations of Tuwim's poems and Zachoder's Vinni Puch songs, Russian readers and viewers internalized not only the foreign texts, but also their translators' stories and personalities. To study production and reception of poetry translations for children is to understand that some of the most familiar Soviet poems, songs, and rhymes have been shaped by complex social and historical factors.

Works Cited

Primary Sources

Busch, Wilhelm. *Plisch und Plum, und Fipps die Affe.* Munich 1944.
Busch, Wilhelm. *Plisch und Plum.* ⟨http://gutenberg.spiegel.de/buch/plisch-und-plum-4189/1⟩ (Accessed November 20, 2017).
Charms, Daniil. *Полное собрание сочинений.* St. Petersburg 1997.
Chukovskij, Kornej. *Собрание сочинений.* Moscow 2001.
Chukovskij, Kornej. *От двух до пяти.* Moscow 1955.
Chukovskij, Kornej and Andrej Fedorov. *Искусство перевода,* Leningrad 1930.
Chukovsky, Kornei. *A High Art,* trans. Lauren Leighton. Knoxville 2004.
Driz, Ovsej. *Зеленая карета,* trans. Genrich Sapgir. Moscow 1972.

Driz, Ovsej. *Di ferte strune*. Moscow 1969.

Letuchij, Vladimir. *Макс и Мориц. Мальчишечья история в семи проделках*. Moscow 2003.

Marshak, Samuil. *Вслух про себя. Воспоминания*. Moscow 1975.

Marshak, Samuil. *Собрание сочинений в восьми томах*. Moscow 1969.

Michalkov, Sergej. *Собрание сочинений в шести томах*. Moscow 1981-1983.

Miln, Alan A. *Винни-Пух и все остальные: О плюшевом медвежонке и его друзьях*, trans. Boris Zachoder. Moscow 1960.

Miln, Aleksandr. *Винни-Пух и все-все-все*, trans. Boris Zachoder. Moscow 1965.

Miln, Aleksandr. *Винни-Пух и все-все-все*, trans. Boris Zachoder. Moscow 1992.

Milne, Alexander. *Winnie the Pooh and Other Stories*. London 1994.

Rabelais, François. *Гаргантюа и Пантагрюэль*, trans. Nikolaj Zabolockij. Moscow 1935.

The Little Mother Goose. New York 1912.

Tuwim, Julian. *Wiersze wybrane*. Wroclaw 1969.

Usachev, Andrej. *Макс и Мориц и другие истории для детей. Истории в стихах и картинках*. Moscow 2011.

Zachoder, Boris. *"Но есть один поэт": Неопубликованное наследие в двух томах*. Moscow 2008.

Secondary Sources

Arzamastseva, Irina. *Век ребенка в русской литературе 1900-1930*. Moscow 2003.

Avtonomova, Natalia and Michail Gasparov. "Сонеты Шекспира – переводы Маршака," in *Вопросы литературы* 2 (1969), 100-112.

Baer, Brian James. *Translation and the Making of Russian Literature*. New York 2016.

Baer, Brian James. "Literary Translation and the Construction of a Soviet Intelligentsia," in Maria Tymoczko, ed., *Translation, Resistance, Activism*. Amherst 2010, 149-167.

Bagno, Vsevolod, and Nikolaj Kazanskij. "Переводческая 'ниша' в советскую эпоху и феномен стихотворного перевода в XX веке," in Vsevolod Bagno, ed., *RES TRADUCTORICA. Перевод и сравнительное изучение литератур: к восьмидесятилетию Ю. Д. Левина*. St. Petersburg 2000, 50-65.

Balina, Marina. "Советская детская литература: несколько слов о предмете исследования," in Marina Balina and Valerij Vjugin, eds., *"Убить Чарскую": Парадоксы советской литературы для детей. 1920-е – 1930-е*. St. Petersburg 2013.

Bogdanov, Konstantin, et al., eds. *Джамбул Джабаев: Приключения казахского акына в советской стране*. Moscow 2013.

Bogdanov, Konstantin. "Право на сон и условные рефлексы: колыбельные песни в советской культуре 1930-1950х годов," in Natalja Borisova, et al., eds., *СССР: территория любви*. Moscow 2009, 79-127.

Borisenko, Aleksandra. "Песня невинности, она же опыта. О новых переводах Винни-Пуха," in *Иностранная литература* 4 (2002), ⟨http://magazines.russ.ru/inostran/2002/4/boris.html⟩ (Accessed November 20, 2017).

Etkind, Efim. "Для маленьких читателей," in *Поэзия и перевод*. Leningrad 1963, 345-379.

Fedorov, Andrej. "К вопросу о переводимости," in V. Ganiev et al., eds., *Актуальные проблемы художественного перевода. Материалы Всесоюзного Симпозиума (25 февраля – 2 марта 1966 г.)*. Moscow 1967, 33-39.

Galanov, B. E., et al., eds. *Я думал, я чувствовал, я жил. Воспоминания о С. Я. Маршаке*. Moscow 1971.

Hellman, Ben. *Fairy Tales and True Stories. The History of Russian Literature for Children and Young People (1574-2010)*. Leiden and Boston 2013.

Hunt, Peter. *Criticism, Theory and Children's Literature*. Cambridge, MA 1991.

Iljicheva, L. V. "Рисованные рассказы В. Буша в переводах Д. Хармса и С. Маршака," ⟨http://www.d-harms.ru/library/risovanniy-rasskazy-busha-v-perevodah-harmsa-i-marshaka.html⟩ (Accessed November 24, 2017).

Inggs, Judith. "Translation and Transformation: English Language Children's Literature in Soviet (Russian) Guise," in *International Research in Children's Literature* 8:1 (2015), 1-16.

Jaccard, Jean-Philippe and T. Grob. "Хармс – переводчик или поэт барокко?" in A. Toddes, ed., *Шестые тыняновские чтения. Материалы*. Moscow and Riga 1992, 31-44.

Jasnov, Michail. *Путешествие в Чудетство. Книга о детях, детской поэзии и детских поэтах*. St. Petersburg 2015.

Jasnov, Michail. "От Робина Бобина до малыша Русселя," in *Дружба народов* 12 (2004), ⟨http://magazines.russ.ru/druzhba/2004/12/ias12.html⟩ (Accessed November 20, 2017).

Karacheva, N. S., "В поисках 'дома в медвежьем углу': В. Руднев vs. Б. Заходер в диалоге с А. Милном," in *Концепт. Научно-методический электронный журнал* 20 (2014), ⟨http://e-koncept.ru/2014/54779.htm⟩ (Accessed November 20, 2017).

Kelly, Catriona. *Children's World: Growing up in Russia, 1890-1991*. New Haven and London 2007.

Khotimsky, Maria. "World Literature, Soviet Style: A Forgotten Episode in the History of the Idea," in *Ab Imperio* 3 (2013), 119-154.

Kirschenbaum, Lisa. *Small Comrades: Revolutionizing Childhood in Soviet Russia, 1917-1931*. New York 2001.

Klein Tumanov, Larissa. "Writing for a Dual Audience in the Former Soviet Union: The Aesopian Children's Literature of Kornei Chukovsky, Mikhail Zoshchenko, and Daniil Kharms," in Sandra L. Beckett, ed., *Transcending Boundaries. Writing for a Dual Audience of Children and Adults*. New York 1999, 129-148.

Kobrinskij, Aleksandr. "О некоторых подтекстах одного Хармсовского вольного перевода," in *История литературы. Поэтика. Кино. Сборник в четь Мариэтты Омаровны Чудаковой*. Moscow 2012, 160-170.

Kukulin, Ilja and Marija Majofis. "Детское чтение советской эпохи: несоветский взгляд. От редакторов," in *Новое Литературное Обозрение* 60 (2003), ⟨http://magazines.russ.ru/nlo/2003/60/ikmm.html⟩ (Accessed November 20, 2017).

Kukulin, Ilja and Marija Majofis. "Семиотика детства. Вступительная заметка," in *Новое Литературное Обозрение* 58 (2002), ⟨http://magazines.russ.ru/nlo/2002/58/m1-pr.html⟩ (Accessed November 20, 2017).

Kuleshov, V. E. "Предисловие," in I. Antipova and V. Kuleshov, eds., *Детский сборник. Статьи по детской литературе и антропологии детства*. Moscow 2004, 2-12.

Lathey, Gillian. "The Translation of Literature for Children," in Kirsten Malmkjaer and Kevin Winde, eds. *The Oxford Handbook of Translation Studies*. Oxford 2011, 198-213.

Lathey, Gillian. "Introduction," in Gillian Lathey, ed., *The Translation of Children's Literature. A Reader*. Clevedon, UK 2006, 3-14.

Lekmanov, Oleg. "О двух редакциях одного перевода Даниила Хармса," in L. Kiseleva, ed., *Лотмановский сборник 4*. Moscow 2014, 495-501.

Leving, Yuri. "Mister Twister in the Land of Bolsheviks: Sketching Laughter in Marshak's Poem," in *Slavic Review* 70:2 (2011), 279-306.

Maeots, Olga. "Jewish Heritage in Russian Children's Literature," in *New Review of Children's Literature and Librarianship*, 6:1 (2000), 77-89.

Marshak, Samuil. "Содоклад С. Я. Маршака о детской литератруе," in *Первый Всероссийский Съезд Советских Писателей, 1934. Стенографический отчёт*. Moscow 1934, 20-37.

Nestjuricheva, Nadezhda. "Английский Spleen на русский лад: 'Винни Пух' Бориса Заходера и Виктора Вербера," in *Филолог* 18 (2012), ⟨https://elibrary.ru/item.asp?id=17334034⟩ (Accessed November 20, 2017).

Nikolajeva, Maria. *Children's Literature Comes of Age. Toward a New Aesthetic*. New York and London 1996.

Oktjabr'skaja, O. S. *Пути развития русской детской литературы XX века (1920-2000-е гг.)*. Moscow 2012.

O'Sullivan, Emer. *Comparative Children's Literature*. New York 2005.

Petrovskij, Miron. "Поэт Корней Чуковский," in Chukovskij, Kornej, *Стихотворения*. St. Petersburg 2002, 5-60.

Pivovarov, Viktor. "Его голос," in T. Michajlovskaja, ed., *Великий Генрих. Сапгир и о Сапгире*. Moscow 2003, 323-330.

Pleshakova, Ol'ga. *Теория литературы и практики читательской деятельности*. Moscow 2012.

Scherr, Barry P. "Chukovsky's Whitmans," in *Russian Literature* 66:1 (2009), 65-98.

Schultze, Brigitte. "Wilhelm Buschs *Max und Moritz* Slavisch: Variantenbildung im Zeichen Von Textverstaendnis, Intermedialitaet und Kultureller Differenz," in *Guttenberg Jahrbuch*, 2007, 211-238.

Shavit, Zohar. "Translation of Children's Literature as a Function of Its Position in the Literary Polysystem," in *Poetics Today* 2:4 (1981), 171-179.

Shavit, Zohar. "The Ambivalent Status of Texts: The Case of Children's Literature," in *Poetics Today* 1:3 (1980), Special Issue: *Narratology I: Poetics of Fiction*, 75-86.

Sherry, Samantha. *Discourses of Regulation and Resistance. Censoring Translation in the Stalin and Khrushchev Era Soviet Union*. Edinburgh 2015.

Shraer, Maksim D., and David Shraer-Petrov. *Генрих Сапгир: классик авангарда*. St. Petersburg 2004.

Shubinskij, Valerij. *Даниил Хармс. Жизнь человека на ветру*. St. Petersburg 2008.

Sil'nyj, Lukjan. "Что такое чуковщина?" in *Вестник литературы* 3 (March 1909), 78-80.

Sokol, Elena. *Russian Poetry for Children*. Knoxville, TN 1984.

Steiner, Evgeny. *Stories for Little Comrades: Revolutionary Artists and the Making of Early Soviet Children's Books*, trans. Jane Ann Miller. Seattle 1999.

Witt, Susanna. "Byron's 'Don Juan' in Russian and the 'Soviet School of Translation,'" in *Translation and Interpreting Studies* 11:1 (2016), 23-43.

Witt, Susanna. "Arts of Accommodation: The First All-Union Conference of Translators, Moscow, 1936, and the Ideologization of Norms," in Leon Burnett and Emily Lygo, eds., *The Art of Accommodation: Literary Translation in Russia*. Bern 2013, 141-184.

Witt, Susanna. "The Shorthand of Empire: Podstrochnik Practices and the Making of Soviet Literature," in *Ab Imperio* 3 (2013), 155-190.

Zachoder, Boris. "Приключения Винни-Пуха. Из истории моих публикаций," in *Вопросы литературы* 5 (2002), ⟨http://magazines.russ.ru/voplit/2002/5/zah.html⟩ (Accessed November 20, 2017).

Zachoder, Galina. *Заходер и все-все-все: воспоминания*. Moscow 2003.

CHAPTER 10

Under the Hypnosis of Disney: Ivan Ivanov-Vano and Soviet Animation for Children

Lora Wheeler Mjolsness

1   Introduction

Ivan Petrovich Ivanov-Vano has been called the father of Soviet animation: over the course of sixty years, he directed over fifty animated films and wrote about his art prolifically and with great insight. Despite the marginalized status of animation in Soviet cinematography, Ivanov-Vano succeeded in bringing it to the fore of scholarly analysis. In his theoretical works, he explored the history of animation and analyzed the technical, narrative and artistic merits of animated films, especially those produced for children. Both his critical analysis and his animated films pushed the boundaries of Soviet animation. One of his most famous films, Конек-горбунок (*The Humpbacked Horse*, 1947), exemplifies the new Soviet aesthetic in animation after World War II. In Конек-горбунок, Ivanov-Vano turned to Russian literature, folklore and representational art as a way of interpreting Russian cultural heritage and translating it into the language of Soviet ideology and culture.[1] At the same time, Ivanov-Vano both adopted and rejected the American animated standard in his approach to filmmaking.

Ivanov-Vano was frequently called the Russian Walt Disney because of his attention to detail and dedication to animating the fairytale. It is true that Russian and Western fairytales, folktales and fables were some of Ivanov-Vano's favorite subjects, just as Western European folktales were the main

---

1 Due to the extreme popularity of the original Конек-горбунок, Ivanov-Vano remade the film in 1975 after the negative of the 1947 original was deemed too poor for rerelease. Technological advancements in restoration have since made it possible to rerelease the 1947 version. Both versions of the film include the folk sense, satire and fantastical escapes established by Petr Ershov's 1834 poem, but the two films differ due to transitions in Soviet animation aesthetics, technical advances, and Ivanov-Vano's creative approaches to storytelling. One of the obvious differences between the films is that the 1975 version is based more closely on the narrative structure of Petr Ershov's poem and hence includes the quest for the Tsar-maiden's ring, omitted earlier.

source of inspiration for Disney. Another reason that justifies critics' comparison of Ivanov-Vano to the American master of animation is their shared technical interests. Like Disney, Ivanov-Vano was attracted to full-scale feature length films that employed full, i.e. cel, animation that normally uses twenty-four frames per second to simulate the reality of movement.[2] Moreover, animated films created by both directors were extravagant, avoided time-saving shortcuts, and were full of spectacular fantasy-filled effects that aimed to catch and hold the audience's attention. There were also dramatic differences between them. To begin with, Disney unfailingly selected tales that would please the general American and his ever-increasing international audience, believing that the choice of a popular tale would appeal to the greatest number of people and thus help the studio generate more profit. Ivanov-Vano, on the contrary, was forced to navigate the strict ideological demands articulated by the Soviet authorities. He had to select fairytales with a specific ideological message. Thus, instead of devising methods for reaching out to the largest number of people imaginable, he was perfecting an Aesopian language of cinematography as well as his own personal style. Secondly, although Ivanov-Vano admired the work of the Disney studio, especially its technical achievements in sound, synchronization and movement, and even was willing to pay tribute to the idiosyncratic Disney style of portraying human characters, animals and inanimate objects, he also fought against what he considered the cheap vulgar disneyfication of Soviet animation. This is why Ivanov-Vano's most noteworthy contribution to his field – achieved both in theory and in practice – appears to be his accomplishment in developing (and urging others to develop) his individual style in animation that, in his opinion, was distinctly Russian. This chapter is dedicated to the discussion of the film director's creative and theoretical accomplishments, as well as to the analysis of his re-interpretation of Disney's heritage in the ideological and aesthetic contexts of Soviet animation.

2 The Early Years: From the Avant-Garde to Animation for Children

Ivanov-Vano was part of the first wave of Soviet animators who, having joined the field after the Revolution of 1917, strove to master the techni-

---

2 For the history of the basic technique of Disney animation, see Maureen Furniss, *Art in Motion: Animation Aesthetics*. Sydney 2008. Ivanov-Vano's basic technique is discussed in Olga Abramova, "Иван Иванов-Вано," in *Мастера советской мультипликации*, Moscow 1972. Ivanov-Vano also explains his own technique in detail in *Рисованный фильм*, Moscow 1950.

cal complexities of animation in order to bring drawings to life on the big screen. Upon graduation from the Higher State Art and Technical Studios (Высшие художественно-технические мастерские – ВХУТЕМАС) in 1923, Ivanov-Vano joined an experimental animation studio at the State Technical School of Cinematography (Государственный техникум кинематографии – ГТК) headed by Zenon Komissarenko, Jurij Merkulov and Nikolaj Chodataev. Still in his early twenties, he learned the basics of animation while working on one of the very first Soviet narrative animated films in support of the Chinese revolution, *Китай в огне* (*China in Flames*, 1925). Ivanov-Vano became interested in animation not only for its story-telling possibilities, but also for the technical process. Both the narrative potential of animated film and its ability to interweave the fantastic with the mundane led him to produce films geared towards younger audiences. Thus, from the beginning of his career, Ivanov-Vano was attracted to the idea of adapting animation in a way that he believed benefited the child. Nevertheless, not all of his early animation was directed at children. For example, *Блэк энд уайт* (*Black and White*, 1932) is a satirical film. Based on the lyrics of Vladimir Majakovskij's famous poem by the same name (1925), it derided American racism in the Cuban sugar industry. And yet, early Soviet animation did reach children, albeit in a round-about way. It was an experimental field influenced by the Russian artistic Avant-Garde, which in its turn had made an enormous impact on Soviet graphic arts and children's literature.[3] In the 1920s in particular, animated films produced in the Soviet Union owed their unique aesthetic appeal to Vladimir Tatlin, Aleksandr Rodchenko, Majakovskij, illustrators like Vladimir Lebedev, and newspaper cartoonists like Viktor Deni. Early animated films, for example, *Советские игрушки* (*Soviet Toys*, 1924) directed by Dziga Vertov, as well as *Блэк энд уайт*, were created with paper and ink cut-outs to resemble graphic collages.[4] They echoed some of the collages in children's books of that era, such as Gustav Klucis's and Valentina Kulagina's black-and-white cutouts in Viktor Gornyj's *Петяш* (*Petjash*, 1926) and S. Senkin's collages in Nikolaj Vladimirskij's *Песня*

---

[3] For example, Laura Pontieri discusses the link between early Soviet animation and the Avant-Garde graphic artist, Michail Cechanovskij. She suggests that Cechanovskij's book illustrations display the directness of poster style, elements of journal graphics, and advertising, and maintains that he was the first animator to use these styles in films. See Pontieri, *Soviet Animation and the Thaw of the 1960s. Not Only for Children*, New Barnet, Herts, UK 2012, 22-29.

[4] *Советские игрушки* draws on the style of Viktor Deni and other newspaper cartoonists of the 1920s. See my "Vertov's *Soviet Toys*: Commerce, Commercialization and Cartoons," in *Studies in Russian and Soviet Cinema* 2:3 (2008), 247-267.

о Тане (*The Song about Tanja*, 1926).⁵ Color collage was a strong influence on Michail Cechanovskij's illustrations to Samuil Marshak's Почта (*The Mail*, 1927) and Семь чудес (*Seven Wonders*, 1926) and Lebedev's collage-like graphic design for Marshak's Мороженое (*Ice-cream*, 1925).⁶ Блэк энд уайт also followed the poster-style of Majakovskij's Окна РОСТА ("The Russian Telegraph Agency Windows," 1919-1921); it was made in the tradition of the Revolutionary poster and agitprop films.⁷

Films for adults like Блэк энд уайт are rare in Ivanov-Vano's career, as he was drawn to the fairytale as a means for appealing to a young audience. Some of his most memorable films are adaptations of fairytales: Сказка о царе Дурандае (*The Tale of Tsar Durundaj*, 1934), Конек-горбунок (1947), Гуси-лебеди (*Swan Geese*, 1949), Снегурочка (*The Snow Maiden*, 1952), Двенадцать месяцев (*The Twelve Months*, 1956), В некотором царстве (*Once Upon a Time*, 1957), and Сказка о царе Салтане (*The Tale of Tsar Saltan*, 1984). But even before Ivanov-Vano began to "translate" folk and literary fairytales into animated films, he was concerned with the power animation exercised over a child viewer. In 1927 in particular, he worked on two animated films which not only featured child protagonists, but also focused on the specific ways animation could be perceived by children in the audience: Каток (*The Skating Rink*, 1927), under the direction of Jurij Zheljabuzhskij, and Сенька-Африканец (*Sen'ka-the-African*, 1927), based on Korneij Chukovskij's tale Крокодил (*Crocodile*, 1916). The latter opens with a live action sequence of a little boy at the zoo and then transitions into the animated imaginary world. Chukovskij's anthropomorphized characters, the elephant, the crocodile and the giraffe, come to life on screen, teaching Senka a moral lesson about proper behavior. Ivanov-Vano's artistic choice – the transition from live action film to animated film – sets the stage for the visualization of a child's active and lively imagination. This thematic focus – children's ability to invent reality and live their fantasy – shifts in Каток, a story of an ice-skating race, which is technically structured around animation's ability to replicate and emphasize the magic of motion. The film's main character is a little boy who accidentally enters and wins

---

5 Both books were published in Moscow by Novaja Moskva. These and other editions are discussed in detail in Michail Karasik's monumental *Ударная книга советской детворы*, Moscow 2010.

6 Samuil Marshak, *Почта*. Leningrad and Moscow 1927; *Семь чудес*. Leningrad and Moscow 1926; *Мороженое*. Leningrad and Moscow 1925.

7 For the discussion of Блэк энд уайт and other satirical films of the 1930s see Pontieri, *Soviet Animation and the Thaw of the 1960s*, 36-37. Anatolij Volkov writes on films influenced by the Avant-Garde in "Мультипликация," in *Кино: политика и люди (1930-е годы)*, Moscow 1995, 112-116.

an ice-skating competition. To overcome the difficulty of depicting the fluid movement of skating, Ivanov-Vano increased the technical difficulty of *Каток* by animating characters in white on a black background, and then finished the sequence by projecting negative images onto a mirror. He argued that this reversal was easier on children's eyes and thus made it easier for them to follow the film's plot.[8] In fact, it was not only the "ease" of perception that seemed to fascinate him, but also the transformative quality of animation itself.

3   The Magical Appeal of the Fairytale

Ivanov-Vano's technical experiments eventually led to his choosing fairytales as an ideal subject of children's animated films. He believed that exposure to the fairytale was the essence of children's future well-being. In an interview given in 1982, at the end of his career, he praised the "consistency" of the genre and suggested that the power of the animated fairytale stemmed from the pedagogical and ethical potential of the fantastical narratives. He also stated that fairytales offer children a type of moral dependability:

> With the fantastical plot and the magic nature of the heroes, the fairytale forces the child's heart to feel and teaches empathy and sympathy. But this happens only when the action of the screen convinces the child of its own authenticity, validity, and outlook of the characters. All of this comes together in an inseparable whole when it is colored by a realistic emotional atmosphere. This is where the educational impact of the tale comes from.[9]

Even in the 1980s, Ivanov-Vano continues to emphasize the real world over the imaginary, despite the fantastic possibilities of the medium of animation already discovered by then. This emphasis could be explained by his familiarity with the Soviet regime's resistance to the proliferation of the imaginative figurativeness and whimsical poetics in literary and cinematic works for children. In the 1920s and 1930s, Soviet pedagogues and party leaders were especially hostile towards the fairytale and fantasy. The director's unwillingness to ac-

---

[8] For more discussion of Ivanov-Vano's *Каток*, see Birgit Beumers, "Comforting Creatures in Children's Cartoons," in Marina Balina and Larissa Rudova, eds., *Russian Children's Literature and Culture*, New York and London 2008, 156.

[9] *Ivanov-Vano's interview to E. Nikitkina. Transcript Interview*, in RGALI, Moscow, Fund 2912, Folder 6, File 245.

cept the reliance on realism they fostered in those years is still evident in the interview he gave so many years later.

Discussing fairytales in the context of the history of early Soviet animation adds to the complexity of interpreting Ivanov-Vano's creative choices. As Marina Balina points out in *Politicizing Magic: An Anthology of Russian and Soviet Fairy Tales*, the Soviets were slow to realize the influential pedagogical advantages of the fairytale and saw enthusiasm for folklore and fairytales as part of the bourgeois mind-set, by then violently eradicated.[10] A collectively authored volume called Мы против сказки (*We are Against the Fairy Tale*, 1928), was edited by leading Soviet pedologists, such as Ivan Sokoljanskij and Aleksandr Zaluzhnyj. They strove to create regulations in children's literature by championing class-oriented content and chastising those authors who "polluted" the imagination of young readers by exposing them to fairytales. This movement had some powerful allies, including Lenin's widow, Nadezhda Krupskaja, who instigated the removal of fairytales from library shelves because of her belief that the fostering of imagination through fantasy directly opposed the utilitarian upbringing necessary for future builders of communism. It was the Decree of the Party's Central Committee that pronounced the fairytale's necessity for Soviet children on September 9, 1933.[11] A year later, Maksim Gor'kij fully rehabilitated the fairytale at the First Soviet Writer's Congress. Gor'kij emphasized the ability of folklore and fairytales to influence social change and insisted on the importance of Soviet readers' familiarity with folklore. Nevertheless, Soviet critics, pedagogues, and ideological workers continued to fear magic, animism, and anthropomorphism – the devices that make the fairytale so attractive to children and thus such a perfect subject matter for animated film. This is especially noticeable in Ivanov-Vano's writing on animation. In his essays and theoretical treatises and in the interview quoted above, he is often torn between praising the fantasy as the foundation of animation and pointing out the need to ground animation in reality.

Ivanov-Vano's career might have changed focus, taking him away from his work for younger audiences and fairytales, had the Soviet State not supported films created specifically for children. In March 1928, just as the struggle against the fairytale was gaining momentum, the ideological validity of cin-

---

10 For a more detailed analysis of the early Soviet fairytale discourse and of Soviet pedologists, including Nadezha Krupskaja's and Maksim Gor'kij's involvement, see Marina Balina, "Introduction," in M. Balina, H. Goscilo, M. Lipovetsky, eds., *Politicizing Magic: An Anthology of Russian and Soviet Fairy Tales*, Evanston, IL 2005, 105.

11 "Постановление ЦК ВКП(б) от 9 сентября 1933 г. 'Об издательстве детской литературы,'" in *Решения партии о печати*. Moscow 1941, 158-159.

ema for children became a focal point of the All-Union Party Congress. Its participants noted that "children's films are almost completely lacking" and advised filmmakers to "make consistent political and pedagogical-artistic, cultural and newsreel films for children's audiences."[12] As animation was still a marginalized art form, the Soviet ideologists spoke predominantly about live action films. And yet, their recognition of cinematic needs of young audiences became instrumental for the development of animated film as a new Soviet art form. That same year, Ivanov-Vano received permission from Sovkino, an influential film organization run by the state, to organize an animation department at the film studio Mezhrabpromfil'm in Moscow. For the first time, the Soviet government allowed animators to have their own dedicated location. With the ideological support for children's animation and the funding of the new animation studio headed by Ivanov-Vano, Soviet animators began to create films for children that both replicated and tried to overcome the standards set by their immediate predecessor, the American film studio headed by Walt Disney.

The organization of this new animation department and the ideological support for children's animation led Ivanov-Vano to peruse animated films for children based on fairytales and children's stories. In the 1930s and 1940s, he directed *Сказка о царе Дурандае* (*The Tale of Tsar Durandaj*, 1934), *Стрекоза и муравей* (*The Dragonfly and the Ant*, 1935), *Котофей Котофеевич* (*Kotofej Kotofeevich*, 1937), *Три мушкетера* (*The Three Musketeers*, 1938), *Мойдодыр* (*Wash 'em Clean*, 1939), *Ивась* (*Ivas'*, 1940), *Краденое солнце* (*The Stolen Sun*, 1943), and *Зимняя сказка* (*The Winter Tale*, 1945) before turning to his first full-length feature *Конек-горбунок* (1947). But in the 1950s he made the most of his practical experience and became a theoretician, passing on to others not only detailed explanations of technical competencies involved in the creation of animation, but also some more abstract perceptions and elucidations of his art, including ideas for the theoretical justification of animated fairytales as a must-have for children in the Soviet Union. In the 1950s, his dedication to animating the fairytale continued. During that decade alone, he created *Гуси-лебеди* (*Geese and Swans*, 1949), *Лесной концерт* (*A Forest Concert*, 1953), another, colored, version of *Мойдодыр* (1954), *Храбрый заяц* (*The Brave Hare*, 1955), and some of his most well-known and timeless tales, *Снегурочка* (*The Snow Maiden*, 1952), *Двенадцать месяцев* (1956), and *В некотором царстве* (1957).

---

12   Richard Taylor and Ian Christie, *The Film Factory and Soviet Cinema in Documents, 1896-1939*, New York 1994, 210-11.

4   Teacher and Theorist: Ivanov-Vano's Ideas on Animation

Ivanov-Vano's critical works make his passion for children's animation more evident. Between 1950 and 1980, he wrote more than a dozen theoretical essays. While writing about animation became more acceptable in the 1970s-80s, in his day and age he was a pioneer in this field. In 1939, Ivanov-Vano, Sergej Koslovskij and Fedor Bogorodskij organized a department at the Soviet State Film School (Всесоюзный Государственный институт кинематографии – ВГИК) to teach both artists and directors the art of animation. Ivanov-Vano's interest in the technical side of animation and his desire to educate others in this art are the key motivations behind his taking on the role as theoretician and historian. Beyond educating others on the technical requirements of animation, he had two main goals in his writings. The first was to legitimize animation as an art form. The second was to encourage his students by making them realize that the limitations of animation lay with the animator. Ivanov-Vano asserted that, in his field, the artist's goal was to develop his or her individuality regardless of the collective aspect of Soviet ideology.

Ivanov-Vano's first book, *Рисованный фильм* (*Drawn Film*, 1950), analyzed animation as an art form especially aimed at children. It consisted of a series of chapters which taught beginning animators technical skills, outlined procedural requirements of their profession, and mapped out the history of animation. In the 1940s-50s, it was already seen as a popular medium, although its target audience – youth – often allowed critics to treat мультфильмы (children's animated films) less seriously than live action films. In his attempt to validate animation, Ivanov-Vano argued that the art form had been born earlier than traditional live action film. Reaching back into history to give animation a decisive head start, he referenced images from ancient Egypt that attempted to reproduce movement and argued, more generally, that, for centuries, humans had been attempting to analyze and recreate movement through images. Writing about the nineteenth century, Ivanov-Vano similarly linked animation to its earlier prototypes, such as фенакистископ (the phenakistiscope) and зоетроп (the zoetrope). He described these early cinematic prototypes as children's toys that produced the illusion of movement by means of a spinning disc with a series of pictures drawn on it. This foray into history proved that for our predecessors, animation was a serious art form worthy of exploration.[13]

---

13 Ivanov-Vano discusses these ideas in the first chapter of his monograph. "Как родилось искусство мультипликации," in *Рисованный фильм*, Moscow 1950, 3-15.

In *Рисованный фильм*, Ivanov-Vano also emphasized the role of the individual artist in the discovery of the limitless qualities of animation, the medium which embraced both realist and fantastic modes of representation. In one passage, he made the animator a magician, a conjuror capable of transforming matter: "He can turn an elephant into a fly and in front of the audiences' eyes turn that fly into an elephant. He can turn a spoon into a fish, and the fish will swim away. He can force a bear and a rabbit to play soccer."[14] Unlike other art forms, this one had no technological confines, Ivanov-Vano suggested. For him, the power of the animator lay in his ability to determine how reality was intertwined with fantasy – or, rather, to imaginatively recreate the world according to the animator's own conventions. In his suggestion that the "animator's fantasy opens up a limitless space," for example, we see how he encouraged his students to realize that they had to overcome limitations by letting their imaginations soar.[15] In the same chapter and elsewhere in the book, Ivanov-Vano asserted that the goal of Soviet animation was to develop the artist's specific means of self-expression (individuality). At that time, such a statement spelled a subtle attack on the collective aspect of Soviet aesthetics.

Ivanov-Vano's ideas on the transformative nature of imagination are similar to the theories of Paul Wells, introduced nearly half a century later. In his groundbreaking *Understanding Animation* (1998), Wells discusses metamorphosis – "the ability for an image to literally change into another completely different image" – as one of animation's most distinctive features. He suggests that animation is not simply art engendering mutation on screen, but the kind of art that leads to a transformative experience in and for a viewer:

> Metamorphosis in animation achieves the highest degree of economy in narrative continuity, and adds a dimension to the visual style of the animated film in defining the fluid abstract stage between the fixed properties of the images before and after transition.[16]

It is clear from this passage that, years before Wells, Ivanov-Vano saw the potential of drawn images to transfigure as one of the distinctive features of animation. And yet, the Soviet director put more of an emphasis on an animator's child-like approach to reality. He stressed the importance not as much of the interrelation of mutating images, as of the freshness and originality of an animator's vision – as these ideas complemented the type of animation he

---

14 Ivanov-Vano, *Рисованный фильм*, 11.
15 Ibid.
16 Paul Wells, *Understanding Animation*, New York 1998, 69.

was creating. By underscoring the connection between the real and the imaginary, Ivanov-Vano pointed out yet another idea that Wells would bring up in his work half a century later – namely, animation's propensity for subversion. Wells focused on the ideological and visual complexity of film narratives, as well as on the shifts between their literary and visual languages that competed for viewers' comprehension to explain political and social subversion.[17] In *Рисованный фильм*, Ivanov-Vano argued that subtle subversion was in the nature of the fairytale as the type of narrative best suited to the transformative medium of animated film, and in children's imagination which was most sharply attuned to perceiving and learning from the films' magical qualities. Ivanov-Vano once again turned to children's imagination and the fairytale as an explanation for subversion in animated films.

Рисованный фильм became one of the foundational works of Soviet animation partly because it explained why targeting animated films to children was so important for Soviet filmmakers. The treatise owed its conclusiveness to Ivanov-Vano's willingness to share his personal experience in it. By then a renowned film director, he justified his dedication to his young audience by suggesting that the power of animation stemmed not only from the artist's, but also from the child's imagination – which, in its turn, it helped to develop.[18] Ivanov-Vano insisted that since we already know the educational role that illustrations play in children's literature, we should not be surprised that animated films also have such a formative effect on children. By using the example of Kornej Chukovskij's tale *Мойдодыр* (*Wash 'em Clean* 1923), he asserted that a child would find an animated film more instructive, engaging, and visually stimulating than a picture book. "For the child it is more convincing to watch the blankets, sheets, a book and a candle escape on the screen from the Dirty Boy in the animated film based on Chukovskij's *Мойдодыр* than to contemplate the same objects and characters drawn in a book. A drawing in animation ceases to be what we understand as a drawing, but rather, becomes specific characters whose actions depend on the film events in which they participate," he wrote.[19]

The essence of animation, Ivanov-Vano noted, lies in its ability to connect perception to imagination.[20] This statement, however, was controversial even

---

17   Wells explains that "Animation legitimizes the social and political ambivalence of ...] narratives by simultaneously approximating some of the conditions of real existence while distancing itself from them by recourse to the unique aspects of its own vocabulary." Ibid., 21.
18   Ivanov-Vano, *Рисованный фильм*, 13-14.
19   Ibid., 14.
20   Ibid., 3-15.

for an accomplished Soviet director of animated films. Aware of ideological constraints of Socialist Realism, Ivanov-Vano struggled with his desire to laud the imaginary as an essence of any artist's work for children. To avoid presenting his approach as an aesthetics that undermined the Soviet ideology's focus on realism, he drew comparisons between animation and other art forms. For example, for him, animated characters had the same power over a child as actors performing in a theater. Known for his interest in audience's response to his films, Ivanov-Vano often snuck into the back of theaters in order to hear the children's reaction first-hand. He noted that the young viewers responded to events on the screen, expressing sympathy for animated characters, in exactly the same manner as they would react to a live theater performance.[21] Although the rehabilitation of the fairytale had already taken place, Ivanov-Vano continued to connect animation to live theater with its actors' more "realistic" portrayals of human action, communication, and emotion. Even his already exalted position in Soviet animation did not allow him to justify his use of imagination and fantasy purely by their visual and narrative potential or by their undeniable appeal to children.

5 Sojuzmul'tfil'm, Cel Animation and Socialist Realism

In spite of the constricting aesthetic policy of the Soviet state, intensifying or slackening with each sociopolitical move of the Soviet government, Ivanov-Vano invariably continued his defense of the imaginary. Like no other director, he was aware of the constraints that Soviet animation had to deal with on a daily basis. Although the industry's transition towards children as its new target audience started in the late 1920s, Soviet animation's relationship with this addressee was framed by the Soviet state's vision of the child as a cog in the ideological machine. As Catriona Kelly notes in "Shaping the 'Future Race': Regulating the Daily Life of Children in Early Soviet Russia," "Bolsheviks' determination to [...] construct a radically different new society meant that, from the first, children were pushed to the forefront of ideological discussion."[22] Authors and film directors, actors and animators had to ideologically inculcate the young, rather than purposelessly entertain them. This is why, in spite of the Soviet ideologues' support of the shift from adult to child-centered ani-

---

21   Ibid., 13-14.
22   Kelly, "Shaping the 'Future Race': Regulating the Daily Life of Children in Early Soviet Russia," in Christina Kiaer and Eric Naiman, eds., *Everyday Life in Early Soviet Russia: Taking the Revolution Inside*, Bloomington, IN 2006, 256.

mated films, the imaginary aesthetics advocated by Ivanov-Vano could not be tolerated in the oppressive and militantly authoritarian 1930s-40s. Instead, indoctrination through animation was one of the early thematic components and structural principles of Soviet cinematic art. No longer a recognizable offshoot of the Russian Avant-Garde, by the end of the 1930s it had been drastically transformed into a medium of Soviet propaganda for children.

Bureaucratic centralization of artistic institutions led to the reorganization of film studios, grouping animators together and changing the dynamic of film production. In 1936, the Mezhrabpomfil'm studio was reorganized, splitting in two; Союздетфильм (Sojuzdetfil'm) was to create live action films for the young, while Союзмультфильм (Sojuzmul'tfil'm) focused on all types of animation, including мультфильмы. The creation of Sojuzmul'tfil'm meant the disbanding of all of the small and relatively independent studios that had previously been part of Mosfil'm, Sovkino and Mezhrabpromfil'm.[23] As animators regrouped, with the majority of them joining Sojuzmult'fil'm, they experienced a loss of creative control and a strict curtailing of artistic initiative. For example, in the early 1930s, Michail Cechanovskij turned to Aleksandr Pushkin's tale "Сказка о попе и о работнике его Балде" ("The Tale of the Pope and his Worker Balda," 1830) for his next animation project. Dmitrij Shostakovich composed the musical score for the animation, which later became his op. 36.[24] However, in 1936 Cechanovskij and Shostakovich were forced to abandon their work on the film as the animation, based on the 1920s graphic style, was considered too experimental, while the music was deemed too formal and too alien to Pushkin's poetic style.

Soviet animators, including those working at Sojuzmult'fil'm studio, not only had to overcome the legacy of the Avant-Garde, but they were also forced to embrace a new artistic model partially based on Walt Disney's distinctive style. In the 1920s and 1930s, an innovative technique and a manifest aesthetic earned Disney wide popularity and compelled animators around the world to take notice. In the Soviet Union, Disney's overwhelming success led to a demand, on the part of viewers and policy-makers alike, to "Give us a Soviet Mickey Mouse."[25] This imperative, announced at the All-Union Conference on Comedy (1933), forced Soviet animators to respond to Disney both stylistically and technologically. The artists' exposure to Disney's smooth, colorful, child-like exaggerations of life-like characters, made their dedication to

---

23   Sjuzanna Bogdanova, "Очерки о жизни и творчестве Александры Гавриловны Снежко-Блотской," in *Кинограф* 19 (2008), 209.
24   Pontieri, *Soviet Animation and the Thaw of the 1960s*, 29-36.
25   Ibid., 39.

the adult-centered, more Avant-Garde, graphic poster imagery from the 1920s seem dated. They now needed to draw differently as well as adopt animation techniques that would permit their characters to walk, jump, run, climb, crawl, and shuffle in a more nuanced and persuasive manner. To achieve this goal, Sojuzmul'tfil'm began to follow the Disney Studio model by making a transition to the newest technique, cel animation. One of the greatest innovations in the industry, it allowed for greater synchronization of sound and movement – an achievement Ivanov-Vano paid particular attention to in his next book, *Рисованный фильм / Особый вид киноискусства* (*Drawn Film / A Special Kind of Cinema*, 1956).[26] Apart from producing a more life-like, convincing visual effect, the new procedure was more efficient and cost-effective. Clear flexible sheets known as cels could be created in an assembly line. This development permitted a large number of people to work on drawing and coloring the thousands of images that would then be layered and filmed. Studios could now create longer and more elaborate animated films quickly. To the chagrin of Soviet animators, Ivanov-Vano included, they were introduced to cel animation only in 1933-34, and even then the outcome of the process could not compare with American animation, partially due to the inferior quality of Soviet cels.[27] Moreover, the method undoubtedly encouraged productivity, but, due to its conveyer-based efficiency, it also reduced animators' individual creative style and made centralized control more possible.

Soviet animation was also marked by the nation-wide, periodically forced adoption of Socialist Realism as the main mode of artistic production, with its imperative to portray nature and society in believable, upbeat, and politically relevant ways. The combination of the new animation technique, cel animation, and Socialist Realism resulted in a greater control over the Soviet animator than ever before. It is not surprising that several artists and film directors who could not tolerate restrictions on their creativity, such as Nikolaj Chodataev, left animation to pursue other careers. And yet there were others who, like Ivanov-Vano, remained creative and even prolific under the changing conditions. In order to thrive, they had to adapt to a multitude of new requirements, from the adherence to a naturalistic, "believable," form and politically charged content to the ever-increasing party control and other administrative reforms at Sojuzmul'tfil'm.

---

26   Ivanov-Vano, *Рисованный фильм / Особый вид киноискусства*, Moscow 1956, 17. Disney and Soviet animation is also discussed by Balina and Beumers, "To Catch Up and Overtake Disney," in Jack Zipes, Pauline Greenhill, and Kendra Magnus-Johnston, eds., *Fairy Tales Films Beyond Disney: International Perspectives*, New York 2016, 151-172.

27   Ivanov-Vano, "Графическая мультипликация," in *Мультипликационный фильм*, Moscow 1936, 170.

Ivanov-Vano's resilience and dedication to a career in animation in spite of the ideological constraints stemmed from the opportunity it gave him to transfer literary, folktales and fairytales from the page to the screen. Despite the early Soviet animosity to the fairytale, the genre held special appeal because of its accessibility to younger audiences, capacity for nationalist and class indoctrination, and other propaganda potential.[28] But although the fairytale could be used as a heavy ideological tool, it could also serve as a foil for subtler artistic endeavors. Drawing from the relatively safe topic of national heritage, animators could focus on moral instruction of a universal timeless type, promoting such values as loyalty to one's friends, love for one's family, courage, and personal honor. Besides Ivanov-Vano, other animators, including the Brumberg sisters, Lev Atamanov, and Cechanovskij, also worked on animated adaptations of fairytales in these years. Some of them, the Brumberg sisters and Cechanovskij in particular, having already tried their hand at adapting fairytales into animated films for children, employed folkloric or magical narratives in order to skirt the issue of overt ideology during the height of the Stalinist terror. Aware that fairytales were not produced by authors strictly following the Socialist Realist canon, they insisted on the propitiousness of their choice by highlighting the fairytales' moral core as the key element in educating young Soviet citizens.

Ivanov-Vano was attracted to the dynamic, expressive nature of fairytale didacticism. In a 1982 interview to Elena Nikitkina, a fellow animator, he extolled the moral educational impact of the fairytale by pointing out its capacity to affect not only the young viewers' minds, but also their hearts:

> Moral teachings should not be abstractly affirmed but must be an organic part of the feature film. This moral core is especially important for the child's emotional growth, because emotional reactions are the most powerful, and sometimes decisive, in the film. The amazing intertwining of fantasy and reality in a story does not confuse the child and it should not bother us, the artists.[29]

Corresponding to the director's earlier pronouncements on the centrality of artistic imagination for the pedagogical influence of an animated film, Ivanov-Vano's statement reveals an insecurity of an artist who, as late as the 1980s, needs to defend the fantastic approach to story-telling on screen from the

---

28 Birgit Beumers addresses these issues in her article "Comforting Creatures in Children's Cartoons," 160-164.
29 *Ivanov-Vano's interview to E. Nikitkina. Transcript Interview.*

ostracism of his doctrinarian critics. His choice of arguments, however, and especially his emphasis on the "emotional impact" of a fantastical narrative, is convincing. As the medium that invited the young viewers' full immersion in the morally valuable story, animated fairytales had a chance to survive and even flourish within the Soviet ideological guidelines. Choosing fairytales and their underlying narratives allowed Ivanov-Vano and other animators to push the boundaries of the doctrine of Socialist Realism and use the moral codes not prescribed directly by the government.

As a theoretician, Ivanov-Vano allowed himself a modest distancing from the Soviet Realist aesthetics in the name of art only in 1962, in his monograph *Советское мультипликационное кино* (*Soviet Animated Film*, 1962). Appearing closer to the end of the "Thaw" era, this publication identified several ways in which animators could sidestep Soviet ideology. One of them was his and his colleagues' new focus on the artistic value of the art form itself. Another was the Russian folk and literary tradition as a safer, politically non-aggressive way to deal with Soviet nationalism. *Советское мультипликационное кино* sheds light on the animators' decisions, in the 1940s-50s, to produce films focused even more heavily on Russian and so-called "classic" fairytales (foreign folk or literary tales in translation). While highlighting timeless morals not directly connected to Soviet life, these source texts were not antithetical to the government's ideological goals, either.[30] It is characteristic of Ivanov-Vano's cautious writing, that, while defending the animators' reliance on timeless moral tales that were devoid of obvious Soviet ideology, he did not state directly that, due to this maneuver, many of the artists managed to evade repercussions during two decades of political terror and oppression.[31]

The trend towards incorporating fairytales in animation coincided with the Soviet government's decision to export more animated films. The post-war invasion of Eastern European countries and the bombardment of the Eastern Bloc with Soviet propaganda as well as the increasing cultural competition with the West on the global Cold War stage were critical factors behind this re-orientation towards a broader international audience. The competition on

---

30 From the 1930s on, themes drawn from Russia's national past became ever-present in Soviet mass culture, including Soviet animation. Heroes from the past joined Soviet heroes in promoting the ideological agenda of the state. Russian folk characters adopted by animators for their films can be seen as part of this trend. The use of Russia's national past in creating new Stalinist heroes is explored in depth in Kevin Platt's and David Brandenburger's *Epic Revisionism: Russian History and Literature as Stalinist Propaganda*. Madison, WI 2006.

31 Ivanov-Vano, *Советское мультипликационное кино*, Moscow 1962, 18-19.

a worldwide scale challenged Soviet animators to perfect their technical competence and outshine American and European studios. Ivanov-Vano's appreciation of Russian folk and literary sources allowed him to produce films that were unique both in form and content and brought about his first international acclaim for *Конек-горбунок* at the International Film Festival in Mariánské Lázně in 1948. He continued to receive international recognition for his films in the 1950s and 1960s, earning awards for *В некотором царстве* in 1958 at Karlovy Vary and for *Левша* (*Lefty*, 1964) at Leipzig in 1964. According to the Soviet director's own estimate, his success was based not only on his own, but also on the Soviet animation industry's commitment to the "national fairytale tradition and Russian arts and crafts."[32] He spoke of this devotion with pride: "I am deeply convinced that the strength of our Soviet animation is that it has always relied on national culture and art. This is our identity and the reason for our success on the world screen."[33] It is, in a way, to be expected that just like Disney, Ivanov-Vano was dedicated to fairytales and their timeless, placeless moral codes. What is more surprising, however, is his awareness of the fairytales' global appeal as a means for Soviet animators – and, more broadly, the Soviet government – to export the Russianized Soviet identity to the world market.

6 Disney's Hypnotic Influence

Кадр за кадром (*Frame after Frame*, 1980), Ivanov-Vano's memoir published seven years before his death, offers an in-depth critical analysis of Soviet animated film. As he had the chance to travel abroad, to meet foreign animators and to view many foreign animated films, the reach of his reminiscences extended beyond the border of the Soviet Union. One of the book's most engaging chapters, "Под гипнозом Диснея" ("Under the Hypnosis of Disney") is dedicated to the influence of the American animator and film producer on early Soviet animation. Ivanov-Vano portrayed Walt Disney as a hard worker, a thoughtful artist and an enterprising businessman. Appreciative of Disney's artistic exuberance, technological risk-taking, and commercial talent, he was nevertheless skeptical of the blind imitation of Disney style, which he believed would not be helpful in the development of animation in other countries, including the Soviet Union.[34] In his opinion, Soviet animators could not copy

---

32   *Ivanov-Vano's interview to E. Nikitkina.*
33   Ibid.
34   Ivanov-Vano, *Кадр за кадром*. Moscow 1980, 84.

Disney-style animation without losing some of the essential qualities of their art, namely, its "Russianness."[35] This idea was not new: in 1947, Sergei Eisenstein commented on the detrimental consequences of imitating Disney, suggesting that Soviet animators should be dedicated scholars of Russian culture. "Our animators use Disney's style. Meanwhile in the images of our animals and in the tracing style of our sketches we can follow our own Russian animal folklore and epic," Eisenstein wrote, ignoring, in his Russo-centric statements, cultural heritages of numerous other nations that were supposed to be an integral part of the Soviet nationhood.[36] And yet, Eisenstein's and Ivanov-Vano's pronouncements did point out an essential feature of Soviet animation – the feature that set it apart from Disney, with his then-focus on Western European literary and artistic tradition. Both recognized the fundamental intent of Soviet animation, namely, its willingness to make the Russian fairytale a literary and visual core of animated films. They also emphasized the need for Soviet animators to distance themselves from Disney's appealing style in spite of their shared interest in the fairytale as a genre. Inspired by their American counterpart, Soviet animators were bound to find their own artistic language to translate Russian fairytales for the screen.

When Disney's *Three Little Pigs* (1933), part of *The Silly Symphonies*, was first shown in 1933 in the Moscow movie-theater "Ударник" ("The Shock Worker"), under the umbrella of the Festival of American Animation, the power of this film over its audiences was palpable. According to Ivanov-Vano, it was this initial viewing that set off the discussion of Disney-style animation at the All-Union Meeting on the Problems of Comedy that same year. Over the next few years, Disney's films were screened at many different festivals in the Soviet Union. But while movie-goers and critics alike admired them, the latter always had to add a cautious note to their generally favorable reviews. Thus, program notes for the 1935 American Color Film Festival in Leningrad prepared the viewers for visual feast while warning them of the ideological pitfalls of American productions:

> The drawing, movement and music are main components of Disney's films, and they subordinate not only characters but also the inanimate objects, trees, flowers, leaves and clouds, which all take part in the whole rhythm. Disney films do not shine because of their narrative content. They are light, happy but frivolous, and their main task is to distract

---

35 Ibid., 85-86.
36 Sergej Ejzenshtejn, "Искусство," in *Избранные произведения в шести томах*, Vol. 3. Moscow 1964, 500.

viewers from evident reality and from the essential causes and social problems of the bourgeois world.³⁷

The program also asserted that Soviet animators should strive to follow the drawing, movement and sound techniques and especially the synchronization of Disney's animated films, but not the story line. The narrative of the *Silly Symphonies* differed significantly from Disney's other narrative shorts. *Silly Symphonies* were whimsically set to music, were not plot-driven and did not feature continuing characters. The Soviet critics of the *Silly Symphonies* chose to focus not on their lack of narrative complexity, but rather, on encouraging Soviet animators to create Disney-style films with ideologically correct storylines.

Ivanov-Vano was similarly impressed by *The Three Little Pigs*. This film, shot in Technicolor, was one of Disney's first efforts at "personality animation," a term used to describe the delineation of individual characters through the development of their idiosyncratic movement and specific voices. Each pig moves in a unique way; each has its own way of speaking. As an animator, Ivanov-Vano could not help noticing that *The Three Little Pigs* had taught him the importance of movement and sound synchronization. In 1933, because of cost constraints, he himself was still working with ink-and-paper rather than cel animation. The fluid, convincing synchronization became an option to many Soviet animators a few years later, when they, too, began to transition to cel. Moreover, Disney had also produced original music for his film, creating an overwhelming success with the song "Who's Afraid of the Big Bad Wolf?" which was translated into Russian for screenings in the Soviet Union.³⁸ According to Ivanov-Vano, within a few days children all over Moscow were singing the catchy jingle in the streets. And yet, just like Soviet critics reviewing the film, Ivanov-Vano was confident that following Disney to a tee would be an artistic dead-end for Soviet animators. In spite of his attraction to *The Three Little Pigs*, he was very strong in his opinion that he and his colleagues should imitate Disney neither in form, nor in idea, and that they should, instead, cultivate an individual style by finding inspiration in their native culture.

Animation, and especially Soviet animation, Ivanov-Vano insisted, was different. Instead of deriving inspiration from comics or caricatures, be they American or Russian, Soviet animators should appreciate and emulate the

---

37   N. Sekundov, ed., *Американские цветные фильмы*, Leningrad 1935, 2-3.
38   According to the Program of the American Color Film Festival, the song title was translated as "Кто боится гадкого большого волка" (Sekundov, *Американские цветные фильмы*, 8). However, in his memoirs Ivanov-Vano refers to it as "Нам не страшен серый волк," ("Who's Afraid of the Big Bad Wolf?") which is what it is widely known as now (*Кадр за кадром*, 80).

humor characteristic of Russian folklore. His other critical statement – and another suggestion that stemmed from it – concerned anthropomorphism, which Disney used so successfully in his Mickey Mouse films. For Ivanov-Vano, borrowing anthropomorphic approach from Disney spelled ignorance on animators' part. In his opinion, Russian traditional folk heroes, especially animals, had unique and complicated personalities, which could inspire Soviet filmmakers to produce funny, convincing, and yet intrinsically Russian animated shorts.[39]

In his memoir, Ivanov-Vano admits that his reaction to Disney changed after he watched *Snow White and the Seven Dwarfs* (1937) in the beginning of 1939. *Snow White* was a serious dramatic work which Soviet animators studied carefully and discussed with passion.[40] In the memoirist's opinion, it contained much of what he had been aiming at in his own animated films, such as an accurate depiction of detail. And of course, *Snow White* was a fairytale, which represented a cinematic translation of the literary genre Ivanov-Vano deemed most propitious for animation. In praising the film, he chose interesting points for analysis. For example, he suggested that Disney was more successful in creating his evil characters than he was at creating Snow White and the prince (this comparison marginalizes the dwarfs who by that time had won viewers' unshakable admiration). The American animators' attention to naturalistic detail also caught Ivanov-Vano's attention. For example, he noticed that when Snow White looked into the water, her reflection was enlivened by a slight ripple effect. Characteristically, in spite of Ivanov-Vano's devotion to the fairytale, the genre embracing the unbelievable and the fantastic, his observations demonstrate his dedication to reproducing life realistically in animated form. His most famous work, *Конек-горбунок*, demonstrated most powerfully that as an artist he did not succumb to Disney's hypnosis. This animated film was his way of proving that Soviet animators could distinguish themselves from the influential aesthetics, while also appreciating some of the American filmmaker's innovations and accomplishments.

7 The Humpbacked Horse (1947)

Ivanov-Vanos's first color full-length feature film, *Конек-горбунок*, is one of the most important animated works of the 1940s. Based on the 1834 narrative poem by Petr Ershov, it is a poetic masterpiece brought to life through

---

39 This is also mentioned in Ejzenshtejn, *Избранные произведения в шести томах*, 1964, 500, n. 30. Ivanov-Vano, *Кадр за кадром*, 86.
40 Ibid., 84.

skillful and imaginative craftsmanship, graphic inventiveness, and compelling sound effects. The director chose Ershov's tale for its folk language, amusing and resourceful heroes, and the fantastical escapades of the protagonist and his loyal magical horse, believing, as he always did, that the imaginary in literature complemented the medium of animation. Ershov's original text is a creative adaptation of several folk tales, remarkable for its appropriation of common Russians' everyday speech, peasants' vernacular, folk beliefs, superstitions, and rituals. Eager to demonstrate that "Russianness" can, indeed, be featured onscreen, Ivanov-Vano follows Ershov's path in imitating folk culture. His version of Конек-горбунок featured Russian folk paintings as well as traditional architecture, ceramics, toys, and wood cuts to create the mood that was both festive and instructive. But the nationalistic visual energy was only part of what made Конек-горбунок such a unique and influential animated film. Ivanov-Vano created a cinematic tale for children, which harkened back to the pre-revolutionary tradition both visually and in its moral message. He was particularly committed to utilizing the color principle, using a warm, intense, red-and-yellow-saturated color palette to unite the film and highlight its folkloric elements. While his indebtedness to Disney is apparent, it is not Disney's influence that distinguishes this attempt to translate cinematically Ershov's fairytale for the Soviet audience. Rather, it is Ivanov-Vano's fascination with pre-revolutionary Russian folk culture and adherence to his own color theory that make this film visually stunning while at the same time very removed from the earlier Avant-Garde convention.

Birgit Beumers suggests in "Comforting Creatures in Soviet Cartoons" that children's animation and specifically animated fairytales were ideologically subversive because they re-instituted the moral value system that the Soviet state had previously replaced with little-meaning propaganda slogans. According to her, animations were conservative in an aesthetic sense.[41] If we look at Soviet animated films of the 1940s, we will notice that by mimicking Disney, they strayed from Russian artistic experiments of the 1920s, choosing to take a more conventional path towards pleasing their audiences. The example of Конек-горбунок makes it clear that Ivanov-Vano emulated Disney in many ways, just as other Soviet animators did at the time.[42] But it also demonstrates

---

41 Beumers, "Comforting Creatures in Children's Cartoons," 161.
42 Disney style can be seen in many Soviet animated films of the 1940s and 1950s, including those produced by the Brumberg sisters, Lev Atamanov, Leonid Amalrik, Vladimir Polkovnikov, Evgenij Migunov, Pantelejmon Sazonov and even Michail Cechanovskij. Many of their characters and animals replicated the typical Disney manner of characterization. The Soviet artists also took on an analytical approach to movement and its relationship to the character's personality, which is a hallmark of Disney style.

how a Soviet animator could forge his own aesthetic that was distinct from the Disney-dominated world of drawn shorts and feature films.

The synchronization of movement and sound was one of the ways in which Ivanov-Vano attempted to emulate Disney. In a certain sense, he failed at his echoing. Although *Конек-горбунок* utilized cel animation, its dance scenes (for example, Ivan dancing with the Firebird or the Humpbacked horse), are not as smooth as they could be and fall short of Disney animations of the late 1940s. There is a possibility that this was an aesthetic choice on Ivanov-Vano's part, but the lack of fluidity speaks more to the lack of time and money: during the era of post-war reconstruction, Sojuzmul'tfil'm did not have the Disney studio's resources. The stilted rhythm and the insufficient fluidity of movement are the reasons why the film was decried in reviews in the Soviet Union and abroad. Some critics liked it nonetheless, praising the director's achievements in other areas. One such reviewer, writing for the Belgian newspaper *Le Courrier du soir*, even noticed the superiority of Ivanov-Vano's work to that of Disney: "Without a doubt the Americans stand higher in terms of technical and rhythmical point of view, but in terms of poetry and aesthetic pleasure the Russian cartoon stands higher," he wrote.[43] Another reviewer, Semen Ginzberg, praised *Конек-горбунок* a few years later in his book, *Рисованный и кукольный фильм* (*Drawn and Puppet Film*, 1957). For him, the film's "Russianness" was refreshing and excluded the possibility of Ivanov-Vano's replicating his American predecessor. Ginzberg called *Конек-горбунок* "nationalistic in form and free from any formalistic tendencies of endless stunts associated with a false direction in animation technique and the imitation of Western and American animation."[44] Another quality Ginzberg praised was Ivanov-Vano's humor. He admired the film's lack of the gag plot that was popularized by Disney in his Mickey Mouse films. What this critic failed to notice, though, was that Ivanov-Vano was following not Mickey Mouse shorts, but the narrative example of Disney's *Snow White*, which, like *Конек-горбунок*, was a feature film.

Starting with the early 1940s, Soviet animators began to follow Disney's lead by including original songs in their films. Ivanov-Vano, again, did not imitate his American colleague blindly. Aware of the potential popularity of the full-length original songs similar to those Disney added to his features in the 1930s and 1940s, Ivanov-Vano refused to include long singing acts in *Конек-горбунок*. There are frequent episodes of singing in his film, but they are brief. For example, Ivan and his brothers sing a few lines at the beginning of the story when

---

43 American animation here refers to Disney animation. MacFadyen, *Yellow Crocodiles and Blue Oranges*, Montreal 2005, 93.

44 Ginzberg, *Рисованный кукольный фильм*, Moscow 1957, 168.

working on the family farm; Ivan hums again as he takes care of the Humpbacked horse in the Tsar's stable; the chants when setting up the noose for hanging Ivan; servants raise their voices in a chorus while washing the Tsar in the bath before his marriage; even the Tsar maiden emits a few siren-like lines. In general, however, Ivanov-Vano's characters sing only when they need to stay focused on their work, which keeps with the Russian folk tradition of peasants singing during labor. In other words, Ivanov-Vano does not mimic the hit song formula that became a feature of Disney films. His focus is instead on the poetic rhythm of the characters' speech, which matches Ershov's original tale written in trochees.

Needless to say, Конек-горбунок was a great step forward for Soviet animated film. Its choice of a master text allowed Ivanov-Vano to not only use visual elements associated with Russian folklore, including wood cuts and *terem*-shaped rooftops, but also to add an emotional tinge to certain scenes with such distinct animation technique as the inventive use of color. Ivanov-Vano worked diligently on improving the film's color scheme so that he could strengthen the psychosomatic impact of certain scenes as well as distance his work from Disney's more naturalist use of color. For example, in the episode where the former Stable Master presents the Tsar with the Firebird feather, Ivanov-Vano's ingenuity in choosing color effects is apparent. The sleeping Tsar is submerged in half darkness. Lit only by the flickering candle, his chamber is depicted in browns, grays and dark reds. But when the Stable Master wakes him to hand over his gift, a blinding light flares from the feather and engulfs the room. Now the chamber glows in yellows, tans and vivid reds, which epitomize the magical power of the Firebird and reinforce the didactic connection of the color red with power. Throughout the film, Ivanov-Vano uses this same technique to visually link the feather not only to the dazzling Firebird, but also to the horse thief Danila, whose identity may otherwise remain a mystery. The starkly contrasting colors immerse these scenes in the atmosphere of fantasy and suspense and allow Ivanov-Vano to enhance the viewers' experience by adding emphasis to the tale's most dramatic plot twists. Thanks to this method, he creates a stylistic whole, which critics praised for its visual and narrative distinctiveness.[45]

The film pleased audiences and inspired other directors of animated films in their own artistic endeavors. Конек-горбунок also brought Ivanov-Vano his first international acclaim, an Honorable Mention at the International Film Festival in Mariánské Lázně in 1948 as mentioned above. Hence the film managed to fulfill two of the important goals the Party's Ideological Committee had

---

45   Sergej Asenin, "Путешествие в мир мультфильма," in Ivanov-Vano, *Кадр за кадром*, 11.

set for Soviet animation in the late 1940s: attaining international recognition and forming a link between the art form inspired by Western prototypes and Russian national heritage.[46] It is important to note that Ivanov-Vano achieved these goals by straying away from realism and embracing the fantastical side of animated film. In this way, he pushed the accepted limit of Soviet ideology during the height of Soviet totalitarianism.

Ivanov-Vano was sometimes very critical of Disney, for example, finding Disney's humor trite and crude. He feared that many Soviet animators had completely forgotten that the tradition of American animation came from American comics, print cartoons, which, according to Ivanov-Vano, served the sole purpose of eliciting as much laughter as possible from the American reader.[47] In his view, American comics had little to do with the cultural traditions of Russia. Moreover, Ivanov-Vano asserted that laughter could not be the main goal of Soviet animation, for it had higher ambitions in mind, such as keeping the audience aware of their cultural heritage and thus of their "Russianness," of teaching moral lessons, and of bringing up loyal citizens. Ivanov-Vano also attempted to distinguish his art from Disney's and gain recognition for his work by claiming that American animation was founded on different satirical principles than Soviet animation. In the chapter "Успехи советской мультипликации" ("Successes of Soviet Animation") of his *Советское мультипликационное кино*, he argued that comics and caricatures effectively lend themselves to the cinema, which was born out of the same desire as print media: to deride the imperfections of life, to indulge in sarcasm, and to appreciate irony as one of the key narrative modes.[48] According to Ivanov-Vano, it was the invention of the movie camera that merged comics and caricatures with movement. Their union gave rise to a new type of art: animated film, with its unprecedentedly sharp and insightful images coming alive and conveying satirical messages in a way not seen before. One particularly useful satirical technique in animated films, he suggested, was the artists' figurative portrayal of people as animals or iconic abstractions, such as allegories of vices. Those extended visual metaphors allowed for more biting parody while softening the reception of the ridicule.[49] To demonstrate the accomplishments of the Soviet animated satire, Ivanov-Vano pointed to the Brumberg sisters' film, *Большие неприятности* (*Big Troubles*, 1961).

---

46   Ivanov-Vano cited these goals in his 1962 monograph, *Советское мультипликационное кино*, 44-47.
47   *Кадр за кадром*, 85.
48   Ivanov-Vano, *Советское мультипликационное кино*, 44-45.
49   Ibid., 46.

Part of Nikita Chrushchev's anti-drinking campaign, it strove to deliver this heavy-handed topic to adult audiences in an entertaining and original form. Valentina and Zinaida Brumberg used child-inspired drawings in the film, and it was narrated from the point of view of a little girl, the victim of adults' incessant arguing, inebriation, laziness, and moral ineptitude. Ivanov-Vano, who found *Большие неприятности* very attractive visually as well as a conceptual triumph, suggested that, unlike Disney's cartoons, the Soviet animation utilized satire as a means to serve a substantial message to the audiences who would not otherwise be reachable by political or ethical didacticism.

Although *Конек-горбунок* is a film aimed at children, it also has a clear satirical side: Ershov ridicules the Tsar's greed and ungainliness, pokes fun at the deferential and idle courtiers, and jeers at Ivan's brothers' indolence and stupidity. Ivanov-Vano recreates Ershov's satirical mood by accentuating his characterization visually. Every character in the film has its own distinct personality; their distinguishing characteristics and mannerisms stand out as a series of graphic "gestures." For example, there is something child-like about the Tsar's way of dressing and walking: his robes look too big on him, they hang over, covering his hands and feet. The sloppy outfits and clumsy strides make the monarch look infantile and capricious. Just like Ivan, who is still an adolescent, the Tsar has a baby-round nose and rosy-fat cheeks – stereotypical marks of childishness. His comical tendency to flap his arms and over-gesticulate with his hands undermines the power that the Tsar wields over Ivan, preparing the viewer for the latter's imminent victory over his immature sovereign opponent. The full-length format of *Конек-горбунок* allows Ivanov-Vano to elaborate the complexity of his characters in these ways. In this feature, he is intent on referencing not only Ershov's original, but also the Soviet ideological stance: the condemnation of autocracy, the presentation of Russia's past rulers as stupid and inept, and the interpretation of the imperial government's relationships with the common people as oppressive. It is obvious that the political commentary in Ivanov-Vano's children's film and its clear ideological message are completely opposite to the artistic and didactic goals of most Disney animated cartoons.

8   Conclusion

Disney, indeed, cast a heavy "spell" over Soviet animation of the 1930s and 1940s, including Ivanov-Vano's films. But even when Soviet animators followed Disney's lead, they did so while striving to find their individual style in a restricting ideological environment. They were battling with Disney's influence while forced to adapt to the constraints of party censorship, the institutional demands of Sojuzmul'tfil'm, and the aesthetic fetters of Socialist Realism. This is why the case of Ivanov-Vano is so exemplary. Not only did he find his own personal style, he also urged other animators to do so as well. His numerous writings on animation technique and on the history and critique of animated film summarized the art form's greatest innovations while inspiring Soviet artists to rely on their cultural background, borrowing from sources closer to home. Although Ivanov-Vano's dedication to children's animated films and the fairytale in particular links him to Disney, his own understanding of how the line between reality and fantasy should be blurred and connected to the child's imagination is truly unique and inimitable. Surprisingly, even Disney himself was aware of Ivanov-Vano's artistic power. According to John Hubley from the Disney Studio, Frank Lloyd Wright once purchased a copy of Ivanov-Vano's *Сказка о царе Дурандае* to show Walt Disney and his artists and animators.[50] This film was made before Ivanov-Vano began to produce cel animation, which means that Wright and the Disney Studio appreciated not the Soviet director's technical skill, but his narrative, imaginative, and visual discoveries, his sheer ingenuity in exploring the possibilities of animated film. It is this ability of animation to empower imagination that encouraged Ivanov-Vano to become its pioneer and advocate. Both as a film director and a scholar of animation studies, he enriched the art form, adopted it for the Russian context, and helped integrate it into Soviet life.

Works Cited

Primary Sources
Films directed by Ivan Ivanov-Vano:
Блэк энд уайт. Moscow, Mezhrabpomfil'm, 1932.
В некотором царстве. Moscow, Sojuzmul'tfil'm, 1951.
Гуси-лебеди. Moscow, Sojuzmul'tfil'm, 1949.
Двенадцать месяцев. Moscow, Sojuzmul'tfil'm, 1953.
Зимняя сказка. Moscow, Sojuzmul'tfil'm, 1945.
Ивась. Moscow, Sojuzmul'tfil'm, 1940.
Котофей Котофеевич. Moscow, Sojuzmul'tfil'm, 1937.
Конек-горбунок. Moscow, Sojuzmul'tfil'm, 1947.

---

50   Tod Polson, *The Noble Approach: Maurice Noble and the Zen of Animation Design*. San Francisco 2013, 18.

Краденое солнце (with Ol'ga Chodataeva). Moscow, Sojuzmul'tfil'm, 1943.

Левша. Moscow, Sojuzmul'tfil'm, 1964.

Лесной концерт. Moscow, Sojuzmul'tfil'm, 1953.

Мойдодыр. Moscow, Sojuzmul'tfil'm, 1939.

Мойдодыр. Moscow, Sojuzmul'tfi'lm, 1954.

Сенька-африканец (with Jurij Merkulov and Daniil Cherkes). Moscow, Mezhrabpromfil'm, 1927.

Сказка о царе Дурандае (with Valentina and Zinaida Brumberg). Moscow, Mezhrabpromfil'm, 1934.

Сказка о царе Салтане. Moscow, Sojuzmul'tfil'm, 1984.

Снегурочка. Moscow, Sojuzmul'tfil'm, 1952.

Стрекоза и муравей. Moscow, Sojuzmul'tfil'm, 1935.

Три мушкетера. Moscow, Sojuzmul'tfil'm, 1938.

Храбрый заяц. Moscow, Sojuzmul'tfil'm, 1955.

Большие неприятности, dir. Valentina and Zinaida Brumberg. Moscow, Sojuzmul'tfil'm, 1961.

Ivanov-Vano, Ivan. "Вечно юное искусство," in *Искусство кино* 11 (1977), 62-63.

Ivanov-Vano, Ivan. "Встреча с Пушкиным," in *Искусство кино* 11 (1987), 86-87.

Ivanov-Vano, Ivan. "Графическая мультипликация," in *Мультипликационный фильм*. Moscow 1936, 101-197.

Ivanov-Vano, Ivan. "Изобразительное решение мультипликационного фильма," in V.V. Vanslov, ed. *О художниках театра, кино и ТВ*. Leningrad 1984, 136-146.

Vanslov, ed. *Кадр за кадром*. Moscow 1980.

Vanslov, ed. *Мультипликация вчера и сегодня* (часть 1). Moscow 1974.

Vanslov, ed. *Мультипликация вчера и сегодня* (часть 2). Moscow 1975.

Vanslov, ed. *Мультипликация вчера и сегодня* (часть 3). Moscow 1976.

Vanslov, ed. *Мультипликация вчера и сегодня* (часть 4). Moscow 1977.

Vanslov, ed. *Очерк истории развития мультипликации до Второй мировой войны*. Moscow 1967.

Vanslov, ed. *Рисованный фильм*. Moscow 1950.

Vanslov, ed. *Рисованный фильм / Особый вид киноискусства*. Moscow 1956.

Vanslov, ed. *Советское мультипликационное кино*. Moscow 1962.

Vanslov, ed. "Эклер – за и против. Стенограмма доклада 'Применение эклерного метода в производстве рисованных фильмов, 1951," in *Киноведческие записки* 80 (2006), 174-187.

Ivanov-Vano's interview to E. Nikitkina. Transcript Interview, in RGALI, Moscow, Fund 2912, Folder 6, File 245.

Каток, dir. Jurij Zheljabuzhskij. Moscow, Mezhrabpromfil'm, 1927.

Китай в огне, dir. Z. Komissarenko. Moscow, Kino Moskva, 1925.

Snow White and the Seven Dwarfs, dir. David Hand. Los Angeles, Walt Disney Studio, 1937.

Советские игрушки, dir. Dziga Vertov, Moscow, Goskino, 1924.

Steamboat Willie, dir. Walt Disney and Ub Iwerks. Los Angeles, Walt Disney Studio, 1928.

The Three Little Pigs, dir. Burt Gillett. Los Angeles, Walt Disney Studio, 1933.

Secondary Sources

Abramova, O. "Иван Иванов-Вано," in *Мастера советской мультипликации*. Moscow 1972.

Asenin, Sergej. *Мир мультфильма: Идеи и образы мультипликации социалистических стран*. Moscow 1986.

Asenin, Sergej. "Путешествие в мир мультфильма," in Ivan Ivanov-Vano, *Кадр за кадром*. Moscow 1980, 7-13.

Balina, Marina and Birgit Beumers. "To Catch Up and Overtake Disney," in Jack Zipes, Pauline Greenhill, and Kendra Magnus-Johnston, eds., *Fairy-Tale Films Beyond Disney. International Perspectives*. New York and London 2016, 124-138.

Balina, Marina, Helena Goscilo, and Mark Lipovetsky, eds. *Politicizing Magic: An Anthology of Russian and Soviet Fairy Tales*. Evanston, IL 2005.

Beumers, Birgit. "Comforting Creatures in Children's Cartoons," in Marina Balina and Larissa Rudova, eds., *Russian and Soviet Children's Literature and Culture*. New York and London 2008, 151-171.

Bogdanova, Sjuzanna. "Очерки о жизни и творчестве Александры Гавриловны Снежко-Блотской," in *Кинограф* 19 (2008), 207-240.

Chukovskij, Kornej. *Мойдодыр*. Petrograd 1923.

Chukovskij, Kornej. *Приключения Крокодила Крокодиловича*. Petrograd 1919.

Crafton, Donald. *Before Mickey*. Cambridge, MA 1982.

Ejzenshtein, Sergej. *Избранные произведения в шести томах*. Moscow 1964.

Ershov, Petr. *Конек-горбунок*. Moscow-Leningrad 1964.

Furniss, Maureen. *Art in Motion: Animation Aesthetics*. Sydney 2008.

Ginzberg, Semen. *Рисованный кукольный фильм*. Moscow 1957.

Karasik, Michail. *Ударная книга советской детворы*. Moscow 2010.

Kelly, Catriona. "Shaping the 'Future Race': Regulating the Daily Life of Children in Early Soviet Russia," in Christina Kiaer and Eric Naiman, eds., *Everyday Life in Early Soviet Russia: Taking the Revolution Inside*. Bloomington, IN 2006, 256-281.

Leslie, Esther. *Hollywood Flatlands: Animation, Critical Theory and the Avant-Garde*. London 2002.

Leyda, Jay. *Kino: A History of Russian and Soviet Film*. Princeton, NJ 1983.

MacFadyen, David. *Yellow Crocodiles and Blue Oranges*. Montreal 2005.

Marshak, Samuil. *Почта*. Leningrad and Moscow 1927.

Marshak, Samuil. *Семь чудес*. Leningrad and Moscow 1926.

Marshak, Samuil. *Мороженое*. Leningrad and Moscow 1925.

Mjolsness, Lora. "Vertov's Soviet Toys: Commerce, Commercialization and Cartoons," in *Studies in Russian and Soviet Cinema* 2:3 (2008), 247-267.

Platt, Kevin and David Brandenberger. *Epic Revisionism: Russian History and Literature as Stalinist Propaganda*. Madison, WI 2006.

Polson, Tod. *The Noble Approach: Maurice Noble and the Zen of Animation Design*. San Francisco 2013.

Pontieri, Laura, *Soviet Animation and the Thaw of the 1960s. Not Only for Children*. New Barnet, Herts, UK 2012.

"Постановление ЦК ВКП(б) от 9 сентября 1933 г. 'Об издательстве детской литературы'," in *Решения партии о печати*. Moscow 1941.

Sekundov, N., ed. *Американские цветные фильмы*. Leningrad 1935.

Sifianos, George. "The Definition of Animation: A Letter from Norman McLaren," in *Animation Journal* 3:2 (1999), 62-66.

Sokoljanskij, I., V. Popov and A. Zaluzhnyj, eds. *Мы против сказки*. Charchov 1928.

Taylor, Richard and Ian Christie, eds. *The Film Factory: Russian and Soviet Cinema in Documents*, 1896-1939. New York 1994.

Volkov, Anatolij. "Мультипликация" in *Кино: политика и люди (30-е годы)*, ed. L. Mamatova. Moscow 1995.

Wells, Paul. *Animation: Genre and Authorship*. New York 2002.

Wells, Paul. *Understanding Animation*. New York 1998.

CHAPTER 11

Embracing Eccentricity: *Золушка* and the Avant-Garde Imagination

Larissa Rudova

1   Introduction

Charles Perrault's fairytale "Cinderella" (1697), a version of the famous coming-of-age folk tale about a downtrodden young girl who finds her true love and extraordinary fortune with the help of magic, has occupied a prominent place in popular culture and inspired numerous literary, musical, and film adaptations. In the USSR, however, the transformation of "Cinderella" had a peculiar history. In the 1930s, its plot was adjusted by Soviet writers and moviemakers to fit the aesthetic and ideological considerations of Socialist Realism. When this new Soviet "Cinderella" was born and made familiar through Grigorij Aleksandrov's musical comedies, its title character exemplified an ideal socialist woman who celebrated moral triumph and achieved good fortune due to her hard work, loyalty, perseverance, and social involvement. However, when in 1947 the film studio Lenfil'm released the motion picture for children, *Золушка* (*Cinderella*), based on the screenplay by the famous children's writer Evgenij Shvarc and directed by Nadezhda Kosheverova and Michail Shapiro, it deviated from the Soviet moviemaking canon and became an instant success with the Soviet critics and moviegoers.[1] The movie's triumph was not necessarily caused by its release during the so-called "малокартинье" ("period of few films"), when every new film drew massive audiences, but primarily because it was unusually creative and different from the numerous shock-worker/collective-farmer "cinderellas" of the Stalinist musical comedies of the 1930s.[2] Kosheverova and Shapiro's *Золушка* was a true, classical enchanted creature; living in a magical

---

[1] According to the official sources, 18,270.000 moviegoers saw *Золушка* in 1947, which placed it fourth among the films released that year. S. Zemljanuchin and M. Segida, *Домашняя синематека. Отечественное кино. 1918-1996*, Moscow 1996, 168.

[2] Soviet film studios released only twenty-two features in 1947. See Peter Kenez, *Cinema and Soviet Society, 1917-1953*, Cambridge, UK 1992, 210-215. On "малокартинье," see Evgenij Margolit, *Живые и мертвое: заметки к истории советского кино 1920х-1960х годов*, St. Petersburg 2012, 353-373.

world free from ideological constraints, and from a retrospective point of view, she became the "most mysterious heroine of the Stalin cinema."[3] *Золушка* also acquired a special status in the history of Stalinist cinematography for its unconcealed non-alliance with Socialist Realist aesthetic at a time when the Communist party was re-establishing tight control over intellectual and artistic life in the USSR.[4]

This chapter examines Kosheverova and Shapiro's film as an artistic project that broke free from the aesthetic and ideological restrictions of Socialist Realism and reaffirmed the playful tradition of the pre-revolutionary and early Soviet Avant-Garde. I analyze *Золушка* through Viktor Shklovskij's concept of "остранение" ("defamiliarization" or "estrangement"), that, according to Svetlana Boym, undergoes a metamorphosis "from a technique of art to an existential art of survival and practice of freedom and dissent" in the broader historical and political context of that time.[5]

Shklovskij defines estrangement as an essential property of true art that breaks down habitual, automatized perceptions and creates new ones. He writes,

> Art exists so that one may recover the sensation of life; it exists to make one feel things [...]. The purpose of art is to impart the sensation of things as they are perceived and not as they are known. The technique of art is to make objects 'unfamiliar,' to make forms difficult, to increase the difficulty and length of perception because the process of perception is an

---

3 Dunja Smirnova, "Золушка," in *Сеанс* 8 (1993), ⟨http://2011.russiancinema.ru/index.php?e_dept_id=2&e_movie_id=8762⟩ (Accessed July 17, 2017).

4 In 1946, the Party launched an "anti-cosmopolitan campaign," masterminded by Andrej Zhdanov, Chairman of the Supreme Soviet and Leningrad Party chief. Zhdanov's campaign targeted "foreign influence" and formalism in Soviet culture. It established strict censorship standards and intolerance of any deviation from the master plot of Socialist Realism. Some of the most outstanding figures of Soviet culture were persecuted and attacked in the press between 1946-1952. For a discussion of this "anti-cosmopolitan" campaign, see Peter Kenez, *Cinema and Soviet Society, 1917-1953*, Cambridge, UK 1992, 215-225. For *Золушка*'s special place in Soviet cinematography of the time, see, for instance, Alexander Prokhorov, "Arresting Development: A Brief History of Soviet Cinema for Children and Adolescents," in Marina Balina and Larissa Rudova, eds., *Russian Children's Literature and Culture*, New York and London 2008, 140. See also Elena Stishova, "Приключения Золушки в стране большевиков," in *Российское кино в поисках реальности*, Moscow 2013, 91-102, and V. Pritulenko, "Золушка на все времена. 'Золушка', режиссеры Надежда Кошеверова, Михаил Шапиро," in *Искусство кино* 3 (March 1997), ⟨http://kinoart.ru/archive/1997/03/n3-article16⟩ (Accessed December 17, 2017).

5 Svetlana Boym, "Poetics and Politics of Estrangement: Victor Shklovsky and Hannah Arendt," in *Poetics Today* 26:4 (2005), 581.

aesthetic end in itself and must be prolonged. Art is a way of experiencing the artfulness of an object; the object is not important.⁶

In the context of Stalinist art, estrangement goes beyond the artistic realm and interacts with politics because, as Boym points out, the device of estrangement emphasizes not only the final product but also the very *process* of making art. In the act of producing art, the artist does not simply displace things from reality in order to create a new sensation, "he also helps to return sensation to life itself, to reinvent the world, to experience it anew."⁷ The reader or the spectator is forced to look at life in a different way—perhaps revisiting his or her buried dreams and aspirations, which in Золушка's case could have manifested suppressed personal happiness and re-actualized the imaginative child's perception of the world that Stalinist culture so methodically tried to destroy.

An "exception to the Stalinist cinematic mainstream" in the late 1940s, Золушка performed what Boym calls a "double estrangement."⁸ In early Soviet Russia, the Bolshevik revolution dramatized and alienated life to the point of turning it into a grotesque art form. By contrast, life in Stalinist Russia in the 1930s "radically defamiliarized the everyday perceptions of Soviet citizens," as the state established control over all spheres of their existence, and for many creative individuals, artistic and actual survival became possible only at the expense of "double estrangement." Sensing that the political machine would crush them together with their art, many talented experimental artists had to distance ("estrange") themselves from the idiosyncrasies of Socialist Realism and flee to children's literature, theater, and cinema which were perceived as a relatively safe territory of creative freedom in the midst of ideological tyranny. The playful tradition of children's literature and folk and fairytales were particularly productive areas of work for talented artists.

2   Fairytales in Soviet Children's Cinema

Fairytales had a precarious position in early Soviet Russia. In 1920, the Bolsheviks began purging libraries of "ideologically harmful and outdated literature," and folk tales and literary fairytales for children were especially targeted in

---

6 Victor Shklovsky, "Art as Technique," in Lee T. Lemon and Marion J. Reis, trans., eds., *Russian Formalist Criticism: Four Essays*, Lincoln, NE 1965, 12.
7 Boym, *Another Freedom: The Alternative History of An Idea*, Chicago 2010, 207.
8 Prokhorov, "Arresting Development," 140; Boym, "Poetics and Politics of Estrangement," 583.

this process.[9] For the Bolsheviks, fairytales in particular were the epitome of bourgeois class-consciousness and therefore culturally unacceptable. This attitude prevailed until the First Congress of Soviet Writers (1934), where Maksim Gor'kij famously spoke about folklore as the most important and inspiring source of all great art and encouraged writers to collect, study, and learn from it.[10] Further, the premier Soviet children's writer, Samuil Marshak, extended Gor'kij's praise of folklore to fairytales, including Western fairytales, and unambiguously argued in favor of their educational value for young readers.[11] What these two prominent writers accomplished went further than reinstating fairytales in the classical canon of children's reading: in the climate dominated by totalitarian art, they stood their ground and ensured the survival, even the flourishing, of the playful artistic tradition in children's literature, theater, and film.[12]

Soviet children's cinema emerged in the 1920s; due to its numerous technical, financial, and organizational problems, however, it could not compete with the enormous popularity of Western adventure films on the domestic market during the NEP years (1921-1928). Yet, the state expected moviemakers to create politically, ideologically, and pedagogically significant films for little comrades, and in 1936 two film studios, Союздетфильм (Sojuzdetfil'm) and Союзмультфильм (Sojuzmul'tfil'm), were opened especially for the pro-

---

9   Ninety-seven names of children's writers were blacklisted and their works were to be destroyed. See *Черная книга имен, которым не место на карте России*, ed. S. V. Volkov, Moscow 2008, 55. For the Bolsheviks' perception of folklore and fairytales, see Marina Balina's introduction to Soviet fairytales in *Politicizing Magic: An Anthology of Russian and Soviet Fairy Tales*, eds. Marina Balina, Helena Goscilo, and Mark Lipovetsky, Evanston, IL 2005, 106-107. See also Ben Hellman, *Fairy Tales and True Stories: The History of Russian Literature for Children and Young Adults (1574-2010)*, Leiden 2013, 133-136; Marija Nikolajeva, "Fairy Tales in Society's Service," in *Marvels and Tales* 16:2 (2002), 171-172.

10 Maksim Gor'kij, *Собрание сочинений в тридцати томах*, Vol. 27, *Статьи, доклады, речи, приветствия (1933-1936)*, Moscow 1953, 305. For the state of folklore in Soviet culture, see Felix J. Oinas, "Folklore and Politics in the Soviet Union," in *Slavic Review* 32:1 (March 1973), 45-58. The use of folklore for propaganda purposes is discussed in Frank J. Miller, *Folklore for Stalin: Russian Folklore and Pseudofolklore of the Stalin Era*, Armonk, NY 1990.

11 Samuil Marshak, "О большой литературе для маленьких," in *Собрание сочинений в восьми томах*, Vol. 6, Moscow 1971, 195-243. See also Balina, *Politicizing Magic*, 108.

12 For instance, Kornej Chukovskij's popular fairytales of the 1920s, "Мойдодыр" ("Wash 'em Clean," 1923), "Тараканище" ("The Big Cockroach," 1923), "Чудо-дерево" ("Wonder-Tree," 1924), "Телефон" ("Telephone," 1925), and "Муха-Цокотуха" ("Fly-a-Buzz-Buzz," 1924), were viciously attacked and not republished until Gor'kij's rehabilitation of the genre. See Balina, *Politicizing Magic: An Anthology of Russian and Soviet Fairy Tales*, 106-107.

duction of children's films.¹³ The significance of this development cannot be overstated. The two film studios became the first world film factories for children whose main curator and censor was the state.¹⁴ In the 1930s and 1940s, children's cinema was more ideologically scrutinized than children's literature, and consequently its normative aesthetic was less playful and diverse, with the exception of the adventure and fairytale genres. In fact, it was unusual to see child characters at play or at rest in Stalinist cinema because they were busy chasing counter-revolutionaries, wreckers, saboteurs, and other enemies of the people, holding meetings, or engaging in socially useful works, such as gardening, raising chickens, or helping the elderly.¹⁵ The child character closely reproduced the "positive-hero" model of Stalinist literature for adult readers and was expected to be socially mature and responsible, or at least to become mature and socially conscious over the course of the plot development. As Katerina Clark has demonstrated, the positive hero had a "dual goal" of either performing a task for the "public sphere," or resolving "within himself the tension between 'spontaneity' and 'consciousness.'"¹⁶ But while children were encouraged to mature quickly, their maturity did not automatically mean independence, especially if independence bordered on individualism and personal interests.

---

13   Alexander Prokhorov's article, "Arresting Development," provides a detailed account of the history of Soviet children's cinema. For a short overview of this topic, see "Детское кино," in *Большая Советская энциклопедия*, Moscow 1969-1978, ⟨http://www.bse.info-spravka.ru/bse/id_24506⟩ (Accessed July 17, 2017).

14   For the discussion of Sojuzmult'fil'm's early years and the fairytale as the prevalent genre in the works of one of its most famous directors, see Lora Wheeler Mjolsness's chapter, "Under the Hypnosis of Disney: Ivan Ivanov-Vano and Soviet Animation for Children," in this volume.

15   See, for instance, L. Ch. Mamatova, *Кино: политика и люди. 30-е годы*, Moscow 1995, 101, 106. Also, see Prokhorov, "Arresting Development," 137. Among ideologically motivated children's films in the 1930s and 1940s was Antonina Kudrjavceva's *Леночка и виноград* (*Lenochka and Grapes*, 1936), in which a group of children investigates a theft of grapes from a collective farm. Igor' Savchenko's adventure film, *Дума про казака Голоту* (*Ballad of Cossack Golota*, 1937), told a story of three Russian boys who saved a Red army commissar from the Whites during the Civil War. Two films, based on Arkadij Gajdar's novellas, *Тимур и его команда* (*Timur and His Team*, 1940), directed by Aleksandr Razumnyj, and *Клятва Тимура* (*Timur's Oath*, 1942), directed by the renowned filmmaker Lev Kuleshov, emphasized Soviet patriotism and collectivism by featuring a group of Young Pioneers committed to selfless humanitarian work in the pre-World War II and wartime Soviet Union. Finally, Margarita Barskaja's ideologically motivated drama, *Рваные башмаки* (*Tattered Shoes*, 1933), focused on working-class children's participation in the revolutionary struggle against the rising Nazi Party in Germany.

16   Katerina Clark, *The Soviet Novel: History as Ritual*, Chicago 1985, 162.

Despite the fact that children's cinema under Stalin was driven by ideological considerations, it also accommodated young audiences' passion for adventure and fairytales. Both genres, while not entirely stripped of ideology, allowed imaginative displacement, escape from mind-numbing political realities, and offered "maximum possible freedom from the power of stereotype."[17] Of particular interest among adventure films are several immensely successful features based on adaptations of Western children's literature. Three of them, Vladimir Vajnshtok's *Дети капитана Гранта* (*The Children of Captain Grant*, 1936), Eduard Penclin's *Таинственный остров* (*The Mysterious Island*, 1941), and Vasilij Zhuravlev's *Пятнадцатилетний капитан* (*A Captain at Fifteen*, 1945), were based on Jules Verne's eponymous novels, whereas Vajnshtok's *Остров сокровищ* (*Treasure Island*, 1937) was a film adaptation of the novel by Robert Louis Stevenson. Although the filmmakers had to make some changes in the original narratives for ideological or political reasons, these films had more affinity with classic Hollywood escapist entertainment than with Soviet didacticism.[18]

But filmmakers' creative vision was most successful in fairytale films. Two masters dominated the genre, Aleksandr Rou (1906-1973) and Aleksandr Ptushko (1900-1973), drawing on Russian folklore and Soviet literary fairytales as their main source material. A key element in both Rou's and Ptushko's films was fantasy, but both of them fully complied with Soviet ideological considerations. Terry Staples observes that their films were always "impacted by revolution, war, political edicts, and issues of national identity."[19] The connection between fairytales and Soviet mythology is hardly surprising if we consider the genre's celebration of human aspirations, dreams, and desires for a positive life transformation. As Jack Zipes elaborates,

> The initial ontological situations in the tales generally deal with exploitation, hunger and injustice familiar to the lower classes in pre-capitalist societies. And the magic of the tales can be equated to the wish-fulfillment and utopian projections of the people, i.e., of the folk, who preserved and cultivated these tales.[20]

---

17 Mamatova, *Кино: политика и люди. 30-е годы*, 108.
18 For ideological changes to the original Western texts, see Julian Graffy, "Literature and Film," in *The Cambridge Companion to Twentieth-Century Russian Literature*, Cambridge UK 2011, 243-244.
19 Terry Staples, "Soviet Fairy-Tale Films," in Donald Haase, ed., *The Greenwood Encyclopedia of Folktales*, Vol. 3 Westport, CT 2008, 901.
20 Jack Zipes, *Breaking the Magic Spell. Radical Theories of Folk and Fairy Tales*, Lexington, KY 2002, 8.

Rou and Ptushko based their fairytale films on traditional folk narratives in which a low-born hero embarks on a successful quest either to find a princess, defeat a monster, or wage a war on behalf of his king or prince. Similarly, if these directors made films based on Soviet literary narratives, they abided by the grand narrative of Socialist Realism and fully validated its values. Marina Balina and Birgit Beumers succinctly identify the following elements of the Soviet cinematic fairytale production that fit the context of Socialist Realism and inform the films of both directors: "the juxtaposition of poor vs. rich with the former's subsequent victory [...] a positive didactic message; a surrogate family with ideological rather than blood ties; and the oppositional war trope, which juxtaposed native vs. foreign and upper vs. lower class. The plot dynamics were motivated by party consciousness."[21]

Among Ptushko's most popular films from the 1930s and 1940s were *Новый Гулливер* (*The New Gulliver*, 1935), one of the world's first full-feature animation films; *Золотой ключик* (*The Golden Key*, 1937), based on Aleksej Tolstoj's adaptation of Carlo Collodi's *Pinocchio*; and *Каменный цветок* (*The Stone Flower*, 1946), based on Pavel Bazhov's *сказы*. Equally well-known were Rou's films, *По щучьему веленью* (*By the Pike's Command*, 1938), *Василиса Прекрасная* (*Vasilisa the Beautiful*, 1939), *Конек-горбунок* (*The Little Humpback Horse*, 1941), and *Кащей Бессмертный* (*Kashchej the Deathless*, 1944). Despite the underpinnings of Soviet ideology, the fairytale film's intrinsic demand was for a fantastic, non-realist world that could be constructed only through special effects, and both directors rose to the occasion and became brilliant technical innovators. Ptushko was among the pioneering film directors to use color and experiment boldly with animation techniques. In his internationally acclaimed film, *Новый Гулливер*, he used over three thousand different puppets, along with stop-motion animation and live action. His other distinguished achievement was the use of color in *Каменный цветок*, which was awarded the International Prize for Color at the Cannes Film Festival in 1946. Rou's contribution to the development of the cinematic fairytale film was also noteworthy, as he was among the first Soviet directors to produce live action fairytale films rather than using traditional animation. Like Ptushko's, his films were full of inventive magical tricks, characters, and creatures. Thus, for the filming of *Василиса Прекрасная*, he famously created the dragon Змей Горыныч as a huge puppet that took twenty people to operate. It looked so horrific that the main hero's horse would stumble in fear at its sight. The power of cinematic

---

21 Balina and Birgit Beumers, "'To Catch Up and Overtake Disney?' Soviet and Post-Soviet Fairy-Tale Films," in *Fairy-Tale Films Beyond Disney. International Perspectives*, New York and London 2016, 125.

magic created by Ptushko and Rou was so irresistible that they continued to be the uncontested fairytale cinema masters for the rest of their careers despite the didactic overtones of their films.

3 Золушка's Art of *Estrangement*

When we turn to Kasheverova and Shapiro's Золушка in the context of Stalinist film production for children, we instantly recognize its aesthetic "otherness." Unlike Ptushko's and Rou's films, it is almost completely ideologically functionless, and its language, characters, and acting shift the balance from the tale's anticipated didacticism to pure entertainment and pleasure. To understand Золушка's special artistic autonomy and ingenuity, we must trace its set of constitutive narrative, musical, theatrical, artistic, and social elements.

3.1 *The Screenwriter*

After folklore and fairytales were officially readmitted into the canon of acceptable literary genres in the 1930s, it was not immediately clear how they could be reinvented for the Soviet context and how they could renegotiate modern life through fantasy and magic. The man who found the most ingenious solution to this problem was Evgenij Shvarc, the famous writer and fairytale playwright who wrote the screen play for Золушка. Shvarc became the inventor of new "modern fairytales" in which he "mixed and matched" old and new elements from a variety of sources, sometimes "foregrounding science and art as the only true magic, updating characterization, and invoking the power of the natural world."[22] Anja Tippner notes that Shvarc's fairytales had a blend of "fantastic allure and antididactic, playful stance" and historical reality.[23] And yet, fantasy never obscured reality in his art and he remained "truthful with the aid of the absurd and the fantastic."[24]

In Золушка, Shvarc masterfully fulfills the double encoding of fantasy and reality. He preserves Perrault's plot but fills it with eccentricity and playful language. The spectator is caught up in the violation of all rules – textual, social, and behavioral – from the very beginning of the film:

---

22 Staples, "Soviet Fairy-Tale Films," 903.
23 Anja Tippner. "Evgenii Shvarts's Fairy Tale Dramas: Theater, Power, and the Naked Truth," in *Russian Children's Literature and Culture*, New York 2008, 308. See also Irina H. Corten, "Evgenii Shvarts as an Adapter of Hans Christian Andersen and Charles Perrault," in *Russian Review* 37:1 (January 1978), 65.
24 J. Douglas Clayton, "The Theatre of E. L. Shvarts: An Introduction," in *Études Slaves et Est-Européennes/Slavic and East-European Studies* 19 (1974), 27.

> King: Greetings to the gatekeepers of the fairytale kingdom!
> Gatekeepers: Greetings to you, your Majesty!
> King: Are you out of your minds?
> Gatekeepers: No, nothing of the kind, your Majesty!
> King (increasingly irritated): What? Arguing with the king? What fantastic swinishness! If I say you're out of your mind, you're out of your mind. Tonight there is a fest at the palace. Do you realize what a great thing it is? To make people have fun, to amuse them, to do something pleasantly surprising for them—what could be greater? I'm working so hard arranging everything, but you? Why aren't the gates opened yet? (Throws his crown to the ground.) Damn it all, I'm going to the monastery! You can all live as you wish. I don't want to be king if my gatekeepers are barely working and besides have sour faces.[25]

The king's language and actions are whimsical and child-like throughout the film, and as his quirky theatricality quickly destroys our idea of royal speech and demeanor, we begin to sense that the artfulness of Kosheverova and Shapiro's film has a close affinity with Shklovskij's concept of estrangement. Boym comments, "Estrangement lays bare the boundaries between art and life but never pretends to abolish or blur them."[26] *Золушка*'s artfulness is laid bare consistently and with gusto not solely through Shvarc's screenplay, but also through unusual casting, additional characters, Avant-Garde acting techniques, eclectic dancing, and random songs. There is almost nothing realistic in this cinematic version of the fairytale. The king who is working hard to entertain his people is an aberration both within the fairytale genre and the Socialist Realist representation of monarchy. His dialogue with guards, an exuberant gesture on the part of the playwright and the filmmakers, sets the stage for the viewer's perception of everything this "non-magical" personage does as whacky and fantastic.

3.2   *Золушка's Cast and Crew*

The narratological estrangement is mirrored by the film's other peculiarities, circumstantial as well as artistic. To begin with, Kosheverova's cast and crew were unorthodox for their time. On the threshold of a new assault against the arts led by the Chairman of the Supreme Soviet, Andrej Zhdanov, Kosheverova

---

25 Evgenij Shvarc, *Золушка. Киносценарий*, in *Сказка о потерянном времени. Сборник*, Moscow 2004, 166. Translation is mine – LR.

26 Boym, "Poetics and Politics of Estrangement," 587.

chose to work with people who were, in some measure, already estranged from the cultural establishment. The new resolutions on the arts reinforced "adherence to ideology, fidelity to the Party, and proximity to the people," and demonstrated little concern for the aesthetic quality of cinema, expecting the artist to be "a soldier, disciplined in obeying orders, seeing to it that those under him obeyed him too."[27] Yet, Kosheverova did just the opposite. She hired artists—although not without a fight in some cases—who had an affinity with the Avant-Garde or had politically undesirable biographies.[28] For instance, her co-director, Michail Shapiro, was married to the author Zhanna Gauzner whose Jewish mother, the famous poet Vera Inber, was related to the "enemy of the people" Lev Trotskij. The film's talented artistic designer, Nikolaj Akimov, studied under the Avant-Garde artist and white émigré Jurij Annenkov. The extraordinary acting genius, Erast Garin, who plays the king, was the favorite actor of the executed "enemy of the people," the brilliant theater director Vsevolod Mejerhold. The list of Kosheverova's "unorthodox" cast also included the Jewish actress Faina Ranevskaja (Cinderella's stepmother) who was a friend of the ostracized poet Anna Achmatova.[29] Vasilij Merkurjev, Cinderella's father in the film, was married to Mejerhold's niece. Aleksej Konsovskij (the Prince) was the son and brother of executed "enemies of the people."[30] Other "cosmopolitans" associated with Золушка were the composer Antonio Spadovekkia, who was Italian; Shvarc, who was half-Jewish; and the production designer Isaak Machlis, who was Jewish and trained in Paris. All these people could have been purged in the post-World War II anti-Semitic

---

27 Mira Liehm and Antonin J. Liehm, *The Most Important Art: Soviet and East European Film After 1945*, Berkeley 1977, 47-48. On the effect of Andrej Zhdanov's policies on Soviet cinema, see Kenez, *Cinema and Soviet Society*, 215-226. Clark discusses "ждановщина" in literature in *The Soviet Novel*. In particular, see her chapter, "The Postwar Stalin Period (1944-53)," 191-209. On "ждановщина" in the arts, see Marina Chegodaeva, *Социалистический реализм. Мифы и реальность*, Moscow 2003, 139-208.

28 For instance, the administration of Lenfil'm was strongly opposed to Kosheverova's selection of Zhejmo for the main role. Among the points against her was her Polish background, age, and eccentricity. "Культурный слой – Золушка," in *5-tv.ru*, January 3, 2009, ⟨http://www.5-tv.ru/video/503084/⟩ (Accessed July 17, 2017).

29 Despite her great talent, Ranevskaja could not get a major role in Soviet films because of her "Semitic" features. In his letter to the Secretary of the Communist Party A.S. Shcherbakov, I. G. Bol'shakov, Minister of Cinematography in post-war USSR, wrote that Ranevskaja's "Semitic features" were too obvious, especially in close-up shots. N. Gogitidze, ed., *Так говорила Фаина Раневская*, Rostov-on-the-Don 2013, 4.

30 Anna Bulgakova and Nikolaj Vershinin-Konsovskij, "Волшебный комсомолец," in *Сеанс* 51-52 (March 5, 2013), ⟨http://seance.ru/blog/dmytriy_konsovsky⟩ (Accessed July 17, 2017).

FIGURE 11.1   Janina Zhejmo as Cinderella

and anti-cosmopolitan campaign described by Richard Stites as the "battle between old and new, Slavic and Western, rural and urban, native and foreign."[31]

The biggest anomaly in Kosheverova's casting was Janina Zhejmo, the actress who played Cinderella. She was 37 years old when she was cast and not as attractive as other actresses who played Soviet Cinderella-type roles in popular musical comedies by Grigorij Aleksandrov and Ivan Pyrjev. Stalin, who was a devoted cinephile and kept the movie industry under his watchful eye, did not like Zhejmo and repeatedly crossed out her name from award nomination lists.[32] To add irony to her "estranged" cast, Kosheverova hired the actress Varvara Mjasnikova for the role of the fairy godmother. The Soviet moviegoer immediately recognized her as the fearless young Red Army machine-gunner Anka from the Socialist Realist blockbuster film *Чапаев* (*Chapaev* 1934), directed by the Vasiljev brothers for Lenfil'm.

---

31   Richard Stites, *Russian Popular Culture: Entertainment and Society since 1900*, New York 1992, 118.
32   Ljudmila Grabenko, "В гостях у сказки," in *Бульвар Гордона* 52 (December 25, 2012). ⟨http://www.bulvar.com.ua/arch/2012/52/50dc0eb72c756/⟩ (Accessed July 17, 2017).

3.3 *The Acting*

Золушка's heightened theatricality also contributed to its strangeness. The acting background of the cast was strongly rooted in Avant-Garde theater. Kosheverova and Zhejmo studied at the Фабрика эксцентрического актера (Factory of the Eccentric Actor, FEKS, 1921-1926)[33] that repudiated traditional acting and found inspiration in such "low genres" as the circus, jazz band, operetta, slapstick, mime, music hall comedy, vaudeville, melodrama, carnival, and cinema. Their artistic method – eccentrism – likewise resonated with Shklovskian estrangement. In the FEKS manifesto, the actors state:

> We cease to recognize the objects that are around us continually. We subconsciously carry out gestures, actions from mere habit, having lost the faculty to "think" them out. [...] In order to truly see things we need to "extract" them from the process of automatization. [...] FEKS worked on the basis of "estrangement" [...] of an object.[34]

Like Sergei Eisenstein "montage of attractions," FEKS's method was aimed at producing a strong sensual and psychological effect on the spectator through a series of calculated techniques. The Formalist critic Jurij Tynjanov described the FEKS's cinematic style in terms of "purely poetic images and metaphors, originating in comedy and fulfilling the role of hyperbole in that genre."[35] Shklovskij also praised FEKS for their "particular artistic approach" and expressionist acting techniques and especially emphasized their improvisational skills and experimentation with eccentrism.[36] Zhejmo's acting in *Золушка* exemplifies her commitment to FEKS-style acting. She plays her role with infectious excitement, pronounced expressiveness, and youthful plasticity. Critics did not fail to emphasize her facial expressions and especially her "wide open, trusting, and happy eyes of a child ready for a miracle to happen."[37]

---

[33] On FEKS, see, for instance, *История отечественного кино*, Moscow 2005, 70-71. Also, see Oksana Bulgakowa, *FEKS: Die Fabrik des extentrischen Schauspielers*, Berlin 1996. In 2003 Lenfil'm released a documentary film, *FEKS*, directed by Oleg Kovalov: ⟨https://www.youtube.com/watch?v=PWuCX9OMuKY⟩ (Accessed December 17, 2017).

[34] Quoted in František Deák, "Two Manifestos: The Influence of Italian Futurism in Russia," in *The Drama Review: TDR* 19:4 (December 1975), 93.

[35] Yuri Tynyanov, "On FEKS," in Ian Christie and Richard Taylor, eds., *The Film Factory: Russian and Soviet Cinema in Documents. 1896-1939*, New York 1994, 258.

[36] Victor Shklovsky, "The Film Language of *New Babylon*," in *The Film Factory*, 311; V.B. Shklovskij, "О рождении и жизни ФЭКС'ов," in *ФЭКС: Григорий Козинцев и Леонид Трауберг*, Moscow 1928, 4.

[37] V. Pritulenko, "Золушка на все времена. 'Золушка', режиссеры Надежда Кошеверова, Михаил Шапиро," in *Искусство кино* 3 (March 1997), ⟨http://kinoart.ru/archive/1997/03/n3-article16⟩ (Accessed December 17, 2017).

3.4 *The Actress*

Shvarc wrote Cinderella's role especially for Zhejmo. As mentioned before, Zhejmo was an unusual choice for the main role, given the fact that playing "Cinderellas" in Stalinist cinema was a high-profile and serious task. In the 1930s, responding to the party's "социальный заказ" ("social demand"), Soviet filmmakers produced numerous *Золушка*-type films, especially musical comedies, in which young heroines of humble origin – peasants, workers, servants – followed the expected Soviet magical-transformation plot and turned into accomplished shock workers, decorated swineherds, or innovative engineers.[38] The most celebrated of the Soviet Cinderella films was Aleksandrov's *Светлый путь* (1940) – originally titled *Золушка* (*Cinderella*) – featuring the beautiful, glamorous, and multi-talented Soviet star Ljubov Orlova. As Anna Wexler Katsnelson demonstrates, it was "a film about a fairytale that became real"; in it, Aleksandrov staged "the ultimate spectacle of Socialist Realism."[39] However, unlike the uncontestable Soviet cinematic icon Orlova, whose most powerful fan was Stalin himself, Zhejmo was never to play iconic heroines. Her lack of stature (4ft 10in) and slender frame doomed her to travesty roles. When she was cast as Cinderella, she was a generation older than her heroine and insisted to be filmed only in the evening, when her face looked "right."[40] Yet Shvarc did not want a standard beauty and insisted that his Cinderella had to be physically inferior to her sisters because she had to be defamiliarized from the traditional visual feminine identity promoted by the Soviet media. As Shvarc's king hints to the audience, all old fairytale characters are "a good thing," but they are "all in the past" because "their fairytales have already been performed, and everybody knows them."[41] Obviously, *this* Cinderella was different and free of clichés. In the king's words, she is "fantastically lovely, supernaturally sincere, and mysteriously modest."[42]

It is truly impossible to define Zhejmo's Cinderella according to the parameters of a new "anthropological type" of beautiful Soviet women.[43] In the

---

38 Among the popular *Золушка*-type films were Grigorij Aleksandrov's musical comedies, *Веселые ребята* (*Jolly Fellows*, 1934), *Цирк* (*Circus*, 1936), *Светлый путь* (*Radiant Path*, 1940), and Ivan Pyrjev's *Свинарка и пастух* (*Swineherd and Shepherd*, 1941; in the US release, the title was *They Met in Moscow*, 1944).

39 Anna Wexler Katsnelson, "The Tramp in a Skirt: Laboring the *Radiant Path*," in *Slavic Review* 70:2 (Summer 2011), 270, 278.

40 Ol'ga Shablinskaja, "Как Золушка," in *Аргументы и факты* 23 (June 3, 2009), 41.

41 Shvarc, "Золушка. Киносценарий," in *Сказка о потерянном времени*, Moscow 2004, 188-189. See also "Культурный слой – Золушка."

42 Shvarc, "Золушка. Киносценарий," 193.

43 Oksana Bulgakova, "Советские красавицы в сталинском кино," in *Советское богатство. Статьи о культуре, литературе и кино*, St. Petersburg 2002, 391.

FIGURE 11.2 Cinderella (Janina Zhejmo) and Prince (Aleksej Konsovskij)

1930s this new "socialist" beauty type was exemplified by movie actresses (e.g., Orlova, Tamara Makarova, Marina Ladynina, Zoja Fedorova, Tatjana Okunevskaja, Valentina Serova, and Ljudmila Celikovskaja) with a set of standard characteristics: a well-proportioned body, physical strength (strong legs and broad shoulders), good health, athleticism, loud voice, precise gestures, and conservative – almost androgynous – clothing. These "blue-eyed blonds" were "monumental like the architecture of that time" and always ready for heavy physical labor on par with their male partners.[44] In fact, in the context of Stalinist cinema, the Soviet beauties were not after love, diamonds, or furs, but rather they aspired to live for collective goals even if it entailed ritual self-denial and self-sacrifice.[45] Again, in this company, Shvarc's Cinderella stood out as an odd creature. She failed the new physical beauty standards and revived old bourgeois – politically incorrect – values of traditional femininity: to fall in love, get married, and be happy. Most of her thoughts were focused on the king's ball and the young handsome prince. Her conduct was also in violation of Soviet "культурность" ("good manners in

---

44   Ibid., 398-399.
45   Clark describes the concept of ritual sacrifice in the Stalinist novel in *The Soviet Novel*, 177-188.

public") norms: she was impish, unrefined, spontaneous, and sometimes she talked back.[46] Zhejmo refreshed the old, worn-out image of Soviet princesses and gave the audience what they craved after the long and exhausting war years: a new form of spontaneous expression and hope for personal happiness.

3.5 The King's Whims, Tricks, and Quirks

Other main actors in Золушка – Garin, Ranevskaja, Konsovskij, and Merkurjev – also worked with Avant-Garde directors at the beginning of their careers and carried on their experimental acting style. Garin in particular was deeply influenced by Mejerhold, whose artistic system differed greatly from the widely accepted and established Stanislavskij method of acting and was not favorably received in Soviet Russia. A famous theater actor and director, Prov Sadovskij, called Mejerhold's theater a "school of formalist quirks."[47] Mejerhold never embraced traditional theater, and his own approach to acting gravitated toward conceptual theater, away from naturalism and realism. He had an affinity for FEKS – the circus had inspired some of his theater productions. Mejerhold's actors were expected to learn how to move on stage according to his method of "biomechanics," a series of exercises that taught them to master the precision of movement on stage or before the camera. They also had to learn acrobatics, mime, dance, and improvisation which their director considered important for the physical expression of emotions.

Garin, the "bumbling king" of Золушка, preserved Mejerhold's theatrical idiom to the end of his career, and in the film his spontaneity, playfulness, and unconventionality are refreshingly quirky and hyperbolically dramatic.[48] His king is full of child-like whims, pranks, and kindness and appeals to the child's

---

46 Vera Dunham argues that the representation of "культурность" was ubiquitous in Soviet middlebrow fiction. She juxtaposes "культурность" – "a proper conduct in public" – and "культура," or culture that describes "higher culture, a synthesis of ideas, knowledge, and memories," associated with the true intelligentsia. To Dunham, "культурность" belongs to the Soviet "мещанин" ("petty bourgeois") identity. See Dunham, *In Stalin's Time: Middleclass Values in Soviet Fiction*, London 1976, 22.

47 Aleksandr Dobrovol'skij, "Смертельная игра мастера," in *Московский комсомолец* 55 (March 16, 2005), 8.

48 Jack Zipes called Garin the "bumbling king" in *The Enchanted Screen: The Unknown History of Fairy-Tale Films*, New York 2011, 182. In Zipes's opinion, the king is the most interesting character in Золушка. Garin's acting was so original that it was considered "abnormal," and for many years he was cast primarily in the roles of negative characters since he did not fit the "positive Soviet hero" type. See, for instance, Andrej Chrzhanovskij, "Ученик чародея," in *Известия* (November 8, 2002). ⟨http://izvestia.ru/news/269395⟩ (Accessed July 17, 2017).

FIGURE 11.3 King (Erast Garin) and page (Igor' Klimenkov)

sense of free play. Apparently, Garin's acting was so eccentric that it rubbed the Lenfil'm administration the wrong way. The studio's director rebuked the actor for making the king unrealistic: "There are no such kings!"[49] But Garin's acting perfectly matches Shvarc's text. The gangly old king is in constant motion: he runs around his kingdom mischievously, dusting the palace, checking on the food in the kitchen, chatting with his subjects, and threatening to abdicate and retire to the monastery each time he hears about injustice or intrigues. Garin's body language, facial expressions, and movements are exaggerated even by fairytale-film standards, and his whole performance effectively intensifies the film's lively theatricality and underscores its departure from the conventions of realist acting. It seems symbolic that Shvarc lets his playful king open and close the story. When at the end of the film Garin takes off his crown and then his wig, he lays bare the device: the spectacle is over, and he is no longer the king, but an old, grey-haired actor with child-like eyes who shows his audience the magic of art. And it is as an actor, not as a fairytale king, that he ends the tale with a praise of human loyalty, honor, and the ability to love ("I adore these magical feelings that will never end"), rather than with a more standard moral message.[50]

---

49   See Ol'ga Filatova, "Zhejmovochka," in *ЛитМир – Электронная библиотека*. ⟨https://www.litmir.me/br/?b=187297&p=1⟩ (Accessed May 10, 2019).

50   Shvarc, "Золушка. Киносценарий," 220.

FIGURE 11.4 Vasilij Merkurjev as Cinderella's father

3.6 Faina Ranevskaja as a Conduit of Shvarc' "Double Encoding"

In his reminiscences, Nikolaj Chukovskij observes that despite the fairytale chronotope in Shvarc's plays, his representation of good and evil is never abstract: "On the contrary, everything in them [Shvarc's fairytale plays – L.R.] seems to be real, concrete, topical, and current, as if the spectator sits at some meeting at work and watches the hidden struggle of passions burning with real anger and pain."[51] In Золушка, we have access to reality through the evil stepmother, played by the extraordinary character actress Ranevskaja. Despite the stepmother's sly, aggressively ambitious, and rude nature, she becomes a conduit of Shvarc's "double encoding." According to the fairytale conventions, the stepmother has to be scheming and malevolent. However, Shvarc's text and Ranevskaja's acting disguise behind this stepmother's traditional vices a grotesque image of the rising Soviet middle-class. The stepmother's speech is strikingly modern, and Ranevskaja, who was notorious for improvising her lines on the set rather than learning them precisely, enhances it even more with her own unscripted remarks. Curiously, the audience loved her impromptu additions and many of her added lines became catch phrases in Soviet culture.

---

51 Nikolaj Chukovskij, "Евгений Шварц," in *Литературные воспоминания*, Moscow 1989, 274.

FIGURE 11.5 Faina Ranevskaja as Cinderella's stepmother

The stepmother is comfortable and seemingly well connected in her fairytale kingdom. She has an ambitious personal agenda and will stop at nothing to have the names of her daughters included in the book of the most beautiful maidens in the kingdom. Soviet reality unfolds in the stepmother's threats to use connections to punish everybody who stands in the way of her plans. To realize her goal to marry one of her daughters to the prince, she writes down the "signs of attention" ("знаки внимания") with which the prince allegedly honors her daughters (looks, sighs, remarks, etc). Once she compiles the list, she can claim that the prince is in love. The displacement from the fairytale world to the real one occurs as the stepmother continues to unleash the uncanny reality of political manipulation, intrigue, information collection, threats, fear, rudeness, and intimidation. Projected mentally onto real life, this fairytale evil becomes threatening, even if the actual Ranevskaja character is not. The main reason Shvarc and Ranevskaja succeed in creating this displacement effect is because they use contemporary language that directly references Soviet life. And although narrative estrangement from the classical fairytale is not unusual for modern adaptations, *Золушка*'s case is special. Its playful dialogues conceal a free, anti-conformist spirit, entertaining the child and slyly carrying a more socially critical message to the adult.[52]

---

52   Mark Lipovetsky writes that the fairytale has an inherent ability "to reveal the utopia's dark secrets, and this ability is what serves as a basis for the *anti-totalitarian vector* of

3.7 The Soundtrack

In his discussion of the Stalinist musical comedy in the 1930s, Evgenij Margolit emphasizes that only acting and music demonstrated "quality," "youthfulness," and "spontaneity" in this tightly structured and clichéd genre.[53] Soundtrack played an important role in Stalinist cinema, but it was never for entertainment only and had many dimensions, the most prominent and predictable of which was ideology.[54] Soviet music and songs were supposed to be a "formula for cultural regeneration" and part of the "quasi-religious aspects of the Bolshevik cultural experiment."[55] Moreover, as any Soviet artistic experience, music was to "enhance or even determine analysis, comment, and judgment 'in the spirit of communism'."[56] Again, on the musical plane, Золушка does not connect to Soviet mainstream songs and instead satisfies its own aesthetic needs of playful theatricality. At the king's ball, Cinderella has to sing and dance for the guests, and she chooses a simple children's song about a kind old bug that never grumbles or complains, and is adored by everyone. When the music starts, old and young join hands, and soon enough the whole court is dancing and singing along with Cinderella: "You are my friend and I'm your friend, your old and kind friend." Music changes adults into children and thus, in a sense, reverses the Soviet "spontaneity/consciousness" dialectic and reaffirms its estrangement from the official style.[57]

4 Золушка's "Knight's Move"

In *Ход коня* (*Knight's Move*, 1923) Shklovskij writes, "The greatest misfortune of Russian art is that it is not allowed to move organically, as the heart moves

---

the fairytale tradition in Soviet culture." See his introduction in *Politicizing Magic*, 234. Jack Zipes also argues that there is an undercurrent in fairytales that tends to subvert dominant ideologies (Zipes, *Breaking the Magic Spell. Radical Theories of Folk and Fairy Tales*, Lexington, KY 2002, especially chapter 1).

53   Margolit, *Живые и мертвое*, 199.
54   Katerina Clark, "Oral Hieroglyphics? Some Reflections on the Role of Sound in Recent Russian Films and Its Historical Context," in Nancy Condee, ed., *Soviet Hieroglyphics: Visual Culture in Late Twentieth-Century Russia*, London 1995, 1-21. Trudy Anderson, "Why Stalinist Musicals?" in *Discourse* 17:3 (Spring 1995), 38-48. David Gillespie, "The Sounds of Music: Soundtrack and Song in Soviet Film," in *Slavic Review* 62:3 (2003), 473-490.
55   Clark, "Oral Hieroglyphics?" 7, 8.
56   Gillespie, "The Sounds of Music," 473.
57   In *The Soviet Novel*, Clark writes, "'Consciousness' means political awareness and the complete self-control that enables the individual to be guided in all his actions by his awareness, whereas 'spontaneity' refers to purely visceral, willful, anarchic, or self-centered actions" (16).

in man's chest: it is being regulated like the movement of trains."⁵⁸ Writing these words well before the onset of Socialist Realism, Shklovskij adumbrated the direction in which Soviet art was moving. For him, as for the creators of *Золушка*, art was clearly synonymous with organic change and development. Yet Shklovskij abstained from apocalyptic pronouncements on the fate of art in Soviet Russia, because he believed that true art would always be able to make its unexpected "knight's move" and checkmate the prescribed official conventions. He believed that "in Russia everything is so contradictory that we have all become witty in spite of ourselves."⁵⁹ It seems that in this context, "witty" means "estranged," "imaginative," "eccentric," Avant-Garde, and thus everything that *Золушка* embodies in its spirit and aesthetics.

It may seem paradoxical that *Золушка* was approved for the official release on Victory Day in 1947, when Zhdanov's "anti-cosmopolitan" campaign was already in full swing and late Stalinist culture had reached its apogee. *Золушка* did not correspond to any ideological standards of the time, and Shvarc and Kosheverova had to run the gauntlet of bureaucracy and censorship to have the film completed and approved by the cultural establishment.⁶⁰ It seems, however, that despite its subversive elements and unique position in Soviet cinema dominated by war and historical-biographical films, *Золушка*'s unbounded theatricality corresponded to the happy and celebratory atmosphere of victory in World War II and the "ideal festive image of peace" that the Stalinist mass media strove to project.⁶¹ It must be for this reason that *Золушка* was released to Soviet audiences. It remains a masterpiece of Soviet cinematography and is admired by both Russian children and adult audiences. In 2009 *Золушка* was restored in color and saw its rebirth on Russian TV.

Works Cited

Anderson, Trudy. "Why Stalinist Musicals?" in *Discourse* 17:3 (1995), 38-48.
Balina, Marina. "Introduction," in Balina, Helena Goscilo, and Mark Lipovetsky, eds., *Politicizing Magic: An Anthology of Russian and Soviet Fairy Tales*. Evanston, IL 2005, 105-121.

---

58 Viktor Shklovsky, *Knight's Move*, trans. Richard Sheldon, Normal, IL 2005, 8.
59 Ibid., 4.
60 See Shvarc' diary entries for 1945-1947: Evgenij Shvarc, *Живу беспокойно... (из дневников)*, Leningrad 1990.
61 Margolit, *Живые и мертвое*, 360.

Balina, Marina and Birgit Beumers. "'To Catch Up and Overtake Disney?' Soviet and Post-Soviet Fairy-Tale Films," in Jack Zipes, Pauline Greenhill, and Kendra Magnus-Johnson, eds., *Fairy-Tale Films Beyond Disney. International Perspectives*. New York and London 2006, 124-138.

Boym, Svetlana. "Poetics and Politics of Estrangement: Victor Shklovsky and Hannah Arendt," in *Poetics Today* 26:4 (2005), 581-611.

Boym, Svetlana. *Another Freedom: The Alternative History of An Idea*. Chicago 2010.

Bulgakova, Anna and Nikolaj Vershinin-Konsovskij. "Волшебный комсомолец," in *Сеанс* 51-52 (2013), ⟨http://seance.ru/blog/dmytriy_konsovsky⟩ (Accessed December 17, 2017).

Bulgakova, Oksana. "Советские красавицы в сталинском кино," in Marina Balina, Evgenij Dobrenko, and Jurij Murashov, eds., *Советское богатство. Статьи о культуре, литературе и кино*. St. Petersburg 2002.

Christie, Ian and Richard Taylor, eds. *The Film Factory: Russian and Soviet Cinema in Documents. 1896-1939*. New York 1994.

Chukovskij, Nikolaj. "Евгений Шварц," in *Литературные воспоминания*. Moscow 1989, 245-279.

Clark, Katerina. "Oral Hieroglyphics? Some Reflections on the Role of Sound in Recent Russian Films and Its Historical Context," in Nancy Condee, ed., *Soviet Hieroglyphics: Visual Culture in Late Twentieth-Century Russia*. London 1995, 1-21.

Clark, Katerina. *The Soviet Novel: History as Ritual*, Chicago 1985.

Clayton, J. Douglas. "The Theatre of E. L. Shvarts: An Introduction," in *Études Slaves et Est-Européennes/Slavic and East-European Studies* 19 (1974), 23-43.

Corten, Irina H. "Evgenii Shvarts as an Adapter of Hans Christian Andersen and Charles Perrault," in *Russian Review* 37:1 (1978), 51-67.

Deák, František. "Two Manifestos: The Influence of Italian Futurism in Russia," in *The Drama Review: TDR* 19:4 (December 1975): 88-94.

Dobrovol'skij, Aleksandr. "Смертельная игра мастера," in *Московский комсомолец* 55 March 16, 2005, 8.

Dunham, Vera. *In Stalin's Time: Middleclass Values in Soviet Fiction*. London 1976.

Filatova, Ol'ga. "Zhejmovochka," in *ЛитМир – Электронная библиотека*. ⟨https://www.litmir.me/br/?b=187297&p=1⟩ (Accessed May 10, 2019).

Gillespie, David. "The Sounds of Music: Soundtrack and Song in Soviet Film," in *Slavic Review* 62:3 (2003), 473-490.

Gogitidze, N., ed. *Так говорила Фаина Раневская*. Rostov-on-the-Don 2003.

Gor'kij, Maksim. *Собрание сочинений в тридцати томах*, Vol. 27, *Статьи, доклады, речи, приветствия (1933-1936)*. Moscow 1953.

Grabenko, Ljudmila. "В гостях у сказки," in *Бульвар Гордона* 52 (December 25, 2012), ⟨http://www.bulvar.com.ua/arch/2012/52/50dc0eb72c756/⟩ (Accessed December 17, 2017).

Graffy, Julian. "Literature and Film," in Marina Balina and Evgeny Dobrenko, eds., *The Cambridge Companion to Twentieth-Century Russian Literature*, eds. Cambridge, UK 2011.

Hellman, Ben. *Fairy Tales and True Stories: The History of Russian Literature for Children and Young Adults (1574-2010)*. Leiden 2013.

Katsnelson, Anna Wexler. "The Tramp in a Skirt: Laboring the *Radiant Path*," in *Slavic Review* 70:2 (2011), 256-278.

Kenez, Peter. *Cinema and Soviet Society, 1917-1953*. Cambridge, UK 1992.

Liehm, Mira and Antonin J. Liehm. *The Most Important Art: Soviet and East European Film after 1945*. Berkeley, CA 1977.

Mamatova, L. Kh. *Кино: политика и люди. 30-е годы*. Moscow 1995.

Margolit, Evgenij. *Живые и мертвое: заметки к истории советского кино 1920х-1960х годов*. St. Petersburg 2012.

Marinelli-König, Gertraud. *Russische Kinderliteratur in der Sowjetunion der Jahre 1900-1930*. Munich 2007.

Marshak, Samuil. "О большой литературе для маленьких," in *Собрание сочинений в восьми томах*, Vol. 6. Moscow 1971, 195-243.

Miller, Frank J. *Folklore for Stalin: Russian Folklore and Pseudofolklore of the Stalin Era*. Armonk, NY 1990.

Nikolajeva, Marija. "Fairy Tales in Society's Service," in *Marvels and Tales* 16:2 (2002), 171-187.

Oinas, Felix J. "Folklore and Politics in the Soviet Union," in *Slavic Review* 32:1 (March 1973), 45-58.

Pritulenko, V. "Золушка на все времена. 'Золушка', режиссеры Надежда Кошеверова, Михаил Шапиро," in *Искусство кино* 3 (March 1997), ⟨http://kinoart.ru/archive/1997/03/n3-article16⟩ (Accessed December 17, 2017).

Prokhorov, Alexander. "Arresting Development: A Brief History of Soviet Cinema for Children and Adolescents," in Marina Balina and Larissa Rudova, eds., *Russian Children's Literature and Culture*. New York and London 2008, 129-152.

Shablinskaja, Ol'ga. "Как Золушка," in *Аргументы и факты* 23 (June 3, 2009), 41.

Shklovskij, Viktor. "О рождении и жизни ФЭКС'ов," in V.V. Nedobrovo, *ФЭКС: Григорий Козинцев и Леонид Трауберг*. Moscow 1928.

Shklovsky, Victor. "Art as Technique," in Lee T. Lemon and Marion J. Reis, trans., eds., *Russian Formalist Criticism: Four Essays*. Lincoln, NE 1965, 5-24.

Shklovsky, Viktor. "The Film Language of *New Babylon*," in Ian Christie and Richard Taylor, eds., *The Film Factory: Russian and Soviet Cinema in Documents 1896-1939*. New York 1994, 311-313.

Shklovsky, Viktor. *Knight's Move*, trans. Richard Sheldon. Normal, IL 2005.

Shvarc, Evgenij. *Живу беспокойно... (из дневников)*. Leningrad 1990.

Shvarc, Evgenij. "Золушка. Киносценарий," in *Сказка о потерянном времени*. Moscow 2004.

Smirnova, Dunja. "Золушка," in *Сеанс* 8 (1993), ⟨http://2011.russiancinema.ru/index.php?e_dept_id=2&e_movie_id=8762⟩ (Accessed July 17, 2017).

Staples, Terry. "Soviet Fairy-Tale Films," in Donald Haase, ed., *The Greenwood Encyclopedia of Folktales*, Vol. 3. Westport, CT 2008.

Stishova, Elena. "Приключения Золушки в стране большевиков," in *Российское кино в поисках реальности*. Moscow 2013.

Stites, Richard. *Russian Popular Culture: Entertainment and Society since 1900*. New York 1992.

Tippner, Anja. "Evgenii Shvarts's Fairy Tale Dramas: Theater, Power, and the Naked Truth," in Marina Balina and Larissa Rudova, eds., *Russian Children's Literature and Culture*. New York and London 2008, 307-324.

Volkov, S. V., ed. *Черная книга имен, которым не место на карте России*. Moscow 2008.

Zemljanuchin, S. and M. Segida. *Домашняя синематека. Отечественное кино. 1918-1996*. Moscow 1996.

Zipes, Jack. *Breaking the Magic Spell. Radical Theories of Folk and Fairy Tales*. Lexington, KY 2002.

Zipes, Jack. *The Enchanted Screen: The Unknown History of Fairy-Tale Films*. New York 2011.

"Детское кино," in *Большая советская энциклопедия*. Moscow 1969-1978, ⟨http://www.bse.info-spravka.ru/bse/id_24506⟩ (Accessed December 17, 2017).

"Культурный слой – *Золушка*," in *5-tv.ru*, January 3, 2009, ⟨http://www.5-tv.ru/video/503084/⟩ (Accessed July 17, 2017).

"Фильм *Золушка*. История создания," in *Made in the USSR*, November 1, 2012 ⟨http://ussr-kruto.ru/2012/11/01/film-zolushka-istoriya-sozdaniya/⟩ (Accessed July 17, 2017).

CHAPTER 12

The Queer Legacies of Late Socialism, or What Cheburashka and Gary Shteyngart Have in Common

Anna Fishzon

1   Introduction

One of the most striking features of Stagnation-era animated films is their preoccupation with the relationship between boy heroes and avuncular companions or, alternatively, between anthropomorphic young characters and older brother figures. Regardless of the prominence of the dyad in the literary source, directors of late-Soviet cartoon favorites arrange to make it the indisputable dramatic focus. Roman Kachanov's Cheburashka and Gena (1969-83) and Fedor Chitruk's Vinni-puch and Pjatachok (1969-72), taken respectively from Eduard Uspenskij's *Крокодил Гена и его друзья* (*Crocodile Gena and His Friends*, 1966) and Alan Alexander Milne's *Winnie-the-Pooh* (1926) are among the best-known examples, as is the eponymous duo of Boris Stepancev's animated films adapted from Astrid Lindgren's Karlsson-on-the-Roof stories, *Малыш и Карлсон* (*The Kid and Karlson*, 1968) and *Карлсон вернулся* (*Karlson Returns*, 1970).

It is not simply that the three cartoon series spotlight older eccentric figures with diminutive sidekicks, but that they portray them queerly, in uneasy relation to gender, identity, social space, and time. Gena, Puch, and Karlson are all decidedly childlike and immature, without access to traditional family units. They are inveterate bachelors ill-suited to their apparent mentoring roles and excluded from procreative life. The queer nature of the older characters emanates from their ambiguous developmental stages and antioedipal positioning: the non-filial register of their interaction with younger mates and their association with other socially marginal or non-reproductive characters – the trouble-making Shapokljak, the tailless depressive Donkey Ia, and the Kid's manifestly unmaternal housekeeper, Freken Bok. The characters' queerness is accentuated also by the art of animation, which separates voices from their original human sources and places them in plastic, temporally promiscuous, and non-normative bodies and unexpected or impossible situations.¹

Here I interrogate the iconic status of failed, queer masculinity in what can be considered late-Soviet popular culture first, by reading Vinni-puch, Karlson, and Gena as fetishistic images that simultaneously masked and registered the trauma undergirding everyday life in the period of "developed socialism." Brezhnev-era society witnessed a shift away from utopian rhetoric and eschatological orientation: by the 24th Congress of the Communist Party of the Soviet Union, convened in 1971, communism had become an asymptotic ideal rather than a realizable goal, and references to "full-scale communist construction" had all but ceased.² Such radical discontinuities of ideology and temporality made the sacrifices and crimes of paternal forebears difficult to symbolize and therefore mourn.

I then turn to Gary Shteyngart's *Little Failure: A Memoir* (2014). Contemporary Russian-American memoirs and autobiographical fiction are proper places from which to explore the silent motivators and illusions of late socialist society because Soviet immigrants like Shteyngart similarly experienced a traumatic breach in their relationship to time. They struggled, as moderns typically do, with the anxiety-provoking loss of "God," or a consummate guarantor of discourse, history, and sense.³ Feeling temporally unmoored, they could neither shed, nor fully integrate, their violent Soviet inheritance and its potentialities. Shteyngart conjures and examines the fetishistic disavowals of late socialism by placing at the memoir's emotional center a lawless and brutal father and then making him into a little failure, a childlike, vulnerable adult or beastly child. The latter image, like those of Stagnation-era animated films, displaces memories of father-son competition and violence, quashing anxiety and allowing space for love and work.⁴

---

1   J. Jack Halberstam has reflected on the queering effects of some forms of animation. He also has commented on the "potential queerness of all allegorical narratives of animal sociality" and called for "creative anthropomorphism" in animated film (fantastical beasts that stage communitarian uprisings, for example) through which it might be possible to "invent new models of resistance [...] in reference to other lifeworlds, animal and monstrous." Judith Halberstam, *The Queer Art of Failure*, Durham, NC 2011, 46, 47, 51; also see 29, 181-186.
2   Mark Sandle, *A Short History of Soviet Socialism*, London, UK and Philadelphia, PA 1999, 225.
3   Psychoanalyst Colette Soler provides a good overview of the ways Søren Kierkegaard, Sigmund Freud, Martin Heidegger, and Jacques Lacan variously conceptualized anxiety as a problem of modernity; they lent the affect ontological import, connecting it to God and the Other, faith and its loss. Soler, *Lacanian Affects: The Function of Affect in Lacan's Work*, trans. Bruce Fink, New York 2016, 18-40.
4   Filmmakers of the 1930s and 1940s already were attempting to cover over or partially represent the Stalin era's unassimilable wounds to the male body and masculinity. Lilya

2   The Odd Couples of Sojuzmul'tfil'm

One way to assess the relative dominance of eccentric male-coded couples in late-Soviet animated film is to draw a quick comparison between the cartoon versions and their literary originals.[5] Chitruk's biggest change to Milne's initial cast was the addition of Pjatachok as a central character. In the Milne story, only Pooh, Christopher Robin, and Rabbit appear in the first two chapters. Piglet is mentioned very briefly in Milne's preface, where he is petty and envious, desperate to be popular like Pooh.[6] In a similar vein, the relationship between the Kid and Karlson is more exclusive and emotionally laden in the Soviet adaptions than in the Swedish original. While in Stepancev's films the Kid's family and dog pose a threat to Karlson, in Lindgren's text the little boy's affections are divided among his parents, Karlsson, and the puppy without jealous tension or rivalry, and the boundary between the world of "children" (Lillebror and Karlsson) and the world of adults (Lillebror's parents) is porous.[7]

Kaganovsky has argued that recurring cinematic images of mutilated and deficient male bodies alluded to both the New Man's submission to Stalin and the relief provided by the exposure and knowledge of one's limitations. Kaganovsky, *How the Soviet Man was Unmade: Cultural Fantasy and Male Subjectivity under Stalin*, Pittsburgh, PA 2008.

5 The abundance of male or vaguely masculine couples consisting of an older mentor and young protégé, has not escaped the notice of recent interpreters of late-Soviet animation, nor has their overt queerness: unusual family structures and living arrangements, alternative life schedules and modes of association, transgender embodiment, and, why not? – nonheterosexuality. Konstantin Kljuchkin goes so far as to call pedophilic, if not homosexual, the relationships of the Kid and Karlson and Gena and Cheburashka; or, at the very least, examples of nonnormative upbringing and moral development in the tradition of the coming-out story and its precursor, the Bildungsroman. Lilya Kaganovsky has written about gender fluidity, transvestism, and self/other confusion of the Wolf and Rabbit in the popular cartoon *Hy, погоди! (Just You Wait!*, 1969-2006). Kljuchkin, "Заветный мультфильм: причины популярности 'Чебурашки'" and Lilja Kaganovskaja, "Гонка вооружений, трансгендер и застой: Волк и Заяц в кон/подтексте 'холодной войны'," in Ilja Kukulin, Mark Lipoveckij, and Marija Majofis, eds., *Веселые человечки: культурные герои советского детства*, Moscow 2008, 360-377 and 378-392.

6 In Milne's stories we never forget that Winnie-the-Pooh is Christopher Robin's toy. Christopher, a human boy, is smarter than Pooh, superior to him in every way. An understanding of Milne's Pooh as an older male protagonist is therefore much more difficult to sustain. Chitruk's replacement of Christopher by Pjatachok will be discussed below.

7 Marija Majofis, "Милый, милый трикстер: Карлсон и советская утопия о 'настоящем детстве'," in Ilja Kukulin et al, eds., *Веселые человечки*, 249-250. The Russian translations of the Milne and Lindgren texts will be discussed briefly below. Generally, the effects I describe are more exaggerated in the animated versions due partly to the visions of Chitruk and Stepancev but also to the possibilities and constraints of their medium.

The importance of the "unlikely (male) friendship" theme for Stagnation-era animators and their audiences becomes even more glaring if we direct our attention back to the immediate postwar years, and then forward to Perestroika and the post-1991 period, both in the Soviet Union and in the West. The anthropomorphic older male/younger protégé component is far less common in the American cinematic canon for children and in animated films of other Soviet eras. One can make the case for Tom and Jerry (1940-58) or Curious George and the Man with the Yellow Hat (1941-66) but the latter duo has a distinctly familial cast, and both lack the queerness and polysemy of their late-Soviet analogues. Tom and Jerry are obvious rivals; their exchanges exhibit none of the features of the mentor-pupil relationship we observe in the *Винни-пух* (Vinni-puch) films. The Man with the Yellow Hat is much more fatherly and self-assured than Gena or Karlson, without the callowness or youthful charm of the latter. Sojuzmul'tfil'm offers even fewer examples. *Мурзилка и Великан* (*Murzilka and the Giant*, 1960), the story of a benighted folktale titan and his much cleverer, technologically savvy little friend, and *Горячий камень* (*The Hot Stone*, 1965), based on Arkadij Gajdar's story about a hoary retired revolutionary's influence over a willful youth, are more earnestly didactic than anything produced in late 1960s and 1970s.[8]

Finally, the sheer popularity and adult appeal distinguish characters like Gena and Cheburashka from many of their Western and Soviet counterparts. We need only to think of Vasilij Livanov's patent husky voice (Gena, Karlson) and the interpenetration of Vinni-puch, Evgenij Leonov, and Leonov's non-animated characters. Livanov, Leonov, and other stars of the stage and screen linked animated heroes to famous feature film roles, broadening the cartoon

---

8   In Stalin's time, many animated films were adapted from Russian fables, folktales, and literary classics: among the most famous were Valentina and Zinaida Brumberg's *Стрекоза и муравей* (*The Dragonfly and the Ant*, 1938), *Ивашко и Баба Яга* (*Ivashko and Baba Iaga*, 1938), and *Сказка о царе Салтане* (*The Tale of Tsar Saltan*, 1943). In the late 1940s and 1950s, directors like Ivan Ivanov-Vano and Ivan Aksenchuk specialized in fantastic tales, developing an original aesthetic rooted in Russian folk arts and architecture: for example, Ivanov-Vano's *Конек-горбунок* (*The Humpbacked Horse*, 1947) and *Снегурочка* (*The Snow Maiden*, 1952) and Aksenchuk's *Ореховый прутик* (*A Walnut Twig*, 1957). During Perestroika, episodes of popular 1970s series like Anatolij Reznikov's *Кот Леопольд* (*Leopold the Cat*, 1975-1987) and *Ну, погоди!* continued to be made; and, notably, Sojuzmul'tfil'm, produced Eduard Nazarov's arch and journalistically styled *Про Сидорова Вову* (*About Vova Sidorov*, 1985). Ivanov-Vano's work is discussed in Lora Wheeler Mjolsness's essay, "Under the Hypnosis of Disney: Ivan Ivanov-Vano and Soviet Animation for Children," in this volume. For a survey of Soviet animation, see David MacFadyen, *Yellow Crocodiles and Blue Oranges: Russian Animated Film Since World War Two*, Montreal 2005. Also see Laura Pontieri, *Soviet Animation and the Thaw of the 1960s. Not Only for Children*, New Barnet, Herts, UK 2012.

characters' renown and expanding their valences.[9] They also instantiated a *queer temporality* – that is, an extraordinary and nonlinear time – through the very materiality of their voices. Because the voice is not merely a vehicle of speech but also an object with timbre and grain, it summons listeners' wayward desire.[10] What scholar Peggy Phelan has asserted about the body in performance can be said about the voice embodied by animation: it is a metonym that alludes not to the subjectivity of the performer, but rather to another element of the performance – a character, a gesture, music, and the like.[11] The raspy prattles of Leonov's Puch and Livanov's characters play precisely this part, metonymically evoking extra-fictional personalities and associations to everyday life. Similarly, the voice of the barely visible Someone from another classic animated film, Jurij Norshtejn's *Ежик в тумане* (*Hedgehog in the Fog*, 1975), stirs one to curiosity by dissolving into a lack to be traversed by the fantasy of the viewer. The animated voice thus functions as a kind of vocal drag that engenders intimacy and queers the libido. It prompts spectators to assume multiple identifications concurrently, and thereby question the self in linear time, or, identity as such.

One wonders why queer thematics and aesthetics, mediated and popularized by famous Soviet actors, became so ubiquitous in animated films and how these issues came to dominate late-Soviet popular culture. I propose several related hypotheses. First, the intense concern with masculine intergenerational couples reflected structural and representational changes in the understanding and function of fatherhood in the post-Thaw period. As the "шестидесятники" (the 60s generation) reached their creative maturity in the late 1960s and 1970s and grappled with the loss of real and spiritual fathers, they also gravitated to the relatively lightly censored animation studios of Sojuzmul'tfil'm, where their strident Thaw-era demands for "socialism with a human face" found more soul-searching and oblique expression. One can well

---

9   For a discussion of the similarities between Leonov's Vinni-puch and the role of Vasilij Charitonov from Georgij Danelija's film *Осенний марафон* (*Autumn Marathon*, 1979), see Anna Fishzon, "The Fog of Stagnation: Explorations of Time and Affect in Late-Soviet Animation," in Larissa Zakharova and Kristin Roth-Ey, eds., *Communications and Media in the USSR and Eastern Europe: Technologies, Politics, Cultures, Social Practices*. Special issue of *Cahiers du Monde Russe* 56/2-3 (2015), 586-590.

10 On the materiality of the voice, see Mladen Dolar, *A Voice and Nothing More*, Cambridge, MA 2006, and Roland Barthes, "The Grain of the Voice," in Jonathan Sterne, ed., *The Sound Studies Reader*, New York 2012, 504-510.

11 Peggy Phelan, *Unmarked: The Politics of Performance*, New York 1996, 150-52. On queer time, see Judith Halberstam, *In a Queer Time and Place: Transgender Bodies, Subcultural Lives*, New York 2005.

argue, on these grounds, that the "father-son" configuration functioned for "шестидесятники" ("men of the sixties") as a representational substitute for what was lacking in their own lives.[12] At the same time, as the regime moved toward stability and away from revolutionary and militaristic imperatives, fathers began to share responsibility for childrearing and the affective bonds of the nuclear family.[13] Even if actual Soviet fathers remained only marginally involved in parenting, a new ideal of domestic life with an emphasis on the father-son tie emerged in advice literature, films, and fictional writings of the period.[14]

Such an explanation does not fully account, however, for the churlishness – and near absence – of women and mothers in the classic Brezhnev-era cartoons. Take, for example, the hardhearted spinsters Shapokljak and Freken Bok from the *Чебурашка* and *Карлсон* series, respectively, the single father-King of Inessa Kovalevskaja's *Бременские музыканты* (*Bremen Town Musicians*, 1969) and its sequel (1973), the nearly all-male world of Kachanov's *Тайна Третьей планеты* (*The Mystery of the Third Planet*, 1981), and the self-absorbed working mother from Vladimir Popov's *Трое из Простоквашино* films (*Three from Prostokvashino*, 1978-84). Nor does the above hypothesis shed light on the mild derision aimed at ineffectual intelligentsia fathers and the fixation on avuncular trickster types. The pusillanimous King from *Бременские музыканты* and the pushover dads of *Карлсон* and *Трое из Простоквашино* immediately spring to mind, as do other characters already mentioned: the well-meaning though hapless Gena, and the mischievous Vinni-puch and Karlson.

---

12 It is risky to paint the diverse "шестидесятники" with a broad brush, especially since their image evolved as subsequent generations attempted to define them. Here I am referencing some of their less disputed "ideals" and hopes: moral renewal, sincerity, lyricism, and a return to a "purer" socialism grounded in collectivism and civic-minded legality in the wake of the terror and the gulag. The fathers of many "шестидесятники" were missing due to symbolic or actual death, often having been both victims and perpetrators of Stalinist purges. On the Thaw generation, see Denis Kozlov and Eleonory Gilburd, eds., *The Thaw: Soviet Society and Culture During the 1950s and 1960s*, Toronto 2013, and Polly Jones, *Myth, Memory, Trauma: Rethinking the Stalinist Past in the Soviet Union, 1953-1970*, New Haven, CT 2013.

13 These new models of fatherhood were disseminated by such children's authors as Viktor Dragunskij and Viktor Goljavkin.

14 On the transposition of ideals of "шестидесятники" into the theatrical and filmic adaptations of Astrid Lindgren's Karlsson books (as well as their critical reviews), see Majofis, "Милый, милый трикстер," in *Веселые человечки*, 241-286. On the prominence of the father-son relationship and male kinship in postwar Soviet film, see Helena Goscilo and Yana Hashamova, eds., *Cinepaternity: Fathers and Sons in Soviet and Post-Soviet Film*, Bloomington, IN 2010.

This point brings me to my second idea, the elaboration of which will require an analysis of Post-Soviet autobiographical writing. I believe that the intense concern with sophomoric protagonists and their younger comrades in animated film enunciated a collective fantasy – a societal wish to posit failed masculinity as a charming and innocuous aspect of late-Soviet family life. The very real violence of the Stalin period and the traumas of World War II demanded a thorough rethinking of maleness and fatherhood, but instead led to a regressive, unconscious procedure of depicting angry, frightening men as harmless and playful, and passionate oedipal conflict as cute sibling rivalry. This symptomatic approach to profound social wounds, in my view, explains the obsession of the most culturally resonant Brezhnev-era animated films with adorable, non-oedipal elders and their pint-sized buddies. Today, the structuring illusions of late socialism remain as memorials to otherwise unspeakable (and often familial) destructiveness. They continue to surface in the cultural production of the last Soviet generation, which compulsively repeats and attempts to master that which its ancestors failed to articulate.

3   Vinni-puch, Pjatachok, and Queer Masculinity

Alan Alexander Milne's *Winnie-the-Pooh* (1926) originated in England and was inspired by stories the author created with his son, Christopher Robin, about Christopher's favorite teddy bear and other toy characters. "Winnie" was the name of a bear relocated from Winnipeg, Canada that Christopher visited at the London Zoo, and "Pooh" the name of a swan the boy saw once on a holiday. While in *Winnie-the-Pooh* Milne appears as the author-narrator and Christopher the reader-protagonist, the text seems to have been forged collaboratively. Milne both observed Christopher's play with a toy bear and participated in it; he then transformed this narrated play into a book, one in which Milne is also occasionally a character, conversing with Pooh as well as Christopher Robin. Perhaps because Milne's *Pooh* is a children's story told humorously from an adult's point of view by a nurturing narrator, it attracts an avid adult readership and even has generated so-called Poohology, a body of texts that mobilized the books, movies, and material culture of *Pooh* for didactic and satirical ends.[15]

The Soviet *Винни-пух*, translated faithfully by Boris Zachoder in the early 1960s and then made into a three-part animated series by Chitruk for Sojuz-

---

15   On "Poohology" and psychoanalytic uses of Milne's text, see Kenneth B. Kidd, *Freud in Oz: At the Intersections of Psychoanalysis and Children's Literature*, Minneapolis 2011, 35-63.

mul'tfil'm between 1969 and 1972, also enjoyed immense popularity with a dual audience of children and adults, proving especially appealing to intelligentsia readers and spectators. Literature scholar Natalija Smoljarova, waxing autobiographical in her article, "Детский, 'недетский' Винни-пух," tells of the warm welcome she received when in 1972 she started her first position as translator in one of the Moscow institutes. Her senior colleague boasted of the friendly atmosphere in the department: "We have here many couples, travel novels, shared children, and a copy of *Винни-пух*." Smoljarova considered herself lucky since Zachoder's *Винни-пух* was in short supply and high demand. There were long queues for the book in libraries and friendship circles; copies changed hands many times and the less fortunate searched for it without success in stores and among speculators.[16]

A comparison of the original illustrated *Winnie-the Pooh* books and the Sojuzmul'tfil'm version highlights the distinguishing features of Chitruk's characterizations and reveals how the *Винни-пух* films reflected and commented on masculinity, the family, and pleasure systems in the Stagnation era, offering insights about the organizing fantasies of late-socialist society.[17] The most obvious changes made by Chitruk are the removal of Christopher Robin and his narrator-father from the story. Christopher's lines are given to Pjatachok (and in places Rabbit) and Milne's to a less intrusive voice-over narration, with the effect that the distance between spectators and characters is narrowed and the self-reflective storytelling duties are transferred to the viewer. The potential for recognition and reflexivity on the part of the spectator is expanded, too, by occasional ruptures in the diegetic frame (Puch pauses during his contemplative walks to stare directly into the camera) and the intertextuality occasioned by gravelly voice of Leonov. The celebrated character actor not only brought to Chitruk's films his trademark natural acting style, slurred speech, warm facial expressions, and clumsiness; he also famously served as Puch's physical model.

The initial chapters of Milne's *Winnie-the-Pooh*, illustrated by *Punch* cartoonist Ernest H. Shepard, revolve around Pooh's insatiable appetite for honey. In the inaugural "We are Introduced to Winnie-the-Pooh and Some Bees and the Stories Begin," Pooh fails to obtain honey from the top of a tree inhabited by bees; in the following "Pooh Goes Visiting and Gets into a Tight Place" our hero climbs through a narrow hole into his friend Rabbit's home and eats so

---

16   Smoljarova, "Детский 'недетский' Винни-пух," in Kukulin et al, eds., *Веселые человечки*, 287.
17   A similar comparison but with a nearly exclusive focus on aesthetics and commentary on Wolfgang Reitherman's first Disney adaptation *Winnie-the-Pooh and the Honey Tree* (1966) has been made by Yuri Leving, "'Кто-то там все-таки есть...': Винни-пух и новая анимационная эстетика," in Ibid., 315-353.

much honey that he gets stuck on his way out. Self-reflective narration is used liberally in these early chapters. Milne initially focuses on Pooh's relationship with Christopher Robin and introduces the good-mannered Rabbit in the second chapter, only briefly previewing other characters. The reader never forgets that Pooh is Christopher Robin's beloved toy, his transitional object, and that Christopher is the narrator's six-year-old son who asks his father "sweetly" to tell Pooh stories about himself – "because he's *that* sort of bear."[18] Parenthetical italicized conversations that readers are led to assume took place between real father/author Milne and his son Christopher appear throughout. These layered metanarratives have been of great importance to the understanding of Pooh stories and one of the principal sources of their appeal. Kenneth B. Kidd, for example, suggests that the structure of Milne's book echoed the development of collaborative play in child psychoanalysis and inspired appropriations of Pooh for philosophical and other, middlebrow, purposes.[19]

Chitruk's first two films, *Винни-пух* (1969) and *Винни-пух идет в гости* (*Vinni-puch Goes Visiting*, 1971), about ten minutes each in length, in many respects are consistent with the original plot, reproducing much of the dialogue verbatim. But Chitruk's narrator, unlike Milne's, has no relationship to Vinni-puch or anyone else, and only serves to unobtrusively introduce the story, offer sparse commentary, and utter a few valedictory lines at the end. By eliminating the metanarratives that Milne uses to evoke the childlike make-believe world of the Hundred Acre Wood – a world of hybrid socialities where naturalistic forest animals, stuffed toys, and a boy congregate and have adventures – Chitruk is able to obviate not only Christopher Robin (much to the dismay of Zachoder), but also human life more generally.[20] Instead, he intensifies and widens the fantasy space, creating a universe where Vinni-puch and his friends are very much alive. They are no longer animals or stuffed toys but, rather, "real" characters that feel more authentic when not placed in scenes with naturalistically drawn humans. The written word does not stand between them and the spectator, and the film induces identification and reflective engagement, implicitly summoning viewers to assume the position of Vinni-puch or the space evacuated of author-narrator Milne. Most obviously, Chitruk's version removes the father-son relationship and shifts its primary focus to a non-oedipal alliance.

---

18 A. A. Milne, *Winnie-the-Pooh*, New York 1926, 4.
19 Kidd, *Freud in Oz*, 35-52.
20 On the strained relations between Zachoder and Chitruk and the differences in their vision for the *Винни-пух* films, see Leving, "Кто-то там все-таки есть...," in *Веселые человечки*, 319-326.

The immediacy and queerness of Chitruk's world is also transmitted through his naïve animation. The scenes resemble children's colored-pencil drawings: flat, laconic, with saturated reds and yellows, and lush greens. Technical difficulties necessitated some of the simplicity in the art, limiting the movements of Puch and Pjatachok (for example, Puch's front and back paws always moved in the same direction) but also enhancing the characters' awkward charm.[21]

Milne rarely chooses to reveal Pooh through his relationships with other characters. The British bear is a child's toy and prefers to play games, sit quietly before a fire, or listen to stories, especially about himself. Chitruk, in collaboration with Zachoder, complicates Puch through an expansion and modification of the role of Pjatachok. By substituting the piglet for Christopher Robin, he gives Puch a companion who, unlike the human Christopher, is not blatantly superior in intelligence or maturity. Pjatachok, in fact, is quite admiring of Puch and he spends much of the films taking orders and breathlessly trying to keep up with Puch's swift pace. Voiced by the film actress Ija Savvina and sped up to a piercing treble, Pjatachok thus reads like an infant or toddler, both eliciting sympathy and enlarging Puch's personality.[22]

The Soviet Vinni-puch is slow-witted though highly impulsive, and his body and actions seem to overrun and race ahead of his thoughts. During his first conversation with Pjatachok he barely makes eye contact and speaks in fitful terse phrases. The piglet eagerly does whatever Puch demands: he fetches props, proffers encouragement, and becomes an accomplice in all of his mentor's schemes. But despite his subordinate position, we occasionally suspect that Pjatachok possesses more knowledge about the world than Vinni-puch – as in the first installment when he expresses concern that Vinni's muddied body looks nothing like a dark cloud, and thus will not fool or distract the bees from whom the cub hopes to steal honey. Or in the second episode, where Pjatachok exclaims in protest that "no one goes visiting in the mornings!"

---

21   Ibid., 328-329; 336-343.

22   I focus on Puch's relationship with Pjatachok here as it threads the three Chitruk films and is clearly the most central; yet it should be noted that Chitruk's bear generally displays a greater interest in human-like contact than Milne's Pooh. He attempts to console the doleful Ia and seems a shade conflicted about his imposition on Rabbit. Moreover, Zachoder and Chitruk subjectify Puch from the opening credits of the series. Before the hero comes into view in the first film, we see his tracks and hear the narrator explain that Vinni-puch is a poet who makes up short songs, and that he always likes a snack. Puch then appears, marching briskly and composing his latest verses to the rhythm of his steps. The bear thus introduces himself and his life philosophy in his own words. Though Pooh's poems punctuate Milne's *Winnie-the-Pooh* and occasionally exhibit self-reflection, they are not used as a narrative framework.

That Pjatachok's presence adds complexity to Puch and helps underscore relationships among characters becomes especially apparent in Chitruk's 1971 film *Винни-пух идет в гости* based on the second Milne chapter. The honey-eating scene in Rabbit's abode is expanded to demonstrate the subtle ways in which Puch's oral drive trumps other impulses. He is not altogether unaware of etiquette, but his superficial grasp of rules of comportment is put only in the service of crude manipulation and ultimate goal of acquiring snacks. Puch's "concern" that Rabbit not find him rude is unaccompanied by an actual capacity for empathy, with the result that he overstays his welcome and eats everything Rabbit has in his cupboard. Yet Chitruk humanizes his Puch through nuanced gestures and interactions. The bear gently bosses around Pjatachok without appearing tyrannical. Like a parent might do to a small child, Puch washes his little friend's face before the meal. He then ties a napkin over Pjatachok's mouth (but without force or malice) so that the piglet is unable to eat or say anything during the whole meal and disrupt his plans. At the end Puch reaches for Pjatachok's hand several times before finally grabbing it and running off with him.

Chitruk's Vinni-puch is surlier and fatter than the British Pooh. His body is huge. It overflows, embarrasses itself, announces its enormity. The tiny and squeaking Pjatachok serves to accentuate his friend's stoutness.[23] Puch's body is a haphazard assemblage of shaggy parts, testimony that errors have been made. Puch cannot help being overweight; he is all hunger and mouth, unable to stop ingesting. He invites our hunger, perhaps even our envy, with his driven and out-of-control orality. His is an infantile mouth, a pre-oedipal body. Neither Puch nor Pjatachok (and in this way they are typical cartoon characters) understand bodies as carriers of shame or as markers of difference – certainly not sexual difference. Puch is innocent of the reality principle and he might never grow up. Chitruk said as much in a letter to Zachoder, explaining that he understood Vinni-puch as a character who is "always bursting with grandiose plans, too complex and unwieldy for the trivialities to which he wants to apply them. This is why the plans fall apart as soon as they come into contact with reality. He is constantly getting into trouble, not because of stupidity, but because his world does not accord with reality."[24]

In the second film, Chitruk and Zachoder take perhaps the most liberties with Milne's text, largely in the service of conveying late-socialist cultural paradigms. While Shepard's Rabbit is drawn in a naturalistic style, Chitruk's is

---

23 Pjatachok's fleshiness suggests "baby fat" rather than gluttony.
24 Leving, "'Кто-то там все-таки есть...'," in *Веселые человечки*, 328.

anthropomorphized – an unmistakable member of the Soviet intelligentsia. With nose in the air, finger raised, large spectacles, thick lisp, and nasal effeminate self-righteousness, he lectures and prevaricates more than Milne's meek creation.[25] Puch's voracious appetite and poor self-restraint in Rabbit's home acquires special relevance in a deficit economy. Rabbit is compelled to yield the entire contents of his kitchen: he shudders at having to serve the condensed milk and honey but seems too spineless and docile to say "no" to Puch. Though Rabbit is cynical and insincere, initially lying to Puch about not being home, he immediately yields to his visitor's demand just as he might satisfy the demands of the state. Puch's drive for pleasure and willfulness is thrown into sharp relief by the inertia and cheerless aridity of Rabbit (and Donkey Ia, another intelligentsia-like character Puch encounters in Chitruk's third installment). If Rabbit's intelligentsia masculinity is more fully achieved than Puch's – more civilized, moral, ambivalent, and self-distanced – it is also devoid of desire: bookish, overly polite, saccharin, longwinded, and without virility. Indeed, Puch's immature and queerly embodied masculinity is rendered endearing and even triumphant in a world where being "mature" means living like the passive Rabbit.

In summary, the Soviet Vinni-puch is not a teddy bear or a naturalistic bear, but a raspy-voiced man who remains a boy or failed adult. The stain of failure is instantly conveyed through the broken-down baritone of Leonov, housed in a naively drawn, clumsily rotund body; and it is elaborated through the bear's not-quite parental, self-serving relationship with Pjatachok, as well as his id-driven, unempathic motivation. Chitruk's work suggests that the relationship between Puch and Pjatachok is vaguely familial due to the loyalty and esteem of the soprano-voiced piglet for the much larger bear. Yet, the films make equally explicit that the infantile Puch is completely incapable of parenting anyone and might be less informed about life than Pjatachok.

Puch, we can safely say, is a pre-ethical being. He exists purely at the level of material reality and mostly ignores social norms. He is preoccupied with taking care of his oral drives – eating and drinking – and throughout the course of the series behaves in a decidedly unheroic fashion. In the third episode, *Винни-пух и день забот* (*Vinni-puch and a Busy Day*, 1972), Puch intends to cheer up the sad Donkey Ia on his birthday by giving him a jar of honey, but on his way to the melancholic predictably gets hungry and, without hesitation or remorse, consumes the contents of the jar. Thus, we see, from the first in-

---

25   Rabbit's resemblance to a late-Soviet *intelligent* is also noted by Leving in Ibid., 332.

FIGURE 12.1 *Винни-Пух идёт в гости*, director Fedor Chitruk, Sojuzmul'tfil'm 1971

stallment to the last, that Puch does not learn; he remains resolutely at the level of instinct, desire – the simple gratifications of the mouth. In one possible reading, the bear exemplifies a lower path, an incomplete realization of subjectivity.

Chitruk and Zachoder nevertheless adopt an indulgent attitude toward Puch. In their world, there seems to be a place for those who cannot attain intellectual and moral heights. Puch's good fortune and harmlessness suggests that a life of consumption and hedonism is not to be disdained – not everyone is bound for genital sexuality or scrupulousness. Though Pjatachok also belongs to the pre-ethical realm, his generosity toward Puch from the start shows he has an empathic potential the bear lacks. Hence we are not surprised, in the last episode, by the Pjatachok's sincere attempt to give Donkey his prized green balloon as a birthday present. In fact, it is arguably because Pjatachok is less driven by the demands of the body and responds to more tender urges than Puch that the latter escapes punishment for his stupidity and boorishness. Through Pjatachok's (and to some degree Rabbit's) forgiveness and indulgence, Vinni-puch is redeemed.

We have arrived, then, at what is perhaps the chief source of Vinni-puch's late-Soviet appeal. The post-Stalinist social body, enfeebled by state violence and warfare, welcomed into its heart a voluptuous innocent, unburdened by moral limits and considerations. Audiences that had placed the bloodthirsty *вождь* (leader) in the position of father and Pavlik Morozov in the role of son, now eagerly embraced a hungry, affable bear and his trusting acolyte. If Zachoder and Chitruk's creation was a reparative gesture, spectatorship of their films was an act of disavowal: witnesses and participants of purge campaigns that had turned child against parent became adoring viewers of Vinni-puch – a troublesome yet resilient figure, supported by a junior sidekick with boundless tolerance for casual abuse.

4   Karlson, Anti-oedipal Hero

The preoccupation of Brezhnev-era culture with charitable boyish protagonists and their regressed older companions is also evident in Stepancev's beloved animated films, *Малыш и Карлсон* and *Карлсон вернулся*.[26] Karlson seems to have no significant attachments other than his younger friend and the pair's relationship is built on the kind of exclusivity, passion, and potential for disaster usually attributed to romantic love affairs. We sense this from the moment the propellered Karlson first lands on the Kid's windowsill: with Karlson's prompting, the two flirtatiously exchange information about age and residency with plenty of shoulder shrugs, giggles, and bashful head tilting.[27] The Kid hesitatingly reveals that he is seven years old while Karlson, theatrically stroking his hair and waving his hand, declaims that he is "in the prime of his life!" Before Karlson's arrival, the Kid longs for a puppy, and though he is temporarily distracted by his new playmate's attention and stimulating shenanigans, the desire resurfaces dramatically during his eighth birthday party. As the Kid weeps bitterly after the party, wrongly believing his parents neglected to grant his most ardent wish, Karlson asks, on his knees and in a stunned half-whisper, "A dog? But what about me? Kid, am I not better than a dog?" When moments later the Kid's parents finally surprise him with a puppy, Karlson cannot bear the competition and disappears, leaving the boy utterly bereft. In the episode's final frame, washed in a grayish blue, the Kid stands motionless with the dog under his arm, waiting and hoping for Karlson's return to the strains of a mournful tune.[28]

---

26   Lindgren's Karlsson books were translated into Russian in 1957 by Liliana Lungina and adapted for the screen most famously by Stepancev.
27   Such gesticulations and affectations are not narrated in Lungina's translation. See Astrid Lindgren, *Три повести о малыше и Карлсоне*, trans. Liliana Lungina, Moscow 1974, 8-10.
28   The streets and roofs of the city are drawn in vaguely gothic style and always in gray tones – until Karlson appears. Everything connected to Karlson and the Kid's positive

As literary scholar Marija Majofis points out, Lindgren's Karlsson is more integrated into Lillebror's (the Kid's) family life, traversing comfortably the worlds of adults, children, and domestic animals. For example, in Lindgren's story, Karlsson meets Lillebror's parents at the aforementioned birthday party, whereas in Stepancev's films, he always vanishes just before the parents' arrival and the party occasions yet another missed encounter.[29] Karlson's departures, in fact, lead the parents to believe that he is the Kid's imaginary friend, an invented alter ego on whom their son can blame his own acts of mischief. While viewers know that Karlson exists beyond the Kid's imagination (he appears to the housekeeper Freken Bok in the second episode), Boris Larin's screenplay not only separates children from adults but also produces de-oedipalizing, and even anti-oedipal, effects. The Kid's ardent love of Karlson, in other words, is both external to the family romance and disruptive of it.

A curious omission in Larin's adaptation demonstrates quite well the anti-oedipal stance of the Soviet *Karlson*. In Lindgren's text the following conversation takes place between the Kid and his mother about his older brother:

> – Listen, mama – when Bosse gets old and dies will I have to marry his wife?
> – What makes you say that, darling?
> – Well, I get all his hand-me-downs – I wear his old pajamas, and skates, and ride his old bicycle ...
> – I will save you from his old wife – this I promise, said his mother seriously.
> – Will I be able to marry you?
> – It's impossible, I'm afraid, said his mother – You see, I'm already married to your father. ...
> – What an unfortunate coincidence that papa and I both love you ...[30]

In the Soviet film version all references to mother-son love are dropped and the dialogue breaks off shortly after the Kid is assured that he will not be forced to marry his old sister-in-law. Instead of proposing marriage, the Kid volunteers that he would much rather have a dog than a wife, his mother promptly leaves, and Karlson appears seconds later to the Kid's sheer delight.

---

emotional investment is bathed in primary and secondary colors, usually red, green, orange, or yellow. Jurij Butyrin and Anatolij Savchenko worked on both Karlson films (1968, 1970) as artistic directors and animators.

29 Majofis, "Милый, милый трикстер" in *Веселые человечки*, 249-250.

30 Ibid., 267. Lungina is faithful to Lindgren here, reproducing the entire dialogue between mother and son. See Lindgren, *Три повести о малыше и Карлсоне*, 96.

It is worth pausing to consider the queering effects of Larin's "censorship" of the Kid's oedipal longings.[31] Larin does not simply edit out the allusion to romantic love between mother and son but also, importantly, the maternal enforcement of the incest taboo through the invocation of the father's name. In their place, he inserts a reference to a dog and, finally, a better alternative: Karlson. As a result, the Kid seems troubled by the thought of heterosexual marriage and exchange rather than the prohibition against marrying his mother – a prohibition that, if we follow Freud, eventually leads, with a dissolution of the Oedipus complex, to a desire for more appropriate female love objects. The Soviet cartoon, then, charts a different, anti-oedipal course. The timing and context of the dialogue implies that the Kid's sudden foray into sexual research is motivated by the horror of conjugal duties and the related anxiety of having to give up his new love, Karlson. The family romance collapses into a single, and very queer, emotional dyad.

But who, after all, is Karlson? And what about him communicates advanced age even as his diminutive stature (he is shorter than the Kid), grandiosity, silly antics, and insatiable appetite for sweets signal pre-pubescence? Does he represent what Eve Kosofsky Sedgwick called the "avunculate" – spaces and relations forged with uncles and aunts whose nonconforming sexualities and life trajectories function for the child as alternatives to the law of the biological domestic father, offering pleasures and futures unavailable within the normative family?[32] Is Karlson, in other words, a gay uncle type?

He certainly is queerly embodied: thick in the waist and carrot-topped, with a propellered back and triangular head, he wears pants held up asymmetrically by one suspender. Karlson's entrances initiate flights of imagination – a campy, queer and exaggerated mode of living attested by histrionic movements and retro aesthetics. Toward the end of the second film, Karlson extracts a top hat and long fur-collared coat from deep inside a closet to impress Freken Bok, and a performative outburst ensues. Raucous dancing is accompanied by a cacophony of whistles, bells, and out-of-tune piano thumping. Operatic poses, flamboyant gesticulation, and costumes from the fin de siècle and NEP hint at sexual license and decadence. The housekeeper yields to the fun, swaying her hips and clapping furiously. Karlson's hijinks incite the other characters to display heightened affects and hurl themselves at each other with a surfeit of blushing and libido.

---

31 In her discussion of this scene, Majofis attributes the elimination of the "Freudian problematic" largely to Soviet censorship.
32 See Eve Kosofsky Sedgwick, "Tales of the Avunculate: *The Importance of Being Earnest*," in Michele Aina Barale, Jonathan Goldberg, Michael Moon, and Sedgwick, eds., *Tendencies*, Durham, NC 1993, 63.

Though much of his dressed body is clownish and infantile in appearance, Karlson is readable as an adult principally because of his hoarse baritone, provided by Livanov. Livanov's is a masculine timbre that finds only tenuous corporeal support in his character's dark, bushy eyebrows and broad-palmed bravado. Moreover, it is precisely such vocal incongruence that seems partly responsible for the Brezhnev-era Karlson's continued popularity. As Majofis discusses at some length, the 2002 Russian release of a dubbed version of the Swedish animated film *Karlsson on the Roof* elicited a flood of very critical reviews and, perhaps inevitably, many invidious comparisons between the familiar Soviet interpretation, deemed definitive, and the latest "foreign" iteration. Critics expressed dismay over most of the performances and yearned for the warm and loving Karlson of Livanov. Nonetheless, they were mildly impressed by the efforts of the well-known actor Sergej Bezrukov, who attempted to imitate Livanov's timbre and intonation.[33]

The attachment of Soviet audiences to the 1968-70 Karlson thus seems to be rooted at least in part in a certain sonority as well as a particular form of vocal drag: by locating Livanov's deep and weatherworn voice in a destructive but ultimately benevolent trickster, the animators at Sojuzmul'tfil'm performed and rejoiced in a failure – a certain excess or heterogeneity – and showed that the vocal object can never reliably be traced to a given body. They also attenuated and domesticated the sound of a much less sympathetic adult Russian masculinity, associated after many years of war and Stalinist policies with arbitrary violence.

Karlson's immaturity is everywhere in evidence. He is an egotistical manchild with no ties to the social world, no family, and no friends his own age. When he is not blithely flying around, having adventures with little boys, or impersonating ghosts and scaring burglars, he lives a drab bachelor existence in a cramped and modestly appointed rooftop house. It is quite fitting that he competes with the dog for the Kid's affections: the puppy and Karlson exist on the same plane or occupy the same position in the boy's imaginary – that of an enlarging and transformative alter ego. The alliance of Karlson and the Kid resembles the many animal-child alliances found in children's literature and culture.[34] Depictions of "animal/child affectionate bondings," are common, per-

---

33 Majofis, "Милый, милый трикстер," 241-244. Börje Ahlstedt's voice in *Karlsson på taket* (*Vibeke Idsøe*, 2002) is decidedly more mellifluous and lighter in timbre than Livanov's.

34 I briefly discuss two iconic representations of child-animal bonds from Soviet animation (*Трое из Простоквашино* and *Бременские музыканты*) below. The best-known examples from Hollywood and American television are probably the Lassie films (1943-2005), the plots of which center on a heroic female collie and her young male master.

FIGURE 12.2 *Малыш и Карлсон*, director Boris Stepancev, Sojuzmul'tfil'm 1968

haps, because, as theorist Kathryn Stockton suggests, they "offer opportunities [...] for children's motions inside their delay" – their pause on the threshold of adulthood – "making delay a sideways growth the child in part controls for herself, in ways confounding her parents and her future."[35] Children, Stockton tells us, sometimes grow sideways rather than up and forge horizontal alliances that eschew parental, domestic, or future-oriented temporality. The family dog, for example, can operate as more than simply a sentimental domestic relation, serving "rather as a loving, growing metaphor for the child itself [...] and for the child's own propensities to stray." The anti-oedipal, non-filial dog, in Stockton's view, "is a vehicle for the child's strangeness [... and] her companion in queerness. As a recipient of the child's attentions [...] and a living screen for the child's self-projections, the dog is a figure for the child beside itself."[36]

In Soviet cartoons animal-child alliances tend to be formed against the backdrop and in contrast to a dull family scenario with an emasculated or

---

35   Kathryn Bond Stockton, *The Queer Child: Growing Sideways in the Twentieth Century*, Durham, NC 2009, 90.
36   Ibid.

ineffectual father.[37] In *Трое из Простоквашино* (1978), for example, an overly serious six-year-old nicknamed Uncle Fedor runs away from the urban home of his narcissistic mother and submissive intelligentsia dad to set up house in the country with the worldly cat Matroskin and the earnest mutt Sharik. Matroskin and Sharik create for Uncle Fedor a temporary detour away from oedipal resolution, expanding the boy's personality through lateral rather than vertical child-parent bonds.

The Kid uses Karlson in a similar way and to a similar end, also in defiance of his working mother and bespectacled, newspaper toting intelligentsia father (who, like the milder and more involved dad of the *Простоквашино* films, sports a chin curtain beard). Karlson, reminiscent of Vinni-puch, is a perfect antidote to colorless and sanctimonious parental maturity.[38] He is analogous to the puppy but more ample and complex, haughty yet pragmatic; his coarseness is touched by lyricism.[39] Most relevant, Karlson knows how to enjoy. Like Puch, he is a great partisan of oral pleasure, pursuing cakes, pastries, and jam with infectious abandon. It is precisely Karlson's queer failures – his failure to grow up, to control his impulses, to marry and reproduce – that make him such an attractive and alive companion for the Kid and, arguably, for a post-Thaw audience increasingly exposed to images of sensual consumption and saccharine masculinity.[40] Dwelling in the in-between space of not-yet and not-quite,

---

37 In *Бременские музыканты*, one of the most popular products of Sojuzmul'tfil'm, a bored Princess runs away from the home of a dotty Baroque King with a hippie Troubadour and his band of animals. The itinerant collective thus takes her away from parental authority to a different temporal order and the open road.

38 Early in the first episode, the Kid is beaten by an older and bigger boy for trying to protect the bully's abused dog. Later at dinner the Kid's parents casually lecture him on non-violent alternatives to conflict resolution. Karlson, by contrast, brings much violence and destruction in his wake, though it is a violence directed toward inanimate objects, more contained and largely symbolic. Karlson also prevents the Kid's internalization of the father's law (weak in any case) and provides an alternative to the mother's tempting and potentially mortifying embrace.

39 Karlson appears to lack control over his own commotion-causing activities and yet always knows to disappear when the Kid's parents return home to discover his mess. We witness Karlson's crude machinations (feigning illness to obtain sympathy and jam, distracting Freken Bok in order to snatch her pastries) and also his expressions of love for the Kid.

40 Oksana Bulgakowa claims that the popular acceptance and critical acclaim of breathy and muffled male voices in Soviet films of the 1950s indexed new postwar images of masculinity – more ambivalent, sensual, gentle, and open to intimacy. Bulgakowa, "Vocal Changes: Marlon Brando, Innokenty Smoktunovsky, and the Sound of the 1950s," in Lilya Kaganovsky and Masha Salazkina, eds., *Sound, Speech, Music in Soviet and Post-Soviet Cinema*, Bloomington, IN 2014, 145-161.

Karlson has access to a *jouissance*, or enjoyment, unknown to the realm of ordinary adults.[41]

5   Gena and the "Avunculate"

The *Чебурашка* four-part series, probably the most widely recognized cartoon produced in the Soviet period, is principally about the relationship between Gena, a lonely crocodile bachelor who seeks friends, and Cheburashka, an animal (or is he a toy?) of ambiguous species, age, and gender affiliation.[42] We know from the start that Cheburashka is queer. He embodies, effects, and performs a radical unknowability. In the first installment, he arrives at a produce store in a crate of oranges with no name, clothes or other identity markers, and promptly is taken to the zoo.[43] After some fuss and inquiry, the zookeeper explains to the store clerk that Cheburashka cannot be accepted because "he is unknown to science" and nobody can figure out "where to place him." Part monkey, part bear, possibly neither, Cheburashka defies categorization – he simply does not fit. Gena's search for "чебурашка" in an encyclopedia yields only a dumb blankness somewhere between "Чебоксары" and "чемодан" ("suitcase"). Cheburashka, too, fails to solve the riddle of his own identity. Characters ask repeatedly about his species in the initial episode, and each "who are you?" elicits from him an unperturbed "I don't know." One might expect that such unintelligibility and ignorance would disable Cheburashka, make him the object of ridicule, social exclusion, judicial action, perhaps even medical scrutiny and scientific experimentation. But nothing of the kind happens. Cheburashka is quite subjectified and self-possessed, unfazed by his biological indeterminacy: he gains the respect and love of Gena and everyone else

---

41   For an examination of the creative, anti-capitalist, and nonconformist applications of failures often attributed to queer people (for example: passivity, unproductivity, and childishness), see Halberstam, *The Queer Art of Failure*.

42   The animated tetralogy produced by Roman Kachanov and designed by Leonid Shvarcman consist of: *Крокодил Гена* (*Crocodile Gena*, 1969), *Чебурашка* (*Cheburashka*, 1971), *Шапокляк* (*Shapokljak*, 1974), and *Чебурашка идет в школу* (*Cheburashaka Goes to School*, 1983). For good plot summaries of the episodes, see Birgit Beumers, "Comforting Creatures in Children's Cartoons," in Marina Balina and Larissa Rudova, eds., *Russian Children's Literature and Culture*, New York and London 2008, 166-167.

43   "Cheburashka" denotes "topple" and is the nickname given to the character by the store clerk when the former falls off a table, dazed and numb after a long stint in the cramped crate. Uspenskij coined the character's name but not the colloquialism "чебурахнуться," meaning "to tumble" or "topple over."

he meets, helps build the House of Friendship and, in general, seems comfortable in his own skin. In fact, Cheburashka's unknowing enables him to evade regimes of truth and injurious ideological interpellation.[44] In a totalitarian society, Cheburashka is free.

What, then, do we make of Gena and his connection to the appealing misfit? Livanov's dark timbre and pipe smoking code the crocodile as an older male, as does the sonic distance between him and the reedy-voiced Cheburashka of Klara Rumjanova.[45] We meet Gena at the zoo, where he works as a Crocodile, and soon observe him beset by loneliness in a cluttered and untidy house, playing chess with an imaginary partner and composing a flyer seeking friendship. Gena's fatherly attitude can be detected in his concern for the welfare of the local children (who inspire him to build a playground) in the second episode (1971) and in his decision to send Cheburashka to school in the last installment of the series (1983).[46] The relationship between Gena and Cheburashka seems, at least at some points, to carry the sort of emotional overinvestment we attribute to parent-child bonds. When Cheburashka accidentally latches onto a launched toy helicopter and perilously flies through the air before landing safely, Gena is beside himself with worry, racing after his buddy and breathlessly inquiring about his physical wellbeing. But at many other moments, the generational difference between Gena and Cheburashka breaks down, along with their filial relationship. For example, in the second episode, it is Cheburashka who shyly gives Gena the toy helicopter for his birthday, and, later in the film, the two aspire to gain entry into a Young Pioneers team as if they were coevals. Gena describes himself as a "young crocodile" in tentative, childlike scrawl at the beginning of the series, but since youth is a relative concept and Gena is an animal, the matter of his age remains unresolved: is he adolescent, unintelligent (and therefore "young") in some specifi-

---

44 My thoughts on Cheburashka's "unknowing" are inspired by Eve Kosofsky Sedgwick's essay, "Privilege of Unknowing: Diderot's *The Nun*," in Michele Aina Barale et al, eds., *Tendencies*, 23-51.

45 Rumjanova voiced several other popular young characters of various genders in animated films and sound recordings of the Brezhnev era: the Kid from both Karlson films, Alisa from Vladimir Vysockij's *Алиса в Стране чудес* (*Alice in Wonderland*, 1977), and the Rabbit from *Ну, погоди!* All her characters speak in the same high soprano and with very similar intonations. By contrast, Livanov's characterizations are distinctive. His Karlson has a mild speech impediment and employs more vocal modulation than Gena.

46 Gena wants to send Cheburashka to school so that he can learn how to read in *Чебурашка идет в школу*, though in the first two films of the series he is portrayed as literate. In the third episode (1974), Gena selflessly carries Cheburashka a long distance after Shapokljak spoils their vacation plans by purloining their train tickets and forcing them to walk home.

cally reptilian way, or, on the contrary, coy, urbane, and self-promoting like the ever-youthful Karlson?

With these multiple readings and tensions in mind, I suggest that Gena's childlike manner, like Karlson's, signals and rejoices in the stereotype of stunted queerness, tacitly referencing the Freudian association of homosexuality with regression. Many aspects of Gena's character support such a view. On the one hand, he has no interest in female companionship or conjugal life, preferring to spend eternity with a toylike orphan. While Shapokljak's pranks might be viewed as disguised or disavowed declarations of love for Gena, the crocodile returns her modest overtures with a formal gentlemanly posture and an absolute indifference to heterosexual romance.[47] On the other hand, as is plain from the two instantly classic songs from *Чебурашка* and *Шапокляк*, respectively, "Пусть бегут неуклюже" ("Gena's Birthday Song") and "Голубой вагон" ("The Blue Traincar"), Gena is not altogether innocent of pain and loss. In the first song, he laments in doleful minor key that no one understands him ("Passersby just don't get why/on this rainy day/I am so happy") and "birthdays come only once a year." The second number, "Голубой вагон" is sung by Gena as he sits, accordion in tow, on top of a caboose with Cheburashka and the anti-heroine Shapokljak:

> Slowly the minutes flow past
> Don't expect to see them again.
> And even though we mourn the past a little bit
> the best, of course, is still ahead.
>
> Smoothly, effortlessly the long path spreads beneath
> and runs straight into the horizon.

---

[47] Old Shapokljak is a woman without family and in gender trouble. She is ancient, wiry, and screechy. Indeed, in the first and fourth episodes she is voiced by a male actor. Her stance toward the world and her place in the narrative evoke a nonconformist politics, external to time and sexuality. Shapokljak is a hopelessly old-fashioned yet meticulously attired androgyne, clad in a turn-of-the-twentieth-century black dress with a white ruffle lace collar and a 1940s half-top hat. She also sports a sizable purse containing her pet rat, Lariska, who is long, thin, sharp-nosed, and phallic, like her owner. Shapokljak seems fonder of rodents than people (or anthropomorphic animals). The old lady's opening ditty bluntly conveys her enthusiasm for misanthropy and delinquency: "Those who help others are wasting their time./You can't get famous by doing good deeds, ha-ha-ha." She spends much of the series devoted to vandalism, petty theft, and verbal abuse. But by the third episode Shapokljak tries to gain social acceptance and promises to reform, flirtatiously returning the train tickets she had stolen from Gena and Cheburashka and helping them rid the countryside of polluters and hooligans.

> Everyone, everyone hopes for the best
> and our blue traincar rolls forward.
> Perhaps we hurt someone gratuitously ...
> the calendar will turn that page for us.
> Toward new adventures let's run my friends.
> Hey, driver, speed it up!
>
> [refrain]
>
> The blue car races and shakes,
> the express train's picking up speed
> But why does this day have to come to an end
> I wish it would last the whole year.
>
> [refrain]

"Голубой вагон" is both overtly about time and against it, situated outside the time and space of the film's narrative and functioning vertically, as a reflective postscript and halt in the action. The lyrics of the song present us with an apparent contradiction as well. The emotionally weighted message at the start seems to be: turn the page. Despite possible loss and difficulty, we must let go of past grievances, direct our attention toward the future, and seek new adventures. Do it now, accelerate, move along; the best is ahead. But almost instantly the impatient, forward-looking optimism is subverted. As the train chugs to a nostalgic minor tonality, Gena and the others sit at the rear of the caboose, looking not to their future, but backward, as it were. The unnecessary "of course" in "the best, of course, is still ahead" raises the sort of skepticism commonly elicited by over-insistence: is it sarcasm or a defensive posture concealing contrary feelings? And in a final, dramatic reversal of sentiment, the lines after "the express train picks up speed" suggest time is passing too quickly: "Why does this day have to come to an end / I wish it would last the whole year." Even more blatantly than in Gena's Birthday Song we encounter here a desire for the postponement of the future, if not a foreclosure of futurity. It is a longing for an eternal moment of reparation and wholeness, a dilated present lived to the fullest.

Gena is a psychological being because he longs, that is, he is gripped by a desire for the impossible or obscure: "Perhaps we hurt someone gratuitously / The calendar will turn that page for us." Longing can be distinguished from wanting by the fact that the one who longs does not have a clear notion of his object. He yearns for a lost object that cannot be recaptured even in the imagination. Longing is thus likely to show itself as a nebulous dissatisfaction

THE QUEER LEGACIES OF LATE SOCIALISM 463

FIGURE 12.3 *Чебурашка*, director Roman Kachanov, Sojuzmul'tfil'm 1971

with one's predicament, an unspecified foreboding. It supplies the catalyst for action, but with an ill-defined intent that lends uncertainty to one's endeavors. Figures burdened by longing are disposed to melancholia and minor tonalities. Gena sings with the longing melancholic's typical ambiguity of purpose: he expresses a wish to move but toward no particular aim. We know that the train is *en route* to Moscow and that Gena's goal is friendship but in this moment Gena himself does not experience his needs in such specific terms. He does not want, as children do, he yearns in the shadow of the disappointment born of lived experience.

The view of Gena as a childlike adult and non-oedipal ally of Cheburashka is supported, finally, by the crocodile's tendency to succeed by failing, or succeed accidentally, through good fortune rather than skill. Gena's grandiose plans, unlike those of Vinni-puch, do not collapse under the strain of reality. His projects are driven by simple and authentic altruism rather than naïve narcissism, gaining social support and recognition that ultimately aid in their realization. While the rigid Pioneers engage in modest and humdrum activities such as marching, scrap metal collecting, and birdhouse fixing, Gena enlists Cheburashka and others in more creative pursuits: building a House of Friendship, constructing a playground, and foiling polluters. And despite falling short along the way – the House of Friendship needs to be repurposed, a compressor is sacrificed to build the playground, and the anti-pollution measure is provisional at best – Gena's efforts forge communities and inspire ingenuity. His achievements are not seamlessly attained, or even successes proper. Perhaps more aptly, they are productive and happy failures that ultimately redefine or lead to success on a plane previously unconsidered. Hence, avuncular Gena, as well as Karlson and Vinni-puch, like Sedgwick's "'artistic' Uncle Harvey, 'not the marrying kind' Cousin David [...] and Aunt Estelle and Aunt Frances, sisters who slept in the same room for most of their eight decades,"[48] carve out in the sterile zone of intelligentsia family hygiene and the rule-bound ethos of the Young Pioneers camp, a queer, non-reproductive space and time, elongated and twisted to accommodate imaginative detours and utopian moments that only desire can enable.[49]

Examining the queer duos of Stagnation-era Sojuzmul'tfil'm is not especially difficult, but specifying the cultural logics and fantasies produced by and reflected in such figures will take us on a more speculative path – one with implications for understanding the Soviet Union's strategies of veiling its traumatic past after the Thaw. It is telling, perhaps, that while Vinni-puch constantly craves honey and Karlson hungers for jam, Gena is ruled by less concrete hankerings. Chitruk and Stepancev's characters, Soviet adaptations of Western types, are governed by drives, while Gena and his open-ended desire are products of Uspenskij's purely domestic Stagnation-era script. Gena's ambivalent longing is tied to the cartoon's meditation on time and expresses an impasse – at once temporal and rhetorical – continually manifested in late-socialist official ideology and artistic forms. The secular eschatology that initially underpinned Soviet life had broken down by the Brezhnev period: the Stalinist past was again relegated to silence, and communism, the once guaranteed happy tomorrow, was deferred indefinitely with the declaration of "developed socialism" by the Constitution of 1977. As Gena informs us in "Голубой вагон," traces of the incompletely mourned past and an abandoned future haunted the joys of the luxurious present.[50]

---

48 Sedgwick, "Tales of the Avunculate," 63.
49 In the second episode of the *Чебурашка* series, Gena and Cheburashka attempt to gain acceptance into the Pioneers and succeed only after displays of extraordinary ingenuity. The Pioneers team, here depicted rather unsympathetically, initially refuses the pair entry due to their ostensible lack of skills (they cannot march, stoke a fire, or build a nesting box, for example), and instead offers Cheburashka a place in their petting zoo ("живой уголок"). Of course, these renderings can be read as unvarnished social satire by screenwriter Uspenskij.
50 As I already touched on briefly, Stagnation-era animated films also staged such queer, nonlinear temporality in exuberant ways through "temporal drag" – sartorial and bodily references to bygone eras and older personages that disrupt straight, continuous maturation and its reproductive rationale, inciting anticipation and surprise. Gena's bowler

I suggest that tropes of gentle, failed masculinity simultaneously masked and alerted audiences to intergenerationally transmitted traumas of male violence: mass murder, rape, and carceral life under Stalin and during World War II. The vastness of these traumatic experiences – their mute and under-memorialized extension into a stagnant present – is what made them especially burdensome and anxiety provoking.[51] In Gary Shteyngart's diasporic memoir, the re-appearance of the childish adult figure and his little sidekick illuminates the continued difficulty of bringing to speech and metabolizing these traumas in the wake of immigration and the Soviet Union's disappearance.

6 Little Failures

Shteyngart's *Little Failure* is framed by the mystery of a panic attack; or, more precisely, a recollection of and working through recurring panic and asthma attacks, with many hints but no definitive conclusions about their psychological causes. Indeed, anxiety and its psychic underpinnings provide the motive force for both the memoir and its author. In the opening chapter, Shteyngart suffers a particularly significant panic attack at the now-defunct Strand Book Annex while thumbing through the coffee table volume, *St. Petersburg: Architecture of the Tsars*. At the sight of the salmon-pink Chesme Church in the Moskovskij District, the neighborhood Shteyngart spent his first six years, he trembles and sweats, gasping for air, for his very life. Why did the candied

---

hat, stiff white collar, and 1920s coat, like Shapokljak's attire, evoke the distant past. The untimeliness of Gena and Shapokljak marks them as allies of the equally infertile and atemporal Karlson and Freken Bok. Faina Ranevskaja's Freken Bok is vain, demonstrative, and dwells in the lower vocal range. Her magisterial contralto is larded with hyperbole and her pantomime is suffused with decadent fin-de-siècle emotionalism. The pastiche aesthetics of these characters add to the works' musical treatment of time as halted, unanchored, or alternately stretched and squeezed in accordionlike fashion. For more on the concept "temporal drag," see Elizabeth Freeman, *Time Binds: Queer Temporalities, Queer Histories*, Durham, NC 2010, 59-65.

51 On the dearth of monuments dedicated to Stalin's victims and the consequent unfinished mourning in post-war Soviet Union and even today, see Alexander Etkind, *Warped Mourning: Stories of the Undead in the Land of the Unburied*, Stanford, CA 2013. There is a large body of literature on intergenerational transmission of trauma, much of it related to the Holocaust. For example, see Vamik D. Volkan, Gabriele Ast, and William Greer Jr., *The Third Reich in the Unconscious: Transgenerational Transmission and Its Consequences*, New York 2002, and Gabriele Schwab, *Haunting Legacies: Violent Histories and Transgenerational Trauma*, New York 2010.

innocence of the church incite a panic attack? Shteyngart intimates that the answer – a childhood memory – holds the key to his entire life story. What happened that day at the Chesme Church? Readers would have to wait until the end of the book to find out.

Early in the memoir Shteyngart only recalls an idyllic scene of closeness between father and son. Papa and five-year-old Igor' are flying a toy helicopter on a string one afternoon and it gets caught between the church spires. But no matter, because they are "better than this, better than the country around [them]. This must be the happiest day of [his] life."[52] Readers are invited to feel the romance of this brief anamnesis, its excruciating tenderness. And yet almost immediately we understand not only that something went terribly wrong (why else the panic?) but that the idyll was always already tainted. Shteyngart notes the "stretch of potholed asphalt in front of the [church's] diminutive entrance. It looked vaguely like a child overdressed for a ceremony. Like a little red-faced, tiny bellied failure. It looked like I felt."[53]

To quell the panic, Gary attempts to remember his father in this scene, twenty-two years younger, bathed in "untrammeled love" for his son. The elder Shteyngart, who "writes in the [infantile] clumsy script of a typical male-Soviet engineer [... is] an awkward man, childish and bright, happy to have a little sidekick named Igor' [...] palling around with this Igoryochik who is not judgmental or anti-Semitic – a fellow warrior, first against the indignities of the Soviet Union and then against those moving to America, the great uprooting of language and familiarity."[54] Shteyngart's recollection extends over a great distance, twenty-two years and beyond, threading together multiple identities and generations. And then the "nesting doll of memory collapses into its component parts leading to someplace smaller and smaller, even as [the author gets] bigger and bigger."[55] The distance between Gary and the scene narrows, and there is no room left for him.

At the conclusion of the memoir, Shteyngart reveals what happened near the Chesme Church. At the moment he was happiest, after the helicopter got caught between the spires, and because it was getting late and home beckoned, or seemingly for no reason at all, his father struck him in the face, making his nose bleed. Why was it *this* memory of paternal cruelty that caused Shteyngart's panic attack? It was not the first or last time the father hit his son. Was it the arbitrariness and unexpected nature of the violence that impressed

---

52 Gary Shteyngart, *Little Failure: A Memoir*, New York 2014, 17.
53 Ibid.
54 Ibid., 12, 9.
55 Ibid., 17.

Gary, making this particular eruption into an *event* – the moment that structured his subjectivity? Or, if this is a dislocated "screen memory" or phantasm that both veiled and partially expressed even more troubling recollections, why was it assembled and cast in the way that it was and for what end?

Before proceeding, it seems to me useful to place Shteyngart's asthmatic panic not only in the context of the family romance but also something loosely called "modernity," for anxiety is the affect of the twentieth century par excellence. Modernity, writes theorist Joan Copjec,

> [I]s often conceived as a definitive break with previous generations, which were no longer recognized as the founders of present-day actions or beliefs. And yet this effective undermining of ancestral authority, though in certain respects freeing, confronted moderns with another difficulty: by rendering their ancestors fallible, they had transformed the past from the container of already accomplished deeds and discovered truths into a kind of repository of all that was unactualized and unthought. The desire of past generations and thus the virtual past, the past that had never come to pass – was not yet finished – weighed disturbingly on twentieth-century thinkers, pressing itself on their attention.[56]

A discussion of psychoanalytic theories of anxiety and its link to this historically new relation to the past is especially pertinent here since Shteyngart searches for meaning and rootedness in a never-completed former Soviet Union. The search, conducted with the help of a psychoanalyst, leads him through his own and then his parents' pasts and, in turn, the traumatic pasts of his parents' forebears.

While some thinkers understood anxiety as the affective response to loss or abandonment, Freud claimed that the proper response to loss would be mourning, not anxiety. In *Beyond the Pleasure Principle* he distinguished anxiety from fear, explaining that the former seized one only in flashes of uncertainty while the latter arose at moments of foreseen and recognized danger. Freud, therefore, conceived anxiety as dependent not "on an actual condition but rather on a *condition that is not*. Anxiety is the experience of awaiting some event," something that may or may not happen.[57]

---

56 Joan Copjec, "The Object-Gaze: Shame, *Hejab*, Cinema," in *Философский вестник* 27/2 (2006), 17.
57 Ibid., 18.

In Seminar X, Lacan also insists that anxiety arises not from the loss of an object but precisely from its overbearing presence – not from lack but the *lack of a lack* that puts distance between the subject and the Other; and between the subject and that which is Other within himself.[58] Anxiety paralyzes and chokes when the subject's constitutive alienation in language and separation from the maternal body and parental desire (castration, in psychoanalytic parlance) is undone. As the symbolic dimension – the "nesting doll of memory" – collapses, and with it the fantasy of our independence from the Other's will, "we are gripped by jouissance, the object-cause of our own actions that we nonetheless experience [...] as an alien object so suffocatingly close that we cannot discern what it is. [...] Anxiety can [thus] be understood as the affect that registers our encounter with the death drive" – the absolute dimension, or our own potentiality as such. This potentiality is not "at the behest of an autonomous will but attaches us, rather, to the ontologically incomplete past into which we are born," all that could have been done by us and those who lived before us. Jouissance, which gives panic attacks their orgasmic appearance, "is the affective result of our relation to ancestral desire."[59]

Gary's panic attack therefore can be understood as an attempt at liberation from the suffocation induced by the memory of an unanticipated encounter with his father's rage and enigmatic desire – the wish for something beyond an asthmatic son, mechanical engineering, and immigration; a desire that bore the weight of transgenerational trauma, impending losses, and a wild yearning for freedom. One hypothesis Freud advances after discussing the repeated nightmares of shell-shocked soldiers in *Beyond the Pleasure Principle* is that the psyche revives a trauma in order to experience it differently. Through the repetition of a traumatic scene we try to insert anxiety into a situation – anxiety as a form of preparedness or readiness where there was none at the outset. That is, we retroactively try to change the way we lived through an event by signaling and anticipating danger. Following Freud's thread, Lacan elaborated that anxiety paradoxically can bring the subject into existence – placing a gap or a pause, and ultimately enabling reflective capacity where there was previously a tidal wave of affect and being (but no thinking).[60] Where the five-year old Igor' was caught unaware, the middle-aged Gary could step in and get ahead

---

58 See Jacques Lacan, *Anxiety: The Seminar of Jacques Lacan, Book X*, ed. Jacques Alain-Miller, trans. A. R. Price, Cambridge, UK 2014.
59 Copjec, "The Object-Gaze," 19-20.
60 Bruce Fink, *A Clinical Introduction to Lacanian Psychoanalysis: Theory and Technique*, Cambridge, MA 1997, 64-65. See Sigmund Freud, *Beyond the Pleasure Principle*, Standard Edition, Volume 18 (1920), 11-13 and Lacan, *Anxiety*, 157-169.

of the event, mitigating its impact and giving it import. By reactualizing his encounter with his father's (or, the Other's) desire that left a fixation in its wake, the panic and asthma attacks also introduce a certain distance retroactively.

We might speculate, too, that the elder Shteyngart hit Igor' precisely because of the unendurable closeness of the outing near the Chesme Church and other such moments – the sensuality of the father-son bond, the voluptuousness of an afternoon spent playing and in love. For the father, the desperate need for and deep fear of both oedipal intimacy and oedipal conflict required discharge. Gary had a somewhat different relationship to this scene of love and violence. For him, the punch in the face ruptured a moment of pure joy. The bloody nose was experienced not as the punishment of a patriarch laying down the law, but as a confrontation with the primal father – the father of obscene enjoyment, hitting against all reason, out of control and without limit. The blow undid the Oedipus complex and loosened an established order. Shteyngart-the-father instantly transformed from an ego ideal into a rival or semblable who is quantitatively different ("I am bigger," the elder Shteyngart liked to say) rather than qualitatively different. The recollection of this rapacious, sadistically competitive father triggered the invasion of an unbridled jouissance. Shteyngart would likely endorse such an interpretation, for he himself acknowledged, that "the family romance ended" when the hitting stopped.[61]

And, yet, this purely intersubjective psychoanalytic reading would be insufficient if it underemphasized the transcendental, multigenerational dimension to which the panic also bears witness. Shteyngart unconsciously seeks escape in anxiety and asthma attacks because he cannot endure being fettered to the overwhelming, opaque desire of his familial and political progenitors, the unfulfilled Soviet promise. When Shteyngart's father strikes him in a moment later perceived as the very definition of love and happiness, he brings Gary into close proximity, without warning, with pain not only his own. The panic attack is thus a retroactive attempt to transcend not just the actual putdowns and constraints imposed by immigrant parents, but also the confining space in which Gary finds himself attached to their inscrutable injunctions and weighty inheritance – the intergenerationally transmitted trauma that produced his parents: the world war that killed his grandfather, the legacy of genocide and the gulag, anti-semitism, the forced choice of mechanical engineering.

How does Gary retreat from panic attacks, bringing himself back from the brink of death? By imagining his father as childlike and cute, a little failure telling stories, writing him funny letters about "a submarine named Arzum

---

61   Shteyngart, *Little Failure*, 202.

that sailed in from Turkey."[62] The invocation of failed masculinity works both to name and limit the oceanic present of trauma spanning several generations. "My life begins" with the death of my paternal grandfather, declares Shteyngart, "later, Grandmother Polya [marries] a man who will all but destroy my father's life and make me into whatever it is I am today."[63]

To return to our initial cartoon heroes, we might venture that they were implicated in a fetishistic disavowal of the pathology of late-Soviet everyday life, a quotidian haunted by the specter of Stalin-era crimes.[64] Vinni-puch, Karlson, and Gena are overgrown children, or male adults made safe. They are quasi-fatherly, avuncular older siblings who both set rules and break them, all the while retaining benevolence. Puch and Karlson spread excitement and mirth as they perversely instrumentalize others for their own pleasure. Gena attempts singlehandedly to build a playground and explodes a compressor, endangering the very neighborhood urchins he is trying to rescue. In Stagnation-era animated films, the failure of paternal law and arbitrary violence were refigured as pre-oedipal inelegance or the death drive broken down into its component parts – oral fixations, seductive banter, and compulsive scheming. Through images of immature and hysterical masculinity, shorn of adult-sized threat, animators and spectators converted fathers into brothers and uncles, too, allowing benign Karlsons, Genas, and Puchs to screen out and block the threat of trauma, loss, and devouring anxiety.

Works Cited

Barthes, Roland. "The Grain of the Voice," in *The Sound Studies Reader*, ed. Jonathan Sterne. New York 2012, 504-510.

Beumers, Birgit. "Comforting Creatures in Children's Cartoons," in Marina Balina and Larissa Rudova, eds., *Russian Children's Literature and Culture*. New York and London 2008, 153-171.

Bulgakowa, Oksana. "Vocal Changes: Marlon Brando, Innokenty Smoktunovsky, and the Sound of the 1950s," in Lilya Kaganovsky and Masha Salazkina, eds., *Sound, Speech, Music in Soviet and Post-Soviet Cinema*. Bloomington, IN 2014, 145-161.

Chitruk, Fedor, dir. *Винни-пух*. Moscow, Sojuzmul'tfil'm 1969.

Chitruk, Fedor, dir. *Винни-пух идет в гости*. Moscow, Sojuzmul'tfil'm 1971.

---

62 Ibid., 13, 345.
63 Ibid., 39.
64 Etkind has shown convincingly how the "warped" mourning of 1930s terror victims, resulting in compulsive repetitions enacted in Russian literature, film, and visual art, has "shap[ed] a temporal zone of indistinction [that] combines the past and the future in a joint effort to obscure the present." Etkind, *Warped Mourning*, 43.

Chitruk, Fedor, dir. *Винни-пух и день забот*. Moscow, Sojuzmul'tfil'm 1972.
Copjec, Joan. "The Object-Gaze: Shame, *Hejab*, Cinema," in *Философский вестник* 27:2 (2006), 11-29.
Danelija, Georgij, dir. *Осенний марафон*. Moscow, Mosfil'm 1979.
Dolar, Mladen. *A Voice and Nothing More*. Cambridge, MA 2006.
Etkind, Alexander. *Warped Mourning: Stories of the Undead in the Land of the Unburied*. Stanford, CA 2013.
Fink, Bruce. *A Clinical Introduction to Lacanian Psychoanalysis: Theory and Technique*. Cambridge, MA 1997.
Fishzon, Anna. "The Fog of Stagnation: Explorations of Time and Affect in Late-Soviet Animation," in Larissa Zakharova and Kristin Roth-Ey, eds., *Communications and Media in the USSR and Eastern Europe: Technologies, Politics, Cultures, Social Practices*. *Cahiers du Monde Russe* 56:2-3 (2015), 571-598.
Freeman, Elizabeth, *Time Binds: Queer Temporalities, Queer Histories*. Durham, NC 2010.
Freud, Sigmund. *Beyond the Pleasure Principle* [Standard Edition], trans. James Strachey, Vol. 18 (1920).
Goscilo, Helena and Yana Hashamova, eds. *Cinepaternity: Fathers and Sons in Soviet and Post-Soviet Film*. Bloomington, IN 2010.
Halberstam, Judith. *The Queer Art of Failure*. Durham, NC 2011.
Halberstam, Judith. *In a Queer Time and Place: Transgender Bodies, Subcultural Lives*. New York 2005.
Idsøe, Vibeke, dir. *Karlsson på taket*. Stockholm, AB Svensk filmindustrie 2002.
Jones, Polly. *Myth, Memory, Trauma: Rethinking the Stalinist Past in the Soviet Union, 1953-1970*. New Haven, CT 2013.
Kachanov, Roman, dir. *Крокодил Гена*. Moscow, Sojuzmul'tfil'm 1969.
Kachanov, Roman, dir. *Чебурашка*. Moscow, Sojuzmul'tfil'm 1971.
Kachanov, Roman, dir. *Шапокляк*. Moscow, Sojuzmul'tfil'm 1974.
Kachanov, Roman, dir. *Чебурашка идет в школу*. Moscow, Sojuzmul'tfil'm 1983.
Kaganovsky, Lilya. *How the Soviet Man was Unmade: Cultural Fantasy and Male Subjectivity under Stalin*. Pittsburgh, PA 2008.
Kaganovsky, Lilya. "Гонка вооружений, трансгендер и застой: Волк и Заяц в кон/подтексте 'холодной войны'," in Ilja Kukulin, Mark Lipoveckij, and Marija Majofis, eds., *Веселые человечки: культурные герои советского детства*. Moscow 2008, 378-392.
Kidd, Kenneth B. *Freud in Oz: At the Intersections of Psychoanalysis and Children's Literature*. Minneapolis 2011.
Kljuchkin, Konstantin. "Заветный мультфильм: причины популярности 'Чебурашки'," in Ilja Kukulin, Mark Lipoveckij, and Marija Majofis, eds., *Веселые человечки: культурные герои советского детства*. Moscow 2008, 360-377.
Kovalevskaja, Inessa, dir. *Бременские музыканты*. Moscow, Sojuzmul'tfil'm 1969.

Kovalevskaja, Inessa, dir. *По следам бременских музыкантов*. Moscow, Sojuzmul'tfil'm 1973.

Kozlov, Denis and Eleonory Gilburd, eds. *The Thaw: Soviet Society and Culture During the 1950s and 1960s*. Toronto 2013.

Lacan, Jacques. *Anxiety: The Seminar of Jacques Lacan, Book X*, ed. Jacques Alain-Miller, trans. A. R. Price. Cambridge, UK 2014.

Leving, Yuri. "'Кто-то там все-таки есть…': Винни-пух и новая анимационная эстетика," in Ilja Kukulin, Mark Lipoveckij, and Marija Majofis, eds., *Веселые человечки: культурные герои советского детства*. Moscow 2008, 315-353.

Lindgren, Astrid. *Три повести о малыше и Карлсоне*, trans. Liliana Lungina. Moscow 1974.

MacFadyen, David. *Yellow Crocodiles and Blue Oranges: Russian Animated Film Since World War Two*. Montreal 2005.

Majofis, Marija. "Милый, милый трикстер: Карлсон и советская утопия о 'настоящем детстве'," in Ilja Kukulin, Mark Lipoveckij, and Marija Majofis, eds., *Веселые человечки: культурные герои советского детства*. Moscow 2008, 241-286.

Milne, A. A. *Winnie-the-Pooh*. 1988 edition. New York 1926.

Phelan, Peggy. *Unmarked: The Politics of Performance*. New York 1996.

Pontieri, Laura. *Soviet Animation and the Thaw of the 1960s. Not Only for Children*. New Barnet, Herts, UK 2012.

Popov, Vladimir, dir. *Трое из Простоквашино*. Moscow, Sojuzmul'tfil'm 1978.

Reitherman, Wolfgang, dir. *Winnie-the-Pooh and the Honey Tree*. Burbank, CA, Walt Disney Productions 1966.

Sandle, Mark, *A Short History of Soviet Socialism*. London, UK and Philadelphia, PA 1999.

Schwab, Gabriele. *Haunting Legacies: Violent Histories and Transgenerational Trauma*. New York 2010.

Sedgwick, Eve Kosofsky. "Tales of the Avunculate: *The Importance of Being Earnest*," in Michele Aina Barale, Jonathan Goldberg, Michael Moon, and Sedgwick, eds., *Tendencies*. Durham, NC 1993, 52-72.

Sedgwick, Eve Kosofsky. "Privilege of Unknowing: Diderot's *The Nun*," in Michele Aina Barale, Jonathan Goldberg, Michael Moon, and Sedgwick, eds., *Tendencies*. Durham, NC 1993, 23-51.

Shteyngart, Gary. *Little Failure: A Memoir*. New York 2014.

Smoljarova, Natalija. "Детский 'Недетский' Винни-пух," in Ilja Kukulin, Mark Lipoveckij, and Marija Majofis, eds. *Веселые человечки: культурные герои советского детства*. Moscow 2008, 287-314.

Soler, Colette. *Lacanian Affects: The Function of Affect in Lacan's Work*, trans. Bruce Fink. New York 2016.

Stepancev, Boris, dir. *Малыш и Карлсон*. Moscow, Sojuzmul'tfil'm 1968.

Stepancev, Boris, dir. *Карлсон вернулся*. Moscow, Sojuzmul'tfil'm 1970.
Stockton, Kathryn Bond. *The Queer Child: Growing Sideways in the Twentieth Century*. Durham, NC 2009.
Volkan, Vamik D., Gabriele Ast, and William Greer Jr. *The Third Reich in the Unconscious: Transgenerational Transmission and Its Consequences*. New York 2002.

Bibliography

Primary Sources

Benua, Aleksandr, and Kornej Chukovskij, eds. *Елка. Сборник. Книжка для маленьких детей*. Petrograd 1918.
Belych, Grigorij, and Leonid Panteleev. *Республика ШКИД*. Moscow 2014.
Bobinskaja, Elena. *Пионерский суд*. Leningrad 1926.
Bogdanov, Nikolaj. *Пропавший лагерь. Подлинные приключения пионерского отряда*. Moscow and Leningrad 1929.
Bogdanovich, Tatjana. *Горный завод Петра Третьего*. Moscow and Leningrad 1936.
Bogdanovich, Tatjana. *Ученик наборного художества*. Moscow and Leningrad 1933.
Boronina, Ekaterina. *Обвал*. Leningrad 1938.
Boronina, Ekaterina. "Вестник осажденного города," in *Костер* 7-8 (1942), 20.
Boronina, Ekaterina. "Горячее сердце," in *Костер* 9 (1941), 36-38.
Boronina, Ekaterina. "Мальчик из Севастополя," in *Костер* 7-8 (1942), 2-4.
Budogoskaja, Lidija. *Как Саньку в очаг привели*. Moscow and Leningrad 1933.
Budogoskaja, Lidija. *Нулевки*. Moscow and Leningrad 1933.
Bykov, E. *Пионеры и прогульщики*. Moscow 1931.
Charms, Daniil. "17 лошадей," in *Еж* 8 (1928), 28.
Charms, Daniil. "Влас и Мишка," in *Октябрята* (1931).
Charms, Daniil. "Во-первых и во-вторых," in *Еж* 11 (1928), 16-19.
Charms, Daniil. "Врун," in *Еж* 24 (1930), 10-11.
Charms, Daniil. "Га-ра-рар," in *Еж* 12 (1929), 5-7.
Charms, Daniil. "Девять картин," in *Чиж* 6 (1941), 22.
Charms, Daniil. "Иван Иваныч Самовар," in *Еж* 1 (1928), 28-29.
Charms, Daniil. "Иван Топорышкин," in *Еж* 2 (1928), 21.
Charms, Daniil. "Из дома вышел человек," in *Чиж* 3 (1937), 18.
Charms, Daniil. "Как Маша заставила осла везти ее в город," in *Чиж* 2 (1934), 20.
Charms, Daniil. *Миллион*. Leningrad 1931.
Charms, Daniil. "Миллион," in *Чиж* 9 (1935), 11.
Charms, Daniil. "Миша Гришу вызывает," in *Октябрята* (1931).
Charms, Daniil. "Новый город," in *Еж* 5 (1935), 21.
Charms, Daniil. "О том, как старушка чернила покупала," in *Еж* 12 (1928), 11-16.
Charms, Daniil. "Песня про пограничника," in *Чиж* 12 (1938), 6-7.
Charms, Daniil. "Первомайская песня," in *Чиж* 4 (1939), 9.
Charms, Daniil. "Письма Борису Степановичу Житкову," October 9, 1936.
Charms, Daniil. *Полное собрание сочинений: В 4-х томах*, ed. V. N. Sazhin. St. Petersburg 1997–2001.

Charms, Daniil. "Почему", in *Еж* 12 (1928), 28.

Charms, Daniil. "Профессор Трубочкин," in *Чиж* 7, 8, 12, (1933), 5-7 (7), 16-17 (8), 20 (12).

Charms, Daniil. "Рассказ о том, как Панкин Колька ездил в Бразилию, а Ершов Петька ничему не верил," in *Еж* 2 (1928), 1-12.

Charms, Daniil. "Сдали в срок," in *Октябрята* (1931).

Charms, Daniil. "Танкист," in *Чиж* 11 (1938), 18-19.

Charms, Daniil. *Театр*. Leningrad 1929.

Charms, Daniil. "Что мы заготовляем на зиму," in *Еж* 19/20 (1931), 12-13.

Charms, Daniil. "Что это значит?" in *Чиж* 12 (1935), 11.

Charms, Daniil. "Это резвый конь ребенок," in *Чиж* 3 (1938), 7.

Charskaja, Lidija. *Игорь и Милица (Соколята): повесть для юношества из великой европейской войны*. Petrograd 1915.

Chlebnikov, Velimir. *The King of Time: Selected Writings of the Russian Futurian*, trans. Paul Schmidt. Cambridge, MA 1985.

Chlebnikov, Velimir. *Собрание сочинений в трех томах*. St. Petersburg 2001.

Chlebnikov, Velimir. *Собрание сочинений В. Хлебникова*. Leningrad 1928.

Chlebnikov, Velimir. *Творения*. Moscow 1986.

Chukovskij, Kornej. "Ваня и крокодил," in *Для детей* 1-12 (1917).

Chukovskij, Kornej. *Мойдодыр*. Petrograd 1923.

Chukovskij, Kornej. *Об этой книжке: Стихи*, Moscow 1961.

Chukovskij, Kornej. *Приключения Крокодила Крокодиловича*, ill. Re-Mi. Petrograd 1919.

Chukovskij, Kornej. *Собрание сочинений в 15-и томах*, Moscow 2001-2010.

Chukovskij, Kornej. *Солнечная*. Moscow 1933.

Danko, Elena. *Китайский секрет*. Moscow and Leningrad 1929.

Daudet, Alphonse. *Тайна дедушки Корнилия*, adapted by Konstantin Vaginov. Moscow and Leningrad 1927.

Dorochov, Pavel. *Сын большевика*. Moscow 1925.

Dorofeev, Nikolaj. *Зажили по-другому*. Moscow 1927.

Driz, Ovsej. *Di ferte strune*. Moscow 1969.

Driz, Ovsej. *Зеленая карета*, trans. Genrich Sapgir. Moscow 1972.

Druzhinin, Vladimir. *Кто сказал, что я убит?* Moscow 1969.

Druzhinin, Vladimir. "Мировой бригадир," in *Костер* 11-12 (1942), 16-17.

Egorov, Pavel. "Праздник труда," in *Юные строители* 9 (1924), 3-4.

Ekaterina II. *О царевиче Хлоре*. St. Petersburg 1790.

Erlich, Vol'f. *О ленивом Ваньке и его щенке*. Moscow and Leningrad 1926.

Ershov, Petr. *Конек-горбунок*. Moscow and Leningrad 1964.

Ezerskij, Milij. *Аристоник*. Moscow 1937.

Ezerskij, Milij. *Власть и народ. Часть 2: Марий и Сулла*. Moscow 1936.

Ezerskij, Milij. *Димитрий Донской*. Moscow and Leningrad 1941.
Finogenov, Anatolij. "Без елки," in *Чиж* 12 (1931), 4-6.
Finogenov, Anatolij. *Кто впереди*. Leningrad 1932.
Fraerman, Ruvim. "Маленький герой," in *Пионер* 6 (1942), 15.
Fraerman, Ruvim. *Дикая собака динго или повесть о первой любви*. Moscow 1939.
Furman, Petr. *Александр Васильевич Суворов*. St. Petersburg 1848.
Furman, Petr. *Григорий Александрович Потемкин-Рымникский*. St. Petersburg 1848.
Furman, Petr. *Наталья Борисовна Долгорукова*. St. Petersburg 1856.
Furman, Petr. *Саардамский плотник*. St. Petersburg 1847.
Gajdar, Arkadij. *Военная тайна*. Charkov and Odessa 1935.
Gajdar, Arkadij. *Военная тайна. Голубая чашка. Тимур и его команда. Чук и Гек*. Moscow 2014.
Gajdar, Arkadij. "Горячий камень," in *Мурзилка* 8-9 (1941).
Gajdar, Arkadij. *Дальние страны*. Moscow 1932.
Gajdar, Arkadij. *На графских развалинах*. Moscow 1929.
Gajdar, Arkadij. *Школа*. Moscow 1930.
Gajdar, Arkadij. *Чук и Гек*. Moscow 1939.
Garbuzov, Solomon. *Фронтовые ребята*. Moscow 1941.
German, Aleksandr. *Слушали-постановили*. Orel 1925.
German, Jurij. *Вот как это было*. Moscow 1985.
Glinka, S. N. *Русская история*. St. Petersburg 1817.
Glinka, S. N. *Русские исторические и нравоучительные повести*. Moscow 1810.
Golubov, Sergej. *Генерал Багратион*. Moscow and Leningrad 1943.
Golubov, Sergej. *Берко-кантонист*. Moscow and Leningrad 1927.
Golubov, Sergej. "Малахов курган," in *Пионер* 3 (1941), 2-18; 4 (1941), 35-53.
Grigulis, Arvid. *Пограничники, два мальчика и собака Марс*. Moscow and Leningrad, 1952.
Grimm Brothers. *Сказки*, narrated by Aleksandr Vvedenskij. Archangel 1939.
Grjaznov, Innokentij. *Искатели мозолей*. Moscow 1931.
Gumilev, Nikolaj. *Стихотворения и поэмы*. Leningrad, 1988.
Gunin, Dmitrij, ed. *Пионеры-герои: Учебное пособие*. Moscow 1982.
Guro, Elena. *Небесные верблюжата*. Rostov-na-Donu 1993.
Gusev, Andrej. *Год за годом... Из пионерской летописи*. Moscow 1964.
Iljina, Elena. *Четвертая высота. О комсомолке Гуле Королевой, участнице Великой Отечественной войны*. Moscow and Leningrad 1946.
Irkutov, Andrej. *Все за одного*. Charkov 1926.
Irkutov, Andrej. "Две мамы," in *Барабан* 4 (1924), 5-8.
Irkutov, Andrej. "На смерть Ильича," in *Барабан* 2 (1924), 24.
Irkutov, Andrej. "Суд над дедом Архипом," in *Барабан* 10 (1925), 5-6.
Ishimova, Aleksandra. *История России в рассказах для детей*. St. Petersburg 1837.

Jakovlev, Jurij. *Девочки с Васильевского острова*. Moscow 1978.

Jakovlev, Jurij. *Жить нам суждено*. Moscow 1979.

Jakovlev, Jurij. *Кепка-невидимка*. Moscow 1987.

Jakovlev, Jurij. "Мистерия. Страсти по четырем девочкам," in Jakovlev, *Избранное*. Moscow 1992.

Jan (Janchivetskij), Vasilij. *Спартак*. Moscow and Leningrad 1933.

Jurjev, V. *Гренадер Леонтий Коренной*. Moscow 1945.

Karaseva, Vera. *Кирюшка*. Kiev 1965.

Kassil', Lev. *Будьте готовы, Ваше Высочество!* Moscow 1965.

Kassil', Lev. "Дорогие мои мальчишки," in Kassil', *Собрание сочинений в пяти томах*, Vol. 2. Moscow 1987.

Kassil', Lev. *Черемыш, брат героя*. Moscow and Leningrad 1938.

Kataev, Valentin. *Сын полка*. Moscow 1945.

Kaverin, Venjamin. *Два капитана*. Moscow and Leningrad 1945.

Kepler, A. *Гвардии мальчик: сборник рассказов*. Stalingrad 1948.

Kharms, Daniil and Katya Arnold. *It Happened Like This: Stories and Poems*. New York 1998.

Kharms, Daniil and Mark Rosenthal. *First, Second*. New York 1996.

Kipling, Rudjard. *Слоненок*, trans. Kornej Chukovskij, ill. Vladimir Lebedev. Petrograd 1922.

Kiselev, Fedor. "Знамя спасли," in *Юные строители* 8 (1925), 3-4.

Kochetkova, E. "Миша," in *Сибирский детский журнал* 2 (1928), 8-9.

Kole, Luiza. *Детство и юность великих людей*. St. Petersburg 1894.

Kolesnikova, Z., ed. *Юные герои Великой Отечественной войны*. Alma-Ata 1985.

Korenkov, Vasilij. *Всегда готов! (Геройский подвиг пионера)*. Moscow 1925.

Korjakov, Oleg. *Формула счастья*. Moscow 1965.

Kozhevnikov, Aleksej. *Шпана. Из жизни беспризорных*. Leningrad 1925.

Kozlov, Viljam. *Президент Каменного Острова*. Leningrad 1964.

Krapivin, Vladislav. *Мальчик со шпагой*. Moscow 1976.

Krestinskij, Aleksandr. *Мальчики из блокады. Рассказы и повесть*. Leningrad 1983.

Kruchenych, Aleksej. *Собственные рассказы и рисунки детей*. [St. Petersburg] 1914.

Kruchenych, Aleksej, and Zina V. *Поросята*. [St. Petersburg] 1913.

Kuznecov, A. (A. I. Kuzmin). *Крепостные мастера*. Moscow and Leningrad 1953.

Kuznetsova, Olga. "Страх," in *Костер* 5-6 (1942), 2.

Larina, Larisa. "Помогла," in *Барабан* 4 (1925), 2-4.

Larina, Larisa. *По-разному*. Charkov 1925.

Larina, Larisa. "Шпион," in *Барабан* 7-8 (1924), 3-8.

Lebedev, Vladimir. *Азбука*. Leningrad 1925.

Lebedev, Vladimir. *Десять книжек для детей*, ed. G.I. Chugunov. Leningrad 1976.

Lebedev, Vladimir. *Золотое яичко*. Petrograd 1923.

Lebedev, Vladimir. *Охота*. Leningrad 1925.

Lebedev, Vladimir. *Приключения Чуч-ло*. Petrograd 1922.

Leonov, Michail. *Радио-Май. Первомайское зрелище*. Moscow 1925.

Levin, Dojvber, and Daniil Charms. "Друг за другом," in *Еж* 9 (1930), 21-25.

Lindgren, Astrid. *Три повести о малыше и Карлсоне*, trans. Liliana Lungina. Moscow 1974.

Linkov, Lev. *Рассказы о пограничниках*. Moscow 1954.

Lipina, Nina. *Бабушка Андрюша*. Moscow 1926.

Lissickij, El. *Про 2 квадрата: супрематический сказ в 6-ти постройках*. Berlin 1922.

Lunacharskij, Anatolij. *Ленин*. Moscow 1924.

Lurje, Solomon. *Письмо греческого мальчика*. Moscow and Leningrad 1930.

Majakovskij, Vladimir. *Полное собрание сочинений в 13-х томах*. Moscow 1955-1961.

Majakovskij, Vladimir. *Сказка о Пете, толстом ребенке, и о Симе, который тонкий*, ill. N. Kuprejanov. Moscow 1925.

Majakovskij, Vladimir. *Советская азбука*. Moscow 1919.

Majakovskij, Vladimir. *Что ни страница, – то слон, то львица*, ill. K. Zdanevich. Tiflis 1928.

Majakovskij, Vladimir. *Эта книжечка моя про моря и про маяк*, ill. B. Pokrovskij. Moscow 1927.

Makarenko, Anton. *Педагогическая поэма*. Moscow 1935.

Mandel'shtam, Osip. *Два трамвая: Клик и Трам*, ill. B. Ender. Leningrad 1925.

Marshak, Samuil. *Вчера и сегодня*, ill. Vladimir Lebedev. Leningrad 1925.

Marshak, Samuil. "Ленинграду – в день Красной Армии," in *Костер* 2 (1943), 1.

Marshak, Samuil. *Мистер Твистер*, ill. Vladimir Lebedev. Moscow 1933.

Marshak, Samuil. *Мороженое*, ill. Vladimir Lebedev. Moscow and Leningrad 1925.

Marshak, Samuil. *Почта*, ill. Michail Cechanovskij. Leningrad 1932.

Marshak, Samuil. *Семь чудес*. Leningrad and Moscow 1926.

Marshak, Samuil. *Собрание сочинений в восьми томах*. Moscow 1969.

Marshak, Samuil. *Цирк*, ill. Vladimir Lebedev. Leningrad 1925.

Marshak, Samuil and Vladimir Lebedev. "Багаж," in *Избранные детские книги советских художников*, ed. Ju. Gerchuk. Moscow 1982.

Marshak, Samuil. "Как рубанок сделал рубанок," in *Избранные детские книги советских художников*, ed. Ju. Gerchuk. Moscow 1978.

Marshak, Samuil. "Охота," in *Избранные детские книги советских художников*, ed. Ju. Gerchuk. Moscow 1978.

Matje, Milica. *День египетского мальчика*. Moscow 1954.

Matje, Milica. *Кари, ученик художника*. Moscow 1963.

Matveev, German. *Зеленые цепочки*. Moscow 1945.

Matveev, German. *Семнадцатилетние*. Leningrad 1954.

Medynskij, Georgij. *Девятый А*. Moscow 1940.

Michajlov, M. *Федька Апчхи*. Charkov 1925.
Michalkov, Sergej. *Все начинается с детства*. Moscow 1972.
Michalkov, Sergej. *Собрание сочинений в шести томах*. Moscow 1981-1983.
Mikitenko, Ivan. *Уркаганы*. Charkov 1929.
Mikson, Ilja. *Жила, была… Историческое повествование*. Leningrad 1991.
Miller, Jakov (Nikolaj Zabolockij). "Восемь лет без Ленина," in *Чиж* 1 (1932), 4.
Miller, Jakov (Nikolaj Zabolockij). "Восток в огне," in *Еж* 15/16 (1930), 1-4.
Miller, Jakov (Nikolaj Zabolockij). "За окном," in *Чиж* 4/5 (1932), 6.
Miller, Jakov (Nikolaj Zabolockij). "На площадку," in *Чиж* 6 (1932), 2.
Miller, Jakov (Nikolaj Zabolockij). "Песня ударников," in *Чиж* 9/10 (1930), 6.
Miller, Jakov (Nikolaj Zabolockij). "У моря," in *Чиж* 7/8 (1931), 3.
Milne Alexander. *Винни-Пух и все-все-все*, trans. Boris Zachoder. Moscow 1992.
Milne Alexander. *Winnie-the-Pooh*. 1988 edition. New York 1926.
Milne Alexander. *Winnie the Pooh and Other Stories*. London 1994.
Minaev, Konstantin. *Назарка-атаман*. Moscow and Leningrad 1925.
Minaev, Konstantin. *Против отца*. Moscow and Leningrad 1927.
Minaev, Konstantin. *Школьники*. Moscow 1926.
Moiseeva, Klara. *В древнем царстве Урарту*. Moscow 1953.
Moiseeva, Klara. *Дочь Эхнатона*. Moscow 1967.
Morozov, Vjacheslav. *Им было по четырнадцать: О Марате Казее, Володе Щербачевиче*. Minsk 1969.
Nabatov, Grigorij. *Юные подпольщики*. Moscow 1963.
Nadezhdina, Nadezhda. "Лара Михеенко," in *Пионеры-герои*. Moscow 1967-1969.
Nikiforov, Georgij. *Наши ребята*. Moscow and Leningrad 1925.
Olejnikov, Nikolaj. "В октябрьскую ночь," in *Чиж* 11 (1935), 1-4.
Olejnikov, Nikolaj. "Красный бант," in *Чиж* 5 (1936), 4-12.
Olejnikov, Nikolaj. "Макар Свирепый в Америке," in *Еж* 4, 6, 10, 14, 19/20, 21, 22 (1931), 8-9, 20-21, 18-19, 20-21, 24-25, 31-31, 17.
Olejnikov, Nikolaj. "Новые приключения Макара Свирепого," in *Еж* 13, 15/16, 17/18, 22/23, (1930), 22, 16, 10, 28.
Olejnikov, Nikolaj. "Отто Браун," in *Еж* 5 (1928), 15.
Olejnikov, Nikolaj. "Полет парашютиста Евсеева," in *Чиж* 1 (1934), 8-10.
Olejnikov, Nikolaj. "Портрет," in *Еж* (Dec., 1934), 22-25.
Olejnikov, Nikolaj. "Праздник," in *Еж* 3 (1928), 15-19.
Olejnikov, Nikolaj. "Сколько тебе лет?" in *Еж* 2 (1928), 22-29.
Olejnikov, Nikolaj. "Удивительные приключения Макара Свирепого," in *Еж* 5-7 (1929), 31-33, 34-36, 30.
Olesha, Jurij. *Зависть. Три толстяка. Рассказы*. Moscow 1998.
Olesha, Jurij. *Три толстяка*, ill. M. Dobuzhinskij. Moscow 1928.
Oseeva, Valentina. *Динка*. Moscow 1959.

Oseeva, Valentina. *Васек Трубачев и его товарищи*. Moscow 1947.
Ostromenckaja, Nadezhda, and Natalija Bromlej. *Приключения мальчика с собакой*. Moscow 1959.
Ostroumov, Lev. *Макар-следопыт*, Vols. 1 and 2. Moscow 1925.
Ovalov, Lev. *Пятеро на одних коньках*. Moscow 1927.
Panova, Vera. *Наши дети. Рассказы, повести и пьеса*. Leningrad 1973.
Panova, Vera. *Сергей Иванович и Таня*, in *Наши дети: Рассказы, повести и пьеса*. Moscow 1973.
Panteleev, Leonid. *Живые памятники*. Leningrad 1966.
Paustovskij, Konstantin. *Рассказы*. Moscow 1935.
Petnikov, G. N., ed. *В огне Отечественной войны: Сборник стихов, очерков, рассказов*. Nalchik 1942.
Pomozov, Jurij. *Блокадная юность*. Leningrad 1989.
Propiak, Zhirar de. *Плутарх для молодых девиц, или Краткия жизнеописания славных жен*. Moscow 1816.
Pushkarev, Gleb. *Два Петра Ивановича*. Novosibirsk 1949.
Pushkarev, Gleb. *Пионер Павлик Гнездилов*. Novosibirsk 1940.
Pushkin, A.S. *Собрание сочинений в десяти томах*. Moscow 1959-1962.
Razumovskij, Lev. "Дети блокады. Документальная повесть," in *Neva* 1 (1999), 4-68.
Rozanov, Sergej. *Приключения Травки*. Moscow 1928.
Rubinshtejn, Revekka. *Глиняный конверт*. Moscow 1962.
Rubinshtejn, Revekka. *За что Ксеркс высек море*. Moscow 1967.
Ruzhanskij, Evgenij. "Молоко," in *Пожар*. Moscow 1940, 55-56.
Ruzhanskij, Evgenij. "Удочка," in *Пожар*. Moscow 1940, 32-39.
Rybakov, Anatolij. *Кортик*. Moscow and Leningrad 1948.
Ryklin, Grigorij. *Рассказы о пограничниках*. Moscow 1937.
Rysakov, Viktor. *Юные русские герои: Очерки и рассказы о военных и довоенных подвигах русских мальчиков*. Petrograd and Moscow 1914.
Ryzhov, Aleksandr. "Заговор барабанщиков," in *Барабан* 5, 1926, 4-8.
Ryzhov, Aleksandr. "Теплушка № 36084," in *Барабан* 12(17) (1924), 3-11.
Saveljev, L. (Leonid Lipavskij). *Штурм Зимнего. Ленин идет в Смольный*. Moscow 1938.
Savin, Viktor. *Шаромыжники*. Moscow 1925.
Sejfullina, Lidija. *Правонарушители*. Novonikolaevsk 1922.
Selivanov, Vladimir. *Стояли, как солдаты: блокада, дети, Ленинград*. St. Petersburg 2002.
Shestinskij, Oleg. "Ангельское воинство. Рассказы," in *Neva* 1 (1999), 69-87.
Shishova, Zinaida. *Блокада*. Leningrad 1943.
Selivanov, Vladimir. *Стояли, как солдаты: блокада, дети, Ленинград*. St. Petersburg 2002.

Shishkov, Vjacheslav. *Странники*. Leningrad 1931.

Shorin, Ivan. "Одногодки," in T. Gabe, L. Zheldin, and Z. Zadunajskaja, eds., *Костер*. Moscow 1934, 53-54.

Shtenygart, Gary. *Little Failure: A Memoir*. New York 2014.

Shvarc, Evgenij. *Золушка. Киносценарии. Сказка о потерянном времени*. Moscow 2004.

Shvarc, Evgenij. *Первоклассница*. Moscow and Leningrad 1949.

Slepuchin, Jurij. *Перекресток*. Leningrad 1962.

Slonimskij, Aleksandr. *Черниговцы. Повесть о восстании Черниговского полка в 1826 году*. Moscow and Leningrad 1928.

Smirnov-Ochtin, Igor'. "Школа судей," in *Нева* 1(1999), 88-101.

Smirnov, Elizar. "Павлик Морозов," in *Дети-герои*. Moscow 1961.

Smirnov, Elizar. "Пионеры-герои," in *Вожатый* 10 (1938), 47-51.

Smirnov, Elizar. *Славный пионер Гена Щукин. Эпизоды из жизни пионера, разоблачившего планы врагов народа и убитого ими*. Moscow 1938.

Smirnov, S. "Таня Савичева," in *Венок славы. Антология художественных произведений о Великой Отечественной войне*, Vol. 3, *Подвиг Ленинграда*. Moscow 1983, 297-300.

Stanjukovich, Konstantin. *Севастопольский мальчик: повесть времен Крымской войны*. St. Petersburg and Moscow 1903.

Suchachevskij, Stepan. *Коля Мяготин*. Moscow 1967.

Sventickaja, M. *Наш детский сад*. Moscow 1924.

Taezhnyj, A. "Ростки," in *Товарищ* 7-8 (1931), 42.

Tajtc, Jakov. *Рассказы*. Moscow 1940.

Tolstoj, Aleksej. *Повесть о многих превосходных вещах: детство Никиты*. Moscow and Berlin 1922.

Tolstoj, Lev. *Новая азбука*. Moscow 1875.

Tolstoj, Lev. *Севастопольские рассказы*. Moscow 1943.

Tuwim, Julian. *Wiersze wybrane*. Wroclaw 1969.

Ushagin, Aleksandr. "Юный герой," in *Юные строители* 5 (1924), 1-3.

Uspenskij, Lev. "Птичка в клетке," in *Дети военной поры*. Moscow 1984, 93-147.

Verejskaja, Elena. *В те годы. Рассказы о революционных событиях 1905-1917 годов*. Leningrad 1956.

Verejskaja, Elena. *Таня революционерка*. Moscow and Leningrad 1928.

Verkin, Eduard. *Облачный полк*. Moscow 2012.

Vigdorova, Frida. *Мой класс: записки учительницы*. Moscow and Leningrad 1949.

Vinnikov, Boris. *Победа*. Leningrad 1932.

Vishnevskij, Vsevolod. "Комсомольцы Ленинграда," in *Костер* 7 (1943), 2-3.

Vladimirov, Jurij. "На яхте," in *Еж* 19/20 (1930), 22-28.

Vladimirov, Jurij. "Барабан," in *Еж* 10 (1929), 28-29.

Vladimirov, Jurij. "На улице," in *Чиж* 10 (1931), 14-15.
Vladimirov, Jurij. "Самолет," in *Еж* 10 (1930), 14-15.
Vladimirov, Jurij. "Самолет," in *Чиж* 6 (1936), 12-13.
Vladimirov, Jurij. "Синяя точка," in *Чиж* 7/8 (1930), 12-13.
Vladimirov, Jurij. "Чудаки," in *Еж* 6 (1930), 20.
Voronkova, Ljubov. *Старшая сестра*. Moscow 1955.
Voskobojnikov, Valerij. *Рассказы о юных героях*. Moscow 2015.
Vygovskij, Vladimir. *Огонь юного сердца*. Moscow 1960.
Vvedenskij, Aleksandr. "1-е мая," in *Еж* 8 (1930), 15-17.
Vvedenskij, Aleksandr. "4 хвастуна," in *Еж* 2/3 (1933), 41-43.
Vvedenskij, Aleksandr. *Конная Буденного*. Leningrad 1931.
Vvedenskij, Aleksandr. "Волк и семеро козлят," in *Чиж* 5 (1935), 23-27.
Vvedenskij, Aleksandr. *Все*, Anna Gerasimova, ed. Moscow 2010.
Vvedenskij, Aleksandr. "Вшестером всю землю обойдем," in *Еж* 7 (1935), 23-27.
Vvedenskij, Aleksandr. "Горшок каши," in *Чиж* 7 (1935), 6-9.
Vvedenskij, Aleksandr. "Два класса учителя Басса," in *Еж* 1 (1933), 46-47.
Vvedenskij, Aleksandr. "Железная дорога," in *Еж* 3 (1928), 12-13.
Vvedenskij, Aleksandr. "Зима кругом," in *Еж* 5 (1930), 18.
Vvedenskij, Aleksandr. "Ивасик-танкист," in *Чиж* 4 (1938), 2-3.
Vvedenskij, Aleksandr. "Коля Кочин," in *Еж* 9 (1929), 29-31.
Vvedenskij, Aleksandr. "Кто?" in *Еж* 3 (1929), 30-33.
Vvedenskij, Aleksandr. "Лагерная песня," in *Еж* 8 (1934), 8.
Vvedenskij, Aleksandr. "Лошадка," in *Еж* 8 (1929), 30-31.
Vvedenskij, Aleksandr. "Маша в гостях у пионеров," in *Чиж* 7 (1935), 1-6.
Vvedenskij, Aleksandr. "Маша на паровозе," in *Чиж* 5 (1935), 1-6.
Vvedenskij, Aleksandr. "Муж и жена," in *Еж* 10 (1935), 26-29.
Vvedenskij, Aleksandr. "Не отдавай сорняку урожай," in *Еж* 4 (1933), 13.
Vvedenskij, Aleksandr. "Не позволим," in *Чиж* 12 (1931), 6.
Vvedenskij, Aleksandr. "Октябрь," in *Еж* 19/20 (1930), 8-10.
Vvedenskij, Aleksandr. "Первое мая и девочка Мая," in *Чиж* 4 (1939), 10-13.
Vvedenskij, Aleksandr. "Письмо бабушке," in *Чиж* 4 (1940), 5.
Vvedenskij, Aleksandr. "Письмо Густава Мейера," in *Еж* 15/16 (1931), 5-6.
Vvedenskij, Aleksandr. "Пограничник," in *Чиж* 2/3 (1933), 4.
Vvedenskij, Aleksandr. "Подвиг пионера Мочина," in *Еж* 14 (1930), 7-11.
Vvedenskij, Aleksandr. *Подвиг пионера Мочина*. Moscow 1931.
Vvedenskij, Aleksandr. "Приезжайте к нам!" in *Чиж* 4 (1933), 1-2.
Vvedenskij, Aleksandr. "Рыбаки," in *Еж* 4 (1929), 11.
Vvedenskij, Aleksandr. "Семеро храбрецов," in *Чиж* 4 (1935), 14-17.
Vvedenskij, Aleksandr. "Силач," in *Еж* 1 (1935), 28-31.
Vvedenskij, Aleksandr. "Соломинка, уголь и боб," in *Чиж* 3 (1935), 1-4.

Vvedenskij, Aleksandr. *Стихи*. Moscow and Leningrad 1940.

Vvedenskij, Aleksandr. "Стихи про орла, про лису, про медведя," in *Чиж* 9 (1940), 16-17.

Vvedenskij, Aleksandr. "Триста семьдесят ребят," in *Еж* 2 (1934), 27.

Vvedenskij, Aleksandr. "Туристы," in *Еж* 12 (1930), 1-3.

Vvedenskij, Aleksandr. "Турксиб," in *Еж* 7 (1930), 23.

Vvedenskij, Aleksandr. "Умный Петя," in *Чиж* 11/12 (1932), 1.

Vvedenskij, Aleksandr. "Фонарь," in *Еж* 6 (1929), 6-9.

Vvedenskij, Aleksandr. "Храбрый портной," in *Чиж* 8 (1934), 1-7.

Vvedenskij, Aleksandr. "Что кому?" in *Чиж* 1 (1933), 5-7.

Vvedenskij, Aleksandr. "Что это вы строите?" in *Чиж* 9/10 (1932), 1.

Zabila, Natalija. *Катруся уже большая*. Moscow 1957.

Zabolockij, Nikolaj. "Автобиография," in *Стихотворения*. Washington 1965.

Zabolockij, Nikolaj. "Гулливер у великанов", in *Чиж* 5 (1935), 7-11; 6 (1935), 1-5; 7 (1935), 9-13; 8 (1935), 9-13; 9 (1935),16-20; 10 (1935), 20-24; 11 (1935), 8-10; 12 (1935), 7-9.

Zabolockij, Nikolaj. "Два обманщика," in *Еж* 12 (1935), 24-26.

Zabolockij, Nikolaj. "Картонный город," in *Чиж* 11 (1933), 1.

Zabolockij, Nikolaj. "Красные и синие," in *Еж* 3 (1928), 1-7.

Zabolockij, Nikolaj. "Кулацкий маневр," in *Еж* 18 (1931), 9.

Zabolockij, Nikolaj. "Маслозавод," in *Чиж* 11 (1930), 3-5.

Zabolockij, Nikolaj. "Ночь в степи," in *Чиж* 12 (1934), 2-3.

Zabolockij, Nikolaj. "Пионеры шведские и пионеры советские," in *Еж* 8 (1928), 22.

Zabolockij, Nikolaj. "Повесть об удивительной жизни Великого Гаргантюа отца Пантагрюэля," in *Еж* 3-7, 9-12 (1934); 1-10 (1935).

Zabolockij, Nikolaj. "Приключения врунов," in *Еж* 4 (1929), 22-26.

Zabolockij, Nikolaj. "Прощание," in *Еж* (Dec., 1934), 27.

Zabolockij, Nikolaj. "Сказка о кривом человеке," in *Чиж* 8 (1933), 10-13.

Zabolockij, Nikolaj. "Хозяин и работник," in *Чиж* 4/5 (1934), 14. 3-7, 9-12 (1934); 1-10 (1935).

Zamchalov, Grigorij. "Харитон," in *Наши дела*. Moscow 1930.

Zamojskij, Petr. "Буржуй," in *В деревне*. Moscow 1928, 14-16.

Zamojskij, Petr. *Вместе веселей*. Moscow 1928.

Zamojskij, Petr. *Деревенская быль*. Moscow 1924.

Zamojskij, Petr. "Еройка," in *Юные строители* 11-12 (1924), 5-8.

Zamojskij, Petr. *Озорник шатущий*. Moscow 1926.

Zamojskij, Petr. *Смутьян*. Moscow 1926.

Zenzinov, Vladimir. *Беспризорные*. Paris 1929.

Zharikov, Andrej. *Подвиги юных: Рассказы и очерки*. Moscow 1960.

Zilver, Lev. *Быть на-чеку! Рассказы о коварных методах агентов фашистских разведок и работе славной совразведки по их разоблачению*. Moscow 1938.

Zlobin, Stepan. *Салават Юлаев*. Moscow and Leningrad 1929.

BIBLIOGRAPHY

Films

Brumberg, Valentina and Zinaida, dir. *Большие неприятности*. Moscow, Sojuzmul'tfil'm. 1961.
Chitruk, Fedor, dir. *Винни-пух*. Moscow, Sojuzmul'tfil'm 1969.
Chitruk, Fedor, dir. *Винни-пух и день забот*. Moscow, Sojuzmul'tfil'm 1972.
Chitruk, Fedor, dir. *Винни-пух идет в гости*. Moscow, Sojuzmul'tfil'm 1971.
Danelija, Georgij, dir. *Осенний марафон*. Moscow, Mosfil'm 1979.
Disney, Walt and Ub Iwerks, dir. *Steamboat Willie*. Los Angeles, Walt Disney Studio 1928.
Hand, David, dir. *Snow White and the Seven Dwarfs*. Los Angeles, Walt Disney Studio 1937.
Idsøe, Vibeke, dir. *Karlsson på taket*. Stockholm, AB Svensk filmindustrie 2002.
Ivanov-Vano, Ivan, dir. *Блэк энд уайт*. Moscow, Mezhrabpromfil'm 1932.
Ivanov-Vano, Ivan, dir. *В некотором царстве*. Moscow, Sojuzmul'tfil'm 1951.
Ivanov-Vano, Ivan, dir. *Гуси-лебеди*. Moscow, Sojuzmul'tfil'm 1949.
Ivanov-Vano, Ivan, dir. *Двенадцать месяцев*. Moscow, Sojuzmul'tfil'm 1953.
Ivanov-Vano, Ivan, dir. *Зимняя сказка*. Moscow, Sojuzmul'tfil'm 1945.
Ivanov-Vano, Ivan, dir. *Ивась*. Moscow, Sojuzmul'tfil'm 1940.
Ivanov-Vano, Ivan, dir. *Конек-горбунок*. Moscow, Sojuzmul'tfil'm 1947.
Ivanov-Vano, Ivan, dir. *Котофей Котофеевич*. Moscow, Sojuzmul'tfil'm 1937.
Ivanov-Vano, Ivan, dir. *Краденое солнце* (with Olga Chodataeva). Moscow, Sojuzmul'tfil'm 1943.
Ivanov-Vano, Ivan, dir. *Левша*. Moscow, Sojuzmul'tfil'm 1964.
Ivanov-Vano, Ivan, dir. *Лесной концерт*. Moscow, Sojuzmul'tfil'm 1953.
Ivanov-Vano, Ivan, dir. *Мойдодыр*. Moscow, Sojuzmul'tfil'm 1939.
Ivanov-Vano, Ivan, dir. *Мойдодыр*. Moscow, Sojuzmul'tfil'm 1954.
Ivanov-Vano, Ivan, dir. *Сенька-африканец* (with Jurij Merkulov and Daniil Cherkes). Moscow, Mezhrabpromfil'm 1927.
Ivanov-Vano, Ivan, dir. *Сказка о царе Дурандае* (with Valentina and Zinaida Brumberg). Moscow, Mezhrabpromfil'm 1934.
Ivanov-Vano, Ivan, dir. *Сказка о царе Салтане*. Moscow, Sojuzmul'tfil'm 1984.
Ivanov-Vano, Ivan, dir. *Снегурочка*. Moscow, Sojuzmul'tfil'm 1952.
Ivanov-Vano, Ivan, dir. *Стрекоза и муравей*. Moscow, Sojuzmul'tfil'm 1935.
Ivanov-Vano, Ivan, dir. *Три мушкетера*. Moscow, Sojuzmul'tfil'm 1938.
Ivanov-Vano, Ivan, dir. *Храбрый заяц*. Moscow, Sojuzmul'tfil'm 1955.
Gillett, Burt, dir. *The Three Little Pigs*. Los Angeles, Walt Disney Studio 1933.
Kachanov, Roman, dir. *Крокодил Гена*. Moscow, Sojuzmul'tfil'm 1969.
Kachanov, Roman, dir. *Чебурашка*. Moscow, Sojuzmul'tfil'm 1971.
Kachanov, Roman, dir. *Чебурашка идет в школу*. Moscow, Sojuzmul'tfil'm 1983.
Kachanov, Roman, dir. *Шапокляк*. Moscow, Sojuzmul'tfil'm 1974.

Komissarenko, Z., dir. *Китай в огне*. Moscow, Kino Moskva 1925.
Kovalevskaja, Inessa, dir. *Бременские музыканты*. Moscow, Sojuzmul'tfil'm 1969.
Kovalevskaja, Inessa, dir. *По следам бременских музыкантов*. Moscow, Sojuzmul'tfil'm 1973.
Popov, Vladimir, dir. *Трое из Простоквашино*. Moscow, Sojuzmul'tfil'm 1978.
Pudovkin, Vsevolod, dir. *Механика головного мозга, или поведение человека*. Gosfilmofond Archive, Moscow 1926.
Reitherman, Wolfgang, dir. *Winnie-the-Pooh and the Honey Tree*. Burbank, CA, Walt Disney Productions 1966.
Stepancev, Boris, dir. *Карлсон вернулся*. Moscow, Sojuzmul'tfil'm 1970.
Stepancev, Boris, dir. *Малыш и Карлсон*. Moscow, Sojuzmul'tfil'm 1968.
Vertov, Dziga, dir. *Советские игрушки*. Moscow, Goskino 1924.
Zheljabuzhskij, Jurij, dir. *Каток*. Moscow, Mezhrabpromfil'm 1927.

Secondary Sources (Select Bibliography)

Alaniz, José. *Komiks: Comic Art in Russia*. Jackson, MS 2010.
Alfonsov, Vladimir and Simon Krasitskij, eds. *Поэзия русского футуризма*. St. Petersburg 1999.
Arzamasceva, Irina. *"Век ребенка' в русской литературе 1900-1930 годов*. Moscow 2003.
Arzamasceva, Irina, and S. A. Nikolaeva, eds. *Детская литература*. Moscow 2005.
Asenin, Sergej. *Мир мультфильма: Идеи и образы мультипликации социалистических стран*. Moscow 1986.
Baer, Brian James. *Translation and the Making of Russian Literature*. New York 2016.
Bagno, Vsevolod, ed. *RES TRADUCTORICA. Перевод и сравнительное изучение литератур: к восьмидесятилетию Ю. Д. Левина*. St. Petersburg 2000.
Balakirsky Katz, Maya. *Drawing the Iron Curtain: Jews and the Golden Age of Soviet Animation*. New Brunswick, NJ 2016.
Balashov, Evgenij. *Педология в России в первой трети XX века*. St. Petersburg 2012.
Balina, Marina, Evgenij Dobrenko, and Jurij Murashov, eds. *Советское богатство. Статьи о культуре, литературе и кино*. St. Petersburg 2002.
Balina, Marina, Helena Goscilo, and Mark Lipovetsky, eds. *Politicizing Magic: An Anthology of Russian and Soviet Fairytales*. Evanston, IL 2005.
Balina, Marina and Larissa Rudova, eds. *Russian Children's Literature and Culture*. New York and London 2008.
Balina, Marina and Valerij Vjugin, eds. *'Убить Чарскую ...': парадоксы советской литературы для детей (1920-е – 1930-е гг.): сборник статей*. St. Petersburg 2015.

Barannikova, N. B., and V. G. Bezrogov, eds. *И спросила кроха: Образ ребенка и семьи в педагогике постсоветской России*. Moscow and Tver' 2010.

Beckett, Sandra, ed. *Transcending Boundaries: Writing for a Dual Audience of Children and Adults*. New York 1999.

Beumers, Birgit. *A History of Russian Cinema*. London and New York 2008.

Beumers, Birgit, ed. *A Companion to Russian Cinema*. Malden, MA and Oxford, UK 2016.

Beumers, Birgit, Stephen Hutchings, Natalia Rulyova, eds. *The Post-Soviet Russian Media: Conflicting Signals*. New York 2009.

Bljum, Arlen. *Советская цензура в эпоху тоталитарного режима, 1929-1953*. St. Petersburg 2000.

Borisova, Natalja, et al., eds. *СССР: территория любви*. Moscow 2009.

Boyd, Brian. *On the Origin of Stories: Evolution, Cognition, and Fiction*. Cambridge, MA 2009.

Boym, Svetlana. *Another Freedom: The Alternative History of An Idea*. Chicago 2010.

Brandenberger, David. "Proletarian Internationalism, 'Soviet Patriotism' and the Rise of Russocentric Etatism during the Stalinist 1930s," in *Left History* 6:5 (1999), 80-100.

Brintlinger, Angela. *Chapaev and His Comrades: War and the Russian Literary Hero Across the Twentieth Century*. Boston 2012.

Budashevskaya, Olga and Julian Rothenstein, eds. *Inside the Rainbow: Russian Children's Literature 1920-1935: Beautiful Books, Terrible Times*. London 2013.

Bulgakowa, Oksana. *Sergei Eisenstein: A Biography*. Berlin 2001.

Carroll, Joseph. *Reading Human Nature: Literary Darwinism in Theory and Practice*. Albany, NY 2011.

Chardzhiev, Nikolaj. *Статьи об авангарде: в двух томах*. Moscow 1997.

Chudakova, Marietta. *Избранные работы в 2-х т*. Vols 1 and 2. Moscow 2001.

Chukovskaja, Lidija. *В лаборатории редактора*. Archangelsk 2005.

Chukovskij, Kornej. *Дневник 1901-1969*, Vols. 1 and 2. Moscow 2003.

Chukovskij, Kornej. *От двух до пяти*, in *Собрание сочинений в восьми томах*. Moscow 1968-1972.

Chukovskij, Kornej. *A High Art*, trans. Lauren Leighton. Knoxville 2004.

Clark, Katerina. *The Soviet Novel: History as Ritual*. Chicago 1981.

Davydov, V. V., A. M. Prochorov, and E. D. Dneprov, eds. *Российская педагогическая энциклопедия*. Moscow 1993.

deGraffenried, Julie K. *Sacrificing Childhood: Children and the Soviet State in the Great Patriotic War*. Lawrence, KS 2014.

Dobrenko, Evgenij. *Формовка советского читателя: социальные и эстетические рецепции советской литературы*. St. Petersburg 1997.

Dobrenko, Evgeny. *Метафора власти: Литература сталинской эпохи в историческом освещении*. Munich 1993.

Dobrenko, Evgeny. *Political Economy of Socialist Realism*. New Haven, CT 2007.

Dobrenko, Evgeny. *Stalinist Cinema and the Production of History*. Edinburgh 2008.

Dubin, Boris. *Семантика, риторика и социальные функции 'прошлого': к социологии советского и постсоветского исторического романа*. Moscow 2003.

Dusinberre, Juliet. *Alice to the Lighthouse. Children's Books and Radical Experiments in Art*. Basingstoke, HA 1987.

Eisenstein, Sergei. *Избранные произведения в шести томах*. Moscow 1964.

Etkind, Alexander. *Warped Mourning: Stories of the Undead in the Land of the Unburied*. Stanford, CA 2013.

Fateev, Andrej. *Сталинизм и детская литература в политике номенклатуры СССР. 1930-1950-е гг*. Moscow 2007.

Fitzpatrick, Sheila. *Everyday Stalinism: Ordinary Life in Extraordinary Time: Soviet Russia in the 1930s*. New York and Oxford 1999.

Fitzpatrick, Sheila. *The Cultural Front: Power and Culture in Revolutionary Russia*. Ithaca, NY 1992.

Furniss, Maureen. *Art in Motion: Animation Aesthetics*. Sydney 2008.

Gibian, George, ed. *The Man with the Black Coat. Russia's Literature of the Absurd*. Evanston, IL 1987.

Ginzburg, Lydia. *The Blockade Diary*. London 1996.

Goscilo, Helena and Yana Hashamova, eds. *Cinepaternity: Fathers and Sons in Soviet and Post-Soviet Film*. Bloomington, IN 2010.

Gottschall, Jonathan and David Sloan Wilson, eds. *The Literary Animal: Evolution and the Nature of Narrative*. Evanston, IL 2005.

Gourianova, Nina. *The Aesthetics of Anarchy: Art and Ideology in the Early Russian Avant-Garde*. Berkeley, Los Angeles and London 2012.

Grinberg, Anna. "О новой детской книге и ее читателе," in *Народный учитель* 9, 1926, 96-99.

Groys, Boris. *Art Power*. Boston 2008.

Günther, Hans, ed. *The Culture of the Stalin Period*. London 1990.

Halberstam, Judith. *The Queer Art of Failure*. Durham, NC 2011.

Hellman, Ben. *Fairy Tales and True Stories: The History of Russian Literature for Children and Young Adults (1574-2010)*. Leiden and Boston 2013.

Beumers, Birgit, ed. *A Companion to Russian Cinema*. Malden, MA and Oxford.

Hunt, Peter. *Criticism, Theory and Children's Literature*. Cambridge, MA 1991.

Iljina, N. "Из истории детских журналов 20-30-х годов," in *Вопросы детской литературы*. Moscow 1958, 24-61.

Inggs, Judith A. "Censorship and Translated Literature in the Soviet Union: The Example of the Wizards Oz and Goodwin," in *Target. International Journal of Translation Studies* 23:1 (2011), 77-91.

Ioffe, Dennis and Frederick White, eds. *The Russian Avant-Garde and Radical Modernism*. Boston 2012.

Ivanov-Vano, Ivan. *Кадр за кадром*. Moscow 1980.

Jaccard, Jean-Phillipe. *Даниил Хармс и конец русского авангарда*. St. Petersburg 1995.

Janecek, Gerald. *The Look of Russian Literature: Avant-Garde Visual Experiments, 1900-1930*. Princeton, NJ 1984.

Janecek, Gerald. *ZAUM: The Transrational Poetry of Russian Futurism*. San Diego, CA 1996.

Jarov, Sergej. *Повседневная жизнь блокадного Ленинграда*. Moscow 2013.

Jasnov, Michail. *Путешествие в Чудетство. Книга о детях, детской поэзии и детских поэтах*. St. Petersburg 2015.

Jones, Polly. *Myth, Memory, Trauma: Rethinking the Stalinist Past in the Soviet Union, 1953-1970*. New Haven, CT 2013.

Joravsky, David. *Russian psychology: a critical history*. Oxford 1989.

Kachurin, Pamela. *Making Modernism Soviet: The Russian Avant-Garde in the Early Soviet Era, 1918-1928*. Evanston IL 2013.

Kaganovsky, Lilya. *How the Soviet Man was Unmade: Cultural Fantasy and Male Subjectivity under Stalin*. Pittsburgh, PA 2008.

Kaganovsky, Lilya, and Masha Salazkina, eds. *Sound, Speech, Music in Soviet and Post-Soviet Cinema*. Bloomington, IN 2014.

Karasik, Michail. *Ударная книга советской детворы*. Moscow 2010.

Kelly, Catriona. *Children's World: Growing Up in Russia, 1890-1991*. New Haven and London 2007.

Kelly, Catriona. *Comrade Pavlik: The Rise and Fall of a Soviet Boy Hero*. London 2005.

Kenez, Peter. *Cinema and Soviet Society, 1917-1953*. Cambridge, UK 1992.

Kind-Kovács, Friederike. *Samizdat, Tamizdat, and Beyond: Transnational Media During and After Socialism*. New York 2013.

Kirschenbaum, Lisa. *Small Comrades: Revolutionizing Childhood in Soviet Russia, 1917-1931*. New York 2001.

Kobrinskij, Aleksandr. *Даниил Хармс*. Moscow 2009.

Kobrinskij, Aleksandr. *Поэтика ОБЭРИУ в контексте русского литературного авангарда*. Moscow 2000.

Kondakov, Igor. "'Убежище-2': 'Детский дискурс' советской литературы в 1930-е годы," in *Ребенок в истории и культуре*, Библиотека журнала Исследователь / Researcher, Vol. 4. Moscow 2010, 70-117.

Kostjuchina, M. S. *Золотое зеркало. Русская литература для детей XVIII-XIX веков*. Moscow 2008.

Kucherenko, Olga. *Little Soldiers: How Soviet Children Went to War, 1941–1945*. Oxford 2011.

Kukulin, Ilja, Marija Majofis, and Petr Safronov, eds. *Острова утопии. Педагогическое и социальное проектирование послевоенной школы (1940-1980-е)*. Moscow 2015.

Kukulin, Ilja, Mark Lipoveckij, and Marija Majofis, eds., *Веселые человечки: культурные герои советского детства*. Moscow 2008.

Kuleshov, Lev and Alexandra Chochlova. *50 лет в кино*. Moscow 1975.

Lancy, David F. *The Anthropology of Childhood: Cherubs, Chattel, Changelings*. Cambridge, UK 2008.

Lathey, Gillian. "Introduction," in Gillian Lathey, ed. *The Translation of Children's Literature. A Reader*. Clevedon 2006, 3-14.

Leslie, Esther. *Hollywood Flatlands: Animation, Critical Theory and the Avant-Garde*. London 2002.

Leyda, Jay. *Kino: A History of Russian and Soviet Film*. Princeton, NJ 1983.

Liehm, Mira and Antonin J. Liehm. *The Most Important Art: Soviet and East European Film after 1945*. Berkeley, CA 1977.

Loseff, Lev. *On the Beneficience of Censorship. Aesopian Language in Modern Russian Literature*. München 1984.

Lukjanova, Irina. *Корней Чуковский*. Moscow 1997.

MacFadyen, David. *Yellow Crocodiles and Blue Oranges: Russian Animated Film Since World War Two*. Montreal 2005.

Margolit, Evgenij. *Живые и мертвое: заметки к истории советского кино 1920х-1960х годов*. St. Petersburg 2012.

Marinelli-König, Gertraud. *Russische Kinderliteratur in der Sowjetunion der Jahre 1900-1930*. Munich 2007.

Marsh, Rosalind J. *Literature, History, and Identity in Post-Soviet Russia, 1991-2006*. Oxford, Bern, New York 2007.

Marshak, Samuil. *Вслух про себя. Воспоминания*. Moscow 1975.

Miller, Frank J. *Folklore for Stalin: Russian Folklore and Pseudofolklore of the Stalin Era*. Armonk, NY 1990.

Miloserdova, Natalja. "Детское кино," in L. Budjak and D. Karavaev, eds., *Страницы истории отечественного кино*. Moscow 2006, 6-133.

Nadtochij, Eduard. "Тимур и его arcana: социально-антропологическое значение советской 'революции детства' в 1920-30-е годы," in *Социология власти* 3 (2014), 81-98.

Neumann, Matthias. *The Communist Youth League and the Transformation of the Soviet Union, 1917-1932*. London and New York 2011.

Nikolajeva, Maria. *Children's Literature Comes of Age. Toward a New Aesthetic*. New York and London 1996.

Noordenbos, Boris. *Post-Soviet Literature and the Search for a Russian Identity*. New York 2016.

O'Dell, Felicity Ann. *Socialization through Children's Literature: The Soviet Example*. Cambridge 1978.

O'Sullivan, Emer. *Comparative Children's Literature*. New York 2005.

Oktjabrskaja, O. S. *Пути развития детской литературы XX века (1920-2000-е гг.)*. Moscow 2012.

Ostashevsky, Eugene, ed. OBERIU: *An Anthology of Russian Absurdism*. Evanston, IL 2006.

Olich, Jacqueline. *Competing Ideologies and Children's Literature in Russia, 1918-1935*. Saarbruecken 2009.

Petrovskij, Miron. *Книги нашего детства*, St. Petersburg 2006.

Platt, Kevin and David Brandenburger. *Epic Revisionism: Russian History and Literature as Stalinist Propaganda*. Madison, WI 2006.

Pontieri, Laura, *Soviet Animation and the Thaw of the 1960s. Not Only for Children*. New Barnet, Herts, UK 2012.

Prokhorov, Alexander. "Arresting Development: A Brief History of Soviet Cinema for Children and Adolescents," in Marina Balina and Larissa Rudova, eds., *Russian Children's Literature and Culture*. New York and London 2008, 129-152.

Prokhorov, Alexander and Elena. *Film and Television Genres of the Late Soviet Era*. New York 2017.

Putilova, Evgenija. *Детское чтение для сердца и разума. Очерки по истории детской литературы*. St. Petersburg 2005.

Putilova, Evgenija. *Очерки по истории критики советской детской литературы, 1917-1941*. Moscow 1982.

Roberts, Graham. *The Last Soviet Avant-garde:* OBERIU – *Fact, Fiction, Metafiction*. Cambridge and New York 1997.

Rowell, Margaret and Deborah Wye, eds. *The Russian Avant-Garde Book*. New York 2002.

Salem, Linda C. *Children's Literature Studies: Cases and Discussions*. Westport, CT and London 2006.

Salova, Julija. *Политическое воспитание детей в Советской России в 1920-е годы*. Jaroslavl 2001.

Sazhin, Valerij, ed. *"Сборище друзей, оставленных субдьбою": А. Введенский, Л. Липавский, Д. Хармс, Н. Олейников: 'Чинари' в текстах, документах и исследованиях: в двух томах*. Moscow 1998.

Schwab, Gabriele. *Haunting Legacies: Violent Histories and Transgenerational Trauma*. New York 2010.

Seton, Marie. *Sergei M. Eisenstein: A Biography*. New York 1952.

Shavit, Zohar. *Poetics of Children's Literature*. Athens, GA 1986.

Sherry, Samantha. *Discourses of Regulation and Resistance. Censoring Translation in the Stalin and Khruschev Era Soviet Union*. Edinburgh 2015.

Shklovsky, Victor. "Art as Technique," in Lee T. Lemon and Marion J. Reis, trans., eds., *Russian Formalist Criticism: Four Essays*. Lincoln, NE 1965, 5-24.

Shklovsky, Viktor. *Knight's Move*, trans. Richard Sheldon. Normal, IL 2005.

Shklovsky, Viktor. "The Film Language of *New Babylon*," in Ian Christie and Richard Taylor, eds., *The Film Factory: Russian and Soviet Cinema in Documents 1896-1939*. New York 1994, 311-313.

Shrayer, Maxim. *Генрих Сапгир: классик авангарда*. St. Petersburg 2009.

Shubinskij, Valerij. *Даниил Хармс. Жизнь человека на ветру*. St. Petersburg 2008 and Moscow 2015.

Sokol, Elena. *Russian Poetry for Children*. Knoxville, TN 1984.

Steiner, Eugene. *Stories for Little Comrades: Revolutionary Artists in the Early Soviet Children's Book*. Seattle 1999.

Stites, Richard. *Russian Popular Culture: Entertainment and Society since 1900*. New York 1992.

Taylor, Richard and Ian Christie, eds. *The Film Factory: Russian and Soviet Cinema in Documents, 1896-1939*. New York 1994.

Todes, Daniel Philip. *Ivan Pavlov: A Russian Life in Science*. Oxford 2004.

Valsiner, Jaan. *Developmental psychology in the Soviet Union*. Bloomington, IN 1988.

von Glasenapp, Gabriele. "'Was ist Historie? Mit Historie will man was': Geschichtsdarstellungen in der neuren Kinder-und Jugendliteratur," in Gabriele von Glasenapp and Gisela Wilkending, eds., *Geschichte und Geschichten: die Kinder-und Jugendliteratur und das Kulturelle und politische Gedächtnis*. Frankfurt am Main 2005, 15-40.

Vvedenskij, Aleksandr. *An Invitation for Me to Think*, ed. and trans. Eugene Ostashevsky and Matvei Yankelevich. New York 2013.

Vvedenskij, Aleksandr. *Собрание сочинений в двух томах*, Vladimir Erl and Michail Mejlach, eds. Moscow 1993.

Weld, Sara Pankenier. *Voiceless Vanguard: The Infantilist Aesthetic of the Russian Avant-Garde*. Evanston, IL 2014.

Zabolockij, Nikita. *The Life of Zabolockij*, ed. R.R. Milner-Gulland, trans. R.R. Milner-Gulland and C.G. Bearne. Cardiff 1994.

Zipes, Jack. *Breaking the Magic Spell. Radical Theories of Folk and Fairy Tales*. Lexington, KY 2002.

Zipes, Jack, Pauline Greenhill, and Kendra Magnus-Johnston, eds. *Fairy Tales Films Beyond Disney. International Perspectives*. New York and London 2016.

Index

Absurdism   32, 110, 127, 131, 132, 157, 160, 163, 167n, 169, 347, 367, 424
Achmatova, Anna   356, 426
Adaptation   7, 15, 21, 51, 62-63, 66, 67, 77, 91, 123n, 164, 165, 166, 190, 198, 341, 343, 350, 353, 371n, 373, 384, 402, 408, 417, 422-23, 434, 445n, 447n, 454, 464
Aesopian language   50, 52-55, 63-66, 122, 193, 361, 390
Aesthetics
   Avant-Garde (see also Avant-Garde, aesthetics)   59, 60-63, 64, 99-101, 102, 105, 106, 111, 113, 114, 115, 116, 117, 122, 124, 128, 129, 131, 133, 134, 135, 199, 391, 399-400, 408, 436
   Socialist Realist   14, 22, 29n, 63, 165, 181, 182, 183, 287, 288, 303, 307, 312, 314, 315, 319, 322-323, 326, 327, 329, 331, 333, 401, 402, 403, 413, 418, 421, 423, 429, 436
Akimov, Nikolaj   426
Aleksandr I   187
Aleksandrov, Grigorij   417, 427, 429
Aleksin, Anatolij   25, 244
Alexievich, Svetlana   34
Altaev, Al. (Margarita Jamshchikova)   186, 188, 204
Ancient history   186-187, 189, 190, 197-204, 205, 206, 207
Andreevskaja, V. P.   219
Animation
   cel   390, 399, 401, 406, 409, 413
   character's personality   375, 376, 390, 398, 400-401, 407, 408, 412, 440, 442, 443, 444, 445, 448, 449, 450, 451, 459, 460, 461, 464
   children as audience   4, 34, 36, 390, 391, 392, 394-395, 396, 398, 399, 402, 413, 443, 447, 453, 456-458
   color principle   392, 401, 408, 410, 423, 449, 454n
   early experiments   391, 392-393, 400, 408, 419, 423
   fairytale (see also, Fairytale, animation)   389, 390, 392, 393, 394, 405

   film-makers' education (see also Film schools)   391, 396, 428, 431
   musical songs   375, 383, 384, 400, 405, 406
   satire   390n, 411, 412, 464n
   Soviet censorship   390, 394, 413, 418n, 421, 444, 455
   Soviet competition with the West   395, 400, 401, 403-4, 405, 406, 407, 408, 410-11, 412
   Soviet history   375-376, 389-416, 441, 442-445, 446-448
   synchronization   390, 401, 406, 409
Annenkov, Jurij   426
Annenskaja, Aleksandra   184, 216
Anthropomorphism   381, 441n, 443, 451, 461n
Anti-illiteracy Campaign   212
Anti-oedipal   453, 454, 455, 457
Anti-semitism   363n, 426-427, 466, 469
Antokol'skij, Pavel   284, 357
Antonovskij, Boris   151, 154
Anxiety   36, 441, 455, 465, 467, 468, 469, 470
Arsenjev, Pavel   25
Arzamasceva, Irina   31, 197, 217
Asanova, Dinara   9
Aseev, Nikolaj   58
Assonance   155
Atamanov, Lev   402, 408n
Auslender, Sergej   27, 182
Avant-Garde
   aesthetics (see Aesthetics, Avant-Garde)   59, 60-63, 64, 99-101, 102, 105, 106, 111, 113, 114, 115, 116, 117, 122, 124, 128, 129, 131, 133, 134, 135, 199, 391, 399-400, 408, 436
   picturebooks (see also Picturebooks, Soviet)   49-50, 59, 60-62, 63, 65, 67
   Russian history   14n, 22, 29, 34, 36-37, 38, 61-62, 63, 74, 77-78, 81, 84, 99-135, 139-171, 199, 223n, 344, 376, 390-393, 400-401, 426, 428, 436
   Russian poetry   37, 99-135, 139-171, 376
Avunculate   455, 459-465

Bachterev, Igor' 140n, 144n, 145, 147n, 163, 164n
Balina, Marina 26, 29, 31, 32, 36, 179-211, 297, 342, 343, 383, 394, 423
Barskaja, Margarita 4, 29, 421n
Barskova, Polina 39, 303-338
Bechterev, Vladimir 85, 86
Belinskij, Vissarion 223
Belych, Grigorij 9, 29, 217, 227n, 313n
Belyj, Andrej 105, 106
Benjamin, Walter 84
Benois, Alexander (see also Benua, Aleksandr) 59, 118
Benua, Aleksandr (see also Benois, Alexander) 59, 118
Beresnev, Nikolaj 16
Berggolc, Ol'ga 162, 163, 164n, 170, 284, 307, 308-309
Berlin, Isaiah 130
Bernard, Claude 81
Bernays, Jakob 86
Beumers, Birgit 32, 402n, 408, 423
Bezrukov, Sergej 456
Bianki, Vitalij 29, 58
Bird, Robert 33n
Bljum, Arlen 192
Blonskij, Pavel 73
Bobinskaja, Elena 238
Bocharov, Anatolij 304n, 305-306
Bocharov, Eduard 290n, 305
Bogdanov, Nikolaj 215, 238
Bogdanova, Nadja 291, 296
Bogdanovich, Tatjana 188, 190
Bogorodskij, Fedor 396
Borisenko, Aleksandra 372
Boronina, Ekaterina 295, 296, 310n, 314-315, 316, 323
Boyd, Brian 51
Boym, Svetlana 418, 419, 425
Bremener, Maks 242
Brezhnev era
  animation (see also Animation, Soviet history) 441, 445, 446, 453, 456, 460n, 464
  nostalgia (see also, Nostalgia, Soviet) 8-9
  stagnation (see also Stagnation era) 8, 135, 440, 443, 447, 464, 470

Brezhnev, Leonid 8
Bromlej, Natalija 203, 205
Brumberg, Valentina and Zinaida 402, 408n, 411, 412, 443n
Bucharin, Nikolaj 75, 80, 260, 261
Bucharova, Darja 12, 13
Budashevskaya, Olga 15n, 33n, 101n, 139n
Budogoskaja, Lidija 215, 232, 233
Bulgakowa, Oksana 458n
Bulychev, Kir 25
Burljuk, David 100, 115
Busch, Wilhelm 2, 151n, 167, 350, 358, 359, 361, 362, 363, 364, 365
Bychkov, Vladimir 32
Bykov, E. 239
Bykov, Rolan 9, 25
Bykov, Vasil' 297, 298

Campaign for the Unified Reading List 11-12
Carroll, Joseph 51
Cartwright, Lisa 81
Catharsis 86, 94, 236
Catherine II (see also Jekaterina II) 56
Cechanovskij, Michail 63, 391n, 392, 400, 402, 408n
Censorship
  self-censoring 52, 54, 67, 68n, 192, 306, 333-334, 358-359, 361
  Soviet picturebooks 30, 37, 49, 50-55, 57, 62-65, 66, 67, 68, 192
  Soviet state policy 57, 127, 221, 285, 305, 327n, 342-343, 344n, 357, 376, 383, 413, 418n, 421, 436, 444
Chardzhiev, Nikolaj 127n, 128-129
Charitonova-Ostrovskaja, Raisa 220
Charms, Daniil (see also Kharms, Daniil)
  arrests and political persecution 29, 38, 64, 102n, 131, 143-145, 146n, 157-158, 160, 162-163, 164, 169, 170, 308, 358
  as author of short stories 103, 132,
  as children's poet 64, 122, 124, 126, 128, 131-132, 133, 146, 148n, 151, 155-156, 158, 160, 167, 168, 169, 171, 359, 363-364, 369
  as contributor to Чиж and Ёж 37, 140, 141n, 143, 145, 146-147, 149n, 151, 154, 155, 158, 160, 164, 165, 167-169, 171, 359
  as member of OBERIU 126, 127n, 128, 140, 143, 147, 148, 162-163, 164, 170, 308, 357

as translator   2, 32, 127, 343, 358-367, 369, 376
"mimetic camouflage"   64, 149, 160, 357-358
verbal inventiveness   106, 148n, 158n, 357, 360, 362, 363-364
Charskaja, Lidija   216, 252n, 310
Cheburashka   15, 21n, 35, 36, 440, 442n, 443, 459, 460-464
Chechov, Nikolaj   223n, 265
Childhood
    Russian, history   194, 195-196, 216, 253-254
    Soviet, history   15, 18, 30, 33-34, 35, 39, 58n, 180n, 216, 227, 275, 283, 303-304, 316, 332
Childlike aesthetic   99, 100, 105-106, 108, 111, 112-116, 122, 128, 129, 132, 133, 134, 199
Children's art
    archaic prototypes   87-88, 90, 93
    book illustrations and animation   105-106, 111, 159n, 412, 449
    drawings   87-90, 93, 105, 111, 159n, 412, 449
Children's film
    about pioneer heroes   15, 16, 91-94, 95, 290n
    after World War II   395, 396, 403-404, 407-412, 417-439, 440-464
    as party propaganda   5, 16, 22, 74, 78, 80-84, 91, 94, 239n, 290n, 400, 402, 403, 408, 420-421, 423
    audience, testing   73-74, 399
    criticism   11, 12, 14, 21n, 25, 28-40, 73, 75, 389-390, 394, 396-399, 402-403, 404-407, 409, 410, 417, 423, 428, 435, 456, 458n
Children's literature
    "education of the senses"   24, 26
    "theory of conflictlessness"   21
    as "loophole" or "refuge"   29, 30, 127n, 357
    contemporary publishing (see also, Children's publishing, contemporary)   5, 7, 8, 10, 11n, 12, 28
    criticism   11, 12, 14, 17-18, 19, 20, 21, 24, 25-27, 28-40, 51, 68n, 101, 115-116, 118-119, 120, 133, 140n, 145n, 146, 148n, 149n, 150n, 152, 156, 157-158, 160, 161, 162-163,

168, 170, 182, 188-190, 193, 196n, 197-198, 215, 221, 242, 243, 253, 265, 269, 284-285, 287-288, 293, 296-298, 305-306, 308, 345-346, 348, 349, 357
    editors   4n, 8, 10n, 21, 29, 33, 50n, 59-60, 68n, 102n, 147, 150-151, 169, 189, 191, 199, 220, 278, 298, 333, 345, 348-349, 356, 359
    gender politics   26, 185, 326, 330, 375n
    humor   37, 110n, 118, 120, 122, 124, 131, 146, 148, 158, 346, 348, 350, 358, 359, 364, 365, 373, 407, 409, 411, 446
    national value   4-6, 9-10, 12, 13, 14, 19, 28, 30-31, 40, 193, 250, 253, 265-266, 292-293, 305-306, 402, 403-404, 411, 422
    Post-Soviet   5n, 8-9, 10, 40, 296-297
    Post-Soviet popularity of Soviet canon   3n, 9-14, 40
    role models   20, 194, 220, 253, 286, 295, 313, 323, 330, 334
    World War II   18, 19, 20, 134, 144n, 192, 193, 195, 199, 204, 243, 244, 256, 270, 272, 282, 286, 287, 288-292, 293, 294, 296-298, 303-335, 356, 389, 421n, 426, 436, 446, 465
Children's periodicals
    The Campfire (Костер)   141n, 224n, 310, 311, 312, 313n, 314, 322n, 327, 328, 329
    The Drum (Барабан)   144n, 215n, 231, 232n, 238n, 261n, 267n
    The Finch (Чиж)   37, 102n, 126, 132, 139, 140, 141, 143, 144, 145, 147, 148, 149, 151, 154, 155, 156, 157, 158, 159, 161, 162, 163n, 164, 165, 166, 167n, 168, 169, 170, 171, 308n, 357, 358, 366
    The Hedgehog (Еж)   37, 102n, 126n, 134n, 139, 142, 143, 146, 148, 149, 150, 151, 152, 153, 154, 155n, 156n, 158n, 159n, 162, 163n, 164, 165n, 166n, 167n, 168n, 170n, 308n, 357-358
    Murzilka (Мурзилка)   10n, 35n
    The New Robinzon (Новый Робинзон)   4, 126, 140, 144n, 147
    The Pioneer Truth (Пионерская правда)   272, 274, 278
    The Sparrow (Воробей)   4, 140, 144n
Children's publishing

Children's publishing (cont.)
  "Marshak's Academy" (see also, Marshak, Samuil)   4, 29, 58, 126-127, 131, 134, 147-149, 191, 199, 205
  Children's Literature Studio   4
  contemporary (see also, Children's literature, contemporary publishing)   5, 7, 8, 10, 11n, 12, 28
  Detgiz   4, 5, 29, 67, 102n, 126, 127n, 134, 140, 143, 145, 146, 147, 148, 149n, 162, 164, 168, 169, 170, 199, 205, 292n, 344, 358, 359
  Detizdat   126, 189, 190, 191, 205
  Raduga   22, 126, 343
Children's speech
  in poetry   113, 114, 125, 346, 374
  research   80, 87, 88, 90
Chitruk, Fedor   36, 371, 374, 375, 376, 440, 442, 446-453, 464
Chlebnikov, Velimir   99n, 100, 102, 104, 105, 106, 107, 109, 112, 113, 114, 115, 124, 125, 131
Chodataev, Nikolaj   391, 401
Christopher Robin   372, 442, 446, 447, 448, 449
Chrushchev, Nikita   8, 201, 412
Chudakova, Marietta   22n, 26, 27, 29, 181, 182, 196
Chukovskaja, Lidija   29n, 131n, 148, 191, 224
Chukovskij, Kornej   1-2, 3, 16, 22, 29, 31, 40, 59, 60, 101, 102n, 103, 106n, 108, 112, 115, 117, 118, 119n, 123n, 124, 125, 126, 147n, 162, 221, 222n, 224, 285n, 343, 344, 345-351, 354, 355, 357, 367, 372, 384, 392, 398, 420
  The Big Cockroach (*Тараканище*, 1923)   7n, 420n
  Crocodile, also *Vanja and Crocodile* (*Крокодил*, 1917)   1, 3, 31, 40, 126n, 221, 392
  Fly-a-Buzz-Buzz (*Муха-Цокотуха*, 1924)   420n
  The Stolen Sun (*Краденое солнце*, 1927)   2, 395
  Sunny Place (*Солнечная*, 1933)   221, 222
  Wash 'em Clean (*Мойдодыр*, 1923)   395, 398, 420n
Chukovskij, Nikolaj   147n, 433
Cinderella, fairy-tale   417

Cinderella, film (*Золушка*, 1947)   32, 38, 417-439
Civil War, Russian   18, 139, 150, 165, 166, 180, 192n, 221, 223, 226, 252, 260, 263, 271, 282, 288, 294, 334, 421n
Clark, Katerina   275, 322, 324, 421, 426n, 430n, 335n
Class consciousness   11, 92, 141, 163, 217, 223, 227, 323, 420, 423, 435n, 240, 267
Class struggle   2, 15, 18, 23, 161n, 162, 163, 180, 187, 188, 190, 191, 199, 200, 201, 220, 224, 258, 264, 267, 271, 333, 356
Cold War   XII, 22, 38, 270, 403
Comic books   33, 151, 406, 411
Communar movement   24, 294
Copjec, Joan   467
Cultural Revolution, Soviet (1928-1932)   144, 161-162, 165, 170, 215
Cvetaeva, Marina   XIII, 122, 123

Danelija, Georgij   444n
Danko, Elena   190
Daudet, Alphonse   142n
Decembrists' Revolt   187, 188, 189
deGraffenried, Julie K.   33
Deni, Viktor   391
Dernova-Jarmolenko, Avgusta   85, 86
Detskie chtenija, journal   XI, 3n, 35, 63n, 263n, 285n
Developed Socialism   461, 464
Disney, Walt   38, 375, 389, 390, 395, 400, 401, 404-407, 408, 409, 410, 411, 412, 413, 447n
Dobrenko, Evgeny   X, 22, 31, 181, 217, 241, 257
Dobrogaev, Sergej   90
Dolzhenko, Ljudmila   25
Donkey Ia   440, 451, 452
Dorochov, Pavel   262
Dorofeev, Nikolaj   238
Double address   348, 355, 357
Double encoding   424, 433, 441
Double estrangement (see also Estrangement)   38, 377, 419
Dovlatov, Sergej   27
Dragunskij, Viktor   25, 321, 424, 445n
Driz, Ovsej   29, 377, 378, 379, 381, 382
Druzhinin, Vladimir   321
Dubin, Boris   180

INDEX

Dubinin, Volodja 250, 287n, 289, 297
Dunham, Vera 431n
Durnovo, Aleksandr 76
Durnovo, Marina (see also Malich, Marina) 151n
Dusinberre, Juliet 55

Egorov, Pavel 256
Ehrenburg, Ilja 100, 121, 285n
Eisenstein, Sergei (see also Ejzenshtein, Sergei) XIV, 36, 74, 84-95, 405, 428
Ejsymont, Viktor 20
Ejzenshtein, Sergej (see also Eisenstein, Sergei) XIV, 36, 74, 84-95, 405, 428
Enlightenment
  European 218
  oppositionist 181, 206
  Soviet 61, 205, 215, 216
Erlich, Vol'f 221
Erofeev, Venidikt 27, 376
Ershov, Petr 360, 389n, 407, 408, 410, 412
Estrangement (see also Double estrangement) 7, 38, 315, 377, 418, 419, 424, 425, 428, 434, 435
Etkind, Aleksandr 465n, 470n
Etkind, Efim 344, 350, 353
Evolution 37, 49, 50-55, 59, 60, 61, 62, 63, 65, 66, 68, 93
Ezerskij, Milij 192n, 198, 205

Fadeev, Aleksandr 12, 291n, 317
Fairytale
  animation 38, 389, 390, 392-395, 398, 399, 402-405, 407, 408, 413
  campaign against 103, 119, 394, 399, 402, 419-420, 424
  interpretation 106, 108, 111, 119n, 129, 185, 200, 349, 402
  Soviet appropriation 21-22, 23, 32, 61, 65-66, 146n, 270, 275, 402, 419, 421, 422-423, 425
  translation 165, 166, 345, 348, 392, 407, 408
Family
  children "reform" parents 212, 215, 235, 236, 238, 245

children renounce parents 227, 229, 238-240, 245, 256, 272-274, 296, 453, 458, 469
  traditional values 216, 219, 237-239, 360
Fantasy
  ideological value 21-22, 119n, 270, 287
  in animation 390, 392, 394, 397, 399, 402, 410, 413, 448
  in children's poetry 99, 346
  in Soviet film 422, 444
Fateev, Andrej 19, 29, 31, 180n, 292n, 296
Fatherhood
  child-state relationship 17, 91, 215, 227n, 229, 237, 240, 241n, 262, 361, 446, 453
  models of 36, 441, 444-446, 448, 455, 458, 460, 466, 468-470
Festivals
  American Animation 405
  American Color Film (Leningrad) 406
Figes, Orlando 33, 216, 240n
Film schools
  Factory of the Eccentric Actor (FEKS) 428, 431
  Higher State Art and Technical Studios (ВХУТЕМАС) 391
  Soviet State Film School (ВГИК) 396
  State Technical School of Cinematography (ГТК) 391
Film studios
  Lenfil'm 417, 426n, 427n, 428n, 432
  Mezhrabpromfil'm 77, 395, 400
  Mosfil'm 400
  Sojuzdetfil'm 4, 400, 420
  Sojuzmul'tfil'm 9, 32, 399, 400, 401, 409, 413, 420-421, 442, 443, 444, 447, 452, 456, 457, 458n, 463, 464
  Sovkino 395, 400
  Walt Disney Studio 390, 395, 400, 401, 409, 413
Finogenov, Anatolij 159n, 215, 229, 230, 231
Firebird 409, 410
Fishzon, Anna XI, 35-36, 375n, 440-473
Fitzpatrick, Sheila 144, 161, 163, 215n, 269n
Five-Year Plan 141, 144, 165, 170
Folklore
  children's 148
  Jewish 377, 382
  national 356

Folklore (cont.)
  Russian   32, 101, 105n, 389, 394, 405, 407, 410, 420, 422
  Western   23, 420
Fraerman, Ruvim   283, 293
Franck, R.   68
Freken Bok   440, 445, 454, 455, 458n, 465n
Freud, Sigmund   68n, 73, 86, 441n, 455, 461, 467, 468
Frez, Ilja   7, 9, 15, 25
Frierson, Cathy A.   34
Furman, Petr   185
Fursikov, Dmitrij   78
Futurism   14n, 34, 99, 101, 105, 106, 108, 109, 111, 112, 115, 119, 123, 124, 126, 128, 129

Gajdar, Arkadij   7n, 12, 13, 19, 21, 26, 27, 28, 29, 217, 220, 240, 241, 242, 259, 263, 265n, 269, 283, 285n, 286, 287, 295, 296, 311, 312, 321, 324, 421n, 443
  Chuk and Gek (*Чук и Гек*, 1939)   7n, 241n
  The Hot Stone (*Горячий камень*, 1941)   242, 443
  Military Secret (*Военная тайна*, 1935)   7n, 240-242, 265n, 295, 312n, 324
  School (*Школа*, 1930)   26-28, 263, 287
  The R[evolutionary]. M[ilitary]. C[ouncil]. (*P. B. C.*, 1925)   220-221, 263
  Timur and His Team (*Тимур и его команда*, 1940)   7n, 12, 19, 286, 295-296, 312, 321, 421n
Garbuzov, Solomon   283
Garin-Michajlovskij, Nikolaj   216
Garin, Erast   426, 431, 432
Gel'mont, Abram   73n, 74
Gena, the Crocodile   15, 21, 36, 440, 441, 442n, 443, 445, 453, 459, 460, 461, 462, 463, 464, 465n, 470
Genette, Gerard   203
German, Aleksandr   226n
German, Jurij   304, 315, 316, 319, 325
Geschichte   186, 190, 191, 193, 194, 196, 200, 201, 203, 204, 205, 206
Ginzberg, Semen   409
Ginzburg, Lidija (Lydia)   188, 307
Glebova, Tatjana   126n, 139, 140, 143n
Glinka, S. N.   184
Gnezdilov, Pavlik   273, 274, 277, 278

Golikov, Lenja   250, 256, 263, 289, 290, 295, 296, 297
Goljavkin, Viktor   25, 445n
Golubov, Sergej   195, 196
Goncharova, Natalija   100, 102, 119
Gordin, Jakov   179, 180, 181, 206
Gor'kij, Maksim   XIV, 3, 101, 103, 117, 118, 119, 394, 420
Gornyj, Viktor   391
Goscilo, Helena   32, 445n
Gourianova, Nina   14n
Granik, Anatolij   20
Granin, Daniil   331, 333, 334
Great Terror (see also Stalinism, violence)   2, 5, 10, 22, 37, 134, 168, 192, 334, 361-362, 402, 403, 445
Grigorjev, Oleg   134n, 135
Grigorjev, Sergej   188, 192n, 193, 194, 204
Grigulis, Arvid   271n
Grimm Brothers   166, 167n
Grinberg, Anna   205n, 265n
Grjaznov, Innokentij   215, 224, 225
Gromova, Olga   5n
Groys, Boris   18
Gubarev, Vitalij   20, 244, 294n
Gulag   12n, 34, 182n, 240, 469
Gumilev, Nikolaj   65
Gunin, Dmitrij   252n
Günther, Hans   181, 250n, 266
Guro, Elena   100, 106, 107, 108, 115, 116n
Gusev, Andrej   251n

Halberstam, J. Jack (Halberstam, Judith)   441n, 459n
Hellman, Ben   31, 56n, 57, 58, 99n, 102n, 119n, 126n, 350, 356, 420n
Hero narratives (see also, Pioneer heroes)   38, 91, 240n, 251, 252, 253-258, 259-266, 267-282, 283, 284-288, 291, 292, 293, 294, 295, 312, 314
Heroism, children's   253-258, 259-256, 267-271, 284-285
Hicks, Jeremy   32
Historical writing for children
  historical everyday tale   183, 186, 188-189, 193, 199, 200
  historical prose   36, 179, 180, 183, 184, 186, 187, 188, 189, 191, 193, 195, 200, 204, 205

INDEX

historical-biographical tale   183, 185, 186, 187, 188, 191, 192n, 193, 195, 196, 205
historical-revolutionary tale   183, 187, 188, 190, 192, 198, 202-203
Historie   186, 190, 191, 193, 194, 196, 200, 201, 202, 203, 204, 205, 206

Identity
  gender   330, 375n, 429, 440, 444, 451, 455-456, 459, 461, 464, 465, 470
  Post-Soviet   5, 9-10, 35-36, 250, 296-297, 446
  Soviet   10, 13, 14-28, 30, 33-34, 370, 404, 422, 431n
Ideogram   87, 88n, 89, 91
Ideological Committee of the Communist Party   410
Ideology
  Post-Soviet   7, 10, 11, 12-13, 14, 35
  Soviet   4, 10, 13, 17-19, 23-24, 26-27, 28-29, 30, 34, 37, 39, 50, 56, 57, 58, 59, 61-63, 66-67, 72-73, 75, 77, 91, 94, 95, 101-102, 119, 141, 148-149, 154, 157, 158, 162, 165, 166, 167, 169-170, 180, 181, 188, 190n, 192, 194, 195, 199, 200-201, 205, 206, 216, 220n, 222, 223, 232, 236, 237, 240, 244, 252, 257, 258, 260, 262, 266n, 267, 272, 275, 277, 281, 285, 286, 290, 291, 298, 303, 304, 306, 307, 310, 311, 313, 315, 323, 327, 331, 334, 335, 343-344, 349-350, 351, 356, 357, 358, 362, 370, 376, 378, 383, 389, 390, 394-395, 396, 399, 402, 403, 408, 411, 412, 417-418, 419, 421, 422, 423, 426, 435, 436, 441, 460, 464
Iljicheva, L. V.   361, 365n
Iljin, Michail   58
Iljina, Elena   19, 243
Inber, Vera   307, 426
Inggs, Judith A.   67n, 342n
Intelligentsia, Soviet   84, 125, 161, 162, 197, 201, 202, 356n, 431n, 445, 447, 454, 458, 464
Intertextuality   193, 195, 447
Irkutov, Andrej   215, 226n, 232, 238
Ishimova, Aleksandra   184, 185
Ivanov-Vano, Ivan   2, 38, 389-413
Ivich, Aleksandr   29, 282n, 287n, 296n

Jakovlev, Jurij   270, 294, 318n, 326-27, 335
Jakovlev, Kolja   274, 279, 280
Jakovleva, Julija   5n, 13n
Jan (Janchivetskij), Vasilij   197-198
Janecek, Gerald   100n, 105n, 109n, 112n, 120n
Jasnov, Michail   99, 342, 344, 383
Jekaterina II (see also Catherine II)   56n
Judin, Lev   140, 143
Judin, Pavel   285n
Jurezanskij, Vladimir   226
Jurjev, V.   192, 195

Kachanov, Roman   15, 21n, 36, 440, 445, 459n, 463
Kaganovsky, Lilya   441-442n, 458n
Karamzin, Nikolaj   184
Karaseva, Vera   321, 323, 330
Karlson (Karlsson)   440, 441, 442, 443, 445, 453-459, 460, 461, 464, 465, 470
Karpenko, Galina   244
Kassil', Lev   7, 16, 29, 241n, 244, 287n, 289, 295, 296, 297, 311
Kataev, Valentin   196n, 243, 282n, 287-288, 292, 296, 311, 312n, 313
Katsnelson, Anna Wexler   429
Kaverin, Venjamin   15, 19, 21, 240n, 312n
Kazej, Marat   289, 290n, 315n
Kelly, Catriona   18, 19, 33, 35, 58n, 94n, 105n, 180n, 239, 250, 253n, 272n, 275n, 286, 295, 342n, 399
Kepler, A.   292
Kharms, Daniil (see Charms, Daniil)   32n
Khotimsky, Maria   XI-XII, 127n, 134n, 167n, 341-388
Kid (*Kid and Karlsson*; see also Lillebror)   440, 442, 453, 454, 455, 456, 458, 460n
Kidd, Kenneth B.   446n, 448
King, Homay   91
Kipling, Rudjard   60-61, 124n, 345, 349, 351-352, 354, 384
Kirov, Sergej   154-155, 164n, 165-166, 279
Kirschenbaum, Lisa   33-34, 58n, 342n
Kiselev, Fedor   264
Klein Tumanov, Larissa   361
Klejman, Naum   91n, 92n, 93
Klimenkov, Igor'   432
Klimov, Elem   29
Kljuchkin, Konstantin   442n

Klucis, Gustav   391
Kobrinskij, Aleksandr   112n, 127n, 143n, 146n, 162, 163n, 164, 169, 361, 363n
Kochetkova, E.   266n
Kole, Luiza   254n
Komissarenko, Zenon   391
Komsomol Organisation   161, 187, 221, 243, 256, 260, 263, 266, 278, 285, 289, 322, 324, 329
Kon, Lidija   14
Kondakov, Igor'   29, 216
Konsovskij, Aleksej   426, 430, 431
Korenkov, Vasilij   268
Korjakov, Oleg   244
Kormchij, Leonard   57, 260
Kornejchik, T. D.   21
Korshunov, Michail   244
Kosheverova, Nadezhda   9, 32, 38, 417, 418, 425, 426, 427, 428, 436
Koslovskij, Sergej   396
Kosmodemjanskaja, Zoja   250
Kostjuchina, M. S.   216n
Kotik, Valja   289, 290n
Kovalevskaja, Inessa   445
Kozhevnikov, Aleksej   215, 227n
Kozlov, Viljam   244
Kozyreva, Marjana   5n
Krapivin, Vladislav   21, 244
Krasnogorskij, Nikolaj   77, 78, 79, 80, 81, 82, 95
Krestinskij, Aleksandr   304, 312, 313, 319-320, 325, 326, 327
Kruchenych, Aleksej   100, 102, 104, 105, 107, 108n, 109, 110, 111, 112, 114, 115, 125, 128, 129
Kruglov, Aleksandr   216
Krupskaja, Nadezhda   57, 80, 102, 119, 126n, 205n, 228-229, 234, 265, 294
Kucherenko, Olga   33, 290n, 295
Kukulin, Ilja   20, 31, 292n, 357n
Kulagina, Valentina   391
Kuleshov, Lev   77, 78, 421n
Kuprijanova, E.   287n, 288
Kurbatov, Konstantin   294
Kurbatov, Valentin   8
Kuznecova, Olga   314-314
Kvitko, Lev   29, 169

Lacan, Jacques   441n, 468
Larin, Boris   454, 455
Larina, Larisa   215, 238n, 264, 267
Larionov, Michail   100, 102, 105, 112
Lathey, Gillian   341
Lebedev, Aleksandr   206
Lebedev, Vladimir   22n, 59n, 60, 61, 62, 63, 68, 101n, 102, 139, 140, 391, 392
Lekmanov, Oleg   150n, 359
Lenin (Uljanov), Vladimir   8, 15, 57, 74, 102, 145n, 154, 161n, 162, 187, 197, 205, 215, 221, 223, 224, 228, 394
Leonov, Evgenij   375, 443, 444, 447, 451
Leonov, Michail   267
Lévi-Bruhl, Lucien   87, 92
Levin, Dojvber   140n, 141n, 144n, 147n
Leving, Yuri   362n, 447n, 448n, 450n, 451n
Lewin, Kurt   84
Leyda, Jay   93
Lidanova, Lidija   216
Lilina, Zlata   228, 229
Lillebror (see also Kid, *Kid and Karlsson*)   442, 454
Lindgren, Astrid   370, 440, 442, 445n, 453n, 454
Lipavskij, Leonid (L. Saveljev)   141n, 146n, 165n
Lipina, Nina   227
Lipoveckij (Lipovetsky) Mark   32, 35n, 434n
Lissickij, El   61, 102, 139
Literary representation, ironic   24, 245, 357, 360, 363, 364, 367, 148, 150, 160, 163
Litovskaja, Marija   35, 250, 258n, 263n, 266
Little Historical Library   190, 195, 205
Livanov, Vasilij   443, 444, 456, 460
Livschiz, Ann   250, 282n, 287n, 290, 291n
Locke, John   222
Lomonosov, Michail   186
Loseff, Lev   50, 51, 52, 53, 54, 55, 67n, 68, 361
Lotman, Yuri   58, 59, 109
Lozinskij, Michail   351n, 357
Lukjanova, Irina   31, 222n
Lunacharskij, Anatolij   16, 72, 80, 103, 117n, 148n, 161, 188, 222, 223, 228
Lungina, Liliana   453n, 454n
Lurija, Aleksandr   36, 84, 85, 87, 88, 89, 90, 93, 95
Lurje, Solomon   199n

INDEX

Machlis, Isaak   426
Majakovskij, Vladimir   32, 62, 391, 392, 101n, 105, 106n, 115, 118, 119, 120, 121, 124, 139, 160n
Majofis, Maria   31, 357n, 442n, 445n, 454, 455n, 456
Makarenko, Anton   24n, 220, 227n, 313n
Mal'chish-Kibal'chish (see also Gajdar, *Military Secret*)   13, 265n
Malachov, Petr   16
Malachov, Sergej   215n
Malich, Marina (see also Durnovo, Marina)   151n
Maljantovich, Kirill   29
Mandel'shtam, Nadezhda   122
Mandel'shtam, Osip   32, 58, 64-65, 100, 105, 121, 122, 123, 124, 126, 139, 179
Margolit, Evgenij   32, 417n, 435
Markish, Shimon   206, 207n
Markova, Lilija   318
Marr, Nikolaj   87, 92
Marshak, Samuil   2, 4, 9, 29, 58, 57-60, 62, 63, 101n, 102n, 103, 117, 123, 124, 126-127, 128, 131, 134, 147-148, 160, 162, 189, 191, 193, 199, 205, 256, 257, 284, 285n, 310, 343, 344, 345, 348-355, 358, 362n, 365-366
Marshak, Samuil, as editor (see also Children's publishing, "Marshak's Academy")   4, 29, 58, 126-127, 131, 134, 147-149, 191, 199, 205
Maslinskaya (Leontjeva), Svetlana   XI, 18n, 35n, 38, 91n, 240n, 250-302, 261n, 287n
Matje, Milica   198, 199, 200, 201, 202, 203, 205
Matveev, German   241n, 270, 313, 329
Max und Moritz   358
Mechanika golovnogo mozga (Механика головного мозга)   36, 75, 76, 77, 79, 80, 81, 82, 83, 95
Medinskij, Vladimir   6, 7, 10
Medvedev, Dmitrij   11
Medynskij, Georgij   215, 241
Medzhibovskaya, Inessa   17
Mejerhold, Vsevolod   71, 78, 84, 426, 431
Mejlach, Michail   140n, 145, 150n, 154
Memory
 collective   9, 149n, 279, 309, 333, 334, 376
 cultural   5, 6, 286, 304, 307, 309, 334

 historical   296, 304, 307, 333, 334
Men of the sixties (шестидесятники)   371, 445
Merkulov, Jurij   391
Merkurjev, Vasilij   426, 431, 433
Meshcherjakova, M. I.   21n
Metamorphosis
 in animation   397
 in interpretation   418
Metatext   155, 187, 197, 198, 199, 203, 357, 448
Mgebrov-Chekan, Kotija   293, 294, 295
Michajlov, M.   262
Michalkov, Sergej   6n, 9, 23, 24, 245, 269, 294n, 343, 351, 367-370, 371, 377, 384
Micheenko, Lara   290, 294n, 295
Mickenberg, Julia L.   180n
Mickey Mouse   400, 407, 409
Mikitenko, Ivan   227n
Mikson, Ilja   304, 318, 326, 327
Miller, Jakov (see also Zabolockij, Nikolaj)   172
Milne, Alexander Alan   124n, 371, 372, 373, 374, 375, 376, 440, 442, 446-450, 451
Miloserdova, Natalja   29
Minaev, Konstantin   226n, 239
Minin, Oleg   XII, 37, 102n, 126n, 134n, 139-176
Mjagotin, Kolja   274, 280, 291
Mjolsness, Lora   XII, 38, 389-416, 421n, 443n
Mogilevskaja, Svetlana   244
Moiseeva, Klara   198
Montage
 film   89, 93
 intellectual   89
 theory   77, 89, 428
Morozov, Pavlik   29, 91, 92, 94n, 239, 243, 250, 256, 271-275, 276n, 278, 286, 291, 294-296, 312, 453
Morozov, Vjacheslav   314n
Morse, Ainsley   XII, 37, 99-138, 357
Motjashov, Ivan   24, 242, 243
Murashova, Ekaterina   5n

Nabatov, Grigorij   294n, 315n
Nadezhdina, Nadezhda   289, 290, 294n
Nadtochij, Eduard   10
Narkompros (Commissariat of Enlightenment)   14, 161, 285
Narodickij, Abram   16

Nationalism, Soviet   4, 180, 363, 402, 403, 408, 409
Natural history   37, 49, 50-55, 65, 68
Nechaev, Leonid   15
Nekrasov, Andrej   29
Neurophysiology   72, 73, 75, 81, 82, 85
New Economic Policy (NEP)   117, 161, 420, 455
New Soviet Man   21, 72, 74
Neznajka (Dunno)   21, 244
Nicholas I   187, 189
Nicholas II   189
Nikiforov, Georgij   226n
Nikitkina, Elena   393n, 402, 404n
Noever, Peter   33n
Norshtejn, Jurij   444
Nosov, Nikolaj   14, 16, 20, 21, 241, 244
Nostalgia, Soviet   7, 8, 9, 10, 11, 28, 179
Noussinova, Natalija   91
Novosadskij, Nikolaj   86

O'Sullivan, Emer   341, 362
OBERIU
   literary-artistic movement   37, 16, 32, 102n, 126-128, 135, 139-140, 143, 146, 149, 150, 161-71
   periodicals   37, 102n, 139-176
   poetics   34, 114, 128-134, 135, 145-148, 155, 157
October Revolution, 1917   1, 2, 3, 4, 9, 25, 28, 34n, 50, 56, 59, 72, 74, 91, 100, 102, 116, 121, 124, 139, 141, 145, 152, 154, 159, 165, 188, 190, 197, 205, 212, 215, 216, 217, 218, 221, 236, 237, 243, 252, 257, 260, 263, 264, 267n, 271, 275, 293, 294, 296, 331, 342, 343, 344, 390, 392, 419, 422, 445
Octobrists (октябрята)   140, 160n, 229, 231, 279
OGPU   160, 162, 269
Olejnikov, Nikolaj   37, 102n, 126, 140, 141n, 144n, 145, 146, 147, 149-152, 154, 155, 158, 163, 164, 165, 169, 170, 357
Olenina, Ana Hedberg   XII, 36-37, 72-98, 100n
Olesha, Jurij   65, 66, 100, 121
Orlova, Ljubov   429, 430
Oseeva, Valentina   7, 15, 240n, 241, 243
Ostashevsky, Eugene   32, 127n, 129n

Ostromenckaja, Nadezhda   203-204, 205
Ostroumov, Lev   221, 265
Ostrovskij, Nikolaj   12
Ovalov, Lev   238

Palindrome   113, 114, 127, 148
Panova, Vera   304, 318, 319, 325
Panteleev, Leonid   7n, 9, 14, 217, 227n, 286, 304, 311, 313, 324, 331-333, 334-335
Para-text   203
Paramonova, Kira   32
Party Congresses   144n, 395
Pasternak, Boris   XII, 58, 100, 121, 123, 124, 139, 356
Patriotism
   in education   34n, 184, 193-196, 220, 293n
   in literary discourse   169, 180, 184, 193-196, 293n, 298, 312
   in pioneer movement   290, 298, 312, 421n
   Post-Soviet value   11, 12, 14, 28
Paustovskij, Konstantin   241
Pavlov, Ivan   36, 75-80, 81, 87
Pedology
   experiments   73n, 74-75, 80
   history   36, 72-74, 75, 80, 87, 92, 94, 102, 126, 394
   theory   73, 80, 85-87, 92
Peer-hero   199
Perestroika   258, 321, 443
Period of few films ("малокартинье")   417
Perlina, Nina   34n
Perrault, Charles   417, 424
Petrosjan, Mariam   5n
Petrov, Vladimir   16
Petrovskij, Miron   4, 15
Phelan, Peggy   444
Picturebook, Soviet   XIV, 30, 32, 33, 49, 50, 54, 57-68, 102n, 398
Piglet (see also Pjatachok, *Пятачок*)   375, 442
Pioneer heroes
   hagiographic narratives   18, 38, 92, 273, 274, 275
   hero narratives (see also Hero narratives)   38, 91, 240n, 251, 252, 253-255, 256, 258, 261, 263, 275, 277, 278, 281, 282, 283, 291, 292, 294, 295, 312, 314

INDEX 503

  literary representation   258, 268-270,
    275-288, 289-292, 293, 294, 295, 296,
    297, 298
  media representation   255, 257, 259,
    260-261, 271-273, 274, 275, 283, 288,
    310-314, 317, 322, 327-329
Pioneer Organization   XII, 37, 144, 228, 231,
  238, 239, 251, 258, 284, 289, 293, 460
Pivovarov, Viktor   135, 378, 382
Pjatachok (*Пятачок*, see also Piglet)   36,
  375, 440, 442, 446, 447, 449-452
Plisch und Plum (*Плюх и Плих*)   2, 358-367,
  369
Plutarch   184, 185, 191
Poetics
  beyonsense (see also, *zaum'*)   37, 108, 109,
    110, 112n, 125, 128, 131, 133, 147, 148
  fantastical elements   119, 129, 148, 158,
    167, 168, 261, 288, 290, 393, 402-403,
    407, 424, 441n, 443n
  metric combinations   113, 123-124, 148,
    353, 381
  nonsense   100, 108n, 110, 114, 124, 125, 126,
    128, 129, 132, 149n, 285n, 346
  playfulness   22, 34, 37, 61, 62, 105, 112, 121,
    143, 147n, 151, 155, 156, 157, 160, 163, 167,
    169, 181, 199, 221, 323, 348, 349, 357, 369,
    370, 373, 381, 382, 418, 419, 420, 421, 424,
    434, 435, 446
  rhyme   113, 114, 120, 129, 133, 143, 155, 169,
    346, 347, 351, 353, 362, 363, 364, 365,
    366, 367, 369, 381
  riddles   113, 118, 141n, 148, 155
  word play   XII, 120, 128, 148, 156, 158, 346,
    348, 362, 364
Pogodin, Radij   29
Pokrovskaja, Anna   265
Political indoctrination   1, 16, 19, 40, 57, 58,
  101, 220n, 232, 234, 240, 303, 400, 402
Pomozov, Jurij   304, 324-325, 329
Ponomarev, Nikolaj and Svetlana   5n
Poohology   446
Popov, Vladimir   294, 445
Poret, Alisa   126n, 139, 140
Portnova, Zina   289, 290n, 294
Positive hero
  in children's film   421
  in children's literature (see also Pioneer
    heroes)   16, 158, 288, 313, 326, 421, 431n
Post-Soviet discussions on children's reading
  10n, 11-14, 26-27
Poznjakov, Nikolaj   216, 253
Pregel, Ja. A.   215n, 339n
Prevarication   146
Prilezhaeva, Marija   241, 244
Prokhorov, Alexander (Aleksandr)   21n, 25,
  32, 418n, 421n
Prokhorov (Prokhorova), Elena   5, 6, 32n
Proletarian internationalism   2, 18, 141, 180,
  293n, 363
Propiak, Zhirar de   184n
Psychoanalysis   XI, 73, 441n, 446n, 448, 467,
  468, 469
Psychology
  cultural-historical approach   36, 73, 85,
    87
  developmental   72, 87, 440
  ethics   77, 81, 84
  experiments (see also Pedology,
    experiments)   78, 79, 80, 81, 82, 83, 88
  theory of perception   73, 74, 84, 87, 93, 95
Ptushko, Aleksandr   422, 423, 424
Pudovkin, Vsevolod   36, 75, 84, 95
Pushkarev, Gleb   212, 213, 214, 237, 245, 272n,
  273, 276n, 277, 281
Pushkin, Aleksandr   105-106, 360, 372, 400
Putilova, Evgenija   26, 27, 99n, 102n, 117n,
  119n, 219
Putin, Vladimir   6n

Queer temporality   XI, 441, 444, 457, 464n
Queer theory   442n, 444, 445, 457, 459,
  464-465n, 467

Rabbit   375, 442, 447, 448, 449n, 450, 451,
  452
Rabelais, Francois   164, 165, 357
Rachtanov, Isaj   147n, 148n, 149n, 158
Rajzman, Julij   25
Rambow, Aileen G.   307
Ranevskaja, Faina   426, 431, 433, 434, 465
Razumovskij, Lev   321
Red Army   2, 149, 154, 160, 165, 166, 169, 182,
  221, 256, 260, 261, 262, 287, 310, 324,
  325, 421, 427

Red Terror   226, 470n
Reflex, associative   85-86
Reflexology   36, 73, 75, 77, 78, 80, 81, 84, 85, 86, 87n, 94, 95
Reitherman, Wolfgang   447n
Remizov, Aleksej   100, 121
Revolutionary Association of Proletarian Writers (RAPP)   102, 161
Reynolds, Kimberley   258
Rodchenko, Aleksandr   391
Rogachev, V. A.   148
Ronen, Omri   29, 183n
ROSTA (Russian Telegraph Agency) windows   61, 160n, 392
Rostockij, Stanislav   25
Rothenstein, Julian   15n, 33n, 101n, 139n
Rou, Aleksandr   20, 32, 422, 423, 424
Rozanov, Sergej   227
Rozanova, Ol'ga   104
Rubinshtejn, Revekka   198
Rudova, Larissa   XIII, 18, 31, 38, 99n, 117n, 181n, 417-439
Rumjanova, Klara   460
Russianness   2, 38, 405, 408, 409, 411
Ruzhanskij, Evgenij   257-258
Rybakov, Anatolij   16, 240n
Ryklin, Grigorij   269-270
Rysakov, Viktor   254n
Ryzhov, Aleksandr   261, 264
Rzheshevskij, Aleksandr   91, 92

Sabitova, Dina   5n
Salova, Julija   240
Samizdat   67, 376
Samojlov, David   357
Sapgir, Genrich   25, 99, 134n, 135, 343, 371, 376-379, 382
Saveljev, L. (Leonid Lipavskij)   141n, 146n, 165n, 188
Savicheva, Tanja   317-319, 325-326, 335
Savin, Viktor   227n
Sedgwick, Eve Kosofsky   455, 460n, 464n
Sef, Roman   29, 371
Segida, M.   417n
Sejfullina, Lidija   227n
Selivanov, Vladimir   330n
Semashko, Nikolaj   80
Serebrjannikov, Abram   162, 163, 164n

Setin, F. I.   182n
Shapiro, Michail   32, 38, 417, 418, 424, 425, 426
Shapokljak   440, 445, 459n, 460n, 461, 464-465n
Shavit, Zohar   53, 54n, 341n
Shchukin, Gena   273, 274, 276, 277
Shengeli, Georgij   357
Shestinskij, Oleg   321
Shishkov, Vjacheslav   227n
Shishova, Zinaida   308, 309
Shklovskij, Viktor   38, 58, 94n, 115, 116, 279, 418-419, 425, 428, 435, 436
Shorin, Ivan   215, 224
Shostakovich, Dmitrij   400
Shrayer, Maxim   377
Shtejner, Evgenij (see also Steiner, Evgeny)   31, 60n, 101n, 121n, 139n, 223n, 344, 362n
Shteyngart, Gary   35, 36, 440, 441, 465-470
Shubinskij, Valerij   31, 131n, 134n, 139n, 143n, 145n, 148n, 151n, 162, 216n, 357-358
Shul'gin, Vladimir   218
Shumjackij, Boris   92
Shvarc, Evgenij   7, 22, 29, 58, 126, 127n, 147, 241, 417, 424-426, 429, 430, 432, 433, 434, 436
Siege of Leningrad
    child victims   303-304, 311, 316, 317, 318-319, 320, 321, 322, 323, 332, 334
    everyday life   303, 306, 307, 308-309, 316, 325, 327-328, 329, 332
    hero narratives   303-304, 305, 307-308, 309, 310, 311-316, 317, 319, 321, 322, 324-325, 327-330, 333-334, 335
    memory politics   303-304, 305-307, 311, 312, 317-318, 324, 333-334
    non-disclosure of facts   306, 310, 330-331, 334
    post-war publications   305-306, 331-335
    starvation   39, 303, 306, 308, 309, 310-311, 312, 318, 319, 321, 322, 327, 328-329, 331-333
Simmons, Cynthia   34n
Slepuchin, Jurij   243
Slonimskij, Aleksandr   188
Sluckij, Boris   377
Smirnov-Ochtin, Igor'   321

INDEX

Smirnov, Elizar   268n, 272n, 273, 276n, 277, 281n, 294n
Smirnov, S.   318n
Smoljarova, Natalija   447
Snow White and the Seven Dwarfs   407, 409
Social demand   159, 160, 181, 429
Socialist construction   13, 39, 144, 146, 154, 158, 159, 162, 164n, 217, 218, 220n, 221, 265, 266, 268, 270, 441
Socialist Realism
  aesthetics (see also Aesthetics, Socialist Realist)   14, 22, 29n, 63, 165, 181, 182, 183, 287, 288, 303, 307, 312, 314, 315, 319, 322-323, 326, 327, 329, 331, 333, 401, 402, 403, 413, 418, 421, 423, 429, 436
  master plots   227, 307, 323, 418n
Sokol, Elena   65n, 99n, 105n, 121n, 124n, 126n, 134n, 147n, 156n, 158, 160n, 181n, 342n
Sokoljanskij, Ivan   394
Soler, Colette   441n
Soviet childhood (see also Childhood, Soviet, history)
  child-state relationship   4, 10-11, 15, 16, 17, 18, 20, 22-24, 31, 39, 58, 72, 91, 116, 215, 216, 218, 222-233, 234, 236, 237, 241-242, 243-244, 258, 272, 277, 282n, 331n, 399, 452-453
  family politics   15, 19, 24, 91, 216-17, 219, 226-227, 228-229, 360, 444-445
  orphans   5n, 25, 33, 36, 76, 85, 86, 226n, 227, 240, 243, 244, 285, 287, 305, 317, 319-318, 330, 461
  party agenda on   14, 16, 19, 57, 58, 101, 189, 214-215, 220, 228-229, 234, 236, 240, 285-286, 303
Soviet education
  academic self-governance   218n, 229, 234
  authoritarian model   39, 217-219, 236, 241-242
  collectivist approach   24, 217, 218, 219, 220, 222, 223, 224, 227, 228-229, 242-244, 245
Soviet holidays   149, 150, 158, 159n, 232
Soviet novel, theory of   26-27, 29n, 421n, 426n, 430n, 435n
Soviet Writers' Congress, Eighth (1986)   24
Soviet Writers' Congress, First (1934)   117, 119n, 134, 189, 349, 394, 420

Spadovekkia, Antonio   426
Spartacus   189, 197, 198, 199, 201, 204
Stagnation era   135, 440, 441, 443, 444n, 447, 464, 470
Stalin, Joseph   2, 3n, 19, 21, 30n, 38, 120, 169, 240, 277, 427, 429
Stalin Prize   287
Stalinism
  history   33, 195, 198, 250n, 269n, 293n, 403n
  (post-)   10n, 19-20, 21, 105, 126, 199, 201-202, 370, 426n, 445n, 446, 452, 464, 470
  violence (see also Great Terror)   2, 5, 10, 22, 37, 64, 73-74, 87, 91, 105, 134, 161n, 168, 192, 217, 240, 271, 312, 334, 361-362, 402, 403, 436, 441-442, 445, 446, 456, 465
Stalinist cinema and animation   402, 403n, 418-419, 421, 422, 424, 427, 429, 430, 435, 436, 443n
Stanjukovich, Konstantin   193, 194, 254n
Staples, Terry   422, 424n
Steiner, Evgeny   31, 60n, 101n, 121n, 139n, 223n, 344, 362n
Stepancev, Boris   440, 442, 453, 454, 457, 464
Sterligov, Vladimir   143n
Stevenson, Robert Louis   226, 259, 284, 422
Stites, Richard   427
Stockton, Kathryn Bond   457
Suchachevskij, Stepan   280
Suzdorf, Elvira   170n, 171n
Sventickaja, M.   220n
Sverdlov, Michail   150n

Taezhnyj, A.   271-272
Tajtc, Jakov   256n
Tarkovskij, Andrej   25, 315n
Tarkovskij, Arsenij   356
Tatlin, Vladimir   139, 140, 391
Temporal drag   464-465n
Thaw
  censorship after   464
  new humanistic policies   20, 39, 134-135, 199, 201-202, 403, 444, 445n
  poetry   105, 134-135

Thaw (cont.)
   transformation in literary representation 20, 126, 134-135, 199-202, 203-204, 270-271, 295, 306, 315, 331, 444, 445n, 458
   translation 343, 370-383, 384
Tichonov, Nikolaj 13, 58, 284, 308
Tippner, Anja 21n, 424
Tolstoj, Aleksej 15, 118, 190, 196, 285n, 371n, 423
Tolstoj, Dmitrij 187
Tolstoj, Lev 105, 116, 193, 194, 216, 219, 254n
Tongue twisters 127, 148, 155, 156
Translation, Soviet 2, 15, 25, 32, 36, 39, 40, 53, 60, 67, 124, 127n, 134n, 151n, 164n, 167n, 169, 190, 284, 341-388, 403, 453
Trauma
   historical XI, 3, 5, 6n, 36, 39, 92, 305-308, 334, 445n, 464, 465
   psychological 24, 38, 85, 285, 293, 304, 306, 307, 315n, 316, 321, 325, 327, 331, 441, 445n, 446, 468, 470
   transgenerational transmission of 465, 467, 468, 469-70
Trotskij, Lev (see also Trotsky, Leon) 144n, 228, 273, 426
Trotsky, Leon (see also Trockij, Lev) 144n, 228, 273, 426
Turgenev, Ivan 91, 92, 93, 271
Tuwim, Julian 367-369, 384
Tynjanov, Jurij 3, 50-51, 113, 114, 123, 428

Ugrjumov, Naum 16
Uncle Fedor 21n, 244, 245, 458
Uncle Stepa 23
Unnatural selection 37, 49, 50, 51, 62, 63, 66, 68
Ushagin, Aleksandr 261
Ushakin, Sergej 30
Ushinskij, Konstantin 182, 218, 220n
Uspenskij, Eduard 15, 16, 21, 244, 245, 322, 440, 459n, 464
Uspenskij, Lev 322
Utopian thinking 1, 19, 21, 72-73, 74, 77, 80, 81, 84, 91, 92, 244, 422, 441, 464

Vaginov, Konstantin 140n, 141n, 144n, 147n
Vasiljev, Boris 9
Vasiljev brothers (Georgij and Sergej) 427
Vasiljeva, Olga 12
Verejskaja, Elena 15, 240n, 264n
Verkin, Eduard 253n, 296-297
Verne, Jules 226, 259, 422
Vertov, Dziga XII, 391
Victory Day 289, 436
Vigdorova, Frida 241, 244
Vilensky, Semyon S. 34
Vinni-puch 36, 371, 372, 374, 375, 440, 441, 443, 444n, 445, 446-453, 458, 463, 464, 470
Vinnikov, Boris 251, 234-237, 239, 240
Vishnevskij, Vsevolod 329
Vjugin, Valerij 31, 35n
Vladimirov, Jurij 37, 126, 140, 141n, 144n, 147n, 148n, 149, 151, 155, 156-157, 158, 170, 171
Vladimirskij, Nikolaj 391
Vocal drag 444, 456
Voice, in animated film 375, 406, 410, 440, 443, 444, 447, 449, 451, 456, 458n, 460, 461n
Vol'pin, Michail 29
von Glasenapp, Gabriele 186
Voronina, Olga XII-XIII, 1-46, 212-249
Voronina, Tatiana XIII-XIV, 39, 303-338
Voronkova, Ljubov 241n
Voskobojnikov, Valerij 253
Voskresenskij, Leonid 78
Voznesenskaja, Zoja 205n, 311
Vvedenskij, Aleksandr 102n, 114n, 122, 126, 127n, 128, 129, 130, 131, 133, 134, 140, 141, 143, 144n, 145-149, 151, 158-167, 168n, 170, 171, 308, 357
Vygockij L. S. (Lev) 36, 73, 85, 87, 88, 89, 90, 92, 95, 100, 119
Vygovskij, Vladimir 315n
Vysockij, Vladimir 460n

Weld, Sara Pankenier XII, 30, 34, 49-71, 100n, 105, 110n, 111n, 112n, 180n
Wells, H. G. 224
Wells, Paul 397-398
Winnie-the-Pooh 371-372, 373, 440, 442n, 446-447, 448n, 449n
World War II
   censorship 192, 305

INDEX

hero narratives   18, 20, 192n, 193, 195, 199, 204, 243, 256, 270, 272, 282-292, 293, 294, 303, 304, 306, 319, 327-330
  victims   18, 244, 310-327, 331-334, 335, 446, 465

Zabila, Natalija   241n
Zabolockij, Nikita   147
Zabolockij, Nikolaj   37, 102n, 126, 127n, 128n, 140, 141n, 144n, 145, 146, 147n, 149, 151, 154-155, 161, 162, 163, 164-166, 170, 356-357
Zabrodin, Vladimir   92n, 94n
Zacharov, Mark   22
Zachoder, Boris   25, 343, 371-376, 382, 384, 446, 447, 448, 449, 450, 452, 453
Zachoder, Galina   376
Zalkind, Aron   72, 80n, 94n
Zaluzhnyj, Aleksandr   73, 222, 394
Zamchalov, Grigorij   239
Zamojskij, Petr   226, 238, 261

Zaum' (see also, Poetics, beyonsense)   37, 108, 109, 110, 112n, 125, 128, 131, 133, 147, 148
Zemljanuchin, S.   417n
Zenzinov, Vladimir   228n
Zharikov, Andrej   315n
Zhdanov, Andrej   418n, 425, 426n, 436
Zhejmo, Janina   426n, 427, 428, 429, 430, 431
Zheleznikov, Vladimir   9
Zhelichovskaja, Vera   216
Zheljabuzhskij, Jurij   392
Zhelobovskij, Ignatij   197n, 265n
Zhemchuzhnyj, Vitalij   75n
Zhitkov, Boris   27, 58, 151n
Zhitomirova, Nataljia   183, 192, 193
Zholkovskij, Aleksandr   114
Zhuravlev, Vasilij   7, 422
Zinovjev, Grigorij   228
Zipes, Jack   422, 431n, 435n
Zlobin, Stepan   188, 190
Zornado, Joseph   192
Zoshchenko, Michail   27, 361n

Printed in the United States
By Bookmasters